Butterworths
Financial Services Law Guide

Butterworths Financial Services Law Guide

Second Edition

General Editor
Dr Andrew Haynes BA (Hons) Law, PhD, Cert Ed, FSALS
Head, Institute of Finance Law, University of Wolverhampton

Associate Research Fellow, Institute of Advanced Legal Studies; Overseas Moderator, Hong Kong Institute of Bankers; Consultant Editor, Journal of Financial Crime; Executive Editorial Committee, European Financial Services Law; Editorial Team, Amicus Curiae; Editorial Board, The Company Lawyer; International Editorial Board, International Journal of Banking Regulation; Editorial Board, International Corporate Law Bulletin

Butterworths
LexisNexis™

Members of the LexisNexis Group worldwide

United Kingdom	LexisNexis Butterworths Tolley, a Division of Reed Elsevier (UK) Ltd, Halsbury House, 35 Chancery Lane, LONDON, WC2A 1EL, and 4 Hill Street, EDINBURGH EH2 3JZ
Argentina	LexisNexis Argentina, BUENOS AIRES
Australia	LexisNexis Butterworths, CHATSWOOD, New South Wales
Austria	LexisNexis Verlag ARD Orac GmbH & Co KG, VIENNA
Canada	LexisNexis Butterworths, MARKHAM, Ontario
Chile	LexisNexis Chile Ltda, SANTIAGO DE CHILE
Czech Republic	Nakladatelství Orac sro, PRAGUE
France	Editions du Juris-Classeur SA, PARIS
Hong Kong	LexisNexis Butterworths, HONG KONG
Hungary	HVG-Orac, BUDAPEST
India	LexisNexis Butterworths, NEW DELHI
Ireland	Butterworths (Ireland) Ltd, DUBLIN
Italy	Giuffrè Editore, MILAN
Malaysia	Malayan Law Journal Sdn Bhd, KUALA LUMPUR
New Zealand	LexisNexis Butterworths, WELLINGTON
Poland	Wydawnictwo Prawnicze LexisNexis, WARSAW
Singapore	LexisNexis Butterworths, SINGAPORE
South Africa	Butterworths SA, DURBAN
Switzerland	Stämpfli Verlag AG, BERNE
USA	LexisNexis, DAYTON, Ohio

© Reed Elsevier (UK) Ltd 2002

A CIP Catalogue record of this book is available from the British Library.

First edition 1997

ISBN 0 406 93913 6

Typeset by Letterpart Ltd, Reigate, Surrey
Printed and bound in Great Britain by Antony Rowe Ltd, Chippenham, Wilts

Visit Butterworths LexisNexis *direct* at www.butterworths.com

Preface

Although this is the second edition of the title it is a totally new volume. The scale of the changes that have been brought about in financial regulation by the Financial Services and Markets Act 2000 and subsequent statutory instruments, together with steps taken by the Financial Services Authority, have resulted in a new regime coming into existence that is fundamentally different from its predecessor. As a result some of the old chapters have disappeared and some new ones, such as market abuse, financial promotions and money laundering have appeared. In addition those chapters retaining the same title now have a different content, in most instances radically so.

In preparing this book the authors have considered both the legal and practical issues arising as a result of this. As a consequence the work will be useful to legal practitioners, compliance officers, accountants, academics and students who require a guide to the complex range of issues arising as a consequence of the new regime. It should also be of interest to those holding a senior position in a financial services business.

Particular thanks to the staff at Butterworths.

The law is stated as at 1 February 2002.

Dr Andrew Haynes
Institute of Finance Law
University of Wolverhampton

Contributors

Charles Abrams

Charles Abrams is Head of the Financial Services Group at S J Berwin and specialises in non-retail banking and securities regulation. He is co-author of a leading textbook on the Financial Services Act, *Guide to Financial Services Regulation* (3rd edn, 1997), and is the author of *A Short Guide to the Financial Services and Markets Act 2000* (2000). He was a member of the APCIMS, CBI and City of London Law Society committees which reviewed the Financial Services and Markets Bill and the Treasury and FSA consultation papers relating to it. Charles was a legal adviser to the Conservative Party's Treasury Team on the Financial Services and Markets Bill, especially in relation to financial promotion, cross-border issues (including the EU single financial market directives), the European Convention on Human Rights and market abuse.

Peter Bibby

Peter Bibby, LLB (Hons), is a partner at the City office of the law firm DLA where he has a lead role in managing the firm's regulatory practice. Peter was previously Head of Regulatory Enforcement at the Financial Services Authority between 1998 and early 2002 where he had particular responsibility for regulation of the retail sector. He was the author of the FSA's Principles and Code for Approved Persons and was instrumental in the development of the FSA's new approach to regulatory enforcement.

Prior to joining the FSA, Peter led a number of high profile contentious regulatory cases including actions in relation to pension transfers, the Maxwell affair and Morgan Grenfell. During his time at the FSA, he was responsible for enforcement cases such as Royal Scottish Assurance, Royal London, United Friendly, Winterthur, Prudential and GAN.

Susan Brownlie

Susan Brownlie BA (Econ), ACCA, is Director, Financial Regulation with KPMG, a leading accountancy and advisory firm providing regulatory services to the financial sector. She specialises in capital markets regulation, in particular capital adequacy and conduct of business requirements, providing advice to finance and compliance departments of banks and other financial services institutions.

KPMG are a leading firm of auditors and advisors to UK and international financial institutions. With over 1000 financial services professionals including over 100 regulatory specialist staff in the UK KPMG is well placed to advise financial services firms in areas such as compliance arrangements, capital adequacy, regulatory reporting, launching new products and money laundering avoidance.

Andrew R Hart

Andrew Hart is the head of the dispute resolution banking and financial services group at Freshfields Bruckhaus Deringer, the international law firm.

The group's practice concentrates on large scale litigation and regulatory disputes in the financial services sector and has been ranked as a leading practice in the area. Andrew acts for a number of prominent investment banks and other financial institutions and has been instructed on significant high profile regulatory actions. He is named as one of the leaders in litigation by *Chambers* in its guide to the legal profession and as an expert in large scale banking litigation in the *Legal 500* guide. He is co-author of *Freshfields Bruckhaus Deringer on Financial Services Investigation and Enforcement* (Butterworths, 2001).

Freshfields Bruckhaus Deringer has a leading financial services practice which advises on a wide range of contentious and non-contentious issues. The financial services team has acted for financial institutions around the world and has advised in relation to numerous inquiries and investigations by regulators.

Dr Andrew Haynes

Andrew Haynes BA (Hons) Law, PhD, Cert Ed, FSALS has written, edited and contributed to a wide range of books, encyclopaedias and articles on the subjects of financial services, financial crime and international banking law. He has also spoken at a large number of academic conferences and delivered training sessions for a range of financial institutions and regulators throughout the world.

The Institute of Finance Law specialises in the study and research of the law and regulations relating to financial services in the widest sense and has carried out a wide range of research into financial regulation, banking supervision, market abuse and financial crime.

Tamasin Little

Tamasin Little, BA, LLM is a partner in S J Berwin's Financial Services Group. She has worked on financial services law matters since she qualified in 1985 and exclusively in that area since acting as the Legal Associate to the Bank of England's Legal Risk Review Panel in 1991/2.

She advises banks, brokers, fund managers, private equity firms, investment exchanges, insurance companies and other investment businesses on a wide range of regulatory and related issues including buyouts and structuring financial services firms for efficient regulatory capital treatment, authorisation and ongoing requirements, Internet and e-commerce developments, cross-border business, market abuse, agreements with customers and service providers (including clearing and custody) and implementing the Financial Services and Markets Act regime. She writes and lectures regularly on financial services law and regulatory matters.

SJ Berwin's Financial Services Group is a key part of the firm's pan European practice. Working from London, Brussels, Frankfurt, Munich, Berlin, Madrid and Paris the firm concentrates on corporate finance in the broadest sense, with leading practices in private equity, competition, funds, property and media finance all of which draw on the Financial Services Group's expertise in financial services regulation.

Peter Milroy

Peter Milroy is a principal in the Financial Services Regulatory Consultancy Group at PricewaterhouseCoopers. He specialises in the regulatory requirements for investment managers.

He has a degree in law from Cambridge University and is a Fellow of the Institute of Chartered Accountants in England and Wales. Since 1986 he has provided advice on compliance matters to a wide range of investment businesses and to regulatory bodies in the UK and overseas. He has written articles and spoken at conferences on regulatory issues.

The PricewaterhouseCoopers' Financial Services Regulatory Consulting Group comprises 125 partners, directors and regulatory specialists in a single group providing a wide range of regulatory solutions and services to the financial services industry. The group comprises individuals with extensive knowledge of the regulatory framework, rules, codes of conduct, prudential and supervision requirements. The group blends the experiences of former senior regulators, compliance managers, industry personnel and staff with an assurance/client facing background.

Simon Orton

Simon Orton is a senior associate in Freshfields Bruckhaus Deringer's dispute resolution group. He specialises in financial services disputes and regulatory enforcement, and has also spent several months on secondment to a leading international investment bank. He is co-author of *Freshfields Bruckhaus Deringer on Financial Services Investigation and Enforcement* (Butterworths, 2001).

Freshfields Bruckhaus Deringer has a leading financial services practice which advises on a wide range of contentious and non-contentious issues. The financial services team has acted for financial institutions around the world and has advised in relation to numerous inquiries and investigations by regulators.

Richard Parlour

Richard Parlour is a partner and Head of Financial Markets at the international law firm of Richards Butler. His team specialises in international financial markets regulation, new product development (particularly derivatives), trading system development and market integrity issues ranging from money laundering and fraud, to insider dealing and market abuse. The team is very strong on the litigation side. Richard has had secondments to LIFFE and to Brussels. He is the editor of *Butterworth's International Guide to Money Laundering Law and Practice*, and *The Derivatives Industry in the UK*, as well as a contributor to *Bond Market Compliance* and the ICC *Guide to Money Laundering Deterrence*. Richard is a member of many working parties of the Centre for European Policy Studies looking at the future of European securities, pensions, capital adequacy and investment management regulation, and an advisor to Cabinet Office, HM Treasury, DTI, and a number of foreign governments on regulation. He has developed the leading A2E compliance model and is a joint founder of the International Financial Fraud Convention.

Richards Butler is a leading international law firm with over 100 partners and 700 staff in ten locations around the globe, and a network of other leading local law firms in over 100 countries. Clients include all types of financial institution from global banks, exchanges, derivatives brokers, investment managers, to investment advisors, insurance companies, commodities houses, custodians, regulators and governments. The firm is also one of the market leaders in commodities, litigation, media, as well as having strong practices in shipping, corporate finance and banking.

Sue Rutherford

Sue Rutherford MA, FSI is Director, Compliance & Internal Controls at Morgan Stanley Quilter, having previously been Head of UK Compliance for HSBC Midland. Before that she worked in both the surveillance and authorisation divisions of the SFA.

Morgan Stanley Quilter specialises in providing personalised investment management and stockbroking services to private clients. It has its head office in London with nine branches around the UK and the Channel Islands, and is part of the Morgan Stanley global financial services group which has a total of $460bn of assets under management and over 700 offices in 28 countries.

Robert Surridge

Robert Surridge LLB, MA, ACII, TEP, chartered insurer, solicitor, is a senior legal adviser in the Legal Department of AXA UK dealing with a wide range of financial services law issues relating to product development and marketing. He also provides advice on a wide variety of issues including trusts and succession issues. He is a co-author of Houseman and Davies, *Law of Life Assurance* (12th edn).

Sun Life Assurance Society was established in 1810 and in 1900 was the first life office to offer life assurance without medical examination. As a result of the takeover by AXA of UAP, the Sun Life Group merged its operations with those of AXA Equity and Law and the resulting organisation AXA Sun Life is amongst the largest life assurance companies in the UK. The AXA Group is the second largest insurance group in the world.

Owen Watkins

Owen Watkins MA, DPhil is a barrister and member of the General Counsel's Division of the Financial Services Authority (FSA). He has worked in financial services regulation since 1990, and advises on a wide range of issues, including compensation, complaints, and financial promotion. He writes in a personal capacity.

The Financial Services Authority is the statutory body established under the Financial Services and Markets Act 2000 as the single regulator within the UK of banking, insurance, and investment business. Its overall aim is to maintain efficient, orderly and clean financial markets and help retail customers achieve a fair deal.

Contents

Table of Statutes

Table of Statutory Instruments

Table of Cases

S

Chapter 1   The Financial Services
Regime

Dr Andrew Haynes

THE NEW REGULATORY STRUCTURE

1.1   The main purpose of the regulatory restructuring which is a consequence of the Financial Services and Markets Act 2000 (FSMA 2000) is to
create a single system of regulation with the Financial Services Authority
(FSA) regulating virtually the entire financial services industry. This process
had already started with the passing of the Bank of England Act 1998 which
transferred the regulation of banks from the Bank of England to the FSA.
The rest of the new regime consists of the FSA being responsible for the
regulation of: investment business; banks; building societies; friendly societies; credit unions; insurance companies; and oversight of Lloyd's insurance
market.

1.2   The other regulators were abolished as the new FSMA 2000 came into
force, with the exception of the Bank of England, which continues to exist
but with a more limited remit[1]. The regulators which disappeared were the
self-regulating organisations (PIA, IMRO and the SFA), the Bank of
England (surveillance and supervision only), the Building Societies Commission, the Insurance Directorate of the Treasury, the Friendly Societies
Commission and the Registry of Friendly Societies.

---

[1]   See para 1.22.

THE FINANCIAL SERVICES AUTHORITY

1.3   The FSMA 2000 provides the FSA with the power to regulate financial
business and also makes it the competent authority for official listing of
securities, which will entail, inter alia, specifying the requirements to be
complied with for listing. The FSA is responsible for maintaining the official
list and applications for listing have to be made to them. The Treasury
maintain the capacity under the FSMA 2000, s 95 to keep the FSA's
performance under review. A detailed analysis of the listing rules is, however,
beyond the scope of this book.

1.4   The purpose of the listing rules[1] is to provide a regulatory framework
for the issuing of new (primary) securities and the selling of existing
(secondary) ones. The aim of these regulations is to keep a balance between
the interests of those in industry who wish to raise capital and those of the

1

public at large who may wish to subscribe. Securities will only be admitted to listing if the applicant is suitable and it is appropriate for the securities concerned to be publicly held and traded. They must be brought to the market in a way that is appropriate to their nature and number and which will facilitate an open and efficient market for trading in those securities. Issuers must make full and timely disclosures about themselves and the listed securities both at the time of issue and afterwards. The continuing obligations imposed on issuers are designed to promote investor confidence in standards of disclosure, in the conduct of listed companies affairs, and in the market as a whole. As a result the holders of equity securities must be given adequate opportunity to consider in advance and vote upon major changes in the company's management and constitution.

---

[1]   Financial Services and Markets Act 2000 (Official Listing of Securities) Regulations 2001, SI 2001/2956 together with SIs 2001/2955, 2001/2957 and 2001/2958.

1.5   The other ingredients of the FSAs powers are:

- controlling insurance business and banking transfers;
- overseeing the regulation of Lloyd's of London;
- combating market abuse;
- recognising and supervising investment exchange and clearing houses;
- overseeing the compensation scheme; and
- overseeing the ombudsman scheme.

1.6   The FSA is placed in a different position to its predecessor, the SIB, in that the FSA has the power to issue rules that will, as far as those that are affected by them are concerned, have the force of law.

1.7   The FSMA 2000 also sets out the FSA's objectives. These are:

- the maintenance of confidence in the UK financial system[1];
- the promotion of public understanding of the financial system[2]. This objective involves the promotion of public awareness of the risks and benefits of investment and financial dealing and also making available the necessary information and advice for the public to be able to do this;
- to secure an appropriate degree of protection for consumers[3]. In considering what to provide in this context the FSA must consider both the degree of risk and experience that consumers may possess, and their need for accurate information;
- the reduction of the extent to which it is possible for financial services business to be used to facilitate financial crime[4]. The FSA is required to make sure that regulated businesses are aware of the risk of their business being used in connection with the commission of financial crime and to make sure that the necessary steps are taken to monitor, detect and prevent financial crime. The main target in this area is money laundering[5].

Although this appears to leave the FSA with an enormous degree of power they are scrutinised by Parliamentary Committee and the Treasury.

[1] FSMA 2000, s 3.
[2] FSMA 2000, s 4.
[3] FSMA 2000, s 5.
[4] FSMA 2000, s 6.
[5] See Chapter 7.

FSA PRINCIPLES FOR BUSINESS

1.8 These are the initial part of the rules and in many respects the most important. The Principles overarch the various detailed regulations and a breach of either can potentially lead to disciplinary steps being taken by the FSA, though a breach of the Principles will not in themselves give rise to potential civil action by clients. This is in contrast to the FSA rules which can give rise to civil liability where the action is at the suit of a private person[1]. The Principles are widely worded and thus can represent an opportunity for the FSA to successfully bring proceedings where the regulations do not themselves precisely deal with the issue that has arisen. In practice however the vast majority of disciplinary actions for breach of a Principle are likely to involve clear breaches of the other rules.

[1] FSMA 2000, s 150(1).

The eleven FSA principles

1.9 The eleven FSA Principles are as follows.

(1) *Integrity*—a firm must conduct its business with integrity.

(2) *Skill, care and diligence*—a firm must conduct its business with due skill care and diligence.

(3) *Management and control*—a firm must take reasonable care to organise and control its affairs responsibly and effectively, with adequate risk management systems.

(4) *Financial prudence*—a firm must maintain adequate financial resources.

(5) *Market conduct*—a firm must observe proper standards of market conduct.

(6) *Customers' interests*—a firm must pay due regard to the interests of its customers and treat them fairly.

(7) *Communications with customers*—a firm must pay due regard to the information needs of its customers and communicate information to them in a way which is clear, fair and not misleading.

(8) *Conflicts of interest*—a firm must manage conflicts of interest fairly, both between itself and its customers and between one customer and another.

(9) *Customers' relationships of trust*—a firm must take reasonable care to ensure the suitability of its advice and discretionary decisions for any customer who is entitled to rely upon its judgment.

(10) *Customers' assets*—a firm must arrange adequate protection for customers' assets when it is responsible for them.

(11) *Relations with regulators*—a firm must deal with its regulator in an
open and cooperative way, and must tell the FSA promptly of anything
relating to the firm of which the FSA would reasonably expect notice.

APPROVED PERSONS

1.10   All significant individuals involved in a business that requires authorisation by the FSA must be 'approved'. This means that the FSA must be
convinced that the person concerned is fit and proper and has suitable
abilities, relevant qualifications and/or experience and an appropriate level of
honesty and integrity. The people concerned fall into two main groups: those
who carry on controlled functions themselves (such as by advising clients or
arranging contracts and those who manage them); and those who are in such
senior positions that the FSA need to be satisfied that they are suitable.
Examples are: the chief executive; directors; partners (if relevant); senior
managers; compliance officers; money laundering reporting officer; and
finance officer.

1.11   Despite this, the regulated firm remains primarily responsible for
compliance with the regulations. There is however a Code of Practice
affecting approved persons that sets out the conduct to be expected of them.
Its main purpose is to make sure that those people realise the legal
obligations being imposed on them in the area of risk based compliance.

The FSA have determined[1] that controlled functions fall into seven
categories of job function.

---
[1]   FSA Consultation Paper 53 (2000), Chapter 5.

Significant influence functions

Governing body functions

1.12   These consist of being:

- a director of either a company or a holding company;
- a non-executive director of a company;
- a chief executive officer. This is widely interpreted and covers joint
chief executives operating under the immediate control of the board
where there is more than one. In the case of a UK branch of a
non-EEA insurer the role includes the principal UK executive;
- partners and limited partners (where appropriate) are all regarded as
carrying on controlled functions where the firm is primarily carrying
on regulated investment business. Limited partners whose role is that
of an investor are excluded. If a partnership's primary business does
not relate to specified investments but a separate part of the business
does, then provided a distinct partner or set of partners deals with that
aspect of the business, only they need be approved;

- directors of unincorporated associations;
- those directing or regulating the specified activities of a small friendly society;
- sole traders.

Required controlled functions

1.13   There are four of these:

- the director or other senior member responsible for apportionment and oversight;
- the director or senior manager responsible for investment business compliance;
- the money laundering reporting officer; and
- in the case of insurance companies, the appointed actuary.

Management functions

1.14   These consist of the members of senior management reporting to the governing body in relation to the following activities:

- the financial affairs of the firm;
- setting and controlling risk exposure; and
- internal audit.

Significant management functions in relation to business and control

1.15   The functions set out below are added to cover those situations where the firm concerned has senior managers whose function is equivalent to that of a member of the firm's governing body. They do not apply if the activity is a specified activity as this would automatically then be an approved persons' role. They fall into five categories of senior management:

- those operating in relation to investment services, such as the head of equities. This will often be a controlled function in any event;
- those operating in relation to other areas of the firm's business than specified investment activity, eg, head of personal lending or corporate lending, head of credit card issues etc;
- those responsible for carrying out insurance underwriting other than in relation to contractually based investments, eg, head of aviation underwriting;
- those responsible for making decisions concerning the firm's own finances, eg, chief corporate treasurer; and
- those responsible for back office functions.

Temporary and emergency functions

1.16   Should the function of undertaking such a role continue for more than eight weeks in a 12 month period then the person primarily responsible will need to be an approved person.

Dealing with customer functions

1.17 There are nine main functions within this category:

- life and pensions adviser;
- life and pensions advisers when acting under supervision;
- pension transfer advisers—such people can also give ancillary advice in relation to packaged products;
- investment advisers, including those advising in relation to packaged products, but not life and pensions advice;
- investment advisers acting under supervision;
- corporate finance advisers;
- advisers to underwriting members of Lloyd's in relation to becoming a syndicate member;
- customers' trading advisers; and
- investment management function.

Dealing with customers' property

1.18 This covers two main types of activity:

(1) those individuals who deal or arrange deals on behalf of customers (it does not extend to execution only business, and feeding orders into automatic execution systems); and
(2) discretionary fund management.

In addition to the firms being subject to the rules and general principles, approved persons are also subject to a series of ongoing requirements in the form of general principles. Principles 5–7 only apply to those in positions of significant influence whereas the first four apply to all those carrying on investment business.

1.19 The Statements of Principle for Approved Persons are as follows.

(1) An Approved Person must act with integrity in carrying out his controlled function.
(2) An Approved Person must act with due skill, care and diligence in carrying out his controlled function.
(3) An Approved Person must observe proper standards of market conduct in carrying out his controlled function.
(4) An Approved Person must deal with the FSA and with other regulators in an open and co-operative way and must disclose appropriately any information of which the FSA would reasonably expect notice.
(5) An Approved Person performing a significant influence function must take reasonable steps to ensure that the business of the firm for which he is responsible in his controlled function is organised so that it can be controlled effectively.
(6) An Approved Person performing a significant influence function must exercise due skill, care and diligence in managing the business of the firm for which he is responsible in his controlled function.

(7)   An Approved Person performing a significant influence function must take reasonable steps to ensure that the business of the firm for which he is responsible in his controlled function complies with the regulatory requirements imposed on that business.

APPOINTED REPRESENTATIVES

1.20   The FSMA 2000, s 19(1) states:

'No person may carry on a regulated activity in the United Kingdom, or purport to do so, unless he is—

(a)   an authorised person; or

(b)   an exempt person.'

1.21   There is a continuation of the exception that existed under the previous regime whereby the FSMA 2000, s 39 exempts appointed representatives. An 'appointed representative' is defined by the FSMA 2000, s 39(1) as being someone who:

'(a)   is a party to a contract with an unauthorised person ("his principal") which—

(i)   permits or requires him to carry on business of a prescribed description, and

(ii)   complies with such requirements as may be prescribed, and

(b)   is someone for whose activities in carrying on the whole or part of that business his principal has accepted responsibility in writing.'

Anyone satisfying this description as qualified by the Financial Services and Markets Act 2000 (Appointed Representatives) (Amendment) Regulations 2001[1] is exempt from the general prohibition in relation to any regulated activity when they are acting within the remit of the area of business for which their principal has accepted responsibility. Thus the principal will be responsible for the appointed representative's acts[2] and will therefore need to be an authorised person. There is some protection for the principal though, the FSMA 2000, s 39(6) states that 'nothing . . . is to cause the knowledge or intentions of an appointed representative to be attributed to his principal for the purpose of determining whether the principal has committed an offence, unless in all the circumstances it is reasonable for them to be attributed to him'.

Under the FSMA 2000, s 40, applications to carry on regulated activities can be made by individuals as well as corporate entities, partnerships and unincorporated associations.

---

[1]   SI 2001/2508.
[2]   FSMA 2000, s 39(4).

RELEVANT BODIES OTHER THAN THE FINANCIAL SERVICES AUTHORITY

The Bank of England

1.22   Since the Bank of England Act 1998 the Bank's main role has been that of central bank to the United Kingdom. Its functions include:

- setting interest rates for sterling;
- advising the government on economic and monetary policy and implementing agreed monetary policy decisions, mainly through the bank's operations in the markets;
- promoting an efficient and competitive framework for financial activity in the UK, particularly through its involvement in payments and settlements systems;
- responsibility for note issue;
- acting as banker to the commercial banks and to the government;
- acting at its discretion to provide assistance to the money market when it is short of funds, both directly and through the discount houses;
- advising on and managing the government's short and long term borrowings, for which it acts as registrar; and
- managing the nation's gold and foreign currency reserves on behalf of the Treasury.

The Bank's involvement in payment and settlement systems includes membership of APACS (the Association of Payment Clearing Services), active participation in the development of new real-time payment procedures, as well as the provision of the Central Gilts Office and the Central Moneymarkets Office services which provide on-line settlement facilities for gilts and money market instruments.

Lloyd's

1.23   Lloyd's is a society, incorporated by statute, which provides the facilities for the Lloyd's insurance underwriting market to carry on business. In so doing it is overseen by the FSA for regulatory purposes, though managing agents and members agents are also regulated directly. The members, whether individual 'Names' or corporate members, write as members of syndicates managed by managing agents. The members of the syndicates are fully liable for their respective shares of the accepted risk. For this reason any loss they suffer as a result does not potentially give rise to an action under the FSA rules[1]. The insurance business itself falls into four main categories: marine; aviation; non-marine; and motor.

---

[1]   Financial Services and Markets Act 2000 (Rights of Action) Regulations 2001, SI 2001/2256.

1.24   The members do not deal directly with the public. Those requiring insurance will approach a Lloyd's broker. They place business both with Lloyd's syndicates and insurance companies. If it is placed at Lloyd's, the broker will first approach a lead underwriter and then follow up by approaching other underwriters to take a share.

1.25   Lloyd's is now a part of the FSA regulatory regime. Lloyd's syndicate capacity and syndicate membership are specified investments; and advising a person to become or cease to be a member of a Lloyd's syndicate, managing the underwriting capacity of a Lloyd's syndicate as a managing agent, or arranging deals in contracts of insurance written at Lloyd's, are specified activities. The Council of Lloyd's retains the capacity under the Lloyd's Act 1982 to make bye-laws regulating the market and has responsibility for the functioning of it.

1.26   In addition, the FSMA 2000 requires[1] the FSA to keep itself informed about the way in which the Lloyd's Council supervises and regulates the Lloyd's market and the way in which regulated activities are being carried out. The FSA's concern will be twofold: protecting policy holders; and protecting the members who underwrite the policies. The Society of Lloyd's has been made an authorised person[2] and consequently has the authority to carry out its basic market activity, namely 'arranging deals' in contracts of insurance on the Lloyds' market[3]. The relationship between the parties can be varied[4] where the FSA believes that the Society of Lloyd's is failing to satisfy its threshold conditions, has failed to carry on a regulated activity for at least one year, or where the FSA believes it is necessary in the interests of consumers. The FSA can also apply the FSMA 2000 to a member of Lloyd's[5] by applying a general prohibition or a core provision[6] to the carrying on of an insurance market activity, or give a direction to the Council or Society of Lloyds'[7].

---

[1]   FSMA 2000, s 314.
[2]   FSMA 2000, s 315.
[3]   FSMA 2000, s 315(2).
[4]   FSMA 2000, s 45.
[5]   FSMA 2000, s 316(1).
[6]   FSMA 2000, s 317.
[7]   FSMA 2000, s 318.

1.27   In addition to the FSA Principles and Principles for Approved Persons there are also a set of Lloyds' Core Principles for underwriting agents. These are as follows.

(1)   *Integrity*—an agent should observe high standards of integrity and deal openly and fairly.

(2)   *Skill, care and diligence*—an agent should act with due skill, care and diligence.

(3)   *Market conduct*—an agent should observe high standards of conduct and should take all reasonable steps to avoid causing harm to the standing or reputation of Lloyd's.

(4)   *Conduct towards members*—an agent should conduct the affairs of each of the members for whom it acts in a manner which does not unfairly prejudice the interests of any such member.

(5)   *Information*—an agent should seek from members or advisers any information about their circumstances and objectives which might reasonably be expected to be relevant in enabling it to fulfil its responsibilities to them. An agent should take all reasonable steps to give members it advises or for whom it exercises discretion, in a comprehensible and timely way, any information needed to enable them to make balanced and informed decisions. An agent should also be ready to provide members with a full and fair account of the fulfilment of its responsibilities to them.

(6)   *Conflicts of interest*—an agent should seek to avoid any conflict of interest arising, but where a conflict does arise, should make comprehensible and timely disclosure of that conflict and of the steps to be taken to ensure the fair treatment of any members affected. An agent should not unfairly put its own interest above its duty to any members for whom it acts.

(7)   *Assets*—an agent should deal with assets and rights received or held on behalf of a member prudently and in accordance with the terms of any applicable trust deed or agreement with the member.

(8)   *Financial resources*—an agent should maintain adequate financial resources to meet its commitments and to withstand the normal risks to which it is subject.

(9)   *Internal organisation*—an agent should organise and control its internal affairs in a responsible manner, maintaining proper records and systems for the conduct of its business and the management of risk. It should have adequate arrangements to ensure that staff and others whom it employs are suitable, adequately trained and properly supervised and that it has well-defined compliance procedures.

(10) *Relations with Lloyd's*—an agent should deal with Lloyd's in an open and cooperative manner and keep Lloyd's promptly informed of anything concerning the agent which Lloyd's might reasonably expect to be disclosed to it.

1.28   The element of duality in the regulation of Lloyd's between the FSA and the Society of Lloyd's necessitates having arrangements in place to make sure that those being regulated do not find themselves in a position of double jeopardy where complaints were concerned. Thus the FSA and the Society of Lloyd's have agreed a set of working arrangements to assist them with regulation of Lloyd's.

1.29   Complaints by members against each other and against underwriting agents are dealt with by Lloyd's Complaints Department. If that does not resolve matters it can be taken to Lloyd's Arbitration scheme. If the complaint relates to the corporation of Lloyd's itself, it will be taken to Lloyd's Members Ombudsman. Compensation arrangements are dealt with separately from the FSA Compensation Scheme.

The London Stock Exchange

1.30   Since the FSMA 2000 made the FSA the official listing authority, the Exchange's primary role is now in relation to trading equities already in existence. The Board is the governing body of the Exchange and has power to manage the property and affairs of the Stock Exchange. Most importantly it governs strategic policy direction. It also has the power to determine the use of the Exchange's facilities and to manage property belonging to the Exchange, including its acquisition, disposal and letting, borrowing money and the investment of surplus funds. Applicants for membership must have obtained appropriate authorisation to carry on investment business from the FSA, unless they are exempt or in some way excluded from the requirement. Special requirements apply to EU and certain other overseas businesses. Branch membership of the Exchange is permitted and is available to any office that is not the main office of the relevant business, where either the company operating the branch, or another company in its group, is a member of another appropriate investment exchange.

1.31   Settlement of transactions in gilt edged securities is effected either on the basis of payment against documents of title and transfers or through the Central Gilts Office (CGO Service). This operates on a cash against delivery basis and incorporates a system of assured payments, by which each member procures that a settlement bank acting on its behalf undertakes to pay at the end of each business day, the amounts due in respect of securities transferred to that member through the CGO Service on that day.

1.32   London traded options are settled through a clearing house or houses provided by the Council. The current clearing houses are the London Options Clearing House (LOCH), (a wholly owned subsidiary of the stock exchange), which clears all options except currency options; and the International Commodities Clearing House (ICCH) which clears currency options.

The Derivatives Exchanges

1.33   There are three main derivatives exchanges in London: LIFFE; the London Metals Exchange; and the International Petroleum Exchange.

1.34   LIFFE provides exchange facilities to deal in a range of financial futures contracts and options on futures. Both types of contract are traded in relation to a range of currencies, the FTSE 100 index and the FTSE 250 index. Futures contracts alone are traded in relation to Japanese government bonds and stop futures in short equities are available in a range of Spanish, Italian, German and UK contracts. Options alone are traded in: FTSE 100 American style; European style; and FLEX together with a range of equities. LIFFE also trades commodity products, both as futures and options covering cocoa, robusta coffee, potatoes, wheat, barley, and white sugar.

1.35   The London Metal Exchange provides a market for futures and options contracts for aluminium (both alloy and prime grade), copper, lead, nickel, silver, tin and zinc. It administers itself functions and formulates the regulations governing trading, investigates complaints, settles disputes and provides conciliation and arbitration facilities for disputes in respect of transactions relating to the Exchange. Trading is carried out on a twice a day open outcry basis and 24 hour inter office trading.

1.36   The International Petroleum Exchange trades contracts in: Gas Oil Futures, Gas Oil Traded Options; Brent Crude Oil Futures; Brent Crude Oil Traded Options; Natural Gas Futures; and Electricity Backload Futures. Trading is carried out by open outcry.

London Clearing House

1.37   This primarily exists to provide independent central clearing services to London based futures, options and securities markets. It does so for all three of the above exchanges.

It also provides clearing for a range of OTC derivatives[1]. In so doing it carries on the business of a commercial clearing house to regulate and assist the smooth running of the contracts traded. It also affords facilities to secure the performance of these contracts and to ensure the performance of registered contracts following default by a member.

---

[1]   US$, Euros, Yen and Sterling.

1.38   A key element of this clearing process is that it guarantees the performance of the contracts concerned. The contractual process involves a two stage contract of novation: the first of which involves the seller transferring ownership to the Clearing House; and the second involves the Clearing House transferring title to the buyer. The process involves the Clearing House guaranteeing the contract by taking cover and other security from members and taking margin payments by way of security from parties to contracts being registered. The guarantees are also supported by the Clearing House's own capital reserves.

EEA authorities

1.39   Businesses established in another European Economic Area member state and who have their head office there, who are recognised by that state as one of their nationals and who do not carry on investment business from a permanent place of business in the UK are treated as authorised to the extent that the investment laws of that state afford protection to investors equivalent to that afforded in this country. Whether such a state of affairs exists will normally be determined by the Chancellor issuing a certificate to that effect. Passport rights are governed by the FSMA 2000, Sch 3 and in this context 'EEA firm' means, where it does not have its head office in the UK[1], as follows:

- an investment firm[2] authorised by its home state regulator[3];
- a credit institution[4] which is authorised[5] by its home state regulator;
- a financial institution[6] which is a subsidiary[7];
- an undertaking pursuing the activity of direct insurance[8] which is authorised by its home state regulator.

Specific details can be found in the Financial Services and Markets Act 2000 (EEA Passport Rights) Regulations 2001[9].

[1]   FSMA 2000, Sch 3, para 5.
[2]   As defined by the European Council Directive on Investment Services in the Securities Field (Investment Services Directive), Council Directive 93/22/EEC, art 1.2.
[3]   Investment Services Directive, Council Directive 93/22/EEC, art 3.
[4]   As defined in the First Banking Co-ordination Directive, Council Directive 77/780/EEC, art 1.
[5]   Also see the First Banking Co-ordination Directive, Council Directive 77/780/EEC, art 1.
[6]   As defined by the Second Banking Co-ordination Directive, Council Directive 89/646/EEC, art 1.
[7]   A 'subsidiary' of the type mentioned in the Second Banking Co-ordination Directive, Council Directive 89/646/EEC, art 18.2 which fulfils the conditions in art 18.
[8]   Within the meaning of the First Life Insurance Directive, Council Directive 72/267EEC, art 1 or of the First Non-Life Insurance Directive, Council Directive 73/239/EEC.
[9]   SI 2001/2511.

WHOLESALE MARKET ACTIVITIES

The Inter-Professionals Code and the London Code of Conduct

1.40   From 2002/3 wholesale market activities will be regulated by the Code on Inter-Professional Conduct (IPC). It exists as a chapter of the Market Conduct Sourcebook within the *FSA's Handbook of Rules and Guidance*. It is primarily aimed at market professionals with a view to promoting market confidence and standards of market conduct in an environment that will remain primarily self-disciplining. In addition it sets out the transitional arrangements for the training and competence regime for 's 43 brokers'. These are brokers and listed money market institutions who, together with their employers, were exempt from the financial services regime provided the firm was on a list issued by the regulator. As this used to be exempt from the Financial Services Act 1986 (FSA 1986) by s 43 it became known as 'the s 43 list'.

1.41   The two main categories of institution operating in the money markets are brokers and market makers. Brokers are those who act to bring together the independent counterparties to a transaction. Market makers, as their name implies, hold themselves out as being willing to make prices in the instruments concerned on a continual basis. There is however no legal commitment on market makers in the wholesale markets to make prices regardless of conditions in the market. Most of these need to be authorised by the FSA as they take deposits. However, not all of them are banks.

1.42   The IPC will also govern wholesale counterparties, who are those who have entered into a transaction above the minimum limits within the last 18 months, with, or as a result of arrangements by a firm on the FSA list. Such a transaction must be on one of the instruments listed in the London Code of Conduct, paras 6–13. A wholesale counterparty cannot be a listed institution.

1.43   Most of the instruments traded on the wholesale markets are short-term and all such instruments are covered by the IPC. However, the FSA is not responsible for supervising transactions in instruments traded by a recognised investment exchange. The rules of the exchange and the Principles, subject to those rules will apply. In addition the FSA could become involved primarily in the fields of market abuse.

1.44   Transactions are exempt where:

- both parties are wholesale counterparties; or
- both are on the s 43 list; or
- one is a listed institution and the other is a wholesale counterparty.

For a sale and repurchase agreement to be exempt, both counterparties must be listed institutions and acting as principal.

1.45   Turning to a comparison of the new IPC with the old London Code of Conduct a number of points become apparent. The main point is that the IPC guidance is less prescriptive and less detailed, eg the guidance on quotes and on brokers visiting each others dealing rooms and sharing confidential and/or market sensitive information. However, the essential behavioural requirements remain essentially the same. A key factor here will be FSA Principles 1 and 5, which together with a degree of guidance in the IPC will control the giving of gifts. The new approach no longer involves specific guidance on dealing mandates and prompt payment of brokerage. There is also a less detailed approach to confirmations and how often they should be checked. There is a slight change in the approach to taping. Currently relevant data must be taped and retained for two months. Under the IPC it should be done where necessary to provide a record and then kept as such. This may involve tapes being kept for up to three years. Market practice is reflected in a level playing field being applied between OTC and on exchange transactions. Activities on exchanges are however stated to be governed by the FSA Principles, subject to the exchange rules.

1.46   The FSA have indicated that isolated departures from the IPC will not normally cause FSA action, though that would of course be determined by what exactly the departure consisted of.

The Non-Investments Products Code (NIPs Code)

1.47   Some of the firms carrying on investment business will also be carrying on other financial business outside the scope of the FSA regime. In the past such activities have been covered by the London Code of Conduct. This is being replace by the Non-Investment Business Code which is intended to articulate good market practice. It has been designed to operate alongside the Inter-Professionals Code and the FSA Conduct of Business Rules as many firms will be carrying on businesses, different parts of which will be covered by each.

1.48   The NIPs Code applies to:

- sterling wholesale deposits;
- foreign currency wholesale deposits;
- gold and silver bullion wholesale deposits;

- spot and forward foreign exchange; and
- spot and forward gold and silver bullion.

It does not affect deposit taking activities or debt securities, the issuance of which amounts to deposit taking.

The FSA expect management to take account of the NIPs Code, where appropriate, in running their business. An analysis of the content of the Code is however beyond the scope of this book.

PROFESSIONALS AND INVESTMENT BUSINESS

Introduction

1.49 The FSMA 2000 has radically altered the arrangements for regulating solicitors, accountants and actuaries whose practices carry on investment business. Under the new regime those carrying on regulated activities[1] need to be regulated by the FSA. However, there are exemptions for professionals carrying on investment business where this arises out of, or is a necessary adjunct to the professional services being provided to the client[2]. Instances where this is likely to arise with solicitors are: probate and trusts; conveyancing; litigation; divorce; and corporate finance and takeovers. In the case of accountants it is likely to be limited to the last two of these.

---

[1] See para 1.52.
[2] FSMA 2000, s 332(4).

1.50 This regulatory approach is largely a continuation of the 'incidental' exception under the pre-FSMA 2000 regime. The nature of 'incidental' is in line with its normal meaning. The existence of this approach is a consequence of the Investment Services Directive[1] which exempts from the definition of 'investment firms' those who are *providing an investment service where that service is provided in an incidental manner in the course of a professional activity*. This may occur either because of the relative scale of the investment work to the legal task concerned, whether or not the investment business had been held out as being a separate task in the first place, and because of how the firm promotes its activities via the media. This also brings into play the financial promotion rules, which are dealt with in Chapter 3.

---

[1] Council Directive 93/22/EEC.

1.51 The old recognised professional bodies are now termed 'designated professional bodies'. Those designated are[1]:

- the Law Society of England and Wales;
- the Law Society of Northern Ireland;
- the Law Society of Scotland;
- the Institute of Chartered Accountants in England and Wales;
- the Institute of Chartered Accountants in Scotland;

- the Institute of Chartered Accountants in England;
- the Chartered Association of Certified Accountants; and
- the Institute of Actuaries.

These bodies are therefore able to supervise firms carrying on exempt regulated activities. If the firm carries on investment work outside the definition of exempt regulated activities then they must be regulated by the FSA.

---

[1] Pursuant to the FSMA 2000, s 326 and the Financial Services and Markets Act 2000 (Designated Professional Bodies) Order 2001, SI 2001/1226.

Exempt regulated activities

1.52   These are determined by the FSMA 2000, ss 325(2). In addition, the FSMA 2000, s 327(3) requires that the professional person concerned should not be taking any fee or other financial benefit for the work concerned other than one which is being accounted for to the client. This means that the funds must be held to the order of the client[1]. The firm can offset any commission received on the client's behalf against any fee owed by that client, but the offset can only be done on or after the date on which a bill of costs has been drawn up to that effect[2]. The rule also requires that the client has given informed consent to this prior to agreement for the solicitor to keep the commission. The client must have had explained to them that the commission belongs to the client[3] and that the full amount(s) have been disclosed. Commission of less than £20 is no longer exempt on a de minimis basis. This is because the Scope Rules, rule 4(c)[4] (passed pursuant to the FSMA 2000, s 327(3)) overrides Solicitors' Practice Rules, rule 10 in this regard.

---

[1] This is a continuation of the principle in the Solicitors' Practice Rules 1990, rule 10.
[2] Solicitors' Accounts Rules 1998, rules 19 and 22.
[3] FSA Perimeter Guidance, Section 1.9.
[4] Financial Services (Scope) Rules 2001.

1.53   As the work concerned must be being carried out as one that is incidental to the professional activity concerned[1] other identifiable legal work must therefore be carried out to which the investment business work must be adjunct. It follows that it is not possible for a firm to carry out even a one-off regulated activity in isolation that is not incidental.

---

[1] FSMA 2000, s 327(4).

1.54   The FSMA 2000[1] also gives power to the Treasury to pass regulations determining the activities that cannot be carried on by those acting under the umbrella of exempt regulated activities. Pursuant to this the Financial Services and Markets Act 2000 (Professions) (Non-Exempt Activities) Order 2001[2] has been passed which excludes:

- accepting deposits;
- effecting and carrying out contracts of insurance;

- dealing in investments as principal,
- establishing, operating or winding up a collective investment scheme;
- establishing, operating or winding up a stakeholder pension scheme;
- managing the underwriting capacity of a Lloyd's syndicate;
- acting as provider of a funeral plan contract; and
- acting as a lender in relation to, or administering a regulated mortgage contract.

The firm must not carry on, or hold itself out as carrying on, such regulated activities.

---

[1]   FSMA 2000, s 327(6).
[2]   SI 2001/1227.

Solicitors' Rules

1.55   The Solicitors' Financial Services (Scope) Rules 2001 have been issued with a view to determining the financial services activities of those firms of solicitors that are not regulated by the FSA. They also set out the conditions and restrictions that apply to such firms. The activities that are prohibited of necessity parallel those set out in the Non-Exempt Activities Order referred to above[1]. However, the Law Society has taken matters a little further in that it debars the activities of:

- buying, selling, subscribing for or underwriting investments as principal where the firm holds itself out as engaging in the business of buying such investments with a view to selling them; or holding itself out as engaging in the business of underwriting investments of the kind to which the transaction relates; or regularly soliciting the public to enter into transaction with the firm; or
- buying or selling investments with a view to stabilising or maintaining the market price of those investments.

---

[1]   Financial Services and Markets Act 2000 (Professions) (Non-Exempt Activities) Order 2001, SI 2001/1227. See also para 1.54.

1.56   If a firm carries on regulated activities, certain conditions must be met. These are:

- the activity must arise out of, or be complementary to, the provision of the professional legal services which the firm is providing;
- the provision of the service must be in a manner which is incidental to the carrying on of professional legal business;
- any financial benefit accruing to the firm as a result must be accounted for to the client;
- the firm must neither hold itself out as carrying out, nor carry out a regulated activity, unless it is either allowed by the Law Society Rules or occurs because the firm is an exempt person; and
- there are no other legal FSA rules or statutory instruments that debar doing so.

Other restricted activities

1.57   There are also a range of five other restricted areas where activities may be carried out but only subject to restrictions.

Packaged products

1.58   Packaged products are life policies, units or shares in regulated collective investments schemes or investment trust savings schemes (whether or not held in an ISA or PEP), or a stakeholder pension scheme. With the exception of personal pension schemes, these cannot be recommended by a firm, except in certain situations. These are: where the firm is recommending or arranging for a client to be assigned the product; where the firm is doing this as a consequence of the firm managing assets; or where a transaction is arranged for a client on an execution only basis.

Personal pension schemes

1.59   A firm cannot recommend that a client buys or disposes of an interest in a personal pension scheme. If the arrangement does not include a pension transfer or opt out, the firm can make arrangements on a client's behalf, but only where there are reasonable grounds for the firm to assume that the client is not relying on them for advice on the merits or suitability of the arrangement concerned.

Securities and derivatives

1.60   A firm cannot recommend that a client buys or subscribes to such a security or arrangement where the transaction would be made with a person who carries on the business of buying, selling, subscribing for or underwriting the investment, regardless of whether that person is acting as agent or principal. This rule applies not only to investments currently being traded on an investment exchange or other market but also to client responses to invitations to subscribe for new issues of such investments.

1.61   There are exceptions to this rule. It only applies where the client is an individual, and where that individual is not; either acting in connection with carrying on a business as a result of which the client would become a controller[1] of that firm, or where that individual is acting as a trustee of an occupational pension scheme.

---
[1]   There is a statutory definition of this in the FSMA 2000, s 422.

Discretionary management

1.62   A firm cannot carry out discretionary fund management on behalf of a client except in certain very limited circumstances. These arise where the firm is a trustee, donee of a power of attorney, or a receiver appointed by the Court of Protection. In any of these instances the day-to-day decisions concerning the fund management must be taken by an authorised person with appropriate permission. Likewise any decision regarding entering transactions and buying or subscribing for investments must be undertaken in accordance with an authorised person's advice. Again the authorisation must be with relevant permission.

Corporate finance

1.63 A firm cannot act as sponsor to a securities issue to be dealt with on the London Stock Exchange, or act as a nominated adviser in relation to a securities issue to be admitted for dealing on the Alternative Investment Market.

Breach of Solicitors' Rules

1.64 The Law Society take into account the guidance they have provided in relation to the rules when determining whether a firm had acted in breach of them. In this respect they mirror the behaviour of the FSA. A breach of the rules could have a number of consequences according to the circumstances. A criminal offence could have been committed under the FSMA 2000[1] and/or the firm could be deemed to be no longer fit and proper[2] and thus be made subject to an order preventing them from carrying on regulated activities.

---

[1] FSMA 2000, s 23.
[2] FSMA 2000, s 329(1).

Areas of a solicitor's work which may be affected

1.65 The areas affected are essentially the same as under the previous regime. They are as follows.

Acting as attorney

1.66 Any power of attorney which grants the right to manage investments will bring the financial services regime into play and the firm would need an appropriate degree of authorisation from the FSA unless they could fit within the limited areas permitted by the Solicitors' Financial Services (Scope) Rules 2001.

Conveyancing

1.67 Land is not a specified investment, but mortgages now are. However, only entering into arrangements as lender or administering are regulated activities in this context. Thus the areas of a solicitors' work affected will tend to be involved in giving advice in relation to mortgages, endowment mortgages and other specialised types of investment related mortgages, since the investment element is covered by the definition of 'specified investments'.

1.68 For such activities to be carried on the firm would need to be regulated by the FSA and the member of the firm providing the advice be authorised to do so. If such a state of affairs does not exist the firm could arrange for advice to be given to the client by a permitted third party. That is the firm could introduce the client to an independent adviser who has the appropriate authorisation and is in a legal position to do so.

1.69   A common problem arises where the client has been recommended to a particular firm of solicitors by a bank or building society. They in turn may have arranged a mortgage which may be an endowment or investment related mortgage. Now that mortgages are specified investments it should be the case that the bank or building society have suggested a mortgage that it is suitable to the needs of that client. However, as most banks and building societies are a part of tied groups, any associated products they recommend will be from within their own range. The solicitor may have reasons to suspect that the client may get a better endowment policy or investment arrangement elsewhere. The solicitor may only provide advice on this if the firm is appropriately authorised and even then the person making the suggestion must be authorised. As the Solicitors' Practice Rules, rule 1 provides an overriding obligation to always act in the client's best interests, the solicitor may well feel that they must do something. The best approach for solicitors whose firms are not authorised by the FSA would be to suggest to the client that they take independent financial advice. If the firm cannot provide this, the client can be told how they may find an independent financial adviser—one could be recommended or an introduction made.

1.70   The solicitor will not be providing independent advice if all that has been explained to the client is the difference between a repayment mortgage, an endowment mortgage, or any other type of mortgage. This generic advice does not require authorised status.

Management companies

1.71   In relation to leasehold companies, it is sometimes the case that a management company is set up and the various lessees utilise it to give them all a controlling interest in the freehold. As shares are a specified investment any specified activity in relation to them would be covered by the regulatory regime. This would include acting, advising, or arranging for a client to hold such shares. However, as such shares would have a nominal value the FSA may accept that it falls within the complimentary to legal services exemption.

Agencies

1.72   Some solicitors act as agencies for building societies. This is normally limited in practice to accepting deposits on the building society's behalf and making repayments. The firm will have to be covered by the building society's authorised status. A further issue arises when a client of the building society agency asks for advice with regard to the investments related to the building society's products. If the building society offers independent financial advice the solicitor could arrange for this to be done. However, if they are tied, the solicitor should either advise the client to take independent legal advice or provide it himself if appropriately authorised.

1.73 Solicitors sometimes act as intermediaries with insurance companies. They must be careful not to carry on any regulated activity in so doing, as insurance business is now a regulated investment activity.

Corporate work

1.74 Shares, debentures and warrants are all categorised as specified investments. Many activities in connection with companies which involve managing, advising or dealing are therefore covered by the regime. There is the exclusion at the Financial Services and Markets Act 2000 (Regulated Activities) Order 2001, art 15(2)[1] which covers dealing in investments as principal where the investments concerned are a holding of over 20% of the shares in a company and the owner seeks to buy the shares of the other shareholders, or sell his shares to them. It is only possible to advise on the purchase of shares where, as a result of the transaction, the buyer becomes a controller of the company. A 'controller' is defined by the FSMA 2000, s 422(2) as anyone who holds 10% or more of the shares in a company or its parent undertaking, or who is able to exercise a significant influence on the company's management.

---

[1] SI 2001/544.

1.75 General corporate work of a legal nature may on occasion require the giving of advice in relation to shares, debentures or warrants. The exception to the need for authorisation by the FSA where the advice is complimentary to the provision of legal services will normally apply here.

Court of Protection

1.76 Solicitors appointed to act as receivers will not be covered by the FSMA 2000 when carrying on portfolio management unless they do so on a discretionary basis.

Litigation

1.77 This is likely to arise as an issue where a client has obtained money by way of damages in court proceedings and now wishes to take advice on how they should be invested. Firms should suggest that the client takes independent financial advice. Those who are suitably authorised will be able to offer to provide it themselves.

Divorce

1.78 In divorce cases, a problem that commonly arises is that solicitors leave clients to surrender life policies on endowment mortgages when the matrimonial home is sold. Such clients should always be advised to seek independent financial advice. In some instances there is also the matter of life policies taken out for the protection of the other party or any children. Any advice in relation to whether these should be cancelled amount to carrying on investment business. In many cases, allowing clients to proceed and cancel policies without suggesting they take advice probably amounts to negligence. It will often make sense to convert joint policies to single ones in these instances. If one is to be terminated there is an active second hand market in the 'with profits' element and arranging to sell these normally secures a higher return than cancellation. In the cases of policies that are well advanced the client will often be better off financially by retaining them due to the high terminal bonuses that often apply.

1.79 The other possibility is that a settlement agreement in relation to a company may involve the transfer of shares, debentures or warrants or a combination of these. Any activity in relation to these beyond the 'complimentary to' exception would require authorisation.

Private client work

1.80 This does not raise any issues other than those already discussed, where they might arise in the private client department. The area that has given rise to some discussion is that of schemes providing investments arrangements to provide for future school fees. Typically these consist of an investment scheme being offered to the public, whereby they can invest funds over a period of years to provide sufficient return to cover the fees of a particular public school. Such arrangements are usually caught by the definition of 'collective investment schemes'. As a result they will be covered by the regulatory regime.

Probate work

1.81 This area of work will normally involve the firm operating within the 'complimentary to' exception and therefore the bulk of it should not give rise to problems.

Trusts

1.82 Acting as trustee may involve carrying on specified investment activities. If so appropriate, authorisation should be sought from the FSA unless the firm is operating within the exemptions. Alternately, the firm could enter into an arrangement with a suitably authorised firm to enable the relevant work to be sub-contracted to them.

Conduct of business

Introduction

1.83 The Solicitors' Financial Services (Conduct of Business) Rules 2001 determine the requirements imposed on those firms that carry on the narrow range of financial services work that can be done by those firms which do not have FSA authorisation. It also applies to those who are regulated by the FSA but the activity being properly carried out is not a regulated activity.

Status disclosure

1.84 Before a firm provides a regulated activity it must provide to the client in writing:

- a statement that they are not authorised by the FSA;
- which regulated activities are being carried out and the fact that they are limited in scope;
- that the firm is regulated by the Law Society; and
- a statement that complaints and redress can be dealt with through the Law Society.

Execution of transactions

1.85 Once a transaction has been decided on, or the firm has a discretion to act and has so decided, this should be done as soon as possible. The firm has a discretion to delay, but only where to do so is in the client's best interests[1].

---

[1] In this context see also the Solicitors' Practice Rules 1990, rules 1 and 15.

Records

1.86 Transaction records must be kept showing the client's name, the terms of the instruction and their date. If the transaction occurs because of instructions given by the firm to a third party the record should show the client's name, the terms, the date and the name of the party instructed by the firm.

1.87 Records of commission received in relation to regulated activities should also be kept. This could be by a file copy of a letter, or the bill of costs. It should show the amount and how the firm has accounted to the client for the money.

1.88 If the regulated activity of safeguarding and keeping the title to investments is carried out, the firm must keep records of the same. They should also retain a copy of the client's instructions to pass to any third party, and a receipt from any person to whom the investments were sent.

1.89 If the firm should arrange a packaged product for a client on an execution only basis, the firm must send written confirmation to the client stating that the client neither sought, nor was given advice by the firm in relation to the transaction. If advice were given within the confines of an exempt regulated activity there needs to be a confirmation that the client then confirmed that the transaction should be carried out. The confirmation should also state that the transaction was carried out on the client's instructions and reflected those instructions.

INVESTMENT BUSINESS IN THE UK

Specified investments

1.90   The Financial Services and Markets Act 2000 (Regulated Activities) Order 2001[1] provides full definitions of specified investments and activities. It should, however, be borne in mind that the distinctions that used to exist between the FSA 1986 regime and the Investment Services Directive still survive[2]. Thus, a firm that is qualified under the Directive must be congniscent of the Directive as well, in particular with regard to any exclusions that might apply[3].

---

[1]   SI 2001/544, Pts II and III.
[2]   HM Treasury, *Financial Services and Markets Bill*, Regulated Activities—Consultation Document, February 1999, part 3, p 1.
[3]   FSMA 2000, Sch 3.

Regulated activities, specified investments and specified activities

Specified investments

1.91   As far as the Financial Services and Markets Act 2000 (Regulated Activities) Order 2001, SI 2001/544, is concerned, the investments that are specified are as follows.

Deposits

1.92   The investment itself is effectively left undefined but there is a definition of 'accepting deposits' at para 1.119 below.

Contracts of insurance

1.93   These are defined in SI 2001/544, Sch 1. The definition covers the following categories of insurance policy: accident; sickness; land vehicles; railway rolling stock; aircraft; ships; goods in transit; fire and natural forces; damage to property; motor vehicle liability; aircraft liability; liability of ships; general liability; credit; suretyship; miscellaneous financial loss; legal expenses; travel assistance; life and annuity; marriage and birth; linked long term; permanent health; tontines; capital redemption contracts; pension fund management; collective insurance contracts and social insurance.

Shares

1.94   This is widely defined as[1]:
> 'shares or stock in the share capital of—
> (a)   any body corporate (wherever incorporated), and
> (b)   any unincorporated body constituted under the law of a country or territory outside the United Kingdom'.

It also includes deferred shares within the meaning of the Building Societies Act 1986, s 119 and any transferable shares in a body incorporated under the UK law relating to industrial and provident societies or credit unions, or under equivalent laws in other EEA states.

---

¹ SI 2001/544, art 76.

1.95 Shares were defined by Farwell J as being 'the interest of a share-holder in the company measured by a sum of money, for the purpose of liability in the first place, and of interest in the second, but also consisting of a series of mutual covenants entered into by all the shareholders inter se'[1]. The definition appears to extend to stock[2].

---

¹ *Borland's Trustee v Steel Bros & Co Ltd* [1901] 1 Ch 279 at 288.
² Companies Act 1985, s 744.

1.96 The definition in SI 2001/544 excludes shares in open ended invest-ment companies, building societies, industrial and provident societies, credit unions or an equivalent entity in another EEA jurisdiction.

Instruments creating or acknowledging indebtedness

1.97 The definition of debenture is a wide one (as was that in the FSA 1986, Sch 1). In addition to normal debentures, loan stock and bonds, it includes certificates of deposit and any other instrument creating or acknowledging indebtedness.

1.98 It is generally accepted that 'debenture' has never been properly defined[1]. The most widely accepted definition is that of Chitty J[2], who described a debenture as being 'a document which either creates a debt or acknowledges it'. This is the wording adopted by SI 2001/544, and as a result of it being so wide certain other financial instruments are excluded, namely:

- an instrument acknowledging indebtedness for money borrowed to provide the cost of goods or services;
- cheques, bills of exchange, bank drafts and letters of credit, but not a bill of exchange accepted by a banker;
- bank notes and bank statements, a lease or other disposition of property or a heritable security; and
- contracts of insurance.

---

¹ See for example Dine *Company Law* (2nd edn, 1994) p 262 and Simon Morris *Financial Services; Regulating Investment Business* (1st edn, 1990) p 128.
² *Levy v Abercorris Slate and Slab Co* (1887) 37 Ch D 260.

Government and public securities

1.99 This covers loan stock, bonds and other instruments issued by central, regional and local governments in the EEA. Excluded are those instruments excluded under 'debentures' above[1] and instruments issued by the National Savings Bank, under the National Loans Act 1968 and under the National Debt Act 1972, s 11(3).

---

[1]   See paras 1.97 and 1.98.

Warrants

1.100   The definition applies regardless of whether the instrument relates to something that is, or is not, already in existence. They have been defined as: 'transferable option certificates issued by companies and trusts which entitle the holder to buy a specific number of shares in that company at a specific price . . . at a specific time in the future'[1]. As is made clear in the definition this state of affairs applies regardless of whether the shares are already in existence.

---

[1]   McHattie *The Investor's Guide to Warrants* (1992) p 1.

Certificates representing securities

1.101   These are certificates providing contractual rights in respect of shares[1], instruments creating or acknowledging indebtedness[2], government and public securities[3], and warrants[4], where the interest is held by someone other than the person on whom the rights are conferred and where the transfer can be carried out without the consent of that person. This paragraph effectively debars the creation of investments which amount to an indirect interest so as to facilitate carrying on business in such investments outside the jurisdiction of the FSA regime.

---

[1]   See para 1.94.
[2]   See para 1.97.
[3]   See para 1.99.
[4]   See para 1.100.

1.102   Excluded are instruments conferring rights in respect of two or more investments issued by different persons, or in respect of two or more types of government or public security issued by the same person. The first of these exclusions covers legal and equitable mortgages because such an arrangement involves a transfer of property interest from the party granting the mortgage to that receiving it[1].

---

[1]   A charge on the other hand only amounts to a proprietary interest.

Units in collective investment schemes

1.103   Such schemes are defined in the FSMA 2000, s 235 as:

'(1) . . . any arrangements with respect to property of any description, including money, the purpose or effect of which is to enable persons taking part . . . (whether by becoming owners of the property or any part of it or otherwise) to participate in or receive profits or income arising from the acquisition, holding, management or disposal of the property or sums paid out of such profits or income.

(2) The arrangements must be such that the persons who are to participate . . . do not have day-to-day control over the management of the property, whether or not they have the right to be consulted or to give directions.

(3) The arrangements must also have either or both of the following characteristics—

(a)   the contributions of the participants and the profits or income out of which payments are to be made to them are pooled;

(b)   the property is managed as a whole by or on behalf of the operator of the scheme.'

1.104   If the property is held on trust for the participants, the fund will be known as a unit trust[1]. An open ended investment company on the other hand is a collective investment scheme where the property concerned belongs beneficially to and is managed by or on behalf of a body corporate[2]. The aim of such a scheme must be to spread investment risk and give the members the benefit. The investment must however appear to a reasonable investor to be one from which he can realise the investment within a reasonable period and be satisfied that the value of that investment would be calculated by reference to the value of property into which the scheme has invested.

---

[1]   FSMA 2000, s 237.
[2]   FSMA 2000, s 236.

Rights under stakeholder pension schemes

1.105   These are defined by the Welfare Reform and Pensions Act 1999, s 1 which in essence states that such a scheme is one which is registered with OPRA (Occupational Pensions Regulatory Authority) and meets a series of conditions which are set out in the Welfare Reform and Pensions Act 1999, s 1(2)–(9) and any others that may be added by statutory instrument.

Options

1.106   The definition covers options to buy or sell:

- a security or contractually based investment;
- UK or foreign currency; or
- palladium, platinum, gold or silver.

1.107   There are two main categories: put options—which involve the party paying a deposit acquiring the right to sell one of the above commodities whilst the counterparty takes on the obligation to buy; and call options— which operate in reverse. The party paying a deposit acquires a right to buy whilst the counterparty must sell. In each instance the party who has the right to perform can also decide to walk away from the contract and the only cost to them will be the loss of the deposit. Their counterparty has no such right.

Futures

1.108   This covers rights under a contract to sell a commodity or property, where the price is agreed now but delivery is in the future, where such an agreement is made for an investment rather than a commercial purpose. A contract will be regarded as being for investment purposes if it is traded on a recognised investment exchange or where it is not but is expressed to be traded as such. A contract will be regarded as being for commercial purposes if delivery is to be made within seven days or where one of the parties is a producer of the commodity or property or uses it in their business, or where delivery is intended.

1.109   The contract must be for sale, hire, loan or bailment. In practice it is usually a contract for sale. The definition has been widened, for example to cover a weakness in the previous definition that did not clearly cover futures contracts in indexes[1].

---

[1]   Compare the Financial Services and Markets Act 2000 (Regulated Activities) Order 2001, SI 2001/544, art 84(3) and (7) with the Financial Services Act 1986, Sch 1, para 8.

Contracts for differences

1.110   This covers agreements, the aim of which is to secure a profit or avoid a loss, by either or both of the parties by reference to fluctuations in the value of property or an index or other factor. There are two types of contract which would potentially appear to be caught by this wording: swaps and forward rate agreements.

1.111   Swap contracts exist in a number of forms, but essentially they all consist of a contractual arrangement whereby two counterparties will agree to notionally swap similar or dissimilar assets or debts. The original type— currency swaps—evolved as a method of circumventing exchange control restrictions prior to their suspension in 1979[1]. Rather than use traditional methods, such as parallel and back-to-back loans, the parties would enter into a spot exchange transaction to sell one currency and use a forward exchange contract to reverse the original contract. As loans were not being made as such it did not constitute borrowing and the transaction could be left off the balance sheet. Any necessary payments between the parties were then made on a net basis, commonly every six months. The net major development was the emergence of the interest rate swap, where one party who had a greater quantity of fixed rate debt that they wished to retain, arranged with a counterparty who had a surplus of floating rate debt to 'swap' the respective debts. The arrangement did not consist of a transfer- ence of the legal title to the debts but the periodic payment of net amounts needed to place the parties in the financial position they would have been had the legal transfer of the debt taken place. Recent years have seen the emergence of a wide range of swap contracts of which the most important are credit swaps where one party exchanges an income stream against another's equity holdings. This can facilitate a transfer of risk that better suits the respective parties' financial needs.

---

[1] Haynes and Penn *The Law and Practice of International Banking* (2nd edn, 2002) Chapter 8.

1.112 Contracts under which delivery is going to take place to one of the parties, and contracts in relation to money deposits where interest or another return will be paid by reference to fluctuations in an index or other factor are excluded from the definition. Also excluded are contracts in relation to deposits at the National Savings Bank, or money raised under the National Loans Act 1968, or under the National Debt Act 1972, s 11(3).

Lloyd's syndicate capacity and syndicate membership

1.113 Lloyd's is an insurance underwriting market. Those who underwrite risks are the underwriters who work in syndicates to spread the risk between them. They do not carry all this risk themselves but spread it to 'names' in return for passing them a share of the premium. These names fall into two categories. The traditional names, who are wealthy individuals, risk all their assets in return for a premium income and the corporate names take on limited liability in return for premium income on behalf of their shareholders. Syndicate capacity and membership are specified investments.

1.114 Largely as a consequence of the problems that beset Lloyd's in the 1990s, the Council of Lloyd's that traditionally ran the market is now subject to oversight by the FSA. The FSMA 2000, s 314 requires the FSA to keep itself informed about the Council's running of Lloyd's and the manner in which regulated activities are being carried out with a view to exercising their own powers if necessary.

Funeral plan contracts

1.115 This issue is discussed below at para 1.138.

Regulated mortgage contracts

1.116 This is arguably the most important addition to the range of investments covered by the financial services regulatory regime. It is for most people the largest or second largest financial investment they make. Although the banks and other main lending institutions had adopted a code of practice with regard to mortgage lending, the involvement of the FSA now means that tighter control can be taken of advice given to those taking out one of the various types of mortgage contract now available.

Rights or interests in investments

1.117 Essentially this covers any right or interest in the above. Excluded are interests under trusts of an occupational pension scheme and certain interests in contracts of insurance or under certain trusts. This is effectively a safety net provision to catch instruments that would otherwise have been covered by one of the above but are technically outside it, for example, because the beneficiary of the investment has a legal or equitable charge or mortgage over the property or a beneficial interest in a trust rather than a direct involvement with the investment.

Specified activities

1.118   The Financial Services and Markets Act 2000 (Regulated Activities) Order 2001, SI 2001/544 also defines the activities that are regulated in the new regime where they relate to specified investments. These activities are as follows.

Accepting deposits

1.119   This covers the receipt of deposits that will be repaid, either with or without interest, and either on demand or at another time agreed by the parties. It does not cover payments referable to the provision of property other than currency, or services or giving security. There are a range of exclusions, namely sums paid by:

- central banks in Europe;
- an authorised person who has permission to accept deposits;
- EEA authorised firms;
- the National Savings Bank;
- a municipal bank;
- Keesler Federal Credit Union;
- a certified school bank;
- local authorities;
- a body which is enacted to issue a precept to local authorities in England and Wales or by requisition in Scotland;
- the European Community, the European Atomic Energy Community or the European Coal and Steel Community;
- the European Investment Bank;
- the International Bank for Reconstruction and Development;
- the International Finance Corporation;
- the International Monetary Fund;
- the African Development Bank;
- the Asian Development Bank;
- the Caribbean Development Bank;
- the Inter-American Development Bank;
- the European Bank for Reconstruction and Development;
- the Council of Europe Resettlement Fund.

Also sums paid by any other party in the course of wholly or significantly carrying on the business of money lending; sums paid by one company to another where they are both members of the same group or when the same individual is a majority shareholder in both of them; or the making of a payment by a person who is a close relative of the person receiving it or who is a close relative of a director or manager of that person or a partner in it. Likewise, a sum received by a solicitor, or anyone dealing in investments, acting as agent in relation to investments, arranging deals in investments, managing investments, or establishing, operating or winding up a collective investment scheme or stakeholder pension scheme. Also excluded are sums received in consideration of the issue of debt securities.

Insurance

1.120 This covers both effecting and carrying out a contract of insurance. Excluded from this are where such contracts are effected or carried out by an EEA firm falling within the FSMA 2000, Sch 3, para 5(d) and motor vehicle breakdown insurance. Contracts of insurance are defined in SI 2001/544, Sch 1 in two main categories—general and long-term insurance. These are explained at para 1.93.

Dealing in investments as principal

1.121 This covers buying, selling, subscribing for or underwriting securities or contractually based investments (other than funeral plan contracts and rights to, or interests in, investments). Excluded are situations where the person concerned holds themselves out as willing to deal at prices determined by him generally and continuously or hold themselves out as engaging in the business of buying or underwriting investments of the type concerned. Also excluded are those who hold over 20% of the shares in a company and who seek to buy the shares of other shareholders or sell those shares to them, or someone acting on behalf of such a person. Finally, there is a general exception for those whose head office is outside the UK and whose ordinary business consists of dealing as principal or agent, arranging, managing, safeguarding and administering investments and advising on investments. Likewise those who are establishing, running or winding up a collective investment scheme or stakeholder pension scheme, and, where relevant, those agreeing to carry on any of these.

1.122 This category does not extend to those who:

- enter into contractually based transactions with or through an authorised or exempt person;
- accept instruments creating or acknowledging indebtedness;
- are companies issuing shares or share warrants;
- are contracting as principal in relation to options and contracts for differences where the counterparties are not individuals and the principal is contracting with a view to limiting an identifiable business risk other than one arising as a result of regulated activities (or matters that would be regulated activities but for the exclusions in SI 2001/544, Pt III);
- trustees;
- contracts for the sale of goods and supply of services;
- groups and joint enterprises;
- sale of a body corporate; and
- overseas persons.

Dealing in investments as agent

1.123   This covers buying, selling, subscribing for or underwriting securities or contractually based investments (other than funeral plan contracts and rights or interests in specified investments) as agent.

1.124   The exclusions are:

- dealing through authorised persons where the transaction is entered into or the advice given to the client by an authorised person, or where it is clear that the client is not seeking and has not sought advice from the agent regarding the transaction. This exclusion does not apply if the agent receives payment from anyone other than the client, for which he does not account to the client;
- transactions relating to options, contracts for differences or rights or interests in either of those, between parties who are not individuals where the sole or main purpose is that of limiting the extent to which the business may be affecting by an identifiable risk other than one arising as a result of carrying on a regulated activity;
- activities carried on in the course of a profession or non-investment business;
- activities carried on in connection with the sale of goods or supply of services;
- groups and joint enterprises;
- activities carried on in connection with the sale of a body corporate;
- activities carried on in connection with employee share schemes;
- overseas person.

Arranging deals in investments

1.125   This covers the making of arrangements for another person to buy, sell, subscribe for or underwrite investments which are either a security, a contractually based investment, an interest in investments or syndicate capacity or membership of Lloyd's. It also extends to making such arrangements with a view to someone participating. It does not extend to merely introducing someone to another party unless it is done for a fee or on a recurrent basis. The wording is clearer here than in the previous legislation[1] in that it makes overt that the act of arranging must be a causative element in the transaction following[2].

---

[1]   Financial Services Act 1986, Sch 1, Pt II, para 13.
[2]   HM Treasury, *Financial Services and Markets Bill*, Regulated Activities—Consultation Document, February 1999, part 3, p 2.

1.126   The exclusions are:

- arrangements which would not bring about the transaction;
- merely providing the means of communication;
- where the person entering into the contract does so as principal, or as agent, for another;

- arranging deals through authorised persons where the client is acting on the advice of an authorised person, or where it is clear that the client is not seeking advice from the person acting (or if he has and it has been refused and the client advised to seek advice from an appropriate person);
- arranging transactions in connection with lending on the security of insurance policies;
- arranging the acceptance of debentures in connection with loans;
- providing finance to enable a person to buy, sell, subscribe for or underwrite investments;
- introducing persons to either an authorised person, an exempt person acting in the course of a regulated activity for which he is exempt, or someone who is lawfully dealing, dealing as agent, arranging, managing, safeguarding and administering investments, sending dematerialised securities, establishing, operating or winding up a collective investment scheme or stakeholder pensions scheme or advising. The introduction must be made with a view to the provision of independent advice;
- arrangements for the issue of shares, share warrants, debentures or debenture warrants by the company issuing them;
- international securities self-regulating organisations who have been approved as such by the Treasury;
- trustees;
- activities carried on in the course of a profession or non-investment business;
- activities carried on in connection with the sale of goods or supply of services;
- groups and joint enterprises;
- sale of a body corporate;
- employee share schemes;
- overseas persons.

Managing investments

1.127 This is a specified activity if the assets concerned consist of or include an investment which is a security or a contractually based investment. It is limited to discretionary management. If there is no discretion it would normally then be covered by 'arranging deals in investments'[1].

---

[1] See para 1.125.

1.128 The exclusions are:

- where the assets are being managed under a power of attorney and all day-to-day decisions are taken by an authorised person acting within the scope of their authorisation;
- trustees;
- activities carried on in connection with the sale of goods or supply of services; and
- groups and joint enterprises.

Safeguarding and administering assets

1.129   This category applies regardless of whether the securities are held in a certified form. The exclusions are:

- where responsibility has been accepted by a qualified third party;
- making introductions to a qualified custodian;
- providing information as to the units or value of assets held, converting currency or receiving documents relating to an investment solely for the purpose of onward transmission to, from, or at the direction of the person to whom it belongs;
- trustees;
- activities carried on in connection with professional or non-investment business;
- activities carried on in connection with the sale of goods or supply of services;
- groups and joint enterprises; and
- employee share schemes.

Sending dematerialised instructions

1.130   The exclusions here are:

- acting on behalf of a participating issuer within the meaning of the 1995 regulations;
- acting on behalf of settlement banks;
- instructions in connection with takeover offers;
- instructions in the course of providing a network;
- trustees; and
- groups and joint enterprises.

Establishing, operating or winding up a collective investment scheme

1.131   The definition of 'collective investments schemes' is considered at paras 1.103 and 1.104 above.

Establishing, operating or winding up a stakeholder pension scheme

1.132   The definition of 'stakeholder pension schemes' is considered at para 1.105 above.

Advising on investments

1.133   This covers giving advice to an investor or prospective investor on the merits of buying, selling, subscribing for or underwriting an investment which is a security or a contractually based investment, or exercising any right conferred by such an investment. It applies whether the advice is given to someone in their own capacity, or as agent, or another. However, generic advice is not covered, so for example it is possible to advise on the relative merits of direct and indirect investments or of investments of a particular nature.

1.134 The exclusions are:

- advice given in newspapers, journals or broadcast transmissions where that media is neither essentially giving advice or leading or enabling people to buy, sell, subscribe for or underwrite securities or contractually based investments;
- trustees;
- activities carried on in connection with professional or on-investment business;
- activities carried on in connection with the sale of goods or supply of services;
- sale of a body corporate; and
- overseas persons.

Lloyd's

1.135 This covers advising a person to become or to cease to be a member of a Lloyd's syndicate, managing the underwriting capacity of a Lloyd's syndicate as a managing agent or arranging deals in contracts of insurance written at Lloyd's. The background to this is discussed at paras 1.23–1.29. The Society of Lloyd's itself is an authorised person[1] and has permission to carry on the following regulated activities[2]:

- arranging deals in insurance written at Lloyd's (basic market activity);
- arranging deals in participation in Lloyd's syndicates (secondary market activity); and
- activities carried on in connection with basic and primary market activities.

---

[1] FSMA 2000, s 315(1).
[2] FSMA 2000, s 315(2).

1.136 However, the FSA retains the legal capacity to involve itself by applying core provisions of the FSMA 2000[1] to a member of Lloyd's or the Society of Lloyd's generally if it thinks so fit bearing in mind the interests of policyholders and potential policyholders[2]. The FSA can do this either by giving a direction to the Council of Lloyd's or to the Society acting through the Council[3].

---

[1] FSMA 2000, Pts V, X, XI, XII, XIV, XV, XVI, XXII and XXIV, ss 384–386 and Pt XXVI.
[2] FSMA 2000, s 316(1) and (3).
[3] FSMA 2000, s 318(1).

1.137 Former underwriting members can carry out each contract of insurance that they have underwritten at Lloyd's whether or not they are authorised[1]. However, the FSA can impose on them such requirements as the FSA thinks fit to protect policyholders against the risk that the underwriter may not be able to meet their liabilities[2].

---

[1] FSMA 2000, s 320(1).
[2] FSMA 2000, s 320(3).

Funeral plan contracts

1.138   This covers contracts under which one person makes payments to another in return for the provision of a funeral on the first person's death provided it is not expected to occur within the first month. The exclusion is that of plans covered by insurance or trust arrangements.

Regulated mortgage contracts

1.139   This covers entering into or administering a regulated mortgage contract. Such an arrangement arises where a lender provides the credit to an individual or trustee in return for an obligation to repay which is secured by a first legal mortgage on land in the UK, at least 40% of which is to be used as a dwelling by the borrower, or (if it is the beneficiary of a trust the beneficiary), a related person. In this context administering means notifying the borrower of changes in interest rates on payments due and taking any necessary steps to collect or recover payments from the borrower. Merely exercising the right to take action does not amount to administering.

1.140   Exclusions cover arranging administration by an authorised person or pursuant to an agreement with one.

Agreeing to carry on activities

1.141   Agreeing to carry on any other specified activity other than accepting deposits, effecting and carrying out contracts of insurance, or establishing, operating or winding up a collective investment scheme or stakeholder pension scheme.

Gaming

1.142   Traditionally gaming contracts were unenforceable as being for an illegal consideration[1] and any monies loaned to another person with the intention that the borrower would use those monies for gambling was also an unenforceable debt[2]. This gave rise to problems with the increased use of derivative contracts (ie futures, options and contracts for differences) which could, in some instances be viewed as having similar characteristics to gaming contracts. Indeed this misconception is reflected in part in Lord Wilberforce's judgement in *Hazell v Hammersmith and Fulham London Borough Council*[3] where he stated:

> 'A swap contract based on a notional principal sum of £1 million under which the local authority promises to pay the bank £10,000 if LIBOR rises by 1% and the bank promises to pay the local authority £10,000 if LIBOR falls by 1% is more akin to gambling than insurance'.

Hopefully, the greater understanding of derivative instruments and their usage that now exists will stop this judicial approach recurring in the future. In any event, to stop contracts of such financial importance being rendered unenforceable, the FSMA 2000 largely reproduces the provisions of the FSA 1986[4] as s 412. The FSMA 2000, s 412 states that:

'(1) No contract to which this section applies is void or unenforceable because of—

    (a)   section 18 of the Gaming Act 1845, section 1 of the Gaming Act 1892 or Article 170 of the Betting, Gaming, Lotteries and Amusements (Northern Ireland) Order 1985; or

    (b)   any rule of the law of Scotland under which a contract by way of gaming or wagering is not legally enforceable.

(2) This section applies to a contract if—

    (a)   it is entered into by either or each party by way of business;

    (b)   the entering into or performance of it by either party constitutes an activity of a specified kind or one which falls within a specified class of activity; and

    (c)   it relates to an investment of a specified kind or one which falls within a specified class of investment.'

In addition the Financial Services and Markets Act 2000 (Gaming Contracts) Order 2001[5] specifically adds that dealing in investments as principal or agent, or agreeing to carry on certain activities (see para 1.141) are excluded from the gaming laws.

---

[1]   Gaming Act 1845, s 18.
[2]   Gaming Act 1892, s 1.
[3]   [1991] 1 All ER 545 at 559, para b.
[4]   FSA 1986, s 63.
[5]   SI 2001/2510.

1.143   The case law following the FSA 1986 would still seem applicable to the new FSMA 2000, s 412. In particular *Morgan Grenfell & Co Ltd v Welwyn Hatfield District Council*[1] where the judge made clear that in this context 'business' would be very widely interpreted and cover any situation where one of the parties was entering into the arrangement for other than recreational purposes.

---

[1]   [1995] 1 All ER 1.

1.144   The definition of 'contracts for differences'[1] is extremely wide and should thus continue the tradition already seen in *City Index Ltd v Leslie*[2] where it was held that a contract in relation to stock market index movements was not a gaming contract and could be enforced as it fell within the definition of 'contracts for differences' and the party seeking to enforce it was properly authorised to carry on the relevant category of investment business. Indeed the definition of 'contracts for differences' in SI 2001/544, art 85 appears wide enough to cover most spread betting.

---

[1]   See paras 1.110 and 1.111.
[2]   [1992] QB 98.

1.145 Perhaps the other issue is that of speculative forex trading which had been suggested as being at risk from the gaming laws[1]. This risk appears to remain as exemption under the FSMA 2000, s 412 and only exists where the activity involves a specified investment. This could give rise to problems as forex contracts do not fall within any of the 16 categories.

---

[1]   See SIB Guidance Release 1/96 at p 16.

Compensation scheme

1.146 The FSMA 2000 requires the FSA to set up a compensation scheme[1]. The purpose of this is to provide a fall back position for those who have a claim against an authorised firm which cannot be satisfied financially by a claim against the firm or their insurers. The compensation scheme applies even if the firm is acting outside or in breach of its authorisation, but not if it is unauthorised[2]. The claim may be for money that has been paid over to an authorised person, money due to be paid by them to an authorised person, or an amount owing as a result of a legal claim or an ombudsman's ruling.

---

[1]   FSMA 2000, ss 212 and 213.
[2]   FSMA 2000, s 213(9).

1.147 As the function of the compensation scheme is to provide cover for those who need it, claims may only be made by a restricted group of people[1], which excludes larger businesses. As is normally the way with compensation schemes there is a limit on the size of pay-outs for any individual claim. The funds that finance the scheme cover three areas of the financial services markets: investment services; deposit protection; and insurance. The authorised firms are required to pay a levy[2] according to which of these areas the business concerned operates in.

---

[1]   FSMA 2000, s 214(1)(f).
[2]   FSMA 2000, s 213(3)(a).

1.148 The scheme manager can require the authorised person against whom a claim is being made, to provide information and documents[1] within a given period, where this is believed by the manager to be necessary to fairly determine the claim. The manager can also inspect documents held by an administrative receiver, administrator or liquidator, or trustee in bankruptcy of an insolvent person, or in Scotland a permanent trustee of an insolvent person, where this is necessary for the manager to discharge his function[2]. This will normally occur where the authorised person against whom a claim has been made is in insolvency. If either type of request is not met it is possible to request a court order to that effect[3].

---

[1]   FSMA 2000, s 219(1).
[2]   FSMA 2000, s 220.
[3]   FSMA 2000, s 221.

Ombudsman

1.149 An ombudsman scheme has been created to assist those who have a complaint against an authorised person or appointed representative, which has not been satisfactorily resolved by complaining to them. Those who are authorised under the FSMA 2000 regime must agree as part of that process to honour rulings by the ombudsman once the complainant has accepted it. Such a ruling may involve a compensatory award up to a maximum figure, or a direction that specified steps be taken[1]. However, the ombudsman could recommend that an additional sum be paid above the maximum, but the extra amount would be unenforceable[2]. The ombudsman has the power to require any of the parties involved in a complaint to provide specified information or documents[3]. Finally, the complainant can if they wish pursue a complaint in the courts even after a ruling of the ombudsman.

[1] FSMA 2000, s 228(5) and s 229(2).
[2] FSMA 2000, s 229(5).
[3] FSMA 2000, s 231(1).

INTERNATIONAL CO-ORDINATION AND REGULATION

Introduction

1.150 Recent years have seen the increasing internationalisation of banking, insurance and other financial services businesses. Coupled with this has been a breaking down of the barriers that traditionally existed between the various parts of the financial services industry. This is against a background of an ever increasing proportion of the world's wealth being reflected in capital flows, some related to international trade but the majority by way of investment. As a consequence, the regulation of financial services has become a task requiring a far wider range of activities than used to be the case. This was a primary reason for the creation of the Financial Services Authority in the UK. In addition, it is necessary in an increasingly inter-linked world for there to be an agreed set of international standards by which financial institutions should be regulated. This does not require total commonality, but a large degree of equivalence is certainly highly desirable to facilitate economic stability and sustained economic growth. A failure to create high quality economic regulation can also both facilitate a financial crisis and aggravate it when it arises. In addition, the extent to which world capital markets have become integrated has limited the ability of national regulators to monitor firms effectively without a considerable degree of international co-operation[1].

[1] Little, Parry and Taylor *Bond Markets: Law and Regulation* (1999) p 221.

1.151 The proposals considered below which help develop a set of international financial regulations articulate five key features[1]. It represents a reform of the nexus of international financial regulation; a bringing together of a group of limited codes and standards; international collaboration

between a disparate set of linked codes and standards; international collaboration between a disparate set of states, markets, financial regulators and
financial institutions. It engages both international and domestic compliance
assessments and there is a clear acceptance that there is a direct relationship
between adopting such regulation and codes, and maintaining financial
stability.

The motivation is also clear. In the words of a G7 Communiqué[2]:

> 'Close international co-operation in the regulation and supervision of
> financial institutions and markets is essential to the continued safe-
> guarding of the financial system and to prevent erosion of necessary
> prudential standards.'

---

[1]   YV Reddy 'Issues in Implementing International Financial Standards and Codes' Centre
for Banking Studies at the Central Bank of Sri Lanka, Colombo (28 June 2001).

[2]   Background Document, *Review of International Financial Institutions* (Halifax summit,
15–17 June 1995) pp 9–10.

Organisations

1.152   A number of bodies stand out as being key players in this process. In
alphabetical order they are as follows.

The Basel Committee on Banking Supervision.

1.153   This provides a meeting place for the central banks of the G10
countries and facilitates co-operation on the regulation of banking.

Committee on Payment and Settlement Systems

1.154   Also created by the G10 central banks this, as its name suggests,
provides a meeting place for those central banks on matters arising in
relation to payment and settlement systems. Their concern is not limited to
domestic considerations but extends to cross border operations and netting.
Much of their work concerns supervisory standards and recommendations
of best practice.

Financial Action Task Force

1.155   Created by the G7, its role is to ascertain the threat to financial
institutions from money laundering and to recommend steps that can be
taken to counter this. There are now 29 member states and a key function of
the Task Force is to monitor the extent to which these countries are taking
appropriate steps to deal with the problem.

Financial Stability Forum

1.156   Following a meeting of the Finance Ministers and Central Bank
Governors of the G7 countries, Hans Tietmeyer the then President of the
Bundesbank was commissioned to draft a report considering what new
structures might be appropriate to improve co-operation between the existing national and international regulatory bodies. The aim was to facilitate

increased stability in the regulation of world finance and financial services. As a consequence of the report he produced the Forum was created.

International Accounting Standards Board

1.157 The aim of this institution is to bring about the convergence of accounting standards. This is of importance, partly in increasing the financial safety by having high common standards, and also in reducing the risk of financial failure or loss to investors due to accounts not representing a true and fair view in the generally understood meaning of the words.

International Association of Insurance Supervisors

1.158 Its purpose is to develop a set of generally accepted standards in this area to increase the effectiveness of insurance regulation. Over 100 states have become members.

International Federation of Accountants

1.159 This is made up of the national accountancy bodies that represent those accountants who are involved in the public sector, large organisations and commerce and industry. Its primary aim is to increase the quality of the accounting regulations and increase their international equivalence.

International Monetary Fund

1.160 This is the body that sets international standards in relation to overseeing the world's monetary system. It has created a range of standards in relation to monetary and fiscal policy and has assisted in creating methods of assessment for the standards used for the supervision of banking and insurance.

International Organization of Securities Commissions

1.161 As its name implies, this is an organisation made up of the securities and derivatives regulators of the member countries. Its main purpose is to create high standards to govern the regulation of the securities markets.

Organisation for Economic Cooperation and Development

1.162 The aim of this body is to promote world economic growth and to this end it promotes the development of financial markets regulation to a high common standard.

The World Bank

1.163 This aims to reduce poverty in the world by facilitating private investment in the regions concerned.

Key standards

1.164   In its role as a facilitator of increased international co-operation the Financial Stability Forum has issued a set of twelve standards which it believes are a pre-requisite to creating a system of stable, well regulated financial systems. These are as follows.

Code of Good Practices on Transparency in Monetary and Financial Policies

1.165   The essence of this is that it highlights the approaches that create the appropriate level of transparency to enable the public to assess what is happening and thus facilitate accountability. The Code specifically highlights four key areas:

(1)   roles, responsibility and objectives should be clearly stated;
(2)   policy decisions should have clearly defined processes determining how they are reached and reported;
(3)   policies and information pertinent to them should be publicly available; and
(4)   accountable systems should exist to guarantee integrity.

Code of Good Practices on Fiscal Transparency

1.166   The role of transparency is critical in that it makes the regulatory authorities more accountable. To facilitate this the code provides four principles:

(1)   that the roles and responsibilities of those involved should be clear;
(2)   there should be access to the information by the public;
(3)   that key financial steps such as budgets, accounts and financial reports should be publicly available; and
(4)   integrity should be underpinned by independent means.

Data dissemination

1.167   There are two key agreements in this area. The first is the Special Data Dissemination Standard issued by the International Monetary Fund (IMF). This was produced to resolve the problem of instability induced, if only in part, by insufficient information being available in the market place. Those countries who subscribe (and the significant economies already do) agree to satisfy this function in four key regards and to do so in standard form:

(1)   that data, particularly regarding reserves and foreign currency holdings should be made publicly available, promptly and at appropriate periods;
(2)   that the public should be informed of the dates on which such data will be available;
(3)   clear laws determining both the above and proposed changes in the same, coupled with government access to data and comment being released by the relevant government officials; and
(4)   the making available to the public of information to articulate how the data should be formulated and of any other material against which it can be assessed.

1.168   The second is the General Data Dissemination System, also issued by the IMF. This is more severe in its demands than the Special Data Dissemination Standard and the developed economies are expected to apply it. It requires that detailed, high quality information relating to financial, economic and social issues be made publicly available on a timely basis. It adopts the same four-stage structure as the Special Data Dissemination Standard.

Principles and guidelines for effective insolvency and creditor rights systems

1.169   The existence of a clear, fair set of rights for creditors is a key ingredient for a stable economy. It also assists commercial lenders in determining the degree of risk they are taking on. This has been driven primarily by the World Bank, the United Nations Commission of International Trade Law, the IMF and INSOL.

Principles of corporate governance

1.170   This is a system of corporate regulation which applies to a company when it determines its objectives, when it seeks to achieve them and in assessing its performance. It is crucial to have such regulation to create a high quality corporate environment to attract international capital. Key issues to be found within corporate governance regulations are:

- shareholder rights;
- stakeholder rights (this is a contentious area in terms of its future development);
- disclosure of information; and
- board responsibility.

International Accounting Standards

1.171   A succession of international accounting standards have been issued to determine the extent of the detail, range, relevance and reliability of the information to be included in the accounts. To represent a true and fair view, accounts must be regulated by clear and detailed regulation. There are specific types of accounts, those relating to banks, securities houses and insurance companies for example, which give rise to specific issues when determining what should be included.

International Standards on Auditing

1.172   If there are to be accepted standards of accountancy then it follows that there must also be internationally accepted standards of auditing to maintain it. The standards on auditing that have been issued cover:

- audit responsibilities;
- audit planning;
- internal controls;
- evidence;
- practice statements relating to international auditing;
- external auditing; and
- audit characteristics and considerations.

Core Principles for Systemically Important Payment Systems

1.173   To function in a stable way financial markets require stable, effective settlement systems. The aim of the Core Principles is to facilitate this by requiring a degree of safety and efficiency in these systems. The Principles themselves require that domestic and international payment systems satisfy criteria relating to design and operation. Guidance is also provided on interpreting the Principles.

The Forty Recommendations of the Financial Action Task Force on Money Laundering

1.174   These were intended to provide a set of recommendations which, if followed, would optimise the response of banking and financial bodies that were being used to launder illegal money. They cover areas such as:

- criminal justice systems;
- law enforcement;
- the banking and financial systems;
- banking and financial regulation; and
- international co-operation.

All member states are subject to periodic mutual analysis to determine whether they are satisfying the recommendations. They must also carry out an annual self-assessment exercise to the same end.

Core Principles for Effective Banking Supervision

1.175   To assist in stabilising the world's banking system the Basel Committee on Banking Supervision have published a set of 25 core principles and additional criteria for banking supervision. These cover issues such as:

- the preconditions for effective banking supervision;
- licensing requirements;
- ongoing banking supervision;
- powers of supervisors; and
- cross-border banking.

Objectives and Principles of Securities Regulation

1.176   The International Organization of Securities Commissions (IOSCO) has published a set of objectives and principles to help bring about a system of sound regulation of the securities markets. The key objectives are:

- protecting investors;
- making sure the markets function in a manner that is fair, efficient and transparent; and
- reducing the risk of systemic failure.

There are also 30 principles relating to securities regulation.

Insurance Core Principles

1.177   As their name implies these were produced to facilitate that the regulatory supervision of the insurance industry is taking place at a suitably proficient and effective manner. The Principles themselves cover key areas such as:

- the role of supervisors;
- licensing insurance companies;
- corporate governance of insurance companies;
- prudential controls;
- market conduct;
- monitoring by the regulator; and
- sanctions for failure to satisfy the regulations.

Monitoring regulatory observance

1.178   Clearly it is insufficient to create a series of desirable standards without some system for ascertaining whether they are being subscribed to in practice. States themselves will sometimes carry out research into the state of affairs within their own jurisdiction. In addition the IMF and the World Bank both produce reports on the extent to which the standards and codes discussed above are being met. The IMF has produced them in relation to the distribution of data and fiscal transparency. The World Bank has done so in relation to accounting, auditing, corporate governance, insolvency and creditors' rights. How well standards in the financial sector are carried out and what the priorities need to be to rectify any shortcomings are dealt with under the auspices of the joint IMF and World Bank 'Financial Sector Assessment Programme'.

Facilitating regulatory observance

1.179   The Financial Stability Forum has suggested[1] that member states could take a number of key steps to facilitate awareness and observance of regulatory standards.

(1)   an ongoing campaign should be run to raise the level of awareness in their financial centres as to the requirements of the standards;
(2)   that the bodies creating the standards in the first place should themselves facilitate and encourage this process of education;
(3)   that the bodies creating the standards and the national regulators should help explain how satisfying the requirements of the standards will help avoid certain types of risk. In this context explaining how past market problems have led to the standards will assist;
(4)   external assessments of the application of standards should be undertaken by the bodies setting the standards;
(5)   peer discussions should be encouraged to facilitate the implementation of standards; and
(6)   technical advice and training should be provided by the more developed states to the others.

There are a number of reasons why this is thought necessary. The importance of the standards is primarily in that they facilitate a sound financial system. To this end it is important that not only the authorities but also relevant private bodies should put them into effect.

---

[1]   *Report of the Follow-up Group on Incentives to Foster Implementation of Standards* (7–8 September 2000).

Key issues other than regulatory observance

1.180   Turning to the regulated financial institutions themselves, there are factors other than the quality of regulation that will determine whether institutions will proceed with a financial arrangement[1]. A suitable legal system and framework are vital. Key elements are efficiency, transparency and a predictable outcome in the sense that it should be determined by clearly stated laws rather than other factors. In some states it can prove difficult to successfully pursue certain parties through their courts due to corruption. Political risk and economic fundamentals also need to be within acceptable levels. If not there will be no point in pursuing a financial arrangement further. In addition parties to complex financial arrangements do not always fully understand how the regulations relate to the risks such transactions create.

---

[1]   Information provided to the Financial Stability Forum by market participants.

1.181   Some firms are by their very nature less concerned with regulatory issues. The international investment portfolios managed by those such as hedge funds, pension funds and insurance companies are more concerned with market analysis that relates to capitalisation.

1.182   Rating agencies are a key source of information and their role in providing assessments will involve an analysis of supervisory and regulatory issues as well as financial and market issues.

Consequences of regulatory failure

1.183   There are instances of countries having lax regulatory controls and surviving for some time with no serious problems. However, the absence of a system of decent controls both increases the risk of a crisis arising and of it becoming systemic, leading to a larger scale problem when it does. The Asian financial crisis of 1998 has generally been regarded as having been partly caused by lax regulation[1]. In addition the crisis was able to develop to a greater extent before it became apparent that it was occurring, than should have been the case, because of poor corporate governance and a lack of transparency. This was exacerbated by the high proportion of businesses in the area that were owned and managed by the same people, which coupled with traditional business practices, resulted in weak corporate governance. Then as the crisis accelerated those outside the countries concerned were unable to draw a distinction between those institutions in the states concerned that were a real risk and those that were not. This resulted in a flight of matured short-term debt and a refusal by those outside the jurisdictions to hold debt and equity securities denominated in those states' currencies due to fear of devaluation[2].

---

[1] 68th Annual Report—Bank for International Settlements (8 June 1998).
[2] See The International Organization of Securities Commissions 'Causes, Effects and Regulatory Implications of Financial and Economic Turbulence in Emerging Markets' (Emerging Markets Committee, September 1998).

1.184 The key steps that were deemed necessary to reduce the risk of such a crisis in the future were[1]:

- increasing transparency;
- enhancing the free flow of capital;
- strengthening states' financial systems;
- leaving the responsibility and risk associated with lending with the private institutions responsible; and
- increasing the involvement of international financial institutions.

It has been suggested that[2] the larger credit rating agencies have an important role to play in this context.

---

[1] 'Strengthening the Architecture of the Global Financial System' (G7, 1998).
[2] Robert Chote 'Crystal Balls in Washington' and Gerard Baker 'Tea Leaves in Jakarta' Financial Times, 17 April 1998.

CO-OPERATION BETWEEN REGULATORS

Introduction

1.185 At a national level co-operation is much less of a problem. Home state regulators have long since had agreements in place to deal with the issues of co-operation. In the United Kingdom the wideness and extent of the FSA's powers reduce the scale of the problem. It can carry out most of the regulatory steps itself. In instances where it cannot do so there are provisions in place to facilitate them. The real issues arise in the context of international and pan European regulation.

Memoranda of understanding

1.186 The main way in which international co-operation has been put in place is through Memoranda of Understanding (MoU). Originally these tended to be bi-lateral, but more recently a multi-lateral approach seems to have gained ground. A considerable amount of work has gone into key issues such as the exchange of information between regulators to arrive at the best design for such memoranda[1]. These agreements do not impose legally binding obligations on the signatories. Nor can they override domestic laws and regulations. What they can do however is give rise to a much freer flow of information between regulators than would otherwise be the case. This facilitates the national regulators building a more accurate picture of the financial scene of which they are regulating one part. It is important to bear in mind that an MoU is not always a pre-requisite to co-operation being provided. For example, the US Exchange Act specifically allows the Securities and Exchange Commission (SEC) to utilise its powers to assist foreign regulators if there is not an MoU in place. They are also mandated to try and develop reciprocal arrangements with states that are not in a position to sign them. Nonetheless they represent the most effective and comprehensive way of proceeding.

---

[1]   Working Party on Enforcement and Exchange of Information (IOSCO, 1990).

1.187   The principles that the IOSCO Report of 1990 suggested as giving rise to an optimal MoU are that the MoU should provide for assistance to an investigation from an overseas state requesting information even if the behaviour under investigation would not be a breach of the laws or regulations of the country from which it is requested. If that is not possible because of the laws of a state signing a memorandum then they should request a change in their domestic law to permit it. This principle overrides what has been a long standing principle of extradition type laws, namely that someone can only be extradited if the offence concerned is one in both the requesting state and the requested. This has to be overridden in the context of financial regulation as otherwise it would be impossible to police international financial organisations effectively. A decision could be made in a part of a financial organisation in one country to do something that was a breach of financial regulation in another. If the regulator in the state where the offence occurred were to find out, there would be little they could do to proceed against the parties responsible without a MoU drafted on the basis of this principle. They could otherwise only take steps against the branch or subsidiary in their own jurisdiction, which may be insufficient.

1.188   This has been a particular issue for the United States. US law does not require that when a non-US regulator seeks assistance, the events concerned must also be an offence in the US. This is important as US securities laws generally tend to be wider than the securities laws of other countries[1]. However, reciprocity arises in another way in that the Exchange Act requires the SEC to consider whether the overseas regulator would reciprocate were the SEC to request assistance from them. If not, assistance should be refused.

---

[1]   Ed Berman *A Practical Guide to SEC Regulation Outside the United States* (2000), p 246.

1.189   The MoU should also provide that information received by a regulator should be treated 'with the highest possible level of confidentiality'[1]. This is stated to mean that the information should be treated with the same degree of confidentiality as domestically acquired information. The MoU should also give the authority asked for information the opportunity to say what degree of confidentiality should be attached to the information provided.

---

[1]   'Principles of Memoranda of Understanding' Report of Working Party No 4, IOSCO, p 1.

1.190 The MoU should also set out the procedures to be followed in requesting information and in responding to such requests. This is a fundamental issue to be agreed, and in most cases one that should not be too difficult for the parties to agree on.

1.191 The MoU should state that when an investigation is going on in one state as a result of a request from a regulator in a second state, it should not impact on the rights that a person has in the first state. This is necessary because otherwise the MoU will find itself inoperable in the first state. In many nations the rights concerned will be constitutional ones, and so the matter is not negotiable.

1.192 The MoU should contain an agreement that the signatories will consult with each other during the period of operation of the MoU. The need for this could become apparent when there is a difference of view as to whether assistance should be provided in a particular case. It is also hoped that the facility for consultation will give rise to a relaxed relationship between the regulators concerned. Highlighted by IOSCO are three situations where consultation is likely to be particularly important, namely:

(1)   where unforeseen circumstances arise;
(2)   where there is an overlap of jurisdiction; and
(3)   where one country's laws or regulations change.

1.193 As a matter of political and legal reality it is accepted that there must be a public policy exclusion. This permits a regulator to refuse to provide assistance to a request where to do so would violate the public policy of its state. The IOSCO Report defines public policy in this context as being 'issues affecting sovereignty, national security or other essential interests'[1]. This may prove a narrower definition than that which some state's judges may give it.

---

[1]   'Principles of Memoranda of Understanding' Report of Working Party No 4, IOSCO, p 3.

1.194 The MoU should provide that the signatories should take all reasonable steps to fully utilise their powers when faced with a request for information. This should include obtaining documents, testimony from witnesses (where appropriate), giving access to any relevant non-public files they may have, and carrying out inspections of the regulated entity concerned in the investigation. This is a particularly important principle given that there have been instances of regulators refusing to provide information that it can obtain from the regulated firm on a voluntary basis because of an unwillingness to enforce requests for information against the firm. In some cases this has occurred for legal reasons.

1.195 There should be an agreement allowing an authority requesting assistance to take part directly in its execution. This can be useful in cases where the investigating authority is the one with most of the background information on the issue concerned. In addition, it may be the case when the investigation proceeds further, that the requesting authority starts to find information that it would not have been able to request in the first place because it could not have known of its existence.

1.196 Finally, the memorandum should allow the regulator being requested to provide assistance to share the costs with the regulator requesting it. This would be important in cases where an investigation were likely to prove expensive, especially where the regulator being requested to provide assistance has limited resources. It could also prove relevant if, over a period of time, one regulator finds itself requesting more information from another than is requested in return. It is useful to have a mechanism for dealing with this.

Chapter 2   Authorisation

Sue Rutherford

INTRODUCTION

2.1 With the Financial Services and Markets Act 2000 (FSMA 2000) replacing the Financial Services Act 1986 (FSA 1986) and the various other statutes which previously governed banking and insurance business in the UK, authorisation is one of the aspects of the regulatory system that has changed the most. From the first announcement of the new regulatory structure by the Chancellor of the Exchequer in May 1997, one of the main benefits of the new structure was perceived to be a streamlined system for obtaining authorisation to undertake financial services activities in the UK. Previously, a person intending to carry on a broad range of financial services activities might have been required to apply to two or more separate regulatory authorities for authorisation. In contrast, the FSMA 2000 establishes the Financial Services Authority (FSA) as the sole regulator, with the authority to grant permission to conduct almost all types of financial services activity in the UK, from deposit-taking to insurance, from investment management to trading in commodity futures.

2.2 The central provision of the FSMA 2000 is that a person must not carry on a 'regulated activity' in the UK without being either an authorised person, or exempt[1]. This is known as the general prohibition, contravention of which is a criminal offence punishable by imprisonment, an unlimited fine, or both. In addition, transactions or other agreements entered into by a firm in the course of carrying on a regulated activity in contravention of the general prohibition are normally unenforceable against the other party. It is a specific offence for any person who is not authorised or exempt either to describe himself as such, or to hold himself out as being authorised or exempt[2].

---

[1] This general prohibition is set out in the FSMA 2000, s 19.
[2] FSMA 2000, s 24.

2.3 The most usual way to obtain authorisation is to apply to the FSA for permission to carry on one or more regulated activities. Since this permission derives from the FSMA 2000, Pt IV it is known as a Part IV permission, and once granted it automatically confers authorisation.

2.4 An applicant for authorisation might be a company, a partnership, an unincorporated association or an individual—the FSA uses the term 'firm' to cover all of these.

2.5   To determine exactly which activities are classified as regulated activities and therefore are covered by the general prohibition, it is necessary to check not only the FSMA 2000 itself, but also a raft of related secondary legislation. It is only possible to establish exactly which activities fall within the definition of regulated activities by considering carefully the interaction between all the relevant provisions.

REGULATED ACTIVITIES

2.6   The definition of regulated activities is principally contained in the Regulated Activities Order[1], Pt II of which specifies those activities which are regulated if they are carried on by way of business. Generally speaking, the Regulated Activities Order consolidates all the provisions relating to banking, insurance and investment business, which were previously found in the various statutes applicable to these businesses[2]. These activities are regulated activities if they relate to 'specified investments', which are those set out in the Regulated Activities Order, Pt III. The term 'specified investments' includes deposits, rights under contracts of insurance, and the same range of investments which were previously covered by the FSA 1986.

---

[1]   Financial Services and Markets Act 2000 (Regulated Activities) Order 2001, SI 2001/544.
[2]   The main statutes previously applicable were the Banking Act 1987; Financial Services Act 1986; Insurance Companies Act 1982; Building Societies Act 1986; and Friendly Societies Act 1992.

2.7   However, as well as including all the investment products which were previously regulated, the government took advantage of the opportunity provided by such a thorough upheaval of the UK regulatory structure to bring some activities within the regulatory net for the first time. In each case, consultation exercises were used to determine that there was a good case for extending the scope of regulation in this way.

2.8   The difficulties experienced by the Lloyd's market during the 1990s led to the conclusion that self-regulation was no longer appropriate, and it was agreed that the FSA should assume responsibility for the regulation of Lloyd's[1]. Hence the Regulated Activities Order includes the activities of advising on participation in a Lloyd's syndicate, managing the underwriting capacity of such a syndicate and arranging Lloyd's insurance contracts. Lloyd's managing agents and members' agents are therefore required to obtain Part IV permission for these activities. The Society of Lloyd's itself is an authorised person by virtue of the FSMA 2000, s 315, with permission to undertake relevant insurance activities.

---

[1]   For a summary of the arguments and issues involved in the regulation of the Lloyd's market, refer to FSA Consultation Paper 16 'The Future Regulation of Lloyd's' (November 1998).

2.9   In January 2000 the government announced its intention to introduce statutory regulation of mortgage lending, as it considered that the previous environment (a combination of the Consumer Credit Act 1974 and self-regulation under the Mortgage Code developed by the Council of Mortgage Lenders) had not been sufficient to protect consumers. The Regulated Activities Order includes the definition of exactly which mortgages are covered by the FSMA 2000, and these are then carved out of the scope of the Consumer Credit Act 1974 to avoid duplication.

2.10 Similarly, it was decided that the provision of prepaid funeral plans and the deposit-taking activities of credit unions, should become regulated activities and be brought under the regulatory wing of the FSA.

2.11 It was decided that the FSA should assume responsibility for this very wide range of activities gradually, allowing it to take on the staff required to provide the regulatory functions (often by transfer from the previous regulator), and to implement the systems and procedures required. The first step was to transfer responsibility for regulating banks from the Bank of England to the FSA, which took place on 1 June 1998, a date known as N1. The FSA assumed responsibility for the regulation of most forms of insurance and investment business, including the Lloyd's market, on the date that the general prohibition in the FSMA 2000, s 19 came into force, which was termed N2—midnight on 30 November 2001. The dates for the FSA to start regulating prepaid funeral plan contracts, deposit-taking by credit unions, and mortgage lending, were set with reference to N2, at January 2002, July 2002, and September 2002 respectively, with the latter date being known as N3[1].

---

[1] However, on 12 December 2001, the government announced a further extension to the FSA's scope: it was to become responsible for regulating mortgage advice and general insurance broking as well as mortgage lending and administration. As a result, the date of N3 was postponed while the FSA's approach to mortgage regulation was reconsidered.

Activities carried on other than by way of business

2.12 An activity is only a regulated activity under the FSMA 2000 if it is carried on by way of business. This is also elaborated in secondary legislation—the Business Order[1]—giving flexibility for future amendments if this should prove necessary. The Business Order makes provision for persons to accept deposits, or carry on certain kinds of dealing and investment activity, without being regarded as doing so by way of business. In contrast, it specifies that a person who manages the assets of an occupational pension scheme will normally be regarded as doing so by way of business, unless certain circumstances apply.

---

[1] Financial Services and Markets Act 2000 (Carrying on Regulated Activities By Way of Business) Order 2001, SI 2001/1177.

Exemptions

2.13 The Regulated Activities Order[1] itself includes certain exemptions, setting out those circumstances in which particular activities are not to be regarded as regulated activities. In addition, the FSMA 2000 provides that the Treasury may issue an Order providing for specified persons or classes of persons to be exempt from the general prohibition. The Exemption Order[2] provides exemption from the need for authorisation for certain persons, such as central banks and international development banks who would otherwise be conducting regulated activities, but for which regulation by the FSA would be inappropriate or unnecessary. In general, persons who were exempt under the previous legislation continue to be exempt under the FSMA 2000. Investment exchanges and clearing houses which are recognised under the FSMA 2000, Pt XVIII are exempt persons in respect of their activities in those capacities.

---

[1]   Financial Services and Markets Act 2000 (Regulated Activities) Order 2001, SI 2001/544.
[2]   Financial Services and Markets Act 2000 (Exemption) Order 2001, SI 2001/1201.

2.14   A firm may also become exempt by becoming the appointed representative of an authorised person. An appointed representative is a person who is employed by an authorised person under a contract for services to carry on certain limited regulated activities, which are set out in the Appointed Representatives Regulations[1]. These are broadly the same activities as were previously permitted of an appointed representative under the FSA 1986—giving investment advice, arranging deals in investments, and arranging for the safeguarding and administration of investments. The authorised person (the principal) is required to enter into a contract with the appointed representative (its agent) which includes the provisions specified by the Appointed Representatives Regulations, and takes responsibility for the regulated activities of the appointed representative.

---

[1]   Financial Services and Markets Act 2000 (Appointed Representatives) Regulations 2001, SI 2001/1217.

2.15   The FSMA 2000, s 38(2) specifically states that any person who has a Part IV permission cannot also be an exempt person. So it is no longer possible, as it was under the FSA 1986, for a single entity to be authorised in respect of one type of business, but exempt in respect of another. This particularly affects firms which had previously taken advantage of the appointed representative exemption under the FSA 1986, such as building societies. These were previously authorised to accept deposits under the Building Societies Act 1986, but were exempted from the authorisation requirements of the FSA 1986 if they became appointed representatives of another authorised firm. Since they must now be authorised under the FSMA 2000 for deposit-taking, the appointed representative exemption is no longer available to them.

2.16   One further exemption is worthy of mention. Although Lloyd's managing agents and members' agents need to be authorised, members of the Society of Lloyd's—ie the individual Names—do not themselves need to obtain Part IV permission in respect of the insurance business they do in this capacity.

Professional firms

2.17   Firms of professionals such as solicitors, accountants and actuaries were particularly affected by the replacement of the FSA 1986 by the FSMA 2000. Approximately 15,000 such firms were regulated for investment business under the FSA 1986. Their professional bodies (such as the Law Society or the Institute of Actuaries) were given the status of Recognised Professional Bodies under the FSA 1986, and as such could grant authorisation to conduct investment business. However, most of these 15,000 firms were only conducting investment business as an incidental part of providing professional services to their clients; it was estimated that only about 2000 firms were conducting any significant investment business such as giving investment advice or providing discretionary investment management or corporate finance services.

2.18   The transition to the FSMA 2000 regime was an opportunity to reduce such precautionary authorisations. Persons providing professional services may carry out regulated activities arising out of, or complementary to, their professional services without the need for authorisation, provided that they meet a number of detailed conditions. These firms are termed 'exempt professional firms', and the main condition is that they must be members of and supervised by a professional body which has been designated by HM Treasury as a Designated Professional Body (DPB). All the professional bodies which were previously Recognised Professional Bodies under the FSA 1986 have now become DPBs under the FSMA 2000[1].

---

[1]   Financial Services and Markets Act 2000 (Designated Professional Bodies) Order 2001, SI 2001/1226.

2.19   Exempt professional firms can conduct regulated activities without authorisation provided that these activities are incidental to their professional services, they do not hold themselves out as undertaking mainstream regulated activities, and they do not receive any remuneration for which they do not account to their clients. Even though such firms are not regulated by the FSA, the FSMA 2000, s 332(1) gives the FSA the authority to make rules applying to them, for the purpose of ensuring that clients are aware that such firms are not authorised persons. If such firms were to state on their letterheading or in other documentation that they were 'authorised' by their DPB, the FSA was concerned that this might confuse consumers, who might be misled into thinking that such firms were in fact regulated by the FSA, rather than being supervised by the DPB. Thus the FSA imposes a specific rule that exempt professional firms may not describe themselves as 'authorised'.

2.20   If a professional firm does wish to carry out regulated activities which are not merely incidental to its professional services, it can no longer obtain authorisation for this from its DPB. Instead, it has to apply to the FSA for a Part IV permission in the same way as other applicants. In order to ensure that certain activities are always subject to regulation by the FSA, the Non-Exempt Activities Order[1] prescribes that certain regulated activities— such as accepting deposits, effecting insurance contracts or operating a collective investment scheme—can never be undertaken by a professional firm without obtaining a Part IV permission.

---

[1]   Financial Services and Markets Act 2000 (Professions) (Non-Exempt Activities) Order 2001, SI 2001/1227.

2.21   If a professional firm does become authorised by the FSA, it has to distinguish between mainstream and non-mainstream regulated activities—the latter being those regulated activities which would have been exempt if they had been the only regulated activities undertaken by the firm. The firm's mainstream regulated activities will fall within the scope of FSA regulation and be governed by the rules in the *FSA Handbook*, but the non-mainstream regulated activities remain outside the scope of FSA regulation and are subject instead to the supervision of the DPB. The FSA's rules and guidance on the distinction between mainstream and non-mainstream regulated activities can be found in the Professional Firms Sourcebook module of the *FSA Handbook*, which applies to both authorised professional firms and exempt professional firms.

Credit unions

2.22   The FSMA 2000 also contained significant implications for credit unions, which had previously been regulated under the Credit Unions Act 1979 as well as being registered under the Industrial and Provident Societies Act 1965. In November 1999, HM Treasury announced that credit unions would be brought within the scope of the FSMA 2000, with the FSA becoming responsible for regulating them[1]. Credit unions potentially have a significant role in the alleviation of financial exclusion, with sound regulation having the potential to boost the public perception of these firms. It was recognised that the move to regulation by the FSA could have been quite onerous for firms operated and managed to a large extent by part-time volunteers, so it was decided that transitional arrangements were required. Instead of becoming subject to FSA regulation at N2, the Exemption Order initially included an exemption for deposit-taking by credit unions, but with an expiry date of 1 July 2002. From that date, credit unions have to obtain from the FSA a Part IV permission for deposit-taking in order to continue accepting savings from their members. When mortgage lending is brought within the scope of the FSMA 2000, those credit unions involved in this activity will also have to apply for a separate Part IV permission to cover that aspect of their business.

---

[1]   Except in Northern Ireland, where credit unions will not be covered by the FSMA 2000 but remain instead subject to the Northern Ireland Registrar of Friendly Societies.

2.23   The FSA introduced the concept of a two-tier system of regulation for credit unions, to reflect the wide range of size and complexity of these firms. A version 1 credit union is one that accepts a requirement that it may not lend more than £10,000 in excess of a member's shareholding. A version 2 credit union, in contrast, has no such requirement but is subject to more onerous regulation[1]. All credit unions, however, will have to comply with those FSA rules which are of general applicability, such as those relating to senior management arrangements, systems and controls, and those relating to the prevention of money laundering.

---

[1]   These distinctions were introduced in the FSA's Consultation Paper 77 (December 2000), and refined in Feedback Statement 77 (July 2001) and Consultation Paper 107 (August 2001).

THE PERMISSION REGIME

2.24   In general, a firm wishing to become authorised under the FSMA 2000 must apply to the FSA for Part IV permission. Once granted, the firm becomes an authorised person and can therefore carry on regulated activities without breaching the general prohibition.

2.25   The regulated activities and specified investments for which a firm may apply to the FSA for a Part IV permission mirror those set out in the Regulated Activities Order, except that the FSA introduces some further sub-divisions. The regulator considers that certain types of activity pose particular risks for consumers, which are distinct from those applying to the related general regulated activity. Accordingly, the FSA identifies these separately and requires firms to apply specifically to undertake these activities. For example, to give advice on personal pension transfers, a firm requires a separate Part IV permission, in addition to any permission it may request for the general activity of giving investment advice. Similarly, operating unregulated collective investment schemes is distinguished from operating regulated schemes, and the activity of arranging safe custody services is separated from that of actually providing such services. Certain specified investments are also singled out for special treatment—applicants wishing to undertake regulated activities in relation to commodity futures and options, spread betting or rolling spot foreign exchange contracts must apply separately for these.

2.26   Whilst the FSMA 2000 creates a single regulator and a single authorisation process, it is important to understand that authorisation does not allow a firm to engage in all regulated activities, only those for which it has been granted permission by the FSA. A firm's Part IV permission is defined with reference to a description of the regulated activities the firm is permitted to undertake, and to the specific investments involved. Once authorised, if the firm were to undertake other regulated activities for which it had not requested and received permission from the FSA, this would be a breach of the FSA rules and subject to the FSA disciplinary procedures. If a firm wishes to amend the range of regulated activities it conducts, it must apply to the FSA to vary its Part IV permission by adding or removing a regulated activity.

2.27   In granting a Part IV permission, the FSA is entitled to impose limitations upon the scope of the regulated activities to be undertaken by the firm, or the type of specified investments involved. A limitation, as might be expected, limits a regulated activity in some way, and is specific to a particular regulated activity. Limitations imposed by the FSA might include, for example, a limitation on the types of customers that the firm may deal with, or on the number of customers that a firm might deal with during its initial period of operation, or on the types of investments or insurance business that the firm may deal in. The scope and extent of these limitations is likely to be agreed between the applicant and FSA during the application process.

2.28   The FSMA 2000, s 43 also gives the FSA to include 'requirements' in a Part IV permission if it considers these to be appropriate. A 'requirement' might require a firm to take, or refrain from taking, a particular action. It might relate to some or all of the firm's activities, including its non-regulated activities, and is a means by which the FSA can control a firm's involvement in certain types of business which are not in themselves identified as regulated activities in the Regulated Activities Order. For example, as part of the application process, a firm is asked to inform the FSA whether or not it wishes to be involved in holding client money, managing Personal Equity Plans or Individual Savings Accounts, operating an investment trust savings scheme or managing a broker fund. Firms that intend to carry on such activities are required to demonstrate their ability to satisfy the FSA's specific regulatory requirements in relation to them, and firms that do not may be given a requirement that specifically excludes these activities.

2.29   The combination of limitations and requirements gives the FSMA 2000 permission regime more flexibility than some of the regulatory arrangements that it replaced. For example, the FSA has proposed[1] that it could operate a separate regulatory regime for wholesale-only deposit takers. Such firms would obtain a Part IV permission to accept deposits, but subject to a limitation that they could accept deposits only from wholesale counterparties such as other credit institutions or large corporate clients. Previously the Banking Act 1987 made no provision for any such distinction; once a firm had obtained authorisation to accept deposits in the UK there was no method of restricting the types of customers with which it could deal. The FSA suggested that wholesale-only deposit takers would not require such close regulatory attention as those banks which accept deposits from private customers, so the costs of regulation would be reduced. This category might therefore be attractive for overseas banks that had previously considered the costs of establishing branches in the UK to be prohibitive.

---

[1]   In FSA Consultation Paper 88 (April 2001). The proposals were then confirmed in Policy Statement 88 in November 2001.

2.30   The FSMA 2000, s 347 requires the FSA to maintain a public register of all authorised firms, which includes information about the services that the firm holds itself out as being able to provide. The register is available on the FSA website, and includes details of each authorised firm's permissions: a description of the regulated activities which each firm has Part IV permission to conduct, together with any limitations or restrictions imposed.

2.31   An authorised firm also needs to ensure that the scope of its Part IV permission is accurate and up-to-date because this determines the fees which it will be required to pay to the FSA—the annual fees which the FSA charges authorised firms are the primary source of its revenue[1]. The FSA defines a series of fee-blocks, based on the types of business conducted, and allocates authorised firms to one or more fee-blocks according to which Part IV permissions they hold. The size of the firm's annual fee is thus determined by the category or categories of business that it undertakes. The fees charged increase with the size of a firm's business, tapering off for very large firms, though there is no maximum fee. The different fee-blocks use different methods of measuring the size of a firm's business—for example, investment management firms are charged according to the value of their funds under management, but for general insurance business the measure of size is gross premium income.

A minimum fee applies to each fee-block—partly to discourage firms from seeking Part IV permissions on a purely precautionary basis when they are not actually undertaking a particular type of business.

---

[1]   The FSA's approach to levying its fees is developed in a series of FSA Consultation Papers, starting with Consultation Paper 56 (June 2000) and followed by Consultation Paper 76 (December 2000) and Consultation Paper 95 (May 2001).

Threshold conditions

2.32   Before granting an application for Part IV permission, the FSA is required to ensure that the applicant firm meets the five threshold conditions set out in the FSMA 2000, Sch 6 and that it is capable of continuing to do so after authorisation.

2.33   The first two of the threshold conditions relate to the legal status of applicants. Although the FSMA 2000 takes the general approach that an authorised person may have any legal form, including that of a natural person, under EU law not all legal forms are permissible in relation to all types of business. The first threshold condition therefore incorporates these restrictions into the FSMA 2000, requiring that firms that wish to undertake insurance business must either be a body corporate, a registered friendly society, or a member of Lloyd's. Similarly, firms that wish to conduct deposit-taking business must be constituted as either a body corporate or a partnership.

2.34   The second condition specifies that if the firm is a body corporate constituted under the laws of any part of the UK, it must have its head office and, if it has one, its registered office, in the UK. In addition, if the firm is not a body corporate and has its head office in the UK, it must carry on business in the UK. This implements the requirement under the post-BCCI directive[1] that authorised persons must have their head office in the same country as that in which they have their registered office, and is intended to ensure that the FSA can identify the location in which a firm's main management decisions are taken, and thus that it can be supervised effectively.

¹   The European Parliament and Council Directive 95/26/EC of 29 June 1995, which was implemented after the collapse of the Bank of Credit and Commerce International highlighted the extent to which the group structure of a financial institution could inhibit effective regulation.

2.35   The remaining three threshold conditions relate to the firm's ability to continue to comply with relevant regulatory requirements after obtaining authorisation.

2.36   The third condition ('close links') also derives from the post-BCCI directive, and is designed to ensure that where a firm is part of a corporate group or is owned or controlled by another person, this structure does not inhibit the FSA's ability to supervise the firm effectively. The FSA gives the example that its ability to supervise a firm effectively might be hindered if part of a group were to be located in a territory with restrictive bank secrecy laws.

2.37   The fourth condition ('resources') requires that the firm must have resources which, in the opinion of FSA, will be adequate in relation to the regulated activities which it seeks to conduct. This covers not only financial resources such as adequate capital and cashflow projections, but also extends to a requirement for the firm to have effective means by which to manage and control risks. These resources must be sufficient in terms of quantity, quality and availability.

2.38   The fifth condition ('suitability') requires the firm to satisfy the FSA that it is a fit and proper person to carry on its proposed regulated activities, having regard to all the circumstances. This condition gives the FSA considerable latitude to take into account a wide range of factors which, in its opinion, would be relevant to its assessment of the firm's fitness and properness, and the FSA provides detailed guidance[1] on its approach to this issue.

¹   The FSA's approach to considering a firm's ability to satisfy the third, fourth and fifth Threshold Conditions can be found in FSA's Consultative Paper 20 and in the Threshold Conditions module of the *FSA Handbook*.

2.39   The FSA can only determine whether an applicant meets the latter three threshold conditions by taking into account the regulated activities that the firm wishes to conduct, since the FSA needs to consider whether the applicant is ready willing and organised to comply with the specific regulatory requirements imposed by the FSA in relation to those activities. These are likely to include the requirements relating to the firm's high level systems and controls, prudential and anti-money laundering provisions and, for most regulated activities, those conduct of business rules which apply in the context of those activities.

2.40   Being considered fit and proper to conduct one type of business does not automatically mean that the firm is fit and proper to conduct other activities as well. If a firm is assessed by the FSA to be fit and proper to conduct the activities requested, it will obtain a Part IV permission to undertake those activities, and hence authorisation. If it later wishes to start undertaking additional regulated activities, it will have to apply to the FSA for additional permissions related to the new activities, and the FSA will at that stage assess whether or not the firm is fit and proper to carry on these new types of business.

Approved persons

2.41   As well as using the threshold conditions to consider the fitness and properness of an applicant firm, the FSA also considers the fitness and properness of the individuals who will manage and run the firm. The FSMA 2000 introduces a regime allowing the FSA to specify certain controlled functions[1] within the firm, and to require that any person fulfilling a controlled function must be individually approved by the FSA. Direct regulation of the individuals filling key roles within an authorised firm is intended to complement the regulation of the firm itself, stressing individual responsibility for compliance with the regulatory regime. This is in many ways very similar to the individual registration regimes operated by several of the previous regulatory authorities under the FSA 1986, but is a new concept for much of the banking and insurance industry, as well as for the newly-regulated sectors such as credit unions.

---

[1]   The FSMA 2000, s 59 provides that the FSA may specify a function as being a controlled function if the person performing the function fulfils any one of three conditions in relation to a regulated activity. A function may be controlled if the person fulfilling the function is likely to exercise significant influence on the conduct of the firm's affairs, or will be involved in dealing with customers of the firm, or will be involved in dealing with the property of customers of the firm. A total of 27 separate functions have been specified by FSA as controlled functions, and these can be found in section 10 of the Supervision Manual module (SUP) of the *FSA Handbook*.

2.42   A firm which wants a person to carry out a controlled function—either for the firm or for its appointed representative—must seek approval from the FSA before allowing that person to carry out that function. A person fulfilling a controlled function would usually be an individual, but could be a legal person such as a body corporate.

2.43   The role of senior management in controlling a firm was highlighted by the collapse of Barings[1], and in designing the FSMA 2000 and the FSA rules one of the key philosophies has been to emphasise the extent to which a firm's senior management must take responsibility for its governance and for controlling the risks to which it is exposed. In general, the members of the firm's governing body—its directors or partners—will be considered to be exercising significant influence over the conduct of its regulated activities, and will therefore require approval by the FSA before they may fulfil this function. In larger firms, the tier of senior management reporting to the governing body may also be in positions of significant influence and thus require approval.

¹   The Report of the Board of Banking Supervision Inquiry into the Circumstances of the Collapse of Barings, published by HMSO in July 1995, provides an excellent description of these events and their implications for the regulatory system.

THE AUTHORISATION PROCESS

2.44   In place of the different authorisation procedures of the various predecessor regulatory bodies, the FSA operates a single application process for all types of firm, whatever type of regulated activity they intend to conduct. The declared purpose is to integrate and simplify the various approaches, and improve the level of consistency involved in assessing applications for authorisation. As the FSMA 2000 gradually evolved from its first consultation draft in July 1998, the FSA adopted a commendabiy open approach and published a large number of consultation papers, feedback statements and policy statements setting out how it intended to meet its new responsibilities, including its approach to the authorisation process[1].

¹   The main ones of relevance to the authorisation process being Consultation Paper 20 'Qualifying Conditions for Authorisation' (March 1999), together with its related Feedback Statement published in October 1999; Consultation Paper 29 'The Permission Regime' (October 1999) and its related Response Paper published in August 2000; and Consultation Paper 63 'The Authorisation Manual' (August 2000), with its related Policy Statement published in May 2001. The Authorisation Manual itself was developed in Consultation Paper 104 (August 2001) and its Policy Statement in November 2001.

2.45   The authorisation process is a fundamental part of the FSA's risk-based approach to regulation, providing the foundation and understanding for its subsequent risk-based supervision regime[1]. The risks that any firm might pose to consumers or to financial markets vary according to the nature and complexity of the activities which it proposes to conduct, and the types of customers involved. The authorisation process should enable the FSA to satisfy itself that the firm is capable of identifying and managing those risks. Only those firms which meet the threshold conditions are granted authorisation, and the FSA states that its assessment is proportional to the risks associated with the particular activities which the firm applies to conduct. The FSA's consideration of an application to undertake activities which are perceived to pose lower risks to consumers will be less onerous than that applied for a higher-risk activity such as deposit-taking.

¹   In 'A New Regulator for the New Millennium', published by the FSA in January 2000, the FSA indicated that it would score firms' risks against a number of probability factors relating to the likelihood of an event happening, and impact factors relating to the scale and significance of the problem if it were to occur. This assessment then informs the way that the FSA supervises the firm after authorisation. Further details are included in the Supervision Manual module of the *FSA Handbook*.

2.46   The steps for achieving authorisation are set out in the FSA's Authorisation Manual module of the *FSA Handbook*. This is a helpful and relatively user-friendly document, which guides the prospective applicant through the complex choices and decisions involved in achieving authorisation in the UK. The Authorisation Manual includes substantial amounts of guidance on the FSA's interpretation of those provisions in the FSMA 2000 and the related statutory instruments relating to the scope of the authorisation requirement, particularly the Regulated Activities Order[1]. It outlines the types of investment covered by the FSMA 2000, the types of activity which require authorisation, the activities which are specifically excluded from the definition of regulated activities, and the circumstances in which a person can be exempted from the need to be authorised. It also includes an explanation of the legal powers in the FSMA which govern the FSA's authorisation procedures. This gives a potential applicant a good initial indication of whether or not it will need a Part IV permission to carry on a particular activity in the UK. However, the Authorisation Manual explicitly states that it offers high level guidance only, and that any potential applicant should refer to the detailed provisions of the FSMA 2000 and its subordinate legislation, and should seek professional advice when necessary.

The Authorisation Manual also helpfully includes the telephone numbers and e-mail addresses of those FSA staff who should be able to answer applicants' detailed questions about the authorisation process—the FSA actively encourages prospective applicants to approach the regulator to discuss their plans.

---

[1]   Financial Services and Markets Act 2000 (Regulated Activities) Order 2001, SI 2001/544.

2.47   The FSA provides an application pack to prospective applicants. All applicants have to complete certain sections, including those covering the basic information such as the applicant's name and address, legal status and group structure, and the regulated activities it wishes to carry on. Other sections are specific to the applicant's intended business sector, and are supplemented by guidance notes relating to that sector. Each section includes details of the particular regulatory requirements which would apply to the activities that the firm seeks to undertake, enabling the firm to produce and submit to the FSA the information necessary for the regulator to assess the application.

2.48   All applicants must provide the FSA with certain basic information as part of the application pack. The central requirement is to provide a detailed business plan which sets out both the regulated activities and the non-regulated activities which the firm proposes to undertake. This must be supplemented by financial budgets and projections demonstrating that the firm is capable of complying with the relevant prudential requirements, details of the systems that the firm intends to use and its compliance procedures, and details of the individuals who will be involved in running the firm.

2.49   The FSA defines a number of categories and sub-categories of firms for the purpose of prudential regulation, determining how much regulatory capital the firm will be required to hold, and what type and frequency of reporting to the FSA will be required[1]. An applicant's prudential category is determined by its main regulated activities—that is, those from which it is expected to derive the most substantial part of its gross income. So as part of the application process, the applicant needs to decide into which of the prudential categories it will fall, and thus how much regulatory capital it will be required to provide. In considering a firm's financial resources, the FSA can also take into account the financial condition of other companies in the same group.

---

[1]   In the period immediately following N2, firms will be governed by one of the five Interim Prudential Sourcebooks. These will set out separate rules governing banks, building societies, insurance business, friendly societies and investment business respectively, and can be found in FSA Policy Statement 6 (January 2001); Consultation Paper 84 (March 2001); and Policy Statement 54 (March 2001). In due course—not before January 2004—these various interim rules will be replaced by a single Integrated Prudential Sourcebook which will set out the prudential categories that will apply to all firms. The first draft of this integrated rulebook was published by the FSA in June 2001 in Consultation Paper 97. Separately, the details of the requirements for financial reporting to the FSA are included in the Supervision Manual module.

2.50   If the applicant is an entity which has its principal place of business in a country outside the EEA[1], in assessing the application the FSA will have regard to the applicant as a whole, not just the proposed UK branch. As part of this process, it is likely to liaise with the overseas regulatory authority with principal responsibility for supervising the firm. The FSA will take into account information from the overseas regulator about the adequacy of the applicant's resources and internal control systems, and its suitability. In general, the FSA regulatory requirements apply to the firm in full—in other words, to all of its activities worldwide. However, for a firm regulated in another country and governed by different regulatory requirements for that part of its business, it would be unnecessary and unduly burdensome for the FSA rules and guidance to apply as well. In practice, therefore, the FSA uses a combination of limitations, restrictions or waivers of its rules, to ensure that its rules apply to such a firm in an appropriate manner.

---

[1]   The EEA comprises the European Union states of Austria, Belgium, Denmark, Finland, France, Germany, Greece, Ireland, Italy, Luxembourg, Netherlands, Portugal, Spain, Sweden and the United Kingdom, together with Iceland, Liechtenstein and Norway.

2.51   As the FSA indicates in the Authorisation Manual, an applicant for a Part IV permission needs to go through a number of steps before submitting its application to the FSA. It needs to consider all its activities carefully and decide the extent to which each of them requires authorisation, and may well require specialised legal advice on this. It must then prepare the detailed business plan outlining its proposed activities and the resources it will employ to conduct these activities. After obtaining the FSA application pack, the firm will consider the detailed range of permissions it will need, and determine which prudential category will be appropriate and thus how much regulatory capital will be required. At this stage the firm may wish to call upon its lawyers, accountants or other professional advisers to assist in preparing parts of the application (for example, in drafting client agreements). The application pack's guidance on the aspects of the *FSA Handbook* that will apply to the chosen activities will enable the applicant to consider what systems and controls will be expected, in order to demonstrate to the FSA that it is ready, willing and organised to comply with the relevant obligations. The FSA will also expect to see that the firm has plans to implement and test these systems and controls before the determination of the application by the FSA. In some cases, auditors' or accountants' reports may be required by the FSA to support the application.

2.52 At the same time as submitting the application for the authorisation of the firm, the applicant has to consider which of its employees will be undertaking controlled functions, and has to prepare and submit applications for the approval of these persons. An approved person is only approved by the FSA to carry out a particular function for a particular firm. Therefore, even if a person has previously been approved by the FSA to carry out a similar function for a different firm, the applicant firm will still need to submit a new application for approved person status to the FSA.

2.53 The FSA may also take into consideration any person who appears to the FSA to be, or to be likely to be, in a relevant relationship with the applicant—a connected person[1]. The FSA may thus ask for information about any other person, if it believes that this will be relevant to the determination of the application. The FSA will assess whether a relationship is relevant in the light of all the circumstances of that application. If a firm is part of a larger group of companies, the FSA requirements will strictly apply only to the entity applying for authorisation, but the position of other group companies could be relevant to the FSA's assessment of the applicant firm, and the FSA could consult with the overseas regulators of affiliated companies in the group.

---

[1]   This authority derives from the FSMA 2000, s 49. The FSA states (AUTH 3.9.22 G) that connected persons could include, but would not be restricted to, controllers of the applicant, companies in the same group as the applicant, members of the governing body of the applicant, a person with whom the applicant intends to enter into a material outsourcing agreement, or any other person who may exert influence over the applicant which might pose a risk to the applicant satisfying the threshold conditions.

2.54 In summary therefore, it can be seen that an applicant for a Part IV permission, unless it is proposing to conduct only the simplest and most limited forms of regulated activities, is likely to be involved in significant work and expense in preparing the application. It will need to have employed at least its principal staff, and to have started to set up its systems and procedures, a considerable time before it can expect to obtain its authorisation and thus before it can start earning any revenue.

2.55 Once the application has been submitted, the FSA starts considering it, using its risk assessment process. During the FSA's review of the application, the firm will need to continue implementing and testing the systems and controls that it has notified the FSA will be in place. The FSA Corporate Authorisation and Individual Vetting and Registration teams may both ask for additional information about various aspects of the application, and it is very likely that FSA staff will wish to visit the applicant's premises and meet its management team as part of their assessment of the application.

2.56   The FSA can take a flexible approach to the application process. For example, as financial services businesses started to operate by way of the Internet and other channels of e-commerce, the FSA reacted by producing a systems questionnaire focusing on the requirements appropriate for e-commerce. This extended the range of information gathered through the application process, addressing such issues as management controls, project management, systems testing and staff training, and systems security.

2.57   The FSMA 2000 requires the FSA to determine applications within six months if they are submitted in complete form, and within 12 months if incomplete. These are the maximum times permitted by the statute however, and the FSA has stated that it intends to process straightforward applications much more quickly than this—within three months whenever possible. The FSA will publish standard response times on its website to indicate the timescales that it expects to achieve in processing the majority of applications for a Part IV permission and for approval under the approved person regime.

2.58   When the FSA grants an application for a Part IV permission, it provides the firm with a single permission which specifies all or some of the following: a description of the activities the firm is permitted to carry on, including any limitations imposed by the FSA, the specified investments involved, and, where appropriate, requirements on the firm to take or to refrain from taking particular actions. If the FSA does propose a limitation or restriction, it gives the applicant formal notice of this, and an opportunity to make representations before the FSA makes its final decision. During the FSA's discussions with an applicant, it may become clear to the FSA that the firm needs permission for a different regulated activity from the ones specified in the application. Therefore in granting the firm's application the FSA may specify a narrower or wider description of regulated activity than that originally sought by the firm, or may grant permission for a regulated activity for which the firm had not applied at all.

THE DECISION-MAKING AND APPEALS PROCESSES

2.59   The FSA publishes details of its procedures for reaching decisions on applications for a Part IV permission[1], and on the processes available for appealing against the FSA's decisions. In addition to setting up the Financial Services and Markets Tribunal for appeals against the FSA's legislative powers, the FSMA 2000 requires the FSA to establish arrangements for the investigation of complaints arising in connection with the exercise of, or the failure to exercise its administrative functions[2]. This gives firms another route for making complaints to an independent Complaints Commissioner about the FSA's handling of applications for authorisation or for approved person status.

---

[1]   The FSA's decision-making powers and procedures are described in the Decision-Making Manual module of the *FSA Handbook*.

[2]   This derives from the FSMA 2000, Sch 1, paras 7 and 8 and the arrangements are described in FSA Consultation Paper 73 (November 2000) and Consultation Paper 93 (May 2001) and confirmed in Policy Statement 93 (August 2001).

2.60   It is generally perceived that the FSA's authorisation process should be simpler and more streamlined than those that it replaced, which will be of particular benefit to firms conducting a range of varying financial services activities. For example, a firm which already conducts one type of financial services activity, such as deposit-taking, may wish to commence a different activity, such as the provision of corporate finance advice. An application to the FSA to vary the firm's Part IV permission should be much simpler than the previous requirement to make a full application to a different regulatory body.

2.61   Under the FSA 1986 it was sometimes less clear whether or not particular activities required authorisation, and a number of firms obtained authorisation on a precautionary basis just in case their activities might be considered to stray into the realms of regulatory authority. In contrast, the FSA actively discourages such precautionary authorisation. Once a Part IV permission has been granted for a particular regulated activity, the FSA expects the firm to start conducting that activity promptly. If the firm does not commence a regulated activity within 12 months of the permission being granted, or later ceases to conduct a particular regulated activity, the FSA may exercise its powers to cancel or vary the Part IV permission, though it would always discuss its intentions with the firm before acting.

APPLICATION FEES

2.62   As well as the periodic fees charged to authorised firms, the FSA also charges fees to process applications for authorisation. These are charged at different rates according to the complexity of the application, which is mainly determined by the nature of the business that the applicant wishes to conduct. For example, assessing an application for permission to accept deposits is likely to be a more complex process than assessing an application for permission only to give investment advice. Depending on the nature of the permissions applied for, the FSA divides applications into three categories—straightforward, moderately complex, and complex applications. At the time of writing, the initial indication is that the FSA intends to charge £2,000 for a straightforward application, £5,000 for a moderately complex one, and £25,000 for a complex application, though there are reductions available for special cases such as small credit unions. Application fees are not refundable if applications are not successful, and the FSA reviews the size of these fees annually as part of its budget process.

It should also be noted that if a firm later submits an application to vary its Part IV permission, and this causes the firm to fall into a new FSA fee-block, the FSA will also charge a fee to process this variation, at a rate of half the fee charged to process the equivalent authorisation fee.

GRANDFATHERING

2.63   In order to ensure that firms and individuals which were already authorised to conduct banking, insurance or investment business in the UK were not required to reapply for authorisation under the FSMA 2000, 'grandfathering' arrangements were put in place[1]. All those firms, which were already authorised or regulated under the FSA 1986 and other statutes governing banking and insurance business, were grandfathered, provided that they continued to undertake the same types of business. It also covered all the individuals working for those firms in capacities that were to become controlled functions at N2, regardless of whether they were already registered/approved before that.

However, in the event that a firm was grandfathered but was subsequently found not to meet the threshold conditions, the FSA was given the power to require certain firms to reapply for authorisation within a period of two years from N2.

---

[1]   The grandfathering arrangements are contained in the Financial Services and Markets Act 2000 (Transitional Provisions) (Authorised Persons etc) Order 2001, SI 2001/2636 and are explained in the FSA policy statement 'Grandfathering of Firms, Individuals and Products', which was published in December 2000 and updated in January 2001.

2.64   The FSA announced its intention to keep the transition to the new regulatory regime as simple as possible for firms which were already authorised, by issuing each firm with two lists. The first detailed all the regulated activities that the firm was understood to be already undertaking, together with any limitations or restrictions which were already in place, thus reflecting its existing authorisation. The second was a list of those individuals employed within the firm, or by its appointed representatives, who were known to be currently undertaking controlled functions, and who would thus become approved persons.

2.65   These lists were sent to most firms about three months before N2, for firms to check and confirm the accuracy of the information—correcting any errors and omissions identified. For larger firms and complex groups this process started much earlier, with firms being asked to start checking their lists in April 2001. It was particularly important for most firms to review and check their list of approved persons, since in many cases the FSA could not be aware of the identity of all relevant employees, particularly those fulfilling functions which were about to become controlled for the first time. The definitions of controlled functions resulted in the scope of the FSA approved person regime being different from that of the various individual registration regime which it replaced, so the numbers and identities of individuals involved in fulfilling these functions changed significantly for many firms.

2.66   The FSA was particularly concerned that the grandfathering process should only enable firms to carry forward their existing authorisations, and that they should not be able to take advantage of the process to extend the scope of their regulated activities—it was stressed that if any new activities were to be undertaken, an application for a Part IV permission would be required in the usual way. Firms that were unable to reach agreement with the FSA about the extent of their current authorisation which was to be carried forward, had to use the appeals procedures to resolve the dispute.

2.67 By reaching agreement with the FSA on the scope of the activities covered by the grandfathering arrangements, the firm was given its Part IV permission for these activities. Firms which were previously operating under limitations or requirements (such as a requirement not to hold or handle client money) had these carried forward in the grandfathering process too. Similarly, firms that were operating with the benefit of formal concessions or waivers granted by the predecessor regulatory bodies were able to have these grandfathered by the FSA, though in this case only for a maximum period of 12 months after N2. To minimise disruption and the costs of the transition, the FSA provided that all pre-existing concessions continued in effect for a period of 12 months after N2. Any firm that wanted to retain the benefit of a grandfathered concession beyond that time, needed to apply to the FSA for a new waiver of the appropriate FSA rule.

As soon as possible after N2, the FSA was required to send each authorised firm a 'permission notice' stating which regulated activities the FSA considered the firm had permission to undertake at N2, together with the associated limitations and restrictions. No fees were charged for the grandfathering process.

2.68 Obviously, firms conducting activities such as mortgage lending were not previously authorised, so were not able to take advantage of the grandfathering arrangements. Professional firms were similarly unable to use the grandfathering arrangements: instead of carrying forward their existing FSA 1986 authorisation from their Recognised Professional Body, they had to decide whether to take advantage of the regime for exempt professional firms, or to apply for a Part IV permission from the FSA.

2.69 Firms which were operating as appointed representatives also had to review their position. If all their activities were within the scope of their status as an appointed representative for an authorised firm under the FSA 1986, these activities remained exempt under the FSMA 2000 and the appointed representative did not need to take any action. But if the appointed representative was also authorised in its own right for a different activity, such as deposit taking under the Banking Act 1987, it had to make a decision. The FSMA 2000 no longer permits a firm to be both authorised for one activity and exempt for another. So if the firm wished to continue conducting both types of activities, it had to give up its appointed representative status and obtain a Part IV permission to cover both the previously authorised activities, and the previously exempt activities.

THE OBLIGATIONS OF AUTHORISATION

2.70 As described above, applicants for a Part IV permission are expected to demonstrate to the FSA that they are ready, willing and organised to comply, on an ongoing basis, with all the regulatory requirements that are applicable to the type of business they are seeking to conduct. In order to do this, a firm has to consider which parts of the *FSA Handbook* of rules and guidance are relevant to its activities. The *FSA Handbook* is divided into six separate sections, the first of which, High Level Standards, applies to all authorised firms.

High Level Standards for Firms and Individuals

2.71   Within this section, the starting point for all authorised firms is the 11 FSA Principles for Businesses[1], which are intended as concise statements of the fundamental standards expected of all firms. The Principles generally apply to all a firm's regulated activities in the UK and in some circumstances the FSA may also take into account a firm's non-regulated activities and its activities outside the UK. The Principles are deliberately couched in very general terms, so that they can cover any circumstances, even where no specific FSA rules or guidance apply.

---

[1]   Set out in full in the first module of the *FSA Handbook*.

2.72   Breach of the Principles for Businesses may render a firm liable to the full range of disciplinary sanctions available to the FSA. However, whereas a breach of an FSA rule is usually actionable at the suit of a private person under the FSMA 2000, s 150, breach of the Principles for Businesses does not expose the firm to such action. Firms which were previously authorised to conduct investment business under the FSA 1986 were already familiar with these concepts, though they were new to firms undertaking banking and insurance activities as well as the newly regulated activities such as mortgage lending.

2.73   After the Principles for Businesses, the authorised firm needs to consider the FSA's approach to senior management responsibilities—the FSA has stated many times that it places particular emphasis on the need for strong management controls. As well as requiring the firm to take reasonable care to maintain effective systems and controls and adequate risk management arrangements, the FSA specifically requires the firm to create a division of roles between its senior management, to ensure that their individual responsibilities for the various aspects of the business are always clear. In particular, the firm is required to give a member of its senior management team the specific responsibility for apportioning its senior management responsibilities, and for the general oversight of the operation of the firm's systems and controls. For most firms, the chief executive officer will be the individual who is responsible for this apportionment and oversight role, though in larger firms it is possible that two or more individuals may jointly have this responsibility.

2.74   As well as the Principles for Businesses which apply to the authorised firm, the FSA has also published separate Statements of Principle which apply to approved persons, and these are supported by a detailed Code of Practice[1]. As with the Principles for Businesses, these Statements of Principle are high level statements of the standards expected of all approved persons, breach of which is an act of misconduct rendering the individual liable to

FSA disciplinary action. The Code of Practice then fleshes these out with examples of behaviour that the FSA suggests would be likely to be held to be in breach of these Principles.

---

[1] The FSA Statements of Principle and Code of Practice for Approved Persons are set out in the Approved Persons module of the *FSA Handbook* and are explained in Consultation Paper 26 (July 1999) and the Policy Statement 'High Level Standards for Firms and Individuals' (June 2000).

2.75 The senior management of an authorised firm will almost always be performing controlled functions, so will fall within the FSA's approved persons regime. They will thus be governed by two interlocking sets of requirements—both by the rules relating to the firm's obligation to have adequate senior management arrangements and by the provisions relating directly to them as approved persons.

2.76 If the firm conducts 'designated' investment business, as distinct from deposit-taking or insurance activities, it must designate an individual as having the responsibility for oversight of its compliance function. This individual must be a director or senior manager of the firm, and is required to report to the firm's governing body on the firm's fulfilment of its responsibilities under the regulatory regime. Strictly speaking, the Compliance Oversight function is required only to extend to monitoring compliance with the Principles for Businesses and the rules relating to conduct of business and market conduct requirements, and those relating to collective investment schemes if relevant. In practice, however, in most firms it would be usual for the compliance function to take responsibility for advising on all aspects of regulatory risk.

Business Standards

2.77 This second section of the *FSA Handbook* contains the main FSA rules and guidance that are likely to be of relevance to the authorised firm's operations from day-to-day[1]. The precise extent to which these various requirements apply to each authorised firm will depend on both the type of business it is conducting, and the types of clients involved. A firm can only ensure that it is aware of all the regulatory provisions that will apply to its business, and therefore all the procedures and controls that the FSA will expect to see in place, by studying each provision in detail. The format of the *FSA Handbook* assists this process, because each chapter of the rules starts with a description of its application, setting out which types of firms and activities will be affected.

---

[1] The Business Standards block of the *FSA Handbook* incorporates the following sets of rules and guidance: the Prudential Sourcebook which prescribes the capital adequacy requirements; the Conduct of Business Sourcebook which governs the relationships between firms and their clients; and the Market Conduct Sourcebook which governs relationships between authorised firms on regulated markets. It also includes the Training and Competence Sourcebook, which applies particularly to firms conducting designated investment business involving private customers; and the Money Laundering Sourcebook which establishes the standards that firms are expected to adopt in implementing internal procedures to prevent becoming involved in money laundering activity.

Other issues

2.78   The next section of the *FSA Handbook* that the firm will want to consider is that on redress. This includes authorised firms' obligations in relation to handling customer complaints, including the obligation to make biannual reports to the FSA about complaints received from certain categories of customer, and their obligation to co-operate with the Financial Ombudsman Service.

2.79   The final two sections of the *FSA Handbook* collect together the various requirements that apply to specialised sectors of financial services business such as mortgage business, credit unions, professional firms, and the Lloyd's market. Firms which intend to undertake these types of activities must naturally study these specialised requirements as well as the sections that apply to all authorised firms.

THE FSA'S RELATIONSHIP WITH AUTHORISED FIRMS

2.80   As a result of the risk assessment process undertaken during the application process (or during the grandfathering process for those firms previously authorised before N2), the FSA allocates each authorised firm to one of four risk categories A, B, C or D. These summarise the FSA's overall assessment of the risk which the FSA believes that the firm poses to its own regulatory objectives, and indicate the nature of the relationship which the FSA expects to have with the firm[1]. Category A firms are considered to be high risk and the FSA expects to maintain close contact with such firms, with frequent visits to the firm and a continuous dialogue between the firm and its regulator. At the other end of the spectrum Category D firms are considered to be low risk and the FSA indicates that it would expect to have a much more remote relationship with such firms with a much lower level of routine monitoring of their activities.

---

[1]   The FSA's approach to assessing these risks and categorising authorised firms is set out in its report 'Building the New Regulator' (December 2000).

2.81   Although firms undertaking activities of similar nature and scale will be assessed by the FSA as having the same impact on the market in the event of regulatory failure, they can reduce the FSA's perception of the probability of such an event occurring, by improving their management controls. Thus the risk category applied by the FSA is to some extent within the firm's own control, giving firms an incentive to strengthen their management controls and thus reduce their risk category. By achieving a lower risk assessment, the firm might expect the FSA to adopt a less intrusive approach, which has the benefit of reducing the amount of management time absorbed in the regulatory relationship.

It should be noted that these risk categories make no difference to the firm's obligation to comply with all the applicable the FSA rules and guidance that relate to the firm's activities. The risk categories only affect the nature of the firm's relationship with the FSA.

THE EUROPEAN DIMENSION

2.82 With so much emphasis on the changes that have been in preparation in the UK for so long, it can be easy to forget that the UK approach to regulation must continue to be viewed in the context of the European legislation arising out of the EU single market programme, which has included a number of directives which aim to harmonise the regulatory requirements applying to financial services activities throughout the EEA[1]. These directives already have a significant effect on financial services businesses in Europe, particularly in respect of authorisation requirements.

---

[1] The main directives of relevance in this context for banks and other deposit-taking firms are the First and Second European Union Council Directives on the Co-ordination of Laws, Regulations and Administrative Provisions relating to the Taking-Up and Pursuit of the Business of Credit Institutions (Council Directives 77/780/EEC and 89/646/EEC)—known as the First and Second Banking Directives (1BCD and 2BCD). For firms undertaking investment business the relevant directives are the European Council Directive on Investment Services in the Securities Field (Council Directive 93/22/EEC)—known as the ISD. For insurance companies the relevant directives are the First, Second and Third European Council Directives on the Co-ordination of laws, regulations and administrative provisions relating to the taking up and pursuit of the business of direct life assurance (Council Directives 79/267/EEC, 90/619/EEC and 92/96/EEC)—known as the First, Second and Third Life Directives (1LD, 2LD and 3LD) and the First Second and Third European Council Directives on the Co-ordination of laws, regulations and administrative provisions relating to the taking up and pursuit of the business of direct insurance other than life assurance (Council Directives 73/239/EEC, 88/357/EEC and 92/49/EEC)—known as the First, Second and Third Non-Life Directives (1NLD, 2NLD and 3NLD).

2.83 There are two main themes behind these directives. The first is the desire to create a 'level playing field' for financial services businesses in the EEA by harmonising the amounts of capital required to support such business. The intention was to reduce the distorting effect of differing capital requirements both as between banks based in different countries, and also as between bank and non-bank financial institutions.

2.84 The second theme is the creation of the 'single passport'. It is the intention of the single market programme that a firm which is properly authorised in any one EEA state should be able to offer financial services in any other country within the EEA, without having to obtain a separate licence to do so. This applies whether the firm wishes to operate through branches established in other EEA states, or simply by offering services on a cross-border basis into other countries. This 'single passport' is made available by different routes: banks and other credit institutions obtain their passport via the First and Second Banking Directives[1]; insurance companies via the First, Second and Third Life and Non-Life Directives[2]; whereas investment firms obtain similar rights from the Investment Services Directive[3].

---

[1] Council Directives 77/780/EEC and 89/646/EEC.
[2] Council Directives 79/267/EEC, 90/619/EEC and 92/96/EEC; and 73/239/EEC, 88/357/EEC, 92/49/EEC.
[3] Council Directive 93/22/EEC.

2.85   The directives introduce the distinction between 'home state' and 'host state' regulatory responsibilities. The home state is generally the country in which the firm is incorporated or has its head office, and the host state is any other EEA member state in which the firm offers financial services, whether via a branch or on a cross-border basis. A firm must obtain authorisation from the appropriate regulatory body in its home state, and it is then free, in theory, to offer its services throughout the EEA. Since the passport is only available from the regulator of the country in which the firm has its registered office (the 'home state regulator'), it follows that it is only available to firms that are incorporated in one of the EEA states and not to those which are incorporated anywhere else in the world. Each member state must establish a 'competent authority' with responsibility for authorising financial services firms—in the UK this is the FSA.

2.86   The directives are based on the general premise that the home state regulator will be responsible for the authorisation of the firm and for supervising its compliance with prudential requirements such as capital adequacy and the handling of client money and assets. The host state regulator will only be responsible for conduct of business issues relating to the business being conducted in that state, such as the requirements relating to the advertising and marketing of services, or those governing the relationship between the firm and its clients.

The effect of these arrangements on the UK's system of authorisation can be viewed from two different perspectives: that of the UK firm wishing to offer services in other EEA states and conversely that of the non-UK firm wishing to conduct financial services business in the UK.

UK firms passporting out of the UK

2.87   Once a UK-based firm has obtained authorisation from the FSA to conduct a particular type of business covered by the single market programme in the UK, it does not then need separate authorisation in order to conduct similar business in any other EEA state. Instead if, for example, it wishes to open a branch in France, it has only to notify the FSA of this intention. The FSA in turn notifies the competent authority in France, which has a period of three months in which to object to the proposal. If no objection is made during that time, the UK firm is free to open its branch in France[1].

---

[1]   The FSA provides guidance on the procedures to be followed by a UK firm wishing to exercise its EEA passporting rights in the Supervision Manual module of the *FSA Handbook* of rules and guidance.

2.88   A firm which is applying for a Part IV permission for the first time may already be aware that it wishes to exercise its rights to passport into one or more EEA states, and in some circumstances it is possible for the applicant to submit a 'notice of intention' to passport to the FSA at the same time as submitting the application for Part IV permission. However, the prerequisite for exercising EEA passport rights is that the firm must already be authorised in its home state, so the FSA cannot grant the required consent to operate in another EEA state until such time as the firm is actually granted its Part IV permission and hence has become authorised in the UK.

2.89 The implementation of the FSMA 2000 has been an opportunity to bring together the procedures under which UK firms may exercise their single market rights to passport into other EEA states, superseding the previous legislation. The FSMA 2000 now sets out the procedures for a UK firm establishing branches in, or providing services on a cross-border basis into, another EEA state. A UK firm wishing to passport into the EEA must be an authorised person and the FSA must be satisfied about matters such as its resources and systems to undertake such business.

EEA firms passporting in to the UK

2.90 A firm which is incorporated in another EEA state and which wishes to open a branch in the UK or offer its services on a cross-border basis into the UK can similarly take advantage of the 'passport' arrangements. Having obtained authorisation from its home state regulator, such a firm will not have to apply to the FSA for separate authorisation. Three categories of firm are automatically authorised under the FSMA 2000, s 31(1) if they meet certain conditions: these are known as EEA firms, Treaty firms and UCITS qualifiers.

2.91 An EEA firm[1] may qualify for authorisation under the FSMA 2000, Sch 3 if it satisfies the establishment conditions (for those firms seeking to establish a branch in the UK) or the service conditions (for those firms wishing to provide services into the UK on a cross-border basis). The EEA firm needs to contact its home state regulator, which will advise it on the procedures required to exercise its passport rights into the UK.

---

[1] An EEA firm is a person whose head office is situated in an EEA state other than the UK, and which is authorised in its home state under the arrangements applicable to the appropriate EC banking, investment or insurance directive.

2.92 However, it is important to note that the FSMA 2000 does not cover exactly the same range of activities as the single market directives, so firms undertaking some activities in the UK will still need to obtain FSA authorisation. Examples of these types of activities are trading in commodity derivatives, and the management of collective investment schemes. Each of these requires authorisation under the FSMA 2000, but is specifically excluded from the scope of the single market directives. As a result, a firm which, for example, is authorised in Germany to trade commodity derivatives, will still require separate authorisation from the FSA to trade such products in the UK. In the same way as it can be a complex process to determine exactly which of a firm's activities need to be authorised under the FSMA 2000, it is similarly difficult to determine which of its activities are within the scope of the single market directives and therefore whether the firm can take advantage of a single passport.

2.93   A firm established in the EEA which cannot exercise passporting rights because its activities are outside the scope of the single market directives, has to apply to the FSA for a Part IV permission in the same way as a UK firm or a firm established in any non-EEA state.

2.94   A firm may be automatically authorised for some of its activities, but require Part IV permission for other activities (such as reinsurance or commodity derivatives business), and in this case the FSA refers to the Part IV permission as a 'top-up permission'. The FSA Authorisation Manual gives guidance to EEA firms on the procedures by which an EEA firm can gain automatic authorisation in the UK, and also includes guidance on the 'top-up permission' required. The FSA's procedures for considering applications for such top-up permissions are the same as those for any other Part IV permission, with the applicant having to satisfy the relevant requirements in relation to the threshold conditions, the approved persons regime, and all other relevant provisions.

2.95   A Treaty firm[1] which has no right to passport under one of the single market directives may anyway qualify for authorisation under the FSMA 2000, Sch 4 if it is authorised under the laws of its home state to undertake the regulated activities it wishes to conduct in the UK. A Treaty firm has to submit an application for authorisation to the FSA, accompanied by confirmation of its authorisation from its home state regulator. In practice, however, it is not expected that this route will be of relevance to many firms.

---

[1]   A Treaty firm is a person whose head office is situated in an EEA state other than the UK and which is recognised under the law of that state as its national, as defined in the FSMA 2000, Sch 4.

2.96   The third category of firm which is entitled to automatic authorisation under the FSMA 2000 is a UCITS qualifier[1]—under the FSMA 2000, Sch 5 these firms may establish, operate or wind up collective investment schemes and undertake ancillary activities in connection with this business. Such firms will also have to refer to the Collective Investment Scheme Sourcebook for guidance on how to obtain recognition of such schemes under the FSMA 2000.

---

[1]   A UCITS qualifier is an operator, trustee or depositary of a recognised collective investment scheme which is constituted in an EEA state other than the UK.

THE FUTURE

2.97   At the time of writing the full implications of the implementation of the FSMA 2000 are still emerging. The FSA continues to respond to concerns and comments both from the financial services industry and from consumers, publishing consultation papers and policy statements almost daily. The EU single market programme is not complete either, with further directives covering matters such as distance selling and the regulation of takeovers still being discussed.

2.98 It is not becoming any easier for firms to establish exactly which of their activities require authorisation and under what circumstances, and to ensure full compliance with all the applicable regulations. However, the FSA's procedures for accepting and considering applications for authorisation in the UK are fully transparent and have been published in considerable detail, and represent a significant improvement over the variety of different approaches adopted by the numerous regulators it has replaced.

Chapter 3   Financial Promotion

Owen Watkins

INTRODUCTION

3.1   In keeping with the general philosophy behind the Financial Services and Markets Act 2000 (FSMA 2000), the financial promotion regime seeks to rationalise and modernise, into a single consolidated whole, the existing requirements applying to investment promotions. In this case, however, the consolidation has also resulted in a new vocabulary. No longer does the statute speak of an 'advertisement' or of an 'unsolicited call'; instead, it covers 'an invitation or inducement to engage in investment activity'—that is, a financial promotion[1].

---

[1]   FSMA 2000, s 21(1). The words 'financial promotion', though not appearing in the actual text of s 21, are used in the heading and the marginal note.

3.2   Given that one of the main purposes behind the FSMA 2000 was the consolidation of existing requirements in banking, financial services and insurance legislation, it seems at first sight strange that the FSMA 2000 should in s 21 seek to change concepts with which firms and their advisers were well familiar, and instead introduce ones that are new. But throughout the consultation process on the new regime, the Treasury emphasised that its aim was to move to a more 'media neutral' concept. Recent technological developments in communications (in particular, the growth of the Internet) had meant that the existing legislation was becoming increasingly strained to accommodate electronic media within 'advertisements' and 'unsolicited calls'. It was a key Government aim that the financial services system in the United Kingdom should be best placed to reflect, and continue to reflect, the opportunities afforded by electronic commerce[1].

---

[1]   See HM Treasury, Financial Promotion—A Consultation Document (March 1999), part 1, paras 1.2–1.3; Financial Promotion—Second Consultation Document: A New Approach for the Information Age (October 1999), part 1, paras 1.2, 3.3; Financial Promotion—Third Consultation Document (October 2000), para 1.7.

THE STATUTORY PROVISION

3.3   The restriction on making a financial promotion (referred to in this chapter as 'the basic prohibition'), and the main circumstances in which the basic prohibition is lifted, are set out in the FSMA 2000, ss 21(1) and (2).

'(1) A person ("A") must not, in the course of business, communicate an invitation or inducement to engage in investment activity.

(2) But subsection (1) does not apply if—

    (a)   A is an authorised person; or

    (b)   the content of the communication is approved for the purposes of this section by an authorised person.'

The FSMA 2000, s 21(5) gives the Treasury the power to create by order further exclusions, by specifying circumstances in which the basic prohibition will not apply. The Treasury has accordingly made an order under this section, the Financial Services and Markets Act 2000 (Financial Promotion) Order 2001[1].

---

[1]   SI 2001/1335, referred to in this chapter as the Financial Promotion Order and discussed further at paras 3.20 ff. At the time of writing the Financial Promotion Order had been subject to two amending orders, the Financial Services and Markets Act 2000 (Financial Promotion) (Amendment) Order 2001, SI 2001/2633 and the Financial Services and Markets Act 2000 (Financial Promotion) (Amendment No 2) Order 2001, SI 2001/3800. SI 2001/1335, art 16 has also been amended by the Financial Services and Markets Act 2000 (Miscellaneous Provisions) Order 2001, SI 2001/3650.

3.4   Breach of the FSMA 2000, s 21 is a criminal offence under s 25.This reflects the previous position regarding advertisements issued in breach of statutory requirements, but is tougher (at least compared to the Financial Services Act 1986 (FSA 1986)) on a person who makes what would previously have been classified as an 'unsolicited call'[1]. A person in breach of the FSMA 2000, s 21 is subject to a maximum sentence of two years' imprisonment and an unlimited fine. The offence is one of strict liability, although it is a defence under s 25(2) to show that the person making the communication believed on reasonable grounds that the communication was prepared or approved by an authorised person, or that he took all reasonable precautions and exercised all due diligence to avoid committing the offence.

---

[1]   Under the FSA 1986, a person who entered into an agreement with an investor following an unsolicited call in breach of s 56(1) did not commit a criminal offence, though in general he could not enforce the agreement against the investor. By contrast, breach of the unsolicited calls provision in respect of deposits was a criminal offence under the Banking Act 1987, s 34(3).

3.5   Any agreements made as a result of a communication that is in breach of the basic prohibition are generally unenforceable against the person who has entered as a customer into the agreement. In addition, the customer is entitled to recover any money or other property that he has paid or transferred under the agreement, as well as compensation for any loss that he has suffered as a result[1]. Likewise, if as a consequence of an unlawful communication a person exercises any rights conferred by an investment, any obligation to which he is subject as a result is unenforceable against him and he has a similar entitlement to recover money, property and compensation[2]. Only if the court decides that in the circumstances it is just and equitable will the agreement or obligation be enforced or the money or property be allowed to be retained[3].

---

[1]   FSMA 2000, s 30(2).
[2]   FSMA 2000, s 30(3).
[3]   FSMA 2000, s 30(4).

The key concepts

3.6   The FSMA 2000, s 21(1) introduces four concepts that are key to whether the basic prohibition applies or not. These are as follows.

(1)   A person must be acting in the course of business

3.7   Under the FSMA 2000, s 21(4), the Treasury has the power to specify by order circumstances in which a person is to be regarded as acting, or as not acting, in the course of business. At the time of writing, this power has not been exercised. The Treasury has indicated that it has no present intention to do so, and that in the absence of such an order the phrase 'in the course of business' is intended to have its ordinary meaning[1]. It will thus be for the courts to decide, in the light of the circumstances concerned, whether or not a person is acting in the course of business.

---

[1]   Financial Promotion—Second Consultation Document: A New Approach for the Information Age (October 1999), part 1, paras 4.5–4.6.

3.8   The requirement to act in the course of business means that personal communications will not fall within the scope of the FSMA 2000, s 21(1). So correspondence from one close relative to another, conversations between friends, and e-mails posted on a bulletin board or sent to an internet chat room will not be covered, provided that there is no commercial motivation behind the communication.

3.9   The requirement to act in the course of business is not limited to the carrying on of a regulated activity. Firms making communications to their employees, for example, may be affected by the FSMA 2000, s 21(1), even if their business is not a financial services business.

(2)   A person must communicate

3.10   Under the FSMA 2000, s 21(13), 'communicate' includes causing a communication to be made. So the range of potential communicators includes the author of the communication, the person who causes the communication to be made (if a different person) and any third party who passes on the communication. But 'communicate' itself is not defined. The Oxford English Dictionary definition of 'communicate' as 'transmit' suggests that the scope of the word is very wide and would cover any process whereby information is passed from one person to another. However, it seems doubtful whether A could, for the purposes of the FSMA 2000, s 21(1), make a communication to B without intending to do so. Thus if B overhears a conversation between A and C, it would appear that neither A nor C are communicating to B. This result is consistent with the 'directed at' test in the Financial Promotion Order, art 12(4)(e)[1] (where the fact that a communication is included in a newspaper or magazine principally accessed in or intended for a market outside the UK is to be taken into account in determining whether the communication is directed at the UK, even if the communication was in fact received by someone in the UK). It also accords with the Treasury's view of the meaning of 'invitation or inducement', discussed below.

---

¹   SI 2001/1335, art 12(4)(e). See further para 3.37.

---

(3)   The communication must consist of an invitation or inducement

3.11   Neither 'invitation' nor 'inducement' is defined in the FSMA 2000, s 21. The Treasury has indicated that the intention:

> 'is to catch only promotions containing a degree of incitement and not communications comprising purely factual information where the facts are presented in such a way that they do not amount to an 'invitation or inducement'[1].

This reflects the views given by a Government Minister during the parliamentary debates on the FSMA 2000, s 21[2], though how large a degree of incitement is required is perhaps open to question. On this interpretation, the facts of the case determine whether a communication is caught or not.

---

¹   Financial Promotion—Third Consultation Document (October 2000), para 2.2.
²   See 613 HL Official Report (5th series) (18 May 2000) cols 387–388 (Lord McIntosh of Haringey) and compare 611 HL Official Report (5th Series) (20 March 2000) col 105 and 612 HL Official Report (5th series) (18 April 2000) col 567.

3.12   The difficulty with the Treasury view is that the dictionary definition of 'inducement' suggests that a communication amounts to an inducement if the result is that a person takes a particular course of action as a consequence, regardless of the intention of the person making the communication[1]. It remains to be seen whether the dictionary definition, or the view of a Minister in Parliament, will prevail if the meaning of the expression falls to be determined by a court[2].

---

¹   See Oxford English Dictionary, 'inducement', 2—'something attractive by which a person is led on or persuaded to action'. The dictionary definition is also consistent with the decision in *Commission for Racial Equality v Imperial Society of Teachers of Dancing* [1983] ICR 473 at 476, where 'to induce' in the context of the Race Relations Act 1976 was held to mean 'to persuade or to prevail upon or to bring about'.
²   Although courts have been able, since the decision of the House of Lords in *Pepper (Inspector of Taxes) v Hart* [1993] AC 593, to look to statements in Parliament in certain circumstances as a guide to the intention of the legislature, this will apply only where the meaning of the text is ambiguous. A court could well conclude that the meaning of 'invitation or inducement' in the FSMA 2000, s 21(1) was abundantly clear.

3.13   Whatever the meaning of 'invitation or inducement', it is clear that the expression covers a far wider area than the 'advertisements' and 'unsolicited calls' of the previous regimes. In particular, and in marked contrast with the regimes that the FSMA 2000, s 21 replaces, it includes circumstances where the invitation or inducement is made orally (for instance, via a personal visit) and is solicited by the recipient of the communication. The thinking behind this is that solicited oral communications are potentially no less harmful than those that are unsolicited, so it would be anomalous to exclude them[1].

---

[1] HM Treasury, Financial Promotion—A Consultation Document (March 1999), part 1, para 3.2.

---

(4) The invitation or inducement must be to engage in investment activity

3.14 'Engage in investment activity' is defined in the FSMA 2000, s 21(8) as:

'(a) entering or offering to enter into an agreement the making or performance of which by either party constitutes a controlled activity; or

(b) exercising any rights conferred by a controlled investment to acquire, dispose of, underwrite or convert a controlled investment.'

The FSMA 2000, s 21(9) and (10) give the Treasury the power to specify what constitutes a 'controlled activity' or a 'controlled investment', and the Treasury has done so in the Financial Promotion Order, Sch 1[1]. In general, controlled activities and controlled investments are the same as regulated activities and specified investments under the Regulated Activities Order[2], but this is not always the case: for instance, the controlled activity of providing qualifying credit, which applies to all secured loans, is far wider than the regulated activity of entering into a regulated mortgage contract as lender, or administering regulated mortgage contracts, which applies only to loans secured by a first legal mortgage on land and which meet other conditions[3].

---

[1] SI 2001/1335.
[2] Financial Services and Markets Act 2000 (Regulated Activities) Order 2001, SI 2001/544.
[3] Compare the Financial Promotion Order, SI 2001/1335, Sch 1, para 10, with the Regulated Activities Order, SI 2001/544, art 61 as amended by the Financial Services and Markets Act 2000 (Regulated Activities) (Amendment) Order 2001, SI 2001/3544.

Authorised persons

3.15 Where a communication that falls within the FSMA 2000, s 21(1) is made by an authorised person, the basic prohibition does not apply. The authorised person does not commit a criminal offence and any contract that results will be enforceable. However, the authorised person will be subject to the FSA's rules in respect of the communication[1].

---

[1] See para 3.72 ff.

3.16 The fact that an authorised person has made a communication to a third party that falls within the FSMA 2000, s 21(1) does not, in itself, relieve the third party from the basic prohibition if he is unauthorised and wishes to communicate the promotion to a wider group of recipients. In order for this to occur, the authorised person will need to approve the content of the communication under the FSMA 2000, s 21(2)(b). Should the third party materially alter the communication after it has been approved, the original approval will no longer apply and the third party will be committing an offence under the FSMA 2000, s 25, unless he can show that an exemption in the Financial Promotion Order[1] applies[2]. In the circumstances, the defence provided by the FSMA 2000, s 25(2)(a) (belief on reasonable grounds that the content had been approved by an authorised person) is unlikely to be available.

[1]   SI 2001/1335.
[2]   HM Treasury, Financial Promotion—Third Consultation Document (October 2000), para 2.18.

Territorial scope

3.17   As far as communications from within the UK are concerned (sometimes referred to as 'outward promotions'), the basic prohibition applies without limitation. Some respondents to the Treasury's consultations on financial promotion had argued that the FSMA 2000, s 21 should not apply to communications made to persons in an overseas jurisdiction, if those communications were lawfully made in that jurisdiction; but the Treasury has maintained the position that although this might extend the scope of regulation when compared to the previous regime, the result is justified on the grounds that this 'will help to maintain the highest confidence in the UK as a safe place to do business' (unsurprisingly, the UK Government attaches the utmost importance to safeguarding the UK's reputation as a financial centre)[1]. Certain communications made to overseas recipients are however excluded under the Financial Promotion Order, art 12[2].

[1]   HM Treasury, Financial Promotion—A Consultation Document (March 1999), part 2, para 1.4; cf. Financial Promotion—Second Consultation Document: A New Approach for the Information Age (October 1999), part 2, paras 2.7–2.9; Financial Promotion—Third Consultation Document (October 2000), para 2.6.
[2]   SI 2001/1335, art 12 and see paras 3.36–3.41.

3.18   Where the communication originates outside the UK, the FSMA 2000, s 21(3) provides that the basic prohibition applies only if the communication is capable of having an effect in the UK. However, since 'capable of having an effect' covers a wide area—it applies even if in actual fact the communication did not have such an effect—it may well be that in practice persons making non-oral communications will rely on the Financial Promotion Order, art 12[1] rather than the FSMA 2000, s 21(3) to provide them with an exclusion.

[1]   SI 2001/1335, art 12.

3.19   The FSMA 2000, s 21(7) gives the Treasury the power to repeal s 21(3). This power should be read together with the power in the FSMA 2000, s 21(6) which allows the basic prohibition to be disapplied to communications of a specified description originating in specified countries or groups of countries outside the UK. The Treasury has indicated that in light of developments in the European Union towards a 'home state' regime for financial services (as illustrated in the 'country of origin' approach to transactions in the e-commerce directive[1]) it wished to retain in the FSMA 2000, s 21 the flexibility to make the financial promotion regime in the UK a pure 'home state' regime when the time is right (that is, when other Member States agree to operate on a 'home state' basis). Whilst in theory the UK could do so unilaterally, this is not in practice acceptable, since it could leave UK consumers vulnerable to unregulated financial promotions communicated from outside the UK. And in any event, since it is unlikely (whatever the ultimate position within the European Union) that all countries will adopt a 'country of origin' approach, it will remain appropriate for s 21 to apply to some communications, at least, made into the UK from abroad[2].

---

[1]   Council Directive 2000/31/EC.
[2]   See HM Treasury, Financial Promotion—Third Consultation Document (October 2000), paras 2.10–2.13.

THE FINANCIAL PROMOTION ORDER

3.20   The FSMA 2000, s 21(5) gives the Treasury the power to specify circumstances in which the basic prohibition does not apply. The order which has been made under this power, the Financial Promotion Order[1], contains 63 different circumstances (and one transitional provision) which constitute exemptions from the basic prohibition, divided into three categories:

(1)   exemptions applying to all controlled activities (Pt IV);
(2)   exemptions applying to deposits and insurance (Pt V); and
(3)   exemptions applying to certain controlled activities (Pt VI).

---

[1]   Financial Services and Markets Act 2000 (Financial Promotion) Order 2001, SI 2001/1335, as amended by the Financial Services and Markets Act 2000 (Financial Promotion) (Amendment) Order 2001, SI 2001/2633 and the Financial Services and Markets Act 2000 (Financial Promotion) (Amendment No 2) Order 2001, SI 2001/3800.

3.21   Under the Financial Promotion Order, art 11[1], exemptions may be combined where the circumstances of a particular communication are such that no one exemption will cover it. However, there are restrictions on the extent to which combinations can be used. Whilst any of the exemptions in the Financial Promotion Order, Pt IV can be combined with any other exemption, a part V exemption cannot be combined with one in part VI.

---

[1]   SI 2001/1335.

3.22   The Financial Promotion Order[1] states, in respect of each exemption, the type of communication to which it applies. Whether an exemption applies depends on whether a communication is 'real time' or 'non-real time'; and if the former, whether it is solicited or unsolicited. For convenience, the application of the exemptions to the various types of communication is summarised in the tables below[2].

---

[1]   SI 2001/1335.
[2]   See paras 3.23–3.25.

Exemptions applying to various types of communication

Solicited real time communications

3.23   All the exemptions in the Financial Promotion Order apply, except:

Article 20	Communications by journalists
Article 22	Deposits: non-real time communications
Articles 24–25	Relevant insurance activity: non-real time communications
Article 28A	One off unsolicited real time communications
Articles 31–33	Overseas communicators: non-real time communications and unsolicited real time communications
Article 55A	Non-real time communication by members of professions
Articles 71–73	Promotions in listing particulars and prospectuses
Article 74	Transitional provision for advertisements approved under the FSA 1986, s 57

Unsolicited real time communications

3.24   In addition to the exemptions that do not apply to solicited real time communications (except SI 2001/1335, arts 28A, 32 and 33), the following do not apply:

Article 14	Follow up non-real time communications and solicited real time communications
Article 30	Overseas persons: solicited real time communications
Article 34	Governments, central banks etc
Article 35	Industrial and provident societies
Article 36	Nationals of EEA states other than the UK
Article 37	Financial markets
Article 40	Participants in certain recognised collective investment schemes
Articles 41–42	Bearer instruments: promotions required or permitted by market rules and to existing holders
Article 43	Members and creditors of certain bodies corporate
Article 44	Members and creditors of open-ended investment companies
Article 48	Certified high net worth individuals
Article 51	Associations of high net worth or sophisticated investors
Article 52	Common interest group of a company

Article 58	Acquisition of interest in premises run by management companies
Article 61	Sale of goods and supply of services
Articles 67–70	Promotions required or permitted by market rules, of securities admitted to certain markets, or in connection with listing applications

Non-real time communications

3.25   All the exemptions in the Financial Promotion Order[1] apply, except:

Article 15	Introductions
Article 23	Deposits: real time communications
Article 26	Relevant insurance activity: real time communications
Article 28A	One off unsolicited real time communications
Articles 32–33	Overseas communicators: unsolicited real time communications
Article 55	Communications by members of professions

[1]   SI 2001/1335.

3.26   The relevant definitions are contained in SI 2001/1335, arts 7 and 8. A real time communication is 'any communication made in the course of a personal visit, telephone conversation or other interactive dialogue' (art 7(1)). All other types of communication are non-real time (art 7(2)). Non-real time communications include 'communications made by letter or e-mail or contained in a publication' (art 7(3)). SI 2001/1335, art 7(3) appears designed to clarify the position over whether communications made by the Internet could constitute real time communications under the Financial Promotion Order; and though not expressly covered in art 7(3), it would seem that other types of electronic communication (such as via WAP phones and to Internet chat rooms) would also constitute 'non-real time communications'. Broadcasts (whether sound or via television) will also be non-real time communications, even when they are live recordings.

3.27   SI 2001/1335, art 7(5) sets out a number of factors which are to be treated as indications that a communication is non-real time. These are:

(1)   the communication is made to or directed at more than one person in identical terms (save for details of the person's identity);
(2)   the system of communication normally creates a record of the communication which is available to the recipient to refer to at a later time; and
(3)   the communication is made or directed by way of a system which in the normal course does not enable or require the recipient to respond immediately to it.

3.28   Although it seems clear that not all of these indicators have to be satisfied for a communication to be classified as non-real time, it is not clear whether a communication that satisfied none of these indicators could still be a non-real time communication. Given, however, that they are indicators only rather than factors that determine the issue, it would appear that in theory at least this should be possible.

3.29   One key characteristic of a real time communication (and one which is not present in a non-real time communication) is that there is interaction between the communicator and the recipient. Thus a communication by telephone where direct contact is established is a real time communication; the same communication left on an answering machine would be a non-real time communication.

3.30   Under SI 2001/1335, art 8, a real time communication is solicited when initiated by or made in response to an express request from the recipient of the communication, and unsolicited in any other case. Article 8(3) provides that the following do not amount to an express request:

(1)   a failure by a person to indicate that he does not wish to receive any or any further visits or calls or to engage in any or any further dialogue; and
(2)   an agreement to standard terms that state that such visits, calls or dialogue will take place, unless he has signified clearly that in addition to agreeing to the terms, he is willing for them to take place.

These provisions are clearly designed to prevent arguments that real time communications are 'solicited' because the recipient has failed to tick a box, or has 'agreed' to pages of small print which contain, among the many terms and conditions, authority for calls to be made upon him. In practice, however, 'signified clearly' may amount to little more than a person providing a separate signature beside the relevant term.

3.31   SI 2001/1335, art 8(3) also prevents a communication being classified as 'solicited' when the call, visit or dialogue is initiated ostensibly with one purpose in mind, but then moves to a different area. For example, a customer may have agreed to visits being made to discuss investments in units in collective investment schemes. If, however, the caller in the course of the communication turned to discuss the possibility of the customer investing in futures, that part of the communication would be unsolicited.

3.32   SI 2001/1335, art 8(4) allows a real time communication to qualify as a solicited communication if it is made to a person who has not requested it, provided that that person is a close relative of, or expected to engage in any investment activity jointly with, a person who has solicited the communication. This will enable, for example, solicited real time communications to be made to both a husband and wife if only one party has asked for the communication to be made.

3.33   A number of exemptions contain details of the 'indications' that the communication is required to contain in order to satisfy the exemption. Thus, for instance, non-real time communications for deposits, or relating to relevant insurance activity[1], will be exempt if they are accompanied by certain indications, such as the name of the depositor/insurer, the place of incorporation, and whether the deposit-taker or insurer is regulated or not[2]. SI 2001/1335, art 9 provides that these indications must be presented to the recipient:

(1)   in a way that can be easily understood; and
(2)   in such manner as, depending on the means by which the communication is made or directed, is best calculated to bring the matter in question to the attention of the recipient and to allow him to consider it.

---

[1]   That is, relating to a contract of insurance that is not a contractually based investment.
[2]   SI 2001/1335, arts 22(2) and 24(2).

3.34   SI 2001/1335, art 9 is designed to prevent 'indications' being made in an obscure and unintelligible way. Clearly, if the basis for the exemption is the disclosure of certain pieces of information to the recipient, it would negate the rationale for the exemption if the relevant information could not be readily obtained from the communication. However, the words 'best calculated' impose a very high standard. Taken literally, they require the person relying on the exemption to find the objectively best way of presenting the material, or else commit a criminal offence. As there will be cases where there may be several ways in which the indications could be conveyed, and where none of these appears 'better' than any other, the strictness of the test seems unhelpful. It remains to be seen whether the FSA will interpret 'best calculated' literally, or whether it will apply the more practical test of what a reasonable person would conclude as likely to bring the matter in question to the attention of the recipient[1].

---

[1]   This is relevant not only to unauthorised persons, but also to FSA regulated firms, as communications which are exempt under the Financial Promotion Order (SI 2001/1335) are outside the FSA's financial promotion rules: see para 3.73.

3.35   SI 2001/1335, art 10 places an additional restriction on communications concerning qualifying contracts of insurance (that is, life policies). In such cases, an exemption applies only if the contract is entered into with:

(1)   an authorised person;
(2)   an exempt person in relation to effecting or carrying out contracts of the type to which the communication relates;
(3)   a company with a head office, branch or agency in an EEA state other than the UK which is entitled to carry on in that State insurance business of the type to which the communication relates; or
(4)   a company authorised to carry on insurance business of the type to which the communication relates in Guernsey, the Isle of Man, the Commonwealth of Pennsylvania, the State of Iowa, and Jersey.

Exemptions applying to all controlled activities

3.36   As we have seen, the FSMA 2000, s 21(3) exempts from the basic prohibition communications originating outside the UK which are not capable of having an effect in the UK[1]. The exemption created by the

Financial Promotion Order, art 12[2] is in keeping with this. In general, it provides that a communication which is made (whether from inside or outside the UK) to a person who receives the communication outside the UK, or which is directed (whether from inside or outside the UK) only at persons outside the UK, is not subject to the basic prohibition. However, if the communication is an unsolicited real time communication, the exemption applies only if the communication is made from outside the UK and for the purpose of a business which is not carried on in the UK.

---

[1]   See para 3.18.
[2]   SI 2001/1335.

3.37   SI 2001/1335, art 12 is therefore capable of applying both to communications designed with a particular person in mind (those which are 'made to' that person) and to those which are addressed to persons generally (communications 'directed at' those persons, for example by means of advertisements). The 'directed at' exemption allows communications to be exempt even if they reach persons for whom the communications were not designed.

3.38   SI 2001/1335, art 12(4) lists five conditions which are relevant to whether the communication is 'directed only at' persons outside the UK. Depending on how many of these conditions are met, satisfaction of the conditions either carries evidential weight as to whether the communication satisfies the exemption (in the words of SI 2001/1335, art 12(3)(c), they will be 'taken into account' in determining the issue), or is conclusive evidence that the exemption is satisfied. Even if none of the listed conditions are met, it will still be possible for the communication to be regarded as directed only at persons outside the UK[1], though given the nature of the conditions, that would seem possible only in exceptional circumstances.

---

[1]   Financial Promotion Order, SI 2001/1335, art 12(3)(c).

3.39   A communication will be regarded as directed only at persons outside the UK if all of the following conditions are satisfied:

(1)   it is accompanied by an indication that it is directed only at persons outside the UK (but a communication which is directed from a place outside the UK does not need to satisfy this condition);

(2)   it is accompanied by an indication that it must not be relied upon by persons in the UK (again, a communication which is directed from a place outside the UK does not need to satisfy this condition);

(3)   it is not referred to or directly accessible from any other communication by or on behalf of the same person which is made to or directed at persons in the UK; and

(4)   there are proper systems and procedures in place to prevent recipients in the UK engaging in the investment activity to which the communication relates with the person directing the communication, a close relative of his or a company in the same group[1]. 'Proper systems and procedures' are not defined, and to some extent will depend on the

facts of the individual case. But they are likely to require in all cases some sort of screening process to identify UK recipients (whether by password protecting the material, if communicated via the Internet, or otherwise).

---

[1] Financial Promotion Order, SI 2001/1335, art 12(4)(a)–(d).

3.40 A further condition which has evidential weight requires the communication to be contained in a website, newspaper, journal, magazine or periodical publication principally accessed in or intended for a market outside the UK, or in a radio or television broadcast or teletext service transmitted principally for reception outside the UK[1].

---

[1] Financial Promotion Order, SI 2001/1335, art 12(4)(e).

3.41 This exemption remains available if promotions are also directed at persons in the UK who are exempt under the exemptions applying to investment professionals[1] and high net worth companies and other persons[2]. If this is so, conditions (1) and (2) above[3] are to be construed accordingly[4]. Given that art 11 makes clear that exemptions in the Financial Promotion Order, Pt IV can be freely combined with other exemptions in Pt IV or Pt VI, the express mention of the art 19 and 49 exemptions in art 12 is odd. Although it might be taken to imply that none of the other exemptions can be combined with art 12, the better view, based on the unqualified wording of art 11, appears to be that this is not the case.

---

[1] Financial Promotion Order, SI 2001/1335, art 19.
[2] SI 2001/1335, art 49.
[3] See para 3.39.
[4] SI 2001/1335, art 12(6).

3.42 The Financial Promotion Order, Pt IV[1] also includes exemptions for:

(1) communications from customers and potential customers (art 13);
(2) real time communications made with a view to or for the purposes of introducing the recipient to an authorised person who carries on the controlled activity to which the communication relates, or to an exempt person whose exemption covers the controlled activity to which the communication relates, provided that certain conditions are satisfied (art 15);
(3) non-real time communications or solicited real time communications made or directed by exempt persons for the purpose of their exempt business, and unsolicited real time communications made by appointed representatives in respect of their exempt business which, if made by their principal, would comply with any relevant financial promotion rules made by the FSMA 2000, s 145 (art 16);
(4) 'mere conduits', such as postal and telecommunications services, and internet service providers, provided that the principal purpose of the business is transmitting or receiving material provided by others, the

content of the communication is wholly devised by another person, and that no control is exercised over the content prior to transmission or receipt (art 18)[2]; and

(5)   communications made to investment professionals, such as authorised persons, exempt persons whose exemption covers the controlled activity to which the communication relates, governments and local authorities (art 19).

---

[1]   SI 2001/1335.
[2]   'Control' here does not include the power to remove material which is or is alleged to be illegal or defamatory, or where required to do so by law or by a regulator: SI 2001/1335, art 18(3). Even so, the nature of the relationship between newspaper publishers and broadcasters, and the third-party advertisements that they communicate, suggests that they will not be able to take advantage of this exemption.

3.43   Four other exemptions in SI 2001/1335, Pt IV are worth treating in more detail.

Under SI 2001/1335, art 14, communications other than unsolicited real time communications are exempt when the communication follows up an earlier communication, provided that the earlier communication was exempt under the Financial Promotion Order because, in compliance with the requirements of another exemption in the Financial Promotion Order, it was accompanied by certain indications or contained certain information, and that the subsequent communication:

(1)   is made by the same person who made the earlier communication;
(2)   is made to a recipient of the earlier communication;
(3)   relates to the same controlled activity and controlled investment[1] as the earlier communication; and
(4)   is made within twelve months of the receipt of the first communication.

---

[1]   For controlled activity and controlled investment, see para 3.14.

3.44   SI 2001/1335, art 14 will not be available if the earlier communication did not require certain indications to be made or information to be contained. As some exemptions which mention indications or conditions do not as such require the communication to be accompanied by them or to satisfy them (since the exemption is available where none of the listed conditions or indications are satisfied or made), the scope of the exemption is more narrow than first appears[1]. Since art 28, dealing with 'one-off' communications, falls into this category, it would seem that the exemptions for 'one-off' and follow up communications cannot be combined. Of course, it may well be that if the earlier communication satisfied a particular exemption, the later communication would do so also. But if the art 14 exemption cannot be used for the later communication, this will mean (as in the case of someone seeking to take advantage of the exception under art 19) that the person making the communication may need to repeat information made earlier to the same customer. This is hardly helpful to either communicator or recipient, and seems to run contrary to the motivation for the exemption in the first place.

¹   The exemption in SI 2001/1335, art 14 will thus not be available where the earlier communication meets the relevant provisions of arts 12 (communications to overseas recipients), or 19 (investment professionals): see arts 12(3)(c) and 19(3). Contrast, for example, communications which are required to satisfy the specified conditions or indication provisions in arts 24 (relevant insurance activity: non-real time communications), 49 (high net worth companies etc) and 50 (sophisticated investors) in order to obtain the benefits of those exemptions.

3.45   SI 2001/1335, art 17 provides an exception for 'generic promotions', that is communications which do not identify directly or indirectly a person who provides the controlled investment to which the communication relates, or any person as a person who carries on a controlled activity in relation to that investment. This enables promotions comparing the merits of, say, ISAs with deposits, or those extolling the virtues of unit trusts in general terms, to escape the basic prohibition. It will also be possible for an unauthorised intermediary to advertise himself and the services that he provides, provided that in so doing he does not carry on a controlled activity. So an intermediary who offered to find the most competitive insurance quotation or the best performing unit trust over a particular period would fall within the exemption, as he would not be identifying anyone that provided a controlled investment or carried on a controlled activity in relation to that investment. But if the communication contained examples which, though disguised to the general reader, would nonetheless be capable of being identified (such as the managers of 'ABC unit trust, the value of which has grown by 189% in the two years to last March'), the communication would fall foul of the wide scope of 'directly or indirectly' and would thus be outside the exemption.

3.46   The exemption for communications by journalists (SI 2001/1335, art 20) has caused the Treasury a good deal of trouble—as shown by the fact that art 20 has been amended since the Financial Promotion Order was initially made[1]. There is a difficult line to draw between the freedom of the press, and the role that responsible journalism can play in improving consumer awareness of financial products on the one hand, and the need on the other to protect the public from the possibility that journalists' 'buy' and 'sell' recommendations may not be entirely impartial. Partly, perhaps, as a response to the 'City Slickers' scandal (where Daily Mirror journalists had tipped shares in which their editor had a financial interest), the Treasury aim was to allow authors of a communication with a material interest in a particular product to write about that product—they may, after all, be very well qualified to do so—and to have the benefit of the exemption, provided that they disclosed any financial interest that they, or a close relative, at the same time and in the same place[2]. However, the present text of art 20 means that disclosure of a financial interest is not inevitably necessary in order to take advantage of the exemption.

¹   See the Financial Services and Markets Act 2000 (Financial Promotion) (Amendment No 2) Order 2001, SI 2001/3800, art 2.
²   HM Treasury, Financial Promotion—Third Consultation Document (October 2000), para 2.37.

3.47   The Financial Promotion Order, art 20[1] can in effect be subdivided into two separate exemptions for non-real time communications. First, there is an exemption where the communication does not relate to shares or to futures, options and contracts for differences relating to shares, and:

(1)   the content of the communication is devised by a person acting in the capacity of a journalist; and
(2)   the communication is contained in a qualifying publication[2].

'Acting in the capacity of a journalist' is not defined, although as it presumably requires a contractual relationship between author and publication, it should not be difficult to decide in each case whether this condition is satisfied or not. 'Qualifying publication' is defined by reference to the Regulated Activities Order, art 54(1) and (2)[3]. It covers newspapers, journals, magazines or other periodical publications, regularly updated news or information services, and television and radio programmes, provided that the principal purpose of the publication, service or programme is not to give advice on the merits of buying or selling, nor to lead or enable persons to buy or sell, securities or contractually based investments. The FSA may certify that the principal purpose test is met and this is conclusive evidence that it is[4].

---

[1]   SI 2001/1335.
[2]   SI 2001/1335, art 20(1)(a)–(b).
[3]   Financial Services and Markets Act 2000 (Regulated Activities) Order 2001, SI 2001/544.
[4]   SI 2001/1335, art 20(5).

3.48   A journalist who authors a communication which constitutes a financial promotion, but whose subject matter does not concern shares, can therefore take advantage of the exemption without disclosing any financial interest that he or his family has in the matter promoted. If such disclosure was required by the publisher, or under codes of practice that cover the publication concerned, the exemption would apply even if the disclosure was not made. It is probably true that the greatest scope for abuse in this area lies in the tipping of shares where the author stands to gain if the tip is followed by others. However, it seems surprising that the Treasury have apparently concluded that there would be no or no substantial risk to consumers from an author tipping other controlled investments in which he has a financial interest.

3.49   The second exemption arises where the communication concerns shares (or futures, options or contracts for differences relating to shares), directly identifies a person who issues or provides the shares (or futures, options or contracts for differences relating to shares), and meets the requirements set out in para 3.47, points (1) and (2). In this case, if the author[1] or a member of his family[2] would be likely to obtain a financial benefit or avoid a financial loss if persons acted in accordance with the financial promotion, the financial promotion may need to be accompanied by an explanation of the nature of that financial interest if the author wishes to take advantage of the exemption[3]. However, this disclosure is not necessarily required. If the author is subject to proper systems and procedures[4] which prevent the publication of communications that require disclosure of financial interests without an explanation of that interest[5], or the publication in which the communication appears falls within the remit of the Press Complaints Commission's Code of Practice, the Programme Code of the Radio Authority, or the Producer's Guidelines issued by the British Broadcasting Corporation[6], there is no obligation to disclose a financial interest in the product promoted. It is worth noting that it is not a condition of the exemption that the communication be in accordance with the Codes or Guidelines; it simply has to fall within their remit. Nor is it a requirement that the Codes or Guidelines require disclosure of a financial interest. The assumption appears to be that in these circumstances it is appropriate for the body concerned to decide whether disclosure is required and, if so, what steps to take if disclosure is not made. Similarly, if the author acts in breach of the relevant systems and procedures, and a disclosure of a financial interest is not made, the communication would still appear to satisfy the condition in SI 2001/1335, art 20(2)(b). (If it were otherwise, art 20(2)(b) would be unnecessary—the position would be covered by art 20(2)(a).)

---

[1]   Under SI 2001/1335, art 20(5)(a), 'author' includes the person who is responsible for deciding to include the communication in a publication. This will typically be the editor, but the language is sufficiently wide to include a particularly 'hands on' proprietor, depending on the circumstances of the case.

[2]   This expression is far narrower than the original text of SI 2001/1335, art 20: it includes only spouse and children under 18, whereas the previous text, by using 'close relative', covered the author's spouse, children of any age, his parents, siblings, and their spouses.

[3]   SI 2001/1335, art 20(2)(a).

[4]   'Proper systems and procedures' are not defined (compare SI 2001/1335, art 12(4)(d)), but they are likely to include the keeping of a list of relevant financial interests of authors and members of their families, and an obligation on authors to notify any changes to those interests.

[5]   SI 2001/1335, art 20(2)(b).

[6]   SI 2001/1335, art 20(2)(c).

3.50   The Financial Promotion Order, art 20A[1] provides a further exemption for communications by directors and employees of an undertaking, where the communication forms part of a television or radio programme or is displayed on a website (or similar system) comprising regularly updated news and information, and the programme or website satisfies the principal purpose test in the Regulated Activities Order, art 54(1)(a) and (b)[2]. The exemption is available where the communication is a financial promotion relating to shares (or options, futures and contracts for differences relating to those shares) issued by the undertaking or another undertaking in the same group, or relating to any controlled investment[3] issued or provided by an authorised person in the same group, and the communication consists only of spoken words, or is displayed in writing 'only because it forms part of an interactive dialogue to which [the director or employee] is a party and in the course of which [he] is expected to respond immediately to questions put by a recipient of the communication'[4]. This rather obscure provision appears designed to cover question and answer sessions held over the internet, involving the exchange of e-mails[5]. In addition, the communication must not be part of an organised marketing campaign[6], and must identify the person making the communication as a director or employee (as the case may be) of the undertaking.

¹ SI 2001/1335. Art 20A was inserted by the Financial Services and Markets Act 2000 (Financial Promotion) (Amendment No 2) Order 2001, SI 2001/3800, art 3.
² SI 2001/544. For the principal purpose test, see para 3.47.
³ See para 3.14.
⁴ SI 2001/1335, art 20A(1) (a) (b) (ii).
⁵ Though if that is the case, the use of the expression 'interactive dialogue' is strange, since communications made in the course of an interactive dialogue are real time, and communications made by e-mail are by definition non-real time. SI 2001/1335, art 20A would thus appear in practice to be confined to non-real time communications, despite the fact that the exemption is not expressly so restricted. See para 3.26.
⁶ See para 3.53.

3.51   This exemption appears to have been motivated by the possibility that company directors and employees might inadvertently make unapproved financial promotions when responding to questions from radio and television interviewers about their company, or as part of a live website question and answer session. However, it is not clear whether the presence of subtitles on television broadcasts would negate the exemption. The strict wording of SI 2001/1335, art 20A(1)(b)(i) suggests that it would, although logic suggests that this cannot have been the intention.

Exemptions applying to deposits and insurance

3.52   The Financial Promotion Order, Pt V[1] contains exemptions that apply to communications that relate to deposits, and to 'regulated insurance activity'—that is, the effecting and carrying out of contracts of insurance which are not life policies[2]. The scope of the exemptions are similar in both types of case: real time communications are unconditionally exempt[3], and non-real time communications are exempt provided that certain information about the insurer or deposit-taker is disclosed (such as name, place of incorporation, and details of applicable complaints and compensation schemes)[4]. Under SI 2001/1335, art 25, non-real time communications concerning contracts of reinsurance, or insurance contracts concerning 'large risks' (defined in art 25(2)) are also excluded.

¹ SI 2001/1335.
² See SI 2001/1335, art 21.
³ SI 2001/1335, arts 23 (deposits) and 26 (relevant insurance activity).
⁴ SI 2001/1335, arts 22 (deposits) and 24 (relevant insurance activity).

Other exemptions

3.53   The largest part of the Financial Promotion Order[1] is Pt VI, which contains a number of exemptions applying to certain types of controlled activity. In some cases the exemption may depend upon the maker of the communication[2]; in others, on the recipient of the communication[3]; or the subject matter of the communication[4]. The exemptions likely to be of more general interest are discussed below.

¹ SI 2001/1335.
² See eg SI 2001/1335, arts 34 (governments, central banks etc), 35 (industrial and provident societies) and 37 (financial markets).

³   See eg SI 2001/1335, arts 31–33 (overseas communicators: communications to previously overseas customers and knowledgeable customers), 45 (group companies) and 47 (persons in the business of disseminating information).

⁴   See eg SI 2001/1335, arts 29 (communications required or authorised by statute), 59 (annual accounts and directors' report) and 70 (promotions in connection with listing applications).

Articles 28 and 28A (one-off communications)

3.54   One-off communications fall outside the FSMA 2000, s 21(1). 'One-off' is not defined, but SI 2001/1335, art 28(3) sets out three conditions, the satisfaction of all of which means that the communication is to be regarded as 'one-off':

(1)   the communication is made to one recipient only, or to one group of recipients in the expectation that they would invest jointly;
(2)   the product or service mentioned in the communication has been determined having regard to the particular circumstances of the recipient; and
(3)   the communication is not part of an organised marketing campaign (that is, it is not one of a series of similar communications designed to acquire customers for a particular investment or service).

3.55   If one or two of the above conditions are satisfied, that fact is to be taken into account in determining whether the communication is 'one-off' or not. But a communication can still be one-off for the purposes of SI 2001/1335, art 28 and art 28A even if none of the conditions are satisfied[1].

---

[1]   SI 2001/1335, art 28(2)–(3). For this three-pronged approach elsewhere in the Financial Promotion Order, see arts 12 (communications to overseas recipients), 19 (investment professionals), 49 (high net worth companies, unincorporated associations etc) and 52 (common interest group of a company).

3.56   The original Financial Promotion Order limited the 'one-off' exemption to non-real time communications and solicited real time communications[1]. This has now been amended[2] so that unsolicited real time communications which are 'one-off' are also exempt, provided that:

(1)   the communicator believes on reasonable grounds that the recipient understands the risks associated with engaging in the investment activity to which the communication relates; and
(2)   at the time the communication is made, the communicator believes on reasonable grounds that the recipient would expect to be contacted by him in relation to that activity.

---

[1]   SI 2001/1335, art 28(1).
[2]   SI 2001/1335, art 28A, inserted by the Financial Services and Markets Act 2000 (Financial Promotion) (Amendment) Order 2001, SI 2001/2633, art 2(a).

3.57   The words 'one-off' are in fact rather a misnomer, as the Treasury has indicated that this exemption can be used on more than one occasion in respect of the same recipient provided that the conditions of the exemption are met on each occasion[1].

Articles 30–33 (overseas communicators)

3.58   The Financial Promotion Order¹ contains four exemptions that are available for 'overseas communicators'—persons who carry on certain controlled activities outside the UK, but not from a permanent place of business maintained by them in the UK.

3.59   Under these exemptions an overseas communicator when acting as such may, without breaching the basic prohibition, make:

(1)   a solicited real time communication to a person in the UK (but not if the controlled activity carried on by the overseas communicator outside the UK is accepting deposits, effecting or carrying out contracts of insurance, advising on syndicate participation at Lloyd's, providing funeral plan contracts or providing qualifying credit);

(2)   a non-real time communication to a customer in the UK with whom he has done business within the previous twelve months and who at that time (or at an earlier time when the same business was done with the customer) was not resident in the UK and did not have a place of business there (a 'previously overseas customer');

(3)   an unsolicited real time communication to a previously overseas customer in the UK, provided that the past dealings between the parties would lead the customer reasonably to expect to receive unsolicited real time communications concerning that type of investment activity, and that the overseas communicator has previously disclosed that the protections of the FSMA 2000 do not apply to the communication and may not apply to any investment activity that results, and described what complaints or compensation scheme (if any) would apply to a transaction between them;

(4)   an unsolicited real time communication with a customer in the UK whom the overseas communicator believes on reasonable grounds to be sufficiently knowledgeable to understand the risks to which the communication relates, provided that the overseas communicator has previously made the disclosures mentioned in (3) above and the recipient has clearly signalled, after a proper opportunity to consider the position, that he understands the warnings and accepts that he will not benefit from the protections of the FSMA 2000.

Article 36 (nationals of other EEA States)

3.60   Communications (other than unsolicited real time communications) made by a national of another EEA State from that state, in the course of a controlled activity lawfully carried on by him in that state, are exempt, provided that the communication conforms with the relevant financial promotion rules made by the FSA¹. Anyone wishing to take advantage of this exemption will need to have a clear understanding of the relevant FSA rules, since a failure to follow the FSA rules to the letter will result in the exemption not applying, and the commitment of a criminal offence. Given that, it seems unlikely that persons will seek to rely on SI 2001/1335, art 36 without the benefit of specialist outside advice.

----

[1]   For these rules, see para 3.72 ff.

Article 48 (certified high net worth individuals) and art 50 (sophisticated investors)

3.61   These two exceptions mark a departure from previous regimes. Prior to the Financial Promotion Order[1], promotions of investments to private individuals were required to be made or approved by authorised persons. However, various working groups were concerned that this was too restrictive. On the basis that private investment (as opposed to institutional investment) is an extremely important source of finance for companies in the early years; that the costs of obtaining approval for promotions could be prohibitively high, compared to the amounts of money that firms wished to raise; and that the protection of the promotional restrictions might be disproportionate for private individuals of greater sophistication and resource than the average investor, they argued that companies should be allowed to promote investment opportunities directly to more sophisticated private investors, often known as 'business angels'[2]. Given the importance the Government attaches to small and medium-size companies having access to the capital necessary to expand their businesses[3], and the fact that other jurisdictions (in particular Australia and the USA) have a similar exemption, it is no surprise that a decision was taken to liberalise this area.

----

[1]   SI 2001/1335.
[2]   See HM Treasury, Financial Promotion—A Consultation Document (March 1999) part 5, para 1.1.
[3]   See HM Treasury, Financial Promotion—Second Consultation Document: A New Approach for the Information Age (October 1999), part 2, para 2.50.

3.62   SI 2001/1335, art 48 applies in cases where the recipient is a person who has a current (that is, signed and dated no more than twelve months before) certificate of high net worth at the date of the communication, and who has also signed, within the twelve months prior to the communication, a statement in a prescribed form acknowledging, among other things, that he is a high net worth individual and that the communication may not be subject to the controls that would apply if it had been made or approved by an authorised person[1]. The prescriptive nature of the statement required suggests that even non-material deviations from the text would result in a failure to satisfy the condition, and thus the exemption. Where such recipients are concerned, communications other than unsolicited real time communications may be made, provided that:

(1)   they relate only to certain investments (broadly speaking, shares and debentures in unlisted companies, options and futures on such investments, and units in collective investment schemes that invest wholly or mainly in such investments);

(2)   the recipient cannot lose more than the amount invested; and
(3)   the communication is accompanied by certain information (including the requirements necessary to qualify as a high net worth individual, a warning that there is a significant risk of losing all the amount invested, and a suggestion that specialist advice be taken if the recipient is unsure about the investment concerned)[2].

---

[1]   SI 2001/1335, art 48(2).
[2]   SI 2001/1335, art 48(4).

3.63   The certificate of high net worth must be signed by the individual's accountant or employer, and must state that the person certified had, in the twelve months before the certificate was signed, an annual income of at least £100,000, or net assets of at least £250,000. 'Net assets' excludes certain items that could be classed as assets (such as the individual's primary residence), but also (more dubiously) excludes certain debts (such as the loan secured on the primary residence). The assumption appears to be that the value of the residence can never be less that the amount of the loan, which in a declining housing market will not be the case. This leaves open the surprising possibility that someone whose net asset position, by any meaningful measure, is close to or less than zero will still be properly classified as a high net worth individual under SI 2001/1335, art 48.

3.64   Despite the widespread support for the principle behind this exclusion[1], and the restricted circumstances in which the exclusion applies, it remains controversial. It equates suitability to receive an unregulated communication with financial standing, presumably on the basis that high net worth individuals have enough money to be able to pay for specialist advice if required, and should have been told about the need to take such advice. The unwritten assumption appears to be that high net worth individuals will be able to identify when they need to take advice and will duly seek it. That seems, at best, an optimistic assumption to make.

---

[1]   See HM Treasury, Financial Promotion—Third Consultation Document (October 2000), para 2.41.

3.65   SI 2001/1335, art 50 provides a similar, though not identical, exclusion for sophisticated investors. All types of communication may be made to a person who has a current certificate ('current' meaning here signed and dated within the past three years) signed by an authorised person to the effect that he is sufficiently knowledgeable to understand the risks associated with the type of investment that is the subject of the communication. As with the high net worth individual, the sophisticated investor must also have signed within the previous twelve months a statement in prescribed form, which requires among other things the investments in respect of which the person qualifies as a sophisticated investor to be expressly listed. The communication must be accompanied by certain information. This, again, is similar to the information given to high net worth individuals, except that the risk warning is of the risk of not only losing all the amount invested, but also of incurring additional liability[1]. (The latter will be true if the investor is certified as sophisticated in respect of derivatives transactions, for example.)

---

[1]   SI 2001/1335, art 50(3)(d).

3.66   There is, however, a potential catch with this exemption. The certificate has to be signed by an authorised person. An authorised person is exempt from the basic prohibition, under the FSMA 2000, s 21(2)(a), so could make the promotion to the investor in any event. In doing so he is, in general, subject to the FSA's financial promotion rules under the FSMA 2000, s 145. However, those rules do not apply to circumstances covered by the Financial Promotion Order[1]. So there would be an obvious incentive for an authorised person to certify someone as sophisticated, if by so doing he could promote his products to the sophisticated investor without the need to worry about the FSA's rules.

---

[1]   SI 2001/1335.

3.67   However, perhaps mindful of the possibility of abuse, the Financial Promotion Order provides that in order to qualify for the exemption, the communication must not invite the recipient to engage in investment activity with the authorised person who has signed the certificate[1]. So if authorised person A signs a certificate, the effect will be that unauthorised persons will be able to promote the products and services of other authorised persons—but not those of A—to the sophisticated investor. At first sight there would appear to be little incentive for A to sign a certificate, except at a very high fee. There is a similar restriction on high net worth individuals carrying on investment activity with the signer of their certificate[2], but as the signers in that instance will be their employer or accountant, the incentive not to sign is significantly less. (The issue there may be how many persons who would qualify will obtain a certificate of high net worth on the off-chance that they would be contacted by someone seeking 'business angels'.)

---

[1]   SI 2001/1335, art 50(2)(b).
[2]   SI 2001/1335, art 48(1)(c).

3.68   Both these exemptions are silent on an important issue: how can persons find out whether a recipient possesses the necessary certificate? On the basis of the wording of the FSMA 2000, s 21(1), it would appear that it would not be a breach of the basic prohibition if the initial communication simply sought to ascertain whether the recipient had a current certificate, as such a communication would not be 'an invitation or inducement to engage in investment activity'[1]. And even if the answer to the question was in the negative, it seems doubtful whether a further communication urging the recipient to obtain a certificate would inevitably be in breach of the FSMA 2000, s 21(1), as that too would not necessarily have the required promotional purpose.

¹   See above, paras 3.11–3.14.

Article 49 (high net worth companies, unincorporated associations etc)

3.69 Any communications made to or directed at high net worth companies, unincorporated associations or partnerships, or trustees of high value trusts, are exempt from the basic prohibition. Unlike the case of high net worth individuals, there is no requirement for these entities to be certified. Indeed, even if the communication is made to persons who do not satisfy the criteria, the exemption will still apply, provided that the persons concerned are believed on reasonable grounds to be of high net worth or of high value, or the communication may reasonably be regarded as directed only at such persons[1].

¹   SI 2001/1335, art 49(1).

3.70 The requirements are:

(1)   for bodies corporate, called up share capital of at least £5 million (or of at least £500,000 if it has more than 20 members or is the subsidiary of a parent with more than 20 members);

(2)   for unincorporated associations and partnerships, net assets of at least £5 million;

(3)   for trustees, the trust must be a 'high value' trust—that is, a trust which has, or had in the previous twelve months, gross assets of at least £10 million.

3.71 SI 2001/1335, art 49(4) sets out three conditions which, if satisfied, will conclusively classify the communication as directed at these entities. The communication must indicate the types of person to whom it is directed; it must indicate that other persons should not act upon it; and there must be proper systems and controls in place to prevent any other person engaging in the investment activity to which the communication relates with the person directing the communication, a close relative of his, or a member of the same group. As we have seen elsewhere, satisfaction of one or two of these conditions is to be taken into account in determining whether the communication is directed at these entities, though a communication can come within art 49 even if it satisfies none of the conditions[1].

¹   SI 2001/1335, art 49(3)(b); for the approach elsewhere, see para 3.55, n 1.

THE FSA'S FINANCIAL PROMOTION RULES

3.72 The FSA's power to make financial promotion rules is contained in the FSMA 2000, s 145. Under the FSMA 2000, s 145, the FSA may make rules governing the communication by authorised persons, or their approval of a communication by others, of invitations or inducements to engage in investment activity or to participate in a collective investment scheme. In particular, the FSA's rules may make provision about the form and content of communications. The FSA's rules are contained in chapter 3 of the Conduct of Business Sourcebook ('COB').

3.73   The FSMA 2000, s 145(3)(a) prevents the FSA from imposing rules on authorised persons in respect of communications to which an exemption applies under the Financial Promotion Order[1]. This reflects the Treasury's desire that authorised persons should not be at a disadvantage in this area when compared to unauthorised persons[2]. In theory, at least, the FSA could bypass this restriction and use its general rulemaking power under the FSMA 2000, s 138 to regulate promotions that are exempt under the Financial Promotion Order, if that seemed 'necessary or expedient for the purpose of protecting the interests of consumers'; but in practice it has not done so, recognising the fact that the FSMA 2000 clearly envisages financial promotion rules being made under the power in s 145, not that in s 138.

[1]   SI 2001/1335.
[2]   The restriction on the FSA's rulemaking power in the FSMA 2000, s 145(3)(b), in respect of the promotion of unregulated collective investment schemes, has a similar effect: see para 3.100.

3.74   In addition to the exemptions contained in the Financial Promotion Order[1], COB 3.2.4–5 provides that the FSA's rules will not apply to a number of other categories of financial promotions. As with the exemptions in the Financial Promotion Order, different exemptions can be combined in respect of the same financial promotion.

(1)   Communications made to persons whom the firm has taken reasonable steps to establish are market counterparties or intermediate customers, or which may reasonably be regarded as directed at them. Promotions to expert private customers classified as intermediate customers are also exempt, provided that the promotion relates to the investments or type of business for which the customer has been so classified. Firms which do not deal with private customers will therefore not need to concern themselves about the financial promotion rules, unless they are approving financial promotions which are made to or directed at private customers.

(2)   Communications from outside the UK which would be exempt under the Financial Promotion Order[2], arts 30–33 if the office from which the communication was made were a separate unauthorised person.

(3)   'One off' non-real time or solicited real time communications. These are already exempt in part under the Financial Promotion Order[3], art 28; the effect of the exemption in the FSA's rules is to extend the Financial Promotion Order exemption to communications relating to deposits and all contracts of insurance.

(4)   'Image' promotions (promotions containing only such items as firm name, address, logo, or brief factual description of the firm's activities and products) or price lists (such as are found in the business sections of national newspapers). In the latter case, the firm's name and contact details may be added.

(5)   Personal quotations or illustration forms (which will be subject to the protections provided elsewhere in COB, such as the requirement to provide suitable advice).

(6)   Promotions in connection with takeovers subject to the Takeover Code or to other EEA requirements.

---

[1]   SI 2001/1335.
[2]   SI 2001/1335.
[3]   SI 2001/1335.

3.75   The FSA's rules apply generally to firms in respect of all financial promotions. However, this principle is subject to a number of qualifications in specific circumstances.

3.76   First, the rules do not apply to an authorised professional firm if the financial promotion is incidental to the promotion or provision by the firm of professional services or of non-mainstream regulated activities, and is not communicated on behalf of another person who could not lawfully make the communication if he were acting in the course of business[1].

---

[1]   COB 3.1.5R.

3.77   Second, only certain rules apply to financial promotions concerning deposits, general insurance contracts, pure protection contracts (long-term insurance contracts without an investment element, such as permanent health insurance) and reinsurance contracts, the most important of which is that the promotion be clear, fair and not misleading[1]. Financial promotions concerning these types of investments are, in particular, exempt from the provisions relating to direct offer financial promotions in COB 3.9, unless the promotion relates to a cash deposit ISA[2].

---

[1]   COB 3.2.3R.
[2]   See COB 3.9.4G.

3.78   Third, mirroring the Financial Promotion Order, art 12[1], the FSA's rules have a territorial limitation on the promotions to which they apply[2], although certain of the rules apply in any event where a firm approves a financial promotion (even if that promotion is a promotion exempt under the Financial Promotion Order)[3].

---

[1]   SI 2001/1335.
[2]   COB 3.3.1R.
[3]   COB 3.3.3R and 3.3.4G.

3.79   The fact that the FSA's rules do not apply to a particular promotion will not inevitably mean that the promotion is free from all restrictions. Apart from regulations or guidelines outside the FSA's remit (such as Advertising Standards Authority or broadcasting codes, and regulations of overseas regulators), FSA's Principle 7 (communications with clients), which requires a firm to pay attention to the information needs of its clients and communicate information to them in a way which is clear, fair and not misleading, and COB 2.1.3R (clear, fair and not misleading communication), may also be relevant.

The detailed provisions

3.80   The FSA's rules adopt the language found in the Financial Promotion Order[1]. Thus the use of the concepts of real time/non-real time, solicited/unsolicited, and 'directed at' is common to both. The main terminological difference is that the FSA rules speak of a 'financial promotion', whereas the Financial Promotion Order and the FSMA 2000 use the word 'communication'; but this is not a distinction of substance, as the two expressions describe the same concept[2]. In keeping with the Treasury's emphasis on the need for the financial promotion regime established by the FSMA 2000 to reflect developments in electronic commerce, the FSA's rules contain a separate guidance section (COB 3.14) on the use of the Internet and other electronic media to communicate financial promotions.

[1]   SI 2001/1335.
[2]   See paras 3.1 and 3.3.

3.81   Before communicating or approving a non-real time communication, a firm must confirm that the communication meets the requirements of the FSA's rules. It must also ensure that the person who confirms that this is so is someone with appropriate expertise. The task of confirmation may be sub-contracted to a third party, but the firm remains responsible for any promotion that it communicates or approves[1].

[1]   COB 3.6.1–2.

3.82   The FSA has said that it will expect a firm to monitor the financial promotions that a firm communicates or approves, and has suggested that each promotion is given a 'shelf life', at the end of which it should be rechecked against the financial promotion rules[1]. However, a firm that merely communicates a financial promotion produced by another will not need to check the promotion against the FSA's rules, provided that it takes reasonable care to establish that another authorised person has done so, the promotion is directed only at those types of person for whom the original promotion was intended, the promotion remains clear, fair and not misleading following the confirmation of compliance with the FSA's rules by the other authorised person, and the other authorised person has not withdrawn the promotion[2].

[1]   COB 3.6.4G(2).
[2]   COB 3.6.5R.

3.83   Firms also need to retain 'adequate' records of all non-real time communications they have confirmed as complying with the FSA's rules (ie both those communications issued by themselves and those whose contents they have approved). The time for which the records should be kept varies depending on the nature of the investment which is the subject of the communication, but it will be for three years in any event[1]. By 'adequate', the FSA means that the record should include, among other things, the name of the person who confirmed that the promotion complied with the rules, the date of confirmation, and the evidence supporting any material factual statements in the promotion. Records may be kept in any form that the firm chooses, provided that they are readily accessible by the FSA when required for inspection. The firm should retain a copy of the final published version where practicable[2].

---

[1]   COB 3.7.1R.
[2]   COB 3.7.2–4.

3.84   The basic obligation for non-real time financial promotions is that the firm must be able to show, in respect of any such financial promotion that it communicates or approves, that it has taken reasonable steps to ensure that the promotion is clear, fair and not misleading. Where the promotion includes a comparison or contrast, the promotion must satisfy various requirements designed to ensure that like is compared with like and that no 'passing off' of other person's investments or services as one's own can occur[1].

---

[1]   COB 3.8.4R, implementing the directive concerning misleading and comparative advertising, Council Directive 84/450/EEC as amended by Council Directive 97/55/EC.

3.85   The remaining rules that apply to non-real time financial promotions in COB 3.8 are little more than expansions of the clear fair and not misleading concept, fleshed out and applied to specified circumstances. So specific non-real time financial promotions—promotions which identify and promote a particular investment or service—must disclose the nature of the investment or service and any holdings the firm might have in the investment, and present past performance figures in a balanced way so as not to give a false impression of what might happen in the future[1].

---

[1]   COB 3.8.8R, 3.8.10R and 3.8.11R.

3.86   The same principle lies behind the FSA's treatment of real time financial promotions. Here there is no risk that the recipient might be influenced by what is included in or omitted from written promotional material. But there is a clear risk that, left to its own devices, a firm might bring unfair pressure to bear on the recipient, particularly in the context of a personal visit. COB 3.8.22R therefore requires the firm to take reasonable steps to ensure that, where a person makes a real time financial promotion on the firm's behalf, a number of requirements are satisfied, such as:

(1)   the promotion is made in a way that is clear, fair and not misleading;
(2)   the promoter does not make untrue claims;
(3)   the promoter respects the right of the individual to terminate matters at any time and to refuse any request for another appointment; and

(4)   the promotion is not made at an unsocial hour, unless the recipient has previously agreed to contact at that time.

3.87 COB 3.10.3R prohibits firms from making unsolicited real time financial promotions (other than promotions which are exempt under COB 3.2.4–5) unless there is an established customer relationship with the recipient under which the recipient envisages receiving such promotions; or the promotion relates to a generally marketable packaged product which is not a higher volatility fund or a life policy linked or potentially linked to a higher volatility fund; or the financial promotion relates to a controlled activity to be carried on by an authorised person or exempt person, and the only controlled investments involved or which reasonably could be involved are readily realisable securities (other than warrants) and generally marketable non-geared packaged products.

3.88 COB 3.9 deals with 'direct offer financial promotions'—non-real time financial promotions which provide the means for the recipient to enter into an agreement with the firm (such as a tear-off slip which the recipient completes). The rules in this section set out various contents requirements, some of which apply to all direct offer financial promotions, others to specific types only. All direct offer financial promotions need, for instance, to contain sufficient information to enable a person to make an informed assessment of the investment or service to which the promotion relates; to set out details of charges and expenses which the recipient might bear and of commission which might be payable by the firm to a third party; and to include a summary of the taxation of any investment to which it relates and the taxation consequences for investors generally[1]. In addition, there are specific contents requirements for promotions relating to such investments as packaged products (where key features are required), investments that can fluctuate in value (where this fact must be made clear in language suitable for the target market—examples of wording that the FSA regards as potentially suitable are provided), and investments that attract cancellation rights[2].

---

[1]   COB 3.9.6R(1), 3.9.7R(5)–(6), and 3.9.19R.
[2]   COB 3.9.10R, 3.9.15–17, and 3.9.21R.

3.89 Firms cannot communicate or approve direct offer financial promotions that relate to broker funds, and can do so where the promotion relates to unregulated collective investment schemes, derivatives or warrants only if the firm has adequate evidence to suggest that the investment may be suitable for the person to whom the promotion is communicated[1]. The FSA's rules therefore prevent indiscriminate mailing to private customers of promotions relating to these latter types of investment.

---

[1]   COB 3.9.5R.

3.90 The FSMA 2000, s 21(2) envisages the possibility that an unauthorised person can make a real time financial promotion that is not in breach of the basic prohibition, by having the content of the promotion approved by an authorised person. However, the effect of COB 3.12.2R, which prevents a firm from approving such a promotion, is to ensure that unauthorised persons can make real time financial promotions only where an exemption exists under the Financial Promotion Order[1]. The reasoning behind this restriction is not stated in the rules, but it is likely to relate to the difficulty of ensuring that the content that was approved by the firm was not altered or embellished when the promotion was actually made. Firms are also prohibited from communicating or approving specific non-real time financial promotions relating to an investment or service of an overseas person, unless they have no reason to doubt that the overseas person will deal with private customers in the UK in an honest and reliable way, and the promotion discloses that the protections under the FSMA 2000 do not apply and contains a statement of the compensation position[2].

---

[1]   SI 2001/1335.
[2]   COB 3.12.6R.

3.91   Finally, COB 3.13 contains provisions that apply where a firm communicates or approves promotions relating to life policies for overseas long-term insurers. The firm must not communicate or approve such promotions unless the insurer falls within one of the categories listed in the Financial Promotion Order, art 10[1].The promotion must also satisfy various contents requirements designed to make it clear to the recipient that the overseas long-term insurer is not subject to regulation under the FSMA 2000 (such as a warning that holders of policies issued by the insurer will not be protected by the compensation arrangements under the FSMA 2000 in the event of the insurer's insolvency).

---

[1]   SI 2001/1335. See para 3.35.

PROMOTION OF COLLECTIVE INVESTMENT SCHEMES

Restrictions on promotion

3.92   Under the FSMA 2000, s 238, authorised persons can communicate an invitation or inducement to participate in a collective investment scheme only if:

(1)   the scheme is authorised or recognised;
(2)   the communication is in accordance with rules made by the FSA which exempt 'promotions otherwise than to the general public' of specified schemes (this phrase appears to include promotions which are in fact made to the general public but which are designed to reduce, as far as possible, the risk of participation in the scheme by persons for whom participation would be unsuitable)[1]; or
(3)   the circumstances of the promotion are exempt under a Treasury order.

---

[1]   See the FSMA 2000, s 238(10).

3.93 This restriction reflects the fact that unlike other controlled investments, units in collective investment schemes are generally subject to extensive product regulation for the protection of those who purchase them. Accordingly, it is not regarded as appropriate, even for authorised persons, to promote to the general public collective investment schemes which are neither authorised nor recognised.

3.94 There is no need to apply the FSMA 2000, s 238 to unauthorised persons, as units in collective investment schemes are controlled investments[1]. Communications in relation to them are therefore subject to the basic prohibition in s 21.

---

[1]   SI 2001/1335, Sch 1, para 19.

3.95 As with the FSMA 2000, s 21, s 238(1) applies to communications originating outside the UK only if they are capable of having an effect in the UK, and the Treasury has the power to move to 'home state' regulation of communications in relation to units in collective investment schemes should other countries do likewise, by exempting communications that originate in specified countries or territories[1].

---

[1]   FSMA 2000, s 238(7); compare para 3.19.

3.96 The FSMA 2000, s 240 provides that an authorised person cannot approve the content of a promotion under s 21 if the authorised person would himself be prevented from making the communication himself, or causing the communication to be made, under s 238(1). This reinforces the principle, seen in the Treasury order, that an unauthorised person should not be in a better position than an authorised person to communicate invitations or inducements to participate in unauthorised collective investment schemes[1].

---

[1]   See HM Treasury, Financial Promotion—Third Consultation Document (October 2000), para 4.6.

The Financial Services and Markets Act 2000 (Promotion of Collective Investment Schemes) (Exemptions) Order 2001 (CIS Exemptions Order)

3.97 The aim of the CIS Exemptions Order[1] is to ensure that the same exemptions as would apply to unauthorised persons under the Financial Promotion Order[2] apply also to authorised persons when making communications relating to collective investment schemes. It would clearly be illogical for unauthorised persons, as a result of exemptions applying under the Financial Promotion Order, to have a more liberal regime applying to them.

---

[1]   SI 2001/1060.
[2]   SI 2001/1335.

3.98 Consequently, there is a large measure of overlap between the exemptions contained in the Financial Promotion Order[1] and in the CIS Exemptions Order[2]. The definitions of real time, non-real time, and solicited and unsolicited real time communications are the same[3]; exemptions can be combined (though in the CIS Exemptions Order, without restriction)[4]; and there are similar exemptions for one-off and follow-up communications[5], and for communications to overseas recipients, investment professionals, certified high net worth individuals, high net worth companies and sophisticated investors[6].

---

[1]   SI 2001/1335.
[2]   SI 2001/1060.
[3]   SI 2001/1060, arts 4–5.
[4]   SI 2001/1060, art 7.
[5]   SI 2001/1060, arts 15, 15A and 11.
[6]   SI 2001/1060, arts 8, 14, 21, 22 and 23.

3.99 The Treasury also has the power to make regulations under the FSMA 2000, s 239 for exempting single property schemes from the prohibition in s 238(1). A single property scheme is a scheme where the property subject to the scheme consists of a single building or group of adjacent or contiguous buildings managed by the operator as a single enterprise, and where the units of the participants in the scheme are either dealt in on a recognised investment exchange, or where their acquisition is made subject to the units being admitted to dealings on such an exchange. If the Treasury makes such regulations, the FSA may impose duties on the operator, and (if it exists) on the trustee or depositary of the scheme. Given that no such schemes were created in response to regulations made under a virtually identical power in the Financial Services Act 1986, it remains to be seen whether this power will in fact be exercised.

The FSA's rules

3.100 As with financial promotion rules generally, the FSA cannot make rules governing the promotion of unregulated collective investment schemes which place authorised persons at a disadvantage when compared with unauthorised persons. So communications which would be exempt under the CIS Exemptions Order[1] are outside the scope of the FSA's rulemaking power[2].

---

[1]   SI 2001/1060.
[2]   FSMA 2000, s 145(3)(b); compare para 3.73.

3.101 Under COB 3.11.2R, authorised persons are allowed to communicate invitations or inducements to participate in unregulated collective investment schemes (that is, schemes which do not fall within the FSMA 2000, s 238(4)) if the communication is made in the following circumstances:

(1)   to a person who is, or has been in the past 30 months, a participant in an unregulated collective investment scheme, provided that the scheme

promoted is the same as, or has underlying property and a risk profile substantially similar to, the earlier scheme, or that the scheme is being liquidated or merged;

(2)   to a person who is an existing customer of the firm, where the authorised person has taken reasonable steps to ensure that investment in the scheme is suitable—if these conditions are satisfied, the authorised person may promote any scheme;

(3)   to a person who is eligible to participate in a scheme constituted under the Church Funds Investment Measure 1958, the Charities Act 1993, s 24 or the Charities Act (Northern Ireland) 1964, s 225, where any such scheme may be promoted (though the class of qualifying persons will be strictly limited to trustees of charities and of certain trust funds, such as the Central Board of Finance of the Church of England and Diocesan Boards of Finance);

(4)   to eligible employees of an employer which is, or is in the same group as, the authorised person (or who has accepted responsibility for the activities of the authorised person in carrying out the designated investment business in question), provided that the communication relates to certain types of employee incentive schemes;

(5)   to Lloyd's names, provided that the scheme is in the form of a limited partnership established for the sole purpose of underwriting insurance business at Lloyd's;

(6)   to exempt persons (though not to appointed representatives), where any scheme may be promoted if the promotion relates to a regulated activity in respect of which the person is exempt;

(7)   to intermediate customers, where any scheme may be promoted.

3.102   These exemptions largely follow the previous exemptions under the Financial Services Act 1986, s 76(3). In practice, the most useful general exemption for authorised persons is likely to be (7)[1], particularly as it includes those expert private customers classified as intermediate customers under COB 4.1.9R.

---

[1]   At para 3.101.

Chapter 4   Market Abuse

Charles Abrams and Tamasin Little

INTRODUCTION

4.1 The new offence of market abuse, which is set out in the Financial Services and Markets Act 2000 (FSMA 2000), Pt VIII, is the only truly novel part of the new regime. It is an offence which can be committed by anyone, not just FSMA 2000-authorised firms, even without any intention to abuse the market or otherwise do anything which involves committing the offence, even merely by unknowingly issuing a misleading takeover offer document or other company circular, and, in the case of markets in or accessed electronically from the UK, even by conduct outside the UK. Accordingly, it can be committed even by honest directors or employees of quoted companies or their subsidiaries and even by non-UK securities firms or banks without a UK branch.

4.2 Market abuse is defined in the FSMA 2000 at a very high level and the FSMA 2000 therefore requires the Financial Services Authority (FSA), which is to be the regulator and prosecutor of market abuse, to set out in a code examples of the kinds of behaviour which will or will not constitute market abuse[1]. The FSA has accordingly issued for consultation several drafts of its proposed Code of Market Conduct (the COMARC) and this Chapter describes the latest version of the COMARC which was issued in December 2001; but if there are any changes, this Chapter must be read in light of them.

---

[1]   FSMA 2000, s 119.

4.3 The important point to make at once is that the COMARC is not comprehensive. Accordingly, even behaviour which is not proscribed by the COMARC can still be prosecuted as market abuse if it falls within the statutory definition (which, as will be seen below, is much wider) unless it is covered by one of the FSA's safe harbours or the FSMA 2000's[1]; however, the particular examples of market abuse given in the COMARC are probably the cases which the FSA is most concerned about and are most likely to be prosecuted and importantly the FSA has incorporated an intent (or at least knowledge of the consequences or a lack of due care) requirement in practically all of them. In addition, the FSMA 2000 makes it clear that the FSA's opinion that particular behaviour constitutes market abuse is not determinative, albeit that it is persuasive. Accordingly, the allegation of market abuse can be rebutted not only by showing that the facts alleged by the FSA are not correct but also by showing that, even if they are correct, they do not amount to market abuse. A finding by the FSA of market abuse can be appealed to the independent Financial Services and Markets Tribunal and then, on a point of law, to the courts; a decision that proven behaviour constitutes market abuse is exactly a point of law which can be appealed against to the courts. For both these reasons, it is important to understand not only what behaviour the COMARC specifies is market abuse but also what the FSMA 2000 itself defines as market abuse.

---

[1]   See para 4.11.

4.4   The COMARC, which forms the first chapter of the Market Conduct section of the *FSA Handbook*, is intended to give 'appropriate guidance to those determining whether or not behaviour amounts to market abuse'[1]. It fulfils a unique function under the FSMA 2000, perhaps even a function unique in all UK legislation. It is a new tool of statutory interpretation under which a body (other than a court or Government department or Parliament itself) gives examples of prohibited and non-prohibited behaviour which are given some statutory force, by the FSMA 2000, s 122. That section provides that generally the COMARC (as in force at the time the 'abusive' behaviour takes place) has a strong evidential character which can be relied on insofar as it indicates whether or not that behaviour should be taken to amount to market abuse. Moreover, if the COMARC positively states that the relevant behaviour does not in the FSA's opinion amount to market abuse, the FSMA 2000, s 122 goes further and provides that such behaviour will not be market abuse for the purposes of the FSMA 2000. The FSA is therefore able in the COMARC to provide definitive safe harbours. In providing them the FSA has gone far further than might have been expected and, indeed, has in effect made the offence much fairer (and narrower) than appears in the FSMA 2000. In particular, the FSA has provided safe harbours for behaviour conforming with selected rules of a recognised investment exchange (an 'RIE') or the Takeover Panel. In addition, certain of the FSA's conduct of business and listing rules expressly state that behaviour conforming with them does not amount to market abuse and, accordingly, they also constitute safe harbours[2]; these are its price stabilisation rules and rules on Chinese walls and its listing rules relating to share buy-backs and announcements or disclosures (MAR 1.7.3E).

---

[1]   FSMA 2000, s 119(1).
[2]   FSMA 2000, s 118(8).

OVERVIEW OF THE STATUTORY OFFENCE

4.5   The new offence will apply not only to firms authorised (that is, registered or licensed) in the United Kingdom under the FSMA 2000 but also to non-UK securities firms, banks and insurance companies and, indeed, any other person (such as even an ordinary trading or manufacturing company, one of its directors or employees, or a private individual) and is not restricted to 'market participants', as the Government had originally indicated[1]. References in this Chapter to 'firms' therefore include not only stockbrokers, broker-dealers, investment or commercial banks and investment or fund managers, and individuals working for them, but also all these other persons. The offence is based on the existing criminal offences of insider dealing (contained in the Criminal Justice Act 1993, Pt V) and market manipulation (formerly in the Financial Services Act 1986, s 47 and now contained in the FSMA 2000, s 397), which will of course continue, but it goes much wider and is more uncertain in scope.

---

[1] But see para 4.9.

4.6 The FSA will police and enforce the new offence and will be empowered to impose an unlimited fine on 'market abusers', or issue public censures in relation to them[1], and obtain injunctions and remedial orders against them[2]. It can also require the 'abuser' to compensate everyone who suffered loss as a result of the market abuse (even if they are not his clients or counterparties) and to surrender any profits made by him[3]. In addition, the FSA can also impose an unlimited fine on (or publicly censure) anyone who has required or encouraged another person to engage in market abuse[4] and, again, can require him to pay compensation and to surrender his profits from the abuse[5]. As in the case of the insider dealing regime, market abuse does not make any transaction void or unenforceable, even if a penalty is imposed[6].

---

[1] FSMA 2000, s 123(1)(a), (3).
[2] FSMA 2000, s 381.
[3] FSMA 2000, s 384(2)(a), (5).
[4] FSMA 2000, s 123(1)(b), (3).
[5] FSMA 2000, s 384(2)(b), (5).
[6] FSMA 2000, s 131.

4.7 The FSMA 2000's normal enforcement procedures will apply if the FSA seeks to impose a fine or issue a public censure, or even impose an order for disgorgement of profits or reimbursement of losses arising from the market abuse. Accordingly the FSA must go through its warning and decision notice procedures and the alleged market abuser can appeal to the independent Financial Services and Markets Tribunal[1].

---

[1] FSMA 2000, ss 127(4), 386(3).

4.8 One of the policies behind the introduction of the new offence is to enable action to be taken (by the FSA) against an offender who is not a FSMA 2000-regulated person, or a member of the relevant market, for behaviour falling short of the criminal offences of insider dealing and market manipulation but which nonetheless is considered to prejudice the integrity of the market; a 'FSMA 2000-regulated person' is a FSMA 2000-authorised firm or someone employed by a FSMA 2000-authorised firm. The FSA will often be able to impose unlimited fines on FSMA 2000-regulated persons, and throw them out of the industry, for failing to comply with its regulatory requirements to conduct their business with integrity and observe proper standards of market conduct. In these cases, it therefore does not need to allege the new offence against them at all. Accordingly, it is likely that the persons who will be prosecuted by the FSA for alleged market abuse will often be outside the regulatory regime and amongst the most likely candidates for allegations of market abuse would therefore be market practitioners who are not FSMA 2000-regulated persons. It should, however, be noted that the FSA has indicated that it will prosecute FSMA 2000-regulated persons for market abuse (or, indeed, insider dealing or market manipulation) if the alleged facts are sufficient.

4.9   There are, in fact, four separate offences relating to market abuse. There are three primary ones:

(1)   misusing inside information and other information not generally available to the relevant market;
(2)   giving false or misleading impressions (which can be referred to in short as 'misleading the market' provided that it is remembered that the offence does not need to have anything to do with the market at all and covers misleading even just one person); and
(3)   distorting the market.

All of these offences are set out in the FSMA 2000, s 118 and cover behaviour which is likely to give a false or misleading impression or distort the market even if it does not and even if the alleged 'abuser' did not even suspect that it might.

There is also a secondary offence: requiring or encouraging someone else to commit market abuse (which appears only in the penalty provisions in the FSMA 2000, s 123(1)); the COMARC makes it clear that, in the FSA's view, merely giving selected recipients information which is material and not yet generally available may in particular circumstances constitute requiring or encouraging market abuse (MAR 1.8.5G). Giving consent to a proposed dealing under the Model Code may also do so[1]. Only the first three offences are technically the offences of market abuse. Importantly, in their case, the offending behaviour is only market abuse if it is likely to be regarded by a reasonable 'regular user' of the relevant market in the kind of investments concerned as 'a failure on the part of the [accused] to observe the standard of behaviour reasonably expected of a person in his position in relation to the market'[2]. This is a very helpful requirement as it means that in many cases non-practitioners will not commit the offence and is the provision which the FSMA 2000 uses to try to restrict the offence to 'market participants'; it in effect amounts to a statutory defence which an alleged 'abuser' can seek to rely on. Nonetheless, it is in itself probably of little help to investment firms, even if they are from outside the UK[3], or to directors of quoted companies which issue misleading company circulars.

---

[1]   FSA Consultation Paper 76 (November 2000), para 4.39.
[2]   FSMA 2000, s 118(1)(c).
[3]   But see para 4.33.

4.10 The FSMA 2000 defines 'behaviour' to cover both action and inaction[1], and therefore any failure to correct a mistake or indeed to file required information (for example, that a particular holding of shares has been bought or sold) could in itself constitute market abuse. Behaviour will constitute market abuse only if it occurs in relation to qualifying investments traded on a prescribed market[2]. However, there is no need for the market abuse to relate to on-market dealings. Indeed, market abuse can be engaged in without any transaction at all, whether on or off market. This was made abundantly clear by the then Economic Secretary to the Treasury (Melanie Johnson MP) in a debate in the 'market abuse' Commons Committee on 2 November 1999[3], when she gave as an example of market abuse the issue of a misleading press release by a UK quoted company. Indeed, the issue of any circular or even individual letter which contains a misleading statement can in itself be market abuse, if for example the misleading statement could lead someone to buy or sell securities. This is why the FSA was given the final word on allegations of market abuse in public takeovers[4].

---

[1] FSMA 2000, s 118(10).
[2] FSMA 2000, s 118(1)(a).
[3] HC Official Report, SC A, 2 November 1999, col 658.
[4] FSMA 2000, s 120 and see para 4.144 ff.

4.11 In addition to the FSA's safe harbours, the FSMA 2000 provides[1] that information that can be obtained by research or analysis is to be regarded as being generally available[2] and accordingly acting on that information is not market abuse. It also provides[3] that behaviour shall not be market abuse if it conforms with an FSA rule which specifies that behaviour conforming with it shall not amount to market abuse. The FSMA 2000 also provides a quasi-exemption if the alleged market abuser believed on reasonable grounds that he would not be committing, or requiring or encouraging, market abuse or he took all reasonable precautions and exercised all due diligence to avoid doing so[4]. It is only a quasi-exemption because the behaviour is nonetheless market abuse or requiring or encouraging market abuse; it is just that the FSA cannot impose a fine or (probably) publicly censure the market abuser and neither the court nor the FSA can require restitution (the surrender of profits or reimbursement of losses arising from the market abuse). The only real exemptions are therefore: the safe harbours provided by the FSA (in the COMARC or its conduct of business or listing rules); the indications given by the FSA in the COMARC that it would normally prosecute market abuse only if it involves intent, recklessness (including knowledge of the consequences of the 'abusive behaviour') or the lack of due care; and, finally, the likelihood that a regular market user would consider there to be a failure in expected standards only in those cases[5].

---

[1] In the FSMA 2000, s 118(7).
[2] See para 4.48 ff.
[3] In the FSMA 2000, s 118(8).
[4] FSMA 2000, s 123(2), s 383(3) and s 384(4).
[5] See para 4.38.

MARKETS AND INVESTMENTS COVERED

4.12   The Treasury can prescribe for the purposes of market abuse any markets they like, even if the market is outside the UK. However, the Treasury have so far prescribed only UK markets, namely the markets established under the rules of a UK recognised investment exchange[1] and, in addition, OFEX[2]. The UK RIEs are at present the London Stock Exchange, LIFFE, the LME, the IPE, OM London, virt-x plc (formerly Tradepoint), COREDEAL and Jiway. The formula used in the Market Abuse Scope Order will pick up new UK recognised investment exchanges as and when they are recognised. The FSA has made it clear, because there were some doubts among market users, that markets established under the rules of the London Stock Exchange include AIM[3] they similarly include SEAQ International.

---

[1]   Financial Services and Markets Act 2000 (Prescribed Markets and Qualifying Investments) Order 2001, SI 2001/996 (Market Abuse Scope Order).
[2]   Financial Services and Markets Act 2000 (Prescribed Markets and Qualifying Investments) (Amendment) Order 2001, SI 2001/3681.
[3]   FSA *Market Watch* newsletter (November 2001) Issue No 2, p 2.

4.13   Behaviour can only constitute market abuse if it relates to qualifying investments 'traded on' a prescribed market[1]. Because there was some doubt as to whether 'traded' meant that there actually had to be a market transaction, rather than being merely a description of the investments like 'quoted', the Government spelled out in Committee in the House of Commons[2] that the latter was the correct interpretation (as indeed seems quite clear from the terms of the offence). In addition, the Market Abuse Scope Order[3] provides that all the kinds of investments specified for the purposes of the FSMA 2000 authorisation requirement are to be treated as 'qualifying investments'. Accordingly, market abuse can be committed in relation to any FSMA 2000 investments which are for the time being traded on a prescribed market[4] and linked investments or other assets[5]. OTC transactions in market-traded investments are therefore covered despite what the FSA implies in its *Factsheet on Market Abuse*[6].

---

[1]   FSMA 2000, s 118(1)(a).
[2]   HC Official Report, SC A, 2 November 1999, col 674.
[3]   SI 2001/996.
[4]   FSMA 2000, s 118(1)(a).
[5]   See para 4.18.
[6]   FSA *Factsheet on Market Abuse* (September 2001), p 4.

4.14   The FSA expands on this in the COMARC by confirming that 'traded on' a prescribed market means 'traded subject to the rules of' that market and by setting out the categories of investments which would be regarded as being 'traded on' a prescribed market[1]. They include not only those which are currently traded on that market but also those which have not yet traded (which will be regarded as traded on that market from the moment that they start trading, including the first trade) and those which have been so traded in the past and can still be traded under the market's rules, even if trading is not active. The FSA has confirmed that securities which are being traded in the grey market (or on a 'when issued' basis) under the rules of a prescribed market, for example the London Stock Exchange, are within the 'market abuse' offence, even though official listing or normal trading have not taken place[2]. However, it also points out (as a matter of guidance only) that generally, unless there is an ongoing market, it is unlikely that behaviour will amount to market abuse[3]. The FSA explains that this is because it is unlikely that the other conditions for the offence will be satisfied, as market partici-pants are unlikely to rely on the relevant market for price discovery or formation, and trading which is not associated with that market is unlikely to damage confidence in the market. Although helpful, this does not seem very persuasive; for example, the price of the market transaction may be misleading (perhaps because of the market's lack of liquidity), and damag-ing confidence in the market is no longer a required part of the offence, as it was in its first draft. Accordingly, this FSA statement must not be regarded as meaning that the possibility of market abuse can safely be ignored if there is no ongoing market.

---

[1]   MAR 1.11.3G.
[2]   FSA Guidance Note No 1 (2001), Answer to Q 1.
[3]   MAR 1.11.4G.

EXTRA-TERRITORIAL EFFECT AND SCOPE

4.15   Importantly for firms outside the UK, the primary offences of market abuse do not have any territorial limitations where the relevant prescribed market is in the United Kingdom (or can be accessed electronically from it). If it is, the offence can be committed by conduct outside the UK[1] and this extra-territorial application goes far further than in the case of the criminal offences of insider dealing and market manipulation. For example, as the prescribed markets include SEAQ International, a misleading announce-ment or statement made in Paris about a SEAQ International company listed only in Paris is covered. This means that even non-UK firms will have to be fully aware of the scope of the market abuse offence.

---

[1]   FSMA 2000, s 118(5)(b).

4.16   If, conversely, the prescribed market is outside the UK (and cannot be accessed electronically from the UK), market abuse can be constituted only by behaviour (or, conduct or a failure to act) which occurs in the United Kingdom[1]. It is unclear whether behaviour will be treated as occurring 'in the United Kingdom' if the primary 'abuser' is outside the United Kingdom when he instructs a UK broker to deal on a non-UK exchange; it is arguable that it will not be (although it will be for the purposes of the criminal offence of insider dealing), but this could only be determined by case law, or if it were spelled out in the COMARC. In practice this is not at present an issue because the Treasury have so far not prescribed any non-UK market, although it is possible that they will at least prescribe NASDAQ and NASDAQ Europe (formerly called EASDAQ), which are already prescribed for insider dealing purposes. As both these markets are accessible electronically from the UK, abusive behaviour relating to them can be market abuse even if it occurs outside the UK. In addition, instructing the UK broker would surely be 'requiring or encouraging' market abuse and this secondary market abuse is arguably not restricted to behaviour in the UK, at least in the case of a prescribed market in, or accessible electronically, from the UK; however, conduct outside the UK is normally not subject to UK statutes unless there is express language making it clear that it is (as indeed there is in the case of UK markets in relation to the primary offences themselves) and there is no clear language in the FSMA 2000 in relation to 'requiring or encouraging'.

---

[1]   FSMA 2000, s 118(5)(a).

4.17   The COMARC accordingly states that behaviour can constitute market abuse if it occurs in relation to qualifying investments traded on a prescribed market which is located in the United Kingdom or which is accessible electronically in [or rather, from] the United Kingdom[1]. There are two important points to note about this statement. First, because there is no territorial limit specified, this means that the COMARC confirms that behaviour in relation to these markets can constitute market abuse wherever in the world it occurs. Second, however, although the COMARC refers as authority for the statement to the FSMA 2000, s 118(5), this is being slightly loose; what it should have referred to is the FSMA 2000, s 118(5)(b), because in cases falling outside that paragraph (in other words, where the prescribed market is outside the UK and not accessible from it electronically) behaviour can constitute market abuse only if it occurs in the United Kingdom[2]. Presumably, the COMARC does not refer to the position where the prescribed market is outside the UK because at the time the COMARC was published the only markets which had been prescribed by the Treasury were UK markets[3].

---

[1]   MAR 1.1.7G.
[2]   FSMA 2000, s 118(5)(a).
[3]   See para 4.12.

4.18   In addition, behaviour is treated as occurring 'in relation to' qualifying investments even if it does not relate directly to the particular investments themselves. The FSMA 2000, s 118(6) spells out that behaviour will be regarded as occurring in relation to qualifying investments even if it relates only to their subject matter (for example, silver, since silver futures are prescribed), or to anything whose price or value is expressed by reference to their price or value (for example, spread betting on securities quoted in London) or, indeed, if it occurs in relation to investments based on, or referenced to, them (for example, stock futures on securities quoted in London). As 'investments' means assets, rights or interests which constitute investments for the purposes of the FSMA 2000's authorisation requirement[1], this last category includes, for example, options, futures or contracts for differences on shares quoted on the London Stock Exchange. Accordingly, as it is a UK market (and therefore behaviour is covered even if it occurs outside the UK) the grant by a broker-dealer in New York to a buyer in Zurich of an option over shares quoted in London can be market abuse if the broker-dealer had inside information about the shares at the time he granted it. Similarly, behaviour in Canada relating to a particular silver mine is covered merely because silver futures are traded on the London Metal Exchange. If, therefore, a silver producer in Canada sells a quantity of silver at below market price, because he needs to find funds quickly to pay a tax bill, and it was reasonable for market players to think that this low price was only because he had a large supply of silver (which he did not) so that the price of silver (and accordingly silver futures) consequently fell (or could have fallen), he could in principle be treated as committing the market abuse of misleading the market. The COMARC states that something can be related in this sense to qualifying investments only if there is a 'clear relationship' between the two, for example, a contractual (as in contracts for differences or other derivatives) or documented[2] link. The COMARC refers to these linked assets as 'relevant products'. Where gilt futures are qualifying investments traded on a prescribed market, the gilts which are deliverable under them are their subject matter and accordingly their relevant products. Importantly, behaviour in relation to a similar investment can also be 'in relation to' a qualifying investment traded on a prescribed market if the behaviour can affect the price of the qualifying investment. For example, if trading in gold has an effect on the price of silver, and accordingly silver futures (which is a qualifying investment traded on a prescribed market) behaviour in relation to gold will constitute behaviour in relation to silver futures[3].

---

[1]   See para 4.13.
[2]   MAR 1.11.10E.
[3]   FSA Guidance Note No 1 (2001), Answer to Q 2.

4.19   Even though all investments for the purposes of the FSMA 2000's authorisation requirement are qualifying investments[1], behaviour occurring in relation to them can only constitute market abuse if (as explained in MAR 1.11.9E):

(1)   they are themselves traded on a prescribed market (for example, gilts (or gilt futures) traded on a prescribed market);

(2)   their subject matter is other qualifying investments which are so traded (for example, gilt futures where only the underlying gilts are traded on a prescribed market[2]);

(3)   they are themselves the subject matter of other qualifying investments which are so traded (for example, gilts where only the gilt futures are traded on a prescribed market[3]); or

(4)   their price or value is based on the price or value of other qualifying investments which are so traded (for example, spread bets on gilts which are traded on a prescribed market[4]).

---

[1]   See para 4.13.
[2]   FSMA 2000, s 118(6)(b).
[3]   FSMA 2000, s 118(6)(a).
[4]   FSMA 2000, s 118(6)(a).

4.20   The FSA's interpretation of the expression 'investments of the kind in question' which appears in each of the three categories of the primary offence of market abuse set out in the FSMA 2000, s 118(2), seems dubious. The FSA has affirmed at para 8.5 in the policy statement issued with the April 2001 version of the COMARC that 'where behaviour occurs in a relevant product, this would be the "investments of the kind in question" '; although para 8.5 relates to the 'distorting the market' category of market abuse, the same interpretation would presumably apply in relation to all three categories of (primary) market abuse. However, when the FSMA 2000, s 118(2) refers to 'investments of the kind in question' it is in our view referring to the 'qualifying investments traded on a market to which this section applies', in the FSMA 2000, s 118(1)(a); the term 'investments' is used as shorthand for those qualifying investments. In addition, as indicated above[1], it is clear that behaviour can be treated as occurring in relation to qualifying investments even if it relates directly only to something which is the subject matter, or whose price or value is expressed by reference to the price or value, of those qualifying investments[2] and this indirect market abuse is not limited (as implied in para 8.5) to where that something (the 'relevant product', as used in the COMARC) is itself an investment. For example, behaviour distorting the silver market is behaviour which would also distort the silver futures market, which is why the FSMA 2000 uses a very wide definition of behaviour occurring 'in relation to qualifying investments'[3]; this is the case even though silver is not an 'investment'.

---

[1]   See para 4.18.
[2]   FSMA 2000, s 118(6)(a).
[3]   FSMA 2000, s 118(6).

4.21   The fact that there is no need for the market abuse to relate to on-market dealings, or indeed any dealings at all, only widens the scope of the offence even more. If a New York newspaper publishes a report about a company quoted in London which is false or misleading, the journalist could be guilty of market abuse, and subject to an unlimited fine, even if he wrote his report when in New York. It is easy to see why non-UK Internet service providers, publishing articles by companies on websites they are hosting, have grounds for concern.

IMPORTANT POINTS ABOUT THE COMARC

4.22   There are a few important points to bear in mind when reading the COMARC.

(1)   It is not an exclusive or exhaustive description of market abuse. Despite its importance as an interpretative tool it is still possible for the FSA, the Financial Services and Markets Tribunal or the courts to find someone guilty of market abuse based directly on the statute (unless his behaviour falls within a safe harbour specified in the COMARC or in the FSMA 2000, Pt VIII).

(2)   Complying with the COMARC does not exempt anyone from compliance with all the other laws, rules and regulations applicable to him,

including, for example, those relating to insider dealing or market manipulation and, in the case of FSMA 2000-regulated persons, the very general Statements of Principle, which require them to act with integrity and comply with high standards of market conduct and which are much more general high level obligations which may not be satisfied by merely avoiding committing market abuse.

(3) The COMARC uses a complex notation system giving different weight to different provisions in it. Paragraphs marked 'C' are full scale safe harbours; they constitute statutory defences[1] and so narrow the scope of the offence. Paragraphs marked 'E' are statements of the FSA's opinion which are given evidential force by the FSMA 2000, s 122(2) but do not necessarily affect the scope of the offence although they, probably, do bind the FSA. Paragraphs marked 'G' are technically not part of the COMARC and cannot be relied on under the FSMA 2000, s 122 but are only guidance given under the FSA's general powers to give guidance under the FSMA 2000, s 157; accordingly they normally do not bind the FSA as the Government refused to accept the amendment proposed by the Conservative Party's Treasury Team that guidance should be binding.

(4) When the COMARC refers to behaviour conforming, or in conformity, with a particular rule, it means that the rule requires or expressly permits the behaviour or that it is delayed as required or permitted by the rule; for example, if a particular event has to be notified within five days there is no market abuse provided that the notification takes place by the end of the fifth day, even though for four days this was misleading because it might have been thought that the event had not actually taken place because it had not been notified. The COMARC spells this out in relation to conforming with an FSA rule[2] but it is quite clear that it applies in relation to all other rules and, indeed, this is expressly stated in relation to rule 4.2 of the Takeover Code[3]. This probably applies also to the statutory safe harbours for behaviour conforming with the 'safe harbour' FSA rules[4] or the 'safe harbour' rules in the Takeover Code[5].

(5) The FSA is obliged under the FSMA 2000, s 124 to issue a statement of its policy on penalties in relation to market abuse. That statement of policy forms part of the Enforcement Manual and is not dealt with in this Chapter.

(6) Although the FSA is a quasi-legislator in issuing the COMARC under the FSMA 2000, s 119, it is also a prosecutor which imposes and enforces penalties under the FSMA 2000, s 123. The accused can refer the case to the independent Financial Services and Markets Tribunal for it to determine the allegation of market abuse itself—this is not technically an appeal because the Tribunal is empowered to hear the case again from scratch (technically, de novo). It is only the possibility of a reference to the Tribunal that prevents the FSA also being a judge; however, even if the accused does not refer the case to the Tribunal, the Government is of the view that the FSA should not be regarded as acting as a judge even though it decides that its allegations are proven and it imposes a penalty (see point (7) below). Appellants to the Tribunal who are individuals can obtain some legal assistance before

the Tribunal if the FSA imposes a penalty[6]. Appeal to the court from the Tribunal can only be made on points of law, although this includes a decision of the Tribunal on whether proven behaviour constitutes market abuse at all.

(7)   There has been extensive debate as to how far the market abuse regime is a 'criminal' rather than (as it purports to be) a 'civil' one and, to the extent that it is, the impact this has on both the standard of proof and the rights which the accused have under the Human Rights Act 1998 and the European Convention on Human Rights (ECHR). This debate is not covered in detail in this Chapter. However, in our view, where the FSA is seeking to impose a fine (or, as the FSMA 2000 calls it, a 'penalty', which sounds less criminal) the regime is more properly classified for ECHR purposes as criminal, rather than civil. Indeed, the Treasury stated in writing on 14 May 1999, in evidence to the Joint Committee (of both Houses of Parliament) on Financial Services and Markets (the Burns Committee), which in a novel form of pre-legislative scrutiny reviewed the draft Bill before it was formally put into Parliament, that it accepted that there was a 'real possibility' that proceedings for market abuse penalties would be treated as criminal for ECHR purposes, even though they were civil for UK domestic law purposes. The FSMA 2000 was therefore written on the basis that the ECHR 'criminal charges' protections would apply in the case of these proceedings (but not in the case of non-penal proceedings, for example for restitution). That is why, for example, there is legal assistance (a special form of legal aid) for individuals in front of the Tribunal if the FSA is seeking to impose a penalty (or to issue a public censure) and evidence obtained by compulsion from an alleged market abuser normally cannot be used against him in these circumstances[7]. It should be noted, however, that the FSA states in the COMARC that it considers that only the civil 'balance of probabilities' standard of proof applies to charges of market abuse. However, this approach does not appear to be clearly justified on the case law even in UK domestic law and it is outlawed by the ECHR where the offence is criminal for ECHR purposes (see above). In addition, the fundamental ECHR 'due process' entitlement of a fair hearing by an independent and impartial tribunal (ECHR, Article 6(1)) applies even if market abuse is civil for ECHR purposes. It is for this very reason that the concept of a Tribunal hearing an appeal from scratch was introduced into the FSMA 2000. For the same reason, in the Government's view (as expressed in formal correspondence between Lord McIntosh, the Government's spokesman in the Lords, and Lord Kingsland, the Shadow Lord Chancellor), the FSA does not have to comply with the 'due process' requirement even if there is no reference to the Tribunal; it is acting only as a prosecutor not as a judge and the accused is entitled to appeal to the Tribunal, even if he does not do so.

(8)   The COMARC correctly spells out the statutory tests which must be satisfied in order to establish (primary) market abuse[8]. These are: (i) the behaviour must occur in relation to qualifying investments traded on a prescribed market; (ii) the behaviour must fall in at least one of the three categories of 'abusive behaviour'[9]; and (iii) the regular market

user must be likely to regard the behaviour as falling below the appropriate standards. In each of its sections dealing with the three categories of abusive behaviour, the COMARC calls the behaviour 'market abuse'. However, as the COMARC states in the first paragraph of each section detailing the categories of abusive behaviour, it is assuming that test (i) is satisfied. It should, of course, also have assumed that test (iii) is satisfied. Unless it is, the behaviour is not market abuse even if it satisfies tests (i) and (ii). This is a rather unfortunate omission, especially as test (iii) is often a helpful statutory defence and the FSA knows that it cannot be satisfied merely because the FSA thinks that it is.

(9)   When the COMARC describes the respective safe harbours for each of the three categories of (primary) market abuse, it states that their effect is that the behaviour does not constitute the relevant market abuse behaviour[10]. However, the COMARC is perhaps a little misleading when it says this. The relevant behaviour will constitute abusive behaviour but, because of the safe harbour, will not amount to market abuse. It is exactly because it does constitute the relevant abusive behaviour that there needs to be a safe harbour in these cases.

---

[1]   FSMA 2000, s 122(1).
[2]   MAR 1.7.2E.
[3]   MAR 1.7.8C.
[4]   FSMA 2000, s 118(8).
[5]   FSMA 2000, s 120.
[6]   FSMA 2000, s 134.
[7]   FSMA 2000, s 174(2).
[8]   MAR 1.1.3G.
[9]   See para 4.23.
[10]   See, in relation to misusing non-public information, MAR 1.4.19E; in relation to giving false or misleading impressions, MAR 1.5.23E; and, in relation to distorting the market, MAR 1.6.19C.

THE THREE CATEGORIES OF MARKET ABUSE

4.23   The three categories of (primary) market abuse behaviour are:

(1)   behaviour which is based on information that is not generally available to those using the market but which, if available to a regular user of the market, would be regarded, or would be likely to be regarded, by him as relevant when deciding the terms on which he would buy or sell (or effect another transaction in) the investments concerned[1];

(2)   behaviour which is likely to give a regular user of the market a false or misleading impression of the supply of, demand for, or price or value of the investments concerned[2];

(3)   behaviour which a regular user of the market would, or would be likely to, regard as likely to distort the market in the investments concerned[3].

---

[1]   FSMA 2000, s 118(2)(a).
[2]   FSMA 2000, s 118(2)(b).
[3]   FSMA 2000, s 118(2)(c).

No need for intention

4.24   None of the three categories of (primary) market abuse have any express requirement that the alleged 'abuser' should have intended (either positively or by reckless or negligent disregard of the possible effect of the behaviour in question) to engage in the abusive behaviour or, in the case of giving false or misleading impressions or distorting the market, even known that he might do so. An element of intention seems, however, to be implied in the first category (misuse of information) in the sense that the behaviour must be 'based on' the information which is not generally available. It is difficult to see how this can be the case unless the accused intended to use the information. Even if it can, however, the FSA has made the position clear by providing a safe harbour where the abusive behaviour is not 'influenced' by the information[1].

---

[1]   MAR 1.4.21C.

4.25   Although the Government was pressed very hard, and repeatedly, by the Conservative Party's Treasury Team, with the argument that no-one should be found guilty of the other two categories of (primary) market abuse unless he had some intention to give a false or misleading impression or distort the market, or at least some anticipation that he might do so, it refused to introduce any such requirement. The Treasury also refused the calls for an intent requirement which were made by three of the main trade associations of market practitioners: the London Investment Banking Association (LIBA); the Association of Private Client Investment Managers and Stockbrokers (APCIMS); and the British Bankers' Association (BBA). The Confederation of British Industry (CBI) also called for an intent requirement because they were well aware of the risks which the new 'false or misleading impressions' offence might pose to their members. The Government, however, insisted that market abuse was to be an 'effect-based' offence rather than an 'intent-based' one. Accordingly, although the FSMA 2000 provides that the penalty can be smaller if the behaviour (that is, hopefully, the market abuse) was not intended or reckless[1], it thereby confirms that even without intention or recklessness the behaviour can still constitute market abuse. The Government affirmed several times that the purpose of the market abuse offence was to protect the market rather than to penalise transgressors. There are, however, very extensive potential penalties and, indeed, the offence is only 'effect-based' in the sense that the 'abusive' behaviour affects market confidence[2], which even behaviour 'likely' to mislead or distort arguably does even if it did not actually do so. On the wording of the FSMA 2000 it is quite possible to be guilty of market abuse if the abusive effect could be said to be 'likely' even if it did not in fact occur, no-one was misled and the market was not distorted in any way. It is evident also from the FSA's consultation papers and remarks by the Economic Secretary in the 'market abuse' Commons Committee that the offence is supposed to be a deterrent rather than merely something which protects the market. What is not abundantly evident is how someone can be deterred from doing something he did not know that he was doing.

---

[1]   FSMA 2000, s 124(2)(b).
[2]   For example, HC Official Report, SC A, 2 November 1999, col 655.

The 'regular market user' test

4.26   Instead of an 'intention' or 'mens rea' requirement, the FSMA 2000 qualifies the three categories of (primary) market abuse by saying that in each case the behaviour in question needs to be likely to be regarded by a regular user of the relevant market in the investments concerned, as a failure to observe the standard of behaviour reasonably expected of a person in the position of the alleged abuser in relation to the market[1]. The 'regular market user' test is the Government's preferred way of trying to ensure that the market abuse offence applies only (or at least mainly) in the case of market practitioners. The test is therefore a very helpful defence for alleged abusers who have not dealt in the relevant market before, although directors of quoted companies are probably going to be regarded by the regular market user as being aware of the effect of their behaviour on the market, at least in the case of formal press releases, company circulars or other public documentation.

---

[1]   FSMA 2000, s 118(1)(c).

4.27   The 'regular market user' in relation to any particular market is defined as 'a reasonable person who regularly deals on that market in investments of the kind in question'[1]. That person may therefore differ depending both on the market in question and on the relevant type of investments. The 'regular market user' is meant to be a sophisticated market equivalent of the 'man on the Clapham omnibus'.

---

[1]   FSMA 2000, s 118(10).

4.28   The 'regular market user' test was introduced by the Government to bring in an 'objective' standard, but it seems actually to introduce a subjective standard by using what someone thinks to be the likely opinion of those firms which are likely to be regarded as 'regular users'. It seems fairer to create a more truly objective test by dropping the 'regular market user' test and seeing instead whether the behaviour falls short of the standards reasonably expected of a person in the position in relation to the market and with the attributes of the accused (which would be similar to the UK test for negligence by a director). The amendment to that effect proposed by the Conservative Party's Treasury Team was, however, rejected by the Government. The 'regular market user' test therefore seems to make the position rather worse for market practitioners who want to determine in advance whether particular behaviour will be market abuse (and, indeed, also for the FSA, which can only succeed on an appeal to the Financial Services and Markets Tribunal against a determination of market abuse if it can establish the view of a hypothetical regular market user to the satisfaction of the Tribunal), but the Government would not move from it. Essentially, therefore, a compliance officer advising his firm (or an FSA prosecutor considering whether to bring a prosecution) has to put himself in the position of a regular market user and then decide what view that regular market user would take of the behaviour. Accordingly, the market abuse offence of 'giving a false or misleading impression' is going to be committed by anyone doing anything which might be misunderstood by a regular user of the market, provided only that the likely view of the regular market user is that he should have known better. The scope for differences of opinion as to what a 'regular user' of a market may think is obvious. Users of the markets, and their views on what is acceptable, vary widely.

4.29   The FSA has tackled this question in the COMARC by setting out its own views on what is required under the 'regular user' test. Many of the FSA's views on what it considers the expectations of a regular market user to be are helpful both in clarifying the offence and in introducing an element of intent[1]. Essentially, at a number of points, it assumes that a regular market user has some moral sense which condemns intentional bad behaviour much more than accidents. The COMARC says that, although intention is not essential for behaviour to fall below the objective standards required, in some circumstances the determination of whether behaviour falls short of those standards will depend on the purpose of the alleged abuser[2]. A mistake is, however, considered by the FSA to be unlikely to fall below the standards required if the person concerned has taken reasonable care to prevent and detect the occurrence of the mistake.

---

[1]   See paras 4.76–4.78 and 4.85 (false and misleading impression) and paras 4.104 and 4.109 (distorting the market).
[2]   MAR 1.2.5–6.

4.30   Nevertheless, one of the points put forcefully in consultation was that it is not appropriate for the FSA as regulator, rather than a market user, to say what a regular market user might or might not expect. The FSA in its response to consultation accepted that it could not set itself up as a regular market user nor could it require a regular market user to act in any particular way, take any particular factor into account, or give any specific weight to a particular factor. However, the FSA considered that it could give guidance on the behaviour which, in its opinion, the regular market user would be likely to consider as amounting to market abuse and the standards he is likely to accept. This must be correct. The COMARC is required to give guidance to those seeking to determine whether or not behaviour amounts to market abuse. The 'regular market user' test is a key element of the definition of market abuse and it would therefore be a serious omission if the COMARC did not address that element.

4.31   It remains, however, dangerous territory. This is partly because of the normative effect of the FSA's statements in the COMARC which could by shifting the expectations of market users, or some market users, diminish market efficiency if inappropriate. At the other extreme, it is also partly because the FSA's views on what the view of the regular market user would be, may clearly be overruled and, even before that, might be widely rejected by the markets. In either case their removal would potentially damage or unbalance the remainder of the COMARC.

4.32   A number of the FSA's general statements about the 'regular market user' test in MAR 1.2 are uncontroversial. It says[1] that a hypothetical reasonable person familiar with the market in question would consider all the circumstances of the behaviour including:

(1)   the characteristics of the market, the investments traded on it and its users. The example given is that the disclosure standards currently expected in equity markets differ from those in commodity markets;
(2)   the rules and regulations of the market in question and any applicable laws;
(3)   prevailing market mechanisms, practices and Codes of Conduct; and
(4)   the position of the person in question in relation to the market and the standards reasonably to be expected of that person at the time of the alleged market abuse in the light of that person's experience, level of skill and standard of knowledge.

It says that accordingly the standards which it would be reasonable to expect from a retail investor are likely to be different from (that is, lower than) those to be expected of an industry professional[2] and when considering the standards to be expected of public sector bodies it is likely to be relevant to take into account their statutory and other official functions[3].

---

[1]   In MAR 1.2.3E.
[2]   MAR 1.2.3E(4).
[3]   MAR 1.2.7G.

4.33   As a matter of guidance only, the FSA says that where relevant behaviour takes place on an overseas market (but has an effect on a prescribed UK market) the regular market user is likely to consider it relevant to have regard to local rules, practices and conventions in the overseas market and whether or not the person concerned is in the UK[1]. It stresses, however, that compliance with such rules (and, presumably, practices and conventions) will not of itself be determinative, especially where the alleged 'abuser' is a member of the prescribed UK market; it is however not at all clear that the regular market user would expect a local firm acting only in its overseas market to have regard to anything other than its local rules, practices and conventions. The COMARC also addresses the situation where an overseas firm or investor deals directly into the prescribed market; it confirms that compliance with local standards 'may' be relevant to the view formed by the regular market user[2]. However, the Economic Secretary (Melanie Johnson MP) stated in the 2 November 1999 debate in the 'market abuse' Commons Committee[3] that the regular market user would expect such a person to deal in accordance (only) with his local standards and the regular market user would probably indeed take that view, unless perhaps the alleged abuser was aware that the behaviour was not allowed in the UK.

---

[1]   MAR 1.2.9G.
[2]   MAR 1.2.3(2)E.
[3]   HC Official Report, SC A, 2 November 1999, col 679.

4.34   In some other respects the pronouncements of the COMARC on the 'regular market user' test are a little more controversial. It adds as a basic consideration that a regular market user would, in its view, always bear in mind: 'the need for market users to conduct their affairs in a manner that does not compromise the fair and efficient operation of the market as a whole or unfairly damage the interests of investors'. While this may be desirable there are plenty of market theorists who would not say that fairness is a necessary part of efficiency nor that all market users should necessarily conduct their affairs to avoid damage to investors, or at least 'unfair' damage, which is presumably damage arising from unfair trading practices.

4.35   This attribution of morality to the markets is taken a step further when the COMARC goes on to say that the regular market user would only find it relevant, not determinative, that the behaviour 'conforms' with standards that are generally accepted by market users. According to the FSA, the fact that the users of a particular market accept a particular standard of behaviour does not necessarily make it acceptable; accepted market practice is not always the same as acceptable market practice. Indeed, the fact that behaviour complies with the rules of the relevant RIE, the Takeover Code or even the FSA's own rules, all of which firms are not merely expected but actually required to obey, is also regarded by the FSA as a matter which a regular market user would only regard as relevant, not determinative, (apart from certain specific rules for which express safe harbours are given[1]). In its response to consultation the FSA gave as an example that a large on-exchange position might form part of a strategy of behaviour amounting to market abuse even though it had been properly built up in accordance with exchange rules (and presumably the Takeover Code, if relevant)[2].

---

[1]   See para 4.143.
[2]   Paragraph 5.9 of the April 2001 policy statement issued with the COMARC.

4.36   In our opinion, the FSA is not in fact saying that behaviour might be abusive even if it conforms with RIE rules. What it seems to be saying in the policy statement is that compliance will not always be determinative, which seems understandable given that the Government refused a Conservative Party's Treasury Team amendment that it would not be market abuse to comply with RIE rules. However, the FSA does state that compliance with RIE rules will be given 'more weight'[1] when they require or expressly permit behaviour; accordingly, behaviour conforming with RIE rules (in other words, doing what a rule requires or expressly permits) is less likely to constitute market abuse and, indeed, we would think that acting in conformity with them (or indeed behaviour sanctioned by RIE guidance or dispensations) would be exactly what a regular market user would expect of market members. When the FSA says that 'compliance with RIE rules will not in itself be sufficient', it seems to mean not compliance as such, but non-contravention; the mere fact that no RIE rule is contravened does not mean that there is no market abuse. The example it gives is not where the behaviour is sanctioned by RIE rules but merely where no express RIE rules have been broken; indeed, in the April 2001 policy statement, the FSA states that it is possible for behaviour to amount to market abuse 'even if no RIE rules have been breached' (para 5.9). We respectfully agree with that approach. Finally, the helpful express statement issued by the FSA that: 'the RIE rulebooks do not permit or require behaviour which amounts to market abuse'[2], should be emphasised. The strategy of behaviour amounting to market abuse would not in our view be required or expressly permitted by RIE rules anyway.

---

[1]   Paragraph 5.9 of the April 2001 policy statement.
[2]   MAR 1.2.12G.

4.37   As indicated above[1], the COMARC takes the line that the 'regular market user' test is looking at whether the behaviour in question is acceptable, not whether it is actually accepted. Where standards are generally accepted (or a range of practices is generally accepted) such standards (or practices) will, in the FSA's view, only be acceptable where they promote the fair and efficient operation of the market as a whole and do not unfairly damage the interests of investors. The FSA has accepted expressly the strategies of short selling and securities lending if they are not used to effect market abuse[2]; this helpfully makes it clear that neither strategy is 'abusive' in itself.

---

[1]   See para 4.35.
[2]   FSA *Market Watch* newsletter (November 2001) Issue No 2.

4.38   In fact the FSMA 2000 does not refer to either 'accepted' or 'acceptable' behaviour. The question is whether the alleged abuser met the standards reasonably 'expected'. It seems reasonable to take the view that regular market users expect what is actually accepted and happens (provided that the 'accepted' behaviour is known to regular market users and probably that acceptance is universal), not what would happen if the world and the markets were 'fair'. The alternative approach adopted by the COMARC is more like a teacher or regulator saying mournfully 'I expected better of you'. Indeed, it is arguable that a regular market user would not regard any behaviour as falling short of expected standards if there is no intent to engage in the activities constituting market abuse, or recklessness or negligence in doing so, or if the behaviour results from an unexpected mistake (even if there were no protective procedures in place as required by the FSA). This is therefore an area where the FSA may be vulnerable to the criticism that, by spelling out what it thinks to be the likely views of a regular market user, it is putting itself in the place of the regular market user.

4.39   The FSA affirms that it does not expect there to be many cases where accepted standards are lower than those expected by the regular market user and indicates that if such a case arises the FSA will consider giving further guidance rather than proceeding direct to enforcement actions. In its response to consultation, however, the FSA said that enforcement action rather than guidance or supervision might be appropriate (only) when the behaviour is 'egregious or heinous and quite clearly abusive'. Indeed, the Government refused to accept an amendment proposed by the Conservative Party's Treasury Team that the fine should be lower if the behaviour constituted accepted market practice.

4.40   It is nonetheless quite clear that the Financial Services and Markets Tribunal can substitute its own view of what a regular market user would expect for that of the FSA. Indeed, it is likely that the accused can appeal to the courts against the Tribunal's view, as that seems to be more a point of law than a matter of fact[1]; however, for the same reason, the FSA can also appeal.

---

[1]   FSMA 2000, s 137(1).

MISUSE OF INFORMATION

4.41   The 'misuse of information' category of (primary) market abuse requires that the alleged abuser engages in behaviour, in relation to qualifying investments traded on a prescribed market, which is based on information which is not generally available to those using the market but which would be likely to be regarded by a regular market user as relevant when deciding the terms on which transactions in those investments should be effected. Although for convenience it may be useful to refer to this category as misusing inside information, there are important differences between this category of market abuse and insider dealing:

(1)   the market abuser does not have to be an insider or tippee, although it is likely that in most cases he would be;

(2)   the information which is not generally available does not need to be price sensitive for market abuse although it does for insider dealing. For market abuse it is sufficient that it is relevant to deciding the terms on which a transaction will be entered into, which in principle does not need to be restricted to terms as to price;

(3)   a transaction can be market abuse even if it is entered into off-exchange and no professional intermediary is involved. In those circumstances, there cannot be insider dealing;

(4)   there is no defence in terms where both parties to the transaction know the information; there is such a defence in the case of insider dealing. Hopefully, the regular market user would take the view that in these circumstances there is no failure in expected standards (so that there is no market abuse);

(5)   the alleged market abuser can be guilty even though he was acting as a market maker on an RIE; there is a defence in these circumstances in the case of insider dealing;

(6)   an alleged market abuser can be guilty even if he did not know that the information was not generally available (although, depending on the facts, a regular market user may think that accordingly he is not falling below expected standards). Conversely, there can be no insider

dealing unless a person 'has information as an insider' which means that normally he must actually know that the information has not been made public;

(7)   for the moment at least, securities traded only on a non-UK market are not subject to the market abuse regime. Conversely, insider dealing can be committed if the securities are quoted on any of the many European markets covered by the insider dealing regime or, indeed, on NASDAQ or NASDAQ Europe;

(8)   as indicated below, information is generally available (and so outside this category of market abuse) even if it has not been made public in the United Kingdom, is communicated only on payment of a fee or is acquired only by observation. In these circumstances, information is still to be treated as non-public for the purposes of the insider dealing regime unless the court decides that it should be treated as made public;

(9)   the market abuse regime can apply to a much earlier stage in a transaction than the insider dealing regime. For example, it applies even where the alleged market abuser merely arranges a transaction (which is not covered by the insider dealing regime unless he can be said to be procuring the transaction) as it applies to 'behaviour' not merely a transaction; and

(10) in contrast to insider dealing, market abuse is a corporate offence. Accordingly, a company can commit the 'misuse of information' category of market abuse (and be subject to an unlimited fine) even though it cannot be guilty of insider dealing. However, an effective Chinese wall, or similar confidentiality arrangements, constitutes a safe harbour, although one may not in fact be needed for the 'misuse of information' offence[1].

The European Commission published in May 2001 a proposal for a market abuse directive, which, among other things, will replace the insider dealing directive on which the insider dealing provisions in the Criminal Justice Act 1993, Pt V are based. The proposal follows the structure used for market abuse in the FSMA 2000 and accordingly off-exchange transactions can be insider dealing even if no professional intermediary is involved. Under the proposed market abuse directive, insider dealing will become a corporate offence and hopefully the proposal will be amended to allow for Chinese walls.

---

[1]   See para 4.49.

4.42   There are four key elements to the 'misuse of information' category of market abuse[1]:

(1)   the behaviour must be based on information;

(2)   the information must not be generally available to the prescribed market concerned;

(3)   the information must be such that, if available to a regular user of the market, it would or would be likely to be regarded by him as relevant when deciding the terms on which transactions in the investment in question should be effected; and

(4)   the information must relate to matters which the regular market user would reasonably expect to be disclosed to users of the particular market involved, whether then or later.

---

¹   MAR 1.4.4E.

4.43   The COMARC indicates that abusive behaviour in this category of (primary) market abuse can (normally) only be dealing or arranging deals. The FSA has clearly taken the view that disclosing information is not misusing it; on balance, we would tend to agree. However, encouraging somebody else to commit the offence will normally constitute the secondary offence of requiring or encouraging market abuse[1] in the same way as encouraging someone else to commit the offence can itself constitute insider dealing[2], even where the person encouraged does not himself know the inside information despite statements to the contrary made by the judge in the *Townsend* case in December 2000[3]. Accordingly, the FSA has sought to treat disclosing information which is not generally available as encouraging market abuse—we respectfully disagree with this analysis although we well understand why the FSA has put it forward.

---

¹   FSMA 2000, s 123(1)(b).
²   Criminal Justice Act 1993, s 52(2).
³   *Department of Trade and Industry v Jonathan Townsend* (December 2000, unreported), Blackfriars Crown Court.

Based on information

4.44   Although in our view this requirement is written into the FSMA 2000 itself, the COMARC makes the position clear by giving a specific safe harbour for dealing or arranging deals where possession of the relevant information did not influence the alleged abuser's decision to deal or arrange a deal[1]. Accordingly, the COMARC says, but not as a formal safe harbour, that it will be presumed that the information did not affect the decision if a firm decision had been taken to deal or arrange the deal before having the information and the terms of the proposed transaction did not alter after the information was received[2]. In addition where the person concerned is a company or other organisation within which only some individuals have the relevant information it will be presumed[3] that such possession had no influence on the organisation's decision to deal or arrange the deal if none of those individuals:

- had any involvement in the decision to deal or arrange the deal;
- behaved in such a way as to influence, directly or indirectly, the decision to engage in the dealing or arranging; or
- had any contact with those who were involved in the decision making whereby the information could be passed on.

---

¹   MAR 1.4.21C.
²   MAR 1.4.22E.
³   MAR 1.4.23E.

4.45 This explanation of circumstances where it can be presumed that the information did not influence the decision making (and therefore the dealing was not 'based on' the information so that there was no market abuse) leads on to a specific safe harbour for effective Chinese walls or (as, for example, in the case of ordinary manufacturing or trading companies) arrangements equivalent to them in relation to the particular information[1]. A Chinese wall is defined in the FSA's Glossary as an arrangement which requires information held by a person (typically, a company) in the course of carrying on one part of its business to be withheld from, and not to be used for, persons with or for whom it acts in the course of carrying on another part of its business. It is worth noting the stress on an 'effective' Chinese wall. A Chinese wall may, in practice, sometimes be broken by the Chief Executive looking over the wall (which in our view is not normally a problem if the Chief Executive regards himself as being behind the Chinese wall as a result), or even by information being passed through the compliance department. In addition, in our view the Chinese wall will not be 'effective' if an individual behind it requires or encourages a person in front of it to deal or arrange deals and does so on the basis of material information which is not generally available, even if the person in front of it does not know the information.

---

[1] MAR 1.4.24C.

4.46 One of the tests used in the 'no influence' safe harbour gives cause for concern. The COMARC states[1] that it will be presumed that the possession of relevant information which is not generally available did not influence the decision to deal or arrange deals (so that the safe harbour applies) if all of the three criteria[2] are satisfied in the case of the individuals who had the relevant information. The third of these is that none of those individuals had any contact with those who were involved in the decision to engage in the dealing or arranging 'whereby the information could have been transmitted'[3]. Taken literally this means that if there was any contact at all between individuals in each category the presumption of non-influence will not apply; this will be the case even if the relevant information was not in fact transmitted to the decision takers provided only that it could have been. This may mean that the FSA requires total segregation between the two categories of individual (even, for example, at lunch). Hopefully the FSA did not intend to set such a high standard. Even if it did, however, and the standard was not attained, this would seem to mean only that the presumption does not apply (rather than that the information is to be taken to have influenced the dealing). Accordingly, the firm is still allowed to establish that the possession of the relevant information by some individuals in it did not in fact influence the decision by other individuals in it to engage in the dealing or arranging in question, for example because there was an effective Chinese wall between them[4].

---

[1] In MAR 1.4.23E.
[2] See para 4.44.
[3] MAR 1.4.23E(3).
[4] MAR 1.4.24C.

4.47 Finally in this context an express safe harbour is given where the dealing or arranging was required in order to comply with a legal (including contractual) or regulatory obligation in circumstances where the obligation existed before the relevant information was in the person's possession[1]. In these circumstances it is not clear whether it matters that the terms of the deal might change after receipt of the information. Logically it should matter and arguably if the terms change it is no longer a 'pre-existing' obligation.

---

[1]   MAR 1.4.20C.

Not generally available

4.48   There was a good deal of debate during the consultation process over what amounted to information being 'generally available'. The FSA has taken a liberal approach to the subject in the COMARC[1]. The FSMA 2000, s 118(7) states that information is to be regarded as generally available if it can be obtained by research or analysis conducted by or on behalf of market users—presumably this should be tested as at the time of the alleged abusive behaviour (so that, for example, information about a proposed takeover bid is not 'generally available' before it is announced). The FSA adds to this that information which has been obtained through any other 'legitimate means', including 'information which is discussed in a public area or can be observed by the public without infringing rights of privacy, property or confidentiality', will be regarded as generally available. The COMARC gives as specific examples information which is regarded as 'generally available' not only formal material such as:

- information disclosed to a prescribed market through an accepted channel for dissemination of information or otherwise under the rules of the market; or
- information contained in records which are open to inspection by the public;

but also much less formal material such as:

- information otherwise made public, including through the Internet or some other publication, or which is derived from information which has been made public; or
- information which can be obtained by observation, for example the famous hypothetical case of a passenger on a train seeing a burning factory and promptly calling his broker to sell shares in the factory's owner.

---

[1]   MAR 1.4.5–8.

4.49   These examples show that 'generally available' is interpreted very widely in the COMARC. Indeed, in our view it is perhaps interpreted too widely, especially in the case of information obtained by observation or which is heard in a public area. Just because someone obtains the information legitimately does not necessarily mean that the information is generally available to those using the market and, indeed, it is hardly information which can at that time be obtained by research or analysis. However, in other cases, the mere fact that most market users do not have the information does not prevent it being 'generally available'. Thus FSA guidance gives, as examples of information which might be obtained by research (and so is generally available), information which is available only overseas and has not been published or otherwise made available in the UK and information which is only available on payment of a fee. Importantly, the COMARC states that 'the fact that in practice other users of the market cannot obtain the information because of limitations in their resources, expertise or competence does not mean that the information cannot legitimately be obtained'. This liberal approach to the meaning of 'generally available' is helpful in encouraging wide ranging research and analysis.

4.50 When considering the offence of insider dealing this was not an issue. Until the price sensitive information was made public (as defined) it could not be used by an insider or tippee. Once it had been made public it could be used by him. However, observing a fire did not make someone an insider or tippee and therefore the insider dealing regime did not apply even if the fact of the fire was not yet 'public'. The line for 'generally available' information is much less clear. The statements in the COMARC that people are free to use information they have obtained by legitimate means implies that they are *not* free to use information they have obtained by illegitimate means and possibly not even information that they know or believe to have been obtained by others illegitimately. But that is not said expressly in the COMARC and is not what the FSMA 2000, s 118(2) says. That section is just concerned with whether the information is 'generally available' or not. Presumably the FSA is of the view that, as would be expected, if the information can only be acquired by illegitimate means that the information is not generally available. As indicated above[1], however, the opposite is clearly not the case, although the FSA (in an attempt to be helpful) thinks otherwise. In addition, merely putting the information on the Internet would seem to make it public, at least if it is on a well-known site or one often visited from the UK for financial information, and therefore 'generally available' even if the information in question was an insider tip of deeply confidential price sensitive information[2].

---

[1]   See para 4.49.
[2]   But see para 4.124 on whether the act of putting it on the Internet would amount to requiring or encouraging others to commit market abuse.

Relevant information

4.51   The COMARC sets out[1] the factors which the FSA thinks a regular market user would consider in deciding whether a particular piece of information was or was not relevant; if it was not, the market abuse offence of 'misuse of information' does not apply. They include how far it is:

*   specific and precise (a term picked up from insider dealing legislation where anything less is not considered to be inside information);
*   material;

- current;
- reliable, including how near the person providing the information is, or appears to be, to the original source of the information and the reliability of that source. Thus, although it is not necessary for the information in question to be 'inside' information for the offence to be committed, if it *is* inside information it is more likely to be 'relevant' and thus involve commission of the offence if it is acted on.

---

[1]   MAR 1.4.9E.

4.52   According to the COMARC[1], a regular market user would also take into account whether:

- there is other material information which is generally available to inform the market;
- the information differs from information which is generally available and can therefore be said to be new or fresh information;
- if it relates to possible future developments, the information provides with reasonable certainty grounds to conclude that those developments will actually happen; and
- if it relates to possible future developments, those developments would be significant for the regular market user if they did occur.

---

[1]   MAR 1.4.9E and 1.4.10E.

4.53   The specific examples of relevant information given in the COMARC[1] are all fairly straightforward:

- in the case of shares issued by a company or derivatives on them, information on the business affairs or prospects of the company or a related company (or, in our view, of one or more companies in the same sector);
- in the case of a commodity derivative, information or events affecting the deliverable supplies of the commodity, such as information on the business operations of major suppliers;
- more generally, information on official statistics which has not yet been published and fiscal and monetary announcements before they are made.

---

[1]   MAR 1.4.11E.

4.54   The COMARC gives two more express safe harbours for dealing or arranging deals based on trading information or (in limited circumstances) in relation to takeover bids. The need for such safe harbours makes it clear that the regular market user would regard the information in question as relevant (as well as not being generally available).

4.55   The first is a safe harbour for dealing or arranging deals based on information about the actual trading or trading intentions of any person (not just one's own dealings and intentions)[1]. Accordingly, those with access to extensive deal flow information from their own transactions and those of their clients can profit from it without risk of committing market abuse. There are two qualifications to this safe harbour. Information on a possible takeover bid is excluded (it has its own more detailed safe harbour[1]). Information about new offers, issues, placements or other primary market activity is also excluded, as primary market activity is regarded as different in kind from secondary market deal flow; some 'new issue' activities are, however, covered by the takeover bids' safe harbour if they are in connection with takeovers[2].

---

[1] MAR 1.4.26C.
[2] See para 4.57.

4.56 It should be noted that, at least as far as FSMA 2000-regulated persons are concerned, even if it will not amount to market abuse there are a number of other rules which have to be considered before deciding whether it is permissible to act on trading information; these include the rules prohibiting front running, governing personal account dealing or requiring deals to be placed fairly and in due turn, with timely and best execution, (which relate to client abuse rather than market abuse).

4.57 The 'takeover bids' safe harbour is similar in substance but different in detail from that given in connection with the takeover bids 'market information' exemption from insider dealing under the Criminal Justice Act 1993[1]. The COMARC provides a safe harbour for dealing or arranging deals in connection with the proposed acquisition or disposal of an equity stake in a company (as defined and including non-equity shares and convertible debt securities) for the sole purpose of making that acquisition or disposal and for the sole benefit of the person making the acquisition or disposal[2]. The safe harbour is available not only to the person concerned but also to his concert parties and those acting for him but it is only available if the information in question is only one or more of the following facts:

- that investments of a particular kind have been, or are to be, acquired or disposed of or their acquisition or disposal is under consideration or being negotiated;
- that investments of a particular kind have not been, or are not to be, acquired or disposed of;
- the number of investments involved in the actual or possible acquisition or disposal;
- the price (or range of prices) involved;
- the identity of the persons involved, or likely to be involved, in any capacity in an acquisition or disposal;
- importantly, information about the target company which the offeror has legitimately acquired (even though the information is outside, and so excludes, the 'market information' insider dealing safe harbour).

---

[1] Criminal Justice Act 1993, Sch 1, para 3.
[2] MAR 1.4.28C.

4.58 Specific examples given of permitted behaviour include seeking irrevocable undertakings to accept or reject an offer, making arrangements for an issue of the securities which are to act as consideration for, or to fund, a takeover offer (including making arrangements for underwriting or placing those securities and hedging arrangements by the underwriters or placees of the consequent exposure) and making arrangements to offer a cash alternative. The COMARC does not, however, allow the safe harbour to cover all types of transaction which might be considered before, or in the course of, a takeover battle. Specifically it says that the safe harbour given for taking certain steps for the purposes of stakebuilding or otherwise directly in connection with the takeover does not mean that the bidder (or its concert parties or agents) may undertake other types of transaction in the target company's shares or linked investments (for example, contracts for differences on securities in other companies in the sector in relation to which the information is also relevant information).

4.59   The COMARC says that a bidder would be engaging in market abuse if it entered into transactions in investments which are not expressly permitted, including in particular transactions which provide merely an economic exposure to movements in the price of target company shares. This is a clear reference to Trafalgar House's takeover bid for Northern Electric in December 1994, after which the FSA (then called the SIB) issued guidance warning against using contracts for differences on a target company's shares to provide an (insider dealing) windfall for the bidder[1]. It also says that those acting for (or, presumably, with) the bidder would be guilty of market abuse if they used the information to deal for their own benefit in securities or related products for which it was relevant.

---

[1]   SIB Guidance Release 4/96.

4.60   There seems to be a problem (which is surely not intended) in the case of the shareholder-recipients of the bidder's request to enter into an irrevocable undertaking to accept the proposed offer (or a similar commitment). The 'takeover bids' safe harbour seems not to apply to the shareholder and the 'trading information' safe harbour is excluded in the case of takeovers even in the case of a target company shareholder[1]. This is not a problem in the case of the insider dealing regime because the bidder of course knows the inside information (that it was going to bid for the target company). This defence, where both sides of the transaction know the inside information[2], does not apply in the case of market abuse. However, the regular market user would hopefully not regard entering into the commitment as a failure in expected standards and accordingly it would not amount to market abuse[3]. In addition, the 'takeover bids' safe harbour is stated to cover hedging arrangements by underwriters or placees of shares used to fund the bid[4], which is a helpful analogy. Conversely, there is a specific exemption for underwriting[5], which seems to be necessary only because primary market activities are excluded from the 'trading information' safe harbour (even where the activity is by the counterparty)[6]. Accordingly, it would be helpful if the 'trading information' safe harbour was stated to be excluded only in relation to the offeror's side of the takeover bid.

1   See para 4.55.
2   Criminal Justice Act 1993, s 53(1)(b), (2)(b).
3   See para 4.41, point (4).
4   MAR 1.4.29E(2).
5   MAR 1.4.31C.
6   See para 4.55.

Regular user would expect disclosure

4.61   The FSA in the COMARC incorporates in the 'misuse of information' category of market abuse, in addition to the three conditions in the
legislation itself, a requirement that information is relevant (so that there can
be market abuse) only if a regular market user would expect it to be
disclosed, either then or later. This is quite a significant further limitation
and it is worth considering why, and how, it has been included in the
COMARC. No explanation is given in the COMARC itself or in the policy
statement published with the version of the COMARC issued in April 2001.
The explanation is to be found in the FSA Consultation Paper 59 (July
2000), which states that, the FSA 'in applying the regular user test . . . has
identified an additional element which has the effect of narrowing the range
of information which is potentially covered by the market abuse regime'. The
FSA says that there will always be times when some market users have
information which is not generally available and that they may be able to
take advantage of that information by trading on it without necessarily
damaging the wider interest of the market. It takes the view that the reality
of markets is that it is impossible for every piece of information to be made
available on an equal and simultaneous basis and the regular market user has
no expectation that it should be so.

4.62   Without stating it in the COMARC, the FSA has therefore reached
the helpful conclusion that a regular market user would not consider
behaviour based on information which is not generally available to have
fallen below expected standards unless the information on which the behaviour is based relates to matters which the regular market user would
reasonably expect to be disclosed to the particular prescribed market either
then or later. Having helpfully inserted this new element[1] the COMARC
then goes on to analyse it in a fairly legalistic way. It distinguishes between:

(1)   information which has (or will in due course have) to be disclosed in
      accordance with a legal or regulatory requirement ('disclosable infor-
      mation'). This would include, for example, information required to be
      disclosed under the Takeover Code, the Substantial Acquisition Rules
      accompanying it, the listing rules or the rules of a recognised invest-
      ment exchange;
(2)   information which normally is (or will in due course become) the
      subject of a public announcement although not subject to any formal
      disclosure requirement ('announceable information'). This would
      include, for instance, information which is to be the subject of official
      announcements by Governments, central monetary or fiscal authori-
      ties or regulatory authorities, changes to published credit ratings and
      changes to the constituents of a securities index. According to the

FSA, it would however not include surveys or research based on information generally available, in which category the FSA would put CBI surveys and MORI opinion polls[2]; they are likely also to include other economic and survey data published by private sector bodies[3].

---

[1] MAR 1.4.4E(4).
[2] MAR 1.4.16G.
[3] FSA *Market Watch* newsletter (September 2001) Issue No 1.

4.63   The COMARC states that where the information concerned is about possible future developments it should normally only be regarded as 'disclosable' or 'announceable' if it provides with reasonable certainty grounds to conclude that the possible future developments will take place and accordingly that a disclosure or announcement will in due course be made[1]. This seems to give some room for manoeuvre to insiders or tippees to buy or sell on that information (although doing so will probably be insider dealing)[2].

---

[1] MAR 1.4.13E.
[2] See para 4.67.

4.64   There is also an attempt to distinguish between information which is disclosable or announceable in different markets so that, for instance, it is suggested that sometimes information about a commodity producer would be disclosable or announceable information in relation to the equity market, so as to prevent dealings based on it in that market, while potentially not being disclosable or announceable in relation to the relevant commodity futures market. Accordingly, dealings could, without market abuse, take place in the commodity futures market using the same information which could not be used in the equity market. This is a difficult area where each case would need to be analysed quite carefully on its facts. In consultation, commodity producers argued strongly that they should be able to hedge (in the commodity derivatives market) their contractual delivery obligations before disclosing the relevant information and also that information required to be disclosed to the equity market would usually not be required to be disclosed to the commodity futures market. Accordingly, its use in dealing on the commodity futures market when the relevant information was not generally available to that market would not be regarded by the regular market user as a failure to meet expected standards. It appears that these arguments have been accepted for the purposes of the COMARC. However the FSA pointed out that obligations under listing rules may require disclosure of significant new developments without delay.

4.65   If, of course, disclosure was made to the equity market, then the information would in any event become 'generally available' to the commodity futures market so that subsequent dealing on the basis of the information could not in any event be market abuse. It seems however that some commodity producers see a window between the time at which something is sufficiently clear to require them to hedge their commodities position and the time at which it is so clear that an announcement is needed to the equity markets.

4.66 It is certainly true that there can be gaps between when the need to hedge arises and when the need to announce arises[1]. The COMARC identifies the example where a listed company would need to make an announcement on entering into a significant contract with a major supplier which might lead to a substantial movement in the price of the listed securities[2]. Information about the negotiations, or proposed contract, would in the FSA's view come into the market abuse regime at an earlier stage, but only once there are grounds to conclude, with reasonable certainty, that the contract will be entered into and that disclosure of the contract will have to be made.

---

[1] See para 4.63.
[2] MAR 1.4.18E.

4.67 It is apparent that, like all instances of market abuse, these will be highly fact dependent and also that the FSA has taken a particular view of what a regular market user might think. Others might take the view that dealings on the basis of inside information about the negotiations could still be market abuse even if it could not at that point be said with reasonable certainty that the contract would be concluded successfully.

FALSE OR MISLEADING IMPRESSIONS

4.68 Just as the 'misuse of information' category of market abuse has some similarities with the offence of insider dealing, so also the 'false or misleading impressions' category overlaps to a considerable extent with the offence of market manipulation[1]. In some senses this category is central to the concept of market abuse; certainly, it is the category of (primary) market abuse which is most likely to be committed by the 'innocent'. As the COMARC states[2] the prescribed markets provide a mechanism by which the price or value of investments may be determined according to market forces and those trading expect the price or value of investments and volumes of trading to reflect the proper operation of market forces, rather than to be the outcome of improper conduct by other market users. Improper conduct which gives market users a false or misleading impression results in their no longer being able to rely on the prices formed in markets or the volumes of trading as a basis for investment decisions, thus undermining confidence in market integrity.

---

[1] FSMA 2000, s 397.
[2] MAR 1.5.3E.

4.69 The elements of the 'false or misleading impressions' category of market abuse are that the behaviour must be likely to give a regular market user a false or misleading impression as to the supply of or demand for, or as to the price or value of, investments of the kind in question. It is vital to be aware that the misleading behaviour (whether a statement or conduct) does not need to be directed to a regular market user. The offence of market abuse will be committed whoever it is directed at or, indeed, if it is not directed at anyone in particular. The 'regular market user' test is brought in to ensure that the false or misleading impression is caught only if it is the sort of impression that would mislead a regular market user. Accordingly, the 'regular market user' test is used to narrow the class of false or misleading impressions rather than to insist that the offence can only be committed if the person who is given the false or misleading impression is actually a regular market user himself. Although it is fair to refer to this category of market abuse as 'misleading the market', it must be appreciated that this is only because the offence involves doing something which is likely to give a false or misleading impression to a regular market user had that person been aware of the behaviour. The offence is most likely to be committed by giving a false or misleading impression to someone who is not a regular market user (for example, the recipient of a company circular or prospectus or a person who hears an inadvertent comment by a company director); it will, however, not be market abuse if a regular market user would not have been misled (although it may well be a criminal offence under the FSMA 2000, s 397) and therefore the 'regular market user' test in the definition of the 'false or misleading impressions' category of market abuse is likely often to be a helpful defence.

4.70   The COMARC in stating the elements of the test[1] elaborates it in four important ways:

(1)   that the behaviour must be likely to actually give rise to a price or value or volume of trading which is false or misleading or to merely give an impression of such price, value or volume. Indeed, the COMARC indicates that the FSA will not bring a prosecution unless the price, value or volume is 'materially' false or misleading;

(2)   that it should be *materially* false or misleading;

(3)   that, in the FSA's view, the word 'likely' does not mean a higher than 50% chance of producing the abusive effect. It would be sufficient in the FSA's view for the 'likelihood' to be 'real and not fanciful'. This approach appears to downgrade the word 'likely' to 'possible' but the FSA has reviewed the case law and considers that its approach is justifiable. Any challenge to the low level of 'likelihood' required by the FSA to generate a charge of market abuse would therefore have to be made in front of the Financial Services and Markets Tribunal or in court; and

(4)   less controversially, that, in the FSA's view, the behaviour in question may be likely to give rise to more than one effect, including the undesirable one of misleading the market. The latter does not have to be the only effect.

---

[1]   MAR 1.5.4E.

4.71   It is unclear why the COMARC states that the offence can be committed if the behaviour gives rise to a false or misleading price, value or volume of trading[1]. It is a perhaps a little misleading. It may well be that the behaviour does give rise to a false or misleading price, value or volume of trading but that is not in itself the offence; the 'false or misleading impressions' offence can be committed only if the behaviour in itself gives a false or misleading impression, whether or not it does in fact result in a false or misleading price, value or volume. The COMARC refers to the reference point of 'supply or demand' as the 'volume of trading'. This is certainly one consequence of 'supply or demand' (as indeed it was in the 1991 London FOX scandal[2]) but in our view it is not the only one.

---

[1]   See point (1) in para 4.70.
[2]   Where the market colluded with certain dealers to transact fictitious bargains and so increase the appearance of liquidity in the new property figures contracts traded on the market, see SFA Board Notice 58 of 17 December 1991.

4.72   The COMARC then divides its analysis of 'false or misleading impressions' between:

- general factors which are considered relevant;
- certain types of behaviour which the FSA considers would amount to market abuse; and
- a few safe harbours for behaviour the FSA considers would (or should?) not amount to this category of market abuse.

It notes that there is an element of overlap between this category of market abuse and distorting the market. This is hardly surprising given the wide definitions of the two statutory offences.

General factors

4.73   The general factors identified by the FSA as relevant to whether a regular market user is likely to be given a false or misleading impression[1] appear completely non-controversial, though a little vague. They are:

(1)   the knowledge and experience of market users;
(2)   the structure of the relevant market including its reporting, notification and transparency requirements;
(3)   the legal and regulatory requirements of the market concerned and accepted market practices;
(4)   the identity and position of the person responsible for the behaviour (if known); and
(5)   the extent and nature of the visibility or disclosure of that person's activity.

---

[1]   MAR 1.5.5E.

Behaviour which the COMARC indicates will amount to market abuse

4.74   The COMARC identifies four types of possible market abuse in the 'false or misleading impressions' category.

Artificial transactions

4.75   The first type of behaviour identified by the COMARC as potential market abuse is artificial transactions[1] where:

(1)   someone enters into a transaction or series of transactions in a qualifying investment or relevant product; and

(2)   the principal effect of the transaction or transactions on the market will be, or will be likely to be, to inflate, maintain or depress the apparent supply or demand, price or value so that a false or misleading impression is likely to be given to the regular user; and

(3)   the person *knows* or could *reasonably be expected* to know that this is the case *unless* the regular market user would regard:

(a)   the principal rationale for the transaction as a legitimate commercial rationale; and

(b)   the way in which the transaction is to be executed as proper.

---

[1]   MAR 1.5.8E.

4.76   Thus in its formulation of an artificial transaction the FSA has brought in a form of intention at two levels. The first is that the alleged abuser knew, or ought to have known, of the likely adverse principal effect of the transaction(s). The second is that his principal rationale for the transaction should not have been a legitimate commercial one where the transaction was executed in a proper way[1]. The FSA has decided not to make 'legitimate commercial rationale' and 'proper execution' a safe harbour but instead to treat them as limiting the scope of the abusive behaviour of effecting artificial transactions[2]. This is probably because the FSA wants to give itself room to allege that particular behaviour nonetheless gives a false or misleading impression amounting to market abuse even if the principal rationale is a legitimate commercial rationale and the way in which the transaction is executed is proper[3].

---

[1]   MAR 1.5.10E.
[2]   MAR 1.5.8E.
[3]   See para 4.81.

4.77   The COMARC then goes into considerably more detail on the elements of its definition of artificial transactions[1]. To begin with simply aiming to make a profit or avoid a loss (directly or indirectly) does not necessarily amount to a 'legitimate commercial rationale' for these purposes. That would be far too easy a get out. More specifically a transaction will rarely be regarded as having a legitimate commercial rationale where the purpose was to induce others to trade or to position or move the price of a qualifying investment or relevant product. This clearly makes sense. It should, however, be noted that the FSA only requires that purpose to be an 'actuating purpose', not the sole purpose for the transaction(s). Thus, even if there was a legitimate commercial rationale for the transaction, it could nonetheless be treated as giving a false or misleading impression if price positioning or a volume increase was also a purpose.

4.78　The term 'actuating purpose' which is defined as 'a purpose which motivates or incites a person to act' is used at a number of places in the COMARC where the word 'intention' (actual or presumed) might have been used had it not been for the extended debates during the legislative process over the incorporation of 'intent' as a required element in the definition of the 'misleading or distorting the market' offence.

4.79　Factors the COMARC identifies[1] as *relevant* (but not necessary, nor determinative) when considering whether there have been one or more artificial transactions include:

(1)　whether the transaction causes or contributes to an increase or decrease in supply/demand/price/value and the person concerned has an interest in the level of that supply/demand/price/value (for example, because he directly benefits by having a holding or short position, or has indirect benefits from a change in the market price or may be rewarded by, or is otherwise in collusion with, those who do benefit);

(2)　whether the transaction involves the placing of buy orders higher than the market price, or sell orders lower, or the placing of buy and sell orders which increase the (perceived) volume of trading;

(3)　whether the transaction coincides with a time at or around which the volume or pricing is relevant, either for the market as a whole or for the person in question, in calculating reference prices, settlement prices or valuations (for example putting in false prices for cash market trades so as to artificially change the concomitant futures prices);

(4)　whether those involved are connected parties;

(5)　whether the transaction causes a change in the market price which immediately thereafter returns to its previous level;

(6)　whether a bid or offer is placed outside the previous bid or offer price only to be removed before it is executed.

4.80　An important factor is whether the transaction opens a new position, creating an exposure to market risk, or closes a position, removing pre-existing market risk. Where this is the case it is a strong indication that the transaction will be regarded as having a legitimate commercial rationale and not amounting to market abuse, provided it is executed 'properly'.

4.81　As noted above[1], proper execution is regarded by the FSA as being just as important in avoiding an 'abusive' artificial transaction as is the requirement that the principal purpose of the transaction should be a legitimate commercial one. Its comments on the subject are, however, not very clear and have circular tendencies. According to the COMARC a transaction will only be executed in a 'proper' way if it is executed in a way which takes into account the need for the market as a whole to operate fairly and efficiently[2]. This would not be the case if a transaction was executed in a particular way with the purpose of giving a false or misleading impression. It notes that the rules of most prescribed markets have a requirement that transactions be executed in a proper way, for example by rules on reporting and executing cross trades, but does not remind the reader at this point that there is no safe harbour as such for complying with exchange rules on cross trades. Compliance with those rules would therefore seem to be necessary but not sufficient to avoid market abuse. However the COMARC does at least state that transactions would not 'necessarily' be considered to be executed in an improper way simply because the way in which they were executed did not disclose the firm's positions or intentions to the market.

---

[1]   At para 4.76.
[2]   MAR 1.5.10E.

4.82   Moving on to circumstances which the COMARC identifies as possibly giving a false or misleading impression without having a legitimate commercial rationale, examples given in the COMARC are[1]:

(1)   arrangements (other than normal repo or stock borrowing or lending) for a sale or purchase where there is no change of beneficial ownership or market risk or the transfer of beneficial interest or market risk is only between persons acting in concert or collusion;

(2)   arrangements (other than normal nominee holdings) designed to conceal ownership of a qualifying investment or relevant product.

The final example the COMARC gives, without further explanation, of an 'artificial transaction' is a 'fictitious transaction'.

---

[1]   MAR 1.5.14.

4.83   Two safe harbours are given in the COMARC for transactions which would not be regarded as artificial transactions offending under this category of market abuse[1]. They are:

(1)   arbitrage transactions which take or unwind a position so as to take 'legitimate' advantage of differences in the taxation of income or capital gains (no reference is made to other taxes such as stamp duty and value added or sales tax) generated by investments or commodities (whether the differences arise by reason of the identity of the recipient of the income or gains or otherwise) or differences in the prices of investments or commodities as traded in different locations; and

(2)   lending or borrowing qualifying investments or commodities to meet an underlying commercial demand for them (for example, from short sellers).

---

[1]   MAR 1.5.24C (but see para 4.84).

4.84 It should be noted, however, that these are very limited, indeed positively rock strewn, safe harbours because they are only available if it can be shown that:

(1)   the principal rationale for the transaction was a legitimate commercial one; and
(2)   they are executed in a proper way.

Since the way in which the safe harbour transactions are defined sets out their purpose in some detail it is perhaps confusing to add a 'legitimate commercial rationale' test since it might suggest that in some cases those purposes (ie tax or other arbitrage or satisfying underlying commercial demand) might *not* be a legitimate commercial rationale. It is to be hoped that such doubt was not intended and that the extra test is only designed for those who actually have an abusive purpose so that arbitrage, or the commercial demand, although it exists, is something of a facade.

Disseminating information (generally)

4.85   The second type of behaviour identified in the COMARC as potentially covered by the 'false or misleading impressions' category of market abuse is where:

(1)   a person disseminates information which is, or if true would be, relevant information; the test for 'relevance' is the same as under the 'misuse of information' category, namely information a regular market user would consider relevant when determining the terms of a proposed transaction;
(2)   that person knows, or could reasonably be expected to know, that the information is false or misleading; and
(3)   that person disseminates it in order to give a false or misleading impression. This need not be the sole purpose of disseminating the information but once again must be an 'actuating purpose'.

Thus here again the COMARC writes in two 'intent' elements, a knowledge test and a purpose test.

4.86   In this context it is relevant when considering the putative abuser's purpose to see whether he has an interest in a qualifying investment or relevant product to which the information is relevant. If he does it will tend to suggest the existence of an improper purpose. However, the COMARC makes it clear that the absence of any such interest does not conclusively prove that there is no market abuse.

4.87   The example given in the COMARC is of posting false or misleading information on an Internet bulletin board or chat room site. No comment is made on the position of the Internet service provider or host of the bulletin board or chat room but the 'purpose' elements which the COMARC has introduced in this context would seem to give them a significant degree of protection provided at least that they had no reason to suppose the information was false or misleading. What is unclear is how far they would need to be ready and in a position to remove information if it became apparent (or likely) that it had been posted in order to give a false or misleading impression. The question of how far policing or censorship of Internet sites by the host is necessary or desirable, or how far repeated intervention will lead to the host being seen as having taken on a 'vetting' role and accordingly positive responsibility for content (and accordingly as excluding the 'mere conduit' exemption from needing approval of its financial promotion communications), is a perpetual tension. It does not seem to have been addressed to any significant extent in the COMARC. In addition, no express mention is made in the COMARC of the potentially false or misleading effect of *failing* to disseminate information, rather than positively disseminating information which is false or misleading[1].

---

[1]   But see para 4.93.

Disseminating information through official channels

4.88   The third type of market abuse the COMARC identifies in the category of 'false or misleading impressions' is a variant of the second. It relates to the submission of information to an 'accepted channel for the dissemination of information'. Such a channel is defined, in relation to any prescribed market, as an approved channel of communication whereby information concerning investments traded on the market is formally disseminated to other market users on a structured and equitable basis. Such channels include but are not necessarily limited to those required to be used under the rules of a particular market (for example, the Regulatory News Service, LIFFE Connect).

4.89   Where relevant information which is likely to give a false or misleading impression is disseminated in this way the COMARC imposes a much lower knowledge/purpose test. The person concerned does not have to know that the information is false or misleading. There is not even a requirement that that person ought to have known. Nor is any level of purpose (actuating or otherwise) required. All that is required is that the person concerned has not taken reasonable care to ensure that the information is not false or misleading[1]. The FSA points out that users of information which is disseminated in this relatively formal way should be able to rely on the accuracy and integrity of information carried through those channels. Those disseminating information through them, whether the company itself, its financial advisers or its public relations advisers, should therefore take reasonable care to ensure that the information is accurate and not misleading.

---

[1]   MAR 1.5.18E.

4.90   This approach is a useful warning to companies and their advisers (including public relations advisers, some of whom can be less careful than others) about the importance of formal releases. It is, however, as interesting for what is left unsaid as for what is said. It seems that press releases not made through 'accepted channels' are subject only to the higher knowledge (actual or deemed) and purpose tests even when they come from 'official' sources such as the company and its advisers.

Course of conduct

4.91   The fourth type of market abuse identified by the COMARC in the category 'false or misleading impressions' could be said to be a variant, or rather a wider description, of the first. It is where a person engages in a course of conduct:

(1)   the *principal effect* of which will be, or is likely to be, to give a false or misleading impression to the regular market user as to the supply/demand/price/value of a qualifying investment or relevant product; and

(2)   the person concerned knows, or could reasonably be expected to know, of this actual or likely principal effect

   unless the regular market user would regard:

   (a)   the *principal rationale* for the conduct as a legitimate commercial one; and

   (b)   the way in which the conduct is engaged in as proper[1].

Once again the COMARC includes two tests in this type of market abuse: knowledge (actual or implied) of likely effect coupled with the illegitimate 'principal rationale'.

---

[1]   MAR 1.5.21E.

4.92   Both examples given of this category of market abuse relate to the commodities markets. They are the movement of physical commodities, or of an empty cargo ship, in a way which might give a misleading impression as to the supply of or demand for, or price or value of, a commodity or the deliverable under a commodity futures contract.

Safe harbour for permitted delays in disclosure

4.93   It is clear under the legislation that 'behaviour' includes inaction as well as action[1] and in the course of the legislative process the example was given of a company or other person which failed to make a required disclosure or failed to correct a particular impression which was known to be current in the market. It is strange therefore that this situation is not addressed expressly in the COMARC. The COMARC does however give a safe harbour where there is a regulatory or statutory requirement to provide certain information provided that the information is given within the required time[2]. In terms the safe harbour is for making a disclosure in accordance with legal or regulatory requirements but the examples given in the COMARC[3] are where a person must make the disclosure within a prescribed period or is allowed to delay disclosure for a specified period. It is clear that what is meant is that it will not be treated as market abuse if the person required to make the disclosure does not do so straightaway, provided that that person makes it within the required or permitted period. For example, a notification is normally required under the Companies Act 1985, s 198 within three business days of the acquisition or disposal of a notifiable interest. The safe harbour makes it clear that it is not market abuse to refrain from making the notification until that third day even though the absence of a notification for the first two business days might be misleading; the regular market user will in theory be aware of the statutory timetable.

---

[1]   FSMA 2000, s 118(10).
[2]   MAR 1.5.25C.
[3]   MAR 1.5.26G.

Safe harbour for Chinese walls

4.94 The COMARC provides a safe harbour for false or misleading impressions given only because the relevant information was kept safely behind a Chinese wall or similar confidentiality arrangements[1], provided that the individual who disseminated the information did not know, and could not reasonably be expected to know, something which would mean that the information was false or misleading. This seems a higher test than knowing something which *might* mean that the information was false or misleading (for example, that something relevant was happening behind a Chinese wall). The FSA is, however, likely to regard merely being put on notice as sufficient for the 'false or misleading impressions offence' to be committed. If a securities firm has established a Chinese wall (as is quite normal) as a result of which confidential corporate information is held behind it and accordingly a stockbroker in front of it in all innocence says something which is clearly misleading (or indeed false) because he did not know the information held behind it, it would be unfair to penalise the firm concerned. Indeed, it is likely that the regular market user would think that, in the circumstances, the making by the firm (through the stockbroker) of a false or misleading statement is not falling below expected standards. Nonetheless, an express safe harbour is clearly very helpful.

---

[1]   MAR 1.5.27C.

4.95 The only problem is that the drafting of the Chinese walls safe harbour is very unclear. The COMARC does not set out specific criteria designed to prove the existence of a Chinese wall in the context of giving a false or misleading impression. Instead, it merely refers back to some of the criteria designed for the 'misuse of information' offence to prove that the dealing or arranging was not influenced by the relevant information[1], which it adopts without amendment for the 'false or misleading impressions' offence. The criteria it uses therefore do not properly fit the 'false or misleading impressions' offence and are as a result somewhat confusing. First, the COMARC provides that the company or other organisation can prove that it did not know, and could not reasonably be expected to know, that the information being disseminated was false or misleading by showing that the requirements of MAR 1.4.22E have been satisfied[2]. However, those requirements are directed only at showing that the information did not influence the decision (to deal or arrange deals) because the decision was taken first; MAR 1.4.22E has nothing to do with the Chinese walls and, indeed, it sets out an alternative way of showing that the decision was not influenced by the information. Perhaps the COMARC should have referred instead to MAR 1.4.24C (safe harbour for Chinese walls). In addition, this concept of information not influencing a decision to deal or arrange deals cannot be duplicated in the 'false or misleading impressions' safe harbour at all as the COMARC tries to do. Even if the decision to make the false or misleading statement had been taken before the individual making it received the information which made it clear that it would be false or misleading, that individual should nonetheless still not make the statement which he now knows would give a false or misleading impression. Second, the COMARC also provides that an effective Chinese wall will be presumed in the circumstances described in MAR 1.4.23E(1) to MAR 1.4.23E(3)[3]. This is more appropriate to the 'false or misleading impressions' safe harbour because it depends on ensuring that no one who knows the relevant information has any involvement (direct or indirect) in the decision to engage in the dealing or arranging or any contact with the people making that decision whereby the information could have been transmitted[4]. There is unlikely to be any abusive dealing or arranging of deals in the context of the 'false or misleading impressions' category of market abuse (except for artificial transactions, which hopefully will not be common). Nonetheless it is quite clear that what is meant is that the firm will not be committing the 'false or misleading impressions' category of market abuse merely because the correct information was not available to the individual making the false or misleading statement, as a result of a Chinese wall (or, where there is no Chinese wall, as a result of similar confidentiality arrangements, for example in the case of ordinary trading or manufacturing companies). Hopefully, the FSA will amend the description of and the required evidence for the safe harbour in due course so as to make the position clear.

---

[1]   See paras 4.44–4.46.
[2]   MAR 1.5.28C.
[3]   MAR 1.5.29E.
[4]   MAR 1.4.23E.

4.96   It should, however, be noted that the Chinese walls safe harbour is not clearly given in the COMARC for where information is disseminated through accepted channels; it is thought, however, that it nonetheless applies, as would surely be acceptable from a policy point of view. Firstly, there is a mismatch in language in that the obligation where information is disseminated through an accepted channel is to ensure that the information given is not false or misleading, whereas the Chinese walls language tracks exactly the 'disseminating information (generally)' type of market abuse which applies where the person who gives the false or misleading impression knows or could reasonably be expected to know that the information disseminated is false or misleading[1]. If as a result of a Chinese wall the individual in front of it unknowingly gives a false or misleading impression, the firm is treated as not knowing or being reasonably expected to know[2]. Secondly, the second Chinese walls safe harbour from the 'false or misleading impressions' category of market abuse is expressly limited to where the impression was created by the dissemination of information (generally), and so does not include the giving of that impression by a statement made through an accepted channel[3]. In our view, an effective Chinese wall would be taken to mean that the information making the statement false or misleading could not be accessed even if the individual making it took reasonable care to verify the statement. It would not be appropriate to expect an individual in front of the Chinese wall to seek verification from people behind it. Accordingly, the safe harbour applies because the individual (and through him the firm) cannot be regarded as being at fault for failing as a result to ensure that the statement is not false or misleading.

---

[1]   MAR 1.5.15E.
[2]   MAR 1.5.27C.
[3]   MAR 1.5.28C.

4.97   However, MAR 1.5.28C is not really a safe harbour in itself—it merely explains how it can be demonstrated that the principal safe harbour[1] can be shown to apply and, indeed, it does not really work in the context of the 'false or misleading impressions' category of market abuse[2]. Conversely, that principal safe harbour is not itself expressly limited. In addition, surely individuals in front of the Chinese wall cannot know or reasonably be expected to know about the information held safely behind the Chinese wall. As a result, the principal safe harbour will apply. The firm cannot reasonably be expected to know the information held behind the Chinese wall; the firm therefore cannot be regarded as failing to take due care to find it out. The Chinese walls safe harbour would accordingly apply even where the information is disseminated through accepted channels (although an express safe harbour for disseminating information through accepted channels would clarify the position). Even if this view is not correct, a regular market user would also not expect people in front of the Chinese wall to ask people behind the Chinese wall whether their proposed statement is false or misleading in light of the information known behind the Chinese wall and accordingly, the regular market user would take the view that there is no failure in expected standards. Everything said above[3] in relation to effective Chinese walls applies equally in relation to other confidentiality arrangements, provided that they also are effective. Indeed, it would seem to be very unlikely that any 'public statement' would be made through accepted channels other than by the corporate finance arm of the firm (and in particular the individuals who know the relevant confidential information), although compliance arrangements providing for this would probably alert people in front of the Chinese wall that something is going on behind it.

---

[1]   MAR 1.5.27C.
[2]   See para 4.95.
[3]   See para 4.94 ff.

4.98   As will be seen from the above, there is no safe harbour for a statement made in all innocence by a stockbroker or other individual in front of a Chinese wall because he did not know the facts held behind the Chinese wall which made what was said false or misleading. The FSA has explained that none is needed; the person did not know (and could not be expected to know) the facts making the statement false or misleading, so that he would not be guilty of giving false or misleading impressions[1]. However, the offence of giving false or misleading impressions can be committed even without knowledge of the true facts, although the FSA's version of the general 'disseminating information' subset of the 'false or misleading impressions' offence cannot[2]. Nonetheless, as indicated above[3], a regular market user would probably not regard it as a failure of expected standards for the individual in front of the Chinese wall not to have checked the position with the people behind the Chinese wall. Accordingly, and given that the FSA are clear that the individual in front of the Chinese wall will not be expected to know the information behind the Chinese wall, the FSA will probably not allege this category of market abuse against the individual in front of the Chinese wall on these facts.

---

[1] FSA policy statement (April 2001), para 7.6.
[2] MAR 1.5.15E.
[3] See para 4.97.

Possible safe harbour for an important LME rule

4.99 Although a safe harbour is given from the 'market distortion' category of market abuse for the rules of the London Metal Exchange arising from its October 1998 report dealing with the behaviour expected of holders of long positions[1], no such safe harbour for complying with those rules seems to be given for the 'false or misleading impressions' category of market abuse. However, there is a slight oddity here in that the provisions of those rules are equally applicable to this category of market abuse. The commentary in the April 2001 policy statement issued with the COMARC did indeed suggest that the safe harbour was being applied to this category as well (para 7.8) but this does not seem to have happened in the COMARC itself.

---

[1] See para 4.114.

MARKET DISTORTION

Main elements

4.100 The main elements of the third category of (primary) market abuse, as elaborated in the COMARC, are:

(1) that the behaviour must be such that a regular market user would, or would be likely to, regard it as behaviour which would, or would be likely to, distort the market in the investment in question;

(2) that the behaviour must interfere, or be likely to interfere, with the proper operation of market forces in order to position prices at a distorted level. This need not be the sole purpose of entering into the transaction or transactions but it must be an actuating purpose;

(3) in order for the behaviour to be likely to distort there must be a real and not just a fanciful likelihood that the behaviour will have such an

effect. However, this effect need not be more likely than not and can be only one of several different effects[1].

---
[1]   MAR 1.6.4E.

4.101   Point (1) in para 4.100 is the statutory definition[1]. Points (2) and (3) are added by the COMARC. It should be noted that there is a double 'likely' in the statutory definition. Although the COMARC addresses only the FSA's view of the meaning of 'likely' when applied to the effect of the behaviour, presumably the FSA would have the same 'less than 50% likelihood is sufficient' approach when considering the likelihood of a regular market user coming to a view on that effect, as it clearly does in the case of the 'false or misleading impressions' category of market abuse[2]. The COMARC again inserts an intention, or 'actuating purpose', test although in this case not a knowledge one (which, however, is surely implied by the intent requirement).

---
[1]   FSMA 2000, s 118(2)(c).
[2]   See para 4.70, point (3).

4.102   The COMARC takes the view that the purpose of this category of market abuse is to prevent behaviour that interferes with the proper operation of market forces, and accordingly supply and demand, with a consequent undermining of confidence in the market and damage to market efficiency. It therefore says[1] that it is unlikely that the behaviour of market users trading at times and in sizes most beneficial to them and seeking the maximum profit from their dealings will of itself amount to distortion. It even adds, in a curious formulation, that it is 'unlikely' that prices trading outside this normal range will 'necessarily' be 'indicative' that someone has engaged in abusive behaviour with the purpose of positioning prices at a distorted level. Although the wording used is double-edged, the general statements about freedom to trade and to make profits without being too concerned about the price range and the recognition that high or low prices relative to a trading range can be the result of the proper interplay of market demand give some comfort on concerns that trying to avoid the 'market distortion' category of market abuse could itself involve distorting the market because it would inhibit proper trading.

---
[1]   MAR 1.6.5E.

4.103   The COMARC goes on to give two examples of behaviour amounting to the 'market distortion' category of market abuse: price positioning and abusive squeezes. The former could often also be caught under the 'false or misleading impressions' category of market abuse. The latter arguably could not, although the FSA is of the view that in some circumstances it can.

Price positioning

4.104   Price positioning is described as entering into a transaction or series of transactions with the purpose (that is, an actuating purpose) of positioning the price of a qualifying investment or relevant product at a distorted level. The COMARC notes that trading in significant volumes for a proper purpose even at the close of trading (for example, index tracking) and in a proper way is unlikely to distort the market even if it causes the market to move[1].

---

[1]   MAR 1.6.10E.

4.105   The COMARC then goes on to list factors which the FSA considers should be taken into account when determining whether someone has positioned the price at a distorted level as follows:

(1)   the extent to which the timing of the transaction(s) coincided with a time at which the price was relevant (whether for the market as a whole or for the person in question) for the calculation of reference prices, settlement prices or valuations;

(2)   the extent to which the alleged market abuser had a direct or indirect interest in the price or value of the investment or relevant product in question;

(3)   the volume or size of the transaction(s) in relation to reasonable expectations of the depth and liquidity of the market at the time in question;

(4)   the extent to which price, rate or option volatility movements and the volatility of these factors for the investment in question occur which are outside their 'normal intraday, daily, weekly or monthly range';

(5)   the extent to which the transaction(s) caused the market price of the investment in question to increase or decrease, following which the market price returned immediately to its previous level;

(6)   whether the alleged market abuser has successively and consistently increased or decreased his bid, offer or the price he has paid for a qualifying investment or relevant product.

The FSA makes it clear that even the presence of one or more of these factors does not necessarily mean that there is 'market distortion'[1].

---

[1]   MAR 1.6.11E.

4.106   It is worth noting that points (1), (2) and (5) in para 4.105 also feature as relevant factors when considering whether there have been artificial transactions giving a false or misleading impression but the other factors diverge significantly. This is because in the 'market distortion' category of market abuse the transaction concerned may well be 'real' in the sense that full commercial risk is taken for the transaction and, indeed, the resulting price may even be said to be 'true' within the conventions of the relevant market. Nevertheless, it has been structured to have a disproportionate effect on the market so that the price is 'distorted' even if it is arguable that it is not misleading.

4.107   Four examples are given in the COMARC of abusive price position-ing[1] all of which are fairly clearly improper. Only the first of them would clearly fall within the COMARC's description of artificial transactions giving a false or misleading impression, although arguably all could fall within the statutory wording for misleading the market as well as for distorting it.

---

[1]   MAR 1.6.12E.

4.108   They are:

(1)   a trader simultaneously buying and selling the same investment which is relevant to the calculation of the settlement price of an option at a price outside the normal trading range. He has a position in the relevant option and the purpose of the dealing is to position the price to give him a profit or avoid a loss on the option;

(2)   a trader buying just before the close of trading a large volume of commodity futures, the price of which is relevant for the settlement value of a derivatives position he holds, again in order to distort the price and profit from the derivatives position;

(3)   a trader holding a short position which would show a profit if a particular investment falls out of the index and placing a large sell order on that investment just before the close of trading in order to reduce its price sufficiently for it to drop out of the index; and

(4)   a fund manager wishing to improve his quarterly performance and doing so by placing a large order to buy relatively illiquid shares of a kind contained in the portfolio just before the end of the quarter.

Abusive squeezes

4.109   The second type of market abuse identified by the COMARC in the category of 'market distortion' is 'abusive squeezes', which is defined as a situation where the alleged abuser:

(1)   has a significant influence over the supply of, demand for or delivery mechanisms for a qualifying investment or relevant product; *and*

(2)   has a position (directly or indirectly) in an investment under which quantities of the relevant investment or product are deliverable; *and*

(3)   engages in behaviour with the purpose (which as usual need not be sole but must be 'actuating') of positioning at a distorted level the price at which others have to deliver, take delivery or defer delivery to satisfy their obligations[1].

The COMARC emphasises[2] that squeezes often occur but, without this purpose, will not constitute 'market distortion'. In addition, merely having a 'significant influence' is also not of itself abusive.

---

[1]   MAR 1.6.13E.
[2]   MAR 1.6.14E.

4.110 Factors which the COMARC says will be taken into account when determining whether or not someone has engaged in an abusive squeeze are:

(1) the extent to which, and price at which, that person is willing to relax his control or influence in order to help maintain an orderly market;

(2) the extent to which the activity causes or risks causing settlement default by other market users on a multilateral basis and not just a bilateral one;

(3) the extent to which prices under the market delivery mechanisms differ from those for delivery of the investment or its equivalent off market;

(4) the extent to which the spot or immediate market, compared to the forward market, is unusually expensive or inexpensive, or the extent to which borrowing rates are unusually expensive or inexpensive[1].

---

[1] MAR 1.6.16E.

4.111 The COMARC states that these factors are not intended to impose new obligations on market users so that, for instance, it does not create an obligation for someone with a long position, even a very significant one, to lend investments. The FSA considers in guidance that other market users should normally also be expected to protect their own interests and put themselves in a position to be able to fulfil their obligations in a manner consistent with the standards of behaviour on that market. In its view (which must surely be correct) the regular market user is likely to expect others not to put themselves in a position where they have to rely on the holders of long positions lending securities or other deliverables to them when they may not be inclined to do so and may be under no obligation to do so[1].

---

[1] MAR 1.6.17G.

4.112 Even so, the COMARC also says that willingness to lend means behaviour is less likely to amount to an abusive squeeze. Although it is not stated in the COMARC, given the prevalence of lending in some markets, it may already be, or become, open to question whether regular market users could sensibly assume that loans would always be available for settlement. What, for instance, would the position be if a person who normally participated in a clearer's automatic lending programme pulled out unexpectedly? If an inappropriate 'actuating purpose' could be found this might be market abuse.

4.113 The example given in the COMARC of an abusive squeeze is, however, much narrower and clearer. It is where a trader, with a long position in bond futures, buys or borrows a large amount of the cheapest to deliver bonds and either refuses to re-lend them or lends them only to those that the trader believes will not re-lend to the market and his purpose in doing this is to position the price at which those with short positions have to deliver to satisfy their obligations at a materially higher level, making the trader a profit[1].

¹   MAR 1.6.18E.

Safe harbours

4.114   The only safe harbour given by the COMARC in the 'market distortion' category of market abuse is for certain LME rules generated by its October 1998 report into market aberrations dealing with the behaviour expected of holders of long positions on that market.

REQUIRING OR ENCOURAGING MARKET ABUSE

Main elements

4.115   The final category of market abuse is the secondary offence of requiring or encouraging market abuse; it is just as important as the three primary categories. There is no need for the 'encourager' to benefit from the market abuse. The FSA can impose unlimited fines on a person, and require him to disgorge profits and reimburse losses arising from the market abuse, not only where the FSA is satisfied that he has engaged in one or more of the three primary categories of market abuse but also where it is satisfied that he has 'by taking or refraining from taking any action required or encouraged another person or persons to engage in behaviour which, if engaged in by [the first person], would amount to market abuse'[1].

¹   FSMA 2000, s 123(1)(b).

4.116   This somewhat convoluted wording is designed to prevent an obvious avoidance technique under which a sophisticated market abuser uses relatively innocent or unsophisticated players to carry out the abusive behaviour. The fact that they may have a defence, under the COMARC or (in particular) under the 'regular market user' test, so that they have not committed 'market abuse' should not prevent the encourager from being held liable. However, this would have been the result if the offence had been written on the basis of requiring or encouraging market abuse (as it originally was), because for one or other of these reasons no market abuse would actually have been committed by the innocent or unsophisticated player.

4.117   All the various provisions of the COMARC (including its safe harbours) will be applied in the normal way when putting the alleged 'encourager' into the shoes of the person encouraged to see if market abuse would have been committed. In addition the COMARC has a few additional pieces of guidance on the subject, mostly relating to situations which the FSA would, or would not, normally regard as requiring or encouraging market abuse. There are no safe harbours given by the COMARC, however, in relation to this offence because the FSMA 2000 does not grant any or allow the FSA to grant them. It should be noted that there is therefore no extra 'regular market user' test applied to whether particular action or inaction amounted to 'requiring or encouraging'. That question is left to the FSA. It should also be noted that the whole of the section in the COMARC on 'requiring or encouraging' is technically just ordinary guidance by the FSA under the FSMA 2000, s 157 and does not have any special status under the FSMA 2000, s 122.

4.118   As a general comment the FSA maintains that whether someone might be regarded as 'requiring or encouraging' will depend on circumstances such as acceptable market practices, the experience, level of skill and standard of knowledge of the person concerned and the control or influence that person has in relation to the person who engages in the behaviour in question[1]. Thus it seems that the FSA will apply to this (secondary) category of market abuse at least some of the elements which in other circumstances it lists as part of the 'regular market user' test for the other (primary) categories.

---

[1]   MAR 1.8.4G.

Examples

4.119   Examples given in the COMARC of behaviour which may be regarded as 'requiring or encouraging' are:

(1)   a director of a company while in possession of relevant disclosable information, other than trading information[1], which is not generally available instructs an employee of the company to deal in qualifying investments or relevant products[2];

(2)   someone simply recommends or advises someone else to do something which, if he had done it himself, would have amounted to market abuse[3] (this would normally include someone with relevant disclosable information advising or encouraging someone else to deal);

(3)   except in limited circumstances[4], making an early or selective disclosure of information which a regular market user would expect market users to have[5] (although we do not agree with this view in the normal case).

---

[1]   See para 4.55.
[2]   MAR 1.8.3G(1).
[3]   MAR 1.8.3G(2).
[4]   See para 4.123.
[5]   MAR 1.8.4G.

4.120   In FSA Consultation Paper 76 (October 2000) the FSA had suggested that an employer would be guilty of requiring or encouraging an employee to engage in market abuse merely because he is aware that the employee is engaged in market abuse but nonetheless permits him to continue to engage in it; this has now been dropped. If the FSA had not dropped this example, it would have meant that in its view a person encourages something merely because they do not stop it happening (which would have been a very worrying view, albeit that on balance it would appear to be wrong). Although the FSA indicated in the consultation paper that an employer who did not stop an employee who he knew was misusing (non-public) information is himself engaging in the primary offence of misusing information (para 2.6), it is difficult to see how this can be the case without more.

4.121   Examples given in the COMARC[1] of behaviour which would not be regarded as 'requiring or encouraging' are:

(1)   in the context of a take-over offer, an adviser to the person considering the relevant acquisition or disposal advising that an acquisition or disposal should be made of a kind which is permitted without breach of the COMARC under MAR 1.4.28C[2]; and

(2)   a stockbroker or other intermediary acting on a transaction where the client appears to have engaged in market abuse, unless the intermediary knew or ought reasonably to have known that the client was indeed engaging in market abuse[3].

---

[1]   MAR 1.8.7G and 1.8.8G.
[2]   See para 4.57.
[3]   See para 4.128 ff.

Early or selective disclosure of information

4.122   Most of the commentary in the COMARC on the 'requiring or encouraging' category of market abuse relates to early or selective disclosure of information which the regular market user would expect other market users to have. The FSA clearly does not like such early or selective disclosure but (as it seems to take the view that disclosure is not misusing information) can only treat the disclosure as a market abuse offence on the basis that it constitutes requiring or encouraging market abuse. However, in our view mere disclosure should normally not be treated as (requiring or) encouraging the person receiving the disclosure to commit market abuse by using it and, indeed, the CBI emphasised this point very clearly in its response to consultation. Nonetheless, the FSA has continued to assume that such disclosure will involve 'encouraging' the recipient of the disclosure to deal on the information before it becomes generally available (in other words, assuming that it is relevant information which is disclosable or announce-able, to engage in the 'misuse of information' category of market abuse[1]).

---

[1]   See para 4.43.

4.123   The FSA says that such disclosure will generally be regarded as abusive[1] unless:

(1)   there is a legitimate purpose for the disclosure. Some examples of legitimate purposes given in the COMARC[2] are disclosures required or permitted under the rules of an exchange, the FSA or the Takeover Code; and

(2)   it is accompanied by a statement at or before the time the information is passed that the information is given in confidence and that the recipient should not base any behaviour in relation to the qualifying investment

or relevant product on the information until the information is made generally available; in our view, this restriction should also apply to any other qualifying investment or relevant product in relation to which the information is relevant information. The COMARC makes it clear that this confidentiality statement can be either express or implied. The FSA has obviously accepted that it would be wrong to treat a permitted disclosure as falling outside the safe harbour merely because the person making the disclosure forgets to obtain a confidentiality statement (typically, because it is obvious that the recipient of the disclosure would not act on it improperly); accordingly, the FSA has sought to avoid this problem by stating in the COMARC that the confidentiality statement can be implied[3].

---

[1]   MAR 1.8.5G.
[2]   MAR 1.8.5G and see para 4.125.
[3]   MAR 1.8.5G.

4.124   It is not clear in this context whether, when the FSA refers to information being made 'generally available' (so that the recipient of the disclosure can properly engage in behaviour in relation to the qualifying investment or relevant product[1]), 'generally available' is to have the extended meaning given to it earlier in the COMARC[2] or whether it should be restricted to the time at which the information is actually released to the market. If it is the former, the restrictions could arguably be circumvented by placing the relevant information on the Internet in an obscure language and place, possibly even on a subscription basis. Arguably, placing information on an obscure website would not constitute making that information public and therefore it will not be treated as being generally available, but this is not certain. In principle, 'disclosing' information in this way (particularly if restricted to a subscription website) should perhaps be regarded as a form of selective distribution which could itself potentially amount to requiring or encouraging market abuse. It is, however, possible that under the COMARC as drafted the information will indeed be treated as generally available.

---

[1]   See para 4.123.
[2]   See para 4.48.

4.125   The COMARC also addresses more traditional situations[1]. It gives as examples of situations where disclosure might be regarded as being for a 'legitimate purpose' (though still needing to be coupled with a confidentiality statement in order to avoid the risk of being regarded as encouraging market abuse):

(1)   giving information to group employees on a 'need to know in order to do their jobs' basis;
(2)   giving information to professional advisers for the purpose of obtaining advice;
(3)   giving information to those with whom a commercial, financial or investment transaction is being negotiated (including prospective underwriters or placees of securities) in order to facilitate the transaction;

(4)   giving information to those from whom irrevocable undertakings or expressions of support are being sought in a takeover, in order to get those commitments;

(5)   giving information to representatives of employees or trade unions in fulfilment of a legal obligation (for example, redundancy consultations); and

(6)   unsurprisingly, giving information to any government department, the Bank of England, the Competition Commission, the Takeover Panel or any other statutory or regulatory authority to fulfil a legal or regulatory obligation or otherwise in connection with the performance of that body's functions. The FSA has modestly refrained from including itself in the list of regulatory authorities but clearly disclosure to it would be permitted, hopefully even without an express confidentiality statement!

In addition, a director or employee of a company quoted on the London Stock Exchange, or of a subsidiary, will not be regarded as requiring or encouraging market abuse merely because he notifies his connected persons (as defined) or investment managers of when he is in a close period or is in possession of price sensitive information, as required by the UKLA's Model Code[2]. A confidentiality statement should also be handed over.

---

[1]   MAR 1.8.6G.
[2]   MAR 1.8.10G.

4.126   It is worth emphasising again the need to state at or before the time the information is handed over that it is given in confidence and is not to be the basis for action by the recipient before it becomes generally available. As indicated above[1], this statement can be incorporated in the express or implied terms of any contract governing the relationship of the persons concerned. In our view, the statement should refer not just to the information not being used by the recipient before it is generally available, but to the information not being used by the recipient before it has been made public for insider dealing purposes and so become generally available.

---

[1]   See para 4.123, point (2).

4.127   In some circumstances it is already normal to have confidentiality agreements in place so that all that is needed is to extend the standard wording of these agreements so that they pick up the requirements of the COMARC. In others, such as employment relationships, it may be that relevant provisions can be implied into the employment contract but an express confidentiality statement would be preferable. In others again, either no formal confidentiality statement has normally been given (for example, disclosures to statutory authorities) or it has not been reduced to writing and recorded. In future, bearing in mind the level of penalties which may be imposed for encouraging market abuse, it will be advisable always to give and record a formal written statement, preferably obtaining written agreement to the restriction.

THE POSITION OF STOCKBROKERS AND OTHER INTERMEDIARIES

4.128 The stockbroking community has been very alarmed by the potential risk of committing market abuse, or being treated as encouraging market abuse, because a client involved it in the client's market abuse. The stockbroker ran the risk of committing market abuse, if the client was using relevant disclosable or announceable information which was not generally available where it dealt on the instructions of its client or issued a false or misleading financial promotion communication on his instructions. Similarly, the stockbroker ran the risk of being regarded as encouraging market abuse if it merely approved the contents of the financial promotion communication for the purposes of the FSMA 2000, s 21. These points were made forcibly by the Association of Private Client Investment Managers and Stockbrokers (APCIMS) and the FSA helpfully responded that in these cases it would normally regard only the originator of the abusive behaviour (in other words, the client) as being guilty of market abuse or of requiring or encouraging market abuse, and not the stockbroker.

4.129 However, the FSA is of the view that the stockbroker (or other intermediary) should be regarded as itself committing market abuse or requiring or encouraging it if it carried out the client's instructions when it knew or reasonably ought to have known that the client was engaging in market abuse[1].

---

[1] MAR 1.8.8G.

4.130 This, although helpful as far as it goes, does not give much assistance to brokers and other intermediaries in establishing how far they have a duty to monitor their clients' activities and may themselves be held guilty of market abuse or requiring or encouraging market abuse if they fail to do so.

4.131 Where the intermediary knows very little about a client or merely executes the transaction on an execution-only basis, it is unlikely that the FSA would think it appropriate to accuse the intermediary of market abuse or requiring or encouraging it. Conversely, if the intermediary knows a lot about the client and in particular is aware of matters in the background which should give rise to the suspicion of market abuse, the intermediary ought to satisfy itself that there would not be market abuse. The FSA has emphasised that 'the new market abuse provisions do not impose any additional duties on intermediaries to regulate their customers nor to enquire as to their intentions'[1] and this could, on balance, be where the FSA will draw the line.

---

[1] FSA Consultation Paper 76 (November 2000), para 2.10.

TRANSACTIONS SUBJECT TO THE MODEL CODE

4.132 The COMARC does not refer to the Model Code except in relation to the 'requiring or encouraging' offence[1]. However, it is very important that quoted companies and their advisers should be aware that market abuse can be committed even in the case of a dealing permitted or consent to dealing given under the Model Code. The FSA explained its thinking about the interaction of the Model Code and market abuse at paras 4.28 to 4.43 of its Consultation Paper 76 (November 2000).

---

[1]   See para 4.125.

4.133   The obvious concern is that a director may enter into a transaction where that is permitted under the Model Code but as a result may nonetheless commit the 'misuse of information' category of market abuse. The Model Code normally prohibits a director of a quoted company from buying or selling shares in his company when he is possession of unpublished price sensitive information or the company is in a close period. The Model Code applies not only to directors of the quoted company but also qualifying employees and, indeed, directors or qualifying employees of connected companies and, in addition, quoted companies can impose more stringent restrictions than those appearing in the Model Code; however, for convenience we refer to all these directors and employees as directors of the quoted company and the dealing restrictions to which they are subject as the Model Code.

4.134   If the director does not have any relevant information which is not generally available (which is not quite the same thing as unpublished price sensitive information) his dealings will fall outside the 'misuse of information' category of market abuse. However, if a director does have relevant information which is not generally available but the transaction falls within one of the special or exceptional circumstances set out in the Model Code (for example, the exercise of an option under an employees' share scheme in the permitted circumstances or where he gets clearance for a sale to meet an urgent financial obligation) so that his dealing is permitted by it, or he is not restricted by the Model Code at all (for example, a sale to his wife), the director's dealing may nonetheless constitute market abuse. The FSA is somewhat sanguine about this because, as it says, the director could equally contravene the insider dealing prohibition even though the dealing is permitted by the Model Code; just as the director has to check that he will not be committing insider dealing, so also he must satisfy himself that he will not be engaging in market abuse. In addition, as the FSA points out, the dealing may fall within one of the safe harbours provided by the COMARC, in particular where the director had already decided to enter into the transaction before he obtained the relevant information and the terms on which he dealt did not alter after receipt of the information[1]. The FSA also says that compliance with regulatory obligations will always be a factor to be taken into consideration when determining whether market abuse has taken place[2]. However, this may not be persuasive in this case because although the director is allowed to deal by the Model Code he is not actually required to do so.

---

[1]   MAR 1.4.22E.
[2]   FSA Consultation Paper 76 (November 2000), para 4.37.

4.135   There is a second, more subtle, risk involved in dealing as permitted by the Model Code. This is because the director is not allowed to deal (even where he is permitted to do so by the Model Code) except with the consent of his chairman. The FSA warns chairmen in FSA Consultation Paper 76 (November 2000) that they also have to be worried about market abuse if they give that consent when they are in possession of relevant information which is not generally available but are allowed to give clearance within one of the Model Code's special or exceptional circumstances. They also have to be worried about market abuse even if, exceptionally, the relevant information is not unpublished price sensitive information (so that the Model Code does not apply, except during a close period). The FSA has decided not to provide a safe harbour for company chairmen in these circumstances but is willing to provide guidance in particular cases. Presumably, the FSA is of the view that the giving of consent is itself abusive behaviour. However, it is our view that in a normal case the chairman's consent would not be 'based on' the information which is not generally available, so the question of market abuse would not normally arise. It is also arguable that by giving consent the chairman is committing the secondary offence of requiring or encouraging market abuse; importantly, an offence would be committed even if the director receiving consent did not know the relevant information, and in the case of the 'requiring or encouraging' offence there is no safe harbour. However, the chairman would normally not be encouraging the director to buy or sell the shares; the director has already decided to do so and that is exactly why he is asking for his chairman's consent. Hopefully, therefore, unless the chairman actually tells the director to buy or sell shares because of the relevant information which is not generally available, the chairman will not in practice need to worry about market abuse and giving his consent to dealing under the Model Code.

4.136   The FSA also indicated in FSA Consultation Paper 76 (November 2000) that there is a third situation in which compliance with the Model Code may fall foul of the market abuse regime. The Model Code requires directors to inform all their 'connected persons' (as defined) and discretionary or advisory investment managers of the periods during which they are not allowed to deal in the company's listed shares. The COMARC in effect gives directors a safe harbour for thereby (in the FSA's view) encouraging the recipient to commit market abuse[1], provided that a confidentiality statement is given with the notification.

---

[1]   See para 4.125.

4.137   However, it will probably be very difficult for the FSA to establish that the director is 'encouraging' anyone to use the information to buy or sell the company's shares. Where the notification relates to the company's close periods, that will not be relevant information as it will not affect the terms of any transaction. Even when the notification relates to when the director is in possession of unpublished price sensitive information, provided that the director merely says that that is the case and does not give any indication as to whether the price sensitive information should lead to a purchase or a sale, the director again can hardly be said to be encouraging a transaction based on that information. In any event, it is (hopefully) inconceivable that the FSA will prosecute a director for market abuse if all he has done is to make a disclosure which the FSA's own Model Code requires him to make.

COMPLYING WITH REGULATORY RULES

4.138   Complying with regulatory rules, even those the firm is bound to obey, is under the COMARC normally not a full defence against a charge of market abuse but only a factor to be taken into account when applying the 'regular market user' test.

4.139   Although the Government initially indicated that behaviour con-forming with FSA rules would not be regarded as market abuse, they subsequently retreated somewhat from that. The FSMA 2000, s 118(8) now provides that this 'safe harbour' only applies if the FSA rule itself includes a provision that behaviour conforming with the rule does not amount to market abuse and this is of course reflected in the COMARC[1]. The reason for this reduced safe harbour is that the Government thought that a safe harbour for FSA rules generally will be too wide. However, it is difficult to see that behaviour 'conforms' with an FSA rule if it consists of dealing on information which is not generally available, or misleading or distorting the market. What the reduced safe harbour means is that, in particular cases, the firm might have to choose between being at risk of an unlimited fine by complying with the rule and consequently committing market abuse and being at risk of an unlimited fine by avoiding market abuse by not complying with the rule. This could put a firm in an intolerable position but the Government refused to move from it.

---

[1]   MAR 1.7.1E.

4.140   Similarly, compliance with the FSA's Code of Market Conduct would not in itself necessarily mean that the firm will not be subject to an accusation of market abuse by so doing. The FSMA 2000 makes it clear that the safe harbour given by compliance will only apply if the COMARC states expressly that the given behaviour, in the FSA's opinion, does not amount to market abuse—if it does not contain such a statement, the COMARC is only evidential in that it may be relied on only insofar as it indicates whether or not particular behaviour should be taken to amount to market abuse. Full safe harbours are given only by the very limited number of provisions in the COMARC which are marked 'C'.

4.141   The restriction of safe harbours under the COMARC is rather more understandable than the position in relation to FSA rules. First, there is no provision that a rule can be taken as evidence as to whether or not behaviour does or does not amount to market abuse. Second, and more importantly, the firm does not have to comply with what is provided for in the COMARC, although of course it is at risk if it does not, but it has no choice as to whether or not to comply with actual FSA rules.

4.142 Despite urging by the Conservative Party's Treasury Team, the FSMA 2000 also does not provide any safe harbour for compliance with the rules of a recognised investment exchange as such or even require the FSA, as they also suggested, to have regard as part of its fining policy to whether the accused was complying with existing market practice. It is again unfair that firms dealing on an RIE should run the risk that complying with RIE rules (for example, the rules of the London Stock Exchange) may constitute market abuse, as the FSA has at least de facto authority over the RIEs.

4.143 In practice the FSA has gone through its rules and given express safe harbours to those acting in compliance with a number of them:

(1)   those relating to price stabilisation (MAR 2);
(2)   those relating to Chinese walls (as noted above, specific safe harbours for effective Chinese walls or equivalents have also been written into the COMARC in a number of places[1]);
(3)   various listing rules on the timing, dissemination or availability, content and standard of care applicable to disclosures, announcements, communications or releases of information; and
(4)   Listing Rule 15.1(b) in relation to share buy-backs.

The FSA understandably does not comment on whether it otherwise regards its own rules as requiring or expressly permitting market abuse (one must assume that it generally does not!). It does say, as a matter of guidance only not officially forming part of the COMARC, that it is satisfied that the RIE rulebooks do not permit or require behaviour which amounts to market abuse[2].

---

[1]   See paras 4.45 and 4.94.
[2]   MAR 1.2.12G.

THE TAKEOVER PANEL

4.144 The last political battle which was fought in Parliament on the FSMA 2000 related to the involvement of the FSA in takeover bids and the position of the non-statutory Takeover Panel (the 'Panel'). The Panel were very concerned that somebody could allege market abuse during a bid and this would require the FSA to get involved in the bid and severely affect the timetable. The Conservative Party's Treasury Team therefore put forward an amendment on behalf of the Panel that the Panel could agree with the FSA that certain provisions of the City Code on Takeovers and Mergers, which is issued and administered by the Panel, (the 'Takeover Code') would constitute safe harbours for market abuse. The Government did not want to allow this (because the FSA is supposed to be the only securities regulator and, perhaps, because the Takeover Panel represents the last important example in the City of London of self-regulation) and therefore insisted that, although the Panel and the FSA could indeed agree safe harbours, the FSA could only agree them with the consent of the Treasury. In addition, and importantly, the Government wanted the FSA to have the last word on what constituted market abuse and therefore on what sort of behaviour was permitted or required by the Takeover Code safe harbours and so fell within whatever safe harbour was agreed. Although the Government lost an important vote on this amendment in the last lengthy debate in the House of Lords, and the amendment giving primacy to the Panel was passed, the Government succeeded in reversing this when the Bill went back to the House of Commons and their own amendment was then passed when the debate went back to the House of Lords.

4.145 The end result was the FSMA 2000, s 120 which gave the FSA (without requiring agreement from the Panel) a *limited* power to include in the COMARC a provision that in its opinion behaviour conforming with the Takeover Code does not amount to market abuse (either generally, or in specified circumstances, or when done by specified persons). The limitations were that the Treasury's consent is required for any such provision (perhaps because for some reason the Government did not trust the FSA's judgment as to what would be acceptable) and that if such provisions are included, the FSA must keep itself informed of the way in which the Panel interprets and administers the relevant provisions of the Takeover Code (which, therefore, seems to constitute a Damoclean sword hanging over the Panel's ability to interpret and administer its own rules if the FSA does not like the way it did it). Ironically, since otherwise the FSA has a general power under the FSMA 2000, s 122(1) to grant safe harbours, this means that in law (if not in practice) it is more difficult to grant a safe harbour for behaviour conforming with the Takeover Code than with, for example, the rules of a foreign regulator such as the National Association of Securities Dealers (the NASD) in the US or with guidance issued by a trade association such as the London Investment Banking Association in the UK. Indeed, the FSA has given safe harbours in the COMARC[1] in relation to the Substantial Acquisition Rules (SARs), which are also produced and interpreted by the Takeover Panel but which do not require Treasury consent for safe harbours as they are not part of the City Code (which is how the FSMA 2000, s 120 refers to the Takeover Code).

---

[1]   See para 4.148.

4.146 Accordingly, if a party to a bid makes misleading statements in its offer or defence document, or engages in a share support operation, the FSA can interfere in the bid (which the other party will probably ask it to do as a delaying tactic) and, in extreme cases, apply to the court for an injunction stopping it—the mere application could stop the bid in its tracks even if it failed. It was in order to prevent this happening, and also because the Takeover Panel is so well regarded, that the House of Lords originally insisted that primary responsibility for takeover bids should remain with the Takeover Panel. The Government did actually agree to this but made it clear that, ultimately, if there was disagreement between the Panel and the FSA as to the meaning of a particular 'safe harbour' rule in the Takeover Code, the final decision as to what it meant lay with the FSA, and not the Panel. Indeed, if the FSA disagrees with the Panel, the FSA will seemingly be able to require the Panel to change its rules, or at least its interpretation of them, with the threat always in the background that the FSA would remove its safe harbours.

4.147   In our view, this whole debate (which was really the last stand of the City against a potential over-mighty regulator) was somewhat misdirected. First, the FSA was not under any obligation to agree any safe harbour at all. Second, the safe harbour is only for behaviour 'conforming with' the Takeover Code. Although the Takeover Code provides that, for example, the offeror normally must issue its offer document within 28 days after announcing the offer, and the issue of the document within that period would therefore conform with the COMARC, it cannot sensibly be argued that the making of misleading statements in that document also conforms with the COMARC. Accordingly, although it has entered into an operating agreement with the Takeover Panel providing for a modus operandi and it has expressly agreed to give 'due weight' to the Panel's views, the FSA can always interfere in a bid. However, it has agreed that during a bid it will only do so before the conclusion of the Panel's procedures in 'exceptional circumstances' (for example, where the Panel cannot itself enforce co-operation or where the alleged offence is 'misuse of information'). The UK will therefore have to become used to the idea of references to the FSA, even if only to double-guess the Panel and delay the bid timetable, becoming a regular part of takeover bids in the UK.

4.148   The FSA has in the COMARC in this area as in many others sought to reduce the risks posed by the breadth of the legislation. As far as the Takeover Code and SARs are concerned it has given specific safe harbours from the 'false or misleading impressions' and 'market distortion' categories of market abuse for:

(1)   various rules relating to the timing, dissemination or availability, content and standard of care applicable to disclosures, announcements, communications or releases; and
(2)   behaviour conforming with Rule 4.2 of the Takeover Code (relating to restrictions on dealings by the offeror and concert parties)

provided, in each case, that the General Principles set out in the Takeover Code, as well as specific rules, are followed. No safe harbours are given in relation to the 'misuse of information' category of market abuse but that is not surprising; the Panel did not even ask for this because insider dealing has always been outside its jurisdiction.

4.149   More generally, and without giving a full safe harbour, the FSA says that it is satisfied that the remainder of the Takeover Code and SARs do not permit or require behaviour which amounts to market abuse[1]; for example, many rules relate to ensuring that an offer or stakebuilding is conducted in an orderly manner or that shareholders in a company are treated similarly. It also says that sometimes the existence of these rules would be taken into account by a regular market user in considering whether behaviour falls below the standards reasonably to be expected. As usual, however, the FSA does not consider that compliance with such rules will necessarily avoid market abuse. It gives as an example a situation where the SARs are followed in building up a stake but the decision to build up that stake was based on a misuse of relevant disclosable or announceable information which was not generally available. Again, this really means only that not contravening the Takeover Code or SARs does not necessarily mean that there is no market abuse.

---

¹   MAR 1.7.6E.

THE STATUTORY DEFENCE

4.150   There is one other defence written into the FSMA 2000. The FSMA 2000, s 123(2) says that the FSA cannot impose penalties if it is satisfied that the alleged market abuser:

(1)   believed on reasonable grounds that his behaviour did not amount to any of the four categories of market abuse; or

(2)   took all reasonable precautions and exercised all due diligence to avoid behaving in a way which amounted to market abuse or requiring or encouraging market abuse.

It is not a full defence because it only prevents a penalty (and probably a public censure), disgorgement of profits and reimbursement of losses, and the behaviour concerned still ranks as market abuse. It may therefore still be regarded as a breach of FSA Principles for FSMA 2000-regulated persons and the FSA can still apply to a court for sanctions, such as injunctions and remedial orders. The reason that the FSA arguably cannot publish a public censure if the statutory defence applies is that it can only publish one where it is entitled to impose a penalty (FSMA 2000, s 123(3)) and as a result of the statutory defence it is not entitled to impose a penalty.

4.151   The defence also has the weakness that in order to rely on the defence it is necessary to have thought about the possibility of committing market abuse. Those who are too innocent or ignorant to do so (and especially company directors or overseas financial services firms) cannot avail themselves of the defence. Those who do think about possible market abuse will often find that the question only arises in situations where they are arguably at fault so that the defence is again not available. The defence does, however, provide a further reinforcement of the COMARC. Establishing systems and procedures which are based on the COMARC and testing proposed actions against the COMARC will be of assistance when seeking to use this defence.

FURTHER ACTION AND GUIDANCE

4.152   Although it is the COMARC alone which has a special statutory function in relation to market abuse, the FSA does plan to give some further assistance to those who are trying to avoid committing market abuse. It will give guidance on individual difficult situations provided full and clear disclosure is made. It will also publish simplified descriptions of market abuse and 'decision trees' on the subject, although it is hard to see how useful these will be except in the simplest situations. It will also continue to consult its specialist Practitioners Group on the subject over the implementation period and is planning to issue a 'Frequently Asked Questions' (FAQ) bulletin. Such a bulletin will be of considerable assistance in bridging the gap between very specific individual cases and the general material in the COMARC. In addition, certain trade associations, notably a joint working group of the BBA and the LIBA, are planning to work on guidance on hypothetical situations and examples which they do or do not regard as market abuse.

4.153 All of these additional initiatives will help in applying the difficult and uncertain area of law which is market abuse. However, as guidance and FAQ bulletins are issued, it would be desirable to have them incorporated as far as possible in a regularly revised version of the COMARC, thus clarifying the level of reliance which can be placed on them.

Chapter 5   Money Laundering

Dr Andrew Haynes

INTRODUCTION

5.1   This is an area that is likely to become of greater importance following the declarations of the British and American governments that the financial structures used to support international terrorism must be closed down. It is not only terrorists who launder money; the drugs trade creates huge reserves of cash from retail drug sales which need to be laundered; heads of state and senior figures in many third world countries also seem to regard their own countries' finances and overseas aid as a source of personal wealth. Organised crime in general also engages in laundering. The purpose of laundering in each instance is to hide the proceeds of crime and get it to re-emerge in a different place, under different apparent ownership, and with an apparently honest source. Such laundering falls into two main categories: that which starts off as cash and that which is already in the banking system. Drug laundering proceeds commence in the former state and laundering by corrupt governments commences as the latter. Thus not all laundering will be of the same nature.

5.2   Money Laundering has been defined as[1]:

> '. . . the process by which criminals attempt to conceal the true origin and ownership of their criminal activities. If undertaken successfully, it also allows them to maintain control over those proceeds and, ultimately, to provide a legitimate cover for their source of income'.

Another, briefer definition is[2]: 'rendering the proceeds of crime unrecognisable as such'.

---

[1]   Joint Money Laundering Steering Group *Guidance Notes for the Financial Sector*, at 1.03.
[2]   Simon Gleeson 'The Involuntary Launderer' in *Laundering and Tracing* (1995).

5.3   However the Joint Money Laundering Steering Committee Guidelines adopt a common mistake which provides false security in many of the larger laundering operations, ie, 'Criminally earned money is invariably transient in nature'. This will often be the case as the criminal organisation concerned will be in need of the funds as soon as possible. However, the vast increases in wealth available to the larger organised crime groups in recent years, and possibly some of the smaller ones, means that it may be possible for them to tie up some of their funds for significant periods of time as part of the laundering process[1].

5.4   The range of methods that can be utilised to launder money are
enormous and anyone needing to have a clear understanding of the subject
needs to read widely around the subject and keep abreast of changes in
laundering patterns. The commonest vehicles for laundering are those where
large amounts of cash or liquid investments of assets are handled. In the
financial markets, banks and investment business firms are the most heavily
used. In the commercial field, businesses dealing in high value goods can
prove attractive as they provide the opportunity for moving money around by
dealing in expensive goods, often across international boundaries. Another
development, and one that has become more heavily utilised as banks and
other financial businesses have attempted to tighten their anti-money laundering operations, is to include a firm of solicitors, accountants or other
professionals in what appears to be a bona fide scheme to invest or transact
money[1]. This provides the attraction of feeding money through a professional's client account to mask the arrangement with a veneer of respectability.
There have been recent suggestions by the National Criminal Intelligence
Service that some of these firms have been assisting criminal clients by
knowingly laundering money[2], though at the time of writing there have been
no arrests. It seems unlikely that many professional firms would take such a
risk. A particular problem in identifying laundering is that most of those with
large amounts of money to launder can construct their operations intelli-
gently enough to avoid them looking suspicious. In almost all instances of
large movements of laundered money the criminals will be employing experts
to advise and assist them.

¹   Financial Action Task Force, 1996 update on the FATF 40 recommendations: see
www.laundryman.u-net.com.
²   Robert Mendick 'Police Probe City Firms Links to Organised Crime' The Lawyer
(24 November 1998), p 1; Richard Tyler 'City Accusations Send Sparks Flying' The Lawyer
(1 December 1988), p 11; Comment and Analysis 'Law Society Laundering Reaction Will Not
Wash' The Lawyer (1 December 1998), p 16.

5.5   The legislation and guidelines follow from the UN Convention on the
subject[1] and thus focus primarily on laundering the proceeds of drug sales.
A consequence of this is that they are not of great assistance in identifying
the laundering of terrorist monies. In the UK, in particular, a dissimilarity
arises between the patterns of terrorist money and many of the other
laundering schemes. There is also a dissimilarity in the legislation in that it is
necessary to report the movement of monies which may be utilised to
commit a criminal act by a proscribed organisation rather than just money
being moved after a crime. This issue is examined more closely below.

¹   UN Convention on Psychotropic Drugs and Narcotic Substances, 1988.

5.6   The imposition of money laundering obligations on financial institutions and certain professionals has created a situation where those parties
must ascertain whether a particular transaction is 'suspicious' and, if so,

potential reporting issues arise. This chapter will consider what circumstances should arouse suspicion, what reporting issues then arise and what to do in borderline situations.

THE CRIMINAL OFFENCES—LAUNDERING DRUG PROCEEDS AND THE PROFITS OF CRIME

Concealing or transferring the proceeds of drug trafficking

5.7 It is an offence for someone to transfer property, convert it, or remove it from the jurisdiction to avoid criminal proceedings, or to conceal or disguise it if there are reasonable grounds to suppose that it is the proceeds of another's drug trafficking or criminal offence. In this context 'criminal offence' includes a confiscation order[1].

---

[1] Drug Trafficking Act 1994 (DTA 1994), s 49 and Criminal Justice Act 1988 (CJA 1988), s 93A.

Assisting another to retain the benefit

5.8 It is an offence to assist someone in retaining the proceeds of drug trafficking or other crime or to place the proceeds of crime so that the criminal can gain access to them. Likewise it is a crime to assist someone in utilising the proceeds of crime to acquire property. The person who is facilitating the crime must know or suspect that the money is either the proceeds of drug trafficking or other crime[1]. Thus the offences do not appear to extend to commercial investment to protect or increase the value of the money concerned[2].

---

[1] DTA 1994, s 50 and CJA 1988, s 93C.
[2] See comments to the Criminal Justice Act 1991, s 51 in *Current Law Statutes* (1993).

Disclosure

5.9 Anyone making a disclosure to 'a constable' is protected[1]. In the case of suspected laundering of drug proceeds the recipient of the disclosure would normally be the National Criminal Intelligence Service (NCIS). In the cases of other general crime the local fraud squad would be more appropriate. However, in the vast majority of cases the person spotting a suspicious transaction is unlikely to have any idea as to the nature of the original crime. Thus a report to NCIS is generally the best option. The law also covers reports being made after the event, as in many instances, suspicion will only arise then. In such cases the party making the report is not committing a criminal offence by not having made a report earlier, provided they did so as soon as was reasonable and on their own initiative[2].

---

[1] DTA 1994, s 50(3).
[2] DTA 1994, s 50(3)(b)(ii).

5.10   Such disclosures are not treated by the law as a breach of any statutory or common law duty of confidentiality, or breach of contract or the laws of defamation. In other words the party who makes the report need not fear civil proceedings as a consequence. In any event it is extremely unlikely that the party to whom the disclosure referred would ever know that it had taken place.

Acquisition, possession or utilising the proceeds

5.11   It is a criminal offence to use or acquire property which the person concerned knows to represent the proceeds of drug trafficking, whether directly or indirectly[1]. If they have paid 'adequate consideration' for the property (ie, consideration which is not 'significantly less than the value of the property') that person will have a defence. The accused would have to discharge the burden of proof in showing that adequate consideration had been paid were this defence to be pleaded.

---

[1]   DTA 1994, s 51.

Failure to disclose suspicion

5.12   This is the one area where there is a significant difference between the law relating to drug money laundering and laundering the proceeds of crime. It is a criminal offence to fail to disclose to the police, in practice the NCIS, a suspicion that someone carrying on 'relevant financial business' (see paras 5.19–5.22 for a definition of this) that someone is engaged in amounts to laundering the proceeds of drug sales[1]. The law only applies if the information came into that person's possession as a result of their trade, profession, business or employment. It does not extend to legal advisers obtaining such information in circumstances of professional privilege. The civil law protections mentioned at para 5.10 apply here as well.

---

[1]   DTA 1994, s 52.

5.13   If the person concerned had a reasonable excuse for not disclosing the information, they have a defence. Unfortunately, the DTA 1994 does not explain what a 'reasonable excuse' is and so far there have been no cases on the point.

Tipping off

5.14   It is a criminal offence to provide someone with information, the nature of which is likely to obstruct a police investigation[1]. It is also an offence if, having disclosed information to the police or the NCIS, further information is released which is likely to prejudice any investigation. Solicitors and barristers are excluded from this where they are giving legal advice in connection with legal proceedings.

---

[1]   DTA 1994, s 53 and CJA 1988, s 93D.

Penalties

5.15 The offences relating to concealing, assisting or acquiring goods are punishable by a fine or up to six months imprisonment on summary conviction, or a fine or up to 14 years on indictment. The penalties for the offences of failing to disclose and tipping off is the same on summary conviction but falls to a fine or up to five years imprisonment on indictment.

TERRORISM

5.16 There are a separate set of laws that apply to terrorist money. These are determined by the Terrorism Act 2000 which, inter alia, creates a series of criminal offences relating to handling terrorist money. The most relevant to those involved in the banking and financial services industries are the following criminal offences:

- to receive money or other property with the intention that it be used, or where there is reasonable cause to believe it will be used for the purposes of terrorism[1];
- to become concerned in an arrangement which facilitates the retention or control of terrorist property by or on behalf of another whether this be done by concealment, removal from the jurisdiction, transfer to nominees or in any other way[2];
- to fail to report to the police (in practice the NCIS) as soon as is reasonably practicable, a suspicion that someone has committed a financial offence in relation to laundering, where this information has come into their possession as part of their trade, profession, business or employment. They must also report the information on which their suspicion is based. There is a defence of having a 'reasonable excuse' for not making the disclosure[3]. Information obtained by a professional legal adviser is exempt if it is obtained in privileged circumstances[4];
- to disclose information to another which is likely to prejudice an investigation or interfere with material which is relevant to such an investigation where there are reasonable grounds to suppose that the police are conducting, or proposing to conduct a terrorist investigation.

---

[1] Terrorism Act 2000 (TA 2000), s 15(2).
[2] TA 2000, s 18.
[3] TA 2000, s 19(2).
[4] TA 2000, s 19(5).

5.17 Terrorist offences by their nature relate to terrorist organisations and the TA 2000 provides a list of 14[1] who are all parties involved in the conflict in Northern Ireland. Since then a statutory instrument[2] has added a rather more cosmopolitan list of 21 additional organisations whose activities relate to overseas conflicts.

---

[1] TA 2000, Sch 2.
[2] Terrorism Act 2000 (Proscribed Organisations) (Amendment) Order 2001, SI 2001/1261.

5.18   The penalties for non-compliance are a fine or up to six months imprisonment on summary conviction and a fine or up to 14 years on indictment[1].

---

[1]   TA 2000, s 22.

RELEVANT PARTIES

5.19   Not everyone is bound by the requirement to report suspicious transactions. Essentially those who are caught are those carrying on 'relevant financial business'[1].

---

[1]   Money Laundering Regulations 1993, SI 1993/1933, reg 4(1).

5.20   This covers:

(a)   specified investment business within the meaning of the Financial Services and Markets Act 2000; deposit taking business, carried on by a person who is for the time being authorised under the Financial Services and Markets Act 2000;

(b)   acceptance by a building society of deposits made by any person (including the raising of money from members of the society by the issue of shares);

(c)   business of the National Savings Bank;

(d)   business carried on by a credit union;

(e)   any home regulated activity carried on by a European institution in respect of which the requirements of the Banking Co-ordination (Second Council Directive) Regulations 1992, Sch 2, para 1 have been complied with;

(f)   any activity carried on for the purpose of raising money authorised to be raised under the National Loans Act 1968 under the auspices of the Director of National Savings;

(g)   any of the activities in points 1 to 12, or 14, of the Annex to the Second Banking Coordination Directive;

(h)   insurance business carried on by a person who has received official authorisation under the First Life Directive, Art 6 or 27.

5.21   Under SI 1993/1933, reg 4(2), specifically excluded from being 'relevant financial business' are:

•   the issue of withdrawable share capital within the limit set by the Industrial and Provident Societies Act 1965, s 6 if within the limits set by ss 6 and 7(3) respectively;

•   the issue of withdrawable share capital within the limit set by the Industrial and Provident Societies Act (Northern Ireland) 1969, s 6 by a society registered under that Act;

•   activities carried on by the Bank of England;

•   the miscellaneous exceptions set out in or pursuant to the Financial Services and Markets Act 2000, of whom the bulk are the holders of certain judicial or other offices.

5.22 The Second Banking Directive referred to above covers:

(1) acceptance of deposits and other repayable funds from the public;
(2) lending;
(3) financial leasing;
(4) money transmission services;
(5) issuing and administering means of payment (eg, credit cards, travellers' cheques and bankers' drafts);
(6) guarantees and commitments;
(7) trading for own account or for account of customers in:

    (a) money market instruments (cheques, bills, CD's etc);
    (b) foreign exchange;
    (c) financial futures and options;
    (d) exchange and interest rate instruments;
    (e) transferable securities;

(8) participation in securities issues and the provision of services relating to such issues;
(9) advice to undertakings on capital structure, industrial strategy and related questions and advice and services relating to mergers and the purchase of undertakings;
(10) money broking;
(11) portfolio management and advice;
(12) safekeeping and administration of securities;
(13) safe custody services.

This definition is of limited use as, in the light of subsequent statutory changes, its content is partly out of date. Firms carrying on any type of investment activity or operating under the NIPs Code should assume that their business activities operate within the remit of the anti-money laundering regime and act accordingly unless they are absolutely clear that the business activity concerned operates outside its remit.

5.23 A draft EU Directive will extend the application of the laws to professionals such as solicitors and accountants and others whose businesses render them particularly at risk as laundering vehicles, such as those owning casinos. Once the Directive is finalised the details will be added to the next edition.

CHECKING IDENTITY

5.24 The Money Laundering Regulations 1993[1] require that the identity of a new client be checked in any of the following situations:

- were it has been decided that a business relationship should be formed with them;
- when the person dealing with the client has reason to suspect that a one off transaction could be part of a money laundering operation;
- where a one off transaction exceeds €15,000; and

- where there are a series of connected transactions exceeding €15,000 in total value.

_____

[1]   SI 1993/1933.

_____

5.25   It would be wise for most financial services firms to require that all new clients have their identity checked at the outset. Failure to do so could give rise to the risk of someone using the firm on an incremental basis and then getting round the identity checking requirement because staff do not remember to do so on breaching the €15,000 barrier. Generally speaking the client's identity should be checked at the outset but the regulations do permit some variation in this, where the nature of the contact with the client may make this impossible, eg, where they are in another country. In any event it should always be done at the first reasonably possible time. If the person dealing with the financial institution appears to be acting for someone else, that person's identity must also be checked in the same way.

5.26   The Money Laundering Regulations 1993[1] require that identity be checked by an approach that is 'reasonably capable of establishing that the applicant is the person he claims to be.' This means seeing original documents that prove that the person is who he claims to be and also that they live at the address they have provided. This will generally mean seeing more than one document. Documents that are useful to prove identity are:

- passport;
- driving licence;
- identity card (if from a country that has them); or
- references.

To prove that the person is resident where they claim to be, it is useful to see:

- utility bills;
- check the electoral roll; or
- check the telephone directory.

_____

[1]   SI 1993/1933.

_____

5.27   Where the proposed client is a company it will be necessary to carry out a company search to ascertain that the company is genuine, who its directors are, their registered address, and to obtain copies of filed accounts. If it is an overseas company it is important to check whether it is registered in a jurisdiction where certificates of incorporation must be reviewed annually. In addition such documents may be in a foreign language. If the firm checking does not have personnel with appropriate language skills it will be necessary to obtain certified translations. Should the company be part of a group it is necessary to check the line of ownership of the company to its ultimate source. It is also necessary to check the identity of any other member of the group whose activities are relevant to the business being transacted by the checking institution for the new client.

5.28 Once these have been carried out and a photocopy of the documents concerned have been placed on file the identity checking requirements have been met. However, it should be borne in mind that any criminal seeking to launder money will have no difficulty at all in satisfying the requirement that they produce such documents. They will either have fake or real documents in the name they are using and searches will rarely distinguish companies used by criminals from genuine ones. This is not a reason for being cavalier about checking identity, but it does mean that possession of 'proof' is not a reason to lower a firm's guard when it comes to suspicious activity by a client.

5.29 It is not necessary to check on identity where:

(1)   there is clear evidence that another person, regulated by a financial services body in the European Union has already done so;
(2)   the applicant is someone who must themselves check clients' identity because they too are a regulated firm;
(3)   it is a one off transaction carried out via an intermediary who have themselves provided an assurance that their client's identity has been checked;
(4)   the person who will receive the money will be re-investing it in another investment or transaction on their own behalf or for their benefit and proper records will be kept; and
(5)   it is an insurance scheme with a single instalment that does not exceed €2,500 or with a periodic premium not exceeding €1,000.

WHAT IS 'SUSPICION'?

5.30 Unfortunately the statutes mentioned above give no guidance on what 'suspicion' means. It probably relates to apprehension or mistrust considering the unusual nature or circumstances of the transaction, or the person or group of persons with whom they are dealing. Whilst there is no case law in this country in the context of the legislation, there is case law on the nature of suspicion. In *Husslen v Chong Fook Kam*[1] Lord Devlin stated that: 'Suspicion in its ordinary meaning is a state of conjecture or surmise where proof is lacking.' He added that:

> 'Suspicion can take into account matters that could not be put in evidence ... Suspicion can take into account matters which, though admissible, could not form part of a prima facie case.'

The Money Laundering Guidance Notes reinforce this[2]: 'Suspicion is personal and subjective and falls far short of proof based on firm evidence'. It goes on to say that 'a suspicious transaction will often be one which is inconsistent with a customer's known, legitimate business or personal activities or with the normal business for that type of account'.

---

[1]   [1970] AC 942.
[2]   See Joint Money Laundering Steering Group *Guidance Notes 2001*, at 6.01.

5.31   Given that the Money Laundering Regulations 1993[1] and the FSA Money Laundering rules require that those covered by the regulations must 'know their customer' and are required to maintain an appropriate level of expertise, we are left with a situation in which the requirement begins to function in a manner much closer to an objective one than the subjective crime that the legislation provides.

---

[1]   SI 1993/1933.

5.32   The guidance comments at para 5.33 give assistance as to what can be regarded as suspicious. In part however there is also an element of common sense as to what looks unusual or abnormal. It is rare that laundering will clearly appear as such.

5.33   Issues to consider would include the following.

(1)   the speed with which cash is being transferred to another form of money and to another place. In particular is money, and in particular cash, paid into an account and then paid out at unusual speed?

(2)   Does the routing of the funds involve a country with close contacts to drug production, processing, or the laundering of proceeds?

(3)   Is the arrangement one which does not make sense from a business point of view? In particular is it an arrangement that did not appear to be designed to make a profit. This is not always an element however. Many criminal organisations now attempt to utilise the laundering process to make a profit, eg, by utilising funds to buy goods which are then re-sold at a mark up.

(4)   Does the arrangement involve offshore shell companies, trusts and tax haven banks, when the purpose of their involvement does not fit in with normal business practice for the type of transaction taking place? Unfortunately it often will as the criminals will have constructed their finances to optimise their tax position on an international basis after taking legal and financial advice. In reality their transactions will tend to replicate legitimate ones.

(5)   Does the transaction involve cash flows in and out of countries where the banking system is heavily permeated by organised crime, eg, Russia? If it does careful note should be made of the exchange rates at which the currency concerned changes from one currency to another. If these appear to be other than market rates, the transaction should be regarded as particularly suspicious[1].

Note should be taken of structures that seem to be designed to make it difficult for outsiders to ascertain exactly what is going on. An abnormally complex structure of companies should arouse suspicion.

---

[1]   Timor Sinuraya 'Integration of Criminal Capital from Russia into West European Markets: An Assessment of Threat' Journal of Money Laundering Control. Vol.1, No.1, 1997, p 32; V P Aksilenko 'Security Concerns' Organized Crime Digest, 27 September 1995, p 5; A Neshyadin 'Seraya ekonomika Rossii' Izvestia 21 September 1994, p 9; I Botovsky 'Koloss prestupnpsti podminaet gosudarstvo' Pravda 1996, No 9, p 3.

5.34 There may be aspects of the client that raise suspicion. This is only likely to occur with the less professional criminals. The rest will have little difficulty in maintaining a credible appearance.

MAKING A SUSPICIOUS TRANSACTION REPORT

5.35 Once a suspicious transaction report has been submitted, the National Criminal Intelligence Service (or in the case of general money laundering, the local fraud squad) will then inform the person who has made the report whether it is acceptable to continue with the transaction. The NCIS normally prefer the transaction to continue to facilitate their observation of the transaction and to provide them with the opportunity to analyse the events concerned. It is necessary to obtain consent to act otherwise the party who made the report will almost certainly be committing a criminal offence such as aiding and abetting or being an accessory after the fact. On the other hand if the firm refused to continue to act for the client they could effectively be 'tipping off' because the client will then realise that the firm is suspicious and assume that a report has been filed[1].

---

[1]   See also para 5.78.

5.36 In cases where there are slight grounds for suspicion but the person concerned does not feel there is sufficient evidence to make a suspicious transaction report, it is a good idea to make a file note of the reasons for concern. It may be that as time goes by a succession of other minor issues may arise and eventually there are sufficient grounds for making a report.

THE FSA'S REQUIREMENTS

Introduction

5.37 In addition to the laws, regulations and guidance notes discussed above, the FSA has also issued a set of rules which apply to those who are approved to carry on investment business and these operate in addition to the above. This has arisen as a result of the Financial Services and Markets Act 2000 (FSMA 2000), which, inter alia, gives the FSA the power to make rules in relation to the prevention and detection of money laundering in connection with the carrying on of regulated activities by authorised persons, with the objective of reducing financial crime[1]. In this context 'financial crime' is interpreted to mean:

'. . . any offence involving—

(a)   fraud or dishonesty;

(b)   misconduct in, or misuse of information relating to, a financial market; or

(c)   handling the proceeds of crime'[2].

It is taken to cover any activity overseas which would have been an offence if it had taken place in the United Kingdom. In attempting to carry out its obligations in this respect the FSMA 2000 requires the FSA to:

'. . . have regard to the desirability of—

(a)   regulated persons being aware of the risk of their businesses being used in connection with the commission of financial crime;

(b)   regulated persons taking appropriate measures (in relation to their administration and employment practices, the conduct of transactions by them . . .) to prevent financial crime, facilitate its detection and monitor its incidence;

(c)   regulated persons devoting adequate resources to the matters mentioned . . .'[3].

---

[1]   FSMA 2000, ss 6 and 146.
[2]   FSMA 2000, s 6(3).
[3]   FSMA 2000, s 6(2).

5.38   Further, the FSMA 2000 also provides the FSA with the power to 'institute proceedings for an offence under prescribed regulations relating to money laundering'[1]. This does not apply in Scotland. In addition, the FSA's suitability requirement for qualification for authorisation includes taking into account 'whether the firm has in place the appropriate money laundering systems and training, including identification, record-keeping and internal reporting procedures'[2]. Finally, the FSA's Principles include the requirement that:

'3. A firm must take reasonable care to organise and control its affairs responsibly and effectively, with adequate risk management systems'[3].

The original draft version of this rule[4] added:

'This will include . . . operating robust arrangements for meeting the standards and requirements of the regulatory system, and for guarding against involvement in market abuse or financial crime (including the detection and prevention of money laundering)'.

In addition, Principle 1 states that 'A firm must conduct its business with integrity' and Principle 5 adds that 'A firm must observe proper standards of market conduct'. There is therefore no doubt as to the ability of the FSA to police the amended anti-money laundering regime they have created.

---

[1]   FSMA 2000, s 402(1)(b).
[2]   FSA Consultation Paper 'The Qualifying Conditions for Authorisation' (March 1999).
[3]   See FSA Principle 3.
[4]   FSA Priciples—Consultation Draft, September 1998, CP13.

5.39   The approach adopted has been heavily influenced by the Basel Committee on Banking Regulations and Supervisory Practices[1], and is therefore likely to be reflected by steps taken by regulators in other Basel countries. The FSA has passed a series of rules that apply to all those whom it regulates. These operate in addition to the statutes, regulations and guidance notes already in existence. However, the FSA states that: 'firms whose systems and controls are already at acceptable levels will be able to comply with the proposed rules with few changes or difficulties, if any'[2].

---

[1] See the 'Prevention of Criminal Use of the Banking System for the Purpose of Money Laundering' (Basel Committee, 1998).
[2] FSA Consultation Paper 46 'Executive summary', p 1.

5.40 The purpose of the FSA rules is stated to be to reduce the opportunities for laundering that are available to criminals through using the businesses of approved persons. They also assist in the promotion of market confidence, increasing public awareness, protecting consumers and combating organised crime.

5.41 The FSA rules apply to 'relevant firms', which are firms engaged in specified activities[1] except those purely involved in general insurance or long-term insurance beyond the scope of the First Life Directive[2]. The rules apply on a host state basis and therefore also impact on UK branches of firms established elsewhere in the EEA.

---

[1] As defined by the Financial Services and Markets Act 2000 (Regulated Activities) Order 2001, SI 2001/544. See paras 1.118–1.141.
[2] Council Directive 73/239/EEC.

Money laundering duties

5.42 Relevant firms are expected to appoint a Money Laundering Reporting Officer. This is part of a wider duty whereby the firm and the officer must make certain that the firm complies with the legal requirements regarding laundering, including the FSA rules. To deliver this, the officer will need to keep himself up to date as to developments in laundering, arrange staff education as necessary, make sure that in-house systems function properly, receive internal reports from staff and send on information to the NCIS as appropriate. In addition they must make an annual report to their own management. These requirements mean that the Money Laundering Reporting Officer must be of sufficient seniority and have the necessary resources to deliver this. As the role is a controlled function[1] their appointment will be subject to FSA approval. In a smaller firm the roles of Compliance Officer and Money Laundering Reporting Officer could be combined.

---

[1] See paras 1.10–1.14.

Customer identification

5.43 Regulated firms must not act without first identifying the identity of each customer[1]. This must be done prior to carrying out a transaction, or even reaching an agreement to do so in future. A 'customer' is defined as[2]:

> 'a private customer, intermediate customer or a market counterparty engaged in, or who has had contact with that firm—(1) on his own behalf; or (2) as agent for or on behalf of another.'

'Transaction' is also widely defined[3] as including 'the giving of advice and any other business or service which is within the scope of a regulated activity.' As with the Money Laundering Regulations[4] identification procedures need not be used in cases that are below the financial limit of €15,000, where the person has been vouchsafed by someone else with a legal responsibility to do so and where the firm has no reason to be suspicious and is not in possession of knowledge that it is a laundering transaction. This is a development from the Regulations in that it extends to any member of staff being suspicious or in possession of knowledge. It appears to amount to strict liability and will apply whenever a firm or anyone within it is in breach, regardless of how thoroughly the firm has attempted to create a suitable anti-laundering regime. Two types of transaction are also exempt: where an isolated recorded transaction involves an investment that may only be re-invested in the client's name or be repaid directly to them, and certain transactions involving a long-term insurance contract below a de minimis figure or which is taken out as part of certain pension schemes.

---

[1]   This has been discussed at para 5.24–5.29.
[2]   FSA Money Laundering Rules, Annex A, p 23.
[3]   FSA Money Laundering Rules, Annex A, p 28.
[4]   SI 1993/1933.

5.44   The evidence that may be accepted regarding identity largely follows the lines of the guidance notes issued by the Joint Money Laundering Steering Group (JMLSG). A couple of points arise however. The first is financial exclusion[1]. This permits firms to make allowance for the fact that some people do not have passports, driving licences or other documents that would satisfy the normal identity checking arrangements. In such instances the firm may accept 'other evidence, such as a letter or statement from a person in a position of responsibility who knows the customer, sufficient to establish to the relevant firm's reasonable satisfaction that the customer is who he says he is, and to confirm his permanent address if he has one'[2]. This is unlikely to put the firm at risk given that the ease with which criminals can obtain false documentation means that they are unlikely to need to adopt this route[3]. The other is that there is no clear guidance on what to do when the client is a limited company or partnership. Such firms will therefore have to fall back on the JMLSG guidelines In the case of listed public companies there is less risk as the stock exchange will have run checks. In other instances it would have been useful for the rules to provide fuller requirements.

---

[1]   FSA Money Laundering Rules, 3.3.5.
[2]   FSA Money Laundering Rules, 3.3.6.
[3]   Haynes 'Anti-Money Laundering Law' in Ed Ashe and Rider *International Tracing of Assets* (1997), p C1/8.

5.45   Identification must be ascertained prior to carrying out a transaction or even reaching an agreement to do so in future.

Know your business

5.46 To try and increase the number of firms who spot suspicious transactions they are now required to utilise the information in their possession about clients to recognise transactions that are abnormal[1]. The rules provide that a firm may choose to establish an internal system to facilitate staff obtaining client information on request. Alternatively, it is proposed that the firm could create a facility where further information would be made available to staff automatically under certain circumstances, such as unusual transactions or dealings.

---

[1]   FSA Consultation Paper 46 (2000) at rule 4.

Reporting

5.47 The reporting requirement is broken into two sub-sections; one dealing with internal reporting and one with external. The internal reporting requirement is that a suspicious member of staff must make a prompt report to the Money Laundering Reporting Officer. The firm is responsible for making sure that there is a system in place to facilitate this. There must be arrangements for taking disciplinary steps against anyone who has failed to do this without good reason.

5.48 The external reporting requirement is, as would be expected, that the Money Laundering Reporting Officer, once in possession of such a report, must promptly make a report to the NCIS if he believes that there are indeed grounds for suspicion. To facilitate this the firm should enable the officer access to any information that could be relevant.

Using national and international findings on material deficiencies

5.49 Firms are required to make proper use of notices published by both the UK and international organisations of which the UK is a member, including the Financial Action Task Force. The notices concerned are those where there has been an examination of the anti-money laundering provisions in a state and that they have been found to be deficient. Proper use means, inter alia, applying that information in the contexts of introduction of a customer for an isolated transaction or the introduction by a customer of a person on whose behalf he is acting. It should be utilised as part of the 'know your customer' process and disseminated as part of staff awareness and training.

Awareness and training

5.50 The rules require that firms make sure that staff are aware of and given regular training in what is expected of them in relation to money laundering, the relevant law including the Money Laundering Regulations 1993[1] and the FSA Rules, the identity and responsibilities of the Money Laundering Reporting Officer and the nature of the consequences to the firm and themselves if they fail to meet the necessary requirements. In particular, the staff should be given information concerning the effect that facilitating a customer in laundering money can have on the firm's bank accounts and other assets. The original Consultation Paper stated: '. . . in particular if a relevant firm decides it is unable to process transactions, because of the risk of committing a money laundering offence'[2]. This is unfortunately worded. A firm should not decide not to process a transaction because it suspects it is a money laundering operation. It should contact the NCIS, report its suspicions, and ask for guidance from the NCIS as to whether to continue acting. The NCIS will usually want them to do so to facilitate watching the suspected laundering operation[3].

---

[1]   SI 1993/1933.
[2]   FSA Consultation Paper 46 (2000) at 7.2.4.
[3]   This has been discussed at para 5.35.

5.51   Information relating to awareness and training need not be recorded in writing but it would be wise to do so, either by hard copy or electronic means, primarily so that the firm can show that the rules are being observed.

5.52   In addition appropriate training must be given to those staff who handle money, or are managerially responsible for transactions which could be utilised to launder money. 'Substantially'[1] all staff should be covered by such training within a period of two years. Although this appears to provide some assistance for a firm that claims it has not been able to provide training for all relevant staff, it does appear to be at odds with the relevant law. There seems no sensible reason why appropriate training cannot be provided to all staff within a reasonable period of joining a firm or changing roles to one in which such training will be needed for the first time. Two years seems a very generous provision, and one without basis in the relevant legislation or statutory instruments. Likewise, the idea that 'substantially' all relevant staff should be so trained seems inadequate. It might satisfy the FSA: it might not satisfy a court.

---

[1]   FSA Consultation Paper 46 (2000) at 7.3.2(1)(c).

The Money Laundering Reporting Officer and compliance monitoring

5.53   The role of Money Laundering Reporting Officer is one that must be filled. To facilitate the officer in being able to do the job properly the person must be senior, be free to act on his own authority, have sufficient resources, be based in the UK and within the firm, and be informed of any relevant knowledge or suspicion within that firm. It is the officer's responsibility to pass on to the NCIS suspicious transaction reports. It is this person who is also responsible for utilising the national and international information referred to at para 5.52. The officer is also responsible for making sure that the awareness and training requirements are fulfilled and making an annual report to the firm's managers. The only exceptions to this requirement are sole traders, and incoming firms which only provide services in the UK from overseas.

5.54 The annual report must assess the firm's compliance with the FSA Rules and show how any new findings under the requirement to learn from national and international findings have been put into effect and state how many internal reports of suspicious transactions have been made by staff to that officer. Internal reports should be broken down in a manner appropriate to the size and nature of the firm's business to facilitate discerning any patterns of reporting so that areas of inadequate reporting can be spotted. It is an obligation that the managers consider the report and take any necessary action to remedy deficiencies.

Record keeping

5.55 Firms must keep a copy of the client identification evidence on file, or where this cannot be done, a note must be kept on file of where that information can be obtained. It should be clear from where records can be obtained. Records must be kept of all regulated activity transactions. In addition, there must be records of any steps taken against insolvent clients to recover monies owed, and internal or external reporting and details of any action taken. This extends to keeping a record of any internal reports that the Money Laundering Reporting Officer decided not to act on.

5.56 Such records must be kept for five years. This time period starts to run with the termination of the firm's relationship with the firm, or the completion of the transaction, or the client's insolvency or the acquisition of the information leading to the creation of the record. In practice, most firms will keep files for at least six years as this will be the limitation period for any breach of contract or negligence action by a client. As the relevant information will normally be kept on client files, it will end up being retained as well.

5.57 There should also be records of the anti-money laundering training given[1] including the names of the staff concerned. There should also be a record of consideration of internal reports of suspicion and any action taken.

---

[1] See para 5.50.

Conclusions

5.58 The FSA requirements are not onerous and, in the case of those currently regulated by recognised professional bodies, only extend to relevant regulated activities. The extension of the role of the Money Laundering Reporting Officer is only bringing the requirement up to what many well run firms will already be doing. However, it is not clear whether the Money Laundering Reporting Officer and Head of Compliance can be carried out by the same person. The areas of operation clearly relate, but in large firms it may be appropriate for the Money Laundering Reporting Officer to be someone who is less senior in rank than the Head of Compliance given that it is part of the latter's function to make sure that the anti-money laundering steps taken are, along with everything else, satisfying the firm's compliance requirements.

5.59   The requirements for staff training are, as discussed at paras 5.50–5.52, potentially less than many firms will currently feel they are required to provide to protect themselves, given the current legal situation.

5.60   There is a benefit to firms in the draft rules in that there is evidence that firms with tight anti-money laundering provisions tend to be better protected against fraud. In addition, if it becomes entangled in a laundering operation the cost to a firm can be very high. Anything that reduces the risk of this has to be in the interests of the firm themselves. Nonetheless, there must be concerns that the approach adopted by the FSA has unnecessarily added an additional tier of regulation to those that are already in place. A simple requirement to satisfy the requirements of the relevant statutes and the Money Laundering Regulations 1993[1] might have been enough, possibly coupled with arrangements for the Regulations to be amended slightly. This could have achieved the same result more simply.

---

[1]   SI 1993/1933.

CIVIL LAW ISSUES[1]

Introduction

5.61   It is not only the criminal law and regulatory issues that pose a threat when an institution launders funds, there is also the potential threat of civil proceedings to recover the funds. For this to occur there must be a real owner of the money in pursuit of it. Two problems occur: the concept of real owner is widely defined and the area of law concerned seems to be going through a period of development, making it unclear.

---

[1]   For a detailed examination of this issue see Paula Reid 'The Civil Law and Money Laundering' in Ed Rider and Ashe *The International Tracing of Assets* (1998), vol 1.

5.62   The position is complicated by the doctrine of constructive trusts. These occur where a court decides to determine after the event that a state of affairs shall be treated as though the parties had set up a trust. Thus the obligations of trustee can be imposed on someone who had not thought of themselves as being in that position. This was traditionally done where someone was behaving in an illegal or immoral fashion. It has also been used to create liability by creating a situation where the trustee is then held to have knowingly assisted in breaching the trust or having knowingly been in receipt of funds from one who has.

5.63   This issue often arises because of the doctrine of tracing. This is an old rule of law that permits someone to pursue money they have lost through the wrongful behaviour of another into the place where it now resides. The common law rule of tracing is of limited use because of old case law that said that once money that had been taken from you had been mixed by a recipient with their own money in a purse, you could no longer use tracing because it was no longer possible to tell which money was which. However, equitable tracing got round this problem by applying relevant maxims of equity which resulted in the court assuming that anyone in possession of the property of another would act to try and repay it. Thus any money they still had should be the injured party's funds. Likewise if they spent all the money, the first money they received back would be held for the benefit of the injured person. The only issue that defeated equitable tracing was where the money had been paid through an overdrawn bank account as there the bank would have been a creditor for the overdraft.

5.64 To obtain equitable tracing it is necessary to prove that the funds were subject to a trust. Thus those who have lost funds usually wish to try and obtain a court declaration that the money was subject to a constructive trust as it was not subject to one in an ordinary sense.

5.65 There is also a jurisdictional problem in that only those jurisdictions that recognise trusts will allow equitable tracing into their jurisdiction. That said it is normally possible to trace through such a jurisdiction into one that does recognise trusts. As a general rule the common law countries (generally ex British Empire states) recognise the concept of trusts.

Grounds for constructive trusteeship

5.66 There are two basic grounds used by the courts:

(1)   knowing receipt; and
(2)   knowing assistance.

The classic exposition of English law on the point was stated by Selborone LC in *Barnes v Addy*[1]:

> 'strangers are not to be made constructive trustees ... unless (they) receive and become chargeable with some part of the trust property or unless they assist with knowledge that it is a dishonest and fraudulent design on the part of the trustees'.

---

[1]   (1874) 9 Ch App 244.

5.67 Unfortunately the cases that have followed have left this area of law in an unclear state. Perhaps the crucial case is *Royal Brunei Airlines v Tan*[1]. Here the airline had appointed Borneo Leisure Travel as its agent for selling seats and cargo space on the airline. The contract stated that Borneo Leisure was to hold any money received on trust for the airline. However, instead of paying these funds into a trust account for their principal, Borneo Leisure paid funds received into their own account. The person controlling Borneo Leisure then allowed the company to use the money for its own purposes. Eventually the firm became insolvent and the airline appeared to have lost its money. It then brought legal proceedings against the managing director and main owner of Borneo Leisure alleging that he had knowingly assisted in breach of trust. In response he claimed that there was only mismanagement, which did not give rise to personal liability. The Privy Council stated that there were certain key issues:

- the liability of an accessory should apply regardless of whether the trustee and the third party have both displayed dishonesty or whether the trustee was innocent;
- that liability could be imposed regardless of whether the third party had procured the breach or dishonestly assisted in it; and
- that the key issue is the state of mind of the third party not the trustee.

In other words, where someone interferes with a trust and deprives the beneficiary of some or all of their property, the beneficiary should be able to get it back.

---

[1]   [1995] 3 All ER 97.

5.68   The Privy Council also approved some earlier cases which could be of particular concern for financial institutions who have laundered funds. One of these cases was *Fyler v Fyler*[1]. Here a firm of solicitors had put funds from a trust into an investment which was unauthorised. They were held liable even though they had believed that the investment would be of benefit to the beneficiary. The other was *Eaves v Hickson*[2]. Here the trustees made a payment on the basis of a forged document that was presented to them and which according to the judge would have fooled anyone not looking for forgery. The person who had produced the forgery was made liable to repay the money in priority to any claim being made against the trustees. However, had they not got the resources to pay, the trustees would then have been liable.

Liability was stated to arise where the person concerned was dishonest rather than unconscionable in their conduct. This consisted of not acting as an honest person would and the test was objective. Interestingly, negligence was held to be insufficient to create liability.

---

[1]   (1841) 3 Beav 550.
[2]   (1861) 30 Beav 136.

Knowing receipt

5.69   There is a dichotomy between two legal issues in many of the cases. This arises between knowing receipt of funds and liability for breach of fiduciary duty. Knowing receipt occurs when property has been received knowingly in breach of trust. Fiduciary duty is a generic term to cover one of a number of situations that occur where someone is held to have particular obligations to another party because of their relationship with them. There does not need to be a trust (though a trust does give rise to a fiduciary relationship) but similar obligations then occur. Again a party who had laundered funds when a fiduciary relationship arose could find themselves faced with a civil claim. To provide such a right the courts have stretched the doctrine further and further over recent years, although surprisingly a thief is not automatically a fiduciary of the true owner.

5.70 The legal consequences of the two states of affairs are different. In cases of knowing receipt an action in equity can be brought to recover the full amount including any capital growth that has occurred since the recipient received it. On the other hand in cases of knowing assistance the liability is for the total amount lost plus simple interest.

5.71 Many of the issues were considered in *Lipkin Gorman v Karpnale*[1] where a solicitor became an obsessive gambler. He started gambling with clients' money. The firm's bank noticed that client account cheques were being paid to a casino but did nothing about it. A claim was brought for constructive trust, quasi-contract, negligence and conversion. The House of Lords held that a recipient of stolen money who was unjustly enriched was under an obligation to pay the same amount back to the victim. There is however a degree of protection for the recipient if he can show that his position had changed as a result of the arrangements and that he would lose out by having to pay the money back. This defence is of value to the financial extent of the change of position that has taken place. Unfortunately, the only issue that was considered on appeal to the House of Lords was a claim for money had and received. However, the Court of Appeal stated that a bank could not be liable to its customer as a constructive trustee unless it was in breach of its contractual duty of care to that customer.

---

[1]   [1992] 4 All ER 409.

5.72 In *Agip (Africa) Ltd v Jackson*[1] a firm of accountants had been acting for a fraudulent client. The accountants received funds from their clients and then passed them on as per instructions received. The true owners eventually appeared and claimed the funds back. As there was no financial sense in pursuing the clients, the wronged parties sued the accountants. It was held that they were not liable as they had not received the funds for their own benefit. However, it was stated that were a bank to receive funds to reduce an overdraft it would be receiving the funds for their own benefit.

---

[1]   [1992] 4 All ER 385.

5.73 In *Polly Peck International plc v Nadir (No 2)*[1] a claim for knowing receipt and knowing assistance was brought against Asil Nadir and the Central Bank of Northern Cyprus claiming that a huge amount of money had been wrongly transferred out of the company concerned. The Bank had received the funds for foreign currency contracts and in the course of this had not made enquiries about the source of the funds. The Turkish Cypriot bank concerned had £45 million on deposit with the Midland Bank in London. The company's administrator sought an order freezing the bank account. The court held that the key issue was whether or not the bank had been involved in any dishonesty or want of probity in that they had actual or constructive notice that they were receiving misapplied funds. The bank did not need to be shown to have been acting fraudulently. One of the judges felt that it was a case of knowing assistance and that the bank would only be liable if they received the money for their own use and benefit. As they received the money as agents and accounted for it to their principals he did not believe that this requirement had been satisfied. Another of the judges, however, believed that most of the funds had been received as banker because the bank received the funds in their own right as a result of a currency transfer and therefore the issue was one of knowing receipt. The appropriate measure to apply was whether there was knowledge that trust funds had been misapplied.

---

[1]   [1992] 4 All ER 769.

Holding property to the order of another

5.74   Sometimes called 'holding in a ministerial capacity' this arises when one person holds property belonging to someone else and mixes it with their own property. This is beyond 'knowing receipt' as discussed at para 5.69 ff unless the agent is setting up their own title to the funds. Two issues arise here. The first is the principle that an agent who uses their principle's money in good faith to pay off a debt owed by the principal can raise the defence of 'payment over'. In *Holland v Russell*[1] an agent paid money to another as agent for a ship owner whose ship had sunk. It later transpired that the policy was void for non-disclosure. By then the agent of the ship owner had paid some of the money over to his principal. The court held that the action would lie against the principal not the agent for this sum as the money had been properly paid over.

---

[1]   (1861) 1 B & S 424.

5.75   However, in *Springfield Acres v Abacus (Hong Kong) Ltd*[1] the defence failed. A company had successfully sued Springfield Acres for a large sum. Whilst the claim was waiting to be settled Springfield's assets were transferred to another company outside the jurisdiction. This money was then advanced to another company via a solicitor's trust account. These funds were then transferred to the defendant who in turn paid them on to other parties. In reality these transactions were for the benefit of one man who was the major shareholder of Springfield and whose family were the beneficiaries of the trusts where the money ended up. The claim succeeded as the defendants were knowingly involved.

---

[1]   [1994] 3 NZLR 502.

5.76   In *El Ajou v Dollar Land Holdings plc (No 2)*[1] the plaintiff had been defrauded of money. The money concerned ended up being used as part of the finance for a building project in England and a claim was then brought against the building company claiming knowing receipt. It was held that a claim could only succeed if enquiry was not made in a situation where an honest and reasonable man would have done so.

---

[1]   [1995] 2 All ER 213.

5.77 In *Cowan de Groot Properties Ltd v Eagle Trust*[1] a claim was brought following an allegation that the directors of a company had sold some of its property at an undervalue. The purchaser was alleged to have been in knowing receipt. The case is not entirely in line with the others but it does appear to accept the doctrine that a defendant's knowledge will be determined on the basis of what a reasonable person would have learned.

---

[1]   [1992] 4 All ER 700.

Suspicious transaction reports and civil liability

5.78 When deciding on how to interpret suspicious behaviour there are problems in the context of civil liability. In theory it can depend on the party concerned failing to carry out a professional level of 'knowing their client' or failing to report suspicious transactions. In practice we seem dangerously close to being in a situation where the courts impose a constructive trust wherever it suits them in order to recover illicit funds. The solution is for firms to be scrupulous in maintaining the requirements of the law and their professional bodies as minimum. Wherever they are in doubt as to whether to make a suspicious transaction report they should do so. From the point of view of both criminal liability and constructive trusteeship they should be safe. However this last issue can then arise in a secondary way.

5.79 A suspicious transaction report may have been made internally in a firm to its Money Laundering Reporting Officer, or an appropriate report made to either the National Criminal Intelligence Service or the fraud squad. Once this is done it could be argued that the firm is knowingly in receipt of illegal funds. Once a report has been made the firm will normally request permission from the body to whom they made that report before they act further. In most cases this will be the course of action which the criminal law enforcement bodies will prefer, so that they have the opportunity to observe the transaction and the client. There is no risk to the firm from the criminal courts in such cases, but neither is there a guarantee that the knowing receipt issue will cease to be a problem. It is possible that such a firm could still be held to be a constructive trustee, a risk exacerbated by the firm potentially ending up in a catch 22 situation. If they refuse to act on the client's instructions whilst waiting for confirmation from the criminal authorities that they can continue, they may be effectively tipping off the client. If however they act on such instructions they could well be held to be a constructive trustee. Rider suggests[1] that in such cases the safest approach would be to apply to the High Court for a ruling under the RSC Ord 85.

---

[1]   Rider BAK 'The Control of Money Laundering—A Bridge Too Far?' E Financial Services LRev (January/February 1998).

THE WOLFSBERG PRINCIPLES

Why were they created?

5.80   A number of leading banks, acting in co-ordination with Transparency International, have agreed to take on board a set of general principles to facilitate improving the standards applied in combating money laundering where private banking relationships are concerned. They also accepted as a formal principle that the responsibility for this rested with the management of the banks concerned. The Principles (named after the town in Switzerland where the working sessions took place) have been issued in the hope that other financial institutions will follow them.

5.81   Banks and other financial institutions have become increasingly concerned that the enormous quantities of money laundering currently taking place could pose a threat to them. This can come about as a result of bad publicity arising as a result of it becoming publicly known that the institution has been caught laundering money. Even where the bank concerned has maintained good standards there is likely to be damage to reputation where the regulator concerned does not believe that disciplinary steps are warranted. In many cases however they will. There are clear signs that the regulators are becoming both more assertive and more proactive in this field[1].

---

[1]   Financial Times (24 March 2001), p 3.

5.82   The primary motivation in adapting the Principles has been a desire to create a new set of standards which it is hoped will become adopted by an increasing number of financial institutions. In the words of Dr Peter Eigen[1]:

> 'We fully expect that other banks will recognise these guidelines and volunteer to accept them . . . We believe it is essential that internationally active investment firms, brokerage houses, insurance companies, property and asset management firms, fully embrace standards similar to those being announced by the banks.'

---

[1]   Chairman, Transparency International (30 October 2000) see http://www.transparency.org.

---

1   Client acceptance: general guidelines

1.1   General

5.83

> *Bank policy will be to prevent the use of its worldwide operations for criminal purposes. The bank will endeavour to accept only those clients whose source of wealth and funds can be reasonably established to be legitimate. The primary responsibility for this lies with the private banker who sponsors the client for acceptance. Mere fulfilment of internal review procedures does not relieve the private banker of this basic responsibility.*

The obvious aim of this is to deal with the issue of criminals in government who steal and then launder the assets of their country and hide them as a personal investment fund. In addition there are others, particularly criminals involved in the drug trade, illegal arms dealing and people smuggling; to name the most remunerative. The Principle 1.1 has the weakness of only being aimed at private clients. In most instances those wishing to launder large amounts will have no difficulty in establishing a network of companies throughout the world and then get the payments that hit the western banking system to be made out to companies in that group. In the case of corrupt government officials receiving bribes, the bribe will often be paid into a corporate bank account which appears to have no connection with the official in any event.

1.2 Identification

5.84

> *The bank will take reasonable measures to establish the identity of its clients and beneficial owners and will only accept clients when this process has been completed.*

This is perhaps all that can be reasonably be expected of a bank, but the effectiveness of such checks is rather limited due to the relative ease with which false documents and real documents in false names can be obtained. In addition, how does a bank ascertain that the beneficial owner is who they appear to be? It is a relatively straightforward matter for one person to create a false identity or to hide behind the identity of another. A bank cannot become, nor be expected to become, a detective agency. The consequence of this is that Principle 1.2 may give a false sense of security to the bank which has taken this step and to others which deal with it.

1.2.1 CLIENT

5.85

> - *Natural persons: identity will be established to the bank's satisfaction by reference to official identity papers or such other evidence as may be appropriate under the circumstances.*

The problem here is the general availability of good forged documents and the relative ease in which it is possible to obtain documents in the wrong name[1]. Apparently safe identity documents such as passports, national identity cards and driving licences are no real guide to identity. To give an idea of the scale of the problem, in the United Kingdom there are also estimated to be between one and a half million more national insurance numbers being used than should be the case.

---

[1] Haynes 'Anti-Money Laundering Law' in Ed Ashe and Rider *International Tracing of Assets* (1997) pp C1/7–1/9.

5.86

> - *Corporations, partnerships, foundations: the bank will receive documentary evidence of the due organisation and existence.*

This will tend to reduce the number of off the shelf companies created specifically to launder money. However, it may well also accelerate the market in buying small, relatively dormant companies that are a number of years old and less likely to attract suspicion. There is evidence that this has been happening in the West Indies. Recent changes in ownership and radical changes in the financial behaviour of a company following acquisition should thus attract close investigation.

5.87

- *Trusts: the bank will receive appropriate evidence of formation and existence along with identity of the trustees.*

This is going to cause particular problems. It is never going to be possible to be certain whether the trustees are running the trust themselves or as a front for others. In some cases, for example the blind trusts available in Cyprus, the vehicle itself seems to have been designed to facilitate this very state of affairs.

5.88

- *Identification documents must be current at the time of opening.*

1.2.2   BENEFICIAL OWNER

5.89

Beneficial ownership must be established for all accounts. Due diligence must be done on all principal beneficial owners identified in accordance with the following principles:

- *Natural persons: when the account is in the name of an individual, the private banker must establish whether the client is acting on his/her own behalf. If doubt exists, the bank will establish the capacity in which and on whose behalf the accountholder is acting.*

While this is an admirable sentiment it seems difficult to see how this is going to be achieved. Those with large amounts to launder should not find it difficult to hire people to front the transactions they need to engage in. Many of the points made above will also apply here.

5.90

- *Legal entities: where the client is a company, such as a private investment company, the private banker will understand the struc-ture of the company sufficiently to determine the provider of funds, principal owner(s) of the shares and those who have control over the funds, eg the directors and those with the power to give direction to the directors of the company. With regard to other shareholders the private banker will make a reasonable judgment as to the need for further due diligence. This principle applies regardless of whether the share capital is in registered or bearer form.*

Clearly this is an area where experience and staff training could make a vital difference. Does the client's corporate group structure make sense in terms of the business transactions being carried on? If not, may it be explicable in terms of the historical development of the corporate group? If neither is the case then the reaction should be one of suspicion and the banker concerned should contact the Money Laundering Reporting Officer.

5.91   A more difficult problem will apply with investment companies. Namely, whose money is being invested? In the case of well known fund managers and investment companies, 'know your client' provisions will normally suffice. However, in cases of firms who are not already known, 'know your client' is going to involve knowing your client's client; or at least being satisfied as to the intermediary's identity checking requirements.

5.92

- *Trusts: where the client is a trustee, the private banker will understand the structure of the trust sufficiently to determine the provider of funds (eg settlor) those who have control over the funds (eg trustees) and any persons or entities who have the power to remove the trustees. The private banker will make a reasonable judgment as to the need for further due diligence.*

The points made at para 5.87 in relation to beneficial owners will apply here as well.

5.93

- *Unincorporated associations: the above principles apply to unincorporated associations.*

This turns to the issues raised at para 5.87 concerning ascertaining who may be standing behind the party dealing with the bank. No guidance is given as to how this should be done. Indeed, the author has yet to come across guidelines issued by any state that have yet satisfactorily done this. It is perhaps a noble sentiment rather than a realisable objective.

1.2.3   ACCOUNTS HELD IN THE NAME OF MONEY MANAGERS AND SIMILAR INTERMEDIARIES

5.94

The private banker will perform due diligence on the intermediary and establish that the intermediary has a due diligence process for its clients, or a regulatory obligation to conduct such due diligence, that is satisfactory to the bank.

The comments made at para 5.91 in relation to investment companies will also apply here.

1.2.4 POWERS OF ATTORNEY/AUTHORISED SIGNERS

5.95

Where the holder of a power of attorney or another authorised signer is appointed by a client, it is generally sufficient to do due diligence on the client.

1.2.5 Practices for walk-in clients and electronic banking relationships

5.96

> *A bank will determine whether walk-in clients or relationships initiated through electronic channels require a higher degree of due diligence prior to account opening.*

This remains a rather vague suggestion. It might be helpful if the banks could agree a clarification to this Principle to reach an agreed minimum standard. There are a number of variables here. How clearly can the proposed customer prove their identity? In regulatory terms how safe is the country they are based in? In short the fact that they contacted the bank by walking into the branch or by electronic contact is not of importance in itself. The key issue is the context and whether this explains the manner of contact. If it does then the degree of due diligence should not need to be higher than for other customers.

1.3   Due diligence

5.97

> *It is essential to collect and record information covering the following categories:*
>
> •   *Purpose and reasons for opening the account*
>
> •   *Anticipated account activity*
>
> •   *Source of wealth (description of the economic activity which has generated the net worth)*
>
> •   *Estimated net worth*
>
> •   *Source of funds (description of the origin and the means of transfer for monies that are accepted for the account opening)*
>
> •   *References or other sources to corroborate reputation information where available.*
>
> *Unless other measures reasonably suffice to do the due diligence on a client (eg favourable and reliable references), a client will be met prior to account opening.*

This could prove particularly helpful. It is unlikely to assist in spotting suspicious clients or funds at the outset unless the launderers are unusually obtuse. However, it will provide the bank concerned with a context into which to place the client's financial activities. It may well be that in the longer term apparently incongruous payments will be made and thus draw the bank's attention. 'Know your customer' has considerably more potential to lead to laundering being spotted than identity checking on opening an account.

1.4 Oversight responsibility

5.98

> *There will be a requirement that all new clients and new accounts be approved by at least one person other than the private banker.*

This is a useful step. It will reduce the risk of a private client banker being too enthusiastic about getting a new, apparently wealthy client who will presumably be helping him hit his financial targets. It will also reduce the risk of corruption, as a new client wishing to subvert a bank into laundering his funds will not be able to achieve this by bribing just one person. Even so, there is evidence that suggests that a greater number of bankers than one might hope will be willing to engage in illegal activity[1].

---

[1] Rachel Ehrenfeld *Evil Money* (1992) pp 44–47. See also Daily Express, International Edition (23 April 1992).

---

2 Client acceptance: situations requiring additional diligence/attention

2.1 Numbered or alternate name accounts

5.99

> *Numbered or alternate name accounts will only be accepted if the bank has established the identity of the client and the beneficial owner.*

2.2 High-risk countries

5.100

> *The bank will apply heightened scrutiny to clients and beneficial owners resident in and funds sourced from countries identified by credible sources as having inadequate anti-money-laundering standards or representing high-risk for crime and corruption.*

This is a useful step, though it would help if the principles referred to a source where up to date information on this could be obtained from time to time. Perhaps an appendix, updated from time to time, on the Transparency International website, or that of a third party would prove useful.

2.3 Offshore jurisdictions

5.101

> *Risks associated with entities organised in offshore jurisdictions are covered by due diligence procedures laid out in these guidelines.*

2.4 High-risk activities

5.102

> *Clients and beneficial owners whose source of wealth emanates from activities known to be susceptible to money laundering will be subject to heightened scrutiny.*

2.5 Public officials

5.103

> *Individuals who have or have had positions of public trust such as government officials, senior executives of government corporations, politicians, important political party officials, etc and their families and close associates require heightened scrutiny.*

This is a particularly important addition given the unfortunate tendency of political leaders in certain parts of the world to regard their country's national wealth as a personal piggy bank from which monies can be removed at will. It will also make it more complicated for such people to launder such monies, though there are no shortage of methods that they could adopt to disguise what was going on. For example, by utilising fake trading transactions involving state entities.

3   Updating client files

5.104

> *The private banker is responsible for updating the client file on a defined basis and/or when there are major changes. The private banker's supervisor or an independent control person will review relevant portions of client files on a regular basis to ensure consistency and completeness. The frequency of the reviews depends on the size, complexity and risk posed of the relationship.*

4   Practices when identifying unusual or suspicious activities

4.1   Definition of unusual or suspicious activities

5.105

> *The bank will have a written policy on the identification of and follow-up on unusual or suspicious activities. This policy will include a definition of what is considered to be suspicious or unusual and give examples thereof.*
>
> *Unusual or suspicious activities may include:*
>
> - *Account transactions or other activities which are not consistent with the due diligence file*
> - *Cash transactions over a certain amount*
> - *Pass-through/in-and-out-transactions[1].*

---

[1]   For a discussion of how these may be used see Haynes, 'Payable-through accounts and money laundering' Jl Banking L, Vol 11, Issue 1, pp 29–31.

4.2   Identification of unusual or suspicious activities

5.106

> *Unusual or suspicious activities can be identified through:*
>
> - *Monitoring of transactions*
> - *Client contacts (meetings, discussions, in-country visits etc)*
> - *Third party information (eg newspapers, Reuters, internet)*
> - *Private banker's/internal knowledge of the client's environment (eg political situation in his/her country).*

4.3 Follow-up on unusual or suspicious activities

5.107

> *The private banker, management and/or the control function will carry out an analysis of the background of any unusual or suspicious activity. If there is no plausible explanation a decision will be made involving the control function:*
>
> - *To continue the business relationship with increased monitoring*
> - *To cancel the business relationship*
> - *To report the business relationship to the authorities.*
>
> *The report to the authorities is made by the control function and senior management may need to be notified (eg Senior Compliance Officer, CEO, Chief Auditor, General Counsel). As required by local laws and regulations the assets may be blocked and transactions may be subject to approval by the control function.*

These guidelines are very useful. The one troubling element is the suggestion that one of the options is to cancel the business relationship. This will simply warn the client that they have aroused suspicion. Their reaction will be to take their business elsewhere and do a better job of disguising it. If the bank is suspicious it should instead be reporting the matter to the relevant authority and taking their guidance as to whether to continue to act. The regulators will normally want the bank to continue acting, thus giving them the opportunity of watching what is taking place[1]. The only potential outstanding issue that could then arise is where the bank suspected it to be a situation where a true owner might later arrive in pursuit of the funds. This is a distinct possibility where large amounts of funds have been pillaged from a state. The bank's fear will be that they may then be made liable to repay the funds even if they have parted company with them[2]. As discussed above the best course of action in such circumstances is to seek a closed sitting at the appropriate civil court, seeking an order that having made a suspicious transaction report, the bank should continue to act.

---

[1] See 'Civil law issues' at para 5.61 ff.
[2] *Agip (Africa) Ltd v Jackson* [1990] BCC 899.

---

5 Monitoring

5.108

> *A sufficient monitoring program must be in place. The primary responsibility for monitoring account activities lies with the private banker. The private banker will be familiar with significant transactions and increased activity in the account and will be especially aware of unusual or suspicious activities (see 4.1). The bank will decide to what extent fulfilment of these responsibilities will need to be supported through the use of automated systems or other means.*

6   Control responsibilities

5.109

A written control policy will be in place establishing standard control procedures to be undertaken by the various 'control layers' (private banker, independent operations unit, Compliance, Internal Audit). The control policy will cover issues of timing, degree of control, areas to be controlled, responsibilities and follow-up etc.

7   Reporting

5.110

There will be regular management reporting established on money laundering issues (eg number of reports to authorities, monitoring tools, changes in applicable laws and regulations, the number and scope of training sessions provided to employees).

8   Education, training and information

5.111

The bank will establish a training program on the identification and prevention of money laundering for employees who have client contact and for Compliance personnel. Regular training (eg annually) will also include how to identify and follow-up on unusual or suspicious activities. In addition, employees will be informed about any major changes in anti-money-laundering laws and regulations.

All new employees will be provided with guidelines on the anti-money-laundering procedures.

9   Record retention requirements

5.112

The bank will establish record retention requirements for all anti-money-laundering related documents. The documents must be kept for a minimum of five years.

10   Exceptions and deviations

5.113

The bank will establish an exception and deviation procedure that requires risk assessment and approval by an independent unit.

11   Anti-money-laundering organisation

5.114

The bank will establish an adequately staffed and independent department responsible for the prevention of money laundering (eg Compliance, independent control unit, Legal).

Conclusions

5.115 These Principles represent a bold and imaginative step forward. The practical limitations bankers and other financial institutions will find themselves faced with in the situations concerned are largely unavoidable. However, it is hoped that an increasing number of financial institutions will adopt the Principles and that this will assist in the struggle to stop the world's financial systems being used to launder illegal funds.

5.116 Reinout van Lennep, head of ABN Amro private banking, recently went on record as saying[1]:

'These principles reflect decent and adequate standards; we neither expect nor wish to see the standards being raised higher.'

The experience of banks since statutory requirements were first brought in during the mid 1980's, suggests that this may be optimistic.

---

[1] See http://www.moneyunlimited.co.uk.

Chapter 6   Customer Relations

Peter Bibby

INTRODUCTION

6.1   The rules relating to the relationships between firms and their customers are to be found principally in the Conduct of Business source book (COB). Essentially COB replaces the Conduct of Business rules previously found in the rulebooks of the Self Regulating Organisations (SROs) (IMRO, SFA and PIA). COB primarily applies in relation to regulated activities, conducted by firms which fall within the definition of designated investment business[1]. COB therefore has only limited application to deposits, pure protection contracts and general insurance contracts[2]. The provisions of COB are at a level of detail which underpin the relevant customer focussed Principles for Businesses[3].

---

[1]   Designated investment business is any one of the activities specified in the Financial Services and Markets Act 2000 (Regulated Activities) Order 2001, SI 2001/544, Pt II (Regulated Activities Order 2001), carried on by way of business. In short, this includes dealing, arranging deals, managing, safeguarding and administering, sending dematerialised instructions, causing such instructions to be sent, establishing operating or winding-up a collective investment scheme, acting as trustee of an authorised unit trust, acting as depository or sole director of an Open Ended Investment Company (OEIC), establishing, operating or winding-up a stakeholder scheme, advising on investments.
[2]   *Deposit*—In summary: a sum of money (other than one excluded by any of the Regulated Activities Order 2001, SI 2001/544, art 6–9) paid on terms: (a) under which it will be repaid, with or without interest or a premium, and either on demand or at a time or in circumstances agreed by or on behalf of the person making the payment and the person receiving it; and (b) which are not referable to the provision of property (other than currency) or services or the giving of security. Money is paid on terms which are referable to the provision of property or services or the giving of security if, and only if: (a) it is paid by way of advance or part payment under a contract for the sale, hire or other provision of property or services, and is repayable only in the event that the property or services is or are not in fact sold, hired or otherwise provided; or (b) it is paid by way of security for the performance of a contract or by way of security in respect of loss which may result from the non-performance of a contract; or (c) without prejudice to (b), it is paid by way of security for the delivery up or return of any property, whether in a particular state of repair or otherwise.
    Pure protection contract—A long-term insurance contract in respect of which the following conditions are met: (a) the benefits under the contract are payable only on death or in respect of incapacity due to injury, sickness or infirmity; (b) the contract provides that benefits are payable on death (other than death due to an accident) only where the death occurs within ten years of the date on which the life of a person in question was first insured under the contract, or where the death occurs before that person attains a specified age not exceeding 70 years; (c) the contract has no surrender value, or the consideration consists of a single premium and the surrender value does not exceed that premium; (d) the contract makes no provision for its conversation or extension in a manner which would result in it ceasing to comply with any of (a), (b) or (c); and (e) the contract is not a reinsurance contract.
    General insurance contract—Any contract of insurance within the Regulated Activities Order 2001, SI 2001/544, Sch 1, Pt 1 (contracts of general insurance), namely: (a) accident (para 1); (b) sickness (para 2); (c) land vehicles (para 3); (d) railway rolling stock (para 4); (e) aircraft

(para 5); (f) ships (para 6); (g) goods in transit (para 7); (h) fire and natural forces (para 8); (i) damage to property (para 9); (j) motor vehicle liability (para 10); (k) aircraft liability (para 11); (l) liability of ships (para 12); (m) general liability (para 13); (n) credit (para 14); (o) suretyship (para 15); (p) miscellaneous financial loss (para 16); (q) legal expenses (para 17); (r) assistance (para 18).

³   In particular—Principle 6 (customer interests): a firm must pay due regard to the interests of its customers and treat them fairly. Principle 7 (communications with clients): a firm must pay due regard to the information needs of its clients and communicate information to them in a way which is clear, fair and not misleading. Principle 8 (conflicts of interest): a firm must manage conflicts of interest fairly, both between itself and its customers and between a customer and another client. Principle 9 (customer relationships of trust): a firm must take reasonable care to ensure the suitability of its advice and discretionary decisions for any customer who is entitled to rely upon its judgment. Principle 10 (clients' assets): a firm must arrange adequate protection for clients' assets when it is responsible for them.

6.2   The regulatory framework seeks to provide a level of protection that is appropriate to the type of investor a firm is dealing with and the rules provide a comprehensive system for the classification of investors. This system of investor classification works:

(1)   by defining what is and is not a customer;
(2)   by drawing a distinction between different classes of customer; and
(3)   by applying specific rules to that class of customer.

   The category into which an investor falls determines which rules apply. Of particular importance is the distinction between private and intermediate customers, since COB compels firms to provide a much greater degree of protection to the former.

6.3   Where relevant to customer relationships, this chapter examines the appropriate sections of the Financial Services and Markets Act 2000 (FSMA 2000), as well as COB together with the Principles for Businesses. In considering the relations between a firm and its customers, this chapter covers:

(1)   categories of client;
(2)   private and intermediate customers;
(3)   execution-only customers;
(4)   conflicts of interest;
(5)   communicating with customers;
(6)   terms of business and client agreements;
(7)   exclusion clauses;
(8)   suitability;
(9)   standards of advice for packaged products;
(10) customer understanding of risk;
(11) suitability letters;
(12) product particulars and key features;
(13) cancellation rights;
(14) dealing;
(15) churning and switching;
(16) transaction reporting;
(17) charges, commission and disclosure of remuneration.

Territorial application

6.4 COB 1.4 sets out the territorial application of COB. In general the whole of COB will apply to an activity which falls within the definition of designated investment business carried on from an establishment maintained by the firm or its appointed representative in the UK. In general, where the activity is carried on with or for a client in the UK but not from an establishment maintained by the firm or its appointed representative in the UK such that it would not be regarded as carried on in the UK then only certain parts of COB will apply (COB 5.5.7 and 5.5.8 relating to overseas business and COB 6.5, 6.7 and 6.8 in relation to long-term insurance business carried on for a customer habitually resident in the UK). There are particular provisions for business carried on by a UK firm from an outwardly pass-ported branch. These provide that for an ISD firm the provisions of COB 9 client assets will apply together with COB 5.5.7 and COB 6.5, 6.7 and 6.8 where relevant.

Transitional provisions

6.5 There are detailed transitional provisions concerning COB. These are necessary because COB replaces the pre-existing SRO rule books. These are to be found in the Transitional Rules for pre-N2 and ex-s 43 (ie of the FSA 1986) firms (TR 1–3). Transitional Rules for ex-RPB firms are found in TR 4 (these are not covered in detail in this chapter). The transitional rules take three distinct forms:

(1) extra time provisions—in general these provide firms with additional time until 30 June 2002 (or for ex-s 43 firms 12 months from commencement) to complete preparations for the impact of certain COB rules;

(2) technical timing provisions—to cover such things as reporting to clients, postponing the impact of these provisions in relation to periods that span N2;

(3) timeless saving provisions—these give indefinite relief to firms allowing them to rely on such things as pre-existing terms of business and client agreements.

It is not the purpose of this chapter to look at the transitional provisions.

The regulations and customer redress

6.6 As noted above at para 6.1 the detailed COB rules underpin the customer focussed Principles for Businesses. There is a distinction between the Principles and the COB rules which is significant in the event that a 'private investor' takes legal action under the FSMA 2000, s 150 (in summary the replacement for the FSA 1986, s 62). The Principles do not give rise to any right of action under the FSMA 2000, s 150 for a private investor, although a private investor can rely on breaches of the underlying COB rules. The Principles can, however, be used by the FSA in taking disciplinary action against an authorised person and, if appropriate, an approved person[1]. In any case, both the Principles and COB, where relevant to customer relationships, are considered in this chapter.

¹   The FSMA 2000, s 66 provides that action may be taken by the FSA against an approved person if that person is guilty of misconduct and the authority is satisfied that it is appropriate in all the circumstances to take action. Misconduct includes knowing concern in a contravention by a relevant authorised person of a requirement under the FSMA 2000. Requirements under the FSMA 2000 on an authorised person include the Principles for Businesses. For an approved person misconduct includes breaching one of the Statements of Principle for Approved Persons.

THE DIFFERENT CATEGORIES OF CLIENT

6.7   The term client includes any person with, or for whom, a firm conducts or intends to conduct designated investment business or any other regulated activity[1]. The majority of COB however provide protection to customers. There is a separate regime for inter-professional business, ie that carried on between market counterparties[2] where the only provisions of COB that apply are:

(1)   Chinese walls (COB 2.4);
(2)   client classification (COB 4.1);
(3)   personal account dealing (COB 7.13)[3].

¹   The glossary of terms in the *FSA Handbook* includes a detailed definition of client.
²   See definition at para 6.20.
³   Not covered in this chapter as it relates to the relationship between employers and employees and not between firms and customers.

The definition of customer

6.8   The starting point when analysing the requirements imposed by COB is to identify whether the client with whom the firm is dealing satisfies the definition of customer. If the entity does not fall within the definition of customer, then minimal obligations under the rules are owed. If the firm is dealing with a customer, the application of the COB rules differs according to whether that customer is classified as a private or intermediate customer.

6.9   A 'customer', as defined by COB, essentially means any person with whom an authorised firm conducts designated investment business other than a market counterparty. A customer can be a natural person or a body corporate. It may be that a firm conducts designated investment business with a trustee acting on behalf of a trust or a partner acting on behalf of a partnership. Trusts and partnerships are customers only in so far as the individual trustee or partner has authority to bind its fellows.

Classification of client

6.10   Under COB 4.1.4 a firm is required to take reasonable steps to establish whether a client is a private customer, an intermediate customer or a market counterparty before it conducts any designated investment business with or for the client.

6.11   The definition of client in COB includes:

(1)   a potential client;

(2)   a client of an appointed representative;

(3)   a person for whom an agent acts or in certain circumstances the agent himself;

(4)   a collective investment scheme—even if it does not have a separate legal personality.

Potential client

6.12   The inclusion of a potential client in the definition of client means that a firm must comply with the rules governing that type of client when marketing investment services. This is also consistent with the Regulated Activities Order 2001, SI 2001/544[1] which includes agreeing to undertake regulated activities within its ambit as a regulated activity.

---

[1]   Regulated Activities Order, SI 2001/544, art 64.

Client of an appointed representative

6.13   A client of an appointed representative of a firm is treated under COB as a client of the principal firm. This is because the firm accepts responsibility under the FSMA 2000, s 39 for specified investment business transacted by the appointed representative. The FSMA 2000, s 39 makes clear that anything done or omitted by an appointed representative as respects business for which the firm has accepted responsibility is to be treated as having been done or omitted by the firm in determining whether the firm has complied with the FSMA 2000 or provisions made under it (that includes in determining whether the firm has complied with COB). Therefore a firm has a responsibility for ensuring its appointed representatives properly classify their clients before undertaking any designated investment business for the client.

Clients for whom agents act

6.14   COB amends the regime that previously existed with regard to the firm's dealings with agent's and to whom duties are owed by a firm. Under the IMRO and SFA rules, the definition of customer included an 'indirect customer'. This was relevant where a firm was dealing with an agent. If the agent disclosed the identity of the principal for whom he acted, the principal became an indirect customer for the firm. If the identity of the principal for whom the agent acted remained undisclosed, then the agent was treated as the customer. Firms were therefore required to consider relations with an agent and decide to whom the obligations were owed and the nature and extent of those obligations.

6.15   Where an IMRO or SFA firm was dealing with an agent acting on behalf of a disclosed principal, particular provisions applied under the rules. Under the SFA rules, a firm providing investment services to an identified principal represented by another authorised firm was required to treat the disclosed principal as his customer, unless there was a written agreement to the contrary between the two firms. Therefore, if the disclosed principal was a private customer, the protections for a private customer would be required.

6.16   Under the IMRO rules, there was wider scope for the treatment of an agent as the customer. A firm could treat the agent rather than the identified principal as customer if the agent was reasonably believed to be an authorised person for the purposes of the FSA 1986 or the Investment Services Directive (ISD[1]); or the agent had refused to answer the firm's enquiries about its principal; or the agent, not being a European investment firm, did not carry on investment business in the UK and the main purpose of the arrangements between the parties was not the avoidance of duties which the firm would otherwise owe to the identified principal.

---

[1]   Council Directive 93/22/EEC on investment services in the securities field (10 May 1993).

6.17   Under the PIA adopted FIMBRA rules, a former FIMBRA member dealing with the agent of a private customer did not need to comply with the rules for private customers where the firm believed the obligations owed to that customer would be met by the agent.

6.18   Under COB the position is now consolidated. Where a firm is aware that the person with or for whom it is conducting designated investment business or related ancillary activities is acting as agent for another person then the agent will be the client of the firm if:

(1)   the agent is another authorised person or is a person authorised in another EEA state by a competent authority or in any country or territory by a body with responsibility for supervision of regulated or financial services which is a member of IOSCO; or
(2)   the agent is any other person provided that avoidance of duties which would otherwise be owed to the principal is not the main purpose of the arrangements between the parties;

Point (1) above will not apply if the firm has agreed in writing with the principal that it will treat him as its customer. In such a case or in a case which falls outside point (2) above (ie where avoidance of provision of duties is the main purpose) then the principal will be the client and the duties owed by the firm will depend on the classification of the principal.

6.19   In cases where the agent is the client then the firm is likely to be dealing on a market counterparty to market counterparty basis (but see the section below on classification of another firm or an overseas financial services institution[1]). The change in the COB rules therefore has been to bring in a presumption that the firm will treat the agent as its client except where there is an agreement to the contrary.

---

[1]   See para 6.25.

Investors falling outside the definition of customer

6.20 Market counterparties are clients but are excluded from the definition of customer. Market counterparties are governments including government bodies and agencies; national monetary authorities; supranationals whose members are countries or central banks or monetary authorities; state investment banks charged with intervening in or managing public debt; another firm or overseas financial institution unless the firm or overseas financial institution is classed as an intermediate customer for that purpose (COB 4.1.7[1]); an associate of a firm (except an OPS firm) or overseas financial institution if it consents; a large intermediate customer when classified as a market counterparty. The definition excludes a collective investment scheme and a person who would be a market counterparty but who under COB 4.1.14 is classed as a private customer[2].

---

[1] See para 6.25.
[2] See para 6.24.

Large intermediate customers

6.21 As noted above, entities that would otherwise be classified as large intermediate customers[1] may in certain circumstances be classified as market counterparties. In order to classify a large intermediate customer as a market counterparty the firm must, before commencing business with the client on a market counterparty basis have:

(1) advised the client in writing that he is being classified as a market counterparty;
(2) given a written warning to the client of the protections he will lose under the regulatory system.

Where the client is a body corporate which is a large intermediate customer due to its size, then the firm must take reasonable steps to ensure the written notices have been delivered to a person authorised to take a decision for the client on its classification. Further, the firm must not have been notified by the client that the client objects to being classified as a market counterparty.

---

[1] See explanation at para 6.33.

6.22 For other large intermediate customers[1], the firm must obtain the client's written consent or otherwise be able to demonstrate that consent has been given to being treated as a market counterparty.

---

[1] Non-body corporates such as local or public authorities; partnerships or unincorporated associations with net assets of at least £10 million; a trustee of a trust (other than an occupation pension scheme (OPS); small self administered scheme (SSAS), or stakeholder pension scheme) with assets of £10 million; a trustee of an OPS, SSAS or stakeholder pension scheme where the trust has, or has had at any time in the past two years at least 50 members and assets under management of at least £10 million.

Trust beneficiaries

6.23   Where investment services are provided to a trust, it is the trustee in a personal capacity who must be treated as a customer. Although the classification of the trust will depend on its size and the nature of its business, this reflects the position under trust law whereby a trustee owes, and can be held accountable for, a duty to beneficiaries. Under the rules, the interests of beneficiaries are protected by requirements that investments be suitable for the purposes disclosed by the trustee.

Market counterparty as a private customer

6.24   COB provides flexibility for firms which only wish to deal with private customers to treat any client (including an intermediate customer or a market counterparty—other than another firm or an overseas financial services institution) as a private customer. The advantage of this for a firm is that it can apply the same systems and processes to all its customer base. The disadvantage for the client is that it may receive protections (such as suitability and best execution) that it does not want and does not wish to pay for. The remedy for the client is to find a firm which is prepared to deal with it as a market counterparty or intermediate customer. To treat a market counterparty or intermediate customer as a private customer the firm must notify the client and explain to that customer that they may not necessarily have rights under the Financial Ombudsman Service or the Financial Services Compensation Scheme because the definition of private customer for eligibility does not include those given private customer status voluntarily.

Classification of another firm or an overseas financial services institution

6.25   A firm or an overseas financial services institution will be a market counterparty of another firm unless it is classified as an intermediate customer under COB 4.1.7. COB 4.1.7 provides that it will be an intermediate customer if the firm (ie the classifying firm) is carrying on what would be inter professional business and the other firm or overseas financial services institution is:

(1)   acting for an underlying customer;
(2)   has decided that to protect that customer it requires itself to have the protections of an intermediate customer; and
(3)   the firm and it have agreed that it will be classified as an intermediate customer when it is acting for that underlying customer or in all circumstances where it acts on behalf of customers.

6.26   It should be noted that the classifying firm can refuse to classify another firm or overseas financial services institution as an intermediate customer and it would then be necessary for the firm or overseas financial services institution to approach another firm that is prepared to provide those protections. This provides the same degree of flexibility to those firms which only wish to deal with market counterparties as is provided to those firms which only wish to deal with private customers.

6.27 When the business transacted is not inter professional business, ie it is not business covered by the inter professional regime then the firm or overseas financial services institution will be an intermediate customer provided it has not indicated that it is acting on its own behalf in relation to that activity, or it is a long-term insurer acting on behalf of its life fund. If the firm or overseas financial services institution is a regulated collective investment scheme it will be a private customer and if it is an unregulated collective investment scheme it will be an intermediate customer.

Corporate finance

6.28 Like the IMRO and SFA rules, COB do not require firms to comply with all the rules for customers where they are carrying on 'corporate finance business', as defined in the FSA Glossary of definitions (the Glossary). Where a firm is carrying on corporate finance business, as defined in the glossary then the only COB rules that apply are COB:

Chapter 1	Application and general provisions.
Chapter 2.1	Clear, fair and not misleading communication.
Chapter 2.2	Inducements and soft commission.
Chapter 2.3	Reliance on others.
Chapter 2.4	Chinese walls.
Chapter 2.5	Exclusion of liability.
Chapter 3	Financial promotion.
Chapter 4.1	Client classification.
Chapter 5.3	Suitability.
Chapter 5.4	Customers understanding of risks.
Chapter 7.1	Conflict of interest and material interest.
Chapter 7.12	Customer order and execution records.
Chapter 7.13	Personal account dealing.
Chapter 9	Client assets.

6.29 Commonly in corporate finance business, business services are provided to clients that wish to raise funds or take over other entities. As part of those services the firm is likely to be involved in preparing documents for issue to individuals or entities with a view to raising finance or proposing the sale and purchase of share capital and may carry on designated investment business with those individuals or entities as a result of the corporate finance business carried on for its client. In such circumstances, those individuals or entities will not be clients of the firm provided certain requirements are fulfilled. These requirements are that:

(1) the firm does not behave in such a way towards the individual or entity to lead him to believe he is being treated as a client; and

(2) the firm clearly indicates to the individual or entity that it is not acting for him and will not be responsible for providing protections that clients of the firm would otherwise receive and will not be advising him on the relevant transaction.

6.30 Accordingly, the firm will owe no specific obligations under the rules to those individuals, persons or entities. The firm will however be required to comply with provisions relating, for instance, to any financial promotions that it may issue to those firms or entities.

THE DEFINITION OF PRIVATE AND INTERMEDIATE CUSTOMERS

6.31   When a firm has established that the client concerned falls within the definition of customer, the exact application of COB will depend on whether the firm is dealing with a private or an intermediate customer. Where the firm is dealing with a private customer then full protection under the rules applies. If the customer is an intermediate customer, then certain rules are disapplied, or apply in modified terms.

Distinction between private and intermediate customers

6.32   Intermediate customers are clients who are not market counterparties[1] and who fall within the following categories:

(1)   a local authority or public authority;
(2)   a body corporate whose shares have been listed or admitted to trading on any EEA exchange;
(3)   a body corporate whose shares have been listed or admitted to trading on the primary board of any IOSCO member country official exchange;
(4)   a body corporate (including a limited liability partnership) which (including any holding company or subsidiary) has (or did have at any time in the preceding two years) called up share capital or net assets of £5 million or more (or its equivalent in any other currency at the relevant time);
(5)   a special purpose vehicle;
(6)   a partnership or unincorporated association which has or had at any time in the previous two years net assets of £5 million (or its equivalent in any other currency at the relevant time) and calculated in the case of a limited partnership without deducting loans owed to the partners;
(7)   a trustee of a trust (other than an OPS, SSAS or stakeholder pension scheme) which has (or had at any time during the previous two years) assets of £10 million or more (before deducting liabilities);
(8)   a trustee of an OPS, SSAS or stakeholder pension scheme where the trust has (or has had during the previous two years): (i) at least 50 members; and (ii) assets under management of at least £10 million;
(9)   another firm or an overseas financial services institution classed as an intermediate customer under COB 4.1.7[2];
(10)   a client classed as an intermediate customer under COB 4.1.9 as an expert private customer[3].

---

[1]   See section on market counterparties at para 6.20.
[2]   See section on classification of another firm or overseas financial services institution at para 6.25.
[3]   See paras 6.35–6.42.

6.33   A regulated collective investment scheme is excluded from the definition of intermediate customer and is a private customer. A client who would be an intermediate customer may be classed as a market counterparty if a large intermediate customer[1]. Note also that any client (other than another firm or an overseas financial services institution) may be classified as a private customer under COB 4.1.14[2].

---

[1]   A large intermediate customer is a client (other than a firm or an overseas financial services institution) who may be classified as a market counterparty if: (i) it is a body corporate (including limited liability partnership) with a called up share capital of £10 million; (ii) it is a body corporate with a balance sheet total of €12.5 million or a net turnover of €25 million or an average of 250 employees during the year; (iii) it is a local or public authority; (iv) it is a partnership or unincorporated association with net assets of £10 million; (v) it is a trustee of a trust (other than OPS, SSAS or stakeholder) with assets of £10 million; and (vi) it is a trustee of an OPS, SSAS, or stakeholder with (either at the time or during the past two years) at least 50 members and assets of £10 million. See also para 6.21.
[2]   See para 6.24.

Treating large intermediate customers as a market counterparty

6.34   A firm may treat a large intermediate customer as a market counterparty if before commencing business with the client it advises the client that it will be classified as a market counterparty; has given a written warning of the protections that will be lost under the regulatory system and has provided the necessary notices in the appropriate way to the customer[1].

---

[1]   For further details see section 'large intermediate customers' at para 6.21.

Expert private customer

6.35   In a similar way to the SRO Rules, COB provides for expert private customers to be treated as intermediate customers. This permits firms to provide such experts more limited protection than they would receive as private customers.

6.36   Under COB 4.1.9 a client who would otherwise be a private customer, may be classified as an intermediate customer if:

(1)   the firm has taken reasonable care to determine that the client has sufficient experience and understanding to waive the protections afforded to private customers and to be treated as an intermediate customer; and
(2)   the client has been given a clear written warning of the loss of regulatory protection; and
(3)   the client has been given sufficient time to consider the implications of being treated as an intermediate customer; and
(4)   the firm has obtained the client's written consent to be treated as an intermediate customer or the firm is otherwise able to demonstrate that informed consent has been given.

Assessing expertise

6.37   The test for assessing expertise has not altered under the new system and reflects that previously found in the IMRO and SFA Rules. The IMRO and SFA rules provided guidance when assessing a customer's experience.

COB guidance indicates that the client's knowledge and understanding of the nature and suitability of the investment and investment service, including the ability to understand the inherent risks are factors to be considered. Likewise COB repeats the SFA guidance by making it clear that the firm should also consider the customer's financial standing and the length of time he has been active in the relevant market, the frequency of dealings and the size and nature of transactions previously undertaken.

6.38   Where an individual is classed as an intermediate customer by reason of his expertise in certain types of investments, then that classification must be specific to the type of investment concerned. Accordingly, just because an individual may deal regularly in equities, and can validly be classified as an expert and be invited to be treated as an intermediate customer for the purpose of equities, this would not itself be sufficient experience for the firm to invite him to be treated as an expert in respect of other securities.

Warning for expert customers

6.39   COB 4.1.11 is an evidential provision[1] that describes the written warning that a private customer should be given before being treated as an intermediate customer by reason of his expertise. The evidential guidance states that the warning given to the customer should draw attention to the protections which will be lost. The rules about which the firm should provide a warning are those concerning financial promotions under COB 3; understanding risk under COB 5; charges and information about remuneration under COB 5; information about packaged products and standard of advice on packaged products under COB 6. Margin requirements under COB 7 and non-exchange traded securities under COB 7.

---

[1]   Where a firm fails to comply with an evidential provision then this will tend to establish a breach of the underlying COB rule.

6.40   In addition to the protections that are lost, the warning should explain the consequences to the client of the rules which are modified in their application to intermediate customers. These are COB 3 (financial promotion); COB 5.1 (status disclosure and polarisation); COB 8.1 (confirmation of transactions) and COB 8.2 (periodic statements). Certain rules are capable of modification in their application to intermediate customers and the warning should explain the possible consequences of modification under COB 7.5 (best execution); COB 9.1 (custody); and COB 9.3 (client money).

6.41   The firm should also warn that, if the customer is classified as an intermediate customer by reason of experience and understanding, he will lose access to the Financial Ombudsman Service (FOS) and that when assessing the requirements of fair, clear and not misleading, the firm may take account of the clients' expertise. In practice this means that in communicating with the customer the firm may assume a greater level of knowledge and understanding than would otherwise be the case.

Review of classification

6.42 Under COB 4.1.15, where a firm treats a private customer as an intermediate customer under COB 4.1.9 (expert private customer) or treats a large intermediate as a market counterparty under COB 4.1.12 then it must review the classification annually. Where no designated investment business has been carried on for a year then the review can be deferred until the next piece of business is undertaken.

Records

6.43 Records of classification including sufficient information to support the classification must be kept for three years after the firm has ceased carrying on business for the client unless it is a pension transfer, opt out or Free Standing Additional Voluntary Contribution (FSAVC) when the records must be kept indefinitely or a life policy or pension contract when the records must be kept for six years.

EXECUTION-ONLY CUSTOMERS

6.44 COB recognise that certain rules will not be appropriate where the service to be provided is limited to merely carrying out the instructions of a customer. There are many examples of this such as dealing-only share services or instructions to a firm to arrange a life policy, the terms of which are specified by the customer. Such transactions are deemed 'execution-only' and many rules are disapplied for execution-only customers. This is the case whether the firm is acting on an execution-only basis for a private or intermediate customer.

What is an execution-only customer?

6.45 There is no definition of an execution-only customer in COB. The focus therefore needs to be on the transaction. The essential element in classifying a transaction as execution-only is that the customer is not relying on the firm for any advice or judgment about the merits of an investment. Accordingly, no investment advice may be given if the transaction is to be properly classified as execution-only. In the case of an execution-only transaction, a firm may wish to obtain written confirmation of the instruction from the customer in order to support its classification as execution-only.

It should be noted that, because certain rules are disapplied in the case of execution-only transactions, the protection available to customers in those circumstances are more limited.

CONFLICTS OF INTEREST

6.46 COB 7.1 concerns conflicts of interest. It applies when the firm is conducting designated investment business with or for a customer. It does not therefore apply when dealing with a market counterparty. Conflicts of interest rules apply where a firm is undertaking corporate finance business. The rules underpin the general requirements of Principle 8 of the Principles for Businesses on conflicts of interest which requires a firm to manage conflicts of interest fairly.

6.47   If an authorised firm has a material interest in a transaction to be entered into with or for a customer, or a conflict of interest when providing investment services for customers, it must take reasonable steps to ensure fair treatment for the customer (COB 7.1.3).

6.48   COB 7.1.4 is an evidential provision that provides four ways in which firms may manage conflicts of interest. These are: disclosure; a policy of independence; by establishing internal rules of confidentiality—such as 'Chinese walls'; or by declining to act for the customer. As this is an evidential provision then failure to adopt one of these approaches where there is a relevant conflict of interest will tend to establish a breach of the rule on fair treatment as it will tend to show that the firm has not taken reasonable steps to ensure fair treatment.

What is covered by the conflict of interest rules?

6.49

(1)   A material interest in a transaction to be entered into with or for a customer. A material interest arises where, for example, the firm acts as principal, or deals in issues which the firm has underwritten. Commission on a transaction that will, in any case, be disclosed by a firm and benefits arising under soft commission agreements are specifically excluded from the definition of material interests.

(2)   A relationship that may give rise to a conflict in respect of a transaction to be entered into with a customer.

(3)   An interest in a transaction that may be in conflict with the interest of any of the firm's customers.

(4)   Customers with conflicting interests in a transaction.

Disclosure to customers

6.50   COB 7.1.5 and 7.1.6 explain the position on disclosure to customers. COB 7.1.5 is an evidential provision which gives examples of material interests that should be disclosed. These include dealing in investments as principal; dealing in investments as agent for more than one party; recommending purchase or sale of an investment where one of the firms' customers has given instructions to buy or sell or where the firm has a long or short position; or acting as broker fund adviser. COB 7.1.6 is a further evidential provision concerning the manner in which disclosure should be made. This provides that disclosure of any material interest or conflict should be given orally or in writing (possibly in customer documentation) before a transaction or an exercise of discretion for that customer. The firm also needs to be able to show it has taken reasonable steps to ensure that the customer does not object to the material interest or conflict.

Policy of independence

6.51 COB 7.1.7 is guidance which provides details of what form a policy of independence may take. If a firm relies on a policy of independence then the policy should:

(1)   require the relevant employee to disregard the material interest or the conflict of interest in giving advice or exercising discretion for the customer. Essentially, this means that the employee must act as if the interest does not exist when carrying out the transaction;

(2)   be recorded in writing and made known to the employee (an ad hoc unwritten application of independence will not be sufficient);

(3)   be disclosed to a private customer stating that the firm may have a material interest or conflict of interest relating to the transaction or service concerned. The disclosure may be made once at the start of the relationship with the private customer.

If a firm wishes to rely on a policy of independence then the key is to ensure that the policy is written down and known to employees.

Internal arrangements

6.52 A firm may manage a conflict of interest by using a Chinese wall[1]. That is an internal arrangement restricting the movement of information within a firm. The essence of a Chinese wall is that it may prevent information held within the firm about a client or potential transaction from being used for the benefit of a customer. For instance Chinese walls will often be established between the corporate finance and client advisory parts of the business. This will ensure that forthcoming deals on the corporate finance side do not influence advice given to clients. A Chinese wall established to meet the requirements of COB 2.4.4(1) provides a defence against action by a customer under the FSMA 2000, s 150 or enforcement action by the FSA based on a breach of a relevant requirement to disclose or use information. Further COB 2.4.6 provides that where the application of a COB rule depends on whether a firm has knowledge, then the firm will not be taken to have that knowledge if none of the relevant individuals in the firm act with knowledge because of the existence of a Chinese wall under COB 2.4.4. Acting in conformity with a Chinese wall under COB 2.4.4(1) provides a defence to proceedings under the FSMA 2000, s 397(2) or (3) (misleading statements and practices). Acting in conformity with COB 2.4.4 is also stated not to amount to market abuse.

---

[1]   See COB 2.4.

6.53 The effect of a Chinese wall will be to limit the individuals within a firm who have knowledge. Therefore if the adviser to a customer does not have information because of the Chinese wall there will be no conflict to disclose or to exercise a policy of independence in respect of.

Declining to act

6.54 If a firm determines that it is unable to manage a conflict of interest using one of the above methods then it should decline to act.

Broker fund adviser

6.55   Where the conflict arises in relation to a broker fund then COB 7.1.10 provides that in addition to the provisions of COB 7.1.3 (fair treatment) the firm must obtain an acknowledgement from any private customer that he understands the dual role of the broker fund adviser as adviser to the private customer and to the operator of the fund.

COMMUNICATING WITH CUSTOMERS

6.56   Firms must comply with specific rules under COB 2.1 when communicating with customers. The specific rules are consistent with the more general requirements imposed by Principle 7 which provides: 'A firm must pay due regard to the information needs of its clients and communicate information to them in a way which is clear, fair and not misleading'.

Communication to be fair and not misleading

6.57   The basic requirement is for communications to be clear, fair and not misleading. This covers not only the wording of a communication but also the manner in which it is presented. For instance, where the investment contains a degree of risk then that risk should be given equal prominence to the reward that may be achieved through good performance.

6.58   In communicating with customers, COB require a firm to take reasonable steps to communicate in a manner that is clear, fair and not misleading. The rule extends to all communications with customers which are not caught by the financial promotion regime[1]. In considering what constitutes clear, fair and not misleading the firm should take account of the customer's knowledge of the designated investment business to which the information relates. This means that if the customer is a private customer classed as an intermediate by virtue of expertise then a different (and lower) standard will be applied in assessing the communication than if the customer were a private customer.

---

[1]   See COB, Chapter 3.

Disclosure of polarisation status

6.59   Polarisation was one of the main concepts of the rules introduced by the FSA 1986 and requires firms selling packaged products to private customers to adopt one of two roles, either that of product provider or independent intermediary. 'Packaged products' are broadly defined as life policies, units in regulated collective investment schemes and investment trust savings schemes. This distinction is still relevant although the FSA is currently reviewing how efficient the distinction is in delivering customer protection.

6.60 Polarisation means that product provider firms must restrict recommendations of packaged products to those available from the firm and any marketing group, while independent firms which do not issue their own products, must offer independent advice on packaged products available from all product providers. In short, firms selling packaged products must be 'tied' or independent.

6.61 Authorised firms must disclose their polarisation status to customers only when advising on 'packaged products'. The requirement to make the disclosure applies only when dealing with private customers. Firms can make the disclosure in any manner, written or verbal. The disclosure is to be made on first contact with a private customer by an independent intermediary or a provider firm. Further details of the requirements in respect of packaged products can be found below[1].

---

[1]   See para 6.107 on 'standards of advice for packaged products'.

TERMS OF BUSINESS AND CLIENT AGREEMENTS

6.62   COB require, with limited exceptions, firms to issue terms of business to a customer before providing investment services. In certain cases firms are required to enter into client agreements with private customers. There are detailed provisions in COB concerning the content of agreements and terms of business. The type of agreement and the circumstances in which it is required will be determined by the investment services to be provided and whether the firm is dealing with a private or intermediate customer.

Terms of business

6.63   Terms of business are required to be provided by a firm to a customer with which or for whom it is intending to, or does, conduct designated investment business unless it falls within an exception[1]. COB 4.2.5 provides that the terms of business (including where appropriate client agreement) must set out the basis on which the designated investment business is to be conducted. Where the business is with or for a specific private customer then terms of business must be provided before any business is conducted unless the business relates to a stakeholder pension scheme or an ISA where the customer has made an oral offer in which case it must be provided within five business days of the offer. Where the customer is an intermediate customer (which could include an expert who would otherwise be a private customer[2]) then the terms of business must be provided within a reasonable period of the firm beginning to conduct designated investment business with or for the customer.

It should be remembered that market counterparties, and certain corporate finance investors fall outside the definition of customer and firms are not required by the rules to issue terms of business to them.

---

[1]   See para 6.66.
[2]   See earlier section at para 6.35 on expert private customers.

Client agreements

6.64 In certain circumstances, COB requires the terms of business to take the form of a client agreement. COB 4.2.7 provides that where a firm intends to conduct, with a private customer, designated investment business involving:

(1)   managing investments on a discretionary basis;
(2)   contingent liability investments;
(3)   stock lending;
(4)   designated investment business involving underwriting;

then it must do so under a client agreement. A client agreement is defined as terms of business which have been signed by the private customer or to which the private customer has consented in writing.

6.65 Discretionary management means that the firm is able to acquire, or dispose of, assets on behalf of a customer without reference to him and is the regulated activity specified in the Regulated Activities Order 2001, SI 2001/544, art 37.

Contingent liability investments are any investments in a derivative such as an option, future or contract for difference, where the client may be required to make further payments upon completion or earlier closing out of the position.

Stock lending is defined as the disposal of an investment subject to an obligation or right to reacquire the same or a similar investment from the same counterparty.

Designated investment business to which terms of business and client agreements do not apply

6.66 Terms of business and client agreements are not required for all designated investment business. No terms of business or client agreement are required where a firm is engaged in any of the following investment activities:

(1)   execution-only transactions, except contingent liability transactions for private customers;
(2)   transactions with a customer as a result of a direct offer or financial promotion;
(3)   providing advice on investments or information provided with a view to providing terms of business or entering a client agreement;
(4)   acting as trustee of a unit trust scheme or depository of an Investment Company with Variable Capital (ICVC);
(5)   services provided by the operator of a collective investment scheme to the trustee or depository of the scheme, which is not part of the operators scheme management activities;
(6)   services provided by the operator of a collective investment scheme as part of its scheme management activity;
(7)   services provided by the operator of an investment trust savings scheme as part of its activities as such;
(8)   the sale or purchase as principal of units in a regulated collective investment scheme by a firm which is the operator of that scheme;

(9) effecting a transaction as principal by a firm which is a life office in relation to a life policy issued by it;

(10) a firm which is the operator of an investment trust saving scheme bringing about a transaction in the shares of any investment trust which is the subject of the scheme;

(11) services performed in pursuance of a customer agreement which is terminated but only for the purpose of fulfilling any obligations outstanding;

(12) supplying published recommendations;

(13) OPS firms who are trustees of an OPS carrying out any designated investment business as part of its OPS activity in relation to an OPS of which it is trustee.

Adequate detail

6.67 Firms are required to ensure that their terms of business and client agreement 'set out in adequate detail' the basis on which services are to be provided. COB provides details of what must be included in the terms of business[1].

---

[1] COB 4.2.15 and 4.2.16 set out the matters about which details must be included.

Client agreements where customer is resident overseas

6.68 Specific provisions apply to private customers resident overseas. Where a client agreement would otherwise be required (see COB 4.2.7 and para 6.64) it will not be needed if the private customer is habitually resident outside the UK and the firm has taken reasonable steps to establish that the private customer does not wish to enter a client agreement. Terms of business should, however, still be provided. The question of what amounts to reasonable steps will depend on the circumstances of the case. The more time the person is outside the UK the less detailed evidence will be required to show that reasonable steps have been taken to establish that the agreement is not wanted.

Amendment of terms of business

6.69 The rules make provision for the amendment of terms of business without consent. COB provide that terms of business may be amended if they provide for amendment without consent. This will allow unilateral amendment. If unilateral amendment of a terms of business is to be made, however, the firm must give ten days' notice before providing any service on the amended terms unless the circumstances dictate a shorter period because it is impractical to wait that long. In judging whether the circumstances dictate a shorter period, IMRO guidance had regard to whether a reasonable investment adviser would consider a shorter period to be justified in all the circumstances. This is likely to be a good guide for the future.

Records of terms of business

6.70   COB 4.2.14 requires a firm to make a record of each terms of business and any amendment to it. The records are to be kept for the same periods as records in relation to customer classification[1]. The time period runs from the date on which the customer ceases to be a customer of the firm and not from the date of the terms of business.

---

[1]   See para 6.43.

Terms of business and rights of action

6.71   The terms of business form the contractual basis on which a firm provides investment services to customers. This is the case whether the agreement is issued as a terms of business or client agreement. A terms of business is particularly important to a customer that does not meet the statutory definition of 'private investor' for the purposes of civil action under the FSMA 2000, s 150 since the terms, rights and obligations under the agreement will be significant when seeking redress if a dispute arises between the customer and the firm.

EXCLUSION CLAUSES

Duties and liabilities under the general law

6.72   COB 2.5 also limits a firm's ability to restrict the rights of customers. Under COB 1 any written or oral notice to a customer in the course of, or in connection with, designated investment business cannot seek to exclude or restrict any duty or liability under the regulatory system (ie the FSMA 2000, the Principles for Businesses, the threshold conditions, the statements of principle, codes and guidance).

6.73   In respect of more general legal duties COB follows the IMRO and SFA rules by stating that firms should not seek to exclude or restrict the liabilities owed to private customers, 'unless it is reasonable for it to do so'. Thus, COB like the IMRO and SFA rules embrace a concept of reasonableness which appears similar to that applied by the Unfair Contracts Terms Act 1977 (UCTA 1977), s 2. The same requirements apply where a firm seeks to rely on an exclusion or restriction in a notice or agreement.

UCTA 1977 and UTCCR 1994

6.74   Customers seeking to avoid unfair terms may also be able to rely on the test of 'reasonableness' under UCTA 1977 and 'good faith' under the Unfair Terms in Consumer Contracts Regulations 1994[1] (UTCCR 1994), although their application to investment agreements is limited. UCTA 1977 applies to contracts for investment advice and investment management, but not to contracts of insurance or contracts for the creation or transfer of securities. The UTCCR 1994 apply, inter alia, to customer agreements for 'the sale and purchase of securities and for the provision of advice and other services, such as portfolio management'.

[1]   SI 1994/3159.

SUITABILITY

6.75   The requirement that firms ensure investments are suitable for customers was a major feature of the system of investor protection introduced by the FSA 1986. That requirement has been retained and further developed in COB 5.3. The framework is designed to achieve suitability of investments for investors through the interaction of a number of rules and principles. This section considers the regulations that must be observed by firms when selecting investments for their customers. It should be noted that additional requirements apply when selecting packaged products and these are considered elsewhere.

6.76   The essence of the COB rules on suitability is that firms are required to take reasonable steps to ensure personal recommendations of investments, and discretionary transactions in them, are appropriate for private customers for whom the investment is selected. The rules also apply to a firm when it manages the assets of an OPS or a stakeholder pension scheme and when it promotes a personal pension scheme by way of a direct offer financial promotion[1] to a group of employees (in the latter case this may well involve a comparison of a group personal pension scheme and a stakeholder since COB 5.3.28 requires a firm to satisfy itself on reasonable grounds that the group personal pension scheme is at least as suitable for the majority of the employees as a stakeholder scheme and to record why it thinks the promotion is justified). Suitability in the case of personal recommendations[2] and discretionary transactions is determined by reference to the facts disclosed by the private customer and other facts about him of which the firm is or reasonably should be aware.

[1]   This is a promotion which: (a) contains: (i) an offer by the firm to enter into a [controlled] agreement with anyone who responds to the financial promotion; or (ii) an invitation to anyone who responds to the financial promotion to make an offer to the firm to enter into a [controlled agreement]; and (b) specifies the manner of response or includes a form in which any response is to be made (for example by a tear off slip). In summary, a controlled agreement is an agreement which constitutes the carrying on of designated investment business.
[2]   Those are recommendations made to a specific person. In order for it to amount to designated investment business the recommendation must go beyond a general recommendation of a type of investment product and must be specific to a particular product.

6.77   The COB rules relating to standards of investment advice are considered below. They are supplemented by the FSMA 2000, s 397 which has replaced the FSA 1986, s 47(1); and by Principle 9 'customers: relationships of trust' which approaches the question of suitability more directly than its predecessors; SIB Principle 4, 'information about customers'; and SIB Principle 5, 'information for customers'.

FSMA 2000, s 397

6.78   This makes it a criminal offence to mislead investors in relation to investment agreements or rights arising from investments. The FSMA 2000, s 397 applies to:

'. . . a person who:

(a)   makes a statement, promise or forecast which he knows to be misleading, false or deceptive in a material particular; or

(b)   dishonestly conceals any material facts whether in connection with a statement, promise or forecast made by him or otherwise; or

(c)   recklessly makes (dishonestly or otherwise) a statement, promise or forecast which is misleading, false or deceptive in a material particular'.

6.79   The FSMA 2000, s 397(2) provides that such a person is guilty of an offence if he makes the statement, promise or forecast or conceals the facts for the purpose of inducing, or is reckless as to whether it may induce, another person (whether or not the person to whom the statement, promise or forecast is made) to enter or offer to enter into, or to refrain from entering or offering to enter into, a relevant agreement or to exercise, or refrain from exercising, any rights conferred by a relevant investment.

6.80   'Relevant agreement' is defined in the FSMA 2000, s 397(9) to mean an agreement, the entering into or performance of which constitutes an activity specified by the Treasury (ie an investment activity) and which relates to an investment. It should be noted that 'any person', not necessarily a person engaged by an authorised firm, may be guilty of an offence under the section. It should also be noted that an offence under the FSMA 2000, s 397(2) can arise if an investor other than one to whom the statements are directed, or from whom facts are concealed, is influenced in relation to an investment agreement or rights under an investment.

6.81   There are two elements to an offence under the FSMA 2000, s 397. First, the offender must have knowingly or recklessly made a 'statement, promise or forecast' which is 'misleading, false or deceptive', or dishonestly concealed material facts. Second, such conduct must be intended to influence, or the person must be reckless as to whether it would influence, an investor to enter, or refrain from entering, into an investment agreement or exercise, or refrain from exercising, rights under an investment. It is not necessary that the investor take action in relation to the investment.

Principle 9—customer: relationships of trust

6.82   Principle 9 is directly aimed at enshrining the concept of suitability in a high level principle. This is a significant development from the SIB principles where Principle 4 required a firm to obtain all information that might reasonably be expected to be relevant to enabling a firm to fulfil its responsibilities to a customer and Principle 5 required a firm to give customers all information they would need to be able to make a balanced and informed decision about an investment. Principle 9 of the Principles for Businesses provides that:

> 'A firm must take reasonable care to ensure the suitability of its advice and discretionary decisions for any customer who is entitled to rely upon its judgment.'

It should be noted that Principle 9 (like the detailed COB rules on suitability) does not apply to market counterparties but only to customers. Further it only applies to customers entitled to rely upon the firm's judgment. A customer will be entitled to rely upon the firm's judgment where the COB Rules impose a suitability requirement and also where there is a suitability obligation in the agreement between the firm and the customer even though the rules may not apply. The obligation will not, of course, apply to execution-only transactions since in such cases the firm is not applying any judgment but is simply following an order. In general, the position is that the suitability obligation applies where the firm is dealing with a private customer. The obligation on the firm under the principle is one of reasonable care to ensure suitability. This is not an absolute requirement and is an objective test, the precise formulation of which will depend on the nature of the customer (including his expertise and understanding of investments) and the information that the firm has about the customer or should have known about the customer.

Suitability under the COB rules

6.83 The rules (COB 5.3.5 in particular) require that firms must take reasonable steps to ensure that personal recommendations to and discretionary transactions for private customers are suitable. Recommendations made to non-private customers do not need to be suitable. This explains for instance why firms must be particularly careful when classifying private customers as intermediate customers due to their expertise. The rules on suitability do not apply to execution-only customers. The suitability rule also applies to a firm which acts as investment manager for a private customer. Here the obligation is an ongoing one in that the firm is required to take reasonable steps to ensure that the private customer's portfolio or account remains suitable. Again, suitability will be tested by reference to the facts disclosed by the private customer himself and other relevant facts about the private customer of which the firm is or reasonably should be aware. Suitability requirements will also apply where, with a private customer's consent, a firm has pooled funds together with a view to taking common discretionary management decisions. Here the firm must take reasonable steps to ensure a discretionary transaction is suitable for the fund having regard to the investment objectives of the fund.

Suitability in practice

6.84 The suitability of an investment for a particular customer will be determined by the particular facts about, and circumstances of, that customer. To ensure investment decisions are suitable, a two-stage process must be undertaken by a firm. First, information concerning the customer's circumstances and investment objectives must be established. Second, the firm must ensure this information is taken into account when deciding which type of investment is suitable. In short, the investment should be appropriate for the customer.

Information about the customer

6.85   The COB rules require firms to obtain information about the customer in order that a suitable investment can be selected. A 'know your customer' requirement is found in COB 5.2.1–5.2.10.

6.86   The rule applies to any firm that:

(1)   gives a personal recommendation concerning a designated investment to a private customer; or
(2)   acts as an investment manager for a private customer; or
(3)   arranges a pension opt-out or pension transfer from an OPS for a private customer.

Under COB know your customer information is not required in respect of an execution-only transaction. It should be noted, however, that know your customer information may be required to satisfy the requirements of the money laundering sourcebook.

6.87   The requirement in COB under COB 5.2.5 states:

'Before a firm gives a personal recommendation concerning a designated investment to a private customer, or acts as an investment manager for a private customer, it must take reasonable steps to ensure that it is in possession of sufficient personal and financial information about that customer relevant to the services the firm has agreed to provide.'

Guidance at COB 5.2.11 indicates that the personal circumstances and objectives of the customer should first be established. This is because the firm must have regard to the facts disclosed by that customer before making a recommendation or effecting or arranging a discretionary transaction. The firm should be able to show a correlation between the information gathered and a personal recommendation given or, where relevant, discretionary management decision taken. The guidance makes clear that the aim of gathering the information is so that a clear identification of the client's needs and priorities can be established and that this, combined with details of a customer's attitude to risk, will enable a suitable investment to be recommended.

6.88   In order that information concerning the customer's circumstances and objectives is recorded, firms typically interview the customer. There is, however, no requirement in the rules that a customer be interviewed in person and it is acceptable that adequate information is established by correspondence or telephone.

6.89   In practice, firms usually complete a 'fact-find' to retain details about a customer. A permanent document such as this also serves as evidence of the information obtained. Reliance by firms on standard pro-forma 'fact-finds' for all investment services, however, may not be appropriate since different investments will require the firm to gather different amounts and types of information to ensure suitability.

6.90   The information required from a customer, and to which a firm must have regard, will vary dependant on the type of transaction under consideration. For instance, details of a customer's rights under an occupational pension scheme will be highly relevant to the question of whether a pension transfer is suitable for the customer, but is unlikely to be relevant to the question of whether a fund managed with discretion for the customer should increase its exposure to particular securities. In those circumstances, the customer's attitude to risk and his investment objectives in terms of income generation or capital appreciation are far more likely to be relevant.

6.91   Information required from the customer for the purpose of compliance with the rules is not just financial, such as affordability (although this is very important particularly where long-term regular premium investments with high penalties are concerned), and may for instance require firms to be aware of a customer's health, domestic and employment circumstances. Information concerning the customer's attitude to risk will be required. If an investment represents a long-term financial commitment to the customer, more information will be needed to ensure suitability. In particular, care will need to be taken to assess whether the customer has access to sufficient short-term funds to warrant his spare cash being tied up in a long-term investment, where early surrender may lead to significant penalties. Savings endowments are good examples of products where surrender penalties may make it unsuitable unless the customer can be sure that he can afford his funds to be tied up for a lengthy period without obtaining access.

6.92   Guidance (COB 5.2.11) makes clear that the record of the personal and financial information gathered by the firm can be retained either electronically or on paper. COB 5.2.9 requires such records to be kept and retained indefinitely in the case of a pension transfer, pension opt-out or FSAVC; six years for a record relating to a life policy or pension contract, and three years in any other case (ie for the same period as customer classification). The guidance also indicates that the customer is not required to sign a copy of the information gathered. If the customer is asked to sign the record then the guidance indicates that there should be a prominent warning advising the customer to read the information before signing his consent that it is accurate.

6.93   With regard to affordability the guidance suggests that due regard should be given to the customer's current level of income and expenditure and likely future changes in income and expenditure. Particular specific guidance is also included in respect of low premium (less than £50 per annum or £1 per week) friendly society life policies. This includes keeping a record of the reasons why this particular transaction is suitable for that individual customer.

6.94   Although the requirement to know your customer does not apply in the case of execution-only transactions, there is a specific rule (COB 5.2.10) dealing with execution-only pension opt-out and pension transfers. This provides that if a firm arranges such transactions on an execution-only basis it must make a clear record to evidence that no advice on investments was supplied to the private customer. This will cover circumstances such as that where a firm acts for an employer in setting up a group personal pension and then arranges a transfer from an OPS for an employee without giving personal advice. It should be noted that in such circumstances COB 5.3.28 will apply if a direct offer promotion has been used and the firm will have to satisfy itself on reasonable grounds that the group scheme is as suitable as a stakeholder scheme for the majority of the employees. It also appears to reflect concerns arising in the context of the industry wide pension review about the number of opt-outs and pension transfers categorised as execution-only where on further examination this turned out not to be the case.

6.95   It should be noted that information about customers retained by a firm remains confidential under fiduciary duties owed by the firm, the rules and, where relevant, the Data Protection Act 1984.

Customers refusal to provide information

6.96   If a customer refuses to give any or all information relevant to proposed investment services, firms should retain documentary evidence of this, preferably signed by the customer. The firm will therefore be able to show that it has taken reasonable steps in attempting to establish the information. A customer declining an invitation to provide information should be advised that suitability cannot be assured and that the lack of such information may adversely affect the quality of services to be provided. In such circumstances, the firm must still rely on whatever information is available in assessing suitability for such a customer. It should be noted that a customer's refusal to provide information does not constitute an execution-only transaction since the customer may still be relying on the firm to give investment advice despite the absence of such information.

'Other relevant facts'

6.97   Besides the information provided by the customer, the COB suitability rules also require the firm to have regard to 'other relevant facts' about the customer of which it is, or reasonably should be, aware.

This effectively puts a responsibility on the firm to establish, on a reasonable basis, information relevant to the proposed transaction even if it has not been disclosed by the customer.

Suitability: selecting an investment

6.98   In the process of selecting an investment that is suitable for a customer, the firm must consider what type of investment is the most appropriate. It may be that the customer is seeking advice on a specific type of investment, in which case the task of the firm (if it is an independent adviser) is to choose the most appropriate provider of that investment.

6.99   Where the firm is determining the type of product that is suitable for a customer, the choice will depend on the needs identified from the information already gathered about the customer, particularly his investment objectives. A firm may decide that, say, a PEP, equities, or a discretionary management service will be suitable for the customer.

6.100   The standard required to comply with suitability is not defined. It should be noted that the rules do not require that the investment chosen be the 'most suitable' for the customer. The standard is, at the very least, that the investment is 'not unsuitable'. An unsuitable investment will be in breach of the requirement. Examples of unsuitable investments include, for instance, those where there is a high degree of risk where the customer is risk averse, or where funds are tied in long-term when the customer has a need for access to the funds in the short to medium-term. Further, more detailed provisions apply in the case of packaged products and these are explained at para 6.107 below.

6.101   It should be remembered that product providers and independent firms must comply with additional requirements if a packaged product is deemed suitable for a customer. As to which see paras 6.107 ff.

What is a 'personal recommendation'?

6.102   COB rules requires a firm to take reasonable steps to ensure suitability when it makes a 'personal recommendation' to a private customer to buy or sell a designated investment. A personal recommendation is defined as a recommendation given to a specific person. This indicates that more general advice given to a group will not be covered. This is understandable since in those circumstances it is unlikely that 'know your customer' information will have been gathered. The IMRO rules also used the term 'personal recommendation'. It was not defined other than by exception. According to the IMRO rules, it did not include generic investment advice since this did not constitute a recommendation. Equally, it does not include published recommendations and direct offer advertisements since they are not personal.

6.103   The question of what constitutes a personal recommendation is a question of judgment in each case. A suggestion that a private customer ought to invest generally in a particular type of investment, such as equities, may not be a personal recommendation since it does not amount to a recommendation to purchase a particular investment.

Suitability: discretionary management

6.104   The application of the suitability rules to investment decisions made at the discretion of the firm, without recourse to the customer, depends on whether the transaction is for a private or non-private customer. Discretionary decisions for private customers are subject to suitability requirements under COB 5.3.5(2). Discretionary transactions for the pooled funds of private customers are also required to be suitable where the suitability will be assessed by reference to the stated investment objectives of the fund.

Suitability: ongoing obligations

6.105   When a firm is required to comply with the suitability rules, it should in the case of each private customer ensure it obtains, in the manner discussed, adequate information to comply with the requirement. Guidance suggests firms should review facts about the personal and financial circumstances of a customer to whom obligations of suitability are owed. IMRO guidance stated that a review should take place at least once a year where there is an ongoing customer relationship, such as when the firm acts as 'investment manager'. It is probably sensible to adopt the same approach under COB. COB 5.2.6 states that information should be kept under regular review and that where a firm acts for a private customer on an occasional basis, then the review should be undertaken whenever the customer seeks advice.

6.106   COB 5.3.5(2) provides an ongoing requirement to ensure that discretionary and non-discretionary portfolios for private customers remain suitable having regard to the facts disclosed, or of which the firm should reasonably be aware. The requirement extends to private customers where the firm monitors and advises on content of portfolios, but does not exercise discretion. This is an important safeguard for private customers since it ensures that the portfolio receives regular reviews to ensure suitability.

STANDARDS OF ADVICE FOR PACKAGED PRODUCTS

6.107   When selecting a packaged product for a private customer, a firm must choose the best product available if the firm is an independent financial adviser, or the best product from its range, if the firm is a product provider (see section on polarisation at paras 6.59–6.61 for further detail).

6.108   Product provider firms will be restricted to advising on packaged products available within their own marketing group and adopted packaged products. Adopted packaged products are stakeholder pension schemes which are packaged products not produced by the firm or in the firm's marketing group but by another producer and on which the firm is able to advise because it has followed the requirements set out in COB 5.1.4[1].

---

[1]   COB 5.1.4 permits provider firms to provide advice to private customers on stakeholder pension schemes which are produced by a person other than the firm or a member of its marketing group. The provider firm will be responsible for the advice and the producer is responsible for the relevant terms and conditions of the adopted packaged products.

6.109   Independent firms (independent intermediaries) must make a selection from packaged products available from all product providers. COB 5.1.16 enforces the need for independence by providing that an independent intermediary is required to act in the best interests of private customers when it gives advice on packaged products and independent intermediaries are prohibited from entering commercial agreements which might be likely to adversely affect its ability to provide independent advice. Where an independent intermediary has appointed representatives then it is required to take reasonable steps to ensure its appointed representatives comply with these requirements.

Duty to keep informed

6.110   COB 5.1.12 requires product provider firms to take reasonable steps to ensure that their representatives are able to sell with advice each of the packaged products on which they may advise private customers (ie packaged products from the limited range that the firm and its marketing group has available).

Duty to select better packaged product

6.111   COB 5.3.6 states that product providers must not advise private customers to buy a packaged product if the firm is aware of a packaged product within the group that better suits the needs of the customer. Having established that there is a suitable packaged product from its restricted range, a product provider must choose the best one available in the range to meet the needs of the customer. COB 5.3.6(2) makes clear that if there is no suitable packaged product within the restricted range then no recommendation may be made. This is an important rule since it emphasises that it is not good enough for the representative of a product provider to offer the most suitable product if it is not actually suitable for the customer concerned. In assessing which is the most suitable product from the restricted range, COB 5.3.7 provides that a product will not be suitable simply because it is available at a more favourable price through an alternative distribution channel or on special terms and its availability is restricted. If the provider firm acts as a non-discretionary investment manager then COB 5.3.6 does not apply since the provider firm will simply be taking instructions.

Independent adviser

6.112   COB 5.3.9 states that independent intermediaries must not advise a private customer to buy a packaged product, if it ought reasonably to be aware of a packaged product generally available that would better meet the customer's needs. The factors to be considered in making a selection should be both quantitative, such as comparative performance (although past performance is not a guide to future returns) and charges, and qualitative, such as the underwriting standards of a life office. In practice, an independent firm may find the packaged products of more than one provider will rank equally 'best' for the private customer. In selecting a packaged product from these equally ranked products, the firm will not breach the rule requirement.

Better than best advice

6.113   COB 5.3.9(2) prevents an independent intermediary from advising a private customer to buy a packaged product issued or operated by an associate[1], if it is or ought to be aware of a packaged product available outside the group which would meet the needs of the private customer just as well. This does not apply when a firm acts as an investment manager.

---

[1]   An associate is an undertaking in the same group as the independent intermediary, an appointed representative of the firm or a member of the group or any other person where the business or domestic relationship might be expected to give rise to a community of interest between them which may involve a conflict of interest in dealing with third parties.

6.114   This has the effect that when an independent intermediary recommends a packaged product from the extended group, a 'better than best' standard applies to the independent intermediary. A packaged product of the group selected for a private customer must not only be suitable but must be demonstrably superior than other available products.

Specific suitability requirements

Manager of OPS and stakeholder pension scheme

6.115   In certain circumstances the suitability rules impose specific requirements. COB 5.3.12 provides that where a firm manages the assets of an OPS or stakeholder pension scheme then the firm must take reasonable steps to ensure the suitability of specific transactions and the investment portfolio overall with regard to the investment objectives in the portfolio mandate.

Broker fund advisers

6.116   COB 5.3.20 provides that broker fund advisers:

(1)   must take account of the charges of the arrangement;
(2)   regularly review the investment objectives of the customer;
(3)   provide annually a recommendation to the customer either to continue with the investment or to withdraw and to supply reasons for it;
(4)   provide an alternative recommendation if the broker fund is no longer suitable;
(5)   notify the customer of any change in the investment strategy of the fund with confirmation of why the fund continues to be suitable for the customer or provide an alternative recommendation.

The additional requirements in respect of broker funds apply because of the dual capacity of the adviser and the added cost to the investor. They also help to mitigate the difficulties caused by the inherent conflict of interest present in a broker fund adviser relationship.

Pension transfers and opt outs

6.117 COB 5.3.21–5.3.27 provide detailed suitability requirements in respect of pension transfers and opt-outs. This reflects the historical problems with pension transfers and opt-outs which resulted in the industry wide pensions review.

Group personal pension schemes

6.118 COB 5.3.28 applies to group personal pension schemes which are promoted by a firm to employees on a direct offer basis (often the case when the firm acts for the employer in setting up the scheme). The Rule requires the firm to be satisfied on reasonable grounds that the scheme is likely to be at least as suitable for the majority of the employees as a stakeholder pension scheme. The firm must also record why it thinks the promotion is justified.

Suitability guidance

6.119 COB 5.3.29 provides guidance on matters to be taken into account when assessing suitability of the following recommendations:

(1) pension transfers and opt-outs;
(2) personal pension schemes and FSAVC's compared to stakeholder pension schemes;
(3) hybrid products including for instance back-to-back products;
(4) industrial assurance policies;
(5) income withdrawals;
(6) ISA or PEP transfers;
(7) contracting out of SERPS.

Reference should be made to the specific guidance when recommending any of the above.

CUSTOMER UNDERSTANDING OF RISK

6.120 Under COB rules firms are required to take reasonable steps to ensure customers are aware of the risks which may be inherent in an investment transaction. The requirement applies to any firm conducting designated investment business with or for private customers. The requirement to ensure the customer understands the nature of any risks does not apply when dealing with respondents to direct-offer advertisements since the advertisement will contain prescribed warnings.

6.121 The text of the rule is as follows (COB 5.4.3):

'A *firm* must not:

(1) make a *personal recommendation* of a transaction; or

(2) act as a discretionary *investment manager*; or

(3) *arrange (bring about)* or *execute* a *deal* in a warrant or derivative; or

(4)   engage in *stock lending* activity;

with, to or for a *private customer* unless it has taken reasonable steps to ensure that the *private customer* understands the nature of the risks involved.'

The essential element is that the firm seeks to ensure the customer understands the nature of any risks in an investment. The steps that must be taken by a firm for each transaction will depend on the customer's ability to understand and their experience. Firms may need to repeat warnings already given to a customer if necessary. It will not be acceptable simply to rely on the issue of a standard key features document. Principle 7 requires a firm to pay due regard to the information needs of a client and communicate in a way that is clear, fair and not misleading.

When should risks be notified?

6.122   Notification of the risks should be made before or at the same time as the recommendation of an investment or, in the case of discretionary management services to be provided by a firm, prior to the service being provided. For packaged products sold by any regulated firm the key features document issued by the product provider will address risk factors (the adviser cannot simply rely on key features to ensure understanding of risks and will need to consider separately whether it is inadequate to explain the risks to that particular customer).

6.123   The risks which should be communicated to a private customer go beyond a mere explanation of potential loss when purchasing an investment of fluctuating value. Explanations may be required concerning, for example: loss of cancellation rights, surrender values of life policies, possible exchange rate losses and, in certain circumstances, potential tax liabilities.

For certain investments, additional risk warnings are required which may need to be written and, where necessary, signed by the customer.

Specific risk warnings

6.124   Evidential guidance (COB 5.4.4) provides that reasonable steps to ensure a private customer understands risks should include certain specific steps in the case of:

(1)   warrants and derivatives;
(2)   non-readily realisable investments;
(3)   penny shares;
(4)   shares subject to stabilisation;
(5)   stock lending activity.

Warrants and derivatives

6.125   COB 5.4.6 sets out evidential guidance indicating that a written notice[1] should be given to private customers in relation to warrants and derivatives. The written notice must be signed by private customers after they have had a proper opportunity to consider the warning. The signed copy must be received by the firm before it recommends, arranges, executes, or acts as discretionary manager in respect of, a warrant or derivative. No such notice is required if the transaction relates to the exercise of warrants already held by the customer or warrants attached to another security. A private customer who is ordinarily resident outside the UK need not be sent a risk warning if the firm has taken reasonable steps to determine that the private customer does not wish to receive the notice. A failure to follow the guidance in COB 5.4.6 will tend to establish a breach of COB 5.4.3 (ie the rule relating to a customers understanding of risks).

---

[1]   COB 5, Annex 1 for details.

Stabilisation

6.126   Stabilisation is the making of bids or effecting of transactions for the purpose of stabilising the price of a recently issued security. Under the rules, a firm may recommend or exercise discretion in relation to securities subject to stabilisation if, before it enters into transactions in securities subject to stabilisation with a private customer, a written notice[1] is sent. The firm need not send a written notice if it has taken reasonable steps to establish that the customer requires an oral explanation only. A failure to follow the guidance in COB 5.4.9 will tend to establish a breach of COB 5.4.3.

---

[1]   COB 5, Annex 2 for details.

Penny shares[1]

6.127   COB 5.4.8 provides that specific warning should be given in respect of any penny shares to the effect that private customers may get back far less than they invested. This is because of the wide bid/offer spread that exists with penny shares. A failure to follow the guidance in COB 5.4.8 will tend to establish a breach of COB 5.4.3.

---

[1]   The risk warning for penny shares is found at COB 3.9.17. Penny shares are defined as readily realisable securities where the bid/offer spread is 10% or more of the offer price. It excludes however government and public securities; a stake in a company quoted on the FTSE 100 index; or a share issued by a company with a market capitalisation of £100 million or more at the time the recommendation is made. In short, penny shares are high risk because of the large bid/offer spread. The increase in value of the share as a proportion of its purchase price will need to be greater than 10% for the investor to recoup his investment on sale.

Non-readily realisable investments

6.128   For non-readily realisable investments, COB 5.4.7 requires specific warnings of the difficulty in establishing a market price to be given to private customers together with a warning that there is a restricted market for the investments. The firm is also required to disclose any position knowingly held by the firm or its associates in such designated investment or in a related designated investment[1]. Again a failure to follow the guidance in COB 5.4.7 will tend to establish a breach of COB 5.4.3.

---

[1]   Related designated investment is one where its value may be affected by a fluctuation in value of the other investment or by any published recommendation that affects the first investment. That may include warrants or perhaps shares in another group company.

Stock lending activity

6.129   COB 5.4.10 requires a firm to notify a customer that stock lending may affect his tax position and that he should consult his tax adviser. It must also warn of the impact stock lending activity may have on the rights of the holder of the designated investments concerned. Again a failure to follow guidance in COB 5.4.10 will tend to establish a breach of COB 5.4.3.

SUITABILITY LETTERS (FORMERLY 'REASON WHY LETTERS')

6.130   In certain circumstances, COB rules require firms to provide customers with written reasons to justify personal recommendations. Suitability letters are required in respect of recommendations concerning schemes[1], life policies, stakeholder pension schemes, the transfer of benefits from an occupational pension scheme and income withdrawals. The requirement does not apply to recommendations to buy or sell units in a regulated collective investment scheme where the firm acts as investment manager for a private customer.

---

[1]   A scheme is defined for this purpose as a regulated collective investment scheme; an investment trust where shares are to be acquired through an investment trust savings scheme, or are to be held within an ISA or PEP which promotes one or more specific investment trusts.

6.131   A suitability letter must be sent not later than the time the post-sale notice of the customers right to cancel is provided, thus giving the private customer an opportunity to consider the implications of the transaction before deciding whether to exercise cancellation rights. If no cancellation notice is required by the cancellation rules, the suitability letter must be sent at the same time as or as soon as possible after the recommendation.

6.132   The suitability letter is required under COB 5.3.16 to explain why the firm concluded the transaction is suitable for the customer having regard to the personal and financial circumstances of the private customer. The suitability letter therefore provides the link between the information gathering stage and the recommendation. The letter must also contain a summary of the main consequences and any possible disadvantages of the transaction. If the recommendation is of a personal pension scheme then it must explain why it is at least as suitable as a stakeholder pension scheme for that customer. Specific requirements apply in the case of an FSAVC where the firm is required to explain why it is at least as suitable as a stakeholder or any in-house Additional Voluntary Contribution (AVC) that may be available. If a stakeholder is not available then the firm is required to explain why the FSAVC is at least as suitable as any option available to make additional contributions to his occupational scheme. The rules require the firm in the letter to identify the individual who is authorised to advise on the type of product recommended. This will help to ensure that advice is only given by those authorised within the firm to do so. COB 5.3.30 gives specific guidance on the content of suitability letters. This guidance is not evidential and therefore a failure to follow it will not tend to establish a breach of the underlying rule.

6.133   Suitability letters are not required:

(1)   if a firm acts as investment manager for a private customer and recommends a regulated collective investment scheme;

(2)   if the customer is habitually resident in another European Economic Area[1] state (EEA) at the time he acknowledges consent to the proposal form for the investment which is the subject of the personal recommendation;

(3)   if the customer is habitually resident outside the EEA and is not present in the UK when he acknowledges consent to the proposal form;

(4)   if the recommendation is for a life policy sold by a friendly society where the premium is £50 a year or £1 a week or less (although see specific guidance at COB 5.2.11 on this where the firm should keep a record of why the investment is suitable for the customer);

(5)   if the recommendation is to increase a regular premium to an existing contract;

(6)   if the recommendation is for additional single premiums or contributions to an existing packaged product to which a single premium or contribution has previously been paid.

---

[1]   As at 21 June 2001: Austria; Belgium; Denmark; Finland; France; Germany; Greece; Ireland; Italy; Liechtenstein; Luxembourg; Netherlands; Norway; Portugal; Spain; Sweden; UK.

PRODUCT PARTICULARS AND THE KEY FEATURES DOCUMENT

6.134   COB requires that written details or 'product particulars' of life and non-life packaged products be issued to private customers by firms which personally recommend, sell, or arrange the sales of certain investments. The requirement is satisfied by issue of the 'key features document'.

6.135   COB 6.1–6.4 sets out the circumstances in which key features are required. In short, key features are generally required in respect of:

(1)   life policies;

(2)   regulated collective investment schemes, investment trust savings schemes, investment trust shares held through an ISA or PEP;

(3)   self-invested personal pension schemes;

(4)   income withdrawals;

(5)   cash deposit ISA's;

(6)   stakeholder pension schemes (except where the firm is advising over the telephone and the firm has adequate evidence that the customer has access to a copy of a decision tree during the conversation).

Nature of a key features document

6.136   COB 6.1.5 states that all firms must ensure that a key features document is in writing and may be either printed or in electronic form. The rule requires the key features document to be of as good quality as the marketing material being used to promote the packaged product or cash deposit ISA. This reflects the concern that the quality of the promotional material will draw the attention of the customer and he will disregard the key features document if it is produced to an inferior standard. Unless the key features document relates to a collective investment scheme or a stakeholder pension scheme then it must be separate from any other material given to the customer. Where it is included as part of another item of sales material (only permitted in the case of collective investment schemes or stakeholder pension schemes) then the key features must appear with due prominence. COB 6.1.6 provides guidance on this.

6.137   Key features must be prepared in accordance with COB 6.5.2. Key features documents must contain standard information in a prescribed order. Key features content requirements for life and non-life products are similar and include descriptions of the nature of the contract, charges and expenses levied, risk factors and a projection of returns. Reference should be made to COB 6.5 for detail of the content requirement. COB also provides details of what the content of decision trees must be for stakeholder pension schemes.

Issue of the key features document

6.138   In practice, the key features document will be prepared by the packaged product provider, such as the insurance company or unit trust operator and firms arranging such products may rely on these key features. This obligation on product providers and stakeholder pension scheme operators to produce key features is at COB 6.1.4.

6.139   The rules concerning issue of key features documents are designed to ensure that it is sent to private customers as early as possible in the process of buying the packaged product. COB requires, in the case of life policies, for the firm to provide the private customer with key features before the private customer completes an application for the policy. Where the private customer acquires a life policy without a written application the firm must ensure that it gives an adequate oral explanation and provide key features within five business days of the date on which the sale recommendation or arrangement was made. Where there is an alteration to the terms of a life policy before the private customer completes the application form then revised key features must be given unless the variation is one of those set out in COB 6.2.12 (ie the premium is changed, the commission is reduced, a rider benefit is added, removed or amended). Changes to the type of packaged product or the underlying purpose will require revised key features. For example, if there is a change from regular to single premiums. If the customer has completed the application form then revised key features must be offered and the customer provided with written details of any change if it amounts to a material change. Guidance in COB 6.2.15 indicates that what amounts to a material change will depend on the circumstances of the case but changes which lead to an increase in the proposed premium of 25% or less can be regarded as not material if the underlying policy conditions remain the same. COB 6.2.16 sets out the requirements in respect of variations of life policies.

Exemption from need to issue key features for life policies

6.140   Firms are not required to provide key features for life policies if at the time the private customer signs the application he is habitually resident in an EEA state other than the UK or outside the EEA and he is not present in the UK.

Post-sale confirmation

6.141   A post-sale confirmation provides information to the customer so that he has details of what he has purchased. COB 6.3.3 requires a long-term insurer to send a post-sale confirmation when a private customer buys a life policy which is a packaged product or varies an existing life policy in a way which would result in the customer having a right to cancel. The long-term insurer must send to, or if an industrial assurance policy, give or send to the private customer an example of how the principal terms of the policy apply to the private customer. The post-sale confirmation must be prepared in accordance with COB 6.5.15–6.5.19; it must contain details of surrender values and the effect of deductions under COB 6.5.23–6.5.28; and details under COB 6.5.38 of the commission and remuneration that will be generated from the sale.

6.142   A post-sale confirmation is not required from the long-term insurer when he has taken reasonable steps to determine that the policy or variation has been purchased for the private customer by an investment manager exercising discretion; or the life policy is purchased by the trustees of an OPS or the trustees or manager of a stakeholder pension scheme; or if a life policy issued pre-1 January 1995 is being varied; or at the time the private customer signs the application for the life policy or variation is habitually resident in an EEA state outside the UK or outside the EEA and was not present in the UK when the application was signed.

Schemes

6.143   COB 6.2.22 provides that where the investment is a scheme holding, key features are to be provided before the private customer completes an application form. Where the private customer is to acquire the scheme without a written application then if the firm provides an adequate oral explanation of the main features of the scheme holding it can send the key features within five business days. Key features are not required in respect of a scheme if the firm is a UK firm and the obligation arises from business in another EEA state through the firm having passported out (ie sales in Europe by a passported provider, since in those cases local rules will apply); the private customer is habitually resident outside EEA and is not present in the UK when he signs the application; it is purchased on an execution-only basis; it is bought by an investment manager exercising discretion for a private customer; or the purchase is made by a non-discretionary investment manager and the private customer has agreed that key features need not be provided. Key features will also not be needed if the customer already has a holding in the scheme; the terms and conditions of the scheme, including all charges, remain the same and the customer received key features at the time of the previous purchase. Likewise, where there is a transfer from accumulation to income units of the same scheme and the customer has already received key features then no further key features are needed.

CANCELLATION RIGHTS

6.144   Under the previous regime, the SIB issued regulations under the FSA 1986, s 51 to allow investors who have entered into, or offered to enter into, an investment agreement with an authorised person to rescind the agreement or withdraw the offer. The FSA 1986, s 51 stated:

> 'The Secretary of State may make rules for enabling a person who has entered or offered to enter into an investment agreement with an authorised person to rescind the agreement or withdraw the offer within such period and in such manner as may be prescribed.'

This was intended, according to the SIB, 'to give investors the opportunity to make considered and well informed investment decisions' and 'to reduce the incentive to adopt "hard-sell" tactics'.

6.145   The new cancellation rules apply to product providers; insurers providing pure protection contracts[1]; independent intermediaries acting as EIS managers or plan managers, or when they sell units to a customer which they bought or redeemed for that purpose; deposit taking firms acting as ISA manager or holding deposits in respect of another firm's cash deposit ISA; the operator of a stakeholder pension scheme.

---

[1]   Essentially life policies with no surrender or cancellation value or rights of conversion.

Rights to cancel

6.146   COB provides private customers with a mixture of rights to withdraw before sale together with post-sale rights to cancel. Rights to cancel are rights to cancel an investment agreement after the agreement has been signed and after the investor has received a post-sale notice[1] from the firm. A right to withdraw applies to certain investments and prevents the firm from accepting the offer for at least seven days after the offer is made. Rights to withdraw and to cancel apply differently to individual customers and to certain products.

They are not therefore limited to private customers and will apply to individual intermediate customers. With some products and customers both a right to withdraw and a right to cancel will apply.

[1]   A post-sale notice is a notice advising the investor of the right to cancel.

6.147   The general position is that for up to two weeks after the purchase of certain investments[1], customers are able to cancel the investment. If the right to cancel is exercised, the firm must refund all moneys paid by the customer, subject—in the case of lump sum investments only—to a potential shortfall deduction. Some cancellation rights only apply where advice is given. They apply where the advice concerns units in an authorised unit trust or an ICVC if held within or outside an ISA or PEP.

[1]   Appropriate personal pensions; cash deposit ISAs; life policies; pension contract; pure protection contract; stakeholder pension scheme; certain variations of existing policies.

Rights to withdraw

6.148   Rights to withdraw apply in the case of a life policy; a pension contract and some variations of existing pension contracts and stakeholder pension schemes. It should be noted that the right to withdraw does not apply to the initial sale of a stakeholder although there is a right to cancel.

6.149   Where advice is given then rights to withdraw apply to all ISA's or PEP's where it is the first sale. There is also the right to withdraw for first sales to an individual of Enterprise Investment Schemes. If the firm advises the customer that rights to withdraw will not apply in subsequent sales then the customer will not have the right to withdraw on subsequent purchases and that will be acceptable under COB. Specific guidance on rights to withdraw and cancellation, and the application to individual products, can be found at COB 6.7.5G.

Pension annuity or pension transfer

6.150   For a pension annuity or pension transfer the firm can choose to operate a pre-sale right to withdraw known as a cancellation substitute; this replaces the post-sale right to cancel. The cancellation substitute will apply if the firm supplies to the customer at least 14 days before the contract is concluded a written notice which states:

(1)   a customer has a period of 14 days to consider pension options;
(2)   the dates for that period;
(3)   the pension options available;
(4)   the steps a customer must take in order to exercise a pension option;
(5)   that the customer is entitled to key features and is advised to check with the firm if the key features have not been received;
(6)   the cost of advice given to the customer in relation to the transaction; and

(7)   the firm has taken sufficient steps to ensure the customer has been made aware of the potential advantages and disadvantages of proceeding and has had an opportunity to consider all other possible alternatives. The firm may reasonably rely upon another firm to supply the notice and upon it to take the sufficient steps referred to.

Post-sale notices

6.151   Where cancellation rights apply firms must give customers pre-sale and post-sale notices setting out their right to cancel the investment agreement. Under COB, the firm must send a post-sale notice within eight days of the agreement for the purchase of a pension contract, a subscription for units in a regulated collective investment scheme and a subscription to invest in an ICVC to which shortfall applies (ie all cases except where the policy has been set-up on a regular premium or payment basis or as a recurring single premium life policy or pension policy or a recurring single payment pension contract or unit savings plan). In all other cases, then the post-sale notice should be sent no later than day 14 after the agreement is concluded.

6.152   Post-sale notices must be sufficiently clear and prominent to enable the customer to exercise the right and where they form part of a document used for promotional purposes the presence of the post-sale notice must be drawn to the customer's attention.

6.153   The content of the post-sale notice is prescribed in COB 6.7.36. Where there is a right to cancel the customer must also under COB 6.7.30 be given a pre-sale notice. The pre-sale notice is required under COB 6.7.32 to contain a summary of the information required in the post-sale notice.

6.154   Under COB 6.7.31, if the policyholder is a trustee and the firm reasonably believes that the policyholder acts on the instructions of an individual beneficiary, a post-sale notice must be sent to both the policyholder (ie the trustee) and the beneficiary or purchaser although only the former may exercise the right to cancel and the notice must remind the beneficiary to give instructions to the trustee.

EXERCISE OF RIGHT TO CANCEL BY CUSTOMER

6.155   Under COB 6.7.42 the customer can cancel by giving, within the period of time set out in COB 6.7.10 of the day following receipt of the cancellation notice (usually 14 days but up to 30 in the case of a life policy), notice of the intention to cancel. Where the notice is sent by prepaid post then it is treated as being served on the day it was posted or sent. Cancellation has the effect of rescinding the investment agreement (or the particular ISA component, or the variation to the policy to which the cancellation arrangements apply).

6.156   Notification of the exercise of the right to cancel can be made by return of the notice sent to the customer or in any other written form, provided it is served on the firm or any of its agents with authority to accept notice. Cancellation rights exercised by one customer on a joint life policy will have the effect of rescinding the entire agreement (provided that policyholder has the right to cancel and irrespective of whether the policy-holder is exercising that right on behalf of all the policyholders). A life policy or unit trust investment remains in full force until service of the cancellation notice is effective. Where a customer makes effective service of the intention to cancel, the firm must return to the customer all moneys paid for the investment, including any charges or commissions deducted by the firm. The firm is entitled to receive any property that became the customer's under the agreement together with any sum the firm has paid under the agreement plus any shortfall.

SHORTFALL

6.157 In summary, a firm may return an amount smaller than that originally invested if the market price of lump sum (usually) unit-priced investments has fallen since the original sale and the firm would suffer that loss as a result of cancelling the agreement. This is known as shortfall and prevents customers making a purchase of a product and gaining a financial advantage by exercising cancellation rights in a falling market. It does not apply to regular premium policies but applies to single premium investments (including life and pension policies, pension contracts, authorised unit trusts and ICVC's and stakeholders, for further details see COB 6.7.57). The manner of calculating shortfall is set out at COB 6.7.55 and further details are at COB 6.7.58. The firm must use an 'offer-to-offer' price basis in calculating any shortfall in value since the investment was purchased. Shortfall is not relevant where withdrawal provisions are operated, since where the customer has exercised the right to withdraw, moneys will not actually have been invested.

Failure to send cancellation notice

6.158 COB 6.7.41 provides that when a firm fails to issue the requisite post-sale notice, or issues it later than the period required by COB, the customer retains the right to cancel for two years from the inception of the agreement. Shortfall provisions cannot be applied by a firm that sends the cancellation notice outside the specified period. Firms need therefore to ensure that cancellation notices are sent within the appropriate period as otherwise customers will be able to recover their single premium investments within two years even where the value has dropped significantly.

Other exceptions to shortfall

6.159 Firms will also be excluded from applying shortfall if:

(1)   the firm failed to make any prominent mention of shortfall in the pre-sale or post-sale notice. COB 6.7.40G gives guidance on the forms of words that will satisfy the requirement for prominence where the post-sale notice forms part of a brochure or is included in a pack of

documents. Even though this guidance is not evidential, firms would be wise to follow it because of the potential cost of being unable to apply shortfall;

(2)   the firm has failed to send a post-sale notice under COB 6.7.30 (in which case, as noted at para 6.158 above, the customer will have two years in which to cancel);

(3)   the customer has served the cancellation notice before the agreement is concluded.

Calculating time periods

6.160   Time limits under COB for cancellation and withdrawal are based on calendar days excluding public holidays. The periods under cancellation notices are extended if a firm or customer cannot meet the requirement due to events that are beyond their control. Any day within the period of such a contingency shall be treated as a public holiday and therefore disregarded for the purposes of cancellation time limits.

DEALING

6.161   Dealing constitutes a regulated activity and includes either dealing as a principal or dealing as an agent. In both cases it includes buying, selling, subscribing for or underwriting securities or contractually based investments[1].

---

[1]   Financial Services and Markets Act 2000 (Regulated Activities) Order 2001, SI 2001/544.

6.162   The COB rules reflect the old SIB Principle 1, 'Integrity', which stated: 'A firm should observe high standards of integrity and fair dealing'. The COB rules on dealing concern good practice in 'buying and selling' for customers and reinforce fiduciary duties owed to customers. The COB rules on dealing ensure that instructions from customers, and discretionary decisions by firms on behalf of customers, are executed fairly and promptly and on the best terms available, and that beneficial ownership is fairly and promptly allocated to the internal records of the firm. In addition, a firm is restricted when dealing in a particular investment prior to publication by the firm of price sensitive material concerning the investment.

Customer order priority

6.163   COB 7.4 requires that firms deal with customer and own account orders fairly and in due turn. The rules on customer order priority apply to private and intermediate customers and to execution-only transactions. They do not apply to dealing on behalf of market counterparties. Firms should execute transactions in the order the instructions to deal are received, unless fairness dictates otherwise. No unfair preference should be given to particular customers or the firm's own account. The requirement that firms execute transactions fairly and in the order received is designed to prevent dealing for favoured accounts out of turn, which may achieve better deals for those accounts in a fluctuating market. Guidance under COB 7.4.4 gives examples of when a firm may deal with its own orders and those of its customers in different order to that in which they were received.

What is an order?

6.164 An 'order' is not defined by COB. In the IMRO and SFA rulebooks an order was defined as an instruction to a firm from a customer to effect a transaction as agent of the customer, or a decision by the firm to transact in the exercise of discretion on behalf of the customer. For the purpose of COB, an order may be assumed to have the same meaning as that given here.

What is an own account order?

6.165 An 'own account order' is defined to mean an order which relates to a transaction executed by the firm for its own benefit or for the benefit of an associate. This includes trading for the profit of the firm via the house account, or on behalf of an account held by a member of the group for the benefit of the group.

What is a current customer order?

6.166 'Current customer order' is defined to include both a customer order[1] for immediate execution and a customer order that becomes effective on fulfilment of a condition—that a share reaches a particular price, for example. The order will become a current customer order where the condition has been fulfilled.

---

[1] Customer order is defined as an order from a customer to execute a transaction as agent; any other order from a customer to execute a transaction in circumstances giving rise to duties similar to those that arise on an order to execute a transaction as agent; a decision by the firm in exercise of discretion to execute a transaction with or for a customer.

Postponing current customer orders

6.167 The rules allow firms to postpone execution of a current customer order where it believes on reasonable grounds that this serves the best interests of the customer. The interests of the customer could be met by the firm deferring a selling order in a rising market, for example. Firms should make a contemporaneous record of the customer's instruction or the discretionary decision to transact and the reason for postponing. Such records will enable the regulator to assess whether proper execution has in fact taken place. COB 7.12 provides details of the record keeping requirements.

Priority for connected transactions

6.168 The general rule is that customer orders are given priority to own account orders. COB 7.4.4 gives guidance as to when a firm may effect an own account order before an unexecuted customer order. This can be done if the firm believes on reasonable grounds that to do so is in the interests of the customer. Current customer orders[1] may be postponed (where it is an order for an associate) when dealing for one associate ahead of another or they may be postponed where the person dealing was unaware of an unexecuted customer order.

---

[1]   In certain circumstances entities with which the firm is connected may be treated as customers. These may be firms which deal solely for connected investment trusts, collective investment schemes, employees and, where the firm itself is an insurance company, for the account of the life fund.

TIMELY EXECUTION

6.169   COB 7.6 applies where a firm agrees or decides in the exercise of its discretion to execute a current customer order in a designated investment. COB 7.6.4 requires the firm to execute the order as soon as reasonably practicable. The obligation to ensure timely execution applies to transactions for private and intermediate customers. COB state that once a firm has agreed, or decided in its discretion, to execute a current customer order in a designated investment it must effect or arrange the execution of the order as soon as reasonably practicable in the circumstances. The requirement does not apply if a firm has taken reasonable steps to ensure that postponing the execution of the current customer order is in the best interests of the customer.

BEST EXECUTION

6.170   Best execution is the requirement to obtain the best available terms on which deals are executed. COB 7.5 provides that best execution applies to a firm when executing a customer order in a designated investment. This means that a firm must take reasonable care so that dealing is undertaken at the price and on the terms most favourable to the customer for transactions of the kind and size concerned. Best execution must be provided to private and, unless it has been excluded in writing, intermediate customers. Best execution applies to most types of dealing, including discretionary transactions. The purchase of life policies and units in collective investment schemes are excluded from best execution requirements. There is no exemption from best execution for execution-only customers.

How is best execution achieved?

6.171   The rules state that a firm will be considered to provide best execution if it takes reasonable care to ascertain the best available price for the customer in the relevant market, considering the size and type of transaction undertaken. Firms must deal at a price which is no less advantageous to the customer unless, in the circumstances, it would be in the best interests of the customer to do otherwise.

6.172   Evidential guidance under COB 7.5.6 states that in assessing whether the terms on which it intends to deal comply with best execution, the firm should exclude any charges to the customer which it, or its agent, would make and which are disclosed to the customer.

6.173 The guidance also confirms that a firm need not have access to competing exchanges in order to provide best execution but if a firm has access to competing exchanges or to access prices displayed by different exchanges and can make direct and immediate comparisons it should execute at the best price available on such exchanges or platforms if it is in the best interests of the customer. The firm should pass on the price to the customer and not take any mark-up or mark down. Where the firm is engaged in programme trading then it should apply best execution to each individual transaction.

6.174 Specific guidance for transactions in euro priced securities and shares traded on SETS is also to be found at COB 7.5.6.

When can the obligation to provide best execution be disapplied?

6.175 Where a firm deals with or for an intermediate customer, best execution need not be provided if the obligation has been waived by agreement in writing with the intermediate customer. This exception does not however apply where the intermediate customer is the trustee of an OPS or an OPS collective investment scheme or where the customer is a trustee of any trust for which the firm acts as 'permitted third party', as defined in the rules[1]. Best execution will also not apply if the customer order is for the purchase of a life policy or the purchase of or sale of units in a regulated collective investment scheme from or to the operator of that scheme.

---

[1]   A permitted third party is an authorised person who has been appointed by a trustee to carry out acts for it in respect of regulated activity.

TIMELY ALLOCATION

6.176 COB require a firm to ensure that a transaction it executes is promptly allocated to a customer or, for own account transactions, the firm itself. The rules on timely allocation apply to dealing for private and non-private customers and are a particularly important protection for customers of firms which act as discretionary investment managers on their behalf. A single bargain may represent the investments of many customers and, possibly, the firm itself and a market counterparty. Beneficial ownership must be recorded in the internal records of the firm prior to execution. Until accurate allocation of ownership has been made in the firm's records, the possibility exists that customers could be disadvantaged if, considering market movements after the transaction, allocations favoured certain accounts and disadvantaged others. It is to avoid any customer being disadvantaged by allocation, intentional or otherwise, that the rules require allocation to be undertaken promptly.

6.177 Timely allocation under COB 7.7.1 applies to all firms which aggregate a customer order with another order. Firms are required under COB 7.7.3 to have a written policy on allocation that is consistently applied and that meets the specific requirements of COB 7.7. Evidential guidance at COB 7.7.6 provides that timely allocation will be achieved where an aggregated order is allocated within one business day. The general requirement is subject to a number of exceptions. Five business days will apply where each customer is an intermediate customer and they have all agreed to the extension. It will be three business days where the aggregated order relates to one or more ISAs or PEPs and it is necessary to execute the transaction in that way to best serve the customer's needs.

Records of allocation

6.178   COB 7.7.14 address the stage at which the allocation of an aggre-gated order should be recorded. The allocation should be consistent with the record made upon receipt of the customer's instructions or, in the case of discretionary management, the firm's decision to transact. Under COB 7.7.14(2), a firm dealing for a number of different customers must record the intended basis of the allocation as soon as is practicable. If the firm has combined customer orders with own account orders, the intended basis of allocation must be recorded 'before the transaction is executed'. If errors in allocation occur and correction is required, this must be undertaken within one business day of the error being identified, and a written record of the reason for the correction should be made. Where an order is only partially filled resulting in an unfilled allocation to some customers the firm may carry out a reallocation provided it is in the best interests of customers (as a whole) for whom it has dealt.

6.179   When allocating the aggregated transaction, including any customer orders, the firm must make a record of:

(1)   the date and time of allocation;
(2)   the investment concerned;
(3)   the identities of each customer and market counterparty;
(4)   the amounts allocated;
(5)   any agreement with intermediate customers to extend the allocation period.

Fair allocation

6.180   Where firms execute combined customer transactions, which may include own account orders, the rules state that, in allocating the deal, a firm must not give unfair preference to its own account or that of any customer for whom it has dealt. If the quantity of the entire order cannot be satisfied, priority must be given to meeting orders for customers. A possible exception to this requirement arises where the firm can demonstrate, on reasonable grounds, that terms as favourable as those achieved would not have been possible without the firm's participation in the transaction.

Fair allocation of connected transactions

6.181 For the purpose of fair allocation, COB allow a firm to treat certain bargains for connected parties as if they were customer transactions. These may be accorded the same priority as other customers when allocating the beneficial ownership of a transaction. The transactions that may be treated as customer orders are transactions:

(1) for the life fund of an insurance company where the latter is in the same group as the firm (or the firm);
(2) for an investment trust or collective investment scheme that is a body corporate in the same group;
(3) for an employee of the firm or its associate or a trustee on his behalf but only if the transaction is carried out on a pre-established and recorded basis;
(4) for the firms occupational pension scheme.

Price of allocation

6.182 COB 7.7.12 provides that aggregated orders must be allocated either at:

- the actual price paid for each designated investment;
- a volume weighted average of the prices of a series of transactions.

The method for calculating volume weighted prices is set out at COB 7.7.13.

DEALING AHEAD OF PUBLICATIONS

6.183 COB 7.3 applies where a firm or an associate intends to publish a written recommendation or piece of research or analysis for customers that relates to a designated investment. COB 7.3.3 provides that firms must not knowingly effect an own account transaction in the investment or any related investment, until the customers for whom publication was intended are likely to have had an opportunity to react to it. The requirement applies to published recommendations for private and intermediate customers. The rules are intended to prevent the mischief of a firm making a profit for its own account by dealing ahead of published recommendations which may encourage customers to deal and so cause price movements of particular securities. The restriction does not apply where the published recommendation could not reasonably be expected to affect significantly the price of the investment in which the firm intends to effect an own account transaction. Likewise the requirement does not apply if:

(1) the firm is a market maker and the transaction is carried out in good faith and in the normal course of market making; or
(2) the firm deals in order to fulfil an unsolicited customer order; or
(3) the firm deals to fulfil customer orders anticipated upon publication, provided the purchases will not result in the market price moving against customers' interests; or

(4)   where the own account transactions proposed or effected are disclosed in the publication.

CHURNING AND SWITCHING

6.184   Remuneration in the investment industry is often commission based and a firm that effects a greater number of transactions is likely to see a commensurate increase in income. 'Churning' or 'switching' is the practice of generating additional income for the firm by recommending, or effecting with discretion, unnecessary transactions for customers. The COB rules are designed to prevent such unjustifiable transactions. The provisions apply where a firm conducts designated investment business with or for a customer (that includes both private and intermediate customers).

Churning: personal recommendations

6.185   In short, the rules at COB 7.2 provide that a firm must not make a personal recommendation to a private customer to deal or to switch within, or between, packaged products, including life policies, unless it has taken reasonable steps to ensure that the switch or deal is in the customer's best interests when viewed in isolation and in the context of earlier transactions.

6.186   The key to assessing whether churning has taken place is whether, in all the circumstances, the dealing would appear to be too frequent. It should be noted that perfectly legitimate switching may take place where tied sales forces become independent and are then in a position where they can advise on a wide range of products. In making recommendations to existing customers to switch to different products, advisers will need to take account of the surrender penalties or charges that may be incurred by the investor.

Churning and switching: discretionary management

6.187   When undertaking decisions with discretion, the COB rules prevent firms effecting transactions for private and intermediate customers if the dealing would reasonably be regarded as too frequent in the circumstances. The requirement applies to firms exercising discretion to switch within, or between, packaged products for private customers. Firms must have taken reasonable steps to ensure that the deal or switch is in the customer's best interests both when viewed in isolation and taking account of other transactions.

TRANSACTION REPORTING

Confirmations

6.188   COB 8 sets out the requirements in respect of transaction reporting. A confirmation is the new terminology for a contract note. The rules generally require firms effecting a sale or purchase of an investment, other than a life policy, to send to the customer a confirmation containing the essential details of the transaction. The requirement to issue confirmations applies where a firm deals with private and intermediate customers. There is no exemption in the case of execution-only transactions. A firm can rely on a third party to issue a confirmation but the firm remains responsible for the provision of the required information in the event that the third party fails to supply it.

6.189 Exceptions to the requirement to send a confirmation are set out in COB 8.1.6 and include a life policy or personal pension contract; where there is an arrangement for a customer to make a series of payments for the purchase of units in a collective investment scheme or shares in an investment trust; where there has been a specific request from the customer; the firm is an investment ISA or plan manager and the investment is not a contingent liability transaction and the firm has taken reasonable steps to determine the customer does not wish to receive confirmations provided the firm complies with COB 8.1.7 and COB 8.1.8; or it would duplicate a confirmation which is to be promptly dispatched by someone else.

Contents of confirmations

6.190 COB sets out the content requirements for confirmations for all transactions (COB 8.1.15), and separate content requirements for confirmations for particular circumstances (COB 8.1.16), and for confirmations for derivatives (COB 8.1.18) with particular requirements for options (COB 8.1.19). There are also specific requirements for transactions in units in a regulated collective investment scheme (COB 8.1.17).

Issue of confirmations

6.191 Confirmations must be issued promptly. Evidential guidance at COB 8.1.5 provides that the confirmation should be sent to the customer on the business day following the day on which the transaction was, executed, or within a period specified by the customer on his own initiative. When a firm is passing on a confirmation issued by a third party, it is to send it 'as soon as practicable' and in any event no later than the business day after receipt. Where the firm has issued or redeemed units in a collective investment scheme then confirmation should be dispatched on the business day following the day the issue or redemption price was determined. Confirmation details may be provided electronically by firms under the rules (see COB 1.8). The requirement to send a confirmation is met if the firm posts the confirmation on its website provided that it is only accessible to the investor who placed the order. Where it is a private customer, then the firm should review its website to ensure the customer has reviewed the confirmation. Where the private customer has not accessed the confirmation within five business days of posting then the firm should send a further confirmation in hard copy or electronically.

Exclusion of detail from confirmations

6.192 When a firm is acting as intermediary and a third party fails to supply details needed to enable the firm to issue a confirmation to the customer, the rules say the details may be omitted. Where a series of transactions (that is a series with a view to achieving one investment decision or objective) has been effected, COB allows the time of the last transaction in the series to be used for the purpose of deciding when the deal is executed, rather than requiring a confirmation for each individual transaction, provided each individual transaction time is recorded by the firm. In addition, the rules allow unconverted currency details to be omitted, provided the details are sent in a supplementary confirmation and the initial confirmation makes clear that the information has been omitted.

Exemptions from need to issue confirmations

6.193   COB provides that in some circumstances, such as certain types of discretionary management and where the customer has requested, firms may transact without the need to send confirmations for each transaction. If the customer is not supplied with the required information in a confirmation, details must be included in a periodic statement issued subsequently, which contains information relating to the transactions executed during the relevant period.

Periodic statements

6.194   COB 8.2 sets out the requirements for periodic statements. Under the COB rules, firms acting as investment managers for customers must generally send the customer a regular statement providing a valuation of their investment portfolio and other details. The rules specify the required contents of such statements and the frequency with which they must be sent. The requirement to issue periodic statements also applies where a firm operates a customer's account containing uncovered open positions in a contingent liability transaction.

What is an investment manager?

6.195   'Investment manager' has two meanings according to the definition in COB. First, it means a firm which exercises discretion, within agreed restrictions, in the composition of a customer's portfolio. Second, it means a firm which has agreed regularly to advise on the composition of an investment portfolio without any powers of discretion.

Content of periodic statements

6.196   Detailed provisions setting out the content requirements for periodic statements are found in COB Chapter 8.

Frequency

6.197   The basic requirement is that a firm acting as investment manager must send a statement of periodic information for a customer at least once every six months. The frequency can be reduced to once in every 12 months if requested by the customer in writing. If the portfolio includes an uncovered open position in a contingent liability transaction then the statement should be sent monthly. Where the customer is an intermediate customer then the periodic statement can be sent at such intervals as the customer has agreed on his own initiative with the firm.

6.198   The rules provide that the statement should be sent to a private customer within 25 business days of the end of the period to which it relates.

For private customers with open positions in derivative transactions, a firm must send a statement monthly, within 10 business days of the period end. Firms whose sole permitted activity is venture capital business should send periodic statements to private customers within 50 business days of the period end.

6.199   Periodic statements should be provided to intermediate customers within such period as the intermediate customer has on his own initiative agreed in writing with the firm as adequate. A firm need not send a periodic statement to an intermediate customer which is not an OPS firm if the customer has requested, or the firm has taken reasonable steps to establish, that he does not wish to receive it.

Periodic statements for customers resident overseas

6.200   Under COB, firms do not need to send periodic statements to a private customer or intermediate customer habitually resident outside the UK. Before a firm can disapply the requirement to issue a periodic statement, the customer overseas must request that no statements be sent, or the firm must have taken reasonable steps to establish that he does not wish to receive them.

CHARGES, COMMISSIONS AND DISCLOSURE OF REMUNERATION

6.201   Remuneration in the financial services industry can be by way of commissions, mark-ups on an investment, periodic management fees levied on a portfolio or charges for time spent providing investment services. The rules prevent firms overcharging for investment services and require automatic disclosure to private customers of commissions earned by a firm from packaged products. For other products, private and some intermediate customers must be told in what manner the firm will be remunerated.

Reasonable charges

6.202   The rules seek to prevent private customers being overcharged by firms for investment services. COB 5.6 deals with excessive charges and applies to a firm that makes a charge to a private customer. A charge includes a mark-up or mark down and can be direct or indirect. COB 5.6.3 states that a firm's charges to a private customer for the provision of investment services must not be 'excessive'.

6.203   The main issues here concern the meaning of charges and the benchmarks that will be used in determining 'excessive'. COB guidance states that prevailing industry charges will be taken into consideration in considering whether charges are reasonable. Further, a firm should consider the degree to which the charges are an abuse of the trust that the customer has placed in the firm and the nature and extent of the disclosure of the charges. This suggests that where the firm has fully disclosed its charges and complies with the charges disclosed then they are less likely to be found excessive.

6.204   If charges for advising or managing a private customer's assets are dependent on the valuation of non-readily realisable securities then the firm must base them on the price that would be agreed between a willing buyer and seller with all available information. This protects customers against unreasonable valuations where a readily available market valuation does not exist.

Disclosure of remuneration

6.205   Firms must disclose to all private customers in writing the basis on which they will be charged and the amount of the charges. The disclosure should cover all income receivable to it as a result and any income receivable by its associate as a result of that business.

Packaged products

6.206   Remuneration from packaged products is usually by way of commission paid by the product provider to the firm or agent. Under COB 5.7.5, the amount of commission to be received by the firm or agent must be disclosed to private customers before effecting a packaged product. The firm must also disclose any payments it or its associate will make to its employees or agents. In practice, disclosure is made by the product provider in the key features document and intermediary firms can rely on this. For the issue of units in a regulated collective investment scheme, disclosure is also made in the confirmation. The disclosure must be made in cash terms. The definition of remuneration is broad and disclosure by product providers must take into account benefits such as contributions to overhead expenses of company representatives, so that the remuneration is disclosed on a basis 'equivalent' to that of independent intermediaries. Evidential guidance for valuing payments for product providers is found at COB 5.7.16. Disclosure must also be made in the case of execution-only transactions and customers responding to direct-offer advertisements. Disclosure for packaged products does not apply in certain cases for instance if the firm is acting as an investment manager or the transaction is for a private customer who is habitually resident overseas or the product is a life policy and the private customer is not present in the UK when the application is made.

6.207   Where the precise amount of remuneration is not known in advance the firm should make an estimate. If a private customer purchases a packaged product on amended terms, such that a cancellation notice becomes issuable, the firm must disclose in writing to the private customer any increase to the remuneration that is receivable as a result of the transaction.

Chapter 7   Retail Products

Robert Surridge

LIFE ASSURANCE

Introduction

7.1   The number of life assurance products available on the market is vast and increasing continually. However, the variety of underlying contracts is quite limited and all life assurance products are essentially only variations or combinations of a few basic types. These are set out at paras 7.5–7.9.

What is life assurance?

7.2   Fundamentally, life assurance involves the payment of money, known as the 'premium' to the life office in return for a payment in the future of a sum of money, on the occurrence of certain events, namely death, expiry of a fixed term ('maturity'), or surrender. The sum paid on death or maturity is known as the 'sum assured' and on surrender a 'surrender value' may be payable. The sum received from the life office is usually in the form of a single lump sum but may occasionally be in the form of regular payments. The premiums paid to the life office may be regular (usually monthly or annually) or a single premium. The various purposes of life assurance are most easily and conveniently considered in conjunction with an examination of the types of life assurance set out at paras 7.5–7.9.

Is there a technical legal definition of life assurance?

7.3   While in most cases there will be no difficulty in deciding what is or is not a life assurance policy, the case of *Fuji Finance Inc v Aetna Life Assurance Co Ltd* [1]investigated in detail an example of one of the contracts set out below under 'Investment bonds'[2]. On appeal, counsel for Aetna argued that a contract, which whilst described as a life assurance policy offered no more on surrender (after the first five years) than it did on the death of the life assured, and which in many respects closely resembled a pure investment contract, was nevertheless a life assurance policy and as there was no insurable interest it was null and void. Counsel for Fuji argued that it was not a life assurance policy and so was not affected by the Life Assurance Act 1774 (LAA 1774) (which contains the requirements relating to insurable interest). Furthermore the effect of the Insurance Companies Act 1982 (ICA 1982), s 16, was not to avoid such contracts but to provide a means for intervention by the Secretary of State for Trade and Industry. The Department of Trade and Industry were also represented at the appeal and, for their part, stated that they recognised such contracts as life assurance policies.

¹   [1997] Ch 173, CA.
²   See para 7.10.

7.4   It was unanimously held that the policy in question was a policy of life insurance. The fact that no greater amount was payable on surrender than on death was not sufficient to prevent the contract being recognised as a policy of life insurance. The important point was that the events on which payment would be made were sufficiently life or death related. As it was a life assurance contract the fact that there was no insurable interest rendered the contract 'null and void' and so the appeal was allowed. Therefore there was no need to consider the ICA 1982, s 16 point (whether the policy was unenforceable as a result of the application of this section). However, opinions were expressed. Morritt LJ said it was not unenforceable. Sir Ralph Gibson said it was unenforceable and Hobhouse LJ declined to express a view except to say that legislation was required. This aspect of the decision is therefore disappointing as the uncertainty currently remains. Leave to appeal to the House of Lords was granted but the case was settled beforehand.

Types of life assurance

Whole of life

7.5   Payment of the sum assured occurs on death whenever that occurs. Alternatively, the policy may be surrendered prior to death for the surrender value (if a surrender value has been acquired). Indeed, single premium investment bonds¹ are designed virtually exclusively as medium to long-term investment products to produce a return on surrender in excess of the premium paid, although this does not necessarily happen. In most cases, with regular premium policies, especially in the early years, the surrender value will be considerably less than the sum assured and very often less than the total premiums paid although in general terms surrender values have tended to increase in recent years following regulatory and consumer pressure.

¹   See para 7.10.

7.6   The purpose of non-investment based whole of life policies is to provide a substantial sum on death whenever that occurs, for example to provide for a spouse and/or family who could otherwise face financial difficulties; or to provide a sum to pay inheritance tax (IHT) in respect of the deceased's estate; or to provide a sum to enable business associates to purchase the deceased's interest in the business; or to enable a company to protect itself against the loss of a key employee ('key man' assurance). Indeed, in any situation where a substantial lump sum is required on death.

Temporary (or term)

7.7   As the name suggests cover only lasts for a limited time. If death occurs during that time then the sum assured will be payable. There are no amounts payable in any other circumstances, eg on surrender, or on death outside the term of the policy. This is generally the cheapest type of life assurance available. Some term assurance policies contain an option to convert into other types of policies.

7.8   Term assurance is suitable where a substantial sum of money may be required as a result of death during a given time period, for example, on the death of the borrower before repayment of the amount of an outstanding loan. Another purpose is to cover death before retirement where the loss of an earner's income prior to retirement (when his pension would otherwise commence) could leave his family in financial difficulties. Temporary assurances can also be suitable in connection with gifts, and more specifically, potentially exempt transfers for IHT purposes. IHT can be due in respect of lifetime gifts or transfers if death occurs within seven years. As a sliding scale applies after three years the ideal type of policy would be what is known as a 'decreasing term assurance'.

Endowment assurance

7.9   This type of policy provides cover during the term of the policy but, unlike temporary assurances, also provides a payment at the end of the term and a surrender value after the early period of the policy. Generally this is the most expensive form of life assurance. It is commonly used in connection with house purchase as a means of repaying the sum borrowed at the end of the term whilst also providing life cover equal to the outstanding amount of the loan during the term. Endowment assurances are also used as pure savings vehicles with the amount of life cover being quite small but the minimum necessary for 'qualification' purposes[1]. Endowment assurances for mortgage repayment purposes have been the subject of regulatory attention recently as a result of concern at amounts payable on maturity not being sufficient to repay borrowings The Financial Services Authority have issued a consultation paper[2] and as a result has now published guidance on handling mortgage endowment complaints[3].

---

[1]   See para 7.52–7.58.
[2]   Consultation Paper 75.
[3]   See also PIA Regulatory Update 89.

Investment bonds

7.10   These are whole of life policies but because of their popularity, specific consideration is merited. These policies are designed purely for investment purposes with the amount of life cover generally being minimal—often an additional one per cent of the surrender value. In some cases the amount of life cover is no more than the ongoing investment value of the bond. In this respect the case of *Fuji Finance Inc v Aetna Life Assurance Co Ltd*[1] is important. At first instance doubt was cast on the validity of life assurance policies with no life cover.

---

[1]   [1997] Ch 173, CA.

7.11   The premium for such policies is invariably a single premium which is invested in one or more of the life office's range of unit-linked investment funds or in its with profits fund. The policy is usually issued as a series of identical policies known as 'segments'. This can have taxation advantages.

Contractual issues

7.12   A life assurance policy is merely one species of contract and the normal contract law rules are applicable. There are, however, certain idiosyncrasies in addition to a range of legislative and common law provisions which are applicable to contracts of life assurance. Life assurance contracts have posed interesting questions in the areas of offer and acceptance. In *Canning v Farquhar*[1] it was made clear that the so-called 'letter of acceptance' from a life office did not necessarily constitute acceptance in terms of contract law. In practice, in modern life assurance contracts the proposer makes an offer by submitting the proposal with the premium which is usually by direct debit instruction for regular premium contracts or a cheque for single premium policies. The life office (if prepared to do so) then accepts and in practice communicates acceptance of this offer by issuing the policy (although it may communicate acceptance separately). However, each case needs to be judged on its own facts and the wording of the proposal/application form is of course crucial.

---

[1]   (1886) 16 QBD 727.

The proposal form

7.13   Although not technically a requirement a prospective policyholder will generally initiate the application process by completing a proposal form supplied by the life office. If the policy in question offers a significant element of life cover it is usual for a range of questions to be asked to assist in underwriting. These questions will deal with such issues as age, sex, medical history and certain lifestyle questions, and information as to previous applications for life assurance. The proposal form is also likely to contain authority to obtain information from any doctor who has treated the proposer. This area is governed by the Access to Medical Reports Act 1988. If the prospective policyholder consents the life office may have access to a medical report on the individual. The individual in question may request sight of the medical report before it is sent to the life office in which case the life office must inform the doctor of that request. On receiving the application the doctor may release the report to the life office either once the individual has had access to it or after 21 days from making the application in the absence of the individual having contacted the doctor. The individual can request amendments to it if he thinks parts are misleading or untrue. If he wishes to see the report before it is passed to the life office the doctor may delete any part of it which he believes would be likely to cause serious harm to his physical or mental health.

7.14   The Statement of Long Term Insurance Practice sets out certain requirements relating to proposal forms. The consequences of failure to disclose all 'material facts' should be set out. 'Material facts' should be the subject of clear questions in the proposal form. Questions which require knowledge beyond that which the proposer could reasonably be expected to possess should be avoided. The proposal form or a supporting document should also include a statement that a copy of the completed proposal form and the policy conditions is available on request.

7.15 It is also possible that proof of identity, in accordance with the Money Laundering Regulations 1993[1], may be requested in the proposal form. Permissions regarding the processing of data under the Data Protection Act 1998, may also be included.

---

[1]   SI 1993/1933 (as supplemented by the Money Laundering Regulations 2001, SI 2001/3641.

7.16   For proposals on the life of someone other than the proposer ('life of another' cases) the underwriting questions are normally answered by the life to be assured who, it should be noted, is not a party to the contract. The proposer would generally be required to declare that the answers are correct to the best of his knowledge and belief. The signature of agents, such as attorneys, in respect of medical questions would not normally be satisfactory to life offices. In many circumstances (eg 'off-the-page' advertisements for policies with modest sums assured) simplified proposal forms are used which require few or possibly no medical questions.

Insurable interest

7.17   As the term implies this is a concept limited to insurance contracts. It became a focus of attention in the life assurance industry as a result of the *Fuji Finance Inc v Aetna Life Assurance Co Ltd*[1] case[2]. Unfortunately, the governing legislation in this area is over two hundred years old. The LAA 1774 was introduced in order to bring an end to gambling on the lives of public figures. The LAA 1774 provides that no life insurance shall be made unless the person effecting the insurance has an interest in the life to be assured and any life insurance made without such interest shall be 'null and void' and no greater sum shall be recovered than the amount or value of the interest of the assured. Also, the name of the person(s) interested should be inserted in the policy.

---

[1]   [1997] Ch 173, CA.
[2]   See also para 7.10.

7.18   Insurable interest need only exist at the outset of the policy and the fact that insurable interest ceases before the time of the claim is not relevant[1].

---

[1]   *Dalby v India and London Life Assurance Co* (1854) 15 CB 365.

7.19   Apart from insurances made by a person on their own life or on the life of a husband or wife, where insurable interest is presumed, the insurable interest must be a pecuniary interest, capable of valuation in money and must be based on an obligation or liability which will, or will be likely to result from the death, or the loss or diminution of any property right which would be recognised at law or equity. A moral obligation or an expectation, for example, the prospect of benefiting under a will, is not sufficient.

7.20   The LAA 1774, s 3 provides that no greater sum shall be recovered from the insurer than the amount or value of the assured's interest. The sum assured at the outset must be supported by an insurable interest of an equivalent amount. Apart from those cases set out above, examples of insurable interest which have been recognised include a creditor on the life of a debtor (to the extent of the debt and accrued interest); employer and employee in each other's lives (where the employer is an individual) to the extent of the value of services to be performed (in the case of an employee's life), or the remuneration for the agreed period of service for fixed term contracts, or notice period in other cases (in the case of an employer's life where the employer is an individual). However, in practice more extensive sums assured are accepted[1]. Other examples are pension scheme trustees on the life of a member (where the member has an enforceable right to death benefits).

---

[1]   See para 7.21 with regard to 'key man' policies.

7.21   In other situations the position may not be so clear although in practice the proposal is often accepted. In 'key man' cases a policy is effected by a company or partnership on the life of a director/partner/manager etc on the basis that the loss of the key man's special services would involve the business in reduced profits and the expense of finding a suitable successor. There must be some doubt in many cases about whether there is technically any insurable interest as there is not necessarily any pecuniary loss, merely an expectation of loss. Nevertheless, this possible objection has not been taken by, for example, the Inland Revenue who permit the premium payments under a key man policy to be deducted as a business expense for corporation tax purposes.

7.22   In the case of co-directors and co-partners again there is no automatic insurable interest. In some cases the articles of association or partnership deed or other agreement will require the purchase of the deceased's shares or interest and this can form the basis for an insurable interest. Even in cases where there is no certainty that pecuniary loss would result, in practice many life offices seem to be happy to issue such policies.

7.23   Trustees of a trust or settlement do not necessarily have an insurable interest in the lives of beneficiaries. However, there are many possible exceptions in theory or practice to this generally accepted position. In view of the fact that the purpose of the LAA 1774 was to prevent 'a mischievous kind of gaming' then it seems inappropriate that this should prevent trustees effecting policies on the lives of beneficiaries when those persons will be those who are ultimately likely to benefit (and in most cases the policy in question will be an investment orientated one with limited life cover). In some cases inheritance tax (IHT) will be payable on the death of a beneficiary who has an interest in possession under the trust. As the trustees would be accountable for any tax payable in respect of that interest in possession then they may effect a policy for the probable amount of tax payable. Also, trustees would have an insurable interest in the life of the settlor during the seven years after the gift where this would be a potentially exempt transfer for IHT purposes.

Parents and children do not, as such, have an insurable interest in each others' lives.

7.24 What is the position where insurable interest does not exist? There is a general consensus that the LAA 1774 is in many respects unnecessary today. Furthermore, many observers view it as a hindrance to the modern commercial transaction of life assurance business. It would be extremely unlikely that if the LAA 1774 were repealed life offices would be prepared to issue 'gaming' contracts.

7.25 The LAA 1774 does not prescribe penalties for infringement. Policies which infringe the LAA 1774 are technically 'null and void' although for life offices it would rarely make sound business sense to raise the lack of insurable interest in refusing to make payment out under such a policy. In many cases life offices are prepared to issue policies where it is clear that no insurable interest exists. In doing so life offices should be aware of the provisions of the Insurance Companies Act 1982, s 16, (and its provisions as restated in the Interim Prudential Sourcebook for Insurers (at 1.3(1))) as contravention of the LAA 1774 (especially on a deliberate and systematic basis) may not constitute insurance business. Also, questions would arise regarding the taxation treatment of such business.

Non-disclosure and misrepresentation

7.26 Unlike other forms of contract the contract of insurance is subject to the principle of 'uberrimae fides' or 'utmost good faith'. The facts on which the risk is to be computed generally lie exclusively in the knowledge of the person proposing. The insurance company must trust the proposer's representations and proceed on the basis that he does not keep back any relevant circumstances in his knowledge or mislead the insurance company.

7.27 In order to satisfy the duty of disclosure the proposer must voluntarily disclose, without misrepresentation, all material facts known to him or which the proposer ought to have known if he had made reasonable enquiries.

7.28 The proposer cannot withhold material information merely because no specific question on the point is asked on the proposal form or in the medical examination. However, the proposer may be justified in inferring from the fact that the question is not asked that the information withheld is not regarded by the life office as material. But generally, it is not a defence to non-disclosure for the proposer to say that he omitted to disclose the fact through carelessness or mistake or that he did not regard it as material.

7.29   The material facts which a proposer is required to disclose are those which would influence a prudent insurer in determining whether it will accept the risk, at what premium and on what conditions. The opinion of the proposer as to whether a fact is material is irrelevant.

7.30   The duty to disclose extends beyond the time of proposal up until the time the contract is binding on both parties. With regard to modern business there is generally a provision in the proposal that the life office will not become bound until receipt of the first premium, and the inclusion of a continuing condition that the information supplied is still accurate at the time the policy is issued.

7.31   The Statement of Long Term Insurance Practice provides that where the proposal form calls for the disclosure of material facts a statement should be included in the declaration or prominently displayed elsewhere on the form or in the document of which it forms part:

'(i)   drawing attention to the consequences of failure to disclose all material facts and explaining that these are facts that an insurer would regard as likely to influence the assessment and acceptance of a proposal; and

(ii)   warning that if the signatory is in any doubt about whether certain facts are material, these facts should be disclosed.'

In addition, those matters which insurers have commonly found to be material should be the subject of clear questions in the proposal form. Insurers should avoid questions requiring knowledge beyond that which the proposer could reasonably be expected to possess. Failure to disclose, or state accurately, a material fact enables the life office to avoid the contract. The policy is not automatically rendered void. In order to avoid a contract in these circumstances the life office must show that it has been induced by the non-disclosure to enter into the contract[1].

---

[1]   *Pan Atlantic Insurance Co Ltd v Pine Top Insurance Co Ltd* [1995] 1 AC 501, HL.

7.32   If the life office avoids the contract then it is set aside from the outset and not merely for the future. Therefore the office would be able to recover any sums paid out (as a mistake of fact). Similarly, any premiums paid would be returnable unless there has been wilful or fraudulent non-disclosure. But if premiums continue to be accepted with full knowledge of the actual facts the life office cannot afterwards repudiate liability on the grounds of non-disclosure[1]. The duty of good faith also requires the insurer to be accurate in its representations.

---

[1]   See *Joel v Law Union and Crown Insurance Co* [1908] 2 KB 863.

7.33   Knowledge gained by the life office concerning the policyholder may be imputed to the life office in respect of other policies effected by the proposer, although the precise circumstances are important. Therefore imputed knowledge may not arise unless the information is received by a person authorised and able to appreciate its significance[1].

A breach of the duty of disclosure may in extreme circumstances amount to fraudulent misrepresentation.

---

[1]   See *Malhi v Abbey Life Assurance Co Ltd* [1996] LRLR 237, CA.

Policy document

7.34   Although in theory it may not be necessary for a policy document to be issued, in practice some form of policy documentation is almost always issued. It will contain, at the very least, the main terms and conditions of the contract between the insurance company and the policyholder.

7.35   A life policy is generally issued under hand, as a 'simple' contract, although it may on occasions be issued as a deed and thus be a 'specialty contract'. The policy must be executed in accordance with the constitution or regulations of the life office. The modern practice is to provide a standard universal printed set of terms with a schedule containing the terms which are of specific application, such as the policy number, the name of the insured and the life assured, the nature and amount of the benefit, when and to whom payable, the amount(s) of premium and when payable. The conditions and benefits of the policy usually form part of the standard printed terms and would include, for example, provision as to payments of claims, days of grace for payment of premiums, protection against forfeiture, surrenders, conversions and options available under the policy, charges and, for unit-linked policies, provisions as to the calculation of fund prices. The Policies of Assurance Act 1867, s 4 requires the policy to specify the principal place(s) of business at which notices of assignment may be given.

7.36   The growth of unit-linked life assurance business led to the introduction of 'cluster' or 'segmented' policies. Therefore, the proposer will receive a number of policies of equal value for his premium rather than one single policy. Such policies offer opportunities for tax planning. The practice evolved whereby one document was issued as the principal policy document together with a number of separate schedules of benefits each representing an individual contract or policy which expressly incorporates the principal contract by reference. However, the perceived requirement for a separate piece of paper to represent each contract seems to have become less prevalent in recent years.

7.37   Other statements and documents such as marketing literature, quotations and proposal forms do not form part of the contract unless they are incorporated in the contract by reference or otherwise. It would be unusual for statements in marketing literature to form part of the contractual terms of the policy, although if there is a misrepresentation this may afford grounds for rescission of the contract and return of the premiums.

Unfair Contract Terms Directive (UCTD)

7.38 The UCTD[1], which came into force in the UK on 1 July 1995 and now takes effect via the Unfair Terms in Consumer Credit Contracts Regulations 1999, SI 1999/2083, provided something novel in insurance contracts—the requirement of fairness. It may also, in time, help remove the public perception of insurance companies being able to rely upon 'small print' to avoid paying legitimate claims, a perception which may in some part be due to the fact that insurers were able to avoid the effects of the Unfair Contract Terms Act 1977 (UCTA 1977), by means of non-statutory adherence to the ABI Statements of Insurance Practice. Unlike UCTA 1977, which applies only to exemption clauses, the UCTD applies to *all* terms of a contract which are subject to the directive.

---

[1]   Council Directive 93/13/EEC.

Exclusions

7.39 UCTD[1], art 4 (2) (and SI 1999/2083, reg 6(2)(a)) effectively excludes from the requirement of fairness terms which reflect the main subject matter of the contract or the question of adequacy of the price, in so far as those terms are in plain intelligible language. A recital to the directive also excludes terms in insurance contracts which define or circumscribe the risk. However, the DTI did not adopt this in the regulations as it considers that it is only one example of the main subject matter exemption.

---

[1]   Council Directive 93/13/EEC.

Unfair terms

7.40 The UCTD[1] provides that:

'A contractual term which has not been individually negotiated shall be regarded as unfair if, contrary to the requirement of good faith, it causes a significant imbalance in the parties' rights and obligations arising under the contract, to the detriment of the consumer.'

From this it is clear that the directive applies to individual terms (not just to contracts in their entirety) which have not been individually negotiated, in contracts between a seller/supplier and a consumer. The regulations define consumer as a 'natural person who in contracts covered by these regulations, is acting for purposes which are outside his trade, profession or business'. A seller/supplier, conversely, is someone acting in the course of their business. Clearly, insurance companies will be dealing in the course of their business but when is a person dealing as a consumer? It is straightforward in most cases but there are potentially difficult situations.

---

[1]   Council Directive 93/13/EEC.

7.41   The UCTD[1] specifically provides that a term shall always be regarded as not having been individually negotiated where it has been drafted in advance and the consumer has therefore not been able to influence its substance. This would appear to apply to almost all insurance contracts where virtually all of the terms will be in a standard printed form and any negotiation will be likely to have been in relation to price (price being excluded from the scope of the directive).

---

[1]   Council Directive 93/13/EEC.

7.42   It can be seen from the definition above of 'unfair' that it has three limbs:

(1)   contrary to the requirement of *good faith*;
(2)   the individual term causes *a significant imbalance in the party's rights* and obligations arising under the contract;
(3)   to the *detriment of* the consumer.

The requirement of good faith in contracts is not something with which English lawyers, unlike many European lawyers, are familiar. There is, of course, the overriding obligation of 'utmost good faith' (uberrimae fides) in insurance contracts but this has historically been used by insurers against policyholders to avoid contracts and it has, in no small way, been responsible for the public perception of insurers relying on 'small print'.

7.43   As the definition of 'unfair' hinges on this requirement of good faith the directive provides in an Annex the following guidance:

'In making an assessment of good faith, particular regard shall be had to:

−   the strength of the bargaining position of the parties;

−   whether the consumer had an inducement to agree to the term;

−   whether the goods or services were sold or supplied to the special order of the consumer; and

−   the extent to which the seller or supplier has *dealt fairly and equitably with the other party whose legitimate interests he has to take into account.*' [emphasis added].

7.44   The essence of the matter, in most cases appears, therefore, to be fairness in relation to a consumer's legitimate interests. Hence, where a consumer takes out a contract to cover a particular loss, then it is presumably not dealing equitably with the consumer's legitimate interests for the insurer to avoid paying at all, or to pay less than the sum insured, whether as an abuse of stronger bargaining position or a technicality. Conversely, it is arguable, where powers expressed in the contract to be exercisable at the discretion of the insurer have to be exercised in a reasonable manner, that the objectivity of the requirement of reasonableness is indicative of the insurer dealing fairly and equitably with the consumer's legitimate interests, particularly where such powers have been disclosed to the consumer before he became bound by the contract.

7.45   The second limb of the definition of unfair terms appears somewhat superfluous, particularly in insurance contracts where the inequality of bargaining power will almost always exist. The requirement of detriment to the consumer is an uncertain concept, as neither the UCTD[1] nor the regulations (SI 1999/2083) define detriment. The requirement of detriment is familiar in issues of contractual consideration or equitable estoppel, in the sense of a financial loss to the innocent party or arranging affairs in an irrevocable way.

---

[1]   Council Directive 93/13/EEC.

Relevance to life contracts

7.46   Clauses in life contracts that might be caught by the directive are as follows.

(1)   Terms excluding liability—limitation clauses or exemption clauses not related to the nature of the risk (ie not covered by the main subject matter exemption).

(2)   Terms requiring payment of disproportionate amounts for failure to fulfil obligations—early surrender penalties.

(3)   Clauses irrevocably binding the consumer to terms with which he had no real opportunity to become acquainted before the conclusion of the contract. This could apply to all terms of an insurer's standard contract which do not circumscribe the risk. It is arguable where cancellation rights exist and the policyholder receives the policy within that period that the consumer is not then irrevocably bound. In addition the policy terms must be made available to the proposer under the Statement of Long Term Insurance Practice.

(4)   Power of unilateral variation—any power of alteration which is discretionary (subject to some possible exceptions).

(5)   Power to change charges—any terms allowing charges or fees to be increased without allowing the consumer a right to cancel could be caught. However, there is an exemption which permits indexation of charges provided the basis is explicitly described.

(6)   Terms requiring formalities—imposing time limits (for example for claims), requirements of notification in a particular form (eg writing) without a valid reason.

Clear disclosure

7.47   A recurrent theme is that if the reason for a particular term is valid, is disclosed to the consumer at the earliest opportunity or the consumer has the right to dissolve the contract when they are notified of a change, then the term will generally be fair. This is coupled with and to a certain extent exemplified by the requirement in the UCTD[1] that all written terms be drafted in *plain, intelligible language*. Where there is doubt about the meaning of a term, the interpretation most favourable to the consumer shall prevail. It should be noted that the requirement of plain, intelligible language also applies to terms dealing with the main subject matter of the contract, as this is a condition of the exemption.

¹   Council Directive 93/13/EEC.

7.48   The European aspect of this should also be noted. If a policyholder is resident in another member state and the law of that country applies then, unless a choice of law is available in that country, the requirement may be that the policy be in, for example, plain intelligible French or German. It should also be noted that member states are required by the UCTD[1] to ensure that if the consumer has a close connection with the territory of a member state, he does not lose the protection granted by the directive by virtue of a choice of law of a non-member state as the law applicable to the contract. However, there is an inference from this wording that where a choice of law is permitted in a member state, the insurer can insert a choice of law clause of another EU member state (namely the UK) and thereby ensure that 'plain intelligible language' means English, although this could be subject to the Third Life Directive[2] 'general good' requirements stipulating that the contract, or parts of it, be written in an official language of the host state.

¹   Council Directive 93/13/EEC.
²   Council Directive 92/96/EEC.

Burden of proof

7.49   The burden of proof that a term has been individually negotiated is on the seller/supplier (ie the insurer) and a term shall always be regarded as not individually negotiated where it has been drafted in advance.

Effect

7.50   As the UCTD[1] applies to contracts made after 1 July 1995 insurers should have reviewed their contractual documents to ensure that they comply with the terms of the directive and, in particular, the requirement for plain intelligible language. The emphasis in sales literature should therefore be to produce an understanding of the contract concerned in a manner which is intelligible to the consumer when he/she is deciding whether or not to enter into the contract.

¹   Council Directive 93/13/EEC.

Early cancellation of policies

7.51   The cancellation rules give investors the opportunity to make considered and well informed investment decisions. The cancellation provisions are now set out in Chapter 6 of the Conduct of Business Sourcebook (COB 6.7) issued by the Financial Services Authority under the Financial Services and Markets Act 2000 (FSMA 2000), and generally provide for at least 14 days in which to cancel.

Concept of 'qualification'

7.52 The concept of qualification is important for income tax purposes. The definition of a qualifying policy is complex but, broadly, the policy must be on the policyholder's or his or her spouse's life and it must secure a capital sum on death, earlier disability or not earlier than ten years after the policy is taken out.

7.53 The premiums must be reasonably even and paid at yearly or shorter intervals. There are additional requirements relating to the amount of the sum assured and sometimes also as to the surrender value. Providing these conditions are satisfied the policy proceeds are tax free (although the underlying fund will be subject to tax). However, where a qualifying policy is surrendered less than ten years after it was effected (or, for endowment policies, before the expiry of three quarters of the term if that is less than ten years) any profit is charged to tax at the excess of higher rate tax over basic rate to the extent that the profit falls within the tax payer's higher rate income tax band (but see later with regard to 'top slicing relief'). There will be no tax liability at the higher rate if the proceeds are no greater than the premiums paid, because there has been no profit.

7.54 For non-qualifying policies the proceeds are not wholly tax free. Whilst free of Capital Gains Tax (CGT), if the capital appreciation on realisation is such as to put the individual within the higher rate tax band when added to income in the tax year in which the chargeable event occurs, it is chargeable to income tax at the excess of higher rate tax over basic rate, subject to certain special provisions. Life policy gains are added in last of all in order to calculate any tax liability.

7.55 'Top slicing relief' is available to lessen the impact of the higher rate charge. The gain on the policy is divided by the number of complete policy years the policy has been held and the amount arrived at is treated as the top slice of income to ascertain the tax rate which is then applied to the full gain. The longer the policy has been held the smaller the annual equivalent on which the tax charge is based.

7.56 Switching investments between underlying funds, for example from an equity fund to a gilt fund, will not have any taxation effects, although there may be an administration charge for doing this.

7.57 Non-qualifying policies often take the form of single premium investment bonds. It is possible to make withdrawals of not more than five per cent of the initial investment in each policy year without attracting a tax liability at the time, such withdrawals being treated as partial surrenders which are only taken into account in calculating the final profit on the bond when it is encashed. The five per cent is a cumulative figure and amounts unused in any year increase the 'tax-free' withdrawal available in a later year. If more than five per cent is withdrawn tax will be charged on the excess but only if (taking this withdrawal into account) the policyholder's taxable income exceeds the basic rate limit, so that if the excess occurs in a year when the taxpayer is solely a basic rate taxpayer no charge will normally arise. Similarly, if final encashment of the bond can be delayed to a time (perhaps in retirement) when the taxpayer's income, even with the addition of the policy profit, will not attract the higher rate no tax will normally be payable. Where the bond is encashed on death any mortality element of the profit as distinct from the surplus on the underlying investments is not taxable and since the income in the year of death will usually not cover a full tax year, even on the taxable portion there may be little tax liability at the higher rate.

7.58 Encashment of the bond or an earlier chargeable event may result in a tax charge with regard to age related allowances even where the taxpayer does not pay tax at the higher rate.

Trusts and uses of life assurance

7.59 In broad terms life assurance is used either for protection or investment purposes (or a combination of these). The former can generally be facilitated by the use of trusts. The subject of trusts is dealt with in depth in the standard works and in relation specifically to life assurance in the *Law of Life Assurance*[1]. One of the better definitions of a trust is given by the Inland Revenue in its 1991 Consultative Document. This is as follows:

> 'A Trust is a legal obligation which binds a trustee (or trustees) to deal with property or income in a particular way, usually for the benefit of another person or class of persons (the beneficiaries). The person who provided the original funds for the trust (the settlor) may also be a trustee or beneficiary'.

The reason why trusts are so important with regard to 'protection' life policies is easily demonstrated by considering what would happen if, for example, a life policy with a sum assured of £292,000 is effected. If that policy is merely left to be dealt with in accordance with the policyholder's estate then, unless for example a surviving spouse benefits from the proceeds, there will be an IHT charge of £20,000 in respect of these proceeds alone, ignoring any other assets which may be contained in his estate. Had this policy been written subject to a suitable trust this charge would have been avoided. The fact that policy monies are payable outside of the taxable estate on death can also be used to provide a convenient fund to pay any IHT which does become due on the death of the testator so that assets (for example, the home) do not have to be sold in order to pay the tax.

---

[1] Houseman & Davies (12th edn, 2001).

7.60 Apart from taxation mitigation trusts are used as an alternative to wills or intestacy in the devolution of assets. Moreover, unlike wills, trusts can become effective during lifetime as well as on death.

7.61 Effecting policies in trust also has an advantage over wills in that provided there is a surviving trustee then on the death of the life assured the trustees can claim the proceeds immediately from the life office on production of the death certificate. If the policy had not been written in trust (or there are no surviving trustees) the beneficiaries of the estate would have to wait until a grant of probate (where a valid will has been left) or letters of administration (where there is no valid will) have been obtained.

7.62 In appropriate circumstances trusts can also be used for the purpose of creditor protection. In these circumstances it will be necessary to satisfy the provisions of the Insolvency Act 1986. It should be noted that there are particular provisions with regard to life policies effected in trust for spouses and/or children under the Married Women's Property Act 1882, so that even if fraud can be proven with regard to placing the policy in trust, the most that can be claimed back is the amount of premiums paid.

7.63 Trusts are also frequently used in connection with business assurance arrangements. Directors or partners effect policies in trust for their co-directors or co-partners so that on death the surviving directors or partners have a fund from which they can purchase the deceased's interest in the company or firm. There will often be an agreement to buy and sell shares, and it is generally advantageous that this be drafted on an 'option' basis for IHT business relief purposes. The issues and planning in this area can be very complex.

Policyholders Protection Act 1975 (PPA 1975)/Financial Services Compensation Scheme

7.64 The PPA 1975 was introduced largely as a response to a number of insurance company failures. The PPA 1975 introduced a compensation scheme to assist policyholders of an insurance company which has been wound up. The scheme was administered by the Policyholders Protection Board.

7.65 The FSMA 2000 provides for the new Financial Services Compensation Scheme, one of the objects of which is to merge all the existing compensation schemes which existed with regard to retail investments and to provide a single point of contact for consumers in the event of a firm being unable to pay claims against it. However, merger does not necessarily mean harmonisation of levels of cover. Indeed, priority was stated to be maintaining the levels of consumer protection offered by the existing schemes and only change arrangements where believed to be clearly justifiable.

The functions under the FSMA 2000, Pt XV are to be undertaken by the scheme manager and the Financial Services Compensation Scheme Limited (FSCS Limited) have been appointed by the FSA for this purpose, who will be independent of the FSA but accountable to it.

The FSMA 2000 sets out the required constitution and essential provisions of the scheme and provides for the FSA to be able to make rules relating to the scheme and also provides for the scheme manager to be able to impose levies. The FSMA 2000, ss 216 and 217 relate to the continuity of long-term policies and the provisions relating to insurers in financial difficulties respectively.

7.66 Chapter 3 of the FSCS Rules contains key provisions for life assurance companies. When an authorised insurer which provides long-term insurance cover is declared in default, FSCS Limited must try to arrange to continue cover with another insurer if this is more cost effective than paying compensation. Such action must only be taken if it is more cost effective than paying compensation. 'Financial difficulties' encompasses provisional liquidation; inability to pay debts under formal insolvency proceedings or an application has been made to court to secure a voluntary creditors arrangement, but the firm is not yet in liquidation or being wound up. Chapter 3 also sets out the qualifying conditions for paying compensation which are explained more fully in following chapters.

Eligibility to claim compensation is set out in the FSCS Rules, Chapter 4. Protection offered by the scheme is aimed at ordinary retail consumers. The provisions work on the basis that all persons are eligible to claim and then sets out a table of exclusions. Essentially, all long-term policyholders will continue to be protected (even if they are large companies) unless they are connected with the insurance company in some way.

The claim must also be a 'protected claim' which is explained in the FSCS Rules, Chapter 5. One of these can be in respect of a 'protected contract of insurance'. This follows the provisions where the establishment of the relevant person is in the UK, another EEA state, the Channel Islands or the Isle of Man. The commitment must also be habitually resident in one of these territories at the time the policy is entered into.

7.67 The 'relevant person' (such as a life assurance company as an 'authorised firm') must also be in default in order for claims to be made against it. Also described in this chapter are the circumstances in which a relevant person is in default. Examples include insolvency or bankruptcy. If compensation is offered the claimant may be required to transfer to FSCS Limited his rights to claim against other parties. The reasoning behind this is to maximise recoveries by FSCS Limited and prevents the affected consumer from taking action against the party(ies) in default. Offers may be withdrawn if disputed or not accepted within 90 days. Offers may be re-issued or varied. The FSCS Rules, Chapter 9 sets out time limits for payment of compensation. The limits on the amount of compensation payable for long-term insurance contracts remain as they were under the PPA 1975, namely at least 90% of the value of the policy, including future benefits declared before the date of default. Unlike bank and building society deposits and retail investments such as unit trusts there is no maximum payment. Payments in respect of life policies are to be made directly to the claimant or on his instructions. Partial payments or payments on account are also permitted where there may be some uncertainty about paying the full amount. Interest may also be payable on compensation payments at the discretion of FSCS Limited.

Guaranteed products

7.68 In most cases this implies a type of single premium investment bond although there are also guaranteed unit trusts and ISAs. The products in their various forms tend for marketing purposes to be aimed at building society investors and persons who (while still nervous of the stock market) would still like some exposure to equities.

7.69   Guaranteed products will generally guarantee a return based on the value of the FTSE 100 or other stock market index. At the same time, the product offers a minimum cash guarantee or other limitation to the potential downside. As stock market indices do not generally allow for the reinvestment of dividends in their day-to-day price the dividend income is effectively forfeited and used to meet the cost of the guarantee, expenses and profit margin of the life office.

7.70   Therefore, at maturity (usually five years) the investor receives an amount either based on the pre-agreed index element of the investment or some fixed, guaranteed, sum. Death benefit is usually stated to be a value no less than the original investment. Surrender values are not, however, usually guaranteed and may well be substantially lower than the original value.

7.71   For the taxation treatment of such products where these are insurance bonds (which are 'non-qualifying' policies) this is described above with regard to 'qualification'[1]. Where the guaranteed product is based on a unit trust vehicle or open ended investment company any gains on encashment from the unit trust (or 'OEIC') would be treated as capital gains and are liable to CGT.

---

[1]   See paras 7.52–7.58.

7.72   In order to provide the guarantee the product will generally combine an equity investment and what is known as a 'put option' with an exercise price equal to the guaranteed amount. A put option gives the purchaser the right to sell the underlying asset in question at a predetermined price. This underlying asset can be any of a wide variety of assets, and for the purpose of guaranteed products is likely to be stock indices. The product provider therefore backs his liabilities by buying a combination of suitable assets and tailored 'over the counter' options from an investment bank.

7.73   The perceived advantages of guaranteed products are probably greater than their real advantages as historically equity performance over five-year periods has almost invariably resulted in at the very least the return of the investor's capital. However, they appear to be popular for persons who have hitherto kept their money on deposit but are now interested in some exposure to equities.

INDIVIDUAL SAVINGS ACCOUNTS (ISAS)

7.74   Personal equity plans (PEPs) were introduced in the Finance Act 1986. The regulations governing PEPs were issued under the Income and Corporation Taxes Act 1988 (TA 1988) and the Taxation of Chargeable Gains Act 1992 (TCGA 1992). The original purpose behind PEPs was to encourage wider share ownership by individuals in UK companies by offering investment tax incentives. This original purpose was diluted to some extent by relaxations, for example, to permit investment in unit trusts which are able to invest in a range of investments. Successive Finance Acts have introduced changes which generally extended further the scope of PEPs in all respects. In 1997 PEPS were, in effect, replaced by ISAs by the incoming Labour Government. An ISA is not an investment in itself but a tax efficient 'wrapper' into which other investments are placed.

7.75 Anyone over the age of 18 and resident in the UK for tax purposes can take out an ISA. Crown employees working overseas and their spouses are deemed to be resident for this purpose. If a plan holder subsequently becomes non-resident, the plan can be maintained and its tax benefits preserved but no further subscriptions can be made in respect of that plan. For cash components of maxi ISAs and cash mini ISAs the minimum age is reduced to 16.

7.76 The tax benefits take the form of total exemption from CGT and income tax on realised capital gains and investment income earned from the underlying investments of the plan. A plan can be terminated at any time and the proceeds withdrawn without loss of the tax benefits.

7.77 There are two types of plan. A 'maxi' account and a 'mini account. A mini account is made up of one of the three specified components—stocks and shares, cash or insurance. A maxi account is a stocks and shares component with or without any of the other components.

7.78 There is no restriction on the investment switches that can be made and no income tax or CGT liability arises as a result. An ISA can be transferred from one account manager to another.

7.79 Currently the maximum investment into a maxi account is £7,000 per tax year and £3,000 into a mini cash ISA, £3000 into a mini stocks and shares ISA and £1,000 into a mini insurance ISA. ISAs also exist for maturing tax exempt special savings accounts ('TESSAS') which have no bearing on subscription levels for maxi or mini ISAs. An ISA can only ever be an individual investment and so it would not be possible to have a joint ISA. It is not possible to have a mini account if you have a maxi. However it is possible to have three individual mini accounts which may be with different account managers.

7.80 Tax relief is not available for investment into the ISA, as it is with pensions. However, the fund is virtually a gross fund in the same way as a pension fund. There is an advantage with ISAs in that all proceeds are tax free whereas at least part of what emerges from a pension scheme will be taxable. The Individual Savings Account Regulations 1998[1], regs 6–9 (the ISA Regulations 1998) prescribe what ISA subscriptions may be invested in.

---

[1]   SI 1998/1870.

7.81   Each plan must be managed by an account manager authorised under the FSMA 2000, or approved in some other way as set out in the ISA Regulations 1998[1], reg 14 and approved by the Inland Revenue. The ISA agreement or terms and conditions will contain various provisions concerning the conduct of the investor's investment, for example, arranging for the investor to receive copies of the reports and accounts of the companies in which he is invested. All records, dealing and other paperwork is the responsibility of the account manager whose function it is to deal with the Revenue on behalf of the investor. Also likely to be included in these terms will be provisions relating to charges and to termination of the plan.

---

[1]   SI 1998/1870.

7.82   The fundamental governing regulations for the operation of ISAs are contained in the ISA Regulations 1998[1], which have been amended on various occasions. Shortly before the withdrawal of PEPs the concept of 'corporate bond' PEPs was introduced which has been carried forward into the ISA regime. These are attractive because of the high rates of interest which attach to such investments. In order to qualify as a corporate bond investment for an ISA the bonds in question must, amongst other attributes, have a minimum of five years to maturity.

---

[1]   SI 1998/1870.

UNIT TRUSTS

Introduction

7.83   As the name suggests the underlying legal basis for this type of investment is the trust. The investors are the beneficiaries and there will be a trustee appointed (which will invariably be a corporate professional trustee) who will look after the trust assets. Unit trusts are, in the eyes of the investor, recognised more particularly by the manager (in whose name the unit trust will be branded and promoted) who will be responsible for the administration of the trust and for the management of the underlying investments. The constitution, management and marketing of unit trusts and the various rights, duties and obligations of the manager, trustee and investors are governed by the applicable trust deed and the various applicable statutes. In 1988 the responsibility for authorisation for new unit trusts passed from the Department of Trade and Industry to what is now the FSA. The regime established by the FSA 1986 concerning regulation, establishment and running of unit trusts, was replaced by the FSMA 2000, ss 235–284.

7.84   The definition of 'collective investment scheme' is wider than, but embraces, the concept of unit trusts (FSMA 2000, s 235). A specific reference to 'unit trust schemes' is contained in the FSMA 2000, s 243. Unit trusts are therefore a variety of collective investment scheme.

Legal nature

7.85 The underlying unit trust deed, as mentioned, is made between the managers, who are the promoters of the scheme and who are responsible for the conduct of the investment and administration, and the trustee (usually a trustee company subsidiary of a bank or building society), which is responsible for ensuring that the managers act in accordance with the trust deed, and which holds the assets of the trust on behalf of the unitholders. The underlying investments are registered in the name of the trustee which also holds any cash forming part of the fund. The trustee receives all income and other distributions in respect of those assets, such as dividends in respect of shares.

7.86 The trust deed and regulations also set out a formula for valuing a trust to determine the prices at which units must be bought back by the manager from unitholders. Additional units may be created to meet demand from investors or existing units may be cancelled as a result of the subsequent repurchase of units from investors. A unit trust is therefore 'open ended' and will expand and contract depending on whether there are more buyers or sellers.

7.87 The ability of a unit trust to borrow (known as 'gearing') is limited to 10% of the value of the property of the Scheme and is not available to geared futures and options funds.

7.88 Subject to the provisions of relevant regulations the trust deed may make provisions as to termination and also specify circumstances in which the approval of unitholders at a general meeting is required. For example, approval is required in order to vary certain provisions of the trust deed, such as to change the investment objectives or to amalgamate with another unit trust.

Authorisation

7.89 The central requirement for authorisation is that a trust deed conforming with the FSA's requirements is executed between a management company and an independent trust corporation to hold the trust's investments and supervise the managers. Both the managers and the trustee must be incorporated under a law of one of the countries within the UK or any other state within the EU, and must maintain a place of business within the UK and must be both authorised and with the relevant permissions under the FSMA 2000.

7.90 The directors of the management company must be approved by the FSA. The trust deed would provide for a number of issues, for example:

(1) managers' investment and borrowing powers and limits on investment of the trust assets;
(2) the manner in which prices and yields are calculated and provisions as to the repurchase of units from investors;

(3)   setting up the register of unitholders, with procedures for issuing certificates and dealing with transfers;
(4)   managers' and trustees' remuneration;
(5)   periodic audits of the trust and the issue of financial statements to unitholders, with reports by the managers, trustees and auditors;
(6)   unitholder meetings.

The consequences of authorisation are that it makes it possible for the managers to advertise units for sale to the public and carries with it certain taxation advantages.

Authorisation under the FSMA 2000, s 243 (unit trusts); FSMA 2000, s 262 (OEICS)

7.91   In order to be marketed to the general public an order under the FSA 1986, s 78 had to be in force with regard to that unit trust scheme. The applicable provisions were summarised in the previous edition of this book. The relevant provisions of the FSMA 2000 are now contained in the FSMA 2000, ss 243 and 262 as appropriate. The general rule (as set out in the FSMA 2000, s 238) is that authorised persons must not promote collective investment schemes but this is subject to exceptions in the case of authorised unit trust schemes and a scheme constituted by an authorised open-ended investment company. Other exceptions relate to 'recognised' schemes which generally means schemes constituted in other EEA states (FSMA 2000, s 264), schemes authorised in designated countries or territories (FSMA 2000, s 270) and individually recognised overseas schemes (FSMA 2000, s 272). Also, if the communication originates outside of the UK the restriction in the FSMA 2000, s 238 only applies if the promotion is capable of having effect in the UK.

Unit trust pricing

7.92   Since 1 July 1988, unit trust managers have been able to deal either on a 'forward price' basis, ie at the next price to be calculated, or at prices already calculated and published, ie an 'historical price' basis. However, in this case if the value of the trust is believed to have changed by more than two per cent since the valuation on which the company is offering to deal a new price must be calculated (using an index if the trustee agrees). Alternatively, the company would have to change to forward pricing.

Purchase of unit trusts

7.93   Individuals, corporate bodies or trustees may all purchase units subject to any limitation which may be imposed on their own investment powers. Unit trusts were specifically mentioned as 'wider range' investments under the Trustee Investments Act 1961. This has now been replaced by the Trustee Act 2000, which introduced a general wide power of investment which would permit investment in unit trusts for all trusts unless there was (unusually) something prohibiting investment in unit trusts in the trust instrument.

7.94   Most unit trusts specify a minimum investment limit with specialist funds tending to have a higher limit. In many cases monthly savings plans are available. As unit trusts are open ended there is no maximum holding though corporate or trustee investors may be restricted by their own investment limitations.

7.95   Non-UK residents may invest in unit trusts subject to the domestic laws and regulations in their countries of residence or domicile. Many UK managers and OEICS will specifically not deal with US residents.

Investments of unit trusts

7.96   Unit trusts must invest their portfolios in accordance with the invest-ment and borrowing powers as set out in CIS 5 of the *Collective Investment Schemes Handbook* which specifically deals with investment and borrowing powers. Managers must also take into account the trust deed and scheme particulars.

7.97   Most unit trusts invest predominately in equity shares although preference shares, gilts and other fixed interest investments, are also held for the purpose of generating a yield.

7.98   Traditional authorised unit trusts generally only invest in securities although new classes of unit trusts are permitted to invest in other financial instruments, or property, and mixed funds invest in several different types, including commodities. These schemes have certain rules and regulations which apply only to those particular schemes. Most unit trusts may make use of traded options (in a prescribed manner) for efficient portfolio manage-ment purposes. Any call options written and put options bought must be covered by the relevant securities held in the trust. It is not currently possible to have 'split' unit trusts under which income accrues to one class of holder and capital appreciation to another.

7.99   Although all unit trusts will have their own particular objectives in terms of stated investment powers in the trust deed itself, all unit trusts share certain general characteristics.

Spread of risk

7.100   An investor can achieve a much wider spread of risk by purchasing a unit trust, which in turn invests in a wide range of securities, than he could himself achieve economically with limited resources. The risks inherent in holding shares in one company or a small number of companies are therefore avoided. The result, in theory, should be a more even progression of income and capital growth. This is reinforced by regulations regarding the maximum investment of a trust's assets in a single company or issue. In practice, unit trusts usually hold between 30 and 100 different securities which is well in excess of the required minimum.

Professional management

7.101   Investment in a unit trust effectively involves a delegation of the day-to-day management of an investor's portfolio to the unit trust managers. Unit trust management companies generally employ a team of investment experts whose function is to seek to maximise the investment returns of the trust(s) for which they are responsible. The advantage to the investor is that his investments are under the continuous supervision of professionals whose business it is to keep under review economic, political and corporate developments.

Simplicity and convenience

7.102   The paperwork involved in owning a portfolio of securities is usually avoided. Decisions relating to rights and scrip issues, mergers and takeovers are all taken by the managers. Dividends are received by the trustee and distributions of the trust income are made to unitholders together with reports on the progress of the trust.

Marketability

7.103   As an open-ended investment, so units can be created or cancelled to meet the requirements of investors. Unit trusts are therefore a generally very liquid investment with none of the restrictions on marketability encountered with some other types of investment.

Types of unit trusts

7.104   There is a wide range of unit trusts which offer a variety of investment objectives designed to suit different categories of investors. The main types are as follows.

(1)   *Balanced*—investment mainly in 'Blue Chip' shares with the aim of achieving steady growth of both income and capital.
(2)   *Income trusts*—aim is to achieve an above average yield to investors seeking a high and growing income. They may purchase convertible shares as a way of achieving their yield objectives.
(3)   *Capital trusts*—these are designed to seek maximum capital growth and the income produced is likely to be low.
(4)   *Fixed interest trusts*—these generally invest in government bonds, corporate bonds and convertible shares. They may be income or capital trusts.
(5)   *Overseas trusts*—investors have the opportunity to invest through these in stock markets in other countries in the world. The complexity involved in overseas investment for the private investor can be avoided by investment via unit trusts. Overseas investment can be rewarding if sterling is weak or economic conditions are more buoyant in overseas regions.
(6)   *Specialist trusts*—these invest in particular sectors of the securities market (eg commodities, smaller companies or new technology companies). They are inherently more risky than more balanced trusts.

(7)   *Accumulation trusts*—certain trusts within all the above categories are structured on the basis that they will accumulate the income rather than distribute it. The income is nonetheless subject to taxation as if it had been received by unitholders.

(8)   *'Tracker' trusts*—certain trusts are structured to imitate the performance of a stock market index.

Taxation

7.105   Authorised unit trusts attract the relevant CGT treatment described below[1]. For taxation purposes an authorised unit trust is one which, for any accounting period, is a unit trust scheme that has been authorised under, currently, the FSMA 2000, s 243. By virtue of the TA 1988, s 468, for taxation purposes an authorised unit trust is effectively treated as a company with unitholders being treated in the same way as shareholders in a company, with distributions of income treated in the same way as dividends paid to shareholders. An exception to this is fixed interest unit trusts. A major advantage for unitholders is that within the unit trust itself there is an exemption from CGT. However, the unitholder would be personally liable for any gains made by him on a disposal of units. The taxation provisions relating to unit trusts have, with certain modifications and exceptions, been extended to OEICS under the Open-ended Investment Companies (Tax) Regulations 1997, SI 1997/1154, regs 3–5.

---

[1]   See para 7.107.

Taxation of the unit trust: income tax

Franked income

7.106   This was income received by a unit trust in the form of dividends paid by a UK company in respect of which that company had paid advance corporation tax (ACT). ACT was effectively a payment by a UK company on account of its own corporation tax liability and made in respect of dividends paid by it. The amount of dividend plus the ACT was known as 'franked payment'. From 6 April 1999, ACT was abolished and the tax credit reduced to 10%. Non-taxpayers are not able to reclaim any of this tax credit. Starting and basic rate taxpayers have no further liability to tax on the dividend if the addition of the 'grossed up' dividend does not create a higher rate tax liability.

Capital gains of unitholders

7.107   Capital gains made on units in authorised unit trusts are treated in the same way as gains made on any other type of security, ie the gain, after allowing for indexation, is added to the taxpayers' income for tax purposes. Currently, capital gains up to £7,500 are exempt from tax.

Charges in respect of unit trusts

7.108   On purchase there is usually an initial charge payable to the managers which is incorporated in the unit price. The trust deed must contain a figure for the maximum permissible charge. Initial charges are normally in the region of 5–6 per cent. More managers are moving to a system of no initial charges but with exit charges on encashment in the early years. Most managers pay commission to authorised agents and intermediaries. This is borne by the managers from the initial charge.

7.109   Annual management fees based on the value of the trust are deducted by the managers from the unit trust income. The maximum permitted level of annual management fees must be laid down in the trust deed. If managers wish to increase fees within the maximum figure, investors must be given 90 days written notice. Increases in the maximum figures must be approved by unitholders in accordance with the trust deed. Fees charged usually vary between 0.75 and 1.00 per cent per annum.

7.110   Certain other costs, for example, custody fees for holding overseas investments and collecting foreign dividends, may be charged to the income of the trust. Stamp duty and broker's fees on the purchase and sale of underlying investments are borne by the trust but are reflected in the unit prices.

Offshore funds

7.111   This is a broad term applied to a range of investment mediums whether it is a unit trust, an investment trust company or an investment oriented life assurance policy which is issued by an insurer outside of the UK, often in a so-called 'tax-haven'. The jurisdictions in which such funds are based are usually those which attract little or no local tax, such as the Channel Islands, Isle of Man, Bahamas, Bermuda, Cayman Islands, British Virgin Islands and Luxembourg. The precise taxation effects depend upon a range of factors, such as residence of the unit trust, investment company or life office, where it invests and the existence, or otherwise, of double taxation treaties.

   Offshore funds may or may not be recognised under the FSMA 2000, ss 264, 270 or 272.

Advertising unit trusts

7.112   The statutory basis permitting the promotion of authorised unit trust schemes is contained in the FSMA 2000, s 238. The provisions relating to Financial Promotion of Collective Investment Schemes is now set out in the Conduct of Business Sourcebook, Chapter 3 (COB 3).

The UCITS Directive

7.113   The Council of the European Community adopted the UCITS Directive[1] in December 1985 (subsequently amended in 1988) which concerned the co-ordination of laws, regulations and administrative provisions relating to undertakings for collective investment in transferable securities. The intention behind the UCITS Directive is to harmonise laws in this area throughout the European Community and to facilitate the cross-border marketing of collective investment schemes which comply with its provisions. In order to qualify as a UCITS certain investment and other limitations must be complied with. The influence of the UCITS Directive in the UK can be seen in the FSA and subsequent legislation.

---

[1] Council Directive 85/611/EEC.

OPEN ENDED INVESTMENT COMPANIES (OEICS)

7.114 At the time of writing the chapter on 'Retail products' in the last edition of *Butterworths Financial Services Law Guide* it was thought that OEICS would substantially replace unit trusts as the most popular collective investment vehicle in the UK. However, whilst there has been a degree of replacement of unit trusts it is probably true to say that this has not been as extensive as was originally anticipated. In terms of spread of risk, professional management, simplicity and convenience, types of investment fund and reasons for investing, OEICS have virtually identical characteristics to unit trusts as set out above.

7.115 Regulations were introduced in order to put in place the regulatory framework for OEICS in the form of the Open Ended Investment Companies (Investment Companies with Variable Capital) Regulations 1996[1].

---

[1] SI 1996/2827.

7.116 OEICS are collective investment schemes under the FSMA 2000. Unlike unit trusts, OEICS are corporate bodies and thus have a separate legal existence unlike a unit trust. OEICS must have an 'Authorised Corporate Director' (ACD) responsible for running it on a day-to-day basis and the ACD will often be the only director of the company. This position has many similarities in practice to that of the unit trust manager. It must also have a depositary responsible for safekeeping of the assets. The depositary must be independent of the OEIC and its directors. It exercises a similar function to that of the trustee under a unit trust. Unlike unit trusts, the beneficial interest in the underlying assets is vested in the OEIC, not its shareholders. Both the ACD and the depositary must be authorised under the FSMA 2000. OEICS are able to offer a variety of share classes whereas unit trusts could only offer two types of units. Whilst unit trusts have tended in the past to operate a dual pricing system, OEICS will all operate 'single pricing'.

7.117 A further advantage of OEICS is that it will be easier to convert or amalgamate them than unit trusts. In addition a more flexible regime applies to OEICs in terms of the extraction of charges, subject always to proper disclosure in the OEIC prospectus.

The Association of Unit Trusts and Investment Funds

7.118   This was originally established by the industry in 1959 as the Association of Unit Trust Managers (later renamed the Unit Trust Association). In 1993 the name was amended to its current title to reflect the interests of its members in PEPs, open-ended investment companies, investment trusts and UCITS funds set up in other EC member states, as well as unit trusts. The Association acts as a consultative body in agreeing industry standards and as a representative body for managers in dealing with governmental and regulatory bodies. Prior to the FSA 1986, the Association acted very much as a Self-Regulatory Organisation supervising such things as advertising, pricing and commission payments to agents. The FSA and the SRO rulebooks (and latterly the FSMA 2000 and COBS) have effectively superseded this particular function.

7.119   However, AUTIF continues to exert significant influence in the area of collective investments and publishes useful information packs, leaflets and other publications.

PENSIONS

7.120   Apart from those provided by the state, pensions can in general terms be divided into occupational schemes and personal schemes. The former relate to an individual's employment and the latter relate to either an individual's self-employment or to situations where no occupational scheme is available, or in rare cases where the employee chooses not to be a member of his employer's scheme. Within each of the above broad categories there are a range of variations. For example, it is possible to have occupational pension schemes with one or two members and group personal pension schemes with hundreds of policyholders. Although all personal pensions are provided by a pension provider (usually an insurance company) the position with regard to occupational schemes can be much more varied. They can be provided fully by an insurance company at one extreme or, at the other, fully self-administered. There can be a range of intermediate schemes where part is insured and part is self-administered (known as 'hybrids').

7.121   The entire framework of private pension provision was fundamentally altered with effect from 6 April 2001. The distinction between occupational schemes and personal pension schemes (which is, however, still useful for other purposes) was replaced by a new system under which schemes now fall within the 'defined contribution' regime or the 'defined benefit' regime. The framework for retirement annuities will not be affected in any way. The introduction of stakeholder pensions has also been a significant recent development and is considered below.

Occupational pension schemes

Introduction

7.122   State pensions only provide a modest income in old age, even though employees' pensions are increased by an earnings-related addition known as the State Earnings Related Pension Scheme (SERPS) unless 'contracted out'.

From 6 April 2002 the second state pension (S2P) will replace SERPS. In order to encourage individuals and their employers to make pension provision for themselves and reduce the burden of pension provision on the state the Government therefore gives generous tax treatment to occupational schemes.

7.123 Provided an employer's scheme provides at least equivalent benefits to SERPS, employees may be 'contracted out' of the earnings-related element of the state scheme, thus paying lower contributions to it. This can now be done by guaranteeing minimum contributions to employees' pensions (contracted-out money purchase schemes (COMPS) or 'Defined Contribution' (DC) schemes) rather than having to guarantee the benefits on retirement (a final salary or 'Defined Benefit' (DB) scheme). Contracted-out employees still receive their basic pension from the state and any additional benefits from their employer's scheme.

7.124 Many employers, particularly smaller ones, prefer to remain contracted in to the state scheme and provide their own pension scheme in addition. The employee then gets full benefits under the state scheme (and pays full contributions) plus the additional benefits provided by his employer's scheme.

7.125 Employees in a contracted-in scheme are able to contract out of SERPS independently while remaining in their employer's scheme, either by setting up and making contributions to a free-standing additional voluntary contribution or through a separate personal pension plan.

7.126 Those in personal pension schemes have been able on retirement to defer using their pension fund to buy an annuity and have some flexibility as to how much income they draw in the meantime. This is termed 'Income Drawdown' or 'Pension Fund Withdrawal'. It is probably fair to say that it has had a mixed reception from commentators but at the very least it does provide some additional flexibility in taking pension benefits. It is now available in connection with occupational schemes although the rules are quite different.

The trust as the basis of occupational pension schemes

7.127 Except in very limited circumstances the underlying structure of an occupational pension scheme is the trust and, in general, this has worked well as the effect of a trust is to separate the pension scheme assets from the assets of the employer. The pension trustees' duties arise not only from the terms of the trust deed but from the general law relating to trusts and increasingly by statute and especially the Pensions Act 1995 and the Trustee Act 2000. The importing of the trust concept into occupational pension schemes has not been universally easy as the law relating to trusts originally evolved in the context of family trusts and not commercial operations. There is a contractual as well as a trust relationship underpinning occupational schemes. Nevertheless, the Goode Committee expressed its faith in trust law as the continuing basis for occupational schemes.

Documentation for occupational pension schemes

7.128   In order to provide an idea of the type of documents encountered in the establishment and running of an occupational scheme the following list sets out the most common ones:

- Interim Document;
- Definitive Trust Deed (the core document);
- Deed of Adherence (to enable associated companies to join in);
- Deed of Alteration/Variation;
- Deeds of Appointment/Retirement of Trustees;
- Winding up documentation (Resolution or Deed);
- Transfer Agreement (eg on a takeover);
- Application for Membership;
- Indemnities;
- Employee Announcement;
- Contracting-Out Notices;
- Reports, etc under disclosure regulations;
- Investment Management Agreements (where outside investment managers are to be employed).

Membership of occupational pension schemes

7.129   Employees cannot be obliged to be members of their employers' schemes, unless the scheme is non-contributory and provides only death benefits. Employees are able to take out personal pension plans instead or rely on the state pension scheme. In practice this would be very rare as it would normally be in the employee's interest to be a member of the employer's occupational scheme. Pension rights from an existing occupational scheme may be transferred to a personal pension plan. It is possible to transfer back from a personal pension plan to an employer's scheme if the receiving scheme so permits.

Inland Revenue approval for occupational schemes[1]

7.130   The underlying taxation approval legislation for occupational schemes is found in ICTA 1988, ss 590–612. This legislation now covers the 'Defined Benefits' regime. It also covers money purchase occupational schemes that chose not to be subject to the DC Rules and other arrangements such as Additional Voluntary Contributions and 's 32 contracts'[2]. Working instructions for DB schemes are provided in the Occupational Pension Schemes Practice Notes—IR12.

To obtain Revenue approval, the employer must contribute to the scheme but the employee is not required to.

---

[1]   Income and Corporation Taxes Act 1988, ss 590–612.
[2]   Finance Act 1981, s 32 (see now Income and Corporation Taxes Act 1988, s 591(2)(g)).

7.131   A scheme obtains automatic Revenue approval provided it conforms precisely to the statutory conditions. The Revenue may, however, approve other schemes on a discretionary basis and nearly all schemes follow the discretionary approval route under which greater benefits can be paid (but of course at a higher cost in contributions). The Revenue issues Practice Notes on the manner in which they exercise their discretion and schemes can therefore be structured so that they will receive the approval of the Pension Schemes Office (PSO). Schemes may be either 'defined benefit' (DB) schemes, under which the benefits depend on final salary, or 'defined contribution' (DC) (money purchase) schemes, under which the contributions are fixed and the benefits depend on those contributions and on the investment performance of the assets of the scheme.

7.132 A pension fund's investment in employer-related investments is generally limited to five per cent of the current market value of the fund (except for small self-administered schemes)[1].

---

[1] Pensions Act 1995, s 40 and Occupational Pensions Schemes (Investment) Regulations 1996, SI 1996/3127.

What is the purpose in obtaining Revenue approval?

7.133 The following sets out the taxation advantages of exempt approved schemes:

(1) the employer's contributions reduce business profits for corporation tax purposes;

(2) the employer's contributions are not treated as a benefit in kind to the employee (and so the employee is not subject to income tax in respect of those contributions), nor do they count as the employee's earnings for national insurance contributions;

(3) an employee's own contributions (up to a maximum of 15% of his remuneration) reduce his earnings for tax purposes (but not for national insurance contribution purposes);

(4) a tax-free lump sum (obtained by commutation of pension benefits) can be paid to the employee on retirement;

(5) provision can be made for a lump sum to be paid on an employee's death in service, which is usually free of IHT;

(6) the income and capital gains of the fund are not taxed, although since 2 July 1997 the government has removed the ability of pension funds to reclaim tax credits in respect of dividends arising from UK companies.

Retirement age

7.134 Normal retirement age may be at any age between 60 and 75. Early retirement may be allowed from age 50 and is also permitted prior to then for incapacity and for certain special occupations.

Maximum contributions

7.135 Maximum contributions depend on earnings, which means the amount on which an employee is chargeable to tax under Schedule E, including benefits in kind but excluding taxable amounts under share option or incentive schemes or lump sum termination payments.

7.136   For final salary schemes, there is no specific upper limit on the amount that an employer may contribute, subject only to the requirement that the benefits provided as a result are within the permitted levels and the contributions are not excessive in relation to those benefits. There are, however, regulations to prevent schemes being overfunded and 'surpluses' arising.

7.137   If an employee joins a scheme late, it is possible to make contributions of several times the employee's current earnings in order to fund the maximum benefits. Special irregular contributions may be made by the employer in addition to the normal annual contributions.

7.138   As mentioned, an employee cannot be required to contribute to a scheme but if the employee does, then contributions (including any additional or special contributions to obtain additional benefits) must not generally exceed 15 per cent of his earnings. For schemes set up on or after 14 March 1989 and for those joining existing schemes on or after 1 June 1989, there is a limit (referred to as the 'earnings cap') on the earnings on which contributions may be paid. This limit is usually increased annually in line with increases in the retail prices index (note—not in line with increases for average earnings). Currently it is £95,400[1].

---

[1]   This figure is expected to change to £97,200 following the next budget.

Concurrent membership of DB and DC schemes

7.139   Where the DB scheme provides death in service benefits only, the legislation allows concurrent membership of a life cover only occupational pension scheme under the DB regime and a money purchase occupational pension scheme under the DC regime in the same way that it was, and still is, possible to be a member of a life cover only occupational scheme and make personal pension contributions. All employees can have benefits on this basis, including controlling directors and those whose earnings exceed £30,000.

7.140   The maximum contribution that can be paid into the DC regime scheme is the greater of:

*   £3,600;
*   the personal pension percentage of net relevant earnings for the relevant basis year subject to the earnings cap.

The cost of the life assurance benefits on the DB side, would not affect the maximum contribution permitted to the DC side.

7.141   The legislation permits the Inland Revenue to approve a scheme partly as a DB regime scheme and partly as a DC regime scheme. Hence, a money purchase occupational pension scheme effected prior to 6 April 2001 would be able to split into two, with part approved under the DC regime and part under the DB regime.

THE DB SCHEME PROVIDES PENSION BENEFITS

7.142   The legislation governing the circumstances in which an individual can be accruing pension benefits under a DB regime scheme and also make contributions to a DC regime scheme, is contained in ICTA 1988 (as added through the Finance Act 2001) and the Personal Pension Schemes (Concurrent Membership) Order 2000[1].

---

[1]   SI 2000/2318.

7.143   The rules are as follows.
A member of a DB regime scheme can contribute to a DC regime scheme (normally a Stakeholder scheme) where:

- the individual has not been a controlling director at any time in the current tax year or in any of the five previous tax years;
- the individual's remuneration from the current employment in any one of the five previous tax years did not exceed £30,000. Where the earnings were for only a part of the tax year, the annualised equivalent is used;
- tax years before 2000/2001 are not taken into account for the above purposes.

The £30,000 limit will not automatically increase in any way. It can only be changed by order of the Treasury. The maximum contribution that can be paid to the DC regime scheme is £3,600.

7.144   In practice it is likely that contributions on this basis will usually be made by employees as an alternative to AVCs within the DB regime rules. However, it is possible for the employer to contribute as well. It is still possible for an employee to contribute up to 15% of earnings to the DB regime scheme and associated AVC arrangements.

7.145   Before contributions can be accepted by the DC regime scheme, it is necessary for the individual to provide a certificate to the scheme administrator which:

- identifies the tax year (any of the five tax years immediately preceding the current tax year, but not going back beyond 2000/2001) in which earnings did not exceed £30,000 (the 'qualifying year');
- confirms that the total contributions to be made to all DC regime schemes in the current tax year will not exceed £3,600;
- confirms that the total contributions to be made to all DC regime schemes in any future tax years which fall within the five tax years immediately following the 'qualifying year' will not exceed £3,600;
- gives the name and address of any person who pays the member the remuneration from the relevant employment.

Additional voluntary contributions (AVCs)

7.146   An employee wishing to increase his potential pension may pay AVCs to the employer's scheme or to a scheme of his choice (a 'free-standing' AVC). Any AVCs paid must not take the employee's total contributions to more than 15 per cent of his earnings (the earnings being subject to the 'cap' where relevant). No part of the additional benefits earned may be taken as a tax-free lump sum, except for AVCs to an employer's scheme under a contract to purchase added years which will produce a precise level of pension and lump sum benefit and AVCs that are paid under arrangements made before 8 April 1987. Some AVCs may have to be refunded on retirement or earlier death if the combined benefits from occupational and free-standing schemes are excessive. Tax is deducted from such refunds in accordance with the ICTA 1988, s 599A.

A free-standing AVC may be used by an employee to contract out of SERPS individually, even though his employer's scheme is contracted in.

Employees: maximum benefits

CALCULATION OF MAXIMUM BENEFITS

7.147 Other than for 'off-the-peg' money purchase schemes, maximum benefits are measured in terms of 'final pensionable remuneration'. This is the greater of the remuneration in any one of the five years before retirement (with averaging for fluctuating payments) or the average of total remuneration for any period of three or more consecutive years ending in the last ten years before normal retirement date.

7.148 Unless the 'final remuneration' is that of the 12 months ending with normal retirement date, each year's remuneration included in the calculation may be 'dynamised', ie increased in proportion to the increase in the Retail Prices Index for the period from the end of the year up to normal retirement date.

Different rules apply to directors of 'close companies'.

MAXIMUM PENSION

7.149 The maximum pension payable under final salary (DB) schemes is two-thirds final remuneration, at the maximum rate of 1/30th for each year's service up to 20 years. The standard formula is however, 1/60th of final remuneration for each year of service ('straight sixtieths'). For members of an existing scheme at 16 March 1987, the maximum can apply after ten years' service. Inflation-proofing may be provided for within the funding of the scheme. Under provisions in the Pensions Act 1995, pension payments under final salary schemes may be inflation-proofed in line with the Retail Prices Index or five per cent per annum if greater. Part of the pension may be commuted for a lump sum.

Pensions from other schemes

7.150 Benefits at the 1/30th per year rate (or accelerated rate for members of the pre-16 March 1987 schemes) may usually be provided in addition to any pension benefits from previous occupations or self-employed pension plans, providing the combined benefits do not exceed two-thirds of final remuneration.

Lump sums

7.151 Part of the available benefits may be commuted for a lump sum. The maximum lump sum is normally 3/80ths final remuneration for each year of service up to 40, giving a maximum of 1.5 times final remuneration, but this may be varied or restricted depending on when the employee joined the scheme.

7.152 For schemes set up on or after 14 March 1989 and those who join existing schemes on or after 1 June 1989, the lump sum cannot exceed 1.5 times the 'earnings cap'. There is also an alternative to the 3/80ths calculation. If it gives a higher figure, the lump sum is calculated as two and a quarter times the amount of the pension before commutation. This enables late entrants to get the maximum lump sum in appropriate circumstances.

7.153 In calculating the maximum lump sum payment, lump sums from earlier employments must be taken into account. If dynamised final remuneration is used to calculate the pension, it may also be used to calculate the lump sum. If a lump sum is to be taken, the maximum pension of two-thirds final remuneration will of course be reduced as a result.

Dependants' benefits

7.154 Provision for dependants may be made both for death in service and for death after retirement. Inflation increases may be provided for in both cases. A pension to a surviving spouse may continue for the spouse's lifetime, but children's pensions must cease when they reach age 18 or cease full-time education.

DEATH IN SERVICE

7.155 If an employee dies in service, a lump sum up to four times final remuneration (which is defined in a more generous way than for other benefits) may normally be paid without attracting IHT. In addition, the employee's own contributions may be repaid with interest. The pension scheme trustees have complete discretion as to who receives the death in service lump sum, but they generally act in accordance with the employee's known wishes as expressed in any completed nomination form. There may be a theoretical IHT problem where the employee dies in service after the earliest age at which he could have retired. The capital value of the pension he could have taken immediately before death may be taken into account for IHT. The Revenue have, however, stated that this will not apply in genuine cases of deferred retirement, and will only apply where there is evidence that the intention behind deferring benefits was to increase another person's estate[1].

---

[1]   Inheritance Tax Act 1984, s 3(3).

7.156 Pensions may also be paid to the surviving spouse and/or dependants. The pension paid to any one person cannot exceed two-thirds of the maximum pension the employee could have received if he had retired on incapacity grounds at the date of death (with potential service up to normal retirement age being taken into account). The total pensions to spouse and dependants cannot exceed the total incapacity pension the employee could have received.

7.157   Provision may be made for an employee's pension to continue for a set period after retirement despite his earlier death (a 'guarantee'). Separate pensions for spouse and dependants can also be provided, subject to the individual pensions not exceeding two-thirds of the maximum pension that could have been approved for the employee and the total pensions not exceeding the whole of that maximum.

Unapproved pension schemes

7.158   In addition to approved schemes it is possible to establish unapproved pension schemes either alongside approved schemes, or on their own. Such schemes became very popular after the budget of 1989 which announced the removal of certain penal provisions and, importantly, the imposition of the 'cap' referred to earlier. Unapproved schemes have both advantages and disadvantages. As with an approved scheme the employer's contributions are usually deductible in arriving at taxable profits. However, they are taxed as a benefit on the individual employees (apart from the amount needed to establish and administer the scheme when they are actually received). National insurance contributions (NICs) were not originally payable. But in June 1997 the government announced that it would introduce legislation to stop relief from NICs in respect of payments made into a 'FURBS' (Funded Unapproved Retirement Benefits Scheme) with effect from 6 April 1999. Somewhat unusually, however, the Contributions Agency of the Department of Social Security (DSS) received legal advice to the effect that legislation already existed to enforce the payment of NICs in these circumstances and a press release was issued on 17 November 1997 to clarify the position. Provided contributions were not made in order to avoid NICs they would not pursue the payment of NICs for contributions made prior to 6 April 1998. But from that date all contributions to an employer's FURBS would be subject to employer's NIC. Also, if the employer agrees to pay the employee's tax the DSS consider that national insurance contributions are due on the amount paid in respect of tax.

7.159   Unapproved schemes can be either unfunded or funded. For funded schemes income and capital gains are taxable according to the normal trust taxation rules. If the trust is confined to the provision of relevant benefits it will be taxed at the lower rate on most of its investment income. The main problem with unfunded schemes is the potential lack of security.

7.160   Death in service payments are usually free of IHT, providing of course they are not paid to the employee's estate. The employee can take the benefits on retirement wholly as a tax-free lump sum. He could take a pension instead, but as the pension would be taxable, it would be better to take the cash and, for example, buy a life annuity, part of which (the capital element) would then be free of tax. Providing the employer's contributions are wholly and exclusively for the purposes of the trade, there is no limit on the amount that can be contributed, and no limit on the tax-free lump sums that can be paid out.

7.161 Measures were introduced to block the use of offshore funded schemes that pay little or no tax to provide increased tax-free lump sums to employees. For offshore schemes established or varied on or after 1 December 1993, tax is charged at the employee's marginal rate on any difference between the lump sum received and the employer's and employee's contributions to the fund.

7.162 Unsurprisingly, unapproved schemes can be much more flexible than exempt approved schemes but there are advantages in having a similar 'structure and operation' to approved schemes.

EFFECTS OF LEAVING SERVICE ('PRESERVATION' REQUIREMENTS)

7.163 When an employee leaves employment, then provided he has been in the pension scheme for at least two years, he will be entitled either to have a preserved pension (within the former employer's scheme) which will become payable on retirement, or a transfer payment to a new scheme (if the scheme will accept it) or to an insurance company in order to purchase a 'buy out' policy (still known colloquially as a s 32 policy after the FA 1981, s 32 under which such policies were originally issued—see now ICTA 1988, s 591(2)(g)) or a personal pension plan. Where there is a preserved pension under a final salary scheme, it must be increased each year in line with the increase in retail prices (or by five per cent if less). These are the revaluation and indexation requirements[1].

Refunds of contributions are not usually available except for periods of employment of less than two years, but where they are made tax is deducted at the rate of 20 per cent.

---

[1]   Pensions Act 1995, ss 51–54.

'SURPLUSES'

7.164 There are special rules for pension scheme surpluses. A fund is technically in surplus where the statutory valuation basis, in accordance with guidelines specified by the Government Actuary, shows that the projected value of the scheme's assets is more than five per cent higher than the projected cost of paying pension benefits to members. The trustees are required to reduce the surplus to the five per cent level by a combination of:

(1)   increases in pension benefits (within permissible limits);
(2)   a reduction or suspension of contributions by the employer and/or employees for up to five years (a contribution 'holiday'); and
(3)   a refund to the employer (subject to stringent conditions, including for final salary schemes, the need to provide for inflation-proofing of pensions).

For final salary schemes, trustees also have the option of paying tax on the surplus.

7.165 If a refund is made, it cannot reduce the surplus to *below* five per cent. The trustees are required to deduct 40 per cent tax at source from any refund they make to the employer and pay it over to the Revenue within 14 days. Interest is charged for late payment. In no circumstances can a company obtain a repayment of the 40 per cent tax because of trading losses or other available reliefs.

7.166 The question as to who actually owns a pension scheme surplus is one which has occupied the time of many lawyers and the judiciary from the mid-to-late 1980s, and continues to do so as is evident from the National Grid and National Power cases.

Small self-administered pension schemes[1]

7.167 A particular variety of occupational scheme is the self-administered pension scheme where the contributions remain under the control of trustees appointed by the company and are not paid to a pensions provider. While it gives maximum flexibility in managing a fund, the pension scheme trustees must invest in the best interests of the members. It is also possible to have what are often called 'hybrid' schemes where the funds are partly managed by a pensions provider. The fund will also usually hold appropriate life assurance cover on the scheme members so that its funds are not unduly diminished by the death of a member.

---

[1]   See Retirement Benefits Schemes (Restriction on Discretion to Approve) (Small-Self Administered Schemes) Regulations 1991, SI 1991/1614.

7.168 A small self-administered scheme (ie one with less than 12 members) is subject to specific regulations that control its format, funding and investment powers. It may borrow up to an amount equal to three times the normal annual contribution which it receives from the company and from scheme members plus 45 per cent of the value of the scheme assets. This could be helpful in boosting its funds for, say, the purchase of premises for use by the company. The borrowing is paid off by future annual contributions from the company and in the meantime the interest cost is covered in such a case by the rent charged by the pension fund to the company.

7.169 Loans to pension scheme members or their families are forbidden, but loans to the company itself, or to buy shares in it, or the purchase by the trustees and leaseback of the company's premises, may be permitted (subject to certain restrictions), providing each member of the scheme is a trustee, and has given written agreement in advance to the proposed investment and is at a commercial rate of interest. Apart from the provision of a pension this sale and leaseback facility is viewed as one of the main attractions of such schemes.

7.170   Anti-avoidance provisions have been introduced to charge tax at 40 per cent on the market value of the scheme's assets if an approved scheme becomes unapproved (for example, by transferring offshore).

Payment of pensions

7.171   Tax on pensions under occupational schemes is taxed as earned income under Schedule E and dealt with under the PAYE scheme, with coding adjustments being made where some or all of the available allowances have been used against other income, such as state pensions.

Personal pensions

Introduction[1]

7.172   The self-employed and those not in an employer's pension scheme are entitled to tax relief on the premiums they pay to provide their own pension (in addition to receiving the state pension via national insurance contributions).

---

[1]   Income and Corporation Taxes Act 1988, ss 630–655.

7.173   The relevant rules were changed from 1 July 1988. Pre-1 July 1988 contracts are known as retirement annuity contracts and the old rules still apply to those contracts. Contracts starting on or after 1 July 1988 are called personal pension plans. Most of the rules for old and new schemes are the same but, for example, new schemes must make provision for transfers on change of employment/self-employment.

7.174   Personal pension schemes may allow members to direct where their funds are to be invested, subject to restrictions to ensure that the scheme still meets the conditions necessary for tax approval.

7.175   With effect from 6 April 2001 the Income and Corporation Taxes Act 1988, ss 630–655 (which were previously the provisions covering personal pensions) now govern the new defined contribution ('DC') regime. However significant amendments are contained in the Finance Act 2000, Sch 13. In addition to new and existing personal pension arrangements this regime also includes new and existing money purchase occupational pension schemes which chose to either come within or, for existing schemes, move to, the defined contribution regime. It also applies to stakeholder pension schemes. Working instructions are also provided in the personal pension scheme guidance notes (including stakeholder pension schemes)—IR76 (2000).

Qualifying individuals

7.176   Those who are self-employed, or who are not members of an employer's pension scheme, may contribute to a pension fund for themselves by paying premiums within stipulated limits to one or more pension providers. A person who has earnings from both a pensionable employment and one that does not carry any pension rights may pay premiums in respect of the non-pensionable earnings.

7.177 Retirement annuity premiums have to be paid to an insurance company, but personal pension contributions can also be paid to any 'personal pension provider'. In addition to insurance companies this includes friendly societies, banks, building societies or unit trust managers. In all cases, the annuity is purchased from an insurance company with the fund at retirement and the 'best buy' available at that time can be selected by exercise of the 'open market option'.

7.178 The fund into which premiums are paid is free of tax on both income and capital gains, although since 2 July 1997 it is no longer possible to reclaim tax credits on dividends in respect of UK companies.

Permissible benefits

7.179 The retirement benefits must commence not later than age 75 nor earlier than age 50 (60 for retirement annuities), except in cases of ill health or where the occupation is one in which earlier retirement is allowed by the Revenue, for example entertainers and athletes.

7.180 At retirement the whole fund may be used to buy an annuity, which will be taxed as income, or a tax-free lump sum may be taken, with the balance used to buy an annuity. For personal pension plans, the lump sum may not exceed one quarter of the fund. There is no overall maximum but the 'earnings cap' for net relevant earnings (currently £95,400[1]) on which premiums can be based will itself limit the size of the pension fund. Payment of the pension may be guaranteed for up to ten years if the taxpayer dies within that time. Should death occur before retirement, the contributions are refunded, with or without interest and bonuses. The refund may be to the personal representatives or to any other person. Alternatively, the death benefits may be held in trust, with the moneys payable at the trustees' discretion. IHT will usually be avoided where the proceeds are held in trust but where someone works on past the earliest possible pension age under the policy with the deliberate intention of benefiting someone else, a charge to IHT may in theory arise (IHTA 1984, s 3(3)).

---

[1]   This figure is expected to change to £97,200 following the next budget.

Deferring personal pension annuity purchase[1]

7.181 For schemes approved or amended after 1 May 1995, those with personal pension contracts may defer buying an annuity until, at latest, age 75. This enables persons to defer buying an annuity when rates may be low which has increasingly been the case. They can still take a tax-free lump sum at retirement and they may make taxable income withdrawals from the fund during the deferral period up to a maximum that is broadly equivalent to the annuity they could have taken (with a minimum income withdrawal of 35 per cent of the maximum). The fund remains fully invested, but further contributions may not be made once any benefits (including income withdrawals) have been taken.

---

[1] Income and Corporation Taxes Act 1988, s 634A.

7.182 If the pension scheme member dies during the deferral period, a surviving spouse or dependant will be able to take the fund in cash (subject to a tax charge of 35 per cent), or buy an annuity immediately, or continue making income withdrawals and buy the annuity at latest when that person reaches age 75 (or when the pension scheme member would have reached age 75 if earlier). If the survivor dies before buying the annuity, the fund may be paid in cash to his or her heirs (net of tax at 35 per cent).

7.183 The ability to defer annuity purchase used only to apply to those with personal pension contracts. This has now been extended to occupational schemes and 's 32' contracts provided this is allowed under the terms of the scheme or contract, although the precise rules are different.

Allowable contributions

7.184 Contribution limits are fixed by reference to 'net relevant earnings'. For a self-employed person, this broadly means his taxable profits, after deducting capital allowances, losses and any excess of business charges over general investment income. For an employee, net relevant earnings are those from an employment not carrying any pension rights. The earnings figure includes the cash equivalent of benefits, but is after deducting expenses allowable against those earnings. In line with occupational schemes, an employee's relevant earnings under personal pension plans exclude earnings under share option and incentive schemes and lump sum termination payments. An overall limit ('earnings cap') applies to net relevant earnings under personal pension plans (but not retirement annuity contracts) as with the limit for occupational pensions. This figure is usually increased annually in line with inflation.

7.185 The maximum contributions which may be allowed as a deduction from relevant earnings in any one tax year is the greater of £3,600 gross (the actual contribution payable being £2,808 net of income tax relief at the basic rate of 22% or for someone aged 35 or under the amount of 17.5 per cent of the net relevant earnings, plus any unused relief for the previous six years. Unused relief is the amount that could have been paid in an earlier year by reference to the net relevant earnings of that year, less what was actually paid in respect of that year's earnings. The percentage limit is increased for taxpayers over 36 at the beginning of the tax year on an increasing basis up to a maximum of 40 per cent at 61 or over for personal pension plans.

7.186 Where someone has pension contracts both under the old and new schemes, the personal pension contribution (PPC) limits are reduced by any retirement annuity premiums paid. The different age limits for personal pensions and retirement annuities and the fact that personal pensions are subject to the earnings cap whereas retirement annuities are not, makes the calculation of maximum available premiums very complex in some cases.

7.187 Employees may use personal pension plan arrangements to contract out of the State Earnings Related Pension Scheme (SERPS) still, however, contributing for a basic retirement pension. It is also possible for an employee in a contracted-in pension scheme to remain in the scheme but contract out of SERPS independently through a personal pension plan. It should be noted that from 6 April 2002 SERPS will be replaced by a new state second pension (S2P) which is generally more widely available than SERPS.

7.188 An employer can contribute to the personal pension scheme of an employee, but the maximum contribution levels (17.5 per cent or higher) cover the combined contributions (but not those by the DSS). Employers' contributions cannot be backdated to earlier years nor can unused relief brought forward be used to cover an employer's contribution.

Stakeholder pension schemes[1]

7.189 All stakeholder pension schemes must be approved by the Inland Revenue as falling within the DC regime, and then by the Occupational Pensions Regulatory Authority (OPRA) as a Stakeholder Scheme. Schemes can be set up either with a 'Scheme Manager' or a board of trustees.

---

[1] Welfare Reform and Pensions Act 1999, ss 1–8, and Stakeholder Pension Schemes Regulations 2000, SI 2000/1403 (and subsequent amending regulations).

7.190 Schemes must permit the payment of contributions from a bank or building society account by either cheque, direct debit, standing order a direct credit (other than standing order). Schemes are not obliged to accept payment by cash or credit card. There can be no restriction on the amount of contributions that can be made to the scheme with the exception that schemes are not obliged to accept contributions below £20. (This is the amount actually paid, ie net of income tax relief at the basic rate for a member, gross for an employer.)

Charges and advice

7.191 The annual management charge for each member must not exceed one per cent of the fund value. This limit is expressed in the legislation as $1/365$ per cent of the fund value for each day the fund is held under the scheme.

7.192 Charges incurred in operating the investments under the scheme (such as dealing charges) can be accounted for in full when determining the value of the fund for the purpose of applying the management charge.

Schemes are not allowed to make any additional charges for administering incoming transfer payments, nor for making transfer payments out of the scheme.

7.193 Schemes are allowed to levy charges to cover the administrative expenses incurred in:

- the purchase of an annuity;
- making payments under income drawdown.

These charges are separate to the 'one per cent' limit.

7.194 Schemes must provide basic information and explanatory material within the one per cent maximum annual management charge. Schemes are not required to make individual financial advice available within the one per cent maximum charge, but they can if they wish. If there is to be an additional charge for advice, it must be in the form of a separate fee. The availability of the advice must be optional for the individual, if the individual is expected to pay the fee.

Contributions on behalf of other people

7.195 It is possible to make contributions on behalf of other people. If such cases, the contribution is treated as having been made by the recipient for tax purposes and thus, if the recipient is a higher rate tax-payer, additional relief can be claimed in the normal way. The donor makes the contribution net of income tax relief at the basic rate even if he or she is a non tax-payer.

7.196 Contributions made in this way are gifts for inheritance tax purposes but the donor's £3,000 annual exemption or the 'normal expenditure out of income' exemption may be available to exempt the gift.

It is also possible for an employer to make contributions in respect of a person who is not an employee—for example a director's wife or child. It seems unlikely that such a contribution would be treated as 'wholly and exclusively for the purposes of the trade' and thus would not be allowed as a deduction when calculating profits liable to corporation tax.

Personal pensions and bankruptcy

7.197 This is an area which has become of increasing concern to personal pension policyholders and their advisers. Unlike with occupational schemes, 'forfeiture clauses' have not in the past been viewed as effective to prevent a trustee in bankruptcy from being able to claim the proceeds of a bankrupt's personal pension (although in effect it is only once the policyholder has reached 50 that the policy is of any value to the trustee in bankruptcy as he can be in no better position than the policyholder himself). This stems from the 'personal' nature of personal pension schemes and the effects of the Insolvency Act 1986. The Pensions Act 1995, s 191 provides for a statutory 'inalienability' clause for occupational schemes whilst omitting personal pension schemes from the ambit of the rule. Concern has been expressed at this apparent unequal treatment afforded to personal schemes. The case of *Re Landau*[1] confirmed that a retirement annuity constituted 'property' in accordance with the definition in the Insolvency Act 1986 and hence was available to the trustee in bankruptcy. It is generally thought that the same principles would apply to personal pensions. The cases of *Krasner v Dennison: Lawrence v Lesser*[2] specifically considered personal pensions. It was held that statutory restrictions on assignment do not restrict the rights of the trustee in bankruptcy and so policies vest in the trustee in bankruptcy. Also it is not necessary to obtain an income payments order to make income available to creditors. Therefore, for these purposes personal pensions are treated in the same way as retirement annuities. Many personal pensions are now being written subject to 'forfeiture clauses' (also known by other names) but it is not absolutely clear whether they are effective. The case of *Lesser v Lawrence* was the subject of an appeal to the House of Lords but this was not ultimately proceeded with. The position could be clarified for the future as the Welfare Reform and Pensions Act 1999 contains a section (s 11) which makes it clear that pension rights (including under personal pensions) would be excluded from a bankrupt's estate. However, the relevant section has not yet been brought into force.

---

[1]   [1997] 3 All ER 322.
[2]   [2000] 3 All ER 234.

Pensions Act 1995 (PA 1995)

7.198   The provisions of the Pensions Act 1995 (PA 1995), were a response to a variety of issues of concern to the pensions industry. However, the late Robert Maxwell's widely reported activities in relation to the Mirror Group's pension funds was probably one of the main catalysts for the PA 1995.

7.199   The Social Security Select Committee conducted investigations into the ownership and control of pension fund assets which led to its call in its March 1992 report[1], for further investigation into the precise structure of a Pensions Act. The government obliged in June of that year and established the Pension Law Reform Committee to:

> 'review the framework of law and regulation within which occupational pension schemes operate, taking into account the rights and interests of scheme members, pensioners and employers; to consider in particular the status and ownership of occupational pension funds and the accountability and roles of trustees, fund managers, auditors and pension scheme advisers; and to make recommendations.'

The Committee's report (the Goode Report) made over 200 recommendations. The main one being for a Pensions Act to 'lay out a properly structured framework of rights and duties, and a Pensions Regulator . . . with overall responsibility for the regulation of occupational pension schemes'. These recommendations were adopted by the government in its White Paper (*Security, Equality, Choice: the Future of Pensions*). The intention being that it would provide for greater pensions security by measures designed to achieve 'the greatest practicable security' and that the new legislation would provide a clear framework of statutory obligation on employers, trustees, managers, professionals and members.

¹   Second Report, *The Operation of Pension Funds* (HC Paper 61–II (1991–92)).

7.200   In brief terms the PA 1995 provides the following main measures:

(1)   it provides for a public regulator of schemes with specific statutory duties and powers for enforcing the terms of the PA 1995. Namely, the Occupational Pensions Regulatory Authority (OPRA) which also replaces the Occupational Pensions Board;

(2)   it provides in statutory form an attempt to crystallise duties and responsibilities of scheme trustees and provisions to tighten up scheme management;

(3)   duties in relation to investment requirements have been made more stringent. The position of the trustee in scheme security and operation is reinforced;

(4)   it obliges professionals involved with schemes to be part of the policing of those schemes—the 'whistle blowing' provisions;

(5)   it provides for a quota of trustees to be made up of those nominated by members;

(6)   it provides for a compensation scheme to be established (the Pensions Compensation Board);

(7)   it requires that men and women be provided with equal benefits and the equalisation of the state pensions scheme;

(8)   stringent requirements as to payment of surplus to the employer;

(9)   obligations with regard to indexation of pensions after retirement;

(10)   new minimum funding, winding-up and transfer value requirements;

(11)   new contracting out provisions;

(12)   provisions regarding pensions and divorce (see below for more detail).

The result was a large and complex statute comprising 181 sections and seven Schedules. It also authorises the making of regulations which provide much of the detail to the PA 1995.

Pensions and divorce

7.201   Prior to the PA 1995, there was not much that divorcing spouses or the courts could do about pensions, other than to take them into account when allocating the matrimonial property. The case of *Brooks v Brooks*¹ brought this issue very much into public focus. The divorce and pensions law reforms in the PA 1995 give a new range of options.

¹   [1996] AC 375.

7.202   In 1993, the Pensions Management Institute (PMI)/Law Society working party reported. Its conclusions were endorsed in the Goode Report. It recommended that pension splitting should be introduced which involved allowing the court to award part or all of the cash equivalent to a spouse on divorce. She could then leave her pension rights with the scheme, or move them to a personal pension. However, many commentators were not keen about pension splitting and the significant problems in practice were set out in a green paper 'Treatment of pension rights on divorce', published by the DSS in July 1996.

7.203   The government agreed to compromise when it was outnumbered during the passage of the PA 1995. In exchange for dropping it, 'earmarking' provisions were agreed. Earmarking is an order given to the pension scheme trustees, which stipulates that at retirement, part or all of any lump sum or pension payable to the member shall be paid instead to the ex-spouse. These provisions appeared as the PA 1995, s 166 inserting new ss 25B and 25C into the Matrimonial Causes Act 1973. They came into force on 1 August 1996, dated back to petitions issued after 1 July 1996. Orders can be made against the pension scheme immediately for lump sum orders and from April 1997 for pension orders.

7.204   Pressure for pension splitting (based largely on the argument that it was preferable because it met the clean-break objectives of modern divorce law) resulted in the introduction of the Welfare Reform and Pensions Act 1999, introducing appropriate new rules. In effect the new rules allow an immediate transfer of benefits rather than simply earmarking deferred maintenance. The relevant order will therefore be unaffected by the members death or the claimant's future remarriage. Other notable aspects of the new rules are that they are not retrospective; earmarking remains an option; all rights (including AVCs) are included; the claimant does not have to transfer (in which case he or she becomes a member of the scheme); the system operates on the basis of 'debits' against the members rights and 'credits' for the claimant; pension sharing provisions must be included in new scheme rules; for SSAS purposes membership resulting from pension sharing does not count in determining whether it is 'small'[1].

---

[1]   See further PSO update No 62, and Finance Act 1999, s 79, Sch 10.

The effects of EC membership

7.205   The UK's membership of the European Community since 1973 has only slowly affected occupational pension schemes, but the *Barber*[1]case in 1990 highlighted the effect of the Treaty of Rome, art 119 (now 141) on occupational pension schemes. Article 119 was confirmed to have direct effect in the UK without the need for national legislation. The judgment held that pensions form part of pay and required normal retirement ages for men and women to be equalised (with effect from 17 May 1990 only as was later confirmed by the Maastricht Protocol in 1993). As many occupational pension schemes mirrored the state retirement ages of 65 (men) and 60 (women), this created major problems in both financial and trust law terms. The later European Court of Justice decision in *Avdel*[2] in September 1994 exacerbated the financial problems by reiterating the EC concept that benefits for the disadvantaged sex should be levelled-up to those of the advantaged sex in order to achieve equality (although they could thereafter be levelled-down for both sexes). The PA 1995 attempts to assist trustees and pension schemes by giving them authority to effect equality and override trust law provisions which in some cases have made equalisation impossible or difficult to achieve.

---

[1]   *Barber v Guardian Royal Exchange Group* C-262/88, [1990] ECR 1-1889, ECJ.
[2]   *Smith v Avdel Systems Ltd* C-408/92, [1994] ECR 1-4435, ECJ.

Equal treatment

7.206   The Council Directive 86/378 of 24 July 1986 regarding the implementation of the principle of equal treatment for men and women in occupational social security schemes resulted in the introduction of the Social Security Act 1989, Sch 5 in the UK. The *Barber*[1] case in 1990 is a landmark case in the history of UK pensions law. Essentially it meant that normal retirement ages for men and women had to be equalised in occupational pension schemes in advance of equalisation of state retirement ages.

---

[1]   See para 7.205.

7.207   The Social Security Act 1989, Sch 5 was based on the Sex Discrimination Act 1975. However, as this was incompatible with the *Barber* judgment, which emphasised that pensions should be treated as pay for the purposes of the Treaty of Rome, art 119, this approach was abandoned. The government has used the opportunity presented by the PA 1995 to remove the restrictions in the Equal Pay Act 1970 applying to pensions. This is achieved by the introduction into occupational pensions of an 'equal treatment rule' similar to the 'equality clause' imported into contracts of employment under the Equal Pay Act 1970.

7.208   The PA 1995, s 62 deems an occupational pension scheme to have an equal treatment rule so that terms relating to access and benefits must be no less favourable for women than the corresponding provisions applicable to them (in very broad terms) in similar employment. The equal treatment must also apply to the exercise of a discretion by the trustees or managers (PA 1995, s 62(5)) and to benefits for dependants (PA 1995, s 63). Discrimination on grounds of marital status is covered in PA 1995, s 63(2).

7.209   The new equal treatment rule will not apply where the trustees or managers of a scheme can prove that the difference in treatment is genuinely due to a material factor which is a material difference between the woman's case and the man's case (other than sex). The PA 1995, s 63(3) allows a scheme to implement the maternity and family leave provisions of the Social Security Act 1989, Sch 5 that otherwise would be discriminatory.

7.210   PA 1995, s 64 sets out two further exceptions to the equal treatment rule. The first allows variations between pensions attributable to differences in state retirement pensions[1]. This appears to protect bridging pensions in line with the European Court of Justice ruling in the *Birds Eye Walls Ltd v Roberts*[2] decision although the scope of the exception is unclear. The second covers variations between men's and women's occupational pensions attributable to the use of sex-based actuarial factors for calculation of contributions to a scheme by employers or for calculation of benefits (PA 1995, s 64(3)). This supports the decision of the European Court of Justice in the case of *Neath v Hugh Steeper Ltd*[3] which allowed sex-based actuarial factors to be used in a final salary scheme since they related to scheme funding. The government has left itself room for considerable manoeuvre in the PA 1995, s 64(4) to add to the list of exceptions or to repeal or amend exceptions.

---

[1]   PA 1995, s 64(2).
[2]   C-132/92, [1993] ECR I-5579, ECJ.
[3]   C-152/191, [1993] ECR I-6935, ECJ.

7.211   Trustees or managers of an occupational pension scheme are given a unilateral discretion to amend their scheme documentation to ensure that equality is achieved (PA 1995, s 65). This only applies if the scheme's own amendment procedures are inadequate or too complex or protracted, or it is difficult to obtain member consents.

7.212   *Barber* left many questions unanswered so in any effort to reduce the uncertainty created the government assisted in the financing of an application by the ECJ of the trustees of the various Coloroll pension schemes concerning issues arising from *Barber*, including the extent of its retrospective effect. The essential points to arise from *Coloroll*[1] were:

(1)   the *Barber* judgment affects accrual in respect of service from 17 May 1990;

(2)   schemes are covered whether they are contracted in or out, contributory or non-contributory;

(3)   when post *Barber* accrual is not equalised, the benefits of the disadvantaged group are levelled up, although future accrual may be levelled down by an appropriate rule change;

(4)   part-timers may have redress if they have been excluded from an employer's scheme and shown discrimination (albeit indirect)[2];

(5)   dependants pensions must also be equalised from 17 May 1990.

---

[1]   C-200/91, [1994] ECR I-4389.
[2]   See also the Part Time Work Directive (Council Directive 97/81/EC) and Employment Relations Act 1999.

Chapter 8   Clients' Money

Susan Brownlie[1]

SOURCE AND GENERAL PRINCIPLES

8.1   The Financial Services and Markets Act 2000 (FSMA 2000) sets the framework for the Financial Services Authority's (FSA) detailed client money rules. The FSMA 2000 makes provision for the FSA to make rules in relation to the handling of money by authorised persons[2]. Broadly, the legislation provides for the FSA to make provision for money to be held on trust. In addition, the legislation covers the treatment of accounts as a single account (see distribution rules) and for rules relating to interest, both payable to clients and retained by the firm. Importantly, the legislation states that[3]:

> 'an institution with which an account is kept in pursuance of rules relating to the handling of clients' money does not incur any liability as constructive trustee if money is wrongfully paid from the account, unless the institution permits the payment—
>
> (a)   with knowledge that it is wrongful; or
>
> (b)   having deliberately failed to make enquiries in circumstances in which a reasonable and honest person would have done so'[4].

---

[1]   Deborah Sabalot of Landwell provided assistance in the preparation of this chapter, particularly in relation to legal sources.

[2]   FSMA 2000, s 139.

[3]   See the FSMA 2000, s 139(2).

[4]   In the application of the FSMA 2000, s 139(1) to Scotland, 'the reference to money being held on trust is to be read as a reference to its being held as agent for the person who is entitled to call for it to be paid over to him or to be paid on his direction or to have it otherwise credited to him', as set out in the FSMA 2000, s 139(3).

8.2   The FSA is required to act in a way which is compatible with its regulatory objectives. These objectives include the protection of consumers[1]. The FSA has defined its principles which are a general statement of the fundamental obligations of firms under the regulatory system[2]. These principles derive from the FSA's rule-making powers as set out in the FSMA 2000. The principle which deals with clients' assets is Principle 10. This states that: 'A firm must arrange adequate protection for clients' assets when it is responsible for them'. Breaching a principle makes a firm liable to disciplinary sanctions[3]. Some of the detailed rules and guidance in the *FSA Handbook* deal with the bearing of the principles upon particular circumstances but the principles are also designed as a general statement of regulatory requirements (for example, in new or unforeseen circumstances).

THE *FSA HANDBOOK* AND THE CONDUCT OF BUSINESS RULES

8.3   The FSA has sought to document all its rules and guidance in a single document known as the *FSA Handbook*. This *Handbook* is divided into sections dealing with high level standards, business standards (ie detailed rules), regulatory processes (eg the authorisation process), redress (eg compensation arrangements), and specialist sourcebooks (eg a sourcebook for collective investment schemes). The principles are located in the high level standards section of the *FSA Handbook*. The detailed rules and guidance relating to the protection of assets for which a firm is responsible are located within the business standards section of the *FSA Handbook*. These rules are known as the 'client asset' rules and are located within the 'Conduct of Business Sourcebook' (COB) within the business standards section of the *FSA Handbook*. The client asset rules are divided into five sections, the first four sections deal with custody, mandates, client money and collateral respectively. The final section deals with client money distribution (that is, the rules applicable when events such as the failure of the firm occur). In this chapter the term 'firm' is used to mean an authorised person[1]. This is the convention adopted within the *FSA Handbook*. Within this chapter no distinction has been made between rules, guidance and evidential provisions although the references in the footnotes show whether the requirement takes the form of a Rule (R), of Guidance (G), or Evidential provision (E)[2].

---

¹   *FSA Handbook*, Glossary.
²   The status of the different types of provisions depends on the terms of the FSMA 2000 and the particular power exercised to create that provision. An introductory description to the terms is provided in the Reader's Guide section of the *FSA Handbook*.

Scope of the client asset rules

8.4   Whilst a few of the conduct of business rules are applicable to firms carrying on all types of regulated activities (including deposit taking and insurance related activities) the majority of the rules in this section of the *FSA Handbook* are limited in their scope to firms which are carrying on designated investment business[1]. In relation to deposits, pure protection contracts and general insurance contracts, COB has only limited application[2]. Individual sections of COB set out the extent of their application to different types of regulated activities. The application rules differ for the client money and custody rules within COB. The client money rules apply to 'a firm that receives or holds money from, or on behalf of, a client in the course of, or in connection with its designated investment business', except where otherwise provided by the rules[3]. The disapplications are as follows:

[1]   The definition of 'designated investment business' is provided in the Glossary section of the *FSA Handbook*. The activities described in this definition derive from activities specified in the Financial Services and Markets Act 2000 (Regulated Activities) Order 2001, SI 2001/544. Note that not all the activities specified in the Order are included within the 'designated investment business' definition.
[2]   COB 1.3.2G(2).
[3]   COB 9.3.1R.

8.5   Broadly, the client money rules do not apply to:

(1)   the permitted activities of a life office or a friendly society;
(2)   coins held for their intrinsic value, although the custody rules could apply to these assets;
(3)   money held by a firm which is an approved bank where this money is held by the bank in an 'account with itself'. This is dealt with in more detail below;
(4)   money held by depositaries[1].

[1]   COB 9.3.2R. The term depositary is defined in the *FSA Handbook*, Glossary and COB 11 deals with trustee and depositary activities.

8.6   The application of the client money rules to European branches of UK firms and to UK branches of European firms is governed by the Investment Services Directive[1]. Where firms are 'passporting'[2] their activities under the Investment Services Directive then the home state is responsible for prudential supervision of investment firms. This 'prudential supervision' includes a requirement for proper client money arrangements. Consequently, where a UK regulated entity opens a branch in an European Economic Area state (eg Germany) then the FSA's client money rules are the rules applicable to the activities of the branch. Similarly, if a German investment firm were to open a branch in the UK then this branch would be subject to German rather than UK requirements in relation to client money arrangements.

[1]   Council Directive 93/22/EEC.
[2]   FSMA 2000, Sch 3.

8.7   A new Inter-Professional Conduct (IPC) regime[1] will apply to dealings which a firm has with a market counterparty where the activity relates to an inter-professional investment. The list of investments is broadly:

• shares;
• debentures;
• government and public securities;
• certificates representing certain securities;
• futures;
• warrants;
• options;
• contracts for differences;
• rights to, or interests in, investments falling within the other categories listed above.

Transactions relating to deposits, general and long-term insurance contracts and units in collective investment schemes will fall outside the inter-professional conduct regime.

---

[1]   *FSA Handbook*, Market Conduct section (MAR 3).

8.8   The IPC regime covers the activities of dealing and arranging deals in IPC investments with advice covered only to the extent that it is given for the purposes of dealing or arranging services that the firm is already providing, or which it wishes to provide[1].

---

[1]   MAR 3.1.2R.

8.9   Whilst most of the provisions in the conduct of business sourcebook (COB) will not apply to inter-professional business, the requirements in COB 9 (customer assets) will apply where a firm provides safekeeping and administration of assets. In particular, the COB requirements in relation to holding money for clients will apply in connection with inter-professional business.

Customer classification[1]

8.10   In order to properly appreciate the FSA's conduct of business rules in general and in particular, their client money rules, it is necessary to understand the FSA's terminology as used to define the different groups of customers and market participants with which they interact. The key definitions used in the conduct of business rules are as set out below[2]. There are various references below to different customer types being reclassified as different types. The rules provide for some clients to be reclassified where certain conditions apply. Consent and/or notification requirements typically attach to these reclassifications.

---

[1]   The full definitions from the *FSA Handbook*, Glossary, should always be used when classifying a client. The text in this section is indicative rather than representing precise definitions. Note that the definitions are frequently varied for COB 3 (financial promotions).

[2]   See paras 8.11–8.14.

Client

8.11   For the purposes of most sections of the *FSA Handbook* including the Conduct of Business Sourcebook the term 'client' means 'any person with or for whom a firm conducts or intends to conduct designated investment business or any other regulated activity'. Every client will be either a market counterparty or a customer.

Market counterparty

8.12   Broadly, the definition of a market counterparty includes:

- governments;
- central banks;

- a supranational whose members are countries or central banks or national monetary authorities;
- a state investment body;
- another firm (ie regulated entity);
- an overseas financial services institution;
- a client when he is classified as a market counterparty in accordance with COB 4.1.12R (large intermediate customer classified as a market counterparty);
- an associate of a firm or associate of an overseas financial services institution, where the firm or institution consents.

The following are excluded:

- a collective investment scheme;
- a client who would otherwise be a market counterparty, when he is classified as a private customer in accordance with COB 4.1.14R (Client classified as private customer).

Intermediate customer

8.13 Broadly, the definition of an intermediate customer includes:

- a local authority or public authority;
- a body corporate with shares listed on an EEA exchange/primary board listed companies on any IOSCO member country official exchange;
- a body corporate with called up share capital or net assets of £5 million;
- SPVs;
- partnerships or unincorporated associations with net assets of at least £5 million;
- a trustee of a trust with assets of at least £10 million;
- a trustee of an OPS, SSAS or stakeholder pension scheme where the trust has not less than 50 members and assets under management of not less than £10 million;
- another firm, or overseas financial services institution, when that firm or institution is an intermediate customer in accordance with COB 4.1.7R (classification of another firm or an overseas financial services institution);
- an unregulated collective investment scheme;
- a client when he is classified as an intermediate customer in accordance with COB 4.1.9R (expert private customer classified as intermediate customer).

The definition excludes:

- a regulated collective investment scheme; and
- a client who would otherwise be an intermediate customer, when he is classified in accordance with COB 4.1.12R (large intermediate customer classified as market counterparty) or COB 4.1.14R (client classified as private customer).

Private customer

8.14   Those clients not satisfying the definition of market counterparty or intermediate customer will be classified as private customers. A firm can treat them as 'experts' (that is, as intermediate customers) if they can demonstrate that the customer has sufficient experience and understanding for this classification.

Identifying client money

8.15   Not all money arising in a regulated entity will automatically fall within the scope of the rules. A key aspect of ensuring compliance with the FSA's client money rules is the correct identification of money which falls within and outside the rules.

8.16   The definition of client money provided in the *FSA Handbook* reads:

'subject to the client money rules, money of any currency which, in the course of carrying on designated investment business, a firm holds in respect of any investment agreement entered into, or to be entered into, with or for a client, or which a firm treats as client money in accordance with the client money rules'[1].

The following notes set out the key criteria to be considered in determining where the client money rules are applicable. In particular the notes examine the terms 'designated investment business' and 'client' which are key to the definition.

---

[1]   *FSA Handbook*, Glossary.

Type of business (COB 9.3.1)

8.17   The client money rules apply to a firm that receives or holds money from or on behalf of, a client in the course of, or in connection with, its 'designated investment business', except where otherwise provided in the rules[1]. Client money can only arise in relation to designated investment business activities, so activities which fall outside this definition such as lending or deposit taking cannot give rise to client money to which the COB client money rules will apply.

---

[1]   COB 9.3.1R.

8.18   Although firms undertaking regulated activities must be authorised under the FSMA 2000, they are not precluded from undertaking activities which are not regulated activities. In addition, a regulated firm may carry out regulated activities which fall outside the definition of designated investment business. Any firm involved in activities other than designated investment business is not considered to hold client money in respect of those activities.

Money which is not client money (COB 9.3.8–9.3.24)

8.19 The initial sections of COB 9.3 (on client money) contain rules and guidance which specify a number of situations in which money arising in the course of designated investment business will not need to be treated as client money.

Money due and payable to the firm (COB 9.3.19–9.3.24)

8.20 Money which is properly due and payable to the firm for its own account is not client money[1]. An evidential provision provides guidance on the term 'due and payable' in the context of fees and commissions[2]. Broadly, fees and commissions can be treated as due to the firm from five business days after a statement showing the fees has been sent to the customer, provided these fees were accurately calculated on a basis previously disclosed to the client and the FSA regulated firm has no reason to believe that the client questions the amount of the fees or commissions shown on that statement[3].

---

[1] COB 9.3.19R.
[2] COB 9.3.20E and COB 9.3.21G to COB 9.3.22G.
[3] COB 9.3.20E.

Money from an affiliated company (COB 9.3.17–9.3.18)

8.21 Affiliated companies are considered to be so closely related to the firm that their money should be treated as the firm's money and should be held separately from any client money. However, where money from an affiliated company belongs to an underlying client the segregation of this money would be in accordance with the principle of investor protection. Hence, the rules specify that the money from affiliated companies should not be given client money protection unless:

(1)   the firm has been notified by the affiliated company that the money belongs to a client of the affiliated company; or
(2)   the affiliated company is a client dealt with at arm's length; or
(3)   the affiliated company is a manager of an occupational pension scheme or is an overseas company and the money has been given to the firm in order to carry on designated investment business for or on behalf of the clients of the affiliated company and the firm has been notified by the affiliated company that the money is to be treated as client money[1].

Whilst the general principle is that group company money should not be treated as client money, in fact the result of these exemptions, in particular those for money belonging to underlying clients of the affiliated company and for situations where the affiliated company is treated on an 'arms length' basis, is that, in fact, most group company money is held in protected accounts.

---

[1] COB 9.3.18R.

DVP transactions (COB 9.3.15–9.3.16)

8.22   Even where a transaction constitutes investment business and, prima facie, client money could arise, it is necessary to consider the settlement process involved in the transaction. Delivery versus payment (DVP) transactions are those transactions where it is intended that the transfer of securities and cash will take place on the same day. Clearly, if a client delivers securities to the firm or pays for the purchase of securities without receiving an asset (in the form of cash or securities) from the firm in exchange, then the client is at risk.

8.23   The client money rules provide a concession where there is a short-term delay in the delivery to, or payment of, a client in relation to a DVP transaction since these delays are not considered to represent a significant risk to the client. Where the client delivers securities or cash to the firm on day one, the firm must provide client money protection to the client's funds only if delivery or payment by the firm has not occurred by the end of day four. Hence the firm effectively has a 'three (business) day window' in which to resolve the mismatch of delivery and payment before it is required to protect the client's money[1].

---

[1]   COB 9.3.15R.

8.24   A similar principle applies for money received by a firm in relation to the issue of units in a regulated collective investment scheme. This money will only need to be treated as client money if the price of the units has not been determined by the close of business on the next business day after receipt. If the money was received by an appointed representative of the firm, some time is allowed by the rules for transmission to the firm. In addition, if money is held in the course of redeeming units it need not be treated as client money if the redemption proceeds are paid within the timeframes specified in the Collective Investment Scheme sourcebook within the *FSA Handbook*[1].

---

[1]   COB 9.3.16R and COB 9.3.49R.

Client opt outs

8.25   The rules recognise the fact that not all clients require the same level of protection and they therefore aim to provide the greatest protection to inexperienced clients. Applying this principle, the client money rules include provisions allowing firms to disapply the rules to certain types of client provided strict conditions have been satisfied.

Private customers—no opt out

8.26   Private customers (eg individuals) require the greatest protection and therefore the firm cannot opt these clients out of client money protection. An exception to this general rule occurs in the case of individuals and small business investors who are classified as 'expert' customers for the purposes of the Conduct of Business Rules and are treated as intermediate customers. The client money rules do not need to be applied to money held for these customers where their written consent has been obtained. The written consent will only be effective if it is in the required form[1].

---

[1]   See para 8.27.

Other clients—two way opt out (COB 9.3.8–9.3.9)

8.27   The client money rules do not need to be applied to money held for intermediate customers and market counterparties if their written agreement has been obtained. This written agreement will only be effective if it contains the matters specified in COB 9.3.9, that is, if it states that:

(1)   the client's money will not be subject to the protection of the client money rules; and

(2)   the client's money will not be segregated from the firm's own money; and

(3)   the client's money will be used by the firm in the course of its own business; and

(4)   the client will rank as a general creditor of the firm[1].

---

[1]   COB 9.3.9R.

Non-European business—one way opt out (COB 9.3.10–9.3.11)

8.28   Where a firm is carrying on designated investment business which is not a core investment service, a non-core investment service[1], or a listed activity[2], and where the counterparty (ie the client) is not an authorised person or a private customer, a one way opt out from client money protection may be used. The written form of the opt out must be the same as that used for the two way notice described above[3]. The FSA is not permitted by European legislation to treat 'ISD type' business of a non-ISD investment firm with branches in the UK any more favourably than business of an ISD firm so two-way opt outs should be used in relation to such 'ISD type' business[4].

---

[1]   Core investment services and non-core investment services are defined in the Investment Services Directive and in the Financial Services and Markets Act 2000 (Regulated Activities) Order 2001, SI 2001/544, Sch 2.
[2]   A listed activity is an activity listed in Annex 1 to the Banking Consolidation Directive, Council Directive 2000/12/EC.
[3]   COB 9.3.11R.
[4]   COB 9.3.10G.

Money transferred—no opt out (COB 9.3.13–9.3.14)

8.29   Where a firm transfers client money to another person, the firm must not allow itself to be 'opted out' of client money protection on either a one way or two way basis[1].

---

[1]   COB 9.3.13R.

Type of bank account—mandated accounts

8.30   Money held in a bank account in the name of an individual client is not client money since it is not 'held by the firm'. There is a normal banker/customer relationship between the customer and the bank with which the money is placed, although for practical reasons the firm will usually have a mandate to transfer money to or from the account. Even though such money is not client money for the purposes of the rules, it should be noted that FSA has specific requirements relating to the operation of mandated accounts: these are set out in COB 9.2.

Money of clients held by banks (COB 9.3.2(3), 9.3.5–9.3.6)

8.31   It should be noted that where a firm is an approved bank and the money is held on behalf of a client 'in an account with itself'[1], then the client money rules do not apply. However, if the firm then transfers money from that account to another approved bank or another authorised person, then that money will have to be treated as client money. Where a bank wishes to rely on this 'banking' exemption it must be able to account to all of its clients for amounts held on their behalf at all times. Normally a bank would comply with this requirement by recording the amount due to a client in a current account on the firm's balance sheet. Such accounts can be 'pooled' accounts but where this is the case the bank must clearly identify the pooled account as an account for clients and must be able to identify individual clients' entitlements within the pool at any time[2]. Specific examples illustrate the extent to which this 'exemption' applies in different circumstances.

---

[1]   COB 9.3.2R.
[2]   COB 9.3.5G.

8.32   Where a bank places money of its investment business clients in accounts with another bank, this may be client money, depending on the way in which and the purpose for which, it has been deposited. Consider the following scenarios.

(1)   Bank A passes money to Bank B in the form of an overnight deposit in the normal course of banking business (eg as part of its treasury management activities)—the money passed to Bank B is not within the scope of the client money rules.

(2)   Bank A opens an account with Bank B for the purpose of depositing money on behalf of its investment business clients (eg because Bank B offers a preferential rate of interest for deposits over £X,000)—the money in this account is within the scope of the client money rules.

(3)   Bank A passes money of its investment business clients to a futures broker in the course of undertaking futures business on behalf of these clients—once passed to the broker, this money is within the scope of the client money rules.

Money passed on in the normal course of banking business is not deemed to be client money—here, it is important to distinguish between the liability (ie the liability of the bank to its account holders) and the underlying asset (which the bank may use in the normal course of banking business).

8.33   Where a firm (which is a bank) relies on this 'banking exemption' it must notify the client in writing that money held for that client will be held by the firm as banker and not as trustee, and as a result the money will not be held in accordance with the client money rules[1].

---

[1]   COB 9.3.2R(3).

8.34   Where the banking exemption does not apply the standard client money rules apply and the usual considerations in respect of the treatment of the money should be addressed; whether the clients have been opted out of client money protection, whether the accounts opened with other banks are in the name of the client only, or in the form 'Bank A, Client account'. Trust status is required as normal.

Segregation

Purpose of segregation and rules applicable (COB 9.3.36–9.3.41)

8.35   The purpose of the client money rules is to keep clients' money separate from the firm's money. In the event of a default, such as the firm's failure, it is important that the money belonging to clients is held in such a way as to distinguish it from the money available for general creditors. Further, the funds belonging to clients must actually be 'ring-fenced' in a way which provides protection from their being distributed to the general creditors.

8.36   The rules explicitly state that the firm must hold client money separate from the firm's money except as specified in the rules[1]. To achieve this a firm must not hold money other than client money in a client money bank account except as follows:

(1)   it is a minimum sum required to keep the account open;
(2)   it is temporarily held in that account in accordance with the rules on mixed remittances[2];
(3)   it represents interest paid into the account in excess of the amount due to clients[3].

---

[1]   COB 9.3.37R.
[2]   See para 8.59.
[3]   COB 9.3.39R.

8.37   A firm is permitted to deposit its own money into a client bank account where it deems it prudent to do this for the protection of clients[1]. These amounts are commonly referred to as 'buffers' and the regulator will expect a firm to be able to explain the reasons for such buffers. The guidance to the rules makes it clear that the use of a 'buffer' does not reduce in any way the firm's responsibility to properly perform the daily calculations of client money requiring segregation[2].

---

[1]   COB 9.3.40R.
[2]   COB 9.3.41G.

8.38   The rules seek to protect client money by ensuring that it can be easily identified as money belonging to clients. The definition of a 'client bank account' demonstrates this. The definition is:

'(a)   an account at a bank which:

(i)   holds the money of one or more clients;

(ii)   is in the name of the firm;

(iii)   includes in its title an appropriate description to distinguish the money in the account from the firm's money; and,

(iv)   is a current or a deposit account; or,

(b)   a money market deposit of client money which is identified as being client money[1].

Merely identifying the money as client money does not represent adequate protection and consequently the rules provide for a trust to be established, as set out below[2].

---

[1]   *FSA Handbook*, Glossary.
[2]   See para 8.39.

Statutory trust (COB 9.3.30–9.3.31)

8.39   The FSMA 2000, s 139 provides that the FSA's rules may make provisions which result in money being held by a firm on trust (in England and Wales) or as agent (in Scotland). The FSA rules provide that:

'A firm (other than a trustee firm) receives and holds client money as trustee (or agent in Scotland) on the following terms:

(1)   for the purposes of and on the terms of the client money rules and the client money distribution rules;

(2)   subject to (3), for the clients for whom that money is held, according to their respective interests in it;

(3)   on failure of the firm, for the payment of the costs properly attributable to their respective interests in it;

(4)   after all valid claims and costs under (2) and (3) have been met, for the firm itself[1]'.

---

[1]   COB 9.3.31R.

Holding client money

General and designated client bank accounts (COB 9.3.32)

8.40   Although different types of client money exist (money held pending investment, money held in the course of settlement etc) all client money can be held in a single type of account known as a general client bank account[1]. Firms may use names such as 'client settlement money' or 'client free money' in naming their client money bank accounts notwithstanding the fact that these accounts all take the form of general client bank accounts. An alternative type of account, a designated client bank account, is available but is rarely seen in practice. The purpose of these designated accounts is to establish different pools of client money in the event of the failure of a bank at which the firm holds client money.

---

[1] COB 9.3.32G.

Currency in which funds are held (COB 9.3.38)

8.41 A firm can hold segregated client money in a different currency from that of receipt. Daily translations must be performed to ensure that the amount held is equivalent to the value in the currency of receipt (or where different, equivalent to the currency in which the liability to the client is due)[1].

---

[1] COB 9.3.38R.

Client bank accounts (COB 9.3.67–9.3.68 and 9.3.74–9.3.79)

8.42 The rules in relation to bank accounts aim to ensure that clients' money is properly protected. With this objective the rules specify that client money can only be held in accounts with approved banks except in specified exceptional circumstances, as described below[1]. A detailed definition of an approved bank is provided in the Glossary section of the *FSA Handbook*. A regulated firm wishing to open a client bank account with an approved bank must carry out a detailed risk assessment of the bank to be used[2]. This assessment must be performed even where the bank is within the same group as the firm[3]. Reviews should then be performed on a continuing basis with a review performed at least once in every financial year. Guidance is provided on the factors to be considered in the assessment[4]. A concession is provided in relation to a bank authorised by an EEA regulator whereby the continuing assessment is not required provided the bank remains authorised[5].

---

[1] COB 9.3.68R. See also para 8.43.
[2] COB 9.3.76R.
[3] COB 9.3.80R.
[4] COB 9.3.78G.
[5] COB 9.3.79G.

8.43 A firm may hold money with a bank which is not an approved bank only where the applicable law or market practice of that overseas jurisdiction prevents the holding of client money in a client money bank account with an approved bank. This 'concession' is available only in relation to the settlement of transactions or the distribution of income. Hence money held pending investment could not be held with a non-approved bank. The use of such a non-approved bank is permitted only for as long as required to effect the relevant transactions and notifications to the client (or consent for a private customer) is required. This type of account must be established as a designated bank account, thereby creating a separate pool of funds for distribution in the event of the failure of the firm[1].

¹   COB 9.3.74R. See also para 8.129.

8.44   Where a firm uses a group bank to hold client money it must disclose this in writing to its client at the outset of the relationship, or not less than 20 days before it begins to hold client money of that client with the group bank, the identity of the bank and that it is a group bank¹. If a client notifies the firm in writing that he does not wish his money to be held at the group bank the firm must either move the money to a client bank account with another bank or return the money to the client².

¹   COB 9.3.80R.
²   COB 9.3.81R.

Euroclear

8.45   Confusion often arises over the treatment of client money held with Euroclear which is commonly used by authorised persons as custodian for their holdings of client investments. Since settlement of securities transactions is effected through Euroclear, cash accounts as well as securities accounts are operated. Money, including client money, held within the Euroclear system is held by Morgan Guaranty Trust Company of New York which is an approved bank for the purpose of the client money rules.

Notifications

Notifications to banks (COB 9.3.82–9.3.85)

8.46   The protected status of a client bank account is established by obtaining from the bank at which the account is held a written acknowledgement of the following matters:

(1)   that the money in the account is held by the firm as trustee;
(2)   the bank cannot combine the money with any other account or offset the money against any of the firm's own accounts;
(3)   the title of the account sufficiently distinguished that account from any account containing money of the firm; and
(4)   the account title is in the form requested by the firm¹.

¹   COB 9.3.82R.

8.47   If a UK bank has not acknowledged the trust status of an account within 20 business days, the account cannot be used for client money and any money held in the account must be removed¹. If a non-UK bank has not acknowledged the trust status of the account within 20 business days the firm must notify the client of this fact².

¹   COB 9.3.83R.
²   COB 9.3.84R.

Notifications to exchanges, clearing houses, intermediate brokers or OTC counterparties (COB 9.3.86–9.3.89)

8.48 A firm which carries out any contingent liability investment for clients through an exchange, clearing house, intermediate broker or OTC counterparty must confirm the protected status of the account. The confirmation must:

(1) notify the third party that the firm is under an obligation to keep client money separate from the firm's own money and is under an obligation to 'hold' client money in a client bank account;

(2) instruct the person with whom the account is to be opened that any money paid to it in respect of a contingent liability investment is to be credited to the firm's client transaction account;

(3) require the person with whom the account is opened to acknowledge in writing that they cannot combine the client transaction account with any other account nor is there any right of set-off available against other amounts owed to them[1].

As with the notifications to banks regarding client money accounts, time limits apply to the receipt of a response to a confirmation request[2].

---

[1] COB 9.3.86R.
[2] COB 9.3.87R.

8.49 It is important to note that the 'trust status' notification in respect of securities accounts which hold safe custody investments does not also cover the client money trust status confirmation required for accounts at custodians which hold client money (ie custodians which are banks).

Notification to clients (COB 9.3.90–9.3.97)

8.50 Where a bank account outside the UK is used to hold client money, clients must be notified (in advance) of the fact that their money may be deposited outside the UK and must be warned that the legal and regulatory regime applicable to such overseas banks will be different from that of the UK and that in the event of default on the part of the overseas bank their money may be treated differently from the position which would apply if the bank were a bank in the UK[1].

---

[1] COB 9.3.90R.

8.51 This disclosure must also warn clients of the additional risks which may result from the use of an overseas account where a bank has *not* accepted that it has no right of set off or counterclaim against money held in a client bank account[1].

---

[1] COB 9.3.90R(3).

8.52 A similar notification is required in relation to the use of an intermediate broker, settlement agent or OTC counterparty outside the UK[1].

¹   COB 9.3.95R.

8.53   In both cases (banks and others) if a client notifies a firm that it does not wish money to be held by a bank or other third party in a particular jurisdiction then the money must be held in a protected account in another jurisdiction (to which the client does not object) or the money must be returned to the client[1].

¹   COB 9.3.93R and 9.3.97R.

Notification to the FSA (COB 9.3.98)

8.54   The client money rules seek to protect investors in situations where there is a failure of the firm. The rules are not intended (nor could they be) to protect investors in the event of a default of a third party such as a bank with which the firm deposits its client money. The rules do require firms to perform reviews of the institution with which funds are deposited, but this checking cannot provide guarantees against subsequent failures of these institutions.

8.55   On the failure of a third party with which client money is held the firm must notify the FSA of the failure and then, as soon as reasonably practical after this time, the firm must inform the FSA whether it intends to 'make good' any shortfall which has or may arise[1].

¹   COB 9.3.98R.

Payments into client money bank accounts

General rule (COB 9.3.42–9.3.44)

8.56   A firm can organise the segregation of client money under one of two approaches. These approaches are known as the normal and the alternative approach[1]. The alternative approach is seen in practice only very occasionally but can be particularly useful to firms holding client money in many jurisdictions/currencies. The alternative approach is dealt with later in this chapter.

¹   COB 9.3.42R.

8.57   The normal approach requires firms to pay client money directly into their client money accounts on receipt. The rules require a firm using this approach to pay money which it receives into a client bank account as soon as possible and in any event no later than the business day following receipt[1].

¹   COB 9.3.44R.

Automated transfers (COB 9.3.45)

8.58   If client money is received in the form of an automated transfer then the firm must take steps to ensure that where possible the money is received directly into a client bank account. In the event that the money is received directly by automated transfer into the firm's account, the money which is client money must be paid into a client bank account no later than the next business day after receipt[1].

---

[1]   COB 9.3.45R.

Mixed remittances (COB 9.3.47–9.3.48)

8.59   Where a firm receives mixed remittances (for example dividend cheques representing the firm's and clients' money) these must be paid into a client money account initially and then the firm's money must be withdrawn within one business day of the date the remittance is expected to be cleared[1]. Where the money is due and payable to the firm in respect of fees and commissions, the firm should follow the specific rules for these amounts[2].

---

[1]   COB 9.3.47R.
[2]   COB 9.3.20E.

Appointed representatives, field representatives and other agents (COB 9.3.49–9.3.52)

8.60   Where a firm has appointed representatives, field representatives and other agents, it must have procedures in place which ensure that any money received by these parties on behalf of the firm is paid into a client bank account no later than the next business day after receipt, or forwarded to the firm (or a specified business address of the firm in the case of a field representative) to ensure that it arrives by the close of the third business day after receipt[1].

---

[1]   COB 9.3.49R.

8.61   Appointed representatives, field representatives and other agents must keep client money separately identifiable from other money until the client money is paid into a client bank account or sent to the firm[1].

---

[1]   COB 9.3.51R.

8.62   For the purpose of the rules on receipt of funds by agents, a firm that operates a number of small branches but handles or accounts for all client money centrally (for example, regional stockbroking operations), may treat its small branches as appointed representatives[1].

---

[1]   COB 9.3.52G.

Client entitlements

Notification of entitlements (COB 9.3.53)

8.63   A firm must take reasonable steps to ensure it receives information on the receipt of client money in the form of client entitlements (eg dividends) promptly[1].

---
[1]   COB 9.3.53R.

Overseas entitlements (COB 9.3.54–9.3.55)

8.64   Firms often receive entitlements (dividends, coupons, and other distributions with similar characteristics) relating to clients' assets into their own overseas bank accounts in order to avoid opening client bank accounts in numerous overseas locations. These dividends must be transferred to client money accounts or paid to clients. The client money rules recognise the fact that it may be difficult to arrange the transfer on a same or next day basis and they provide a window of five business days following receipt of notification from the overseas bank for the transfer to be effected[1].

---
[1]   COB 9.3.55R.

Allocation of entitlements (COB 9.3.56–9.3.57)

8.65   A firm should allocate client entitlements due to the individual clients within a period of ten business days[1].

---
[1]   COB 9.3.56R and 9.3.57E.

Payments out of client money bank accounts

Timing of payments to clients (COB 9.3.58–9.3.59)

8.66   Where a firm is liable to pay money to a client then it must make this payment as soon as possible, and no later than one business day after the money is 'due and payable', either by paying the money into a client bank account or by paying it to the client or to the order of the client[1].

---
[1]   COB 9.3.58R.

Interest (COB 9.3.60–9.3.62)

8.67   Any interest due to a client is client money. The FSA regard interest on client bank accounts to be a matter of contract between the firm and its clients. All clients, except private customers, are deemed able to negotiate their own arrangements regarding interest. In relation to private customers, the firm must specify in writing its policy on the payment of interest and whether interest is or is not payable and, if so, on what terms and at what frequency. A firm does not need to disclose actual rates prevailing at any particular time to the customer, rather it must explain its policy for the payment of interest[1]. The example given by the *FSA Handbook* is libor plus or minus 'X' percent. If a firm does not provide a private customer with the required information then the firm must pay all interest earned on client money of a customer to that customer[2]. The inference here is that a firm may, provided they have made the proper disclosure, pay a rate of interest to private customers which is less than that actually earned by the firm on the client money bank accounts.

---

[1]   COB 9.3.62G.
[2]   COB 9.3.60R.

Payments of money to a third party (COB 9.3.63–9.3.66)

8.68   The rules in relation to payment of money to a third party are designed to address situations where the firm passes money to a third party without discharging its fiduciary duty to the client. The specific circumstances in which a firm may allow money to be held or controlled by an exchange, clearing house or intermediate broker are:

(1)   where the firm transfers the money for the purpose of a transaction for a client through or with that person;
(2)   where the firm transfers the money to meet a client's obligation to provide collateral for a transaction (eg initial margin for a derivative transaction);
(3)   in the case of a private customer, where the customer has been notified that the client money may be transferred to the other person[1].

---

[1]   COB 9.3.64R.

8.69   The guidance to this section of the rules states that firms should not hold excess client money in its client transaction accounts with intermediate brokers, settlement agents, and OTC counterparties[1].

---

[1]   COB 9.3.66G.

Money which ceases to be client money (COB 9.3.133–9.3.136)

8.70   Money ceases to be client money if it is paid:

(1)   to the client;
(2)   to a third party on the instruction of the client;
(3)   into a bank account of the client;
(4)   to the firm itself, when it is due and payable to the firm;
(5)   to the firm itself, when it is an excess in the client bank account[1].

---

[1]   COB 9.3.133R.

8.71   When a firm draws a cheque, or equivalent payable order, to discharge its fiduciary duty, it must continue to treat the sum concerned as client money until the cheque or order is presented and paid by the bank[1]. Similarly, where a firm makes payment to, or on the instruction of a client, from an account other than the client bank account, no equivalent sum may be removed from the client bank account until the payment has cleared[2].

---

[1]   COB 9.3.135R.
[2]   COB 9.3.136R.

Allocated but not unclaimed money (COB 9.3.138–9.3.140)

8.72   A firm may cease treating money as client money it if can demonstrate that it has taken reasonable steps to trace the client concerned and to return the balance[1]. An evidential provision sets out the steps which the FSA would consider to be reasonable steps. These steps include undertaking to make good any valid claim against any released balances[2]. Where a firm makes such an undertaking it should make arrangements authorised by the firm's relevant controllers that are legally enforceable by any person with a valid claim to the previously unclaimed money[3].

---

[1]   COB 9.3.138R.
[2]   COB 9.3.139E.
[3]   COB 9.3.140G.

DAILY CALCULATION OF CLIENT MONEY RESOURCE AND REQUIREMENT

Overview

8.73   In order to ensure that sufficient client money is held in the client bank account(s), firms must perform a daily calculation[1] which compares the aggregate balance on the firm's client money bank accounts with the 'client money requirement' calculated in accordance with the rules.

---

[1]   COB 9.3.99G to COB 9.3.118G.

8.74   The 'client money requirement', calculated using end of day figures, is compared with the 'client money resource' being the total value of money held in protected accounts as recorded in the firm's own accounting records, ie the firm's cash book (not the firm's bank statement). If the client money requirement exceeds the client money resource, then the firm must transfer its own money into the client bank account by the end of the following business day to remove the shortfall. If the client money resource exceeds the client money requirement then the firm must transfer money from the client bank account into its own accounts by the end of the following business day to remove the surplus.

Calculation of the client money requirement (COB 9.3.105–9.3.120)

8.75   The client money requirement is:

Total of clients' credit balances	+	Total margined transaction requirement

The margined transaction requirement will apply only to firms which hold clients' money in relation to margined transactions (ie futures and options business). Where the total margined transaction requirement is negative it should be taken as zero in computing the client money requirement.

8.76   Money held in relation to all other types of investment business is taken into account in determining the figure for the total of clients credit balances. The calculation is described in COB 9.3.107.

8.77   The calculation is best performed in a number of stages, as follows.

Stage 1:   Calculate each client's individual client money balance ignoring all margined transaction balances.

Stage 2:   Sum the individual client's client money balances which are positive to obtain a total figure for individual client balances.

Stage 3:   Calculate the total margined transaction requirement (applicable only to firms with derivatives business).

Stage 4:   Add the total for individual client balances to the total margined transaction requirement to determine the client money requirement.

Stage 1: Calculate each client's individual client money balance

8.78   The individual client balance is composed of four elements. These are discussed in detail below:

(1)   free money held for the client; *plus*
(2)   money relating to principal transactions; *plus*
(3)   money relating to agency transactions; *minus*
(4)   money relating to free deliveries.

(1)   FREE MONEY HELD FOR THE CLIENT

8.79   This may be money held pending investment or dividends which are due to the client.

(2)   MONEY RELATING TO PRINCIPAL TRANSACTIONS

8.80   The two parties to any principal transaction are the firm and the client. If the client has released assets (cash or securities) to the firm, without receiving payment or delivery of securities then he is clearly at risk. The client requires protection and this protection is provided by including in the individual client's client money balance a value reflecting the client's exposure. The value included is:

(a)   sale proceeds due to the client for a client sale where the client has delivered designated investments[1] to the firm but has not received the cash in return; or

(b)   purchase money received from the client for a client purchase where the client has paid cash but has not received designated investments in return.

---

[1]   The term 'designated investment' refers to assets such as shares, debentures and government securities. A full definition is provided in the Glossary section of the *FSA Handbook*.

---

(3)   MONEY RELATING TO AGENCY TRANSACTIONS

8.81   *Sale by the client*   The sale proceeds due to the client must be included in the individual client's balance where:

- either—the client has delivered designated investments to the firm which the firm has then delivered to the market[1] in exchange for cash, but the firm has not paid the cash on to the client;

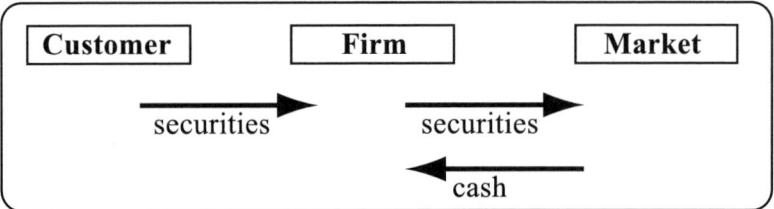

- or—the client has delivered designated investments to the firm which it is holding and the firm has not paid the client.

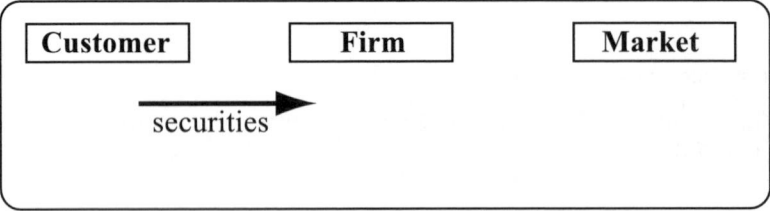

---

[1]   The *FSA Handbook* uses the term 'counterparty' to refer to the market side of an agency transaction. COB 9.3.107 R. 'Counterparty' is not a defined term for this purpose.

8.82   *Purchase by the client*   The cost of purchases which have been paid for by the client must be included in the individual client's client money balance where:

- either—the client has paid the firm and the firm has passed this money to the market in exchange for designated investments, but the firm has not yet delivered the designated investments to the client;

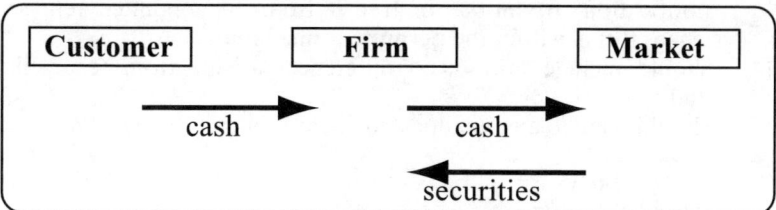

- or—the client has paid the firm and the firm is holding this money as it has not yet paid the market or received the designated investments required for delivery to the client.

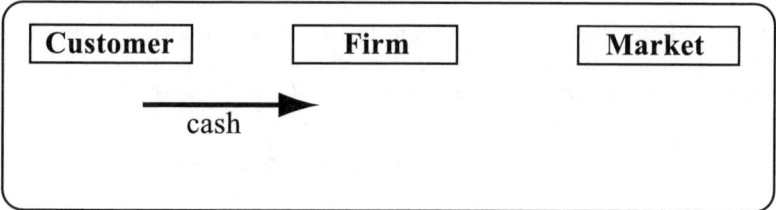

8.83   The firm may choose to segregate designated investments rather than cash. This is permitted for:

(1)   all client sales; and
(2)   all client purchases, except agency deals paid for by the client where the firm has not remitted cash to the market.

   Where designated investments have been segregated then the amount to be included in the individual client's client money balance is nil.

(4)   FREE DELIVERIES

8.84   The amount to be deducted is:

(1)   money owed by the client for any purchases where the firm has delivered designated investments to the client;
(2)   money paid to the client for any sales where the client has not delivered the designated investments.

8.85   The result of the calculation (1) + (2) + (3) – (4) will be a net positive or negative balance for each client.

8.86   In calculating the individual client balances a firm;

(1)   should include dividends received and interest earned;

(2)   may deduct outstanding fees, calls, rights and interest charges and other amounts owed by the client;

(3)   need not include overseas dividend amounts in the five days following notification[1] or money in transit from an appointed representative where this is within the permitted time limits[2];

(4)   should include unresolved differences arising from reconciliations[3]; and

(5)   should include any unallocated client money.

---

[1]   COB 9.3.55R(2).
[2]   COB 9.3.51R.
[3]   COB 9.3.129R.

Stage 2: Calculate the total of clients' credit balances

8.87   All positive individual client's client money balances calculated at stage 1 are added together to give the total of client's client money balances. Negative balances must be ignored.

8.88   Where a firm holds no client money in relation to derivatives business then the total of all client's positive client money balances will equal the client money requirement (ie stages 3 and 4 can be ignored).

Stage 3: Calculate the total margined transaction requirement

8.89   Broadly, a firm must segregate an amount equal to the sum of all the positive client equity balances shown by its records. A client's equity balance is the amount which the firm is due to pay to a client in respect of his margined transactions if all the client's positions are closed out at the prevailing market prices.

8.90   Hence the equity balance of a client may include:

(1)   any futures initial margin paid by the client;

(2)   any realised profits less realised losses not yet paid over to the client; and

(3)   any unrealised profits less unrealised losses on the client's open positions.

8.91   Firms generally act as agent in respect of on-exchange traded margined transactions, standing between the client and the exchange (or intermediate broker where the firm is not an exchange member). Hence the balance on the firm's client transactions account with the exchange reflects the balance due to or from the clients as a group rather than any individual client.

8.92   Typically, the firm's records will show:

(1)   liabilities to individual clients reflecting each client's equity balance (deposits plus profits less losses);
(2)   assets representing the firm's overall equity balance with the exchange or intermediate broker (reflecting the pooled deposits plus profits less losses of the firm's clients in total); and
(3)   off-balance sheet holdings of collateral received from clients against loss-making open positions.

8.93   The following table shows the positive and negative equity balances of clients A to E. Clients D and E have negative balances and have therefore passed collateral to the firm as security against their potential debts.

Clients' equity balances

Client	Positive	Negative	Collateral (Off-B/S)		Balance with Exchange
	£	£	£		£
A	300				300
B	400				400
C	500				500
D		300	100		(300)
E		500	400		(500)
Total	**1200**	**800**	**500**		**400**
	CR	**DR**			**DR**

8.94   The total margined transaction requirement is calculated as follows:

		£
(a)	The total of all the clients' equity balances which are positive	1,200
Less		
(b)	The total of approved collateral held against negative client equity balances	(500)
(c)	The net of the firm's equity balance on client accounts with exchanges, clearing houses, intermediate brokers and OTC counterparties	(400)
	Total margined transaction requirement	300

In this example the firm is required to segregate £300 representing the uncovered losses of clients D (£200) and E (£100).

Where the firm's total margined transaction requirement is negative the firm should treat it as zero for the purpose of calculating the overall client money requirement of the firm.

8.95   To meet a shortfall which has arisen in respect of the margined transaction requirement a firm may utilise its own approved collateral provided it is held:

(1)   on terms specifying when it is to be realised for the benefit of clients;
(2)   it is clearly identifiable for the firm's own property; and
(3)   the relevant terms are evidenced in writing by the firm.

Further, the proceeds of the sale of the collateral should be paid into a client bank account.

Stage 4: Calculate the total client money requirement

8.96   The total client money requirement is calculated by adding the total value of all of the clients' individual client balances to the total margined transaction requirement.

Segregation

8.97   Having calculated the requirement the firm must compare this with the total of the balances on the client money bank accounts (as reflected in the firm's accounting records). Where the requirement exceeds the amount held in the client money accounts (ie the client money resource) the bank accounts must be 'topped up' by a transfer of money from the firm's own bank account. Where the requirement is less than the amount in the client money bank accounts the firm must transfer money from the client bank account to its own accounts.

Reduced client money requirement option

8.98   Where a firm has in respect of the same client:

(1)   a positive individual client balance; and
(2)   a negative client's equity balance;

or vice versa, the firm may offset these to give either a smaller individual client balance or a smaller client's equity balance[1].

---
[1]   COB 9.3.119R.

8.99   Many firms have different computer systems for their margined and other business and where this is the case they are unlikely to be able to take advantage of this concession.

Problems with the client money calculation

Notification requirements (COB 9.3.121–9.3.122)

8.100   If the firm is unable to perform the daily client money calculation, or for any other reason does not perform it, it must notify the FSA immediately[1].

---
[1]   COB 9.3.121R.

8.101   If a firm becomes aware that it may not be able to satisfy any shortfall of client money in the client money bank accounts arising from the comparison of the client money requirement with the client money resource, then it must notify the FSA by the close of business on the day that the calculation is performed[1].

---

[1]   COB 9.3.122R.

Reconciliations

Method and frequency (COB 9.3.123–9.3.131)

8.102   Reconciliations must be performed at least once every 25 business days by comparing independent third party statements (such as bank statements) to the firm's own records for the following:

(1)   client money bank accounts;
(2)   client transaction accounts with exchanges, clearing houses and inter- mediate brokers; and
(3)   approved collateral holdings where these are held in accordance with the client money rules[1].

---

[1]   COB 9.3.123R and COB 9.3.126R.

8.103   A firm must identify the reason for any discrepancy resulting from a reconciliation. Corrections must be made as soon as possible except where differences result solely from timing differences[1]. Firms should perform reconciliations more frequently if the risks to which the business is exposed (eg the volume of business) warrant this[2]. The firm must make this judgment in the context of its overall risk management systems.

---

[1]   COB 9.3.128R.
[2]   COB 9.3.124G.

8.104   Where, however, the FSA regulated firm is unable to resolve a difference arising from a reconciliation and it appears that one of the sets of records indicates that there is a need to 'top up' the relevant client bank accounts or approved collateral, the FSA regulated firm must assume that this set of records is correct and pay its own money into the client bank account until such time as the matter is conclusively resolved[1].

---

[1]   COB 9.3.129R.

8.105   All these reconciliations must be performed within ten business days of the date to which they relate[1].

---

[1]   COB 9.3.125R.

8.106 Where a firm is unable to comply with the rules on the timing of reconciliations, dealing with discrepancies and unresolved differences, it must notify FSA as soon as possible[1].

---

[1]   COB 9.3.131R.

Alternative approach

Benefits and requirements of this approach (COB 9.3.42–9.3.43, 9.3.46 and 9.3.103)

8.107 As noted above, a firm which is holding client money in many jurisdictions may find that significant savings in operational costs can be achieved by adopting the 'alternative approach'. Under this approach client money is received into and paid out of the firm's own bank accounts[1]. In order to achieve the necessary protection of client money, a single transfer is made to or from a client money bank account each day. The balance which the firm must hold in the client money bank account and therefore the amount of each day's transfer necessary to achieve this balance, is determined by the client money calculation described above[2].

---

[1]   COB 9.3.43G.
[2]   See paras 8.73–8.97.

8.108 If a firm wishes to use the alternative approach it must provide the FSA with a report from its auditor that the firm has in place systems and controls adequate to enable it to operate the alternative approach effectively[1].

---

[1]   COB 9.3.42R.

8.109 In addition, a firm wishing to use this approach must appoint a manager with responsibility for client money rules[1]. A firm can chose to operate the alternative method for some types of business (eg overseas equities) whilst adopting the normal approach for other types of business (eg derivatives)[2]. A firm would need to be able to demonstrate that its systems were adequate to permit these two approaches to apply in parallel.

---

[1]   COB 9.3.42R.
[2]   COB 9.3.46R(5).

8.110 The client money calculation operates in the same way where the alternative method is used except in relation to uncleared cheques paid to clients. Where a firm uses the alternative approach and draws cheques on its own account, it must add the value of these undrawn cheques to the client money requirement calculation. This will ensure that an amount equal to the value of these cheques is segregated in the client money bank account. This mirrors the effect created under the normal method since under that method an amount equal to the value of the undrawn cheques will remain in the client money bank account, notwithstanding the lower cash book balance. A firm adopting the alternative method may use a historic average calculation to estimate the value of uncleared cheques rather than separately calculating this value each day[1].

---

[1] COB 9.3.103G.

Commodity futures trading commission Part 30 exemption order

Special requirements (COB 9.3.141–9.3.144)

8.111 Those firms who are subject to a CFTC Part 30 exemption order in relation to trading on behalf of US customers on non-US futures and options exchanges are generally required by the CFTC to offer all US customers segregation in accordance with the client money rules[1]. These firms trade on behalf of US customers on non-US futures and options exchanges and have obtained an exemption under Part 30 of the General Regulations of the US Commodities Exchange Act. Where firms trading as clearing members on the London Metals Exchange (LME) have LME bond arrangements in place they must exclude the US clients' equity balances from the calculation of the sum of all the positive client equity balances (as described in 'stage 2' of the daily calculation of client money, described at para 8.87)[2].

---

[1] COB 9.3.141R.
[2] COB 9.3.142R.

8.112 Firms which have a bond arrangement in place must not reduce the amount of, or cancel, a letter of credit issued under an LME bond arrangement where this will cause them to be in breach of their Part 30 exemption order[1]. In addition, firms must notify the FSA immediately if they arrange the issue of an individual letter of credit under an LME bond arrangement[2].

---

[1] COB 9.3.143R.
[2] COB 9.3.144R.

Client money and Europe

Inward passports (European institutions branching into the UK)

8.113 Article 10 of the Investment Services Directive (ISD)[1] provides that each home member state is responsible for drawing up prudential rules which investment firms must observe at all times. These prudential rules, mandated by the Directive, require each member state to require each investment firm to have, inter alia, adequate arrangements for funds belonging to investors with a view to safeguarding the investor's rights and, except in the case of credit institutions, preventing the investment firm from using investors' funds for its own account. The basic principle then is that the prudential regulation of clients' money is the responsibility of the home state regulator (eg FSA rules do not apply to a German Bank's UK branch investment business activities—these are subject to German requirements).

¹   Council Directive 93/22/EEC.

8.114   It is important to note that these provisions only apply to investment firms subject to the ISD and to client money held in respect of investment services within the passport.

8.115   Non-ISD firms 'branching' into the UK continue to be subject to the FSA's client money rules and in respect of services outside the passport (eg commodities derivatives) the FSA's client money rules will continue to apply.

Outward passports

8.116   On the principle stated in the Investment Services Directive, art 10¹, all UK incorporated banks or investment firms are subject to and should apply the relevant UK client money rules to their activities in branches outside the UK unless the activities are non-ISD activities for which the firm is not authorised in the UK and the services are therefore outside the passport.

¹   Council Directive 93/22/EEC.

Default provisions

8.117   The FSA's client money distribution rules apply to any firm which holds client money. The stated objective of these rules is to facilitate the timely return of client money to a client in the event of the failure of a firm or third party at which the firm holds client money¹.

¹   COB 9.5.3G.

8.118   The client money rules provide protection to clients whose money is in properly established segregated accounts in the event of the failure of the firm. The rules cannot provide protection against the failure of any bank at which client money is held, since the assets (ie bank balance) may no longer be available to the firm. Where a bank at which client money is being held fails, the rules seek to provide for a standardised approach to the division of remaining funds and their prompt payment.

Pooling events

8.119   The client money distribution rules apply to a firm when a 'pooling event' occurs. There are two types of 'pooling event' which can trigger the operation of the distribution rules. A primary pooling event occurs in the following situations:

•   the failure of the firm;

- on the vesting of assets in a trustee in accordance with an 'assets requirement' imposed under the FSMA 2000, s 48(1)(a);
- on the coming into force of a requirement imposed under the FSMA 2000, s 43(2) for all client money held by the firm; or
- when the firm is unable to identify and allocate in its records all valid claims arising as a result of a secondary pooling event[1].

---

[1]   COB 9.5.5R.

8.120   Where certain pooling events, such as the failure of the firm, occur there should be sufficient client money available for all clients to whom money is owed to be paid in full. This outcome is dependent on the daily client money calculation being properly performed and appropriate transfers being made to client money accounts. It is possible that where there has been a breach of the client money rules there may be insufficient funds available even in the event of a primary pooling event. This could also occur where the primary pooling event has been triggered by a secondary pooling event.

8.121   In relation to the final bullet point in para 8.119 (concerning the firm's records), a pooling event will not occur where the firm is taking steps, in consultation with the FSA, to establish those records and there are reasonable grounds to conclude that the records will be capable of rectification within a reasonable period[1].

---

[1]   COB 9.5.6R.

8.122   A secondary pooling event occurs on the failure of a third party to which client money of the firm has been transferred[1]. When a bank fails and the firm decides not to make good the shortfall in the amount of client money held at that bank, a secondary pooling event will occur[2].

---

[1]   COB 9.5.14R.
[2]   COB 9.5.18G.

8.123   In the event of a secondary pooling event it is likely that there will be insufficient funds available to pay in full all those to whom client money is due. In this event the distribution rules seek to provide a mechanism for determining how the remaining funds are distributed.

Objective and operation of the pooling rules

8.124   The basic principle of the client money rules is that when a pooling event occurs the client money held in different client money accounts of the firm is 'pooled' and money from the pool is then distributed to clients on a 'pro-rata' basis[1]. If 80% of the total pooled funds remain at the time of the pooling event each client will receive 80% of their full entitlement.

---

[1]   COB 9.5.7R and COB 9.5.22R.

8.125   If a secondary pooling event occurs but the firm 'funds' the shortfall at the third party using its own funds, then the 'pooling' rules set out below will not apply[1]. The FSA explains in the guidance to the distribution rules that when client money is passed to a third party a firm continues to owe a fiduciary duty to the client. The guidance explains that a firm will not be held responsible for the shortfall in client money caused by a third party failure if it has complied with its fiduciary responsibilities under general law[2]. The guidance explains that in order to comply with its duties the firm should show proper care in selecting the third parties and in monitoring the performance of the third parties[3].

---

[1]   COB 9.5.15R and see para 8.128.
[2]   COB 9.5.16G.
[3]   COB 9.5.17G.

8.126   Assuming initially that there are no 'designated client bank accounts' or 'designated client fund accounts' (these terms are explained at paras 8.129 and 8.130), then the rules require the following approach in the event of a 'pooling event'.

8.127   Where a primary pooling event occurs, client money in each client money account of the firm is treated as pooled and the firm must distribute that money so that each client receives a sum calculated on a 'pro-rata' basis[1].

---

[1]   COB 9.5.7R.

8.128   Where a secondary pooling event occurs as a result of a failure of a bank, intermediate broker, settlement agent or OTC counterparty, then every client bank account and client transaction account of the firm must be pooled. Any shortfall must be borne by all clients rateably in accordance with their entitlements. The firm must make and retain a record of each client's share of the shortfall until the client is repaid (say by the firm funding the shortfall). The firm must recalculate the client money entitlements for each client to reflect the reduced entitlement (ie reduced to reflect the shortfall). These lower values are then used in calculating the ongoing daily client money calculation[1].

---

[1]   COB 9.5.22R.

Designated client bank accounts

8.129   There are two types of 'designated' account. A designated client bank account is an account which is opened for the money of one or more clients who have consented in writing to the use of a particular bank[1]. The key characteristic of this type of account is that in the event of a failure of the bank at which the account is held the account is not pooled, so the full loss would be suffered by the clients whose money is held in the designated client bank account[2]. Further and importantly, in the event of the failure of any other bank at which the firm holds client money subject to the client money rules, then the designated client bank will again not be subject to pooling. The account is effectively 'ring fenced' so that clients who have requested that their money is held in this way are exposed only to the credit risk of their selected bank, not to that of other banks, intermediate brokers, settlement agents or OTC counterparties used by the firm for the holding of client money. In setting up a designated client bank account the firm must include the word 'designated' in the title, to ensure the account can be properly distinguished from other client bank accounts[3].

---

[1]   COB 9.3.69R.
[2]   COB 9.3.69R and COB 9.5.24R.
[3]   COB 9.3.69R.

Designated client fund accounts

8.130   A designated client fund account represents one or more client bank accounts. Clients must consent to their money being held in the same bank accounts and at the same banks as other clients whose client money represents part of the fund. The accounts representing the fund will be separately 'pooled' if one of the banks at which an account is held fails[1]. The accounts in the fund represent a separate pool. They are 'ring fenced' from other accounts including 'client designated bank accounts'.

---

[1]   COB 9.3.70R and COB 9.5.25R.

8.131   In setting up a designated client fund account the firm must ensure that the words 'designated fund' are included in the title of the account to ensure that account can be properly distinguished from other client bank accounts[1].

---

[1]   COB 9.3.70R.

Client money received after a primary pooling event (COB 9.5.9–9.5.12)

8.132   Client money received after a primary pooling event must not be pooled with client money held in any client money account at the time of the primary pooling event. It must be placed in a new client money bank account opened after the primary pooling event. This money must be treated in accordance with the client money rules and must be returned to the relevant client 'without delay'. There are two exceptions to this general rule, firstly money relating to an unsettled transaction and secondly situations where the client owes the firm money[1].

---

[1]   COB 9.5.9R.

8.133   Where money is received in relation to an unsettled transaction it should be used to settle the transaction[1].

---

[1]   COB 9.5.10G.

8.134 Mixed remittances received after a primary pooling event must first be paid into a client bank account and then the money which is not client money must be transferred to a firm's bank account within one business day of the date on which the firm would expect the remittance to be cleared[1]. Wherever possible the firm should seek to split a mixed remittance before the relevant accounts are credited[2].

---

[1]   COB 9.5.11R.
[2]   COB 9.5.12G.

Client money received after the failure of a bank (a secondary pooling event) (COB 9.5.27–9.5.29)

8.135 Client money received after the failure of a bank must not be transferred to the failed bank unless specifically instructed by the client in order to settle an obligation of that client to the failed bank. The money must be placed in a separate client bank account and either transferred to a bank other than the one which has failed on the written instruction of the client or returned to the client as soon as possible[1].

---

[1]   COB 9.5.27R.

8.136 Where mixed remittances are received after this type of secondary pooling event which consist of client money which would have been paid into a general client bank account, a designated client bank account or a designated client fund account maintained at the bank which has failed, the firm must pay the full sum into a client bank account other than the one operated at the bank that has failed and must then pay money that is not client money out of that client bank account within one business day of the day on which the firm would normally expect the remittance to be cleared[1]. Wherever possible the firm should seek to split a mixed remittance before the relevant accounts are credited[2].

---

[1]   COB 9.5.28R.
[2]   COB 9.5.29G.

Client money received after the failure of an intermediate broker, settlement agent or OTC counterparty (COB 9.5.32)

8.137 Client money received after the failure of an intermediate broker, settlement agent or OTC counterparty that would otherwise have been paid into a client transaction account at that intermediate broker, settlement agent or OTC counterparty, must not be transferred to the failed third party unless specifically instructed by the client in order to settle an obligation of that client to the failed third party. The money must be placed in a separate client bank account that has been opened after the secondary pooling event and then either transferred to a third party other than the one that has failed on the written instruction of the client or returned to the client as soon as possible[1].

---

[1]   COB 9.5.32R.

Chapter 9   Financial Rules

Peter Milroy

INTRODUCTION

9.1   Investment businesses regulated under the Financial Services and Markets Act 2000 (FSMA 2000) have to comply with the Principles for Businesses issued by the Financial Services Authority (FSA). Principle 4 concerns financial prudence: 'A firm must maintain adequate financial resources.'

9.2   The fundamental requirement to maintain a minimum level of financial resources is supported by a number of other financial rules in the Interim Prudential Sourcebook for Investment Businesses and in the Supervision Manual. These cover financial reporting and notification, accounting records and systems and the audit rules. All these topics are examined in this chapter, but the related rules on client money and assets are addressed in Chapter 7. It has been necessary to summarise the rules and omit much of the detail, so the reader may need to refer to the *FSA Handbook* in order to obtain an up-to-date picture of all the nuances and exceptions.

9.3   The financial rules apply to a firm regardless of whether it is a company, a partnership or a sole trader. The requirements differ on points of detail depending on the nature of the firm's business and, in particular, on which regulator it was authorised by before N2.

9.4   This chapter covers the financial rules that apply from N2 to investment management firms (ie those formerly regulated by the Investment Management Regulatory Organisation (IMRO)), personal investment firms (formerly regulated by the Personal Investment Authority (PIA)) and securities and futures firms (formerly regulated by the Securities and Futures Authority (SFA)). The financial rules of these Self-Regulating Organisations (SROs) were substantially revised in order to implement the Capital Adequacy Directive (CAD) in 1996[1]. Although the CAD need only be applied to firms whose activities bring them within the scope of the Investment Services Directive (ISD)[2] (see Chapter 11), the SROs took the opportunity to amend some of the rules applicable to non-ISD firms too. At N2, these rules were replaced by the FSA's Interim Prudential Sourcebook—Investment Businesses. The FSA's drafting approach was to use the old rulebooks as the basis for the interim prudential regime. In general, it has made changes only where specifically required by the FSMA 2000 and the statutory rule-making process, eg since the FSA has less discretion to vary the rules than the SROs had, such provisions have been removed (in some cases, waivers may be used instead). The FSA also took the opportunity to reclassify the old requirements into rules, evidential provisions and guidance. In practice, there has been little change to the substance of the financial rules of the former regulators.

---

[1]   Council Directive 93/6/EEC.
[2]   Council Directive 93/22/EEC.

9.5   However, the FSA's future strategy is to reorganise the prudential requirements on a risk-by-risk basis across the whole of the financial sector, replacing the current sector-by-sector approach. It is seen as a major benefit of having a single regulator that there can be one set of financial rules covering all investment firms, and also banks, insurance companies, etc. This major revision will also take account of proposed amendments to the CAD and the Basel Committee's review of the Capital Accord. The FSA plans to introduce an Integrated Prudential Sourcebook in 2004.

FINANCIAL RESOURCES RULES

9.6   The financial resources rules seek to ensure that investment firms have adequate capital and liquidity. The basic test is that the firm must ensure that its 'financial resources' equal or exceed its 'financial resources requirement' at all times. The definition of these terms varies according to the nature of the firm's business and therefore the risks to which it and its customers are subject. There are differences in the detail of how the rules are drafted for each category of investment firm. These are explained below after a general description of the main principles.

Financial resources requirement

9.7   The financial resources requirement addresses the risks facing a firm in carrying out its investment business activities. These activities cover a broad spectrum from providing investment advice to managing portfolios and from broking to securities trading. A distinction is made between 'trading book' and 'non-trading book' business. The trading book covers the activity of buying and selling investments as principal (eg market making) or agent; the non-trading book covers the other activities of the firm. Financial resources requirements in relation to the trading book cover position risk (ie a market risk that a firm will lose money because the value of its investment holdings falls) and counterparty risk (ie a credit risk that a debtor will be unable to pay). The other trading book risks relate to exposures to movements in interest rates and in foreign exchange rates and to 'large exposures', ie where a substantial proportion of a firm's assets depends upon the solvency of a single investment or counterparty. Some of these requirements also apply to the non-trading book.

9.8   In addition, there are some absolute minimum requirements that a firm must always meet. These comprise a fixed sum (ranging from £5,000 to £4 million) and an expenditure-based requirement (4/52nds to 13/52nds of annual expenditure). The expenditure-based requirement is designed to ensure that firms will always have sufficient liquid resources to carry on trading for an appropriate period (ie four to 13 weeks) even if new income ceases, during which time it can wind up the affairs of its customers in an orderly fashion. Some elements of the financial resources requirement remain constant for a year or more, eg the expenditure-based requirement and the fixed sum. Others will fluctuate each day depending on the firm's balance sheet (and off-balance sheet) position, eg the position risk and counterparty risk requirements.

Financial resources

9.9   Having calculated its total financial resources requirement, a firm must then be able to demonstrate that it has sufficient 'financial resources' to meet that requirement at all times. Again, the definition of 'financial resources' varies according to the category of investment firm. The calculations are based on the net assets in the balance sheet of the firm, which must be drawn up in accordance with normal accounting principles, eg after making proper provisions for bad and doubtful debts. The simplest definitions of financial resources include gross capital (ie share capital and reserves, less intangible assets such as goodwill) and net current assets. The CAD introduced the concept of 'own funds', which is similar to gross capital but subject to restrictions on the inclusion of preference shares and unaudited profits. The harshest test is liquid capital: at this level, a firm must exclude all tangible fixed assets and any debtors over 30 days.

Lead regulation

9.10   Some firms carry out other regulated activities in addition to investment business, eg there are banks that are also investment managers or intermediaries. They will be prudentially regulated by the FSA under the banking rules or by an overseas banking supervisor, rather than be subject to the Interim Prudential Sourcebook for Investment Firms. This arrangement is an example of lead regulation.

Financial resources rules for investment management firms

9.11   The financial resources rules affect most investment management firms that are not lead-regulated. In determining which rules apply, a basic distinction is drawn between firms whose activities are within the scope of the ISD and those outside.

ISD firms

9.12   An investment management ISD firm is subject to two tests. Firstly, it must have 'own funds' of not less than its 'own funds requirement'. Own funds mainly comprise ordinary share capital and audited reserves, together with certain types of preference share capital and subordinated loans, after deducting intangible assets. A subordinated loan is a form of loan capital in which the lender agrees not to call for repayment if to do so would cause the borrower's financial resources to fall below its financial resources requirement. Investment management firms are restricted by some ratio requirements as to the proportion of own funds that can be made up from subordinated loans and cumulative preference shares.

9.13   The own funds requirement for an ISD firm is the sterling equivalent of an euro-denominated amount that depends on the nature of the firm's activities. If the firm's permitted business includes dealing in investments for its own account or underwriting new issues, the amount is €730,000. For a firm whose permitted business includes holding customers' money or assets, but not dealing or underwriting, the own funds requirement is €125,000. Firms whose permitted business does not include holding customers' money or assets, dealing nor underwriting, have a requirement of €50,000. There are two exceptions to this basis of determining the financial resources requirement. First, if the firm was authorised before 1 July 1995, it may be able to apply lower figures on a transitional basis. Second, an ISD firm which is the trustee of an authorised unit trust or the depository of an investment company with variable capital has a requirement of £4 million.

9.14   The second test for an ISD firm is that it must have 'liquid capital' of not less than its 'total capital requirement'. Liquid capital essentially comprises own funds plus interim trading book profits, less illiquid assets such as tangible fixed assets and debtors, accruals and loans due after 90 days. It should be noted that, because of the nature of their businesses, only a few investment management firms will have trading book profits; interim non-trading book profits may only be included if they have been reviewed by the auditors.

9.15   The total capital requirement for an ISD firm comprises five elements. The expenditure-based requirement is calculated as a fraction of the previous year's fixed overheads: 13/52 if the firm holds customers' money or assets or procures the appointment of a non-bank associate as custodian; and 6/52 in other cases.

9.16   The position risk requirement applies to the firm's own holdings of investments and comprises a percentage of their market value. This varies depending on the marketability and volatility of the investment, eg two per cent for short-dated gilts, 25 per cent for listed equities and 100 per cent for unlisted stocks. There are further rules for physical commodities and derivatives held as investments by investment management firms.

9.17   The counterparty risk requirement is applied to any debts due in respect of the firm's own account trading, but this is comparatively rare for investment management firms. The foreign exchange requirement is calculated on the net exposure denominated in foreign currencies. Finally, the 'other asset requirement' applies to all other debts, accruals and prepayments, but not cash at bank. It varies between nil and 8 per cent depending on the category of the debtor and also applies to off-balance sheet items such as guarantees.

9.18 All five requirements, where applicable, are aggregated to form the total capital requirement. However, if a firm is subject to an expenditure-based requirement of only six weeks, its requirement must be calculated as the sum of the five requirements or, if higher, a 13 week expenditure-based requirement.

9.19 ISD firms must also calculate their 'large exposures'. These comprise any exposure (debt or investment) to a single counterparty or group of connected counterparties, which amounts to more than 10 per cent of own funds. Firms are generally not allowed to have any such exposures that exceed 25 per cent of own funds, or 20 per cent if the exposure is to an associate.

Non-ISD firms

9.20 'OPS firms', whose only investment business is managing the investments of their group's occupational pension scheme or welfare trust, are exempt from the financial resources rules. Other non-ISD investment management firms are subject to either an own funds test or a liquid capital test.

9.21 The own funds test applies if the firm does not hold customers' money or assets and does not execute transactions or otherwise arrange deals, ie firms that act only as advisers. Certain venture capital firms are also included in this category. The requirement is £5,000 unless the firm is a trustee of authorised unit trusts or the depository of investment companies with variable capital, in which case the requirement is £4 million. The calculation of own funds for a non-ISD firm permits the use of a higher proportion of subordinated loans than for an ISD firm and is not subject to the same restrictions on the use of preference share capital.

9.22 The liquid capital test applies to other non-ISD firms, including unit trust operators and authorised corporate directors. The calculation is similar to that for an ISD-firm, but without the 13/52 minimum and the restrictions on the use of unaudited interim profits.

Financial resources rules for personal investment firms

9.23 The rules applicable to personal investment firms depend on their category of membership. The first distinction is between category A (ISD firms) and category B (non-ISD firms). Each of these is sub-divided into three:

- categories A1 and B1 may deal as principal and hold client money;
- categories A2 and B2 may deal as agent and hold client money;
- categories A3 and B3 are advisers who are not permitted to deal or hold client money.

All these firms are subject to the test that they must be able, at all times, to meet their liabilities as they fall due.

Category A firms

9.24 Category A firms have to comply with three further financial resources requirements:

(1)   test 1 (own funds);
(2)   test 1A (adjusted net current assets); and
(3)   test 2 (expenditure-based).

For test 1, own funds mainly comprise ordinary share capital and audited reserves, less intangible assets. Cumulative preference shares and subordinated loans may be included to a limited extent. The own funds requirement is the sterling equivalent of a euro denominated amount: €730,000 for category A1; €125,000 for category A2; and €50,000 for category A3. Firms which were in business before 1 July 1995 and which have obtained consent from the FSA may use a lower requirement for a transitional period under the 'grandfathering' provisions.

9.25 Test 1A requires firms to maintain adjusted net current assets of at least £1. Net current assets are adjusted by excluding assets that cannot be realised within 12 months and certain inter-company debts, and revaluing investments using bid prices.

9.26 The financial resources requirement under test 2 depends on the sub-category and other factors such as the number of sales staff and whether the firm is a network. The requirement for a category A1 firm is the highest of 13/52nds of annual expenditure, £400 per member of the sales staff and £10,000. In some cases, the measure is the higher of 13/52nds of annual expenditure or the aggregate of 4/52nds and the 'special adjustments'. The latter comprise the position risk, counterparty risk and foreign exchange adjustments. The position risk and counterparty risk adjustments are normally dealt with in the calculation of financial resources[1]. The foreign exchange adjustment applies to net foreign exchange exposures.

---

[1]   See para 9.27.

9.27 The firm must meet the requirement described above with 'financial resources' which are calculated by adjusting the assets and liabilities in the balance sheet. The effect is harsher, in some respects, for category A1 firms than for firms in categories A2 and A3. The main adjustments to assets are to exclude those which are illiquid (fixed assets, old debts) and to discount the value of investments (the position risk adjustment) and debtors (the counterparty risk adjustment). The amount of the position risk adjustment reflects the market risk and liquidity of the investment and varies from 2 per cent to 100 per cent. The counterparty risk deduction depends on the nature of the debtor: no deduction is required if the debtor is an EC government, 1.6 per cent applies to amounts due from other investment firms and 8 per cent to any other debtor. The main adjustments to liabilities are to deduct eligible subordinated loans and to add provisions for the claw-back of commission received on indemnity terms and for contingent liabilities. Partnerships and sole traders must provide for income tax liabilities.

9.28 Category A firms must calculate their large exposures, ie debts due from or investments in another entity (or group of connected entities) which exceed 10 per cent of own funds. In general terms, firms must ensure that such exposures do not exceed 25 per cent of own funds, or 20 per cent if the counterparty is in the same group as the firm.

Category B firms

9.29 The rules for category B firms are similar in structure, but less severe. Test 1 requires the firm to have own funds of at least £10,000 and the calculation of own funds is not subject to the same restrictions on the use of preference shares and subordinated loans. Test 1A (adjusted net current assets) is the same as for category A. Category B3 firms which do not carry out discretionary portfolio management and have less than 26 sales staff are exempt from tests 1A and 2 unless they are networks.

9.30 The financial resources requirement under test 2 varies from the highest of 13/52nds of annual expenditure, £400 per member of sales staff and £10,000 (for a category B1 firm) to the higher of 4/52nds of annual expenditure and £400 per salesperson for a category B3 firm with more than 25 sales staff. The calculation of the financial resources to meet these requirements (liquid capital for category B1 firms and adjusted capital for category B2 and B3 firms) involves making adjustments to the balance sheet assets and liabilities. The structure of these calculations is similar to the rules for category A firms, but the deductions for disallowed assets are generally lower.

Financial resources rules for securities and futures firms

9.31 For securities and futures firms, different sets of financial resources rules apply depending on whether the firm is an ISD or non-ISD firm. The rules summarised below relate to firms on a 'solo' basis, but an ISD firm may also be subject to consolidated supervision to ensure that its group's externally generated financial resources are in excess of a group financial resources requirement.

ISD firms

9.32 The ISD financial rules impose an 'initial capital' test and a 'financial resources requirement' test. The first of these means that a firm must maintain 'own funds' in excess of the 'initial capital requirement'. The main elements of own funds are ordinary share capital and audited reserves, less intangible assets, to which can be added (to a limited extent) cumulative preference shares and long-term subordinated loans. The loan must be drawn up in accordance with the FSA's standard terms and have an original maturity of at least five years. Interim net profits may only be included if the auditors have reviewed them. The initial capital requirement is a euro amount, the value of which depends on the category of firm. For category C and D firms (which are not permitted to handle client money or assets), the requirement is €50,000; for category B firms (which may hold client money and assets but generally may not deal as principal), the amount is €125,000; and other, category A, firms have a requirement of €730,000.

9.33   The second test requires the firm to have financial resources in excess of its financial resources requirement. Financial resources are calculated by making further adjustments to own funds: illiquid assets, charged assets and contingent liabilities must be deducted, but short-term subordinated loans (with an original maturity of at least two years and subject to gearing limits) and interim net trading book profits may be added. The liquidity adjustments include intangible assets and tangible fixed assets (which must be deducted in full) and non-trading book debts over 90 days (which may deducted in full or discounted by a lower percentage according to the nature of the counterparty).

9.34   The financial resources must meet the sum of the primary and secondary requirements. The primary requirement includes the base requirement together with requirements for position risk, foreign exchange risk, counterparty risk and large exposures (the initial capital requirement must be substituted if this is higher). The base requirement is essentially expenditure-based (13/52nds, or 6/52nds for certain category D firms), but subject to scaling down depending on the size of the other requirements.

9.35   The FSA has complex rules on the calculation of the position risk requirement for trading book positions of securities and futures firms. These seek to cover all the types of investment that a firm may hold and to account for the different levels of market risk involved. Allowance is made for netting of long and short positions and for the spread of risk through diversification and hedging. Alternative methods are available and choosing the right approach will enable a firm to minimise its position risk requirement. Firms must be able to monitor their positions at all times (on an intra-day basis) and often use computer models to assist with the calculations, especially for complicated derivative instruments.

9.36   The foreign exchange requirement is based on net exposures in each foreign currency. The counterparty risk requirement depends on the type of debtor (cash against documents, free deliveries, repurchase agreements etc); balances may be reduced by netting or the use of collateral in certain limited circumstances. A firm's requirement may also be reduced if it can demonstrate to the FSA that it has an adequate credit management policy in operation. The final component of the primary requirement relates to large exposures, ie those exceeding 20–25 per cent of own funds.

9.37   The secondary requirement is an additional liquidity adjustment together with amounts that the FSA may specify depending on its assessment of the firm's risk profile and the adequacy of the firm's management of its operational risks.

Non-ISD firms

9.38 Similar financial resources rules apply to non-ISD firms, but there are a number of exemptions for lower-risk activities. Venture capital firms have an expenditure-based requirement of 6/52nds. A corporate finance advisory firm must meet two different tests: tangible net worth (share capital and reserves, less intangibles) and net current assets must each exceed £10,000. Advisers, locals and traded options market makers must show tangible net worth that is positive.

FINANCIAL REPORTING RULES

9.39 The FSA requires investment firms to submit financial returns so that it can monitor whether they are complying with the financial resources rules and gain a general view of their financial health. In addition, firms are under an obligation to make immediate notification of certain financial events. The scale and frequency of the reports required will depend on the nature of the firm's business and the risks to which it is exposed. Late submission of a report may result in a fine or other disciplinary action. The FSA will usually require the annual financial return to be audited[1] but may not require returns from firms that are lead-regulated[2].

---

[1] See para 9.60.
[2] See para 9.10.

9.40 Some firms may need to prepare financial statements more frequently than specified by the rules, in order to check that they are complying with their financial resources requirements. This will particularly be the case where a firm does not have a comfortable surplus of financial resources.

Financial reporting rules for investment management firms

9.41 Investment management firms have to submit an audited annual financial return for each 12-month period. The format of the return is set out in the *FSA Handbook*. It comprises a profit and loss account and balance sheet, a statement of the financial resources surplus or deficit at the year end and a calculation of the expenditure-based requirement for the following year. The annual financial return also includes details of funds under management and statements as to whether the firm has held client money or assets or traded in securities on its own account. ISD firms must report their large exposures. The return must be accompanied by the firm's annual accounts (ie for a UK company, the financial statements prepared under the Companies Act 1985) and the two documents must together give a true and fair view of the state of affairs of the firm and its profit or loss. The return must be signed by the directors and submitted to the FSA within four months of the year end.

9.42 Firms subject to a liquid capital requirement (ie ISD firms and all non-ISD firms other than those which do not hold client money or assets and do not arrange or execute deals) must also submit a quarterly financial return. This must also be prepared on a standard FSA form and comprise balance sheet, profit and loss account and financial resources statement. The quarterly form is also used to report the value of funds under management and whether the firm has held client money or assets or traded in securities on its own account. ISD firms must provide details of all large exposures. The directors must state whether the firm complied with its financial resources requirements throughout the quarter and whether it will be able to meet its liabilities as they fall due. The quarterly return must be received by the FSA within a month of the end of the quarter.

9.43   All ISD firms subject to an own funds requirement of €730,000[1] must also submit a monthly return by the end of the following month, except at quarter ends.

---

[1]   See para 9.13.

9.44   Investment management firms that are part of a group may be required to submit financial information on a consolidated basis.

9.45   Firms subject to lead regulator arrangements are exempt from these requirements and need only submit a copy of their annual accounts prepared under the appropriate legislation. OPS firms (which just manage the investments of their group's occupational pension scheme or welfare trust) must submit their own annual accounts within four months and the accounts of the pension schemes (and any common investment funds) they manage within seven months.

9.46   In addition to the periodic reporting requirements, investment management firms are subject to the ad hoc financial notification rules. For example, a firm must tell the FSA as soon as it is aware that it is, or will shortly be, in breach of the financial resources rules. Other requirements include the need to notify the FSA if the firm will be unable to submit a financial return on time, or if the auditor intends to qualify his report.

Financial reporting rules for personal investment firms

9.47   All personal investment firms other than small personal investment firms (ie non-ISD firms which are not networks and have 25 or fewer sales staff) have to submit annual financial statements. The statements comprise a balance sheet and profit and loss account prepared in accordance with generally accepted accounting principles so as to present a true and fair view. The formats set out in the *FSA Handbook* must be used, but supplemented by additional information on accounting policies and any claw-back of commission received on indemnity terms. Any balances on client money bank accounts must be shown separately by way of note; they must not be included in the firm's own balance sheet. The FSA requires a note on any contingent liabilities, including, if applicable, a statement that there are none. In addition to the balance sheet and profit and loss account, the firm must complete a statement showing the calculation of financial resources as at the balance sheet date. The forms must be signed by the directors or partners and submitted within four months of the year end. The annual financial return must be accompanied by an auditor's report. The FSA has the power to require certain category A firms that are part of a group to submit financial information on a consolidated basis.

9.48 If the firm is a sole trader, the financial statements should include only those items that relate to its business. Sole traders must also submit a separate statement certifying that their total business and personal assets exceed their business and personal liabilities.

9.49 Category A2 and A3 firms must also submit quarterly reports, including a statement of large exposures. Category A1 firms have to submit monthly reports. Category B1 firms have to submit monthly reports; category B2 firms must prepare quarterly reports, but need only submit them to the FSA if they have over 25 sales staff; category B3 firms who are networks or have over 25 sales staff must also submit quarterly reports. The deadline for all these reports is three weeks after the end of the period.

9.50 Certain events must be notified to the FSA urgently, eg where a firm may not be able to meet its financial resources requirements, discovers that previously submitted information was inaccurate, or suffers a breakdown in its accounting systems. Category A firms must notify the FSA if a large exposure exceeds 25 per cent of its own funds (20 per cent for exposures to group companies).

Financial reporting rules for securities and futures firms

9.51 Securities and futures firms must submit an annual reporting statement, comprising the balance sheet, profit and loss account and financial resources calculation. Unless special permission has been received, the annual reporting statement must be submitted electronically using the FSA reporting software, but accompanied by a written statement signed by the directors. The statement must also be accompanied by the annual accounts (eg those prepared under the Companies Act 1985) and must be drawn up so as to present a true and fair view. The FSA specifies that the accounts should reflect the substance of the underlying transactions and balances, not merely the legal form, and that firms must use trade date accounting. The FSA will grant permission, where appropriate, for firms to use a reporting currency other than sterling. The submission deadline is three months.

9.52 Certain ISD firms (categories A and B) and non-ISD firms (broad scope) must submit monthly financial statements within 15 business days. Category C and D firms and arrangers submit quarterly returns instead. These firms must include with their annual reporting statement a reconciliation between that balance sheet and the balance sheets in the monthly or quarterly return and the annual accounts. ISD firms must also report large exposures quarterly. ISD firms may have to provide financial reports on a consolidated basis.

9.53   The financial notification rules include the need to report immediately any breach or expected breach of the financial resources requirements. ISD and broad scope firms must notify the FSA if their financial resources fall below 110 per cent of the requirement.

ACCOUNTING RECORDS RULES

9.54   The FSA has rules requiring firms to maintain proper accounting records and to have proper systems of control over the records. The purpose of these rules is to ensure that investment firms can monitor their financial resources, prepare the reporting statements that have to be sent to the FSA and account properly to their clients. The rules are therefore more wide-ranging than the accounting records requirements set out in the Companies Act 1985. The accounting records must disclose all the transactions, assets and balances of the company itself (ISD firms must distinguish trading book and non-trading book items) and of the clients. They must be sufficient to enable the firm to disclose, with reasonable accuracy, its financial position at any time and to demonstrate compliance with the financial resources rules. There must be sufficient information for the firm to prepare the necessary financial reports to the regulator.

9.55   The rules require that the records should normally be maintained in English and kept up to date. They must be maintained in hard copy (or capable of being printed out within a day) and must be retained for six years. There must be an audit trail and full access for both the auditor and the FSA.

9.56   The accounting records rules also contain or refer to requirements to record client money and custody assets (see Chapter 7).

AUDIT RULES

9.57   Compliance with the rules on financial resources, financial reporting and accounting records has to be checked by the firm itself and by the FSA through its inspection visits and desk monitoring of the financial returns. However, the FSA also requires most investment firms to appoint an auditor (even if the firm is a partnership or sole trader) who will report annually to the FSA on compliance with certain of the financial rules.

Appointment of auditors

9.58   Most investment firms must appoint an auditor, although small personal investment firms are exempt. The auditor must normally be registered under the Companies Act 1985 or under equivalent overseas requirements. The auditor must be independent of the investment business and the FSA has the right to reject an auditor if they are not satisfied as to his knowledge and experience.

9.59 The auditor's rights and duties must be set out in an engagement letter. He must be given full access to all the firm's records and have the right to make enquiries of all the staff. If an auditor resigns, or is not re-appointed, the firm must tell the FSA and the auditor must make a statement as to whether there are any circumstances relating to his departure which should be brought to the attention of the FSA. If it is considered necessary, the FSA may appoint a second auditor, or 'skilled person'[1], at the firm's expense and the original auditor must provide full co-operation.

---

[1]   See para 9.66.

The annual audit report

9.60 Investment firms must arrange for a report from the auditor to be submitted to the FSA annually. The report is addressed to the FSA and is not intended to be disclosed to or relied on by any third parties. It will confirm that the audit has been conducted in accordance with auditing standards and that the auditor has carried out procedures having regard to the practice note on investment businesses. This practice note (PN21), developed by the Auditing Practices Board (APB) in consultation with the FSA, contains guidance on the audit of investment businesses. It covers the form of the report, procedures for the audit of client money and other assets and the role of the auditor in relation to the conduct of business rules.

9.61 The audit report usually contains four main opinions (subject to exceptions for lead-regulated companies) covering the financial statements, financial resources, accounting records and systems, and client money and other assets. The report on the first three matters must be submitted within the three or four month deadlines applicable to financial returns.

9.62 The first opinion is whether the financial statements give a true and fair view of the firm's state of affairs at the balance sheet date and of its profit or loss for the year then ended. The auditor must report whether these financial statements have been drawn up in accordance with the FSA's rules and agree with the accounting records. For personal investment firms and securities and futures firms, the report must also contain an opinion as to whether the financial statements have been properly reconciled to the quarterly or monthly returns if applicable.

9.63 The second opinion concerns the statement of financial resources. The auditor must report whether the statement of the resources and the requirement has been properly prepared and whether the firm met its financial resources requirement at the balance sheet date. The auditor must also report on the calculation of the expenditure-based requirement for the following year.

9.64 Thirdly, the audit opinion covers whether the firm has kept proper accounting records during the year in accordance with the rules.

9.65 The fourth opinion relates to client money and to other custody assets, ie documents of title held in safe keeping. Here the auditor must report whether the firm maintained throughout the year systems which were adequate to enable it to comply with the client asset rules and whether the firm was in compliance with the rules at the balance sheet date. In addition, the auditor must report any other breaches of the client asset rules which came to his attention. If a firm has not held client money or custody assets, the auditor should carry out review procedures and report whether anything came to his attention that caused him to believe that the firm did hold client money or custody assets. This fourth opinion may, at the firm's request, cover a 12 month period different from the accounting period and must be delivered within four months.

It is not unusual for auditors to have to qualify their reports in some respect.

Other reports from auditors

9.66 There are other circumstances when the auditor may have to submit a report to the regulator. The FSA requires a report from the auditor when a firm applies for authorisation. This report covers the financial forecasts submitted with the application form and the adequacy of the accounting and reporting systems. A firm may also ask its auditor to prepare a review report on interim profits if these are to be included in the financial resources calculations[1]. As part of its supervision process, the FSA may commission an auditor (or other 'skilled person') to report on any other aspects of a firm's business.

---

[1]   See paras 9.14 and 9.32 on 'ISD firms'.

9.67 The auditor will normally send the firm a management letter commenting on any weaknesses in internal control which came to his attention during the audit and making recommendations for improvements. The FSA requires the auditor to undertake to do this. If the auditor has no such comments to make, he must send the firm a statement to that effect.

Ad hoc reporting

9.68 In addition to the annual and other reports referred to above, the auditor may also have to report to the regulator on an ad hoc basis under the 'whistle-blowing' provisions. These are set out in the FSMA 2000 itself[1], regulations made by the Treasury, an auditing standard (SAS 620) and an APB practice note (PN21). The effect of these requirements is that, if the auditor identifies an issue that would be of material significance to the regulator, he must bring it to the attention of the regulator without delay. For example, if the auditor discovers that the financial position of the investment firm is so precarious that its ability to continue operating is in doubt, he should report that finding to the FSA immediately, without waiting for the submission of the annual audit report. Another example of where the reporting requirement might be triggered is where the auditor believes that the firm is about to misappropriate client assets. In some cases, eg where the issue casts doubt on the integrity of the directors, the auditor may have to inform the FSA without telling the firm that he is doing so.

---

[1]   FSMA 2000, ss 342 and 343.

Chapter 10   Enforcement

Andrew R Hart[1]
Simon Orton[2]

INTRODUCTION

10.1 Regulatory enforcement in the financial services sector has assumed increasing importance over recent years, particularly following a number of high profile cases such as the collapse of Barings, the issues that arose relating to certain Morgan Grenfell unit trusts and the Sumitomo copper trading affair. There have also been more general problems addressed on a sector-wide basis like pensions misselling or, more recently, the misselling of endowment policies. Until now, though, enforcement has in many cases necessarily been a fragmented process, with different responsibilities and powers being vested in different bodies and, often, no single regulatory authority having the ability to take an overall view on a particular matter. Thus it was, for example, relatively common to see a particular market trading issue being dealt with by one of the exchanges, such as the London Stock Exchange, so far as the firm (as a member of the exchange) was concerned, with one of the self-regulatory organisations then taking enforcement action against any of the firm's employees involved who were registered with it, and any criminal law aspects (for example, prosecutions for the criminal offences of insider dealing or market manipulation) being considered separately by the Department of Trade and Industry. The result, from the perspective of the regulated community, has been a complicated regime leaving firms facing the prospect of multiple investigations by different bodies, using different powers, into different aspects of the same matter. From the perspective of the regulators, this has made for an inefficient enforcement process, as well as one which it has been difficult to operate effectively.

---

[1]   Partner, Freshfields Bruckhaus Deringer.
[2]   Senior Associate, Freshfields Bruckhaus Deringer.

ENFORCEMENT UNDER THE FSMA 2000: AN OVERVIEW

10.2 The Financial Services and Markets Act 2000 (FSMA 2000) sweeps away many of these distinctions. It consolidates, into the FSA, much of the pre-existing range of investigation and enforcement powers, allowing in many cases a single investigation to take place, as a result of which one body, the FSA, has the ability to consider in the round what action it is appropriate to take in relation to the particular matter, and against whom.

10.3   Whilst enforcement is perhaps most often associated with disciplinary action, the FSA's powers are by no means confined to disciplining firms. A range of enforcement powers is available to the FSA to address different aspects of a particular problem. That range encompasses not only disciplining a firm, but also varying its permission (previously referred to as 'intervention'), or in very serious cases cancelling its permission, requiring it to pay restitution to those who have suffered loss or to disgorge profits it has made, disciplining any approved persons who were involved, removing their approval, or imposing a prohibition order preventing a particular individual from being involved in the industry (or specified parts of it), and extends also to bringing criminal prosecutions. These different powers may generally speaking be exercised individually or in combination, depending upon the circumstances.

10.4   This simplifies the previous position, and should bring not only more consistency of approach but also more clarity as to when particular powers are likely to be exercised. It also, though, requires the regulated community to appreciate the range of action that can be taken by the FSA and not to view enforcement purely as a matter of discipline.

10.5   The language of many of the relevant provisions of the FSMA 2000 may be familiar, because to a large extent the FSMA 2000 consolidates provisions previously found in a variety of legislation, such as (among others) the Financial Services Act 1986, the Banking Act 1987, the Building Societies Act 1986, the Friendly Societies Act 1992 and the Insurance Companies Act 1982. However, the effect of drawing together this range of powers, and vesting them all in one body, may, as Howard Davies, the Chairman of the FSA, put it, look intimidating[1]. In addition, on a closer examination the FSA's powers are in some respects more extensive than those of the regulators it replaces. Certain provisions which previously applied only to certain types of financial services business have now been introduced more generally (for example, the ability to require a bank to commission an expert report under the Banking Act 1987, s 39 now applies more generally under the FSMA 2000, s 166). Furthermore, in some cases the language of the consolidated provision is more favourable to the FSA (compare the Banking Act 1987, s 42 ('reasonable grounds for suspecting') and the FSMA 2000, s 168(2) ('circumstances suggesting')).

---

[1]   Quoted in the Financial Times (13 November 1998).

10.6   Moreover, there is one significant extension to the range of regulatory enforcement powers, which requires specific mention, namely the new 'civil offence' of market abuse, which enables misconduct in the financial markets to be addressed. The criminal prohibitions against insider dealing (under the Criminal Justice Act 1993, Pt V) and misleading statements and practices (under the Financial Services Act 1986, s 47) remain (the latter can now be found in the FSMA 2000, s 397). Market abuse complements the criminal regime, allowing a wider range of conduct to be dealt with, including conduct which does not constitute a criminal offence or which it would not be appropriate to pursue through the criminal justice system. It also brings greater clarity to the basis for taking regulatory action against members of the regulated community who engage in inappropriate market practices. These issues are discussed in more detail below[1].

---

[1]   See para 10.108.

10.7   The other major change brought about by the FSMA 2000 is that the investigation and enforcement regime now has a statutory basis. The primary effect of this is two-fold. First, certain safeguards have been introduced, also on a statutory basis, for those subjected to the investigation and/or enforcement process. These include: a limited privilege against self-incrimination[1]; a protection for, broadly, legally privileged information[2]; a limited protection for banking confidence[3]; and, most notably, various procedural safeguards relating to the FSA's decision-making process when exercising its powers and, ultimately, a right to refer many enforcement decisions to the Financial Services and Markets Tribunal. These issues are discussed below[4].

---

[1]   FSMA 2000, s 174.
[2]   FSMA 2000, s 413.
[3]   FSMA 2000, s 175(5).
[4]   See para 10.121.

10.8   Second, there are various statutory provisions supporting the investigation and enforcement provisions, and allowing them to be enforced, including the ability to bring proceedings for contempt of court against those who fail to comply[1]; the ability to obtain a warrant to search premises and seize documents[2]; and the criminal offences of knowingly or recklessly providing false or misleading information[3]; and falsifying, concealing or destroying documents[4]. Again, these are outlined below[5].

---

[1]   FSMA 2000, s 177(1) and (2).
[2]   FSMA 2000, s 176.
[3]   FSMA 2000, ss 177(4) and 398.
[4]   FSMA 2000, s 177(3).
[5]   See para 10.54.

Overlapping enforcement powers of other bodies

10.9   Whilst the FSA is now the primary body responsible for enforcement of financial services and the financial markets, it is by no means the only body with enforcement powers in this area. Various other bodies have responsibility for regulatory enforcement in particular respects, which potentially overlap with those of the FSA.

10.10   These include other UK regulators such as the recognised clearing houses and investment exchanges, including the London Stock Exchange (which have primary responsibility for enforcing trading on their own markets), the Takeover Panel (which retains its responsibilities for the City Code on Takeovers and Mergers and the Rules Governing Substantial

Acquisitions of Shares), Lloyd's (which retains various responsibilities for the regulation of the insurance market), and the designated professional bodies (which are responsible for the regulation of financial services activities by their members, under the FSMA 2000, Pt XX). In relation to most of these, the FSA has an overall supervisory role under the FSMA 2000. In addition, the FSMA 2000, Pt VI confers various duties and powers on a body called the competent authority, or UK Listing Authority, which is responsible for the admission of securities to the UK's official list and has various enforcement powers in support of its functions. The FSA has been appointed to that role and the powers of the UK Listing Authority are therefore vested in the FSA.

10.11 Overseas regulatory authorities may also have a role in enforcement, particularly where the matter concerns an EEA firm exercising its passport rights in the UK and authorised under the FSMA 2000, Sch 3 or 4, or a UCITS scheme, the operator of which may be authorised under the FSMA 2000, Sch 5, or where the matter relates to the conduct of a UK regulated firm in its business overseas.

10.12 Where criminal offences may have been committed, a number of different bodies may potentially be involved as well as or instead of the FSA, including: the Department of Trade and Industry (which retains a role in relation to insider dealing, has a residual prosecution role generally under the FSMA 2000, and may also become involved where Companies Act 1985 issues are involved); the Serious Fraud Office (where criminal fraud is involved); the Crown Prosecution Service (where other criminal offences are involved); and the National Criminal Intelligence Service (in relation to money laundering).

10.13 Finally, the powers of the Financial Services Ombudsman Scheme and the Financial Services Compensation Scheme must not be overlooked.

10.14 Given the range of UK and overseas bodies that may potentially be interested where an issue arises relating to a firm, cooperation and information sharing between regulators, which has been a feature of regulation for some time, is likely to continue, and indeed to increase, particularly as the various European regulators develop their relationships and try to keep pace with the ever more international nature of financial services businesses. The FSMA 2000 and the secondary legislation made under it provide the necessary framework, often reflecting the provisions of the Single Market Directives, by allowing the FSA to, for example:

- exercise investigation powers at the request of an overseas regulator[1];
- vary the permission of UK regulated firms at the request of an overseas regulator[2];
- impose requirements on overseas firms at the request of an overseas regulator[3]; and
- share information with both UK and overseas regulators in many situations[4].

For its part, the FSA has signalled its recognition of the importance of this process[5].

---

[1] FSMA 2000, s 169.
[2] FSMA 2000, s 47.
[3] FSMA 2000, s 195.
[4] FSMA 2000, s 349 and see the Financial Services and Markets Act 2000 (Disclosure of Confidential Information) Regulations 2001, SI 2001/2188.
[5] See for example, the FSA's 2000/2001 Annual Report under 'International policy developments'.

FSA enforcement policy

10.15   Before turning to the specific provisions of the FSMA 2000, it is worth briefly explaining the FSA's approach to enforcement. The backdrop against which all of the FSA's functions and powers must be viewed is the regulatory objectives prescribed for the FSA under the FSMA 2000[1], namely maintaining confidence in the financial system, promoting public understanding of the financial system, securing appropriate protection for consumers, and reducing the extent to which it is possible for financial services businesses to be used for financial crime. These four objectives provide the underlying rationale for the FSA's actions and the FSA regards the effective and proportionate use of its enforcement powers as playing an important role in the pursuit of these objectives[2]. Consumer protection and market confidence may particularly be important considerations in enforcement situations.

---

[1] For the details, see the FSMA 2000, ss 2–6.
[2] See *FSA Handbook* at ENF 1.2.1G.

10.16   Whilst the FSA's enforcement function is clearly an important part of its role, it is not the only means of securing regulatory compliance or, more widely, pursuing the regulatory objectives. The FSA has what it refers to as a regulatory 'toolkit', which includes, among other things, the vetting of firms and individuals at entry, supervision and consumer education. Enforcement thus needs to be seen in context.

10.17   The FSA has provided three broad principles underlying its approach to the exercise of its enforcement powers[1]:

(1)   the need for an open and cooperative relationship between the FSA and those whom it regulates. This is reflected in the Principles for Businesses, Principle 11, and the Statements of Principle for Approved Persons, Statement of Principle 4 (these are outlined at para 10.23 below) and is amplified in the FSA's rules[2], and it is one of the main practical considerations for those who are subjected to FSA investigation or enforcement;

(2)   that the FSA will seek to exercise its enforcement powers in a manner that is transparent, proportionate and consistent with its publicly stated policy; and

(3)   that the FSA will seek to ensure fair treatment when exercising its enforcement powers. Primarily, this is sought to be achieved through the FSA's decision making processes, outlined at para 10.121 below.

As may already be apparent, the FSA's powers of information gathering and investigation are the cornerstone of all its enforcement powers. These are considered first, followed by, second, an outline of each of the enforcement powers available to the FSA, and, third, a brief introduction to the various other relevant bodies.

---

[1]   See *FSA Handbook* at ENF 1.3.1G.
[2]   See the Supervision Manual, Chapter 2.

INFORMATION GATHERING AND INVESTIGATION

10.18   'Information is the key to effective regulation'[1]. When a problem arises, the FSA will first need to obtain sufficient information to understand the problem, before it is in a position to decide what, if any, action is appropriate (although, as will be seen, in some cases, particularly where there is an immediate and serious risk to consumers or the financial markets, it may wish to take urgent action before all of the details are known). The FSA's powers of information gathering and investigation are thus central to its enforcement functions. They are, essentially, fact finding powers[2].

---

[1]   Financial Secretary to HM Treasury, in SC A (Financial Services and Markets Bill), 23 November 1999.
[2]   See *FSA Handbook* at ENF 2.11.1G.

10.19   The FSMA 2000 contains a raft of investigation powers, exercisable by the FSA (many can also be exercised by the Secretary of State, but this power is in practice only residual). The main provisions are to be found in the FSMA 2000, Pt XI, and the FSA's policy on the use of these powers is found in its Enforcement Manual at Chapter 2.

10.20   The statutory provisions are complex, there are large areas of overlap between the various powers of investigation, and the detailed investigation provisions vary depending upon which investigation power is invoked. Hence, among other things, the extent of the investigation permitted in any particular case depends upon the statutory provision under which that investigation was commenced. The complexity of the statutory scheme arises partly from the fact that many of these provisions are derived from earlier legislation and partly because the different types of circumstances in which an investigation can be commenced may require a different set of powers to be available to the investigator. The statutory provisions are also complemented by the FSA's rules, which impose obligations on the regulated community to comply with what might be termed informal investigations by the FSA.

10.21 Not every rule breach requires an exhaustive investigation into all aspects including whether there were any underlying systemic causes. The nature and extent of the FSA's investigation in any case depends upon the circumstances, particularly the nature and seriousness of the FSA's concerns and the attitude of the firm concerned. In many cases, particularly where more minor breaches are concerned, the FSA will not need or wish to exercise any of its formal investigation powers in order to obtain the information it requires[1].

---

[1] For a further discussion of FSA policy on the use of its powers, see *FSA Handbook* at ENF 2.5.

10.22 The investigation powers can usefully be divided into three groups, namely informal FSA investigations, formal information gathering by the FSA, and formal investigations. They are considered in turn.

Informal FSA investigations

10.23 In practice, the FSA obtains much of the information which it needs from the regulated community by simply asking for it, without apparently exercising any of its statutory powers. Authorised firms owe the FSA a duty under Principle 11 of the Principles for Businesses[1] to deal with its regulators (which includes not only the FSA but also any other relevant regulators) in an open and cooperative way. Approved persons owe a similar duty under Statement of Principle 4[2]. The FSA has provided, in the Supervision Manual, Chapter 2.3, guidance on the extent of the firm's obligation. This makes clear that there is little that it cannot ask of firms, for example meetings, access to records and systems, and answers to questions. The firm's obligation extends to take reasonable care to ensure that members of its group, and those who work for it, provide similar assistance. The FSA has also made a rule[3] requiring firms to permit access to their premises, with or without notice. Similar obligations apply to approved persons[4].

---

[1] See *FSA Handbook* at PRIN.
[2] See *FSA Handbook* at APER.
[3] See *FSA Handbook* at SUP 2.3.5.
[4] See *FSA Handbook* at APER 4.4

10.24 There are, however, limits on the extent to which Principle 11 and/or Statement of Principle 4 can be used as a means of investigation. Among other things, the FSA can obtain information in this way only from within the regulated community. From the firm's perspective, the basis for and scope of an investigation conducted in this way may be unclear, the statutory safeguards[1] applicable to formal investigations do not apply (although some may in practice be conferred by the FSA and others may in any event be available as a matter of law) and, moreover the firm may need to consider whether the provision of information in compliance with its obligations under Principle 11 overrides any duties of confidentiality it may owe to third parties.

---

¹   For example, the requirement for notice of an investigation (see para 10.33) and the protection against self-incrimination (see para 10.57).

Formal information gathering by the FSA

Information gathering under FSMA 2000, s 165

10.25   Short of commencing a formal investigation (which, as will be seen, involves the appointment of an investigator), the FSMA 2000, s 165, allows the FSA to obtain from authorised persons and certain others¹ specified information or documents, or documents or information of a specified description. The FSA may specify a reasonable time within which the document or information is to be provided and a place at which it is to be provided. It can also require the documents or information to be verified or authenticated. The requirement is normally imposed by written notice, although this is not always required: an officer of the FSA who has written authority to do so may require the person concerned to provide information or documents without delay.

---

¹   Former authorised persons, recognised investment exchanges and clearing houses and the manager, trustee or depositary of certain recognised overseas collective investment schemes, as well as various types of persons connected with an authorised person.

10.26   The information or documents must be reasonably required by the FSA in connection with the exercise by it of functions conferred on it by or under the FSMA 2000. This is a wide test, and allows the provision to be used to obtain information not only in relation to a particular enforcement issue which has arisen relating to a firm, but also more generally for use in relation to the FSA's other functions, such as supervision or consumer education¹.

---

¹   For the FSA's policy on the use of this power, see *FSA Handbook* at ENF 2.5.3G.

Reports by skilled persons under the FSMA 2000, s 166

10.27   The FSMA 2000, s 166, effectively extends to the whole of the regulated community the former powers contained in the Banking Act 1987, s 39. It allows the FSA to require an authorised person, and certain types of connected persons, to commission an expert report for submission to it.

10.28   The report may be on any matter about which the FSA has required or could require the provision of information under the FSMA 2000, s 165. It may therefore relate to any matter reasonably required in connection with the exercise by the FSA of functions conferred on it by or under the FSMA 2000. It must be prepared by a person nominated or approved by the FSA and who appears to the FSA to have the skills necessary to make a report on the matter concerned. A 'skilled person' thus encompasses not only accountants and actuaries but might also include, for example, lawyers or those with particular business or technology skills.

10.29 Whilst the FSA imposes the requirement to appoint a skilled person, and nominates or approves the particular individual, it is for the firm to contract with that person, and particularly, to bear the cost of that person's work. The FSA has imposed various requirements on the terms of the appointment. In particular, there must be a term[1] requiring and permitting the skilled person to cooperate with the FSA and to report to the FSA, broadly, any matters of potential enforcement consequence which that person comes across in the course of his duties and the firm must waive any duties of confidentiality which might limit the provision of information or opinion by the skilled person to the FSA. The contract must also expressly give the FSA the right to enforce these terms directly against the skilled person (under the Contracts (Rights of Third Parties) Act 1999). It is thus envisaged that the person appointed will not only report on the particular matter concerned but also will inform the FSA about any other matters of concern which that person comes across in the course of his work.

[1]   See *FSA Handbook* at SUP 5.5.1R.

10.30 The firm concerned is expected to take reasonable steps to ensure that a report responsive to the terms of appointment is delivered[1]. Firms are required under the FSA's rules to provide all reasonable assistance to the skilled person[2]. Moreover, the FSMA 2000 imposes a duty on the firm's normal actuary, auditor or other skilled person, to provide all such assistance as the appointed person may reasonably require (and this is enforceable by court injunction)[3].

[1]   See *FSA Handbook* at SUP 5.5.12G.
[2]   See *FSA Handbook* at SUP 5.5.9R for the rule as well as guidance on what this involves.
[3]   FSMA 2000, s 166(5) and (6).

10.31 The FSA has provided, in the Supervision Manual, Chapter 5.3, extensive guidance on its policy on the use of this power. It is clearly a broad power, exercisable in a wide range of circumstances[1] and will be used not only in the enforcement context but also for a range of supervisory purposes. In the enforcement context particularly, in deciding whether to exercise this power, the FSA will consider the objectives of its enquiries and the relative effectiveness of its different powers to achieve those objectives[2]. Thus, for example, it is unlikely to require the firm to commission an expert report where its objectives are limited to gathering historic information or evidence for determining whether enforcement action is likely to be appropriate, but it may do where it needs to obtain expert analysis or recommendations for remedial action. It is also notable that the fact that the firm must bear the cost of such a report being produced is an exception to the general rule[3], that a firm under investigation does not bear the cost of the investigation. Cost is therefore a relevant consideration in whether the power should be exercised[4].

[1]   Some examples can be found in the Enforcement Manual, Chapter 5, Annex 1G.
[2]   See *FSA Handbook* at ENF 2.5.6G.

³   FSMA 2000, Sch 1, para 16. This contrasts with the position under the former regime operated by the self-regulatory organisations, where firms were normally required to pay the cost of the investigation and enforcement process.

⁴   For details of the FSA's policy on cost considerations, see *FSA Handbook* at SUP 5.3.8G.

Formal investigations

10.32   The FSMA 2000 allows a formal investigation to be carried out in a range of circumstances. The nature and extent of the investigation depends upon the circumstances and the statutory provision under which the investigation was commenced. Such formal investigations involve the appointment of one or more investigators, who can be (and normally are) a member of the FSA's staff. It is they who carry out the investigation, subject to directions from the FSA on, among other things, the scope, timing, conduct and reporting of the investigation, and they are obliged to provide a report at the end of the process[1]. (In the case of most types of investigation, the Secretary of State is also entitled to appoint an investigator, although this is a residuary power and unlikely to be commonly used in practice.)

¹   FSMA 2000, s 170.

10.33   The FSA is, generally speaking, required to notify the person under investigation that an investigator has been appointed under a particular statutory provision, and to give the reasons for the investigator's appointment. However, there are exceptions. Particularly:

(1)   the FSA need not do so in relation to an investigation which is commenced under the FSMA 2000, s 168(1) or (4)[1], if it believes that the notice would be likely to result in the investigation being frustrated;

(2)   it need not do so in the case of any investigation commenced under the FSMA 2000, s 168(2) (this includes in particular market abuse investigations and perimeter enforcement[2]);

(3)   it also need not do so in the case of investigations into collective investment schemes or OEICs[3].

¹   See para 10.39.
²   See further para 10.42.
³   See para 10.48.

10.34   No publicity will normally arise from the investigation process nor will the information found in, or conclusions of, the investigation be made public[1]. There are, however, exceptions to this. The FSA may in exceptional circumstances make a public announcement that it is or is not investigating a particular matter, for example where the matter has become the subject of public concern, speculation or rumour and it is desirable for the FSA to make the announcement in order to address this. The findings or conclusions of the investigation may become apparent if the FSA successfully takes enforcement action against the person concerned, because, as discussed below[2], that enforcement action is likely to be publicised. In exceptional circumstances, those findings or conclusions may themselves be made public, for example, if the FSA concludes that the concerns that prompted the investigation were unwarranted in a situation where it had made an announcement that it was investigating.

---

[1] For a more detailed discussion, see *FSA Handbook* at ENF 2.13.
[2] See para 10.133.

10.35 The main investigation powers are outlined in turn, followed by a discussion of whether firms must comply with requirements imposed by investigators. It should be noted that there are various ancillary provisions supporting the investigation provisions, primarily found in the FSMA 2000, s 175. The FSA's procedures when conducting interviews can be found in the Enforcement Manual at Chapter 2.14.

FSMA 2000, s 167: general investigations

10.36 The FSA (and the Secretary of State) has the power to commence a general investigation into the business or ownership of authorised persons under the FSMA 2000, s 167, if it appears to it that there is good reason for doing so. Business includes any part of the person's business even if it does not consist of carrying on regulated activities, and the investigation may extend to other group members of the person under investigation or a partnership of which that person is a member. The provision also applies to former authorised persons.

10.37 The FSA has indicated that this power will be used where there are general concerns about a firm or appointed representative requiring further investigations to be carried out using the FSA's compulsory powers, but the circumstances do not at that stage suggest any specific breach or contravention[1].

---

[1] See *FSA Handbook* at ENF 2.5.9G.

10.38 The powers of an investigator appointed under the FSMA 2000, s 167 are found in the FSMA 2000, s 171. The investigator may require the person who is the subject of the investigation, and certain types of connected persons, to attend before him at a specific time and place and answer questions or otherwise to provide such information as the investigator may require. The investigator has a limited power in relation to unrelated third parties, namely to require them to produce at a specified time and place any specified documents or documents of a specified description. The investigator may only impose such requirements insofar as he reasonably considers the question, provision of information or production of the document, to be relevant to the purposes of the investigation. The investigation power is therefore extensive as against the person under investigation, and those connected with him, but more limited as against unconnected third parties.

FSMA 2000, s 168(1) and (4): regulatory or criminal offences

10.39 The FSMA 2000, s 168(1) and (4) are the main investigation provisions applicable for investigating specific suspected regulatory breaches and suspected criminal offences under the FSMA 2000. The power to appoint an investigator arises where it appears to the FSA that there are circumstances suggesting certain regulatory breaches or criminal offences[1]. The Secretary of State has concurrent powers, but only in relation to criminal offences, not regulatory breaches.

---

[1]   For a full list, see the FSMA 2000, s 168(1) and (4).

10.40 These investigations are not confined to the regulated community, although in most instances they are likely to relate to authorised firms and those who work for them. The test of 'circumstances suggesting' is a low one; there need not be, for example, reasonable grounds for suspicion that a breach or criminal offence has occurred.

10.41 An investigator appointed under the FSMA 2000, s 168(1) or (4) has the same powers as one appointed under s 167, as outlined above[1], but also has additional powers under the FSMA 2000, s 172 to obtain information from third parties unconnected with the person under investigation. In particular, the investigator may require a person who is neither the subject of the investigation, nor a person connected with the person under investigation, to attend before him at a specified time and place and answer questions or otherwise to provide such information as the investigator may require for the purposes of the investigation. Such a requirement can only be imposed if the investigator is satisfied that it is necessary or expedient for the purposes of the investigation.

---

[1]   See para 10.38.

FSMA 2000, s 168(2): serious criminal offences and market abuse

10.42 The FSMA 2000, s 168(2) allows the FSA (or the Secretary of State) to appoint an investigator where it appears to it that there are circumstances suggesting that certain serious criminal offences may have been committed, or market abuse may have taken place. The criminal offences are: unlawful financial promotion[1]; the perimeter offences of breach of the general prohibition[2] and falsely claiming to be authorised or exempt[3]; and the market misconduct offences of insider dealing (under the Criminal Justice Act 1993, Pt V) and misleading statements or practices[4].

---

[1]   FSMA 2000, ss 21 or 238.
[2]   FSMA 2000, s 23.
[3]   FSMA 2000, s 24(1).
[4]   FSMA 2000, s 397.

10.43 The powers of an investigator appointed under this provision are similar to the former provisions relating to insider dealing investigations under the Financial Services Act 1986, s 177 and they are probably the most extensive of the investigation powers found in the FSMA 2000. In particular, under the FSMA 2000, s 173, if the investigator considers that any person is or may be able to give information which is or may be relevant to the investigation, he may require that person:

- to attend before him at a specified time and place and answer questions;
- otherwise to provide such information as he may require for the purposes of the investigation;
- to produce specified documents or documents of a specified description which appear to the investigator to relate to any matter relevant to the investigation; and/or
- otherwise to give the investigator all assistance in connection with the investigation which the person is reasonably able to give.

10.44 As already indicated, there is no statutory requirement for the appointment of an investigator under the FSMA 2000, s 168(2) to be notified to the person under investigation. The rationale is that in many instances the FSA will at the outset be investigating not a particular person, but rather a situation, such as a suspicious movement in the price of particular securities. The FSA has, however, given guidance[1] indicating that it will consider notifying the persons under investigation when it becomes clear who those persons are and will normally notify them when it proceeds to exercise its statutory powers to require information from them. It will also give an indication of the nature and subject matter of its investigation to those who are required to provide information to assist with the investigation.

---

[1] The FSA's policy on notification to the person under investigation can be found in the *FSA Handbook* at ENF 2.12.

FSMA 2000, s 169: assistance to overseas regulators

10.45 The FSA may appoint an investigator to investigate any matter (or may exercise its power under the FSMA 2000, s 165[1]) at the request of an overseas regulator, under FSMA 2000, s 169. In some instances, the FSA will be required to investigate in response to the request because of its obligations under EC law, particularly the Single Market Directives[2]. In other cases, where the exercise of its power is not necessary in order to comply with such an obligation, the FSA has a discretion whether or not to investigate in response to the request and the FSMA 2000 prescribes various factors which it may take into account[3].

---

[1] See para 10.25.
[2] The Banking Consolidation Directive (2000/12/EC), the Insurance Directives (79/267/EEC, 90/619/EEC, 92/96/EEC (life) and 73/240/EEC, 88/357/EEC and 92/49/EEC (non-life)) and the Investment Services Directive (93/22/EEC).
[3] See the FSMA 2000, s 169(4).

10.46   The power to appoint an investigator in response to a request from an overseas regulator is thus different from the other investigation powers, in that there is no particular test for the appointment of the investigator, such as a suspected breach of a particular rule. The FSA simply has to receive a request from an overseas regulator and then has a discretion whether or not to investigate in response to that request (or, where its EC obligations so dictate, no discretion).

10.47   An investigator appointed under this provision has, under the FSMA 2000, s 169(2), the same powers as one appointed under the FSMA 2000, s 168(1)[1]. In addition, the FSA has the power to direct that the overseas regulator be permitted to attend and take part in any interviews conducted for the purposes of the investigation. In deciding whether or not to make such a direction, the FSA takes into account various factors[2] and it may not give such a direction unless satisfied that any information obtained by the overseas regulator as a result of the interview will be subject to safeguards equivalent to those in the FSMA 2000, Pt XXIII (the provisions prohibiting the disclosure of confidential information, subject to the so-called gateways). The FSMA 2000 requires the FSA to publish its policy on the conduct of such interviews and this can be found in the Enforcement Manual, Chapter 2, Annex 2G.

---

[1]   See para 10.41.
[2]   These can be found in the *FSA Handbook* at ENF 2.11.8G.

FSMA 2000, s 284: collective investment schemes

10.48   Unit trusts and other collective investment schemes raise particularly strong consumer protection issues and the FSMA 2000 contains separate provision for investigations into them. In particular, the FSA or the Secretary of State may, under the FSMA 2000, s 284, appoint an investigator to investigate, broadly, the affairs of a unit trust, a recognised collective investment scheme[1] (so far as relating to activities carried on in the UK), or any other collective investment scheme except an open-ended investment company (OEIC), or the affairs of the manager, trustee, operator or depositary, as appropriate, of such a scheme. The FSA may commence such an investigation if it appears to it that it is in the interests of the participants or potential participants to investigate or that the matter is of public concern. This is therefore a broad power, the use of which is largely within the FSA's judgment. There is no requirement to notify the person under investigation that such an investigation has been commenced.

---

[1]   A recognised collective investment scheme means a UCITS scheme recognised under the FSMA 2000, s 264, a scheme constituted in designated territories recognised under the FSMA 2000, s 270 and an individually recognised overseas scheme recognised under the FSMA 2000, s 272.

10.49   The person appointed has extensive powers of investigation, comparable to those applicable to investigations under the FSMA 2000, s 168(2). The investigator may require any person whom he considers is or may be able to give information which is relevant to the investigation, to produce to him any documents in that person's possession or control which appear to the investigator to be relevant to the investigation, to attend before him, and otherwise to give him all assistance in connection with the investigation which that person is reasonably able to give. The investigator may also, if he thinks it necessary for the purposes of the investigation, investigate the affairs of other connected schemes or those involved in the management of such schemes.

10.50 The FSA has a very similar power in relation to OEICs, under the Open-Ended Investment Companies Regulations 2001, SI 2001/1228, reg 30.

10.51 Since those who are involved in the management of collective investment schemes or OEICs will usually be authorised persons, these powers overlap significantly with the FSA's more general investigation powers discussed above[1]. Indeed, suspected breaches of the FSA rules that apply to collective investment schemes could be investigated under the FSMA 2000, s 168(4). Therefore, when considering investigating a matter that relates to a collective investment scheme, the FSA may be able to choose which statutory investigation provision to use. The specific provisions relating to investigations into collective investment schemes are, generally speaking, wider than the general investigation provisions and enable a broader range of information to be obtained.

---

[1] See paras 10.23–10.44.

FSMA 2000, s 97: investigations by the UK Listing Authority

10.52 In its capacity as UK Listing Authority under the FSMA 2000, Pt VI, the FSA may appoint investigators under the FSMA 2000, s 97 to conduct an investigation on its behalf if it appears to it that there are circumstances suggesting, broadly, that there may have been a breach of the listing rules or that one of the criminal offences under Pt VI (failure to register listing particulars under the FSMA 2000, s 83; offering securities to the public in the UK before the prospectus has been published under the FSMA 2000, s 85; or issuing advertisements or other information without FSA authorisation or approval under the FSMA 2000, s 98) may have been committed.

10.53 An investigator appointed under this provision has the same powers as one appointed under the FSMA 2000, s 167, as outlined above[1].

---

[1] See para 10.38.

Compliance with requirements imposed by investigators

10.54 As the discussion above generally highlights, the statutory investigation powers are very broad, they cover most of the different types of information that might exist and there are few apparent limits on the information that a person could be asked to provide. There are, though, certain limits to the investigator's powers, both under the FSMA 2000 and as a matter of general law. These are briefly outlined, followed by a discussion of how a person might make good an objection to complying with a requirement to provide information and the consequences of not providing information in response to requirements to do so.

Limitations on the material that can be obtained

10.55   The FSMA 2000 contains two main limitations on the material that people can be asked to provide. Most importantly, a person cannot be required under the FSMA 2000 to produce, disclose or permit the inspection of an item defined as a 'protected item' under the FSMA 2000, s 413. A protected item is, broadly, one that is protected by legal professional privilege (including both 'legal advice privilege' and 'litigation privilege'). However, the FSMA 2000 does not adopt the common law definition of legal privilege, but instead uses its own definition. That definition is static, whereas the classes of legal privilege protected by common law may evolve and, whilst the definition is unclear in some respects, it is not necessarily wholly consistent with the common law. Notably, there is no statutory protection for without prejudice communications (which the law treats in a similar way to privileged material).

10.56   A secondary limitation is the rather limited protection for banking confidentiality, contained in the FSMA 2000, s 175(5). However, this does not apply where the person by whom or to whom the obligation of confidentiality is owed is the person under investigation (or a member of the same group), where the person to whom the duty is owed consents, or where the imposition of the requirement to produce the information or document has been specifically authorised by the FSA. The breadth of these exceptions means that in practice this is unlikely to be of material assistance to firms or a material obstacle to the FSA.

10.57   There is no right to refuse to provide a document or information or to answer a question on the ground of any privilege against self-incrimination. The statutory protection for self-incrimination[1] is limited to the use which can be made of statements made under compulsion. In particular, it prevents such statements from being used in criminal proceedings (or proceedings for market abuse) against the maker of the statement, with certain exceptions. It does not prevent the FSA from using the statement to obtain further evidence which would be admissible and does not affect the admissibility of any other material, for example documents.

---

[1]   FSMA 2000, s 174.

10.58   Beyond the statutory limitations, the public law duties of the FSA and/or the investigator impose a number of additional limitations. Very broadly, investigators are required to act fairly (see *Re Pergamon Press Ltd*[1]), although all the requirements of natural justice do not apply (see *Herring v Templeman*[2] and *Moran v Lloyd's*[3]), they must not act irrationally (in the *Wednesbury* sense[4]) and, in accordance with the FSA's stated policy outlined above at para 10.17, they should act proportionately and consistently. In addition, they must consider the right to respect for privacy under the European Convention on Human Rights (ECHR), art 8, certainly when exercising their powers in respect of individuals and probably also firms[5]. This can be overridden but only for certain specific reasons and, very broadly, the investigator must consider among other things the extent of the intrusion that is merited in the particular case.

---

[1]   [1971] Ch 388.
[2]   [1973] 3 All ER 569.
[3]   [1981] 1 Lloyd's Rep 423.
[4]   *Associated Provincial Picture Houses Ltd v Wednesbury Corpn* [1948] 1 KB 223.
[5]   It is currently unclear whether corporate bodies have rights under the ECHR, art 8.

Objecting to providing information

10.59   If the person asked to provide information feels there is a genuine reason for not complying, then there are several courses of action available. That person does not, though, have any right to refer to the Financial Services and Markets Tribunal the FSA's decision to initiate a particular investigation or the investigator's decision to impose a particular requirement. The first potential course of action would be simply not to comply, to wait for the investigator to take action to enforce his request and then to plead the reason in his defence, primarily (as discussed in para 10.60 below) as a 'reasonable excuse' why the court should not treat him as being in contempt. This, however, carries the risk that the court may disagree and therefore treat the person as in contempt. Second, the person asked to provide the information could bring a judicial review or other legal proceedings to impugn the decision to impose the requirements, or in some cases bring a civil claim for the same purpose. Third, the person asked to provide the information may be able to complain about the FSA's conduct to the independent complaints commissioner under the statutory complaints scheme (although this is unlikely to provide an adequate remedy, particularly on a real-time basis)[1].

---

[1]   For details, see the *FSA Handbook* at COAF.

The consequences of non-compliance

10.60   If a person does not, for some reason, comply with a requirement to provide information imposed under one of the statutory investigation powers, there are a number of possible consequences. The primary consequence[1] is that the investigator may certify to a court that the person has not complied, in which case the court, if satisfied that the person failed without reasonable excuse to comply, may deal with that person as though they were in contempt of court. The person could, therefore, be fined or in some cases even imprisoned or have their assets sequestrated. The need for the court to consider whether the person failed 'without reasonable excuse' potentially gives the person concerned an opportunity to object to the requirement. The FSA may also be able to obtain a warrant, under the FSMA 2000, s 176, authorising the police to search relevant premises and seize any relevant material.

---
[1]   Under the FSMA 2000, s 177(1) and (2).

10.61   If the person concerned is an authorised firm, or an approved person, then the failure to comply may also carry regulatory consequences. In particular, it could lead to enforcement action in the same way as any other breach of requirements imposed under the FSMA 2000. It may also demonstrate that an approved person is not a fit and proper person to be carrying on a particular controlled function and therefore lead to the withdrawal of that person's approval. This, and the other regulatory enforcement action that may be available, is considered below[1].

---
[1]   See para 10.63.

10.62   In addition, the person may commit a criminal offence if that person knowingly or recklessly provides false or misleading information in purported compliance with the requirement[1]. There is also a criminal offence under the FSMA 2000, s 177(3) of falsifying, concealing, destroying or otherwise disposing of documents which a person knows or suspects may be relevant to an investigation which is being or is likely to be conducted, or causing or permitting this to happen (unless the person shows he had no intention of concealing the facts disclosed by the documents from the investigator).

---
[1]   FSMA 2000, s 177(4).

FSA ENFORCEMENT ACTION

10.63   The FSA has, under the FSMA 2000, a range of enforcement powers, each aimed at addressing different aspects of regulatory issues. Thus, whilst some of the FSA's enforcement powers are disciplinary, others are aimed at for example preventing further harm or compensating those who have suffered losses from the firm's actions. Generally speaking, the FSA can exercise these powers individually or in combination. Action can be taken against firms, against employees of firms (primarily but not exclusively approved persons[1]), and in some circumstances against third parties. Armed with the results of its investigation, therefore, the FSA needs to consider what enforcement action it is appropriate to take in the light of what it seeks to achieve in the circumstances of the particular case. Thus, from the perspective of the regulated community, it is important to have in mind the range of possible action and not to focus purely on the potential disciplinary consequences of the matter.

---
[1]   As will be seen, a prohibition order can be made against any person, whether or not an approved person, and the FSA could potentially apply for an injunction or restitution order against any person who was knowingly concerned in a regulatory contravention by the firm.

10.64   In this section, the main enforcement measures are reviewed (the FSMA 2000 provides for a number of other measures applicable in specific areas which are not reviewed here), followed by an outline of the procedures involved where the FSA proposes to take such measures.

Enforcement measures under the FSMA 2000

Disciplinary action against firms

10.65 Under the FSMA 2000, Pt XIV, the FSA may, if it considers that an authorised person has contravened a requirement imposed on him by or under the FSMA 2000, impose on that person a fine and/or a public censure. The ability to fine firms for rule breaches will be familiar to those firms formally regulated by one of the self regulatory organisations, for whom disciplinary fines were in practice the main enforcement mechanism.

10.66 The phrase 'contravene a requirement imposed by or under' the FSMA 2000 requires further explanation, as it reoccurs throughout the enforcement regime. It is a wide concept, encompassing requirements imposed directly by the FSMA 2000 (such as the requirement on firms under the FSMA 2000, s 59 to take reasonable care to ensure that no person performs a controlled function unless they are approved by the FSA and, probably, requirements under the FSMA 2000 the breach of which also constitutes a criminal offence), as well as requirements imposed indirectly under the FSMA 2000 (for example under the FSA's rules made under powers granted to it under the FSMA 2000, or requirements to provide information imposed by an investigator appointed to conduct a formal investigation), or by the FSA using its powers under the FSMA 2000 to impose certain requirements (for example requirements imposed on a firm's permission under the FSMA 2000, s 43).

10.67 The FSA is required under the FSMA 2000, s 210 to issue a statement of its policy with respect to the amount and imposition of penalties and, in exercising or deciding whether to exercise its powers in any case, to have regard to the policy in force at the time when the relevant contravention occurred. The FSA's policy, which can be found in the Enforcement Manual at Chapters 11–13, outlines various factors which the FSA may take into account in deciding whether to impose a fine and, if so, in deciding the amount of the fine. There is no tariff of fines for particular types of breaches (with the exception of the late submission of reports). In deciding on the amount of the fine, the FSA considers all the relevant circumstances of the case. The main factors are: the seriousness of the contravention; the extent to which it was deliberate or reckless; in some circumstances the size and resources of the firm concerned; the amount of any profits accrued or loss avoided from the conduct; the firm's conduct following the contravention; its disciplinary record and compliance history; previous action taken by the FSA in relation to similar behaviour; and whether any action has been taken by any other regulatory authorities. These factors are not, though, exhaustive.

10.68 One of the exceptions to the general rule that enforcement powers can be used in combination is that the FSA cannot both fine a firm and withdraw its authorisation (FSMA 2000, s 206(2)). In practice, the FSA may be able to vary a firm's permission to prevent it from carrying on any regulated activities, but without going as far as to cancel its permission and withdraw its authorisation. This has substantially the same effect, except that the firm remains authorised and can, among other things, be fined.

10.69   Where the FSA imposes a fine, it will normally publicise the action it has taken, as with any other successful enforcement action. Fines and public censures are not therefore truly alternatives.

Disciplinary action against approved persons

10.70   One question which was the subject of much debate is whether and when the FSA would take enforcement action directly against those individuals working for firms who were involved in rule breaches by the firm. The FSMA 2000 brings within the regulatory system those individuals who carry out controlled functions for the firm, and one result of this is that such persons are amenable to the FSA's enforcement jurisdiction.

10.71   Disciplinary action can be taken against approved persons under the FSMA 2000, s 66 provided that two conditions are fulfilled. First, it must appear to the FSA that the person concerned is guilty of misconduct, which means that the person, while an approved person, failed to comply with one of the Statements of Principle for Approved Persons (made under the FSMA 2000, s 64), or was knowingly concerned in a contravention by the relevant authorised person of a requirement imposed on that authorised person by or under the FSMA 2000. The approved person must therefore either have breached the regulatory general principles applicable to approved persons or have been involved in some way in the firm's breach. The concept of 'knowingly concerned' was previously used in the Financial Services Act 1986, ss 6 and 61 (provisions relating to injunctions and restitution orders) and is also common in the criminal law. In brief summary, it requires actual knowledge of the facts and some degree of active involvement (see *SIB v Scandex Capital Management A/S*[1], *SIB v Pantell (No 2)*[2], and *R v Shivpuri*[3]). This provision also allows a former approved person to be disciplined, in relation to his conduct while he was an approved person.

---

[1]   [1998] 1 All ER 514.
[2]   [1992] 1 All ER 134.
[3]   [1986] AC 1.

10.72   The second condition is that the FSA must be satisfied that it is appropriate in all the circumstances to take action against the approved person. This will be the key question in many cases. The FSA has indicated that primary responsibility for regulatory compliance rests with the firm itself and the FSA's main focus, in considering disciplinary action, will therefore normally be on the firm[1]. Broadly, whether it will take action against the individual depends upon whether that person is personally culpable for the breach, which it interprets as meaning whether that person acted deliberately or whether their standard of behaviour fell below that reasonably to be expected from that person in all the circumstances[2].

---

[1]   See *FSA Handbook* at ENF 11.5.1G.
[2]   See *FSA Handbook* at ENF 11.5.3G. For a further discussion of the FSA's policy, see the Enforcement Manual, Chapter 11.5.

10.73 Where it is appropriate to take disciplinary action for misconduct, the FSA may either impose a financial penalty or publish a statement of the person's misconduct. In practice, successful enforcement action is normally publicised; hence, as with firms, the two are not truly alternatives. The FSA is required under FSMA 2000, s 69 to issue a statement of its policy with respect to the amount and imposition of fines for misconduct and in exercising, or deciding whether to exercise, its powers in any case to have regard to the policy in force at the time the misconduct in question occurred. The FSA's policy, which can be found in the Enforcement Manual at Chapters 11–13, outlines various factors that the FSA may take into account in deciding whether to impose a fine and, if so, the amount of the fine. The amount of the fine is summarized above[1] in the context of disciplinary action against firms.

---

[1]   See para 10.67.

10.74 There is a two year limitation period for taking action for misconduct. The warning notice (which initiates the regulatory proceedings: see para 10.128 below) must be given to the person concerned before the end of the two year period beginning with the first day on which the FSA knew of the misconduct (which includes having information from which it could reasonably be inferred).

Variation of permission

10.75 'Variation of the firm's permission on the FSA's own initiative' is the new, somewhat long-winded terminology for most of the powers formerly referred to as 'intervention'. Although in the past the self regulatory organisations had extensive powers to intervene in the business of firms regulated by them, in practice those powers were very largely used as a blunt instrument to require firms to cease carrying on investment business. The FSA's powers under the FSMA 2000 are capable of being used in a more sophisticated way.

10.76 The new terminology arises from the means by which intervention is now imposed. Since firms now have a single, unitary permission under the FSMA 2000, Pt IV, tailored to their specific circumstances, intervention action is taken by means of the FSA varying that permission to impose limitations, restrictions or requirements on it, thereby directly affecting the business that the firm is permitted to do. Hence, the firm's permission is varied, not on an application by the firm but on the FSA's own initiative, under the FSMA 2000, s 45.

10.77 The power to vary a firm's permission can be exercised as a matter of urgency. This is therefore the power likely to be used where there is a need for immediate action by the FSA in order to protect consumers or if the firm is not complying with the fundamental regulatory requirements found in the threshold conditions. For that reason, as outlined below[1], the procedure for exercising this power is different from that applicable to many of the other enforcement powers. Among other things, where urgent action is taken, the firm concerned may have the right to be involved in the process only after action has been taken.

<hr>

[1]   See para 10.134.

<hr>

10.78   Where the FSA varies a firm's permission, this can include:

- adding or removing a regulated activity from the firm's permission, or varying the description of a regulated activity;
- incorporating limitations in the description of a regulated activity (for example as to the circumstances in which the regulated activity may or may not be carried on); and/or
- imposing such requirements as the FSA considers appropriate (for example, requiring the firm to take or refrain from taking specified action, and even extending to the firm's non-regulated activities).

Variation of permission is thus a flexible tool. Particularly, there are no limitations on the types of requirements that can be imposed on firms. They may, for example, place restrictions on the use of the firm's assets or require assets to be transferred to a trustee[1].

<hr>

[1]   Where requirements are imposed placing restrictions on the disposal of assets or requiring assets to be transferred to a trustee, the FSMA 2000 contains ancillary provisions, found in the FSMA 2000, s 48, among other things dealing with, respectively, the position of third party institutions notified of the requirement not to dispose of assets, and the position of the trustee.

<hr>

10.79   There are three main bases for varying permission, under the FSMA 2000, s 45, namely that it appears to the FSA that the firm is failing or likely to fail to satisfy the threshold conditions[1], that it has failed to carry on a regulated activity for which it has permission for a period of at least 12 months (in line with the general policy of preventing firms from holding on a precautionary basis permission to carry on activities which they do not in fact carry on), or that it is desirable to vary the firm's permission in order to protect the interests of consumers or potential consumers. There is a similar power to vary a firm's permission in support of an overseas regulator, under the FSMA 2000, s 47. The grounds for the exercise of the power are thus widely drawn. The FSA has provided guidance on the circumstances when in practice it will seek to vary a firm's permission and this can be found in the Enforcement Manual at Chapter 3.5.

<hr>

[1]   The threshold conditions (found in the FSMA 2000, Sch 6) are the fundamental requirements underlying the firm's permission and its authorisation under the FSMA 2000.

<hr>

10.80   A similar power exists in relation to overseas firms authorised under the FSMA 2000, Schs 3 or 4, which do not have a Pt IV permission. This is found in FSMA 2000, Pt XIII and the terminology of 'intervention' is still used in that context. (To the extent that an overseas firm does have a Pt IV permission, for example a top-up permission, that permission can be varied in the normal way.) The power in relation to overseas firms that do not have a Pt IV permission is similar to the power to vary permission but limited to imposing requirements. In practice, this still gives the FSA a great deal of flexibility. There is one significant difference in the statutory grounds for the exercise of the power, arising principally from the fact that compliance with the threshold conditions is, from the FSA's perspective, irrelevant in relation to overseas firms that do not have a Pt IV permission. Hence, the first ground for the use of the power is that the firm has contravened, or is likely to contravene, a requirement imposed by or under the FSMA 2000 (in a case where the FSA is responsible for enforcing compliance in the UK), rather than that it is failing to satisfy a threshold condition.

Cancellation of permission

10.81 The most serious exercise of the own initiative power to vary a firm's permission under the FSMA 2000, s 45, is the power to cancel that permission. In practice, this is reserved for the most serious cases, where the concerns which the FSA seeks to address by varying the firm's permission are so serious or extensive that the most appropriate course is for it to cancel the permission altogether. The FSA's policy on the use of this power can be found in the Enforcement Manual, Chapter 5.5.

10.82 The cancellation of a firm's permission cannot be achieved as a matter of urgency, although in practice the same effect can be accomplished by varying the firm's permission to prevent it from carrying on any of its regulated activities, and this can be done as a matter of urgency[1].

---

[1]   See the discussion in the *FSA Handbook* at ENF 5.5.5G.

10.83 If the FSA does cancel the firm's permission, and as a result there is no regulated activity for which it has permission, the withdrawal of the firm's authorisation will follow under the FSMA 2000, s 33. Once its authorisation has been withdrawn, the firm is outside the regulatory arena for most purposes (although some of the statutory powers can still be exercised against it, for example as a former authorised person). Because of this, the FSA recognises that there may be benefit in varying a firm's permission to prevent it from carrying on any further activity but not actually cancelling that permission and it has indicated that it may, in practice, act in this way in appropriate circumstances[1]. As already noted[2], the FSMA 2000 cannot both fine a firm and withdraw its authorisation (FSMA 2000, s 206).

---

[1]   See the *FSA Handbook* at ENF 5.5.6G.
[2]   See para 10.68.

Withdrawal of approval

10.84 The equivalent for approved persons of cancelling a firm's permission is to withdraw the approved person's approval under the FSMA 2000, s 63. The basis upon which the FSA may do so is simply that the person is not a fit and proper person to perform the function to which the approval relates (this is the corollary of the criterion for the grant of approval under the FSMA 2000, s 61).

10.85 The withdrawal of approval is a blunt instrument. The FSA does not have any ability to vary the terms of a person's approval; it can only grant or withdraw it. The effect of withdrawing approval is to prevent the person from performing the particular controlled function for which he was approved, but it does not prevent that person from carrying on other controlled functions for the firm, the approval for which was not withdrawn, or other functions for which no approval is required.

10.86 The FSA's policy on when in practice it will consider withdrawing a person's approval can be found in the Enforcement Manual at Chapter 7.5.

Prohibition orders

10.87 The power to make prohibition orders against individuals is more far reaching than the power to withdraw the approval of an approved person. Withdrawal of approval is effective only in relation to those individuals who carry out functions that are required to have FSA approval and, in any event, does not prevent the relevant person from undertaking other functions for the firm for which no approval is required. Further, the consequences, for both the firm and the individual, of the person carrying out a function for which approval is required following the withdrawal of that approval, are solely in the regulatory arena. Prohibition orders do not suffer from the same limitations and, moreover, can be used in a rather more flexible way.

10.88 Under the FSMA 2000, s 56, the FSA may make a prohibition order against an individual if it appears to it that he is not a fit and proper person to perform functions in relation to a regulated activity carried on by an authorised person. Fitness and propriety is, thus, the key concept.

10.89 A prohibition order means an order prohibiting an individual from performing a specified function, any function falling within a specified description, or any function. The order may (it is not clear whether 'may' in this context is permissive or exclusive) relate to a specified regulated activity, any regulated activity falling within a specified description, or all regulated activities, and authorised persons generally or any person within a specified class of authorised person.

10.90 A prohibition order can therefore be made against any individual involved with a regulated firm, whether or not an approved person. The extent of the prohibition can be tailored to the particular circumstances: it can range from a prohibition from performing a particular function relating to one regulated firm to a general prohibition against performing any regulated function (or, possibly, any function) for any authorised person. The FSA's policy on the use of prohibition orders can be found in the Enforcement Manual at Chapter 8.

10.91   The enforcement of prohibition orders is treated as a serious matter under the FSMA 2000. It is a criminal offence, under the FSMA 2000, s 56(4), for a person to perform or agree to perform a function in breach of a prohibition order, unless that person shows that he took all reasonable precautions and exercised all due diligence to avoid committing the offence. The breach could also result in regulatory enforcement action against the firm concerned and/or, depending upon the scope of the prohibition order, against the individual.

Restitution orders

10.92   The FSMA 2000 provides a mechanism for the payment of restitution to the victims of regulatory breaches, through the imposition of restitution orders. Similar powers were contained in the Financial Services Act 1986, and these powers are also comparable to the former powers of the self-regulatory organisations to make compensation orders. In practice, very significant sums have in the past been paid by way of compensation.

10.93   The FSA may impose a restitution order, under the FSMA 2000, s 384, but only on an authorised person[1]. Alternatively, the court has the power to impose a restitution order against any person (whether or not authorised or approved) under the FSMA 2000, s 382, on the application of the FSA.

---

[1]   But note that the FSA may make a restitution order against any person in a market abuse case, as discussed further at para 10.117 below.

10.94   A restitution order may be imposed upon a person who has contravened, or been knowingly concerned in the contravention of, a requirement by or under the FSMA 2000, or a requirement imposed by or under any other Act the contravention of which is a criminal offence which the FSA has the power to prosecute under the FSMA 2000 (principally, this latter ground refers to insider dealing under the Criminal Justice Act 1993, Pt V, and breaches of the Money Laundering Regulations 1993[1]). Profits must have accrued to the person as a result of the contravention, or one or more persons must have suffered loss or been otherwise adversely affected.

---

[1]   SI 1993/1933.

10.95   The restitution order is an order requiring a person to pay such amount as appears to be just having regard to, as appropriate, the profits or losses or other adverse effects. The body that imposes the restitution order (in other words, either the FSA or the court, depending upon the power used) determines how the money is to be distributed. Assessing the amount that should be paid, and how it should be distributed, can cause serious difficulties in practice, particularly where very large numbers of consumers are involved or where the nature of the problem makes it difficult to assess what losses have been suffered. Determining how profits should be distributed may also cause practical difficulties.

10.96   It will not always be an effective use of the FSA's resources to be seeking a restitution order on behalf of investors who have suffered losses. Some investors, particularly large corporates or market counterparties, have the sophistication and resources to seek compensation in the normal way through the civil courts. In other cases where there are small numbers of consumers involved, the Ombudsman scheme may represent an appropriate means of obtaining redress. The FSA therefore needs to consider in each case whether the use of its power to make or apply for a restitution order is an appropriate regulatory response and whether the costs would be justified by the likely benefits, particularly since it may, if it does do so, become embroiled in a contested process. Factors that may be relevant to this decision include the sophistication, resources and numbers of investors involved, the extent of the losses suffered and the availability of other means for obtaining redress. The FSA's policy on making restitution orders can be found at the Enforcement Manual, Chapter 9.6. In practice, firms may seek to agree a restitution order with the FSA, to try to pre-empt the bringing of civil claims or claims through the Ombudsman scheme. Whether a firm has sought to compensate investors may also be a relevant factor when the FSA decides whether any other enforcement action should be taken against it in respect of the matter.

Civil injunctions

10.97   Civil injunctions were formerly available in support of regulatory enforcement under the Financial Services Act 1986 and the Banking Act 1987 and were used primarily in relation to perimeter enforcement. The FSMA 2000 contains similar provisions, albeit slightly more extensive, allowing courts to make civil injunctions in support of the FSA's enforcement function. Injunctions are also available in cases of market abuse, as discussed below[1].

---

[1]   See para 10.117.

10.98   Under the FSMA 2000, s 380, a court may grant three types of injunction, in each case on an application by the FSA[1]:

- restraining breaches, or further breaches, of regulatory contraventions, where the court is satisfied that there is a reasonable likelihood that a person will contravene a requirement imposed by or under the FSMA 2000 or one imposed by or under any other Act, the contravention of which is a criminal offence which the FSA has the power to prosecute under the FSMA 2000, or that a person has contravened such a requirement and there is a reasonable likelihood that the contravention will continue or be repeated;
- to require a person to take steps to remedy or mitigate the effect of a contravention, where it is satisfied that he has contravened such a requirement and that there are steps which could be taken for remedying it or mitigating its effect; or
- to restrain a person who it is satisfied has contravened or been knowingly concerned in the contravention of such a requirement, from

disposing of or otherwise dealing with any assets belonging to that person which it is satisfied that person is reasonably likely to dispose of or deal with.

Such injunctions can also be granted on application by the Secretary of State, but only in relation to the contravention of requirements imposed by or under the FSMA 2000 the breach of which constitutes a criminal offence.

---

[1] FSMA 2000, s 381 contains similar provisions in relation to market abuse cases, as discussed further at para 10.117 below.

10.99 The first type of injunction, restraining breaches, should not in the normal course be required to be obtained against authorised firms, since they ought to comply without the need for an injunction and, if they do not, they could be restrained by the FSA varying their permission (which it can do as a matter of urgency). It is most likely to be seen in perimeter enforcement, in the same way as, formerly, injunctions under the Banking Act 1987 or the Financial Services Act 1986.

10.100 The second type of injunction, requiring a person to take steps to remedy a contravention, clearly overlaps with restitution orders. It can be used in perimeter enforcement cases, but could also be used to require a firm that has committed a breach to take a step not involving the payment of money, for example to transfer assets or unwind a position in the market. In some circumstances, it may otherwise be difficult for the firm to take the step because of its contractual obligations to other parties.

10.101 The third type of injunction, preventing the disposal of or dealing with assets, is effectively a freezing order. It overlaps significantly with the court's inherent jurisdiction to make such orders. Such an order will normally be granted only in support of some other proceedings which may lead to an order being made against the firm (for example, a restitution order, or a judgment against the firm in civil proceedings), the purpose being to ensure that the firm's assets are not in the meantime dissipated so as to defeat the enforcement of that order.

10.102 In practice, injunctions are often granted on an interim basis in the first instance, in theory to preserve the position until the matter can be determined at a full trial. In deciding whether or not to grant an interim injunction, the court is involved in a balancing exercise, taking into account, very broadly, the prospects of a final injunction being granted when the matter comes to be determined at a full trial and the consequences of granting or refusing interim relief. In practice, the interim injunction usually accomplishes the objective and the question whether an injunction should finally be granted does not fall to be determined.

10.103 The grant of an injunction, whether on an interim basis or on a final basis, is within the discretion of the court. It may not, therefore, be sufficient for the FSA to show simply that the statutory grounds for granting an injunction are satisfied.

Claims for breach of statutory duty

10.104   The FSMA 2000 contains various provisions, similar to that previously contained in the Financial Services Act 1986, s 62, making firms potentially liable to civil claims for breach of statutory duty as a result of regulatory contraventions. The main provision is the FSMA 2000, s 150, which provides that a contravention by an authorised person of a rule (but not the listing rules, the financial resources rules, or any other rule which so specifies[1]) is actionable at the suit of a private person who suffers loss as a result of the contravention, subject to the defences and other incidents applying to actions for breach of statutory duty.

---

[1]   Most significantly, this includes the Principles for Businesses.

10.105   'Private person' is defined in the Financial Services and Markets Act 2000 (Rights of Action) Regulations 2001, SI 2001/2256, to mean individuals not acting in the course of carrying on regulated activities and others not acting in the course of carrying on a business and to exclude governmental organisations. Non-private persons may in certain, very limited, circumstances also bring claims under the FSMA 2000, s 150.

10.106   The provision that any claim is subject to defences and other incidents applying to actions for breach of statutory duty applies the normal common law rules applicable to breach of statutory duty claims. Thus, for example, the person making the claim must show that they have suffered loss, that the loss was caused in legal terms by the breach, is not too remote and is of a type that a court will compensate with an award of damages, and, moreover, various defences may be available to the firm.

10.107   The same provision is applied to certain specific contraventions relating to collective investment schemes[1]. Similar rights of action arise elsewhere in the FSMA 2000, most notably where a firm fails to take reasonable care to ensure that no person performs a controlled function who is not approved for that function or that a prohibited person does not carry out a function from which they are prohibited[2], where a firm carries on a regulated activity otherwise than in accordance with its permission[3], where a passported firm breaches a requirement imposed upon it by the FSA[4], and for contravention of the listing rules requiring a prospectus to be published before securities are offered to the public[5].

---

[1]   See the FSMA 2000, ss 241 and 257 and the Open-Ended Investment Companies Regulations 2001, SI 2001/1228, reg 25(6).
[2]   FSMA 2000, s 71.
[3]   FSMA 2000, s 20(3) and see the Financial Services and Markets Act 2000 (Rights of Action) Regulations 2001, SI 2001/2256.
[4]   FSMA 2000, s 202(2) and see the Financial Services and Markets Act 2000 (Rights of Action) Regulations 2001, SI 2001/2256.
[5]   FSMA 2000, s 85(5).

Market abuse

10.108

> 'We are determined to ensure that the financial markets are open and clean places to do business. London's reputation depends on that.'[1]

The FSMA 2000, s 118 contains a new 'civil offence' of market abuse, complementing the existing criminal regimes for insider dealing under the Criminal Justice Act 1993, Pt V, and misleading statements and practices under the FSMA 2000, s 397 (formerly under the Financial Services Act 1986, s 47). The market abuse provisions allow the FSA to deal with a wider scope of market misconduct than falls within the criminal offences, as well as conduct which is not suitable to be dealt with under the criminal justice system.

---

[1] Economic Secretary to HM Treasury, in SC A (Financial Services and Markets Bill), 2 November 1999.

10.109   The statutory definition of market abuse has to be read in conjunction with the Code of Market Conduct, which the FSA is required to issue under the FSMA 2000, s 119, to give guidance to those determining whether or not behaviour amounts to market abuse. The Code specifies behaviour that in the FSA's opinion amounts to market abuse, that which in its opinion does not, and the factors which are to be taken into account in determining whether or not behaviour amounts to market abuse. To the extent that it describes behaviour as in the FSA's view not amounting to market abuse, that behaviour is to be taken as not amounting to market abuse (FSMA 2000, s 122). Otherwise, the Code has the status of evidential guidance.

10.110   The enforcement of market misconduct was under the previous regime a paradigm example of the fragmented approach to regulatory enforcement, with different regulatory authorities (including the self-regulatory organisations, the exchanges, the Takeover Panel and the Department of Trade and Industry) having responsibility for different aspects and often none having the ability to address all of the consequences of the particular misconduct. The system under the FSMA 2000 should mark a significant change. The FSA has the primary role. It is able to investigate the misconduct and to take a range of action aimed at addressing the different implications of the matter. The recognised investment exchanges, the Takeover Panel and/or overseas regulators may, however, still be involved, and to that extent some overlap remains.

10.111   Market abuse can be enforced on a number of different levels. First, the FSA may impose a civil penalty for market abuse or make a public statement that a person has engaged in market abuse, under the FSMA 2000, s 123. Penalties and public statements can be imposed against any person, whether or not within the regulated community, and they can also be imposed against a person who encourages or requires another person to commit market abuse (in a situation where that person would have committed market abuse if they had done the behaviour themselves). The FSA is required, under the FSMA 2000, s 124, to prepare and issue a statement of its policy with respect to the imposition and amount of penalties for market abuse and in exercising, or deciding to exercise, its power under s 123 in any case is required to have regard to the policy in force at the time when the behaviour concerned occurred. The FSA's policy can be found in the Enforcement Manual at Chapter 14. The FSA will not generally speaking both prosecute one of the criminal offences outlined below[1] and impose a civil fine against the same person for market abuse[2].

---

[1]   See para 10.114.
[2]   See *FSA Handbook* at ENF 15.7.4G.

10.112   It is a defence to the imposition of a fine[1] that the person believed on reasonable grounds that his behaviour did not amount to market abuse or took all reasonable precautions and exercised all due diligence to avoid behaving in a way which amounted to market abuse. The FSA's policy is required to include an indication of the circumstances when the FSA is to be expected to regard a person as falling within these defences, and this can be found in the Enforcement Manual, Chapter 14.5.

---

[1]   Or a restitution order, but not an injunction: see para 10.117 below.

10.113   Proceedings for a financial penalty for market abuse attract additional safeguards under the FSMA 2000 because the Government recognised the risk that such proceedings might constitute a criminal charge for ECHR purposes. As a result, in accordance with the ECHR, art 6(2), legal assistance is available for Tribunal proceedings in relation to market abuse (FSMA 2000, s 134) and the statutory protection against the use of statements made in compulsory interviews applies in such proceedings (FSMA 2000, s 174).

10.114   The second level of enforcement is criminal prosecution. Market abuse overlaps significantly with the criminal offences of insider dealing (under the Criminal Justice Act 1993, Pt V) and misleading statements and practices (FSMA 2000, s 397). Insofar as conduct constitutes one of the criminal offences, and is appropriate to be dealt with through the criminal justice system, it may result in a criminal prosecution and it may be the FSA that acts as the prosecutor. The FSA's policy on the prosecution of criminal offences and, particularly, these two criminal offences, can be found in the Enforcement Manual at Chapter 15.7.

10.115   The third level of enforcement is regulatory. Market abuse or other misconduct occurring in relation to an authorised firm may be indicative that there are broader matters of regulatory concern relating to the firm. For example, it may indicate defects in the firm's systems and controls or issues about the training and competence of employees. It may also indicate that particular individuals are not fit and proper to be involved in regulated activities for the firm. As a result, the FSA may wish to take other regulatory enforcement action. Depending upon the situation, this might include disciplinary action (although whether the firm or person had been subjected to a penalty for market abuse would clearly be relevant to whether it was appropriate also to discipline it in relation to the same matter), as well as other action such as varying the firm's permission or withdrawing the approval of an approved person.

10.116 Moreover, if an authorised firm or approved person commits market abuse, that may amount to a breach of the regulatory general principles requiring firms and individuals to observe proper standards of market conduct (respectively, Principle 5 of the Principles for Businesses and Statement of Principle 3 for approved persons). The FSA has indicated[1] that where the principal mischief is market abuse, or requiring or encouraging market abuse, the FSA will take action under the market abuse regime rather than for a breach of Principle 5. However, a breach of the Principles may be committed even where the conduct does not technically amount to market abuse. In such cases, the FSA may take action to enforce the Principles, and any specific rules breached.

---

[1] See *FSA Handbook* at ENF 14.8.1G.

10.117 Finally, injunctions and restitution orders may also be available in cases of market abuse. Under the FSMA 2000, s 381, the FSA can seek an injunction to restrain threatened market abuse, require a person to take steps to remedy it, or freeze assets. The provisions are similar to the injunction provisions discussed above[1]. The two defences to a fine for market abuse do not apply in the context of injunctions, so that an injunction can be granted notwithstanding a civil penalty could not be imposed. So far as restitution orders are concerned, the provisions (found in the FSMA 2000, ss 383 and 384) are similar to the restitution order provisions already discussed, with the notable difference that the FSA may itself make a restitution order in relation to market abuse against any person, not just an authorised person.

---

[1] See para 10.98.

Criminal offences

10.118 The FSA also has a role as a criminal prosecutor under the FSMA 2000. In particular, under the FSMA 2000, ss 401 and 402, it has the power to prosecute the various criminal offences constituted under the FSMA as well as the offences of insider dealing under the Criminal Justice Act 1993, Pt V and offences under the Money Laundering Regulations 1993[1]. These powers overlap with those of other criminal prosecutors, such as the Crown Prosecution Service, and the Secretary of State has the same powers.

---

[1] SI 1993/1933.

10.119 A general criminal prosecution function represents a new role for the regulator and it reinforces the FSA's ability to address all of the consequences of a regulatory issue. The FSA has agreed with various other

criminal investigating and prosecuting bodies guidelines to ensure coordination and liaison between them in relation to criminal investigations and
prosecutions, which can be found in the Enforcement Manual, Chapter 2,
Annex 1G. Notably, these do not suggest that there will never be overlapping
investigations. In summary, there is a distinct regulatory criminal arena,
within which it is likely to be the FSA that has the responsibility for
prosecution in particular cases.

Enforcing the City Code

10.120   The City Code may be relevant to the FSA's enforcement role for a
number of reasons. The FSMA 2000, s 143 allows the FSA to endorse the
City Code and the Rules Governing Substantial Acquisitions of Shares, and
the FSA has done so[1]. As a result, at the request of the Takeover Panel, the
FSA can exercise the enforcement powers outlined above in order to enforce
the City Code, including rulings made under it by the Takeover Panel. This
gives statutory support to the Code. In addition, failure by an authorised
firm to comply with the City Code may have wider enforcement consequences for the firm concerned, insofar as it indicates there are other matters
of regulatory concern. Finally, there is a potential overlap between the role
of the Takeover Panel and the FSA's policing of the market abuse regime.
The FSA has provided detailed guidance on how it will act where there is
such an overlap, and this can be found in the Enforcement Manual at
Chapter 14.9.

---

[1]   See *FSA Handbook* at MAR 4.

FSA DECISION MAKING

10.121   One of the major issues of debate during the bill stages of the
FSMA 2000 was the nature of the process which the FSA would undertake
before reaching a decision on enforcement action in each case. Historically, a
significant proportion of enforcement cases have been resolved by agreement
between regulator and regulated and it was largely the aim of all concerned
to ensure that this remained the case. Among other things, this allows for
enforcement action to be taken effectively and efficiently, as well as relieving
the FSA of the uncertainties inherent in any tribunal procedure. Firms also,
on the whole, have tended to welcome the ability to bring enforcement issues
to a close on agreed terms, provided they have a proper opportunity to put
their side of the case. The concern was to ensure that firms would not
emerge from the process feeling that they had been unfairly treated, with the
risk of damaging the FSA's relationships with firms over the longer term and
perhaps encouraging the more frequent use of the tribunal process (which
would make enforcement more costly and less efficient).

10.122   The process devised, which can be found in a combination of the
FSMA 2000 and the *FSA Handbook*, aims to promote fair settlements,
whilst at the same time giving firms the option of undergoing a full tribunal
process[1]. Essentially, the FSMA 2000 requires the FSA to issue various

notices when it proposes, and then decides, to take enforcement action, with the firm having the right to enter into settlement discussions and ultimately the right to refer the matter for a de novo hearing before the Financial Services and Markets Tribunal. Save in relation to certain types of powers which can be exercised urgently, the enforcement action does not take effect until the full process has been undertaken, where the firm requires this to be done. A slightly different procedure is involved in relation to certain types of enforcement action which may in some cases need to be exercised as a matter of urgency.

---

[1] An important consideration is the need for the process to be ECHR compliant. For a recent case on the application of the ECHR in this context (albeit under the former regime) see *R v Securities and Futures Authority Ltd, ex p Fleurose* [2001] EWHC Admin 292, [2001] All ER (D) 189 (Morrison J, first instance) and [2001] EWCA Civ 2015, [2001] All ER (D) 361, CA.

10.123   In some cases, the FSA may decide that although a breach has taken place, it is not appropriate to exercise any of its formal powers. In such cases, it may issue a private warning, informing the person concerned that in the FSA's view a breach was committed (but without any determination of this having been made) and letting them know that they came close to formal action being taken. Such warnings are retained on the compliance history of the relevant person and may be relevant when the FSA comes to decide in future cases whether to take enforcement action. No particular procedure is required in order for the FSA to issue a private warning. A more detailed discussion of private warnings can be found in the Enforcement Manual at Chapter 11.3.

Warning/decision notice procedure

10.124   The main decision-making procedure, known as the warning/ decision notice procedure, applies to those enforcement powers which the FSMA 2000 prescribes involve the FSA issuing a warning notice to the person concerned when it proposes that the action should be taken and a decision notice when it decides to take that action. This applies, for example, to disciplinary measures against firms and individuals, the cancellation of a firm's permission, the withdrawal of an approved person's approval, prohibition orders, and restitution orders made by the FSA. A full list of the enforcement action which involves warning and decision notices can be found in the Decision Making Manual at Chapter 2, Annex 1G.

10.125   Under the FSMA 2000, s 395, the FSA is required to publish its procedures in relation to the giving of warning and decision notices and in each case to follow its stated procedure (although a failure to do so in any particular case does not invalidate the notices given). The procedure must be designed to secure that the decision to issue the warning and/or decision notices is taken by a person not directly involved in establishing the evidence upon which that decision is based. There must, therefore, be a separation of functions within the FSA between the investigator and the decision maker. The FSA has accordingly set up a Regulatory Decisions Committee (RDC) which has the responsibility of taking most decisions to issue such notices.

The RDC is a committee of the FSA Board, accountable to the Board but independent from the FSA's executive. Details are contained in the Decision Making Manual at Chapter 4.2. Among other things, a record of its meetings is kept by its Secretariat.

10.126   The first stage in the decision making process is when the FSA enforcement staff responsible for the investigation consider whether to recommend the issue of a warning notice proposing the enforcement action concerned. Prior to this, the FSA's investigation will have been completed, and in many instances the firm will first have received a preliminary findings letter from the investigator, setting out the factual findings considered relevant to the matters under investigation and inviting the firm to confirm that those facts are complete and accurate before the investigation is concluded[1].

---

[1]   See *FSA Handbook* at ENF 2.5.12G.

10.127   Based on the factual findings of the investigation, the FSA enforcement staff will decide whether to recommend that a warning notice is issued proposing particular enforcement action[1]. Where they recommend action, that recommendation is put before, generally, a panel of the RDC, for a decision on whether to issue the warning notice. In deciding whether or not to issue a warning notice, the RDC applies the FSA's policy on the use of the particular enforcement power concerned.

---

[1]   The procedures for issuing warning notices can be found in the *FSA Handbook* at DEC 2.2 and DEC 4.2.

10.128   If the RDC decides to issue a warning notice, the notice is sent to the person concerned. In general (under the FSMA 2000, s 387), the warning notice will be in writing, state what action the FSA proposes to take, give reasons for that action, explain the firm's rights of access to FSA material and specify the period within which the firm may make any representations (the latter two points are discussed below[1]). In certain circumstances, third parties who are identified in the warning notice and to whom it is in the FSA's opinion prejudicial are entitled to be given a copy of it, under the FSMA 2000, s 393, and have certain rights in respect of it.

---

[1]   See para 10.129.

10.129   The warning notice gives the person concerned three rights:

(1)   a right, under the FSMA 2000, s 394, of access to the material relied upon by the RDC in taking the decision that gave rise to the obligation to issue the warning notice and certain types of secondary material[1];

(2)   a right to make representations to the RDC, within the period specified in the warning notice (at least, and normally, 28 days), with a view to influencing the decision whether to issue a decision notice in due course[2];

(3)   a right to enter into settlement discussions with the FSA staff, overseen by the RDC, and if those settlement discussions lead to deadlock, then in many cases to enter into a formal mediation in order to try to reach a mutually satisfactory settlement[3].

The firm also has the option of not taking any action in response to the warning notice, although it will be rare that it wishes to do so.

---

[1]   This is discussed in more detail in the *FSA Handbook* at DEC 2.4.
[2]   For a more detailed discussion, see the *FSA Handbook* at DEC 4.4.
[3]   The provisions relating to settlement and mediation can be found in the Decision Making Manual, Appendix 1.

10.130   Assuming no agreed resolution can be reached, the RDC considers any representations made by the person and decides whether to take the action proposed in the warning notice. It may alternatively decide to take action within the same part of the FSMA 2000 as that action. Thus, for example, if the warning notice proposed a fine, it could decide in its decision notice to impose a greater or lesser fine or a public censure, but it could not decide to take some other type of action such as varying the firm's permission. If the RDC decides to take the enforcement action proposed in the warning notice (or other action under the same part of the FSMA 2000), then it must issue a decision notice. If it decides not to take the action, then it must issue a notice of discontinuance.

10.131   A decision notice is required, under the FSMA 2000, s 388, to be in writing, to give the FSA's reasons for the decision to take the action, to explain the person's rights of access to the FSA's material and to explain the right to refer the matter to the Financial Services and Markets Tribunal (the 'Tribunal'). It must in certain circumstances also be provided to third parties, under the FSMA 2000, s 393, and the third party concerned then has certain rights.

10.132   The decision notice does not of itself give effect to the enforcement action, but gives the person concerned two further rights. The person has a further right of access to the FSA's material under the FSMA 2000, s 394 and, most significantly, a right to refer the matter to the Tribunal, which it must normally do within 28 days. If the firm refers the matter to the Tribunal, then the decision notice does not take effect until the Tribunal process, and any appeal, has been completed, at which point the FSA issues a further statutory notice, under the FSMA 2000, s 390, called a final notice, on taking action in accordance with the Tribunal's decision. If the person does not exercise the right to refer the matter to the Tribunal, then the FSA may take the action referred to in the decision notice and, when doing so, must issue a final notice.

10.133   There is a prohibition, under the FSMA 2000, s 391, against either the FSA or the person concerned publishing a warning or decision notice or any details concerning one, but the FSA may publish information relating to a final notice and the expectation is that it will do so. Publicity ought not, therefore, generally to arise until the enforcement process is complete, at which stage the FSA's general policy is to publicise successful enforcement action. Publicity is, though, likely to arise if the person concerned decides to refer the matter to the Tribunal, because, as discussed below[1], the Tribunal proceedings are likely to be in public.

---

[1]   See para 10.139.

The supervisory notice procedure

10.134   A slightly different procedure applies to certain types of enforcement action which the FSMA 2000 allows to be imposed as a matter of urgency. Principally, this relates to variations of permission and similar intervention action in relation to overseas firms, but it also includes a number of other, specific powers, normally those which involve the FSA giving directions for particular purposes[1]. Rather than warning and decision notices, this procedure involves the FSA giving notices known as supervisory notices (typically, a first and then second supervisory notice).

---

[1]   A full list can be found at the FSMA 2000, s 395(13).

10.135   The procedure is broadly similar to the warning/decision notice procedure. The main differences are that:

(1)   the action need not wait to take effect until the entire decision making process has been completed, but it may, in specific cases where this is necessary, take effect immediately on giving the first supervisory notice or on a date specified in the notice (or, in any other case, will take effect when the decision making process has been completed);

(2)   there is no formal procedure for settlement discussions and mediation is not available;

(3)   the person does not have any right of access to the FSA's material;

(4)   however, the person does have the right to refer the matter to the Tribunal immediately on issue of the first supervisory notice (whether or not the action is specified to take effect immediately);

(5)   in some cases, including very urgent cases where RDC members cannot be obtained, the RDC will not be involved, but decisions are instead taken by FSA executive procedures, which means by senior FSA staff members. In the case of urgent decisions which would otherwise be taken by the RDC, this relates only to the initial decision to issue a first supervisory notice.

Other procedures

10.136   Certain types of enforcement decisions by the FSA, notably to apply to a court for an injunction or restitution order or to use its insolvency powers, or to institute a criminal prosecution, do not involve any specific procedure specified in the FSMA 2000. The safeguards from the firm's perspective are found in the procedures of the civil or criminal court concerned. The FSA has, however, stipulated that such decisions will normally be taken by the Chairman of the RDC[1]. This gives some protection for firms in a situation where the mere institution of such proceedings can cause significant cost and disruption.

[1]   Unless it is particularly urgent: see *FSA Handbook* at DEC 4.6.

The Financial Services and Markets Tribunal

10.137   One of the key safeguards for firms is the ability to refer cases to the Tribunal. For example, it is in the Tribunal that the ECHR fair trial safeguards are fulfilled. The Tribunal is an independent body constituted under the FSMA 2000, s 132 and Sch 13, and operated by the Lord Chancellor's Department under rules and a budget set by that Department. It is entirely separate from the FSA and has no regulatory agenda as such. The Tribunal is not an appeal body, but a first instance tribunal able to consider any evidence, whether or not available to the FSA, and to reach its own decision on what action it is appropriate for the FSA to take in relation to the matter referred to it. It can also make recommendations about the FSA's procedures. The burden of proof in the Tribunal is on the FSA, not on the person against whom the FSA's enforcement action is being taken.

10.138   The Tribunal's procedures are found in the Financial Services and Markets Tribunal Rules 2001[1]. They do not prescribe in any detail the procedure to be adopted, leaving it largely to the Tribunal appointed to hear each case to decide on the process appropriate for the just expeditious and economical determination of that case. Broadly, a Tribunal is appointed to hear each case, drawn from a panel of legally qualified chairmen and a panel of lay members with relevant experience. The person commences the process by issuing a simple notice referring the matter to the Tribunal. It is then for the FSA to take the first step in explaining what the case is about, by issuing a Statement of Case, and the person concerned responds to that in its Reply. At the same time, there is a process of disclosure of relevant documents. Generally, the Tribunal will allow the parties to make submissions, will hear evidence from witnesses and where appropriate experts and has powers to summons witnesses and to order the disclosure of documents. It also has the power to dispose of cases summarily.

[1]   SI 2001/2476.

10.139   Proceedings before the Tribunal are normally held in public and judgment pronounced publicly, in accordance with the requirements of the ECHR. This may be an important consideration for firms considering whether or not to refer a particular case to the Tribunal. There is a right of appeal to the Court of Appeal, with permission, but only on points of law arising from the Tribunal's decision disposing of the reference, and from there to the House of Lords.

Chapter 11   European Law Considerations

Richard Parlour

INTRODUCTION

11.1   This *Butterworths Financial Services Law Guide* has so far focused on
the regulatory implications of UK financial services law. However, the UK
financial market, despite its size and importance, cannot operate in a
vacuum in today's global marketplace and it is vital to consider the impact
of international regulatory developments on it. There is a growing body of
global regulatory initiatives promulgated by such bodies such as IOSCO,
the Basel Committee, IAIS, G7, G10, OECD, FATF, the tripartite group,
and others[1]. Of more immediate relevance since the UK joined the
European Community in 1972, is the recognition of the supremacy of
European law[2] which that decision entailed. This clearly means that a work
such as this has to cover certain European law considerations which are
relevant to the financial services sector. Potentially this is a rather large task
since there are a sizeable number of measures to address[3]. In addition, there
are a number of general principles of European law which have an
important impact on the financial services sector, flowing from the treaties,
as interpreted by the Court of Justice of the European Communities
(CJEC). For the sake of brevity, it has been decided to limit coverage to the
consideration of three key financial services directives:

(1)   Investment Services Directive (ISD)[4];
(2)   Capital Adequacy Directive (CAD)[5];
(3)   Investor Compensation Scheme Directive (ICSD)[6].

---

[1]   See Chapter 1.
[2]   Treaty of Rome.
[3]   See Appendix.
[4]   Council Directive 93/22/EEC.
[5]   Council Directive 98/31/EC.
[6]   Council Directive 97/9/EC.

11.2   There has been considerable discussion since the first edition of
Butterworths Financial Services Law Guide on how the single market in
financial services is working. This debate has been encapsulated in a
number of documents ranging from the Lamfalussy and CEPS Reports on
the future of European Capital Markets, to the EU Financial Services
Action Plan and Second Consultation Document on *Review of Regulatory
Capital for Credit Institutions and Investment Firms*. This chapter focuses on
what the current law is, but readers should be aware that there are a number
of proposals for change, which as they had not been decided at the time of
going to press, are not covered here.

INVESTMENT SERVICES DIRECTIVE (ISD)

Key concepts

Single European market and the 'passport' concept

11.3 The overall intention of the ISD is to create a single market in investment services across the European Economic Area (EEA) (a territory formed following an agreement between the European Union and the European Free Trade Association, which includes all member states of these two organisations, save for Switzerland where a referendum rejected EEA membership)[1], in a similar manner to that in which the Second Banking Directive[2] was intended to create a single European market for the banking industry, and the Third Generation Insurance Directives[3] were intended to create for the insurance industry. The way in which the single market is created is by permitting investment firms authorised to provide investment services in one EEA member state, to provide investment services in other EEA member states, whether on a cross-border services basis or by establishing a local branch, without the need for further authorisation in the host member state. This freedom is known as the 'investment services passport'. It should be recognised that the passport only relates to authorisation, and that local conduct of business and other rules which may be applied 'in the general good' still need to be complied with, along with other local laws, such as advertising requirements.

---

[1] European Economic Area member states consist of: Austria; Belgium; Denmark; Finland; France; Germany; Greece; Iceland; Ireland; Italy; Liechtenstein; Luxembourg; Netherlands; Norway; Portugal; Spain; Sweden; and the UK. The EEA essentially consists of an agreement between the European Community and the European Free Trade Association (EFTA). Switzerland was the only member of EFTA not to ratify the EEA Treaty and therefore did not become an EEA member state, even though much of its legislation follows European Union legislation.

[2] Council Directive 89/646/EEC.

[3] Council Directives 92/49/EEC and 92/96/EEC.

11.4 The passport is only available to investment firms which are authorised in accordance with the ISD, rather than any local regulation which may allow for other types of financial institution which are not covered by the ISD. The passport is only available to EEA entities, ie those which are incorporated under the laws of an EEA member state and have their head office, registered office or principal place of business within the EEA. This has been the subject of some debate since not all member states recognise the same test of incorporation. For the UK, Denmark and Ireland it is one of establishment under local law and registration which confer legal personality. However, in France there have been four cases where the nationality of an English subsidiary of a North American company has been called into question since the place where all the management decisions is made is outside the EEA, and therefore does not comply with the French test (which is one of the head office or principal place of business being within the EEA). That being said, none of these cases has resulted in the exclusion of such a subsidiary from France.

11.5 It is not essential to obtain a passport to conduct investment services in the EEA, and it is still possible to establish operations on a state-by-state basis if that is what is required. Even if a financial institution has a passport, it may not want to make full use of it, and wish to establish subsidiaries in other member states, perhaps for tax reasons which may outweigh the advantages which might otherwise flow from expanding such operations through a branch network or on a cross-border services basis. The vast majority of financial institutions, however, appear to be using the passport out of preference, though there is nothing to stop the institution subsidiarising if it prefers.

Authorisation is subject to compliance with the minimum standards set out in the ISD and the CAD[1].

---

[1]   See paras 11.11–11.136.

Home member state supervision

11.6   As with the passport regimes in the banking and insurance sectors, it is the authorities of the home member state which are given primary responsibility for the supervision of investment firms within the EEA. The home member state is the member state in which the head office is situated, if it is a natural person, and the member state of the registered office, or head office, if it is a legal person.

Harmonisation

11.7   The authorities claim to have given up on detailed rules requiring harmonisation (though this claim is particularly difficult to maintain in the light of the complexity of the CAD[1]), and prefer to adopt directives which provide for minimum standards. Member states are, in accordance with general European principles, allowed to establish stricter rules on the financial institutions which they are responsible for, but not on those authorised by other member states, the idea being that member states are unlikely to regulate any stricter than necessary for directive implementation purposes, since this would put their own institutions at a competitive disadvantage as compared to those from other member states. For the most part this has occurred, though Germany has taken particular exception in the field of deposit protection. In other examples, the member state concerned has merely repeated the text of directives almost verbatim with no attempt to put any flesh on the skeleton of regulation provided for in the directive concerned.

---

[1]   See paras 11.37–11.136.

Cultural differences

11.8   Whereas implementation of the Second Banking Directive[1] across the EEA essentially represents the introduction of Germanic 'universal' banking concepts, the ISD represents the introduction of Anglo-Saxon investment culture across Europe. This cultural difference at least partly explains the difficulties the UK experienced in implementing the Second Banking Directive, and the fact that only a third of EEA member states managed to implement the ISD on time. In many EEA member states, however, investment services regulation had previously been minimal, unsophisticated, or even non-existent, though all member states did at least have some banking regulatory history.

---

[1]   Council Directive 89/646/EEC.

Scope

11.9 It is important to note that the ISD, and indeed the CAD and the ICSD, are directives which apply across the EEA.

General good

11.10 The investment services passport, like the passports in the banking and insurance sectors, only avoids the need for authorisation in the host member state, and not the requirement to comply with host member state rules relating to provision of investment services. Those host member state rules do, however, have to be made in the interests of the general good. Under European law, the requirements of the general good test means that local host member state rules must not be discriminatory, nor duplicate equivalent home member state rules to which the firm is subject, be objectively necessary and proportionate to the objective pursued. In addition, they must not relate to matters which might already have been harmonised. That being said, it appears that most member states have taken the view that the majority of their local rules, if not all of them, are being applied in the general good, leaving it to individual investment firms to challenge whether or not they really meet the test.

Introduction

11.11 The ISD has two main objectives, being the protection of investors and the stability of the financial system. It relates primarily to the authorisation of investment firms, and is closely allied to the CAD which covers the capital which investment firms and others must maintain in order to carry on investment business. It also contains some key market access provisions.

Principal provisions

Scope of the ISD

11.12 Certain institutions providing investment services are exempted from the ISD and do not therefore gain the passport. These include:

(1)   institutions regulated under certain other European directives (credit institutions, insurance companies, collective investment undertakings and the managers and depositories of those undertakings);

(2)   institutions which provide services to certain types of person only (such as group treasury companies and administrators of employee share participation schemes);

(3) commodity dealers, and locals on financial derivatives markets;
(4) institutions which act solely as introducing brokers in transferable securities and UCITS, provided they do not hold client money or assets or provide any other investment services and act only as introducers to other investment firms or credit institutions (including EEA branches of non-EEA credit institutions) and certain UCITS;
(5) those providing an investment service in an incidental manner in the course of a regulated professional activity;
(6) central banks and other bodies performing similar functions.

11.13 Credit institutions authorised to provide investment services under the Consolidated Banking Directive will be subject to those ISD rules relating to prudential supervision, conduct of business, market access and transaction reporting, as well as to the capital rules in the CAD. ISD rights do not extend to those providing services as counterparty to the state, central bank, or other similar body.

Those investment firms which were already authorised by their home member states and which happened to comply with the ISD authorisation requirements are 'grandfathered' into the new regime.

Investment services

11.14 The ISD covers the services and non-core services in the instruments listed in the Annex to the ISD.

Section A: Services

(1) (a) Reception and transmission, on behalf of investors, of orders in relation to one or more of the instruments listed in Section B.
     (b) Execution of such orders other than for own account.

(2) Dealing in any of the instruments listed in Section B for own account.
(3) Managing portfolios of investments in accordance with mandates given by investors on a discretionary, client-by-client basis, where such portfolios include one or more of the instruments listed in Section B.
(4) Underwriting in respect of issues of any of the instruments listed in Section B and/or the placing of such issues.

Section B: Instruments

(1) (a) Transferable securities.
     (b) Units in collective investment undertakings.

(2) Money market instruments.
(3) Financial futures contracts, including equivalent cash-settled instruments.
(4) Forward interest rate agreements (FRAs).
(5) Interest rate, currency and equity swaps.
(6) Options to acquire or dispose of any instruments falling within this section of the Annex, including equivalent cash-settled instruments. This category includes in particular options on currency and on interest rates.

Section C: Non-core services

(1) Safekeeping and administration in relation to one or more of the instruments listed in Section B.
(2) Safe custody services.
(3) Granting credits or loans to an investor to allow him to carry out a transaction in one or more of the instruments listed in Section B, where the firm granting the credit or loan is involved in the transaction.
(4) Advice to undertakings on capital structure, industrial strategy and related matters and advice and services relating to mergers and the purchase of undertakings.
(5) Services related to underwriting.
(6) Investment advice concerning one or more of the instruments listed in Section B.
(7) Foreign exchange services where these are connected with the provision of investment services.

11.15   The passport is only available for those services and instruments for which the investment firm is authorised by its home member state authority. There is therefore no automatic right to conduct services in the instruments listed.

11.16   The passport may also extend to the non-core services provided core services are carried on. However, the passport will not be available to those investment firms whose business consists only of non-core services. This will be important for those investment firms which conduct such services through a subsidiary which conducts no core services but wishes to co-ordinate such activities across Europe. A number of investment activities under local legislation, such as the Financial Services and Markets Act 2000 in the UK, will not be covered by the passport and therefore authorisation to conduct such activities in other EEA member states will have to be obtained locally.

11.17   The method of construction of the Annex to the ISD therefore gives rise to a number of limitations, including:

(1) commodity and (other than as a non-core service) foreign exchange dealing;
(2) marketing of non-UCITS funds;
(3) dealing in government debt (see the ISD, Article 2.4); and
(4) the requirement that securities which are listed in an EEA member state may have to be dealt in on a regulated market there if the resident investor is a resident of that member state.

11.18   For the first time in European legislation there is a full definition of 'transferable securities'. This includes shares in companies and other equivalent securities, and bonds and other forms of securitised debt which are negotiable on the capital market, and any other securities normally dealt in giving the right to acquire any such transferable securities by subscription or exchange or giving rise to cash settlement, excluding instruments of payment. There will be many problems with this definition, but at least it is an improvement on its circular predecessor, being 'securities which are transferable'.

Authorisation

11.19 All those carrying on a core service in the instruments mentioned must be authorised. This authorisation may also cover the non-core services, but an authorisation cannot be given for the provision of non-core services alone. Investment firms have to have their head office and registered office in the same member state, pursuant to the 'BCCI Directive'[1], and if the investment firm does not actually have a registered office, then the head office and the principal place of business must be in the same member state.

---

[1]   Council Directive 95/26/EC.

11.20 The investment firm also has to have sufficient initial capital and those who effectively direct the business of the investment firm must be of sufficiently good repute, have sufficient experience and number at least two. Authorisation shall be refused if the countries of those who have close links with the investment firm prevent the exercise of effective supervision. The competent authorities also have to establish the identities and holdings of shareholders, whether direct or indirect, natural or legal persons, and must be satisfied as to their suitability. Authorisation of branches of non-EEA investment firms is to be no less rigorous. Where an investment firm is related to another investment firm or credit institution authorised in another member state, then the respective competent authorities must communicate with each other on authorisation of the applicant.

11.21 Applications for authorisation have to be accompanied by a detailed business plan which includes the organisational structure of the investment firm. Investment firms should be informed of their authorisation within six months of the submission of the application, or reasons given for their refusal, and naturally business may be commenced as soon as authorisation has been received.

11.22 Authorisation may be withdrawn if the investment firm:

(1)   does not make use of the authorisation within twelve months;
(2)   renounces the authorisation;
(3)   ceased to provide investment services more than six months previously;
(4)   no longer fulfils the conditions under which authorisation was granted;
(5)   no longer complies with the CAD;
(6)   has seriously and systematically infringed the provisions relating to prudential supervision and conduct of business;
(7)   falls within any of the cases where national law provides for withdrawal.

Prudential supervision

11.23   During negotiation of the ISD, it was decided at a fairly early stage that it would be extremely difficult to obtain agreement on the application of common European conduct of business rules. Accordingly, conduct of business rules were relegated to a possible future directive, though the ISD does contain certain principles of prudential supervision and conduct of business.

11.24   In particular, an investment firm must:

(1)   have sound administrative and accounting procedures, control and safeguard arrangements for electronic data processing and adequate internal control mechanisms, including rules for personal transactions by its employees;

(2)   make adequate arrangements for instruments belonging to investors with a view to safeguarding those investors' ownership rights, especially in the event of the investment firm's insolvency, and to preventing the investment firm using investors' instruments for its own account, except with the investors' express consent;

(3)   make adequate arrangements for funds belonging to investors with a view to safeguarding the latter's rights and, except in the case of credit institutions, preventing the investment firm from using investors' funds for its own account;

(4)   arrange for records to be kept of transactions executed which shall be at least sufficient to enable the home member state authorities to monitor compliance with prudential rules for which they are responsible for applying;

(5)   be structured and organised in such a way as to minimise the risk of clients' interests being prejudiced by a conflict of interest whether as between the firm and its clients or as between clients. Nevertheless, where a branch is established, the compliance arrangements may not conflict with the conduct of business rules laid down by the host member state to cover conflicts of interest.

Conduct of business principles

11.25   Certain principles have been agreed in relation to the conduct of investment business. Accordingly, an investment firm must:

(1)   act honestly and fairly in the conduct of its business activities in the best interests of its clients and the integrity of the market;

(2)   act with due skill, care and diligence in the best interests of its clients and the integrity of the market;

(3)   have and employ the resources and procedures that are necessary for the proper performance of its business activities effectively;

(4)   seek from its clients information regarding their financial situation, investment experience and objectives as regards the services requested;

(5)   make adequate disclosure of relevant material information in its dealings with clients;

(6)   attempt to avoid conflicts of interest, and where they cannot be avoided, ensure that clients are fairly treated;

(7)   comply with all regulatory requirements applicable to the conduct of business activities so as to promote the best interests of its clients and market integrity as a whole.

11.26   It is certain that these conduct of business principles will be interpreted differently in different member states. It should be pointed out that although a policy for lighter regulation of cross-border services has been recognised, together with the relaxation of rules in relation to professional investors, this has largely only been applied in the UK and not in other member states[1]. However, continental member states are beginning to recognise that professionals do not need, nor want, the same regulatory protection as may be appropriate for private investors. However, since there is no definition of 'professional investor' in the ISD, there will be considerable difficulty in applying the exemptions in practice.

---

[1]   ISD, art 11(1).

11.27   The ISD excludes rules relating to marketing and distribution of investments covered by the Annex. Investment firms will therefore need to comply with local solicitation and marketing rules.

11.28   In addition, it ought to be pointed out that general legal standards in host member states will apply and that general civil and criminal law standards and regulations which govern locally will continue to apply and have not been harmonised. This will have an indirect effect on the conduct of investment business and may include such matters as investigation, standards and burden of proof, and capacity of investors to enter into particular transactions.

Using the passport—notification

11.29   Once the passport has been obtained, this does not mean that the services can be provided into host member states without further action. Investment services 'visas' must be applied for, but from the home member state. Under the notification procedures, the home member state has responsibility for ensuring that the investment firm is able to provide the services for which the passport is requested. The host member state cannot refuse provision of the service in its state, but can and should notify the investment firm of the local conditions under which business should be carried on. The procedure differs depending on whether the services are to be offered cross-border or through a local establishment. If they are to be offered cross-border, the home member state regulator, having been notified by the investment firm, has one month to forward the notification to regulators in the relevant host member states. The investment firm can start to provide the cross-border service upon that notification being made or after one month, whichever is the earlier.

11.30   If it is decided to open a branch, the home member state regulator has three months in which to review the notification and pass it on to its opposite number in the host member state. The host member state then has two months in which to prepare for the new business, after which the investment firm can establish the branch. Establishment of a branch can therefore take up to five months, as compared to one month for the provision of cross-border services.

Exchange access

11.31   A second main aim of the ISD is to allow investment firms to obtain membership of EEA securities and derivatives exchanges. This will abolish the restrictions on the ability of non-domestic investment firms and credit institutions to join local exchanges and clearing houses. However, the access of credit institutions to domestic exchanges, where it was prohibited at the time of finalisation of the ISD, was maintained until 1997 (2000 in Greece and Portugal) and may have been subject to a local presence requirement as well as, in respect of certain clearing houses, additional capital requirements.

Enforcement

11.32   It is the competent authorities of the home member state which will be responsible for taking enforcement action against investment firms which do not comply with either the rules of the home member state, or with those of the host member state into which it conducts business. If a host member state regulator complains to the regulator of the home member state, then it is the latter which must require the investment firm concerned to rectify the situation. If it fails to do so, then the host member state can again complain and the home member state regulator should then take action against the investment firm. If these measures fail, then the host member state can take action itself. At first sight this procedure appears to be somewhat unwieldy and bureaucratic and will require extremely close liaison between respective enforcement authorities.

11.33   Relations with third countries are also covered in the ISD as it is thought to be a good opportunity to use the freedoms given under the directive to open up the markets of non-EEA states where at all possible. Reports are to be made to the Commission of any difficulties pertaining to certain countries, and in the most extreme case, authorisation can be delayed by up to three months unless the Council decides to extend the period.

Circumventing non-implementation

11.34   Not all member states implemented the ISD in time. However, the intention of the Commission, which was recognised by a number of non-implementing member states, was that provided the investment firm was authorised in its home member state to conduct investment services cross-border or through a local establishment, then it could go ahead and do so, notwithstanding the fact that the host member state had still to implement the directive. This ties in with general principles of European law which state that those having rights under the treaties and directives can take advantage of those rights and freedoms, notwithstanding delayed implementation, though the exact parameters of this principle remain unclear. Its application to the situation where one member state has implemented the ISD, but another has not, as advocated by the Commission and the competent authorities of various member states, was that investment firms located in member states which had implemented the ISD would be able to provide cross-border services or establish branches into member states which had still to implement. However, the reverse situation was not allowed to happen, even if the investment firm concerned has received authorisation from some other body exercising a regulatory function, such as an investment exchange, and even though that exchange may have been recognised in the implementation of the ISD by the member state having implemented. This aspect can be expected to recur on future amendment of the ISD and CAD.

Key issues

Place of provision

11.35   Difficulties arise from the fact that the ISD contains no definition of when it is that cross-border services are regarded as being provided. The matter is not helped by there being two different tests being used by the member states. One test focuses on whether there has been solicitation of the client or counterparty by the investment firm. If there has, the services are regarded as being provided in that member state.

11.36   The second test looks at where the service is really being provided. For example, a share transaction where the shares are listed on an exchange of a home member state would be regarded as occurring in the home member state even though the order was solicited from a counterparty based in a host member state. On the other hand, the sale of unlisted securities would be regarded in the example as occurring in the host member state since it amounts to a sale to the client or counterparty based there. A Commission Communication on the freedom to provide services and the interest of the general good in the Consolidated Banking Directive attempted to resolve this issue by stating that the cross-border service under the Consolidated Banking Directive will in the main be considered as provided in the jurisdiction in which the client is located if the service is solicited by that firm. However, this test can be considered inappropriate as in any client relationship, certain services could be solicited by the client, and others by the firm, which may occur in different member states. No consensus has yet been reached. Accordingly, investment firms may find themselves in the difficult position of having to comply with two separate and contradictory rules in relation to the provision of the same service, depending solely on whether it is the client or the firm which has initiated the business.

CAPITAL ADEQUACY DIRECTIVE (CAD)

Key concepts

The need for capital adequacy requirements

11.37   The crash of October 1987, in both securities and derivatives markets around the globe, served to highlight the increasing interdependence of the world's financial markets.

11.38   Attention became focused on the ability of market participants to respond to such developments, and on the need for all markets to have an adequate regulatory system in place for the prudential supervision of those markets, in order to ensure their continued financial and operational integrity. Other pressures include the globalisation of markets, the growing use of derivatives, new information technologies, decreasing barriers to competition and market access.

11.39   Capital adequacy is a vital component of the protection of the financial and operational integrity of every financial market. It should aim to produce an environment where market participants are able to enter, participate in and withdraw from the marketplace without breaching that integrity. It should enable this to happen with minimum disturbance to the market or loss being suffered by customers of the market generally. It should be fair, strong yet flexible, well supervised, encourage competition between market participants and stimulate market growth. Finally, the requirements should be designed to avoid the danger of a default in one market affecting either the rest of that market, or any other markets.

11.40   Capital adequacy standards are often seen as amounting to a component of investor protection, though it is strongly arguable that this reason for their imposition does not hold the same validity in markets where investors are perhaps better protected by requirements for segregation of their money and investments, and/or being able to claim on an investor compensation fund in the event of a default. The appropriateness of these other two methods of protecting the investor depends on the nature of the investor concerned. To be effective, compensation funds for professional investors would have to be massive. It is perhaps for this reason that professional investors are no longer covered under the compensation schemes operating in the UK. Professional investors are not felt to require as much protection as private investors and for this reason are also allowed to opt out of the segregation requirements. Many do opt out of the protection, though it should be noted that many of these swiftly opted back into segregation when rumours of the impending Drexel Burnham Lambert collapse, for example, reached the markets.

11.41   Capital adequacy standards are also needed for counterparty reassurance. Markets operate more efficiently where participants are aware that the financial integrity of their fellow players is centrally monitored, than where participants have to check out their counterparties on a transaction-by-transaction basis. This helps to explain the dramatic growth of European derivatives markets, in particular.

11.42   Capital adequacy requirements are therefore primarily needed to protect a market's financial integrity. With increasing globalisation there is a need to ensure that there is some common approach not only as between jurisdictions, but also as between market sectors, so that, for example, investment firms can compete on an equal footing against banks for the same business, all the more so in the light of increasing conglomerisation of financial institutions (a recent study suggested that there are now well over

800 financial conglomerates in Europe, though a similar study for the European Commission put the figure at a little over 200). The capital adequacy debate is an important one and is being addressed not only at European level, but also by the Basel Committee, International Organisation of Securities Commissions (IOSCO) and International Association of Insurance Supervisors (IAIS). Capital requirements now have a dramatic effect upon a financial business' profitability and investment activities, all the more so since increasing competition is driving margins down, such that where such institutions always used to examine the tax efficiency of financial products, they now need to examine their capital efficiency in much the same way.

The risks to be considered

11.43   Capital adequacy requirements should be related to the risks faced by market participants. Unsophisticated capital adequacy regimes which do not track risk adequately, tie up capital unnecessarily and lead to market inefficiency, distort competition and also increase the systemic risk of the financial market as a whole. Similarly, politicians and regulators need to recognise that capital adequacy regimes which may be suited to one part of the financial sector may not be suited to other parts of the financial sector (eg banking cf investment services cf insurance).

11.44   What are the capital related risks faced by market participants and what factors should be considered when calculating the impact of those risks? The risks faced depend on the type of business being conducted by the financial institution concerned. The risks may be numerous (one analysis identifies around forty different types of risk facing financial institutions) and are given numerous and differing labels, but they essentially fall into the following three categories:

(1)   'position' or 'market' risk;
(2)   'counterparty' or 'settlement' risk;
(3)   base risk.

'POSITION' OR 'MARKET' RISK

11.45   This risk takes a variety of forms. It may be subdivided into risks which may affect the market participant directly, such as the market generally moving in the opposite direction, and other risks which may affect participants more indirectly. Such indirect risks may include adverse movements in foreign exchange rates or interest rates which nevertheless have an impact upon the positions maintained by the participant.

11.46   Calculation of position risk should be related to the size and nature of the positions maintained by the participant and the particular dimensions of risk to which those positions are subject. Clearly, some instruments carry a greater intrinsic risk than others depending on the design of the financial instrument in question. Some sophisticated systems differentiate between the holdings of different securities by giving them different weightings or ratings, for example. Full use of these systems should be encouraged, provided the methodology behind the setting of the ratings is sound and the rating itself can be objectively justified.

11.47   The risk to which a market participant is exposed by virtue of having concentrated his positions in any one particular instrument or sector also needs to be considered. Against this, allowance should be made for the diversification of investment and for use of hedging techniques and risk assessment models, again provided that such techniques and models are able to be justified on an objective basis. This allowance should be calculated to encourage market participants to employ risk-reducing strategies rather than risk-increasing ones, and ensure the transfer of risk from one party to another in such a manner as to reduce the overall risk to the market. Finally, full account should be taken of margin, collateral or security put up to cover positions. There should also be some assessment of the risks faced by the firm overall, rather than simply summing the particular exposures in particular instruments.

'COUNTERPARTY' OR 'SETTLEMENT' RISK

11.48   Common to all markets is the possibility that the counterparty or client of a market participant will fail or delay in performing a contract whether in whole or in part. The risk that this will happen is known as counterparty or settlement risk.

11.49   Counterparty risk depends to a large extent on the nature of the clearance and settlement system in the market concerned. Calculation of the counterparty risk requirement will therefore have to take into account the settlement system relevant to the particular market or instrument. The requirement should encourage the use of systems where considerable risk is removed or at least reduced by the existence of an efficient book entry method or by a central clearing house guaranteeing trades. Accordingly, the counterparty risk requirement should not only address the risk of a counterparty failing to honour its obligations, but should also encourage the development of efficient clearing and settlement systems.

11.50   The requirement should also take account of unsecured claims and free deliveries, namely where securities may be delivered before cash is received, and vice versa. The role of market makers should also be taken into consideration in the calculation of the counterparty risk requirement. The requirement should be reduced where there is a liquid market which would enable positions held by a defaulting market participant to be quickly transferred.

11.51   Finally, it should be recognised that cross-border trading may pose particular problems in the calculation of the counterparty risk requirement bearing in mind the major differences in settlement cycles and procedures between markets.

BASE RISK

11.52 The base risk encompasses a wide variety of other risks essentially of an administrative or purely commercial nature which are difficult to measure with any real degree of accuracy. One element of this risk is the level of overheads sustained by market participants and this is usually known as the expenses requirement. This should be set at a low level and have the effect of covering market participants against the risk of reduced revenues, but stationary or increased overheads. There are a number of other types of risk including execution errors, misunderstandings or disagreements, which are largely unmeasurable (though use of a suitable dark number technique can be used to ascertain the general extent of the risk). These need to be taken into account by a measure of capital based on the scale of a market participant's activities. The base risk requirement should be structured so as to encourage market participants to adopt efficient and effective compliance systems and procedures.

11.53 These are the main risks to which investment firms are exposed. Flexibility should be built into the capital adequacy system adopted which should accommodate a wide variety of investment firms, instruments, markets, investors, settlement systems and market customs and practices. For example, firms which only provide investment advice, or firms whose trades are guaranteed by others (such as locals on derivatives markets), may not need to be subject to any capital adequacy requirement at all. On the other hand, firms which may be acting for private customers and running large positions in a restricted range of high risk stocks, unhedged, on a non-centrally cleared market with a long settlement period would clearly be taking on a large amount of risk and should be required to commit an appropriate amount of capital to cover this risk.

11.54 Finally, it should be recognised that there are a variety of ways to protect the financial and operational integrity of a market and investors, besides imposing capital adequacy requirements. For example, protection can also be achieved by requiring segregation of client money and assets, ensuring that market entrants are indeed fit and proper to conduct business not merely in the financial sector, but also in the particular market under consideration. Imposition of appropriate conduct of business rules, monitoring and the provision of appropriate compensation schemes should also be considered. This should all be considered in the round and proper compliance chain analysis undertaken to ensure that all requirements are effective and lead to market efficiency.

Differences in culture

11.55 To understand the more peculiar provisions of the CAD requires an examination of the cultural differences between European financial markets. Unfortunately, the CAD was not compiled on the basis of financial market technical needs, but was subject to a considerable amount of political distortion.

11.56   The European Union contained a variety of cultural differences in relation to the provision of financial services. At the one extreme is the Anglo-Saxon system, involving a risk-based approach to capital adequacy, and at the other is the Germanic system involving a largely unsophisticated high entry barrier approach to capital adequacy regulation, with a Napoleonic system lying somewhere in between the two. These differences are starting to ease as markets grow and techniques cross-fertilise, but an understanding of the history eases understanding of the requirements and can help to explain differences in interpretation and implementation of the Directive from member state to member state.

11.57   The traditional Anglo-Saxon financial market culture displays a clear preference for markets as the source of finance and opportunity. This relies on equity capital, strong shareholders and open markets. There are a great variety of participants including securities houses, brokers, portfolio managers, investment advisers and market-makers, as well as banks. This is reflected in a great variety of markets including stock exchanges, derivatives exchanges and many specialised professional markets. There is also a wide variety of investors ranging from private individuals to highly specialised professionals and an increasingly wide variety of investment products to choose from.

11.58   By contrast, the traditional Germanic culture relies on banks as sources of finance and opportunity. This culture is dominated by the power of universal banks which offer a range of services under one roof. These banks are substantial shareholders in industry. This direct influence is increased by private shareholders generally lodging their bearer shares with banks. In addition, there is considerable cross-membership of the boards of banks and corporates. Germanic investors have traditionally shunned risk and preferred fixed income assets. There is therefore a restricted range of investment products to choose from and, as most investment services are provided by banks, a restricted range of distribution channels. Finally, the Germanic culture regards the provision of investment services as involving deposit-taking and therefore involving the need for a banking licence.

11.59   There has therefore been a tremendous difference across the European Union in terms of investment service culture, which has made the drafting and implementation of the CAD an extremely tortuous and demanding exercise. On top of this, the differences between banking and investment services regulation have made that task even more challenging.

Differences in regulatory approach

11.60   An examination of the differences in the nature and regulation of banking and investment services provision is essential to achieve an understanding of the workings of the CAD.

11.61   The fundamental difference is that banks typically hold assets to maturity, whereas investment firms trade assets, holding them in the short-term only. Banks generally hold illiquid commercial loans as opposed to investment firms holding highly liquid assets. This fundamental difference is reflected in a fundamental difference in the risks that are faced in the two types of activity, being credit risk for banks, and position risk for investment firms.

11.62   Banks' loan portfolios change very gradually, as does their credit risk. They have stable balance sheets and slow-changing capital ratios. They are evaluated as going concerns and their accounting treatment is based on original cost.

11.63   Investment firms' asset portfolios may change very rapidly, as may their position risk. They have large movements in their balance sheets and quickly-changing capital ratios. They are evaluated on a liquidation basis and their accounting treatment is carried out on a mark-to-market basis.

11.64   Banks rely heavily on retail deposits for non-capital funding. For investment firms, reliance is placed on money markets.

11.65   Given these differences, it can be seen that there must be a funda-mental difference in the treatment of the two types of financial institution and the two types of financial business if they run into trouble. For banks, the regulator's objective is to keep the bank afloat as a going concern, to allow it to raise new capital and conserve financial resources. This is because in the event of a run on the bank, if it were not to be kept afloat, the bank's illiquid loan portfolio could only be disposed of at a dramatic undervalue, exposing creditors and depositors to losses. For investment firms, the regulator's objective is to wind the investment firm down completely. The investment firm has a highly liquid asset portfolio, which should be capable of liquidation without giving rise to heavy losses.

11.66   These differences are reflected in the different rationale for regula-tory capital. For banks, capital should be permanent to support the bank as a going concern should it run into difficulties, whereas for the investment firm, capital need only be temporary. Leading on from this, banks clearly require high quality core capital and should only be allowed to rely on long-term subordinated debt as secondary capital. By contrast, investment firms can be allowed to rely heavily on short-term subordinated debt.

11.67   What does all this mean for capital adequacy regulation? Generally speaking, it will mean that banks will require higher long-term capital of a restricted nature and that, as their loan portfolios change slowly, monitoring need not be frequent. For investment firms, on the other hand, lower short-term capital of a wider nature is acceptable, but with increased monitoring as compared to banks, since investment firms have quickly-changing portfolios.

11.68   Finally, one crucial point which should not be overlooked is that the above exploration of the differences between banks and investment firms essentially relates to the types of financial service which they traditionally provide, rather than the type of financial institution which they happen to be classified as. In other words, should banks provide investment services, then the capital adequacy treatment to which they should be subject in the provision of that service is that for investment firms. Similarly, should investment firms offer deposit-taking services, then the capital adequacy treatment to which they should be subject in relation to that service is that of the banks.

11.69   This contrast is between banks and investment firms. However, it should not be forgotten that these are but two of the four pillars of the financial sector as a whole and that, for example, the capital treatment of insurance companies and pension funds is different again.

Introduction

11.70   The CAD is part of a package with the ISD in the same way as the Own Funds Directive and Solvency Ratio Directive formed part of a package with the Second Banking Directive (now brought together as the Consolidated Banking Directive[1]). The CAD has since been amended by the Second Capital Adequacy Directive ('CAD II') in 1998. CAD II was aimed at introducing refined and more accurate capital requirements for market risk and to bring the EU regime into line with the international regime under the Basel Capital Accord. In particular, CAD II enabled member states to recognise risk models developed by the financial institutions they regulate and introduce a more refined capital treatment of trading positions subject to commodities price risk, both underlying and derivatives positions. It also required positions in gold and gold derivatives to be treated similarly to FX positions. A proposal for CAD III is expected in the autumn of 2001.

---

[1]   Council Directive 89/646/EEC.

11.71   The aims and objectives of the CAD are:

(1)   to set common capital conditions for investment firms operating in the EU;
(2)   to achieve a level playing field as between banks and investment firms in the provision of investment services;
(3)   to enhance the international competitiveness of EU markets;
(4)   to provide adequate investor protection; and
(5)   to ensure the continuity of EU financial institutions.

11.72   The CAD seeks to achieve these aims by means of the following provisions:

(1)   it sets out different levels of initial capital for investment firms depending on the investment activities which they carry on;

(2)   it provides for a system of evaluation of investment positions (trading book);

(3)   it contains provision against a variety of market risks;

(4)   it establishes what may be allowed to count as regulatory capital;

(5)   it contains provision for consolidated supervision;

(6)   it contains provision for large exposures;

(7)   it sets out the requirements for competent authorities and their duties; and

(8)   it sets out various reporting requirements.

Principal provisions

Capital

11.73   The basic initial capital requirements vary according to the investment activity:

(1)   investment firms holding clients' money or securities, offering reception, transmission or execution of investors' orders, or management of individual portfolios, but not dealing in instruments for their own account (with certain exceptions) or underwriting €125,000;

(2)   investment firms not authorised to hold clients' money, to deal for their own account or to underwrite €50,000;

(3)   locals and investment firms which only receive and transmit orders on behalf of clients, without acting as custodians €50,000;

(4)   all other investment firms €730,000.

Grandfathered firms or mergers of grandfathered firms may continue with lower levels of capital in certain circumstances.

Trading book versus banking book

11.74   The trading book consists of shorter-term trading as compared to the banking book, which consists of longer term-trading, deposit-taking and the investment book. The elements of the trading book are detailed, but in essence consist of:

(1)   proprietary positions in financial instruments held in the short-term, including arbitrage, matched and hedged positions;

(2)   unsettled transactions, free deliveries, OTC derivatives, repos and reverse repos, and securities lending and borrowing; and

(3)   related fees, commission, interest, dividends and margin.

Provisions against risks

11.75   The CAD contains provisions which require capital to be allocated against a number of risks arising from trading book activities. These include the 'building block methodology' approach to position risk, settlement and counterparty risk, foreign exchange risk, large exposures and other risks. The own funds requirement is never to be less than the other risks requirement. Banks and investment firms are required to set up systems to monitor interest rate risk and calculate their financial positions with reasonable accuracy at any time, and their systems are to be supervised by the competent authorities.

11.76   Banks and investment firms may opt out of the CAD and calculate their capital requirements in accordance with the Consolidated Banking Directive instead, provided their trading book does not normally exceed five per cent of total business or €15 million, and never exceeds six per cent or €20 million.

Position risk

11.77   Positions are first of all classified and netted. The net position is the excess of an institution's long (short) positions over its short (long) positions in the same equity, debt and convertible issues and identical financial futures, options, warrants and covered warrants. Positions in derivatives are allowed to be treated as positions in the underlying or notional security. Net positions are to be converted into the reporting currency at the prevailing spot rate and marked to market on a daily basis. Position risk is calculated according to various general rules for debt instruments, equities and under-writing. Specific rules apply to particular instruments such as interest rate futures, forward rate agreements (FRAs), options, warrants, swaps and units in collective investment schemes.

11.78   Position risk is split into specific risk and general risk. Specific risk is the risk of loss resulting from price changes related to factors specific to the issuer. General risk is the risk of price change due to market factors such as changes in interest rates and other factors unrelated to specific instruments. Thus all the factors are examined in isolation, as 'building blocks', a risk element calculated and aggregated to form the overall position risk requirement. The specific and general risk are examined for traded debt instruments and for equity and the general risk for traded debt instruments examined on a maturity based or duration based approach. Underwriting is also covered.

11.79   Thus for the calculation of the position risk requirement, all finan-cial instruments follow essentially the same approach:

(1)   positions are classified according to currency denomination;
(2)   positions are netted;
(3)   capital requirements are calculated for general and specific risk incurred in each currency separately;
(4)   capital requirements are converted at current spot rates.

11.80   *For traded debt instruments specific risk:*

(1)   net positions in all issues are calculated;
(2)   the appropriate weighting for each position is identified and multiplied by the net position;
(3)   the weighted net positions (whether they are short or long) are aggregated.

Item	Residual maturity	Weighting
Central government		0.00%
Qualifying	Up to 6 months	0.25%
	6–24 months	1.00%
	Over 24 months	1.60%
Other		8.00%

11.81 *For traded debt instruments general risk on the maturity based approach:*

(1) maturity based weighted positions are calculated for each instrument or position held by multiplying the net position against the weighting factor;

(2) opposite weighted positions are then matched, first within each maturity band, then within each maturity zone, and finally between maturity zones;

(3) the capital requirement is then calculated based on weighted positions and the relevant matched position rules.

Zone	Maturity band		Weighting	Assumed interest rate change
	Coupon of 3% or more	*Coupon of less than 3%*		
One	0–1 month	0–1 month	0.00	–
	1–3 month	1–3 month	0.20	1.00
	3–6 month	3–6 month	0.40	1.00
	6–12 month	6–12 month	0.70	1.00
Two	1–2 years	1–1.9 years	1.25	0.90
	2–3 years	1.9–2.8 years	1.75	0.80
	3–4 years	2.8–3.6 years	2.25	0.75
Three	4–5 years	3.6–4.3 years	2.75	0.75
	5–7 years	4.3–5.7 years	3.25	0.70
	7–10 years	5.7–7.3 years	3.75	0.65
	10–15 years	7.3–9.3 years	4.50	0.60
	15–20 years	9.3–10.6 years	5.25	0.60
	over 20 years	10.6–12 years	6.00	0.60
		12–20 years	8.00	0.60
		over 20 years	12.50	0.60

11.82 The capital requirement of the institution is then calculated as the sum of:

(1) 10 per cent of the sum of the matched weighted positions in all maturity bands;

(2)   40 per cent of the matched weighted position in Zone 1;
(3)   30 per cent of the matched weighted position in Zone 2;
(4)   30 per cent of the matched weighted position in Zone 3;
(5)   40 per cent of the matched weighted position between Zones 1 and 2 and Zones 2 and 3;
(6)   150 per cent of the matched weighted position between Zones 1 and 3;
(7)   100 per cent of the residual unmatched weighted positions.

11.83   *For traded debt instruments general risk on the duration based approach:*

Institutions may be allowed in general or on an individual basis to use a system for calculating the general risk capital requirement on a duration basis, rather than a maturity basis:

(1)   the market value of each instrument is taken and its yield to maturity calculated;
(2)   the modified duration of each instrument is then calculated;
(3)   each instrument is then allocated to the appropriate zone;
(4)   duration weighted positions are then calculated for each instrument by multiplying its market price by its modified duration and by the assumed interest rate change;
(5)   duration weighted long and short positions are then calculated within each zone and matched.

11.84   The capital requirement is then calculated as the sum of:

(1)   2 per cent of the matched duration weighted position for each Zone;
(2)   40 per cent of the matched duration weighted positions between Zones 1 and 2, and 2 and 3;
(3)   150 per cent of the matched duration weighted position between Zones 1 and 3;
(4)   100 per cent of the residual unmatched duration weighted positions.

$$\text{Modified duration} = \frac{\text{duration (D)}}{(1 + r)} \text{ where:}$$

$$D = \frac{\displaystyle\sum_{t=1}^{m} \frac{t\, C_t}{(1 + r)^t}}{\displaystyle\sum_{t=1}^{m} \frac{C_t}{(1 + r)^t}}$$

r = yield to maturity
C_t = cash payment in time t
m = total maturity

11.85 Of the maturity and duration based approaches, the duration based method allows more generous set-off since modified duration tracks sensitivity to interest rate movements more closely than the maturity approach.

Zone	Modified duration (in years)	Assumed interest rate change
One	0–1.0	1.00
Two	1.0–3.6	0.85
Three	Over 3.6	0.70

11.86 *For equities specific risk:*

(1) net positions (both long and short) in all issues are calculated, the sum of both figures being the overall gross position and the difference is the overall net position;
(2) the overall gross position has a 4 per cent weighting applied;
(3) the specific risk capital requirement may be 2 per cent (rather than 4 per cent), for those portfolios of equities held by institutions meeting the following criteria, if allowed by the competent authority:

   (a) equities are not those of issuers which have issued only traded debt instruments that attract an 8 per cent requirement above or that attract a lower requirement only because they are guaranteed or secured;
   (b) equities judged highly liquid by the competent authorities;
   (c) no individual position comprising >5 per cent of the institution's equity portfolio (but individual positions of up to 10 per cent may be authorised provided in total they are no more than 50 per cent).

11.87 *For equities general risk:*
the capital requirement is equal to 8 per cent of the overall net position.

11.88 *For stock index futures:*
(meaning the delta weighted equivalents of options in stock index futures and stock indices as well as stock futures) may be broken down into positions of their constituents and may be netted against opposite positions in the underlying equities. Institutions shall have adequate capital to cover tracking risk (the difference between the underlying and the derivative market). Exchange traded stock index futures which are broadly diversified attract an 8 per cent general risk capital requirement, but no specific capital risk requirement. They are included in the calculation of the overall net position, but ignored for the calculation of the overall gross position. If a stock index future is not broken down into its underlying positions, it is treated as an individual equity and specific capital risk can be ignored if the future is exchange traded and the index is a broad one.

11.89 *For underwriting:*

(1) net positions are calculated by deducting underwriting positions which are subscribed or subunderwritten by third parties on the basis of formal agreements from the total underwriting position;

(2)   the net position is reduced by the relevant factors during the first five working days after the day on which the institution becomes unconditionally committed (working day zero);

(3)   the capital requirement is calculated based on the reduced net positions.

Working day	Reduction factor
0	100%
1	90%
2 and 3	75%
4	50%
5	25%
thereafter	0%

11.90   *For particular instruments:*

(1)   Interest rate futures, FRAs and forward commitments to trade debt instruments are treated as combinations of short and long positions. The instrument is split into treatment of a borrowing, and an asset holding or the debt instrument. The former is calculated according to the Central Government column of Table 1[1], as is the latter, unless it is a debt instrument, in which case reference to the appropriate debt instrument category is made. For exchange traded futures (and until 31 December 2006 OTC derivatives contracts cleared by a recognised clearing house), the capital requirement may be allowed to be the same as the relevant margin requirement if it is at least equal to the capital requirement for a future that would result from a calculation of position risk or applying the internal models method in the new Annex VIII to the CAD. This applies similarly to exchange-traded and OTC options, save that the competent authorities may allow the requirement on a bought exchange-traded or OTC option to be the same as that for the instrument underlying it, subject to the constraint that the resulting requirement does not exceed the market value of the option. The requirement against a written OTC option shall be set in relation to the instrument underlying it.

(2)   Options on interest rates, debt instruments, equities, equity indices, financial futures, swaps and foreign currencies are to be treated as positions in the underlying, multiplied by the appropriate delta (the 'delta' being the expected change in the price of the option as a proportion of a change in the value of the underlying). These positions may be netted off against positions in the underlying. The delta may be that of the exchange, the competent authority, or the institution. The capital requirement may be the same as the margin requirement set by the exchange for written options, and the same as that for the underlying for bought options.

(3)   Warrants relating to debt instruments and equities are to be treated in the same way as options.

(4)   Swaps are to be treated for interest rate purposes as on balance sheet instruments. Thus a swap where floating rate interest is received and

fixed rate paid, is treated as a long position in an equivalent floating rate instrument and a short position in a fixed rate instrument.

(5) Institutions may use sensitivity models provided the model and its use by the institution is approved by the competent authority.

(6) The transferor of securities in a repo and the lender in a securities lending shall include these in the calculation of its capital requirement.

(7) Positions in units in collective investment schemes are subject to the capital requirements of the Solvency Ratio Directive[2].

---

[1] See para 11.80.
[2] Council Directive 89/647/EEC.

Settlement and counterparty risk

11.91 Settlement and counterparty risk is split into the trading book and the banking book. The banking book is governed by the provisions of the Solvency Ratio Directive (now subsumed into the Consolidated Banking Directive) and outside the scope of this chapter. The trading book is split into settlement (or delivery) risk and counterparty risk, the latter being subdivided first into free deliveries, second into repos, reverse repos, securities or commodities lending and borrowing, and third into OTC derivatives.

11.92 Settlement risk is assessed by:

(1) calculating the institution's exposure to price differences (calculated as the agreed settlement price less the current market value, where the difference could involve a loss for the institution) on transactions in debt instruments, equities or commodities (excluding repos, reverse repos, securities or commodities lending and borrowing) not settled after the due delivery date;

(2) calculating the capital requirement using one of two methods[1]:

    (a) method 1—based on the price difference multiplied by the Column A factors;

    (b) method 2—based on the settlement price multiplied by the Column B factors.

---

[1] As set out at para 11.93.

11.93 Counterparty exposure (for free deliveries and unsecured payments) is assessed by:

(1) aggregating the value of the securities or commodities or the cash owed;

(2) calculating the capital requirement based on 8 per cent of the exposure multiplied by the relevant counterparty risk weighting (see the Solvency Ratio Directive [1], now subsumed within the Consolidated Banking Directive[2]).

Working days after due settlement	*Column A*	*Column B*
5–15	8%	0.5
16–30	50%	4.0
31–45	75%	9.0
46+	100%	Method 1 only

[1]   Council Directive 89/647/EEC.
[2]   Council Directive 2000/12/EC.

11.94   For repos, reverse repos, securities or commodities lending and borrowing:

(1)   calculating the difference between the market value of the securities or commodities and amounts borrowed or lent or the market value of the collateral;

(2)   calculating the capital requirement based on 8 per cent of the exposure multiplied by the relevant counterparty risk weighting, where the difference is positive.

11.95   For OTC derivatives, Annex II to the Solvency Ratio Directive[1] (now subsumed within the Consolidated Banking Directive[2]) is applied to interest rate and exchange rate derivatives and bought OTC equity options and covered warrants are treated as exchange rate contracts under that Annex, and the relevant counterparty risk weighting applied. Until 31 December 2006, the competent authorities may exempt from this treatment OTC contracts cleared by a clearing house where the clearing house acts as the legal counterparty and all participants fully collateralise on a daily basis the exposure they present to the clearing house, provided the competent authorities are satisfied that the posted collateral gives the same level of protection as collateral which complies with Art 6(1)(a)(7) of the Solvency Ratio Directive[3] and that the risk of a build-up of the clearing house exposures beyond the market value of the posted collateral is eliminated. Otherwise, for exposures in the form of fees, commission, interest, dividends and margin, not covered by Annexes I and II, nor deducted from the own funds requirement and which are directly related to items in the trading book, the relevant counterparty risk weighting is applied.

[1]   Council Directive 89/647/EEC.
[2]   Council Directive 2000/12/EC.
[3]   Council Directive 89/647/EEC.

Foreign exchange risk

11.96   Foreign exchange risk applies to both trading and banking books, and the capital requirements are calculated using one of four methods.

METHOD 1

11.97

(1) Calculate the net open position in each currency (including the reporting currency) and gold (this consists of the sum of the net spot position, the net forward position, irrevocable guarantees that are certain to be called, net future income and expenses not yet accrued but already fully hedged, the net delta equivalent of the total book of foreign currency and gold options, the market value of other options. Any positions which the institution has taken to hedge against adverse exchange rate movements on its capital ratio may be excluded). Competent authorities may allow financial institutions to use net present value in their calculations.

(2) For each currency other than the reporting currency, and for gold, convert at spot rate net long and short positions into the reporting currency.

(3) Aggregate all net short positions and all net long positions separately, the higher of the two totals amounting to the net foreign exchange position (NFEP).

(4) If the NFEP/NGP > two per cent of its total own funds, the capital requirement is equal to eight per cent NFEP/NGP. Until 31 December 2004, the competent authorities may allow financial institutions to calculate the capital requirement by multiplying the amount by which the sum of the overall NFEP/NGP > two per cent total own funds, by eight per cent.

METHOD 2

11.98

(1) Calculate NFEP for all currencies, as outlined in Method 1.

(2) Calculate the matched position in closely correlated currencies by:

    (a) converting net open positions into the reporting currency;

    (b) taking the lower of the net open positions in each pair of closely correlated currencies as the matched position in the correlated currencies (MPCC).

(3) The capital requirement on matched positions is equal to four per cent of the MPCC.

(4) The capital requirement on unmatched positions in closely correlated currencies, and all positions in other currencies is eight per cent of the higher of the sum of the net short or long positions in those currencies after the removal of the MPCC.

(5) Currencies may be deemed to be closely correlated if the likelihood of a loss, calculated on the basis of the daily exchange rate for the previous three or five years, occurring on equal and opposite positions in such currencies over the following ten working days, which is four per cent or less of the value of the matched position in question (valued in terms of the reporting currency), has a probability of at least 99 per cent when a period of three years is used and 95 per cent when a period of five years is used.

METHOD 3

11.99   Until 31 December 2004, competent authorities may allow the capital requirement to be equal to the larger of (provided they set and review the calculation formula and the correlation coefficients):

(1)   the losses that would have occurred in at least 99 per cent of the rolling ten day working periods over the previous three years;

(2)   two per cent of the NFEP/NGP as calculated in Method 1.

METHOD 4

11.100

(1)   Positions in any currency which is subject to a legally binding intergovernmental agreement to limit its variation relative to other currencies from the three above methods are removed.

(2)   Matched positions in such currencies are calculated and subject to a capital requirement of 50 per cent of the maximum permissible variation in the agreement.

(3)   Unmatched positions in those currencies are treated in the same way as other currencies.

Capital requirements on matched positions in currencies of member states participating in the second stage of EMU may be calculated as 1.6 per cent of the value of such matched positions. Net positions in composite currencies may be broken down into the component currencies.

Other risks

11.101   Investment firms must hold capital not less than 25 per cent of their preceding year's fixed overhead costs, or of the figure projected in their business plan. This requirement is not additional to the other requirements set out in the CAD, but sets a floor to the overall capital requirement.

Own funds

11.102   Capital, for own funds calculations, is defined in accordance with the Own Funds Directive[1] (now subsumed within the Consolidated Banking Directive[2]) and is divided into three separate tiers. Competent authorities may allow those financial institutions obliged to meet the own funds requirements laid down in Annexes I–VIII (save for Annex V) to use an alternative definition of own funds.

---

[1]   Council Directive 89/299/EEC.
[2]   Council Directive 2000/12/EC.

TIER 1: CORE CAPITAL

11.103   This consists of:

(1)   share capital;
(2)   share premium account;

(3)   prior year profit and loss account reserves;
(4)   current year's retained profit (verified by external audit);
(5)   current year's losses.

TIER 2: SUPPLEMENTARY CAPITAL

11.104   This consists of:

(1)   current year's retained profit (verified by internal audit);
(2)   hybrid (debt/equity) capital instruments;
(3)   subordinated term debt.

TIER 3

11.105   This consists of:

(1)   trading book profit net of any foreseeable charges or dividends, less net losses on other business, provided that none of these amounts have been included as Tier 1 or Tier 2 capital;
(2)   fully paid subordinated loan capital with an initial maturity of at least two years, provided that:

    (a)   neither principal nor interest will be repaid if this would cause own funds to fall below 100 per cent of the institution's overall requirements;
    (b)   it does not exceed 150 per cent of own funds left to meet the requirements laid down in Annexes I–VIII (save for Annex V), except with the agreement of the competent authorities where it may reach 200 per cent or 250 per cent if the deductions referred to below are not made, or the institution is a credit institution;

(3)   less (if required by the competent authorities) illiquid assets such as tangible fixed assets, deficiencies in subsidiaries, loans due in more than 90 days, physical stocks, deposits to be repaid in more than 90 days or which are used as margin, holdings and other investments which are not readily marketable, and holdings in credit and other financial institutions which may be included in the own funds of such institutions.

Those investment firms in a group where consolidated supervision has been waived are subject to a modified definition of own funds.

Consolidated supervision

11.106   Under the CAD the capital requirements should be applied on a consolidated basis to any institution which has a credit institution, investment firm or another financial institution as a subsidiary or which holds a participation in such an entity. They should also be applied on a consolidated basis to any institution, the parent undertaking of which is a financial holding company, though there are circumstances where this obligation to consolidate may be waived (provided each investment firm meets the own funds and market risk requirements on a 'solo' basis and sets up systems to monitor and control the sources of capital and funding of all other financial institutions within the group). The principles of consolidation essentially mirror those contained in the Second Banking Consolidated Supervision Directive[1] (now subsumed into the Consolidated Banking Directive[2]). This is an area of great complexity and certain issues have been left to future debate and future directives. There is particular difficulty in consolidation of group exposure where different types of financial institution or indeed non-financial institutions are included, essentially for reasons of the different types of risk which they face, as described above.

[1] Council Directive 92/30/EEC.
[2] Council Directive 2000/12/EC.

11.107   The basis of the principle is that large exposures, foreign exchange and net positions in the trading book of one institution may be set off against those of another, subject to certain rules. This principle may also be extended to non-EEA states provided certain conditions are met.

Large exposures

11.108   Large exposures are to be monitored and controlled in accordance with the Large Exposures Directive (now subsumed into the Consolidated Banking Directive[1]) subject to any modifications which may be applicable in Annex VI to the CAD. A large exposure is defined as an exposure to individual clients or groups of connected clients which is greater than or equal to 10 per cent of a firm's Tier 1 and Tier 2 capital. Large exposures arising from non-trading book activities must not exceed 25 per cent of the own funds of an investment firm. Large exposures arising from trading book activities may exceed this limit, subject to regulatory approval, provided that the firm holds sufficient capital to cover an additional risk requirement.

Aggregate large exposures may not exceed 800 per cent of Tier 1 and Tier 2 capital in total.

[1] Council Directive 2000/12/EC.

11.109   The exposure to individual clients or to groups of related clients is the total of:

(1)   any excess, where positive, of long over short positions in financial instruments issued by a client or group of related clients;
(2)   net underwriting exposures on debt and equity instruments reduced by the underwriting factors set out above; and
(3)   settlement and counterparty exposures without application of the counterparty risk weightings.

The overall exposure to individual clients or groups of connected clients shall include both the trading book and the non-trading book.

Reporting requirements

11.110   Naturally there must be requirements relating to monitoring of the system, and financial institutions are obliged to report all necessary information to the competent authorities and put internal control mechanisms and administrative and accounting procedures in place to enable verification of compliance at all times. This reporting requirement is monthly for those investment firms with an initial capital requirement of €730,000, quarterly for those with an initial capital requirement of €125,000, and twice yearly for those with an initial capital requirement of €50,000. Consolidated information for all investment firms need only be provided twice yearly. Immediate reporting of counterparty default is required for repos and reverse repos, and for securities lending and borrowing transactions.

Commodities

11.111　Three methodologies for calculating capital requirements for commodities are provided in CAD II:

(1)　a simplified method imposing a conservative flat capital hit designed to ensure that banks and investment firms engaging incidentally in commodities business have a reasonable capital cushion;
(2)　a maturity ladder approach, which generally gives a lower hit than under the first method and which at present is considered the most appropriate approach for banks and investment firms;
(3)　internal models, the development of which is 'encouraged' by CAD II.

11.112　The spot price in each commodity is expressed in the reporting currency. Positions which are purely stock financing may be excluded from the commodities risk calculation. When a short position falls due before a long position, institutions need to guard against the risk of a shortage of liquidity.

11.113　Positions in each commodity are netted. Positions in derivatives may be treated as positions in the underlying commodity. Positions in different sub-categories of commodities where the sub-categories are deliverable against each other, and positions in similar commodities if they are close substitutes and if a minimum correlation of 0.9 between price movements can be clearly established over a year, may be regarded as positions in the same commodity.

11.114　Commodity futures and forward commitments to buy or sell individual commodities are incorporated as notional amounts and assigned a maturity with reference to the expiry date. The competent authorities may allow the capital requirement for an exchange-traded future to be equal to the margin required by the exchange if they are fully satisfied that it provides an accurate measure of the risk associated with the future and that it is at least equal to the capital requirement for a future that would result from a calculation made using the method set out in the remainder of this Annex or applying the internal models method. Until 31 December 2006, the competent authorities may also allow the capital requirement for an OTC commodity derivatives contract cleared by a recognised clearing house to be equal to the margin required by the clearing house it they are fully satisfied that it provides an accurate measure of the risk associated with the derivatives contract and that it is at least equal to the capital requirement that would result from a calculation made using the method set out in the remainder of this Annex or applying the internal models method.

11.115   Commodity swaps where one side of the transaction is a fixed price and the other side the current market price, are incorporated into the maturity ladder approach set out below[1]. Positions are long positions if a fixed price is paid and a floating price received and short positions if vice versa. Commodity swaps where the sides of the transaction are in different commodities are reported in the relevant part of the maturity ladder.

---

[1]   See para 11.118.

11.116   Options on commodities or commodity derivatives are treated as if they were positions equal to the amount of the underlying, multiplied by its delta. Positions may be netted off in identical underlying commodities or commodity derivatives. The delta may be of the exchange, the competent authorities or, where none of those is available or for OTC options, as calculated by the institution itself, subject to approval of the competent authorities.

11.117   Competent authorities must require that other risks associated with commodity options are safeguarded against. They may allow the requirement for a written exchange-traded commodity option to be equal to the margin required by the exchange if satisfied that it is an accurate measure of the risk and that it is at least equal to the capital requirement that would result in using the method set out in the remainder of this Annex, or applying the internal models method. Until 31 December 2006 the competent authorities may also allow the capital requirement for an OTC commodity option cleared by a recognised clearing house to be equal to the margin required by the clearing house, if satisfied that it provides an accurate measure of the risk and that it is at least equal to the capital requirement for an OTC option that would result using the method set out in the remainder of this Annex, or applying the internal models method. They may also allow the requirement on a bought exchange-traded or OTC commodity option to be the same as for the underlying, subject to the resulting requirement not exceeding the market value of the option. The requirement for a written OTC option is set in relation to the underlying. Warrants on commodities shall be treated as commodity options. The transferor of commodities or guaranteed rights relating to commodities in a repo and the lender of commodities in a commodities lending agreement include such commodities in the calculation of its capital requirement.

Method 1

11.118   A separate maturity ladder is used for each commodity. All positions are assigned to the appropriate maturity bands. Physical stocks are assigned to the first maturity band.

Maturity band	Spread rate (in %)
0 ≤ 1 month	1,50
> 1 ≤ 3 months	1,50
> 3 ≤ 6 months	1,50
> 6 ≤ 12 months	1,50
> 1 ≤ 2 years	1,50
> 2 ≤ 3 years	1,50
> 3 years	1,50

11.119 Competent authorities may allow positions in the same commodity to be offset and assigned to the appropriate maturity bands on a net basis for positions in contracts maturing on the same date and positions in contracts maturing within 10 days of each other, if the contracts are traded on markets which have daily delivery dates. The sum of the long positions and the sum of the short positions in each maturity band is calculated, positions are matched and the residual position is the unmatched position. That part of the unmatched position for a maturity band that is matched by the unmatched position for a maturity band further out is the matched position between two maturity bands. That part that cannot be thus matched is the unmatched position.

11.120 The capital requirement for each commodity is calculated as the sum of:

(1) the sum of the matched positions, multiplied by the appropriate spread rate as indicated in the second column of the above table at para 11.118 for each maturity band and by the spot price;
(2) the matched position between two maturity bands for each maturity band into which an unmatched position is carried forward, multiplied by 0,6% (carry rate) and by the spot price for the commodity;
(3) the residual unmatched positions, multiplied by 15% (outright rate) and by the spot price.

Method 2

11.121 The capital requirement for each commodity is the sum of 15% of the net position, multiplied by the spot price, and 3% of the gross position, multiplied by the spot price.

Risk models

11.122 The competent authorities may allow the use of their own internal risk-management models instead of, or in combination with the above methods. Recognition is only given if the model is conceptually sound and implemented and that the following standards are met:

(1) the model is integrated into the daily risk-management process and serves as the basis for reporting risk exposures to senior management;

(2)   the risk control unit is independent from business trading units and reports directly to senior management. It must be responsible for designing and implementing the model and produce and analyse daily reports on the model and on appropriate trading limits;

(3)   the board of directors and senior management must be involved in the risk-control process and daily reports are reviewed by an approved level of management;

(4)   sufficient staff in the trading, risk-control, audit and back-office areas;

(5)   established procedures for ensuring compliance with a documented set of internal policies and controls concerning the model;

(6)   the models have a proven track record of reasonable accuracy in measuring risks;

(7)   frequent conduct of a rigorous programme of stress testing and review by senior management;

(8)   there must be an independent review of the model to include the activities of the business units and the risk-control unit and its overall risk-management process:

(a)   the adequacy of the model documentation and organisation of the risk-control unit;

(b)   integration of market risk measures into daily risk management and the integrity of the management information system;

(c)   the model approval process and front and back office valuation systems;

(d)   the scope of market risks captured by the model and validation of any changes in the risk-measurement process;

(e)   the accuracy and completeness of position data, volatility and correlation assumptions, and valuation and risk sensitivity calculations;

(f)   the verification process of the independence, consistency, timeliness and reliability of data sources used to run the models;

(g)   the verification process for back-testing to assess the model's accuracy.

Competent authorities examine the capability to perform back-testing on both actual and hypothetical changes in a portfolio's value. Back-testing on hypothetical changes is based on a comparison between the end-of-day value and, assuming unchanged-positions, its value at the end of the subsequent day.

11.123   For calculating capital requirements for specific risk associated with traded debt and equity positions, competent authorities may recognise the use of a model if, in addition, the model:

• explains the historical price variation in the portfolio;

• captures concentration in terms of magnitude and changes of composition of the portfolio;

• is robust to an adverse environment;

• is validated through back-testing to assess whether specific risk is being accurately captured.

Unrecognised models are subject to a separate capital charge for specific risk.

11.124   The multiplication factor is increased by a factor of between 0 and 1 in the table, depending on the number of overshootings for the most recent 250 business days as evidenced by the back-testing. Competent authorities require the calculation of overshootings on the basis of back-testing either on actual or on hypothetical changes in a portfolio's value. An overshooting is a one-day change in the portfolio's value that exceeds the related one-day VaR measure generated by the model. For the purpose of determining the factor, the number of overshootings is assessed at least quarterly.

Number of overshootings	Factor
Fewer than 5	0,00
5	0,40
6	0,50
7	0,65
8	0,75
9	0,85
10 or more	1,00

11.125   Competent authorities can waive the requirement to increase the multiplication factor by the factor in the table, if the increase is unjustified and the model is basically sound. If numerous overshootings indicate that the model is not sufficiently accurate, the competent authorities revoke recognition or impose appropriate measures. Overshootings from a back-testing programme that would imply an increase of a factor must be promptly notified.

11.126   If the model is recognised, the capital requirement shall be increased by a surcharge of either the specific risk portion of the VaR measure which should be isolated, or the VaR measures of sub-portfolios of debt and equity positions that contain specific risk. Competent authorities may waive the surcharge if it is shown that the model accurately captures event and default risk for traded debt and equity positions.

11.127   The higher capital requirement of the previous day's VaR number and an average of the daily VaR measures on each of the preceding 60 business days, multiplied by the relevant factor. The calculation is scaled up by a multiplication factor of at least three.

11.128   Calculation of VaR is subject to the following minimum standards:

(1)   daily VaR calculation;
(2)   a 99th percentile, one-tailed confidence interval;
(3)   a 10-day equivalent holding period;

(4)   an effective historical observation period of one year except where a shorter observation period is justified by a significant upsurge in price volatility;

(5)   three-monthly data set updates.

11.129   Competent authorities require the model to capture all material price risks of options or option-like positions accurately and that any other risks not captured by the model are covered by own funds. They also require the model to capture sufficient risk factors, depending on the level of activity in the markets. As a minimum, the following provisions shall be respected:

(1)   for interest rate risk, the model must incorporate a set of risk factors corresponding to the interest rates in each currency in which there are interest rate sensitive on-or off-balance sheet. For material exposures to interest-rate risk in the major currencies and markets, the yield curve is divided into at least six maturity segments, to capture the variations of volatility along the curve. The model must also capture the risk of less than perfectly correlated movements between different yield curves;

(2)   for FX risk, the model shall incorporate risk factors corresponding to gold and the individual foreign currencies;

(3)   for equity risk, the model shall use a separate risk factor for each of the equity markets in which there are significant positions;

(4)   for commodity risk, the model shall use a separate risk factor for each commodity where there are significant positions. The model must also capture the risk of less than perfectly correlated movements between similar, but not identical, commodities and the exposure to changes in forward prices arising from maturity mismatches. It must also take account of market characteristics, delivery dates and the scope to close out positions.

Competent authorities may allow use of empirical correlations within and across risk categories if satisfied that the model for measuring correlations is sound.

Proposed changes

11.130   The CAD is already due to be revised again. It was known that this would have to occur when CAD II was being agreed as the Basel Committee deliberations were known about at the time, but the decision was made not to wait for the outcome. This piecemeal approach is unfortunate and will increase systems costs unnecessarily, but will persist until such time as Basel and EU processes are streamlined, potentially with IOSCO too.

11.131   CAD III is already being mooted. This may cover certain points where there are differences between Basel and the EU, such as:

(1)   specific risk (Basel capital hits are eight per cent for liquid portfolios, four per cent for diversified portfolios and two per cent for liquid indices, as opposed to CAD hits of four per cent, two per cent and zero respectively);

(2) high yield debt instruments (Basel has special treatment, but CAD does not);

(3) duration method for debt instrument instruments (there are differences between the disallowance factors and the maturity bands);

(4) pre-processing of derivatives (use of sensitivity models is limited to swaps by Basel, but not by CAD);

(5) options (Basel describes various alternatives which are not specified by CAD).

Key issues

11.132 Has a level playing field between non-bank investment firms and bank's securities subsidiaries really been created? One of the effects of the creation of two regimes is that there are two separate and distinct definitions both of capital and of capital adequacy which apply to different parts of a bank's business. This means that banks' securities businesses are potentially subsidised by cheap capital from the bank's deposit base.

11.133 The CAD has also resulted in the creation of market distortions. It does not necessarily lower the capital requirements for investment firms which have diversified portfolios. Indeed, when the CAD was being negotiated, similar securities houses ran the then proposed CAD through their books to see what the impact on their capital adequacy requirement would be. It was found that the effect really related directly to the actual structure of the trading book, it being impossible to predict the outcome depending on the type of securities house. The CAD will also have the effect of distorting certain types of product. For example, a loan to a public company would attract an eight per cent haircut, whereas debt (qualifying) would attract a three per cent requirement, as compared to a ten per cent equity requirement. The capital treatment of products has therefore become as important as their tax treatment. Banks will also be encouraged by the capital requirements to prefer securitised lending to traditional loans, which is clearly not in their mindset. Is this wise?

11.134 The process will inevitably involve some substantial systems costs. Financial institutions will have to invest in suitable models of trading and capital.

11.135 Risk management procedures are also likely to need some attention as the CAD regime now provides an incentive for modelling of products, pricing and trading simulations. Consolidated minimum capital requirements will have to be met at all times and this has obvious ramifications for risk management procedures. Financial institutions will have to look at far more than simply the likely effect on their overall capital requirements, and can be expected to investigate the mix of own funds, to incorporate capital efficiency into their product development, business planning and strategy formulation decisions, collating the information from the various different systems centrally.

11.136 The importance of capital efficient hedging will be increased, and the cost of capital may well influence pricing. The overall complexity of the new regulations will result in the need for considerable training of staff, and not merely in the back office, but also in front office support. Reporting systems will have to be considerably more sophisticated to provide continuous compliance monitoring on an efficient basis and the speed and efficiency of clearing and settlement systems will become ever more important.

INVESTOR COMPENSATION SCHEME DIRECTIVE (ICSD)

General concepts

11.137 The ICSD has a rather more precise objective than that of investor protection—which was the driving force behind the ISD and CAD. The ISD and CAD provide for, what is hoped, will be the effective front line defence of the financial and operational integrity of EEA markets. These two directives provide for an assessment of the fitness and properness of investment firms to operate in Europe's financial market place and attempt to ensure that these firms have sufficient capital resources to do so.

   In addition, separate rules require client money and investments to be kept apart from those of the investment firm, and conflicts of interest to be avoided.

11.138 The ICSD operates after the last lines of defence have been breached, its principal objective being to compensate investors should other supervisory methods fail and an investment firm collapses leaving investors unable to recover their money or investments.

11.139 Financial markets depend for their success and growth on investor confidence. The ICSD compensation rules enabling investors to recover a proportion of their money or investments in the event of the collapse of an investment firm, represent an attempt to ensure at least a minimum level of confidence in the investment services market. However, the ICSD is not wholly based on the principle of protecting fools from being parted with their money and there is a cap on the amount recoverable, such that the need for investors to choose their counterparty with care is not eliminated.

11.140 Before introduction of the ICSD, compensation schemes across the European Union varied tremendously. For example, the UK had a comprehensive scheme, covering both stock exchange members and other types of intermediary; other member states had schemes covering stock exchange members alone; and yet other member states had little or nothing in place with the aim in mind of compensating investors. Schemes were funded in a variety of ways. Schemes covered either all investors, only private investors, or no investors. The level of cover ranged from nothing, to 30 per cent of the bank's equity capital per client, or €379,500, and could vary depending on whether cash or securities were lost. Claims may have been restricted to exchange traded securities only, or may have to have been made within a certain time frame.

11.141 Co-ordination at European Union level is intended to enable investors to have greater confidence in European markets as a whole, since they should have broadly similar rights to compensation whether they deal with a firm incorporated in their own member state, or with one established in another member state which provides services either directly or through a local branch. Co-ordination is also intended to help to put in place a broadly level playing field in competition terms as between investment firms from different member states.

11.142 The issue of compensation for investors was originally approached in negotiations on the ISD. However, the technical complexities of operation of investor compensation schemes were beyond their incorporation in the ISD and compensation measures were therefore omitted to be dealt with at a later date, as indeed were conduct of business rules (though conduct of business rules have not yet become the subject of a proposal for a directive).

Under the ISD, investor protection should be organised by the home member state, in line with the general principle of home member state control and supervision of institutions which it authorises.

11.143 Finally, the ICSD is intended to provide not only a level playing field as between investment firms of different member states, but also as between investment firms and other types of financial institution, particularly credit institutions. Accordingly, the ICSD to a large extent follows principles already laid down in the Deposit Guarantee Directive (DGD)[1] drawn up for the banking sector, in a similar fashion to that in which the ISD follows principles laid down in the Consolidated Banking Directive and the CAD follows principles laid down in the Consolidated Banking Directive.

[1] Council Directive 94/19/EC.

11.144 Funding of investor compensation schemes is left up to the member state concerned, though financing capacity should be in proportion to liabilities and not jeopardise the financial markets, nor distort it in competition terms. Curiously, and as an incentive for member states to implement, it is an objective of the ICSD that member states and their competent authorities should not be liable in respect of investors provided they have introduced schemes in accordance with the ICSD. Competent authorities include not only those defined under the ISD, but also, if appropriate, those defined under the Consolidated Supervision Directive[1] (as now replaced by the Consolidated Banking Directive[2]).

[1] Council Directive 92/30/EEC.
[2] Council Directive 2000/12/EC.

Application of the ICSD

Scope of the ICSD

11.145   The ICSD requires both that one or more investor compensation schemes be introduced in a member state and that the investment business of an investment firm be covered by a compensation scheme established in the home member state of the investment firm. The definition of 'investment firm', for these purposes, covers not only investment firms as defined in the ISD, but also credit institutions which are authorised under the Consolidated Banking Directive[1] to engage in one or more core investment services.

---

[1]   Council Directive 2000/12/EC.

11.146   'Investment business' means any of the services set out in Section A of the Annex to the ISD including reception and transmission of orders, agency brokerage, principal dealing, portfolio management and underwriting and placing of investments. In addition, the non-core service of safekeeping and administration of investments[1] is also covered. The reason for this is that this non-core service clearly involves the handling of client money and investments. Investments are those listed in Section B of the ISD Annex. Member states are given the ability to exclude certain categories of investments if they do not consider that they need special protection.

---

[1]   See Section C of the Annex.

11.147   The ICSD aims to provide confidence in European financial markets principally to private investors, though the scope of the ICSD is not expressly limited to this category of investors. Certain categories of investor have been listed in Annex I to the ICSD, following similar principles adopted in relation to the DGD (Deposit Guarantee Directive). These investors include professional and institutional investors (including credit institutions, investment firms, insurance companies, collective investment schemes, and pension and retirement funds), as well as supranational institutions, government, provincial, regional, local and municipal authorities, group companies and directors, managers, partners of investment firms and their close relatives and advisors. Member states are given an option to exclude these types of investors from coverage, or alternatively to provide that a lower level of compensation should apply to them as they are thought to have the ability to judge the risks themselves.

11.148   Member states are under a duty to check whether branches in their jurisdiction of non-EU investment firms have equivalent cover to that required under the ICSD. Member states may require such branches to join their schemes.

11.149   Should an investment firm not meet the compensation scheme obligations, then the relevant competent authorities are to take all appropriate measures to ensure that it does. Investment firms may make alternative equivalent compensation provision but if they cannot their authorisation should be terminated, though cover will continue to be provided up to the time of termination.

Compensation schemes introduced will also cover investors or branches opened by the firm in other member states.

Relationship with banking sector protection

11.150   In principle, the ICSD also covers credit institutions carrying on investment business. In the case of investment services, there is no overlap between the ICSD and the DGD, as the DGD does not apply to investment services. However, where funds are paid to a credit institution, there is some risk of double coverage as there is little distinction between monies deposited in a credit institution and monies given to the credit institution for the purpose of carrying out an investment service.

11.151   A member state may exempt a credit institution from the need under the ICSD for it to belong to a compensation scheme where that credit institution is already exempt under the DGD, provided that the protection and information given to depositors are also given to investors on the same terms and investors therefore have equivalent protection.

11.152   It has also been provided that a credit institution need not belong to two different schemes, provided that the scheme it does belong to meets the requirements of both the ICSD and the DGD. Accordingly, no claim in respect of the same transaction is eligible for compensation under both ICSD and DGD. Member states are able to decide which regime should apply where it may be difficult to distinguish between deposits covered by the DGD and money held in connection with investment business and subject to the ICSD.

Disclosure of schemes

11.153   It is clearly essential to the objective of investor protection for investment firms to be required to disclose to investors, in a readily comprehensible manner, the existence and nature (including the amount and scope of cover) of the compensation scheme or alternative arrangement of which it and its branches are members, before entering into a business relationship. Information should also be made available on request concerning the conditions and formalities governing compensation. All information should be made available in the language of the member state where the branch is established.

11.154   References to compensation schemes in investment advertising should not be allowed to occur on an unregulated basis, in such a way as to distort market competition. Member states are required to lay down more detailed rules to limit the use of advertising so as to prevent its use affecting the stability of the financial system, or investor confidence.

Where compensation is payable

11.155   Compensation (covering claims for client money or investments) should be payable to investors following a decision by the competent authorities or the courts, whichever is earlier, of the relevant member state that the investment firm in question is unable to meet its commitments and has failed or is bankrupt. The ICSD does not then have immediate automatic effect. If any other remedies are available to investors, such as bringing proceedings for return of client money or investments, then these remedies must be exhausted before a claim can be made on the compensation fund. In addition, calculation of the claim should take account of set off and counterclaim as appropriate. Claims arising out of transactions where a criminal conviction under the Money Laundering Directive[1] has been secured are excluded from compensation.

---

[1]   Council Directive 91/308/EEC.

Level of minimum cover

11.156   The minimum level of compensation is €20,000 per investor and this covers both client money and securities. This level is exactly the same as that in the DGD. However, as with the DGD, member states may provide for a higher level of cover should they so wish. Member states may limit the cover to a percentage of the claim, but not less than 90 per cent and only as long as the amount to be paid under the scheme is less than €20,000. The ICSD will only operate to reimburse claims in respect of client money and securities and will not provide any coverage for claims of a different nature, such as negligence. The operation of the ICSD is also without prejudice to the rules and procedures relating to insolvencies of investment firms, applicable in each member state.

11.157   The cover applies to the investor's aggregate claim on the same investment firm irrespective of the number of accounts, currencies and location within the EEA. However, member states can provide that cover in non-EEA currencies shall be excluded from cover or subject to lower cover. Partnerships or similar joint groupings may be treated as the same investor.

11.158   This then is how the ICSD structure is intended to apply across the EU. As with the vast majority of directives, only a skeletal framework is provided and member states are left to implement the ICSD in whatever manner they see fit, provided that it complies with the minimum requirements laid down in the directive. The member states therefore have some latitude to decide how implementation should occur, in line with local market practice. Member states are allowed to introduce more stringent rules or provide greater or more comprehensive cover, as they see fit. However, since the cost of funding the compensation schemes must be borne by the investment services sector, and therefore ultimately by investors, it is unlikely that any member state will substantially increase the amount of cover, as this will of course detract from the competitiveness of its investment services sector.

Harmonising compensation schemes—'topping up' and 'export bans'

11.159   Nevertheless, it has been recognised there may still be some difference between the levels of compensation available in different member states
giving rise to unequal conditions of competition. Therefore, the ICSD allows
for a branch of an investment firm to join in the compensation scheme of
the host member state, should it so wish. This 'topping-up' arrangement
follows the same principle adopted in the DGD.

11.160   For the time being there is a ban on investment firms offering a
higher level or scope of cover of compensation than that available in the host
member state (known as the 'export ban' clause). Essentially these two
clauses represent a failure to find a workable solution. They will therefore be
monitored over the next few years and any market distortions which appear
will reopen this part of the ICSD. Certain guiding principles are set out in
Annex II to the ICSD. These include supervision by the scheme of the host
member state, co-operation between schemes and charging. In theory at
least, it will still be possible to obtain higher compensation in one member
state than another, for the same size and nature of loss.

Claims

11.161   Investors are given a minimum of five months (the compensation
scheme can extend this period) from the determination of the competent
authorities or the ruling of the courts that the investment firm is no longer in
a position to meet its liabilities, to make their claim. The fact that the period
has expired cannot, however, be invoked by the compensation scheme to deny
an investor his right to compensation where he has been unable to assert his
right in time. The compensation must be paid as soon as possible, and in any
event within three months of establishment of the investor's entitlement
(though in exceptional circumstances, the time limit may be extended for a
maximum extra three months). If the investor has been charged with a money
laundering offence, then the payment may be suspended pending court
judgment.
   Investors are to be allowed to bring an action against a compensation
scheme and schemes have the right of subrogation to the rights of those
investors in liquidation proceedings for amounts equal to their payments.

General

11.162   It did not prove possible to introduce the ICSD at the same time as
the ISD and CAD. The ICSD came into force in the member states on
26 September 1998. Germany appealed to the CJEC against the DGD as it
felt the DGD would weaken the protection available to investors in Germany, and voted against the ICSD. Germany lost this case. Article 12 of the
ISD on compensation schemes was repealed by the ICSD.

Appendix

EUROPEAN UNION FINANCIAL MARKETS LEGISLATION RELEVANT TO CHAPTER 11

Expected	Prudential Treatment of Commodities Risks Directive
Expected	Netting Interpretation Communication
Expected	Accident Insurance/Vehicle Insurance Directive
Expected	Third Capital Adequacy Directive
Expected	E Commerce in Financial Services Communication
Expected	Second Netting Directive
Proposed	UCITS Amending Directive
Proposed	UCITS Further Amending Directive
[Proposed]	Listing and Admissions Consolidation Directive
Proposed	Pension Funds Directive
[Proposed]	ISD Conduct of Business Rules Communication
[Proposed]	ISD Upgrade Communication
Proposed	Prospectus Directive
Proposed	Market Abuse Directive
Proposed	Financial Services Distance Marketing Directive
[Proposed]	Retail Payments Communication
Proposed	Financial Collateral Directive
Proposed	Financial Conglomerates Directive
Proposed	Risk Capital Communication
Proposed	Financial Services Action Plan Implementation Communication
Proposed	Fraud in Non-Cash Payments Communication
Proposed	E Commerce in Financial Services Communication
2001/24/EC	Winding Up of Credit Institutions Directive
2001/17/EC	Winding Up of Insurance Companies Directive
2000/46/EC	Electronic Money Institutions Directive
2000/35/EC	Late Payments Directive
2000/28/EC	Banking Amending Directive
2000/12/EC	Consolidated Banking Directive (amended the Self Employed Activities of Banks Directive 73/183/EEC; First Banking Directive 77/780/EEC; Own Funds Directive 89/299/EEC; Second Banking Directive 89/646/EEC; Solvency Ratio Directive 89/647/EEC; Second Banking Consolidated Supervision Directive 92/30/EEC; Large Exposures Directive 92/121/EEC)
1999/61/EC	WTO Negotiations of Financial Services Decision
98/78/EC	Supplementary Insurance Supervision Directive
98/33/EC	Banking, Solvency Ratio and Capital Adequacy Amending Directive
98/32/EC	Third Solvency Ratio Directive
98/31/EC	Second Capital Adequacy Directive
98/26/EC	Settlement Finality Directive
97/9/EC	Investor Compensation Scheme Directive

97/5/EC	EU Credit Transfers Directive
96/10/EC	Netting Directive
95/198/EC	Late Payments Recommendation
95/26/EC	Prudential Supervision of Financial Institutions 'BCCI' Directive
94/19/EC	Deposit Guarantee Directive
94/18/EC	Admissions Directive
EC/3605/93	Protocol on the Excessive Deficit Procedure Regulation
EC/3604/93	Prohibition of Privileged Access to Financial Institutions Regulation
EC/3603/93	Prohibition of Privileged Access to Financial Institutions Regulation
93/22/EEC	Investment Services Directive
93/6/EEC	Capital Adequacy Directive
92/121/EEC	Large Exposures Directive
92/96/EEC	Third Life Assurance Directive
92/49/EEC	Third Non-Life Insurance Directive
92/48/EEC	Insurance Intermediaries Recommendation
92/30/EEC	Second Banking Consolidated Supervision Directive
92/16/EEC	Third Own Funds Directive
EEC/1534/91	Insurance Agreements Regulation
91/675/EEC	Insurance Committee Directive
91/674/EEC	Insurance Company Accounts Directive
91/633/EEC	Second Own Funds Directive
91/323/EEC	Motor Liability Insurance Directive
91/308/EEC	Money Laundering Directive
91/31/EEC	Second Solvency Ratio Directive
90/619/EEC	Second Life Assurance Directive
90/618/EEC	Second Non-Life Insurance Directive
90/605/EEC	Consolidated Accounts Directive
90/232/EEC	Motor Liability Insurance Directive
90/211/EEC	Listing Mutual Recognition Directive
90/109/EEC	Cross-border Financial Transactions Recommendation
89/647/EEC	Solvency Ratio Directive
89/646/EEC	Second Banking Directive
89/592/EEC	Insider Dealing Directive
89/299/EEC	Own Funds Directive
89/298/EEC	Listing Particulars Directive
89/117/EEC	Publication of Annual Accounting Documents Directive
EEC/1969/88	Medium Term Financial Assistance Regulation
88/627/EEC	Listing Particulars Directive
88/590/EEC	Payment Systems Recommendation
88/361/EEC	Free Movement of Capital Directive
88/357/EEC	Direct Insurance Services Directive
88/220/EEC	UCITS Amending Directive
87/598/EEC	Electronic Payments Code of Conduct Recommendation
87/373/EEC	Commission Implementation Powers Decision
87/345/EEC	Admissions Directive

87/344/EEC	Legal Expenses Insurance Directive
87/343/EEC	Credit Surety Insurance Directive
86/635/EEC	Bank Accounts Directive
86/566/EEC	Free Movement of Capital Directive
85/611/EEC	UCITS Directive
85/583/EEC	Free Movement of Capital Directive
84/253/EEC	Eighth Accounts Directive
83/349/EEC	Seventh Consolidated Accounts Directive
79/279/EEC	Admissions Directive
79/267/EEC	First Life Assurance Directive
78/660/EEC	Fourth Company Accounts Directive
77/780/EEC	First Banking Directive
77/91/EEC	Public Limited Company Directive
73/239/EEC	First Non-Life Insurance Directive
73/183/EEC	Self-employed Activities of Banks Directive
64/225/EEC	Reinsurance Directive

Each of the above type of measure, and others which do not figure in the above table, have a different impact, and a guide to the differences is set out below.

TYPES OF EUROPEAN UNION LEGISLATIVE MEASURES

Regulation

Initiator	Commission.
Scope	Specifically addressed to member state governments. Creates binding legislation which automatically enters into force in all member states on a given date, usually within days of official publication.
Publication	First as COM document, then as proposal in Official Journal (OJ) C Series, then on adoption, in OJ L Series.

Directive

Initiator	Commission.
Scope	Defines the objectives to be achieved in the area concerned while leaving it to member states to decide the mode and form of implementation. Implementation of directives usually requires local implementation (some directives are directly effective, as regulations are) and usually within two to three years of adoption.
Publication	First as COM document, then as proposal in Official Journal (OJ) C Series, then on adoption, in OJ L Series.

Decision

Initiator	Council or Commission.
Scope	Can be directed at member states or companies, either individually, or collectively. Decisions are binding on addressees. Generally they are used for the administrative implementation of EU law.
Publication	In OJ C or L Series.

Recommendation and opinion

Initiator	Commission, Council, Parliament, Economic and Social Committee.
Scope	These give non-binding EU views, normally to encourage best practice throughout the EU. Can be addressed to member states and economic operators.
Publication	First as COM document, then in OJ C Series.

Resolution

Initiator	Council and/or Parliament.
Scope	Intended to establish the fundamental principles on which EU action shall be based and to set a time limit. They are only declarations of the Council's intentions.
Publication	As a COM document.

Green and White Papers

Initiator	Commission.
Scope	Green Papers focus on an area of interest where there is as yet no legislation. They are intended to operate as a consultative document, for which a time limit is set. Usually, a Green Paper will lead to a Communication, which may lead to a proposal for legislation. White Papers are similar to Green Papers, but usually focus on broader areas covering more than one industry.
Publication	As a COM document.

Communication

Initiator	Commission.
Scope	Communications are usually produced as a result of comments received in relation to Green Papers. Communications are usually followed up by an actual proposal in the area in question. The Commission has also issued Communications on the interpretation of court cases.
Publication	As a COM document, then in OJ C Series.

Notice

Initiator	Commission.
Scope	Notices indicate and interpret EU policy. Their purpose is purely informational. While they provide guidelines as to how the Commission may interpret legislation, they are of persuasive authority before the national courts only. They are used particularly in the area of competition.
Publication	In OJ C Series.

Study

Initiator	Commission.
Scope	Studies are designed to represent an overview of a particular area of activity within the EU. They may lead to legislative proposals.
Publication	Not required.

EUROPEAN UNION LEGISLATIVE PROCESS

The European Union clearly has a number of possible instruments at its disposal to carry out its legislative function. The role of the various interested institutions varies depending upon which pillar of EU law is relevant. The measures outlined above relate to the first pillar of EU law, which is principally concerned with business matters. Different procedures come into play when other pillars are addressed, such as foreign or security policy and home affairs.

The Commission has the sole right to initiate legislation. The relevant directorate-general will circulate a draft text within the Commission. This is published as a Commission working document, with a SYN or SEC reference or an internal number. Once agreement on the proposed text has been reached within the Commission ('adopted'), it is then published as a COM document, showing the date of issue. This is the first public stage for the proposal. A COM document usually contains an Explanatory Memorandum which sets out the Commission's aim. At any moment the Commission may amend or withdraw the proposal.

After a short interim period and translation of the proposal into the eleven official languages of the European Union, the proposal is published in the 'C' Series of the Official Journal and simultaneously seeks endorsement by the European Parliament and the Economic and Social Committee and/or the Council of the Regions before being finally approved by the Council of Ministers. The EU currently has four different decision-making procedures:

- consultation—this requires an opinion from the European Parliament;
- co-operation—this requires two readings by the European Parliament, before the second reading, the European Council will have to adopt a Common Position. Since entry into force of the Treaty of Amsterdam, the co-operation procedure applies only to EMU issues;

- co-decision—this procedure grants extensive powers to the European Parliament, giving it the right to oppose, amend or veto (by absolute majority) a Common Position of the European Council. If the European Parliament opposes the Common Position of the European Council, the European Council may call a Conciliation Committee (half Council, half European Parliament) to explain its position. If the point of contention remains unresolved after talks in the Committee, the European Parliament can veto the proposal. The Treaty of Amsterdam extended the use of co-decision and introduced a 'simplified' procedure, which cut the number of European Parliament hearings from three to two;
- assent—this procedure is used for all constitutional acts, such as accession to EU membership. If the European Parliament does not give its assent, then an act cannot come into force.

A measure may be adopted after the opinions set out above have been given. Where the European Parliament has given the first of its two opinions, the European Council adopts a common position—this is a political agreement followed by final adoption or rejection after the second Parliamentary reading. The European Council has different voting options:

- unanimity;
- simple majority (eight out of 15) Member States;
- qualified majority (62 votes out of 87).

In the case of issues not proposed by the Commission (eg Common Foreign and Security Policy, justice and interior affairs) the 62 votes have to represent the wishes of at least ten Member States. Now, in the event of between 23 and 27 votes (a blocking minority) against an issue, there will be a delay during which the European Council will attempt to secure a qualified majority. The distribution of votes is as follows:

- ten votes—France, Germany, Italy, United Kingdom;
- eight votes—Spain;
- five votes—Belgium, Greece, Netherlands, Portugal;
- four votes—Austria, Sweden;
- three votes—Denmark, Finland, Ireland;
- two votes—Luxembourg.

Once a proposal is formally adopted, it is published in the 'L' Series of the Official Journal, with full details of the implementation and scope of the legislation.

Index